New Perspectives on Human Development

Developmental theorists have struggled with defining the relations among biology, psychology, and sociocultural context, often reducing the psychological functions of a person to either biological functioning or the role of sociocultural context – nature or nurture – and considering each area of human development separately. *New Perspectives on Human Development* addresses fundamental questions of development with a unified approach. It encompasses theory and research on cognitive, social and moral, and language and communicative development, in various stages of life, and explores interdisciplinary perspectives. *New Perspectives on Human Development* revisits old questions and applies original empirical findings, offering new directions for future research in the field.

NANCY BUDWIG is a professor in the Hiatt School of Psychology at Clark University. She is an associate editor of the *British Journal of Developmental Psychology*.

ELLIOT TURIEL is a professor in Education at the University of California, Berkeley, where he holds the Jerome A. Hutto Chair in Education.

PHILIP DAVID ZELAZO is currently the Nancy M. and John E. Lindahl Professor at the Institute of Child Development, University of Minnesota. He is the recipient of a Boyd McCandless Young Scientist Award from the American Psychological Association and a Canada's Top 40 Under 40 Award.

New Perspectives on Human Development

Nancy Budwig
Clark University

Elliot Turiel
University of California, Berkeley

Philip David Zelazo
University of Minnesota

With
Stephanie M. Carlson (cognitive development)
Cecilia Wainryb and Na'ilah Suad Nasir (social development)
Katherine Nelson (language and communicative development)

CAMBRIDGE
UNIVERSITY PRESS

CAMBRIDGE
UNIVERSITY PRESS

University Printing House, Cambridge CB2 8BS, United Kingdom

One Liberty Plaza, 20th Floor, New York, NY 10006, USA

477 Williamstown Road, Port Melbourne, VIC 3207, Australia

4843/24, 2nd Floor, Ansari Road, Daryaganj, Delhi – 110002, India

79 Anson Road, #06–04/06, Singapore 079906

Cambridge University Press is part of the University of Cambridge.

It furthers the University's mission by disseminating knowledge in the pursuit of education, learning, and research at the highest international levels of excellence.

www.cambridge.org
Information on this title: www.cambridge.org/9781107112322
DOI: 10.1017/9781316282755

First published 2017

Printed in the United States of America by Sheridan Books, Inc.

A catalogue record for this publication is available from the British Library.

ISBN 978-1-107-11232-2 Hardback
ISBN 978-1-107-53182-6 Paperback

Contents

Part III: Language and Communicative Development

(Edited by Nancy Budwig and Katherine Nelson)

Figures

Color versions of figures 3.3 and 3.4 are available online at www.cambridge.org/9781107112322

Maps

Tables

Contributors

NICOLE BARDIKOFF, Queen's University

RADU J. BOGDAN, Tulane University

NANCY BUDWIG, Clark University

JOAN Y. CHIAO, Northwestern University

COLETTE DAIUTE, The Graduate Center, City University of New York

MATTHEW GINGO, Wheaton College

JOAN E. GRUSEC, University of Toronto

GAIL D. HEYMAN, University of California, San Diego

EVA JABLONKA, Tel-Aviv University

JANICE JOHNSON, York University

PETER H. KAHN, JR., University of Washington

ANNETTE KARMILOFF-SMITH, Birkbeck, University of London

AMY KYRATZIS, University of California, Santa Barbara

CAROL D. LEE, Northwestern University

KANG LEE, University of Toronto

LYNN S. LIBEN, The Pennsylvania State University

ROBERT LICKLITER, Florida International University

MAXINE MCKINNEY DE ROYSTON, University of Wisconsin, Madison

NA'ILAH SUAD NASIR, University of California, Berkeley

KATHERINE NELSON, The Graduate Center, City University of New York

JUAN PASCUAL-LEONE, York University

PAUL C. QUINN, University of Delaware

HOLLY RECCHIA, Concordia University

LEOANDRA ONNIE ROGERS, Northwestern University

MARK SABBAGH, Queen's University

SOLACE SHEN, University of Washington

THOMAS R. SHULTZ, McGill University

RICHARD A. SHWEDER, University of Chicago

MARGARET BEALE SPENCER, University of Chicago

ELLIOT TURIEL, University of California, Berkeley

CECILIA WAINRYB, University of Utah

NIOBE WAY, New York University

PHILIP DAVID ZELAZO, University of Minnesota

Preface

In 1970, Jean Piaget participated in a workshop that instigated vigorous discussion in higher education circles about the importance of traversing the boundaries between the disciplines. The workshop, entitled "L'interdisciplinarité – Problèmes d'enseignement et de recherche dans les universités," was held in Nice, France, in September of 1970 and the Proceedings were published in 1972 as a monograph entitled *Interdisciplinarity: Problems of Teaching and Research in Universities.* (Paris: Organization for Economic Cooperation and Development). This workshop and the book that resulted from it set the stage for ongoing debates about how best to view work going on at the intersection of disciplinary boundaries. Piaget's remarks made clear that new conceptual frameworks were needed, frameworks that underscored the importance of augmenting disciplinary knowledge in order to address enduring challenges of our times. Whether to do so from multi-, trans-, or interdisciplinary bases, and what precisely each of these constructs adds to disciplinary discussions, has been hotly debated for the ensuing four decades. What Piaget was wrestling with in 1970 and many others have been pursuing since then are two enduring issues: the complexity of knowledge and the importance of viewing knowledge construction as a process embedded in real time. Piaget understood early on what has become more obvious now, namely the importance of going beyond disciplinary limitations, both theoretically and methodologically. This insight has shaped modern thinking on knowledge and development in significant ways.

Around the same time as Piaget spoke at the Organisation for Economic Co-operation and Development (OECD) workshop, a new society was formed. The Jean Piaget Society was founded in 1970, and has since provided an internationally recognized forum for inquiry and advances about significant problems in the developmental sciences. The Society has had a longstanding commitment to developmental perspectives and has been deeply concerned with theories and conceptualizations of development and the ways developmental perspectives connect to and influence research. Since renamed The Jean Piaget Society for Knowledge and Development, the Society organizes and sponsors a book series, an annual meeting of plenary addresses and scholarly presentations, a special issue of a scholarly journal, and a website (www.piaget.org). Across venues, participating scholars come from a range of disciplines, including departments of psychology, anthropology, linguistics, sociology, biology, philosophy, and education.

The Society has had a longstanding dedication to the publication of books that address core problems in the developmental sciences. For more than thirty years,

Lawrence Erlbaum Press (currently Psychology Press/Taylor and Francis) published a book series from the yearly convenings, and this was later carried on by Cambridge University Press. Each of the volumes in the Jean Piaget Series has engaged influential scholars on a set of themes that bring together divergent disciplinary perspectives. The series, which has included more than forty published volumes, has dealt with topics such as human understanding, developmental psychopathology, concept formation, and relations between learning and development.

Following the tradition of our prior book series, this three-part volume began as a conference series. Unlike the prior volumes, this particular book is the culmination of an effort to plan a three year conference series to take stock of where the study of human development is and to consider holistically across three conferences new perspectives on human development. This has resulted in a three-part volume with more than twenty distinct chapters organized around three interrelated conference themes: cognitive development, social development, and language and communicative development. In the introductory chapter, the editors offer insights into what holds the separate parts together. As such, this book continues to represent the goals of the Jean Piaget Society in important ways by paving the road to further interdisciplinary scholarship at the frontiers of new knowledge about human development. We note with sadness that in the final stages of editing, we learned of the death of Annette Karmiloff-Smith. Always at the frontiers of interdisciplinary scholarship on human development, her writings leave a rich legacy to the study of human development and makes her contribution to this volume all the more poignant.

A large effort such as this could not be done without the assistance of many. We particularly want to thank our collaborators who assisted in the conceptualization and convenings that paved the way for this volume: Stephanie M. Carlson (cognitive development), Cecilia Wainryb and Na'ilah Saud Nasir (social development), and Katherine Nelson (language and communicative development). These individuals helped identify important new directions in developmental research and theory, provided crucial logistical support, and contributed in important ways to the exciting discussions that emerged at the meetings. In addition, we are grateful for the wise council and support of the current and past presidents of the Jean Piaget Society, including Cynthia Lightfoot, Philip David Zelazo, and Geoffrey Saxe, whose support in planning and implementing the three-year linked conference was critical to our efforts. In addition, the conceptualization of the meetings was substantially improved thanks to the work of the conference planning committee, and in particular we single out Larry Nucci's feedback and leadership. We found feedback from members who attended all three conferences valuable to our thinking. Publications committee members and several anonymous reviewers went beyond the call of duty in providing peer reviews on tight turn-around. Cambridge University Press was helpful from start to finish, with David Repetto taking a risk on the volume idea and Emma Collison, Jeevitha Baskaran, and Claudia Bona-Cohen willing to help us through the final phase of editing. Closer to home, each of us was aided by a remarkable fleet of students who attended to the details in the final months of editing, including Jessica Carr, Nicole Stucke, and Jacqueline Jimenez-Maldonado.

1 Developmental Processes, Levels of Analysis, and Ways of Knowing: New Perspectives on Human Development

Nancy Budwig, Elliot Turiel, and Philip David Zelazo

This volume, with three parts, addresses fundamental issues in the study of human development. Typically, theories of human development are framed in terms of either/ or, mutually exclusive alternatives such as: what is the source of development – nature or nurture? Is development characterized by quantitative or qualitative changes? Is there one universal course of development, or are there many that differ by cultural context or even unique personal and environmental circumstances? Developmental theorists have also struggled with defining the relations between biology, psychology, and social-cultural context, often reducing psychological function of the person either to biological functioning or to conditioning by the sociocultural context. These discussions have also played out in slightly different ways for different areas of human development – whether cognitive, social, or pertaining to language and communicative development.

Over the last two decades, with the growth of developmental neuroscience, epigenetics, and embryology, as well as the creation of evolutionary developmental biology (evo-devo) and cultural psychology, more complex ways of ways of understanding development have emerged that force developmental psychologists to reconsider these questions and transcend the dichotomies traditionally offered as solutions. Indeed, it becomes increasingly common – and even required – for developmental psychologists to transcend their traditional disciplinary boundaries and consider evidence and collaborate with colleagues from neighboring disciplines. In this manner, old questions are reformulated. The developmental organism is nowadays seen as a relational matrix with different levels of functioning, each subject to a multitude of influences that operate in different timescales. At the same time, technological and societal changes (globalization) raise new questions that call for new and often practical answers. While shifts have been occurring, again these have not necessarily played out in the same ways in different areas of developmental research, and little discussion has occurred to examine commonalities and differences in such considerations.

It is for these reasons that this book addresses a pressing need in the field of human development. Periodically, the cumulative research evidence and shifts in the technological landscape require entire fields of scientific study to step back and assess where the field is headed, and how potential new directions extend, modify, or move entirely away from historical paradigms. In recent years the emergence of the neurosciences and genetics, advances in the computational power of computers, and rapid changes in our ability to study human development around the globe, among other factors, have caused the study of human development to enter a phase of rapid change requiring such a period of reflection and reassessment.

This book addresses these issues in a comprehensive way that structures the discussion of contemporary research and theory by following the core paradigms of developmental inquiry across the three primary substantive foci of the field: cognition, social development, and language and communicative development. The theoretical lines of argument include the foundational core of developmental science: positivism, constructivism, nativism, and cultural psychology.

Part 1: Cognitive Development

While all aspects of human development are being reconceptualized, cognition serves as an excellent example with which to begin this series, in part because the study of cognition was the first to be substantially transformed by the emergence of new technologies and techniques (e.g., for studying complex interactions among genes and environment, for measuring neural activity in children, for measuring cognitive development across the lifespan, and for modeling complex cognitive changes). Research on cognitive development has entered an era of unprecedented pluralism, and the range of topics, methods, and theoretical approaches is staggering. New questions are being asked: How does environment, including culture, interact with genes and behavior to yield a developing person? What is the role of intentional, goal-directed processes, such as executive function skills, in cognitive development, and how might these skills affect other aspects of development? How can we capture complex relations among processes occurring at multiple levels of analysis, across multiple timescales?

Formal models are increasingly needed to characterize the wide variety of potentially interacting influences on cognition and cognitive development that are now being identified, and these models provide a powerful tool for generating empirical predictions and interpreting empirical results. In Chapter 2, Shultz describes novel ways of modeling cognitive development computationally. In particular, he reviews research using *constructive* neural networks to simulate phenomena in cognitive development. Constructive neural networks involve learning/developmental algorithms that allow the networks to grow in representational and computational power. Like the brain, these networks grow in complexity in the process of problem-solving, adapting to challenges. In these networks, knowledge is depicted in terms of patterns of neural activation, and the process of cognitive development occurs with age and experience via two mechanisms: connection weight adjustment (akin to synaptic potentiation) and hidden unit recruitment (akin to synaptogenesis and neurogenesis). It is this latter feature that allows constructivist learning algorithms to construct increasingly complex networks as needed in order to adapt to the environment and develop. Shultz reviews a rich set of studies, addressing developmental changes in language acquisition, math, learning, theory of mind, and performance in various Piagetian tasks, showing that constructive neural networks capture the cognitive developmental data better than fully designed static neural networks and symbolic rule-based systems.

Pascual-Leone and Johnson (Chapter 5) also provide an excellent illustration of the value of formal modeling of the mechanisms of developmental change. Like Piaget, they argue that problem-solving ("invention") is the real driver of cognitive development – the active synthesis of new schemes out of old schemes, resulting in novel cognition or behavior. In their organismic-causal modeling of problem-solving, Pascual-Leone and Johnson show how new schemes emerge from organismic processes and demonstrate the value of formulating models from the perspective of an individual's cognitive processes, such as the executive processes (*organismic schemes*) that vary in (metasubjective) complexity because they are self-constructed hierarchical coordinations of existing schemes.

Bardikoff and Sabbagh (Chapter 4) also address developmental changes in top-down, goal-directed processing, and focus specifically on the development across childhood, adolescence, and early adulthood of executive function skills, the attention-regulation skills that allow for shifting (or cognitive flexibility), updating (maintaining and manipulating information in working memory), and inhibition (aka inhibitory control of attention and behavior). From the perspective of the influential Interactive Specialization model of brain development (Johnson, 2011), Bardikoff and Sabbagh review behavioral evidence and show that it clearly reveals the differentiation of executive function performance from a unitary construct, to a two-factor construct, and finally to a three-factor construct, with the differentiation of the updating component between 6 and 10 years, and separation of inhibition and shifting between 11 and 15 years.

Bardikoff and Sabbagh (Chapter 4) then present a careful review of the neurodevelopmental literature, showing a remarkably close correspondence between the differentiation of executive function and the differentiation of specific neural networks underlying them. For example, in early childhood – when executive function skills are undifferentiated, and correlations among all three aspects of executive function are high – children rely heavily on the same network of regions, centered on ventrolateral prefrontal cortex, during all three types of executive function task. When the updating component separates itself from a combined inhibition-shifting factor, between the ages of 6 to 10 years, the neural areas recruited during updating tasks undergo *quantitative* changes, including increases in the focalization of activation, and *qualitative* changes involving longer range connections that make the neural correlates of updating distinct from areas important for both inhibition and shifting.

Research on executive function illustrates the simultaneous consideration of multiple levels of analysis, including multiple levels of cognitive process (automatic vs. controlled; reactive vs. reflective) and multiple levels of function (from behavior to brain to genes), all considered over developmental time. Lickliter (Chapter 6) adds an evolutionary level of analysis to his consideration of developmental change as an organismic process. Indeed, Lickliter describes an important shift in thinking about evolution, a move away from the neo-Darwinian view, with its emphasis on random genetic variation and natural selection, and toward a new view that focuses on epigenetic processes contributing to both individual development and evolutionary change. This new view aims to capture the complexity of the bidirectional interactions that occur between organism and environment, that yield individual developmental changes as well as transgenerational effects on physiology and behavior, and that produce both stability and variability in developmental and evolutionary timescales. Lickliter illustrates the need for this view using a variety of keen examples.

Research on cognitive development has also begun to consider a wide range of interactions between cognition and other aspects of human function, including social processes (Kang Lee, Quinn, & Heyman), culture (Carol Lee), and technology (Kahn & Shen). Kang Lee, Quinn, and Heyman (Chapter 3) address the cognitive developmental foundations of a topic traditionally studied by social psychologists: implicit racism, which refers to unconscious racial stereotypes, prejudices, and discriminatory behaviors. The authors propose a novel Perceptual-Social Linkage Hypothesis to explain the emergence and development of racial bias as a consequence of early experience with own- versus other-race faces. Importantly, they also shed light on new ways to prevent or attenuate implicit racism. Their research found that Chinese children between 4 and 6 years who were trained to recognize other-race African faces showed a reduction in racial bias, compared to children who were trained to recognize same-race faces.

Carol Lee (Chapter 8) emphasizes the role of context in development, in particular the interplay between cultural contexts and cognitive development at multiple levels of analysis. She describes a Cultural Modeling framework that incorporates three interdisciplinary themes: (1) the intertwining of culture and biology in human development, (2) adaptation through multiple pathways, and (3) interdependence across levels of context. In her chapter, Lee considers the implications of this framework for education in both formal and informal settings, and underscores the need for a more nuanced approach that avoids normative assumptions, takes seriously the complexity of human development, and recognizes the wide variety of contextually appropriate ways in which it may unfold.

One particular context that has become more pervasive in recent years is that of technology, including the creation of social robots. Kahn and Shen (Chapter 7) review data on human interactions with a particular social robot (Robovie), who/that was controlled remotely, a Wizard of Oz–style technique, and spoke with a natural-sounding feminine voice. Their research shows that after a brief (15 minute) interaction with Robovie, a majority of children and adolescents believed that Robovie had mental states, was a social being, deserved fair treatment, and should not be harmed psychologically. They did not, however, believe that Robovie had free will or was entitled to her/its own liberty or civil rights. The authors argue that social robots of the near future will not map onto one of the traditional ontological categories of person vs. machine, and that a new, intermediate ontological category is currently being created.

Part 2: Social Development

This section of the volume focuses on social development and covers the main theoretical perspectives in the literature, but with presentation of contemporary analyses that include convergence on key topics and provide potential ways of finding commonalities within the context of differences in theories. Traditionally, explanations of social development have revolved around differences in the roles of environment, biology, reasoning, and emotions, as well as differing conceptions of processes of social interactions and development. Whereas there still exist differences in emphases on environment (including culture), biological influences, and the role of reasoning, recent research and theorizing has taken more nuanced approaches to each of the topics that can result in better integration among them. All the chapters in this section take the approach that development entails the formation of complex systems of thought and involves multifaceted social interactions.

First, consider theory and research on socialization that has often taken the perspective that social development is primarily due to cohesive parental practices resulting in the acquisition of standards and behaviors consistent with societal expectations. By contrast, Grusec (Chapter 10) presents a socialization perspective that draws distinctions among different types of social interactions within families involving a variety of parental goals and child outcomes differentiated by domains. In her perspective, parent–child interactions are bidirectional and include a significant role for children in processes of socialization.

A somewhat different approach to bi-directionality, taken by those influenced by Piagetian theory, views development as a process of constructing social and moral thought out of social interactions in early life. These include positions taken by Turiel and Gingo; Liben; and Wainryb and Recchia. The chapter by Wainryb and Recchia (Chapter 11) makes direct connections with Grusec's formulations. These authors carefully analyze a corpus of data based on records of conversations between parents and children – demonstrating the back-and-forth and mutual influences that typically occur between parents and their children. Turiel and Gingo delve into (1) the origins of children's social development in direct, everyday social experiences starting in early life, (2) the different domains of judgment developed, and (3) how decisions in social situations involve coordination of different considerations and goals from different domains.

As also considered in all the chapters, cultural contexts need to be part of analyses of social interactions and development. Culture is a central topic, in a variety of ways, in several chapters. Shweder, a proponent of cultural psychology, traces contemporary work on moral psychology to the philosophical writings of Montaigne (16th century) and Sidwick (19th century). Shweder proposes a developmental theory of social intelligence, including forms of rationality, connected with customary ways of life and attachment to social norms in cultural groups. Several other chapters also address the question of culture and social development. Chiao (Chapter 17) examines cultural orientations in relation to neuroscientific findings. She considers evidence pertaining to cultural and genetic influences on the developing brain during adolescence. In her analyses of gender development, Liben combines a constructivist-relational view of development with ecological developmental theories that also account for cultural contexts. Liben takes a cultural perspective on gender stereotypes that can entail prejudices as well.

Liben's prescriptions for the design of interventions and social policies to counteract the forces of gender stereotyping implicitly include a critical perspective on aspects of cultural practices contributing to unfairness to females. Critical perspectives of this sort imply that cultural orientations and practices can be evaluated from moral points of view, and that cultures cannot be adequately defined as forming agreed-upon, shared meanings. Four of the chapters in this section also analyze the heterogeneity of cultures, including the inequalities and injustices embedded in them. Spencer (Chapter 15), and McKinney de Royston and Nasir (whose perspective includes a Vygotskian historical-cultural view), each address social problems in their chapters, as well as perspectives bearing on social privilege and injustices associated with race. One focus of Spencer's analysis is on the ways Critical Race Theory addresses social inequalities, privilege, and racism. As is evident in the title of the chapter by McKinney de Royston and Nasir (Chapter 14), development and learning processes require greater attention to inequalities and injustices in ecologies that are "racialized." Accordingly, these authors maintain that development and learning, particularly in schools, need to be understood in accord with how they are affected by how race organizes societies. In a related fashion, Way and Rogers (Chapter 13), as well as Turiel and Gingo (Chapter 12), go beyond development as accommodation to or acceptance of cultural norms and practices, to considerations of acts of opposition and resistance. They maintain that in the process of social and moral development individuals come to understand societal inequities, patterns of social domination, and power relations involving unfairness and, thereby, form ways of challenging and attempting to change norms and practices.

Part 3: Language and Communicative Development

The final section of this volume on new perspectives on human development focuses on the topic of language and communicative development and is intended to draw the series of three interrelated sections to a conclusion. In addition to covering this area of theory and research, the chapters on language and communicative development aim to address themes that have emerged across the volume, thereby helping gain perspective on studying human development more broadly.

Almost all children learn at least one language during the first five years of life that then becomes a central tool for cognitive and social development. Over recent decades the study of the diverse processes involved in these developments has been intense. New technologies and methodologies, and interdisciplinary research – whether in the areas of evolution, neuroscience, or cultural anthropology – have significantly strengthened our understanding of these complex processes. Furthermore, it is widely agreed that the study of language and communicative development must be viewed holistically, in contrast to text-book depictions where language development is described in terms of additive models of development using a metaphor of building blocks with sounds becoming words which then link into sentences.

The focus of this third section is on the intricate relations amongst language, mind, and culture and the roles that language and communicative development play in the human capacity for learning from others and building complex conceptual systems. The authors in this section collectively take the stance that the development of language and communication is best conceptualized as a driving force in the process of these essential aspects of human activities, as well as in the social construction of everyday interactions and the support of advances in knowledge.

Language and communicative skills are not achieved within one major period of development – infancy, early childhood, childhood, or adolescence – but instead span the entire range of human development, including adulthood. Although a handful of chapters cannot encompass all of the developments taking place over this broad range, the attempt here is to highlight some of the major problems of their development in each of these four major developmental periods. It also includes comparison with the development of individuals whose development in these areas is delayed or atypical.

There are many views today about the evolution of language, which has been a "hot" subject since the 1990s, with some people taking a more Chomskian view (e.g., Longa, 2013) and others a more Piagetian one (e.g., Christiansen & Chater, 2008). Jablonka (Chapter 18) outlines a view of language evolution that tends toward the Piagetian end of the spectrum, describing the evolution of linguistic communication in terms of phenotypic accommodation mediated through cultural evolution and followed by genetic accommodation.

Karmiloff-Smith (Chapter 20) examines a topic that has been central to both linguistic and conceptual development – namely, domain-specific vs. domain-general explanations of human development – and suggests a third alternative: the domain-relevant explanation underlying neuroconstructivism, which allows for a greater degree of constrained flexibility. She argues that a developing organism needs to be both constrained and flexible (Karmiloff-Smith, 1992, 1994), and achieving that dynamic balance is what ontogenesis is all about.

Bogdan (Chapter 19) argues for the importance of meaning-making as central in the acquisition of intuitive psychology. He suggests that the ability to represent and interpret one's own and others' mental states guides appropriate reactions by way of thought, speech, and action. New pressures are exerted on the young child's goal strategies, and this leads the child to scaffold new cognitive abilities. Using patterns he has called templates, matrices, assemblies, escalators, and infrastructures, Bogdan argues for the central role of meaning-based communication, word learning, and predicative communication in the process.

Nelson (Chapter 21) examines the important role that language and culture have played in the development of the human mind, highlighting how cultural changes in semiotic and communicative tools have impacted human development. She argues that current laboratory research would be well served by being supplemented by naturalistic studies of individual children over time, as well as by larger longitudinal samples that can address both cultural and individual patterns of development, noting the importance not only of time course (slower vs. faster acquisition) but also of the range of different pathways of development.

Examining pre-school-age children's sensitivity to patterning in the languages they speak, Kyratzis (Chapter 22) views language as both developing in terms of forms and functions, and also as a tool for development. In the first part of her chapter, she reviews a significant amount of literature showing how children first use language forms in particular social contexts that are meaningful from their point of view. To this extent, preschool and school-age children's social and cognitive development is deeply connected to their patterning of linguistic structure. A second section examines the dynamic unfolding of meaning-making as children co-construct meaning and build grammatical constructions collaboratively in their everyday discourse.

Daiute (Chapter 23) follows up on the claim made in previous chapters of the ways in which language, social, and cognitive development interact across the lifespan. Her focus examines the use of language by adolescents and young adults as they interact in increasingly complex environments, often using multiple languages to mediate conflict, migration, and unequal access to resources. She argues that by this point, typically developing humans have mastered basic linguistic skills, and that adolescents and adults come to use language to integrate cognitive processes in social context.

Taken together, the chapters in this section of the volume highlight the ways language learning and learning in and through language are too often left out of discussions of human development and yet are one of the most important hallmarks of human development.

Orientation to the Volume: From Past to Future

What new perspectives and directions are brought to bear in this volume? A collective reading of the chapters in this edited volume lead us to propose three areas of focus: first, an emphasis on complex developmental processes; second, an examination of multiple levels of analyses and their interactions across developmental time; and third, a consideration of ways of knowing and the implications of these ways for the interdisciplinary study of knowledge and development. We turn to each of these now.

Emphasis of Psychological and Developmental Processes

One reason the contributions provide new directions is that the emphases in the volume, as a whole, are on analyses of complex psychological and developmental processes – as contrasted with all-too-common concerns with development as adjustment to social and environmental conditions, automatic hard wired reactions, and assessments of skills, capacities, or achievements based on numerical, evaluative comparisons among individuals.

There have long been calls for greater attention to psychological and developmental processes. For instance, in 1931 Kurt Lewin maintained that too much of the field of psychology was tied to evaluative comparisons (which he referred to as valuative concepts) of better and worse or superior and inferior as measured by performance on psychological tests. As he put it (Lewin, 1931, p. 143), "Psychology speaks of the 'errors' of children, of 'practice,' of 'forgetting,' thus classifying whole groups of processes according to the value of their products, instead of the nature of psychological processes involved."

Perhaps the most common application of value of products was the ubiquitous formulation and use of tests aimed at yielding an intelligence quotient (IQ) in place of the study of processes of "intelligence." In contemporary times the approach of "valuative concepts" is more likely to be applied to what are proposed to be relatively stable individual differences in characteristics such as self-control and grit (see Turiel, Chung, & Carr, 2016). The contrast between, on the one hand, the use of IQ tests as valuative concepts or as numerical, evaluative comparisons, and, on the other hand, psychological processes were clearly evident in the work of Jean Piaget. Early in his career, while studying in a laboratory working on the Binet-Simon tests of intelligence, Piaget came to the conclusion that such tests failed to provide understandings of or explanations for the nature of intelligence – that is, of the epistemological bases of children's concepts or of the mechanisms and processes *of curiosity.* of thinking. As opposed to the simple counting of wrong and right answers on tests, Piaget sought to investigate the ways children arrived at their answers. His research was always aimed at explaining processes of thinking and the developmental transformations in those processes. In a variety of ways the contributors to this volume carry those goals forward.

Several long-standing issues regarding human development are considered by most of the contributors. These include biology, environment, constructivism, socialization, domain generality and specificity, culture, reasoning, emotion, and parenting. What is new is that the contributors approach these issues from the perspective of analyzing psychological and developmental processes, couch their analyses in epistemological considerations, and examine relations among these variables. The emphasis on epistemology entails careful consideration of definitions of the constructs analyzed in relation to psychological processes. This results in characterizations of children as active in their relations with the physical and social environments. For example, in the context of the different approaches to social development represented in one section, children are no longer regarded as solely adjusting or accommodating to the social environment. Dynamic explanations of culture, parenting, and social relationships, and epigenetic and/or neurological processes, characterize the contributions.

Levels of Analysis

A common theme in this volume, and in developmental research more generally, is a movement away from what Overton (2010) calls a "split metatheory," with its emphasis on traditional dualisms (e.g., mind/brain, cognition/emotion, individual/society, nature/nurture), and a movement toward a more holistic, developmental systems view of human beings as dynamic, multidimensional phenomena that are simultaneously behavioral and neural, cognitive and emotional, individual and social. This systems view aims to understand the way in which processes operating at many levels of analysis (cultural, social, cognitive, neural, and molecular) work together to yield human behavior and changes in human behavior (Zelazo, 2013). Consideration of multiple levels of analysis highlights the extent to which the effect of any particular influence on psychological development depends on the context in which it occurs, and it reveals the need to capture multiple, simultaneous, and interacting causal influences on behavior and development that are often reciprocal in nature.

The chapters in this volume address a number of distinct levels at which human function can be analyzed: genetic, epigenetic, neural, cognitive, conceptual, behavioral, linguistic, social, cultural, economic. Research on cognitive, social, and language development have all illustrated the importance of multiple levels of analysis by allowing us to observe how children's behavior co-occurs with dynamic patterns of neural activation, and how behavioral development co-occurs with systematic reorganizations in neural function and structure, and is influenced by experience.

When researchers began more routinely to assess phenomena at multiple levels of analysis, and started deliberately to vary the boundary conditions of traditional paradigms (e.g., examining cognitive or social development across cultures [Chiao; Lee; Shweder; and Turiel & Gingo, this volume] or across species [Lickliter, this volume]), it became more obvious that psychological phenomena may be influenced by variations or manipulations at different levels of analysis. Indeed, such interactions among influences are pervasive. Developmental science has a sad history of ignoring unmanipulated boundary conditions (e.g., sociohistorical context, culture, and ethnicity) and making generalizations based on limited, unrepresentative samples and a limited number of assessments in particular situations that turned out be unfounded. But research has now revealed, convincingly, that context matters.

Ways of Knowing: Coming Full Circle in the Interdisciplinary Study of Knowledge and Development

The focus on process and levels of analysis begs the question of whether and how our ways of knowing about human development have stayed the same and how the perspectives expressed in this volume have developed. The question itself is not a new one – for instance, in the early 1980s, Overton (1983) edited a volume in the Jean Piaget Society book series on the relation between social and cognitive development and much focus was placed on the question of changes in our ways of knowing about social and cognitive development. While the question may not be new, there are some subtle shifts in the answers taken in the chapters in the current edited volume.

In Overton's volume, authors debated whether separate development mechanisms are needed and whether differences in ways of knowing in these two domains could be isolated. First, it is important to recognize that for the most part there was consensus that these represented separate but related domains of study. Second, there was a sense that they were related in important ways. Debated was whether cognitive development paved the way for social understanding, whether social relations were necessary for cognitive development, or whether they were separate domains. Language and communication received little explicit focus.

In the present volume, one finds a more nuanced discussion that suggests that, for the most part, authors view the cognitive social, and language division more as one of different lenses to otherwise deeply related areas. In short, the chapters in the current volume take a more relational or systems perspective of development. Many of the chapters could have easily been placed in multiple sections (see, for instance, Lee's discussion of cognitive, social, and language development). Furthermore, the way cognitive, social, and language development are connected is nuanced, and the mechanisms proposed are equally complex. In the section on cognitive development, Lickliter (Chapter 6, p. 93) argues:

> Contrary to the still commonplace assumption that phenotypic stability is "biologically" based and phenotypic variability is "experience" based, a growing body of evidence indicates that there are not separate or distinct processes responsible for stability on the one hand and variation on the other. Both are the products of the bidirectional traffic among the various networks, resources, and levels of the organism-environment system…

Similarly, Jablonka (Chapter 18, p. 364) sums up her argument by stating: "Taking this view means that in order to understand the complex evolution of human linguistic communication we need to consider cultural evolution, behavioral transmission through social learning and through self-reconstructing hormonal modulations, epigenetic inheritance, and genetic inheritance."

Over the years, a second way the modern study of human development has dramatically changed is in the recognition of the importance of the need to study human development – whether cognitive, social, or language development – within context. This perspective involves more than looking at human interaction in context or studying within- and between-cultural variation in human development. Rather, the more holistic, relational perspectives found in this volume have not only shifted the study of human development within everyday practice and experience, but simultaneously look at those experiences as a place for bidirectional developmental influences to take place. As Wainryb and Recchia (Chapter 11, p. 184) note when speaking of moral development:

> But conversations that parents and children have about moral experiences not only illustrate but constitute the critical features of the moral socialization process as we have defined it – its bidirectional quality, the prevalence of interpretations and meaning-making, the coexistence of multiple goals and perspectives, and its embeddedness within a relational context. Further, conversations are an essential vehicle through which the business of moral socialization is transacted.

As the study of human development has integrated more relational and dynamic perspectives, we would argue that the boundaries and ways of knowing of neighboring disciplines have informed theory and research in human development. While the questions about human development have been enduring, the authors in this volume have increasingly drawn upon work outside psychology per se, turning to advances in philosophy, evolutionary biology, neuroscience, and cultural anthropology. While early on in the field neighboring disciplines influenced theoretical perspectives, in these chapters authors have drawn upon tools and ways of knowing from those interdisciplinary areas as well.

Variability and stability are fundamental aspects of the developmental process. We believe this volume both connects with the rich past and simultaneously begins to chart a way forward by illustrating more complex and nuanced advances in the study of human development. The cover of this volume depicts an original work of art painted by Philip David Zelazo entitled *E Unum Pluribus*. The abstract representations suggest not only the multiple developmental perspectives captured in this volume, but also a central challenge for the study of development – namely, that out of many form one, and vice versa.

References

Christiansen, M. H., & Chater, N. (2008). Language as shaped by the brain. *Behavioral and Brain Sciences, 31*, 489–558.

Johnson, M. H. (2011). Interactive specialization: A domain-general framework for human functional brain development? *Developmental Cognitive Neuroscience, 1*, 7–21.

Karmiloff-Smith, A. (1992). *Beyond modularity: A developmental perspective on cognitive science*. Cambridge, MA: MIT Press/Bradford Books.

Karmiloff-Smith, A. (1994). Transforming a partially structured brain into a creative mind. *Behavioral Brain Sciences, 17*(4), 732–745.

Lewin, K. (1931). The conflict between Aristotelian and Galilean modes of thought in contemporary psychology. *Journal of General Psychology, 5*, 141–177.

Longa, V. M. (2013). The evolution of the faculty of language from a Chomskyan perspective: Bridging linguistics and biology. *Journal of Anthropological Sciences, 91*, 1–48.

Overton, W. (1983). (Ed.). *The relationship between social and cognitive development*. Hillsdale, NJ: Lawrence Erlbaum Publishers.

Overton, W. F. (2010). Life-span development: Concepts and issues. In W. F. Overton (Ed.) & R. M. Lerner (Ed. in Chief), *The handbook of life-span development, Vol. 1: Cognition, biology, and methods* (pp. 1–29). Hoboken, NJ: John Wiley & Sons, Inc.

Turiel, E., Chung, E., & Carr, J. A. (2016). Struggles for equal rights and social justice as unrepresented and represented in psychological research. In S. S. Horn, M. D. Ruck, & L. S. Liben (Eds.), *Equity and justice in developmental science. Advances in Child Development and Behavior* (J.B. Benson, Series Ed.), *Vol. 50*.

Zelazo, P. D. (2013). Developmental psychology: A new synthesis. In P. D. Zelazo (Ed.), *Oxford handbook of developmental psychology (Vol. 1: Body and mind; Vol. 2: Self and other)* (pp. 3–12). New York: Oxford University Press.

PART I

Cognitive Development

(Edited by Philip David Zelazo and Stephanie M. Carlson)

2 Constructive Artificial Neural-Network Models for Cognitive Development

Thomas R. Shultz

This chapter provides an overview of research using constructive neural networks to simulate phenomena in cognitive development. These algorithms are described, and their application to developmental issues and phenomena are reviewed in both breadth and some depth. When contrasted against fully designed static neural networks or symbolic rule-based systems, constructive neural networks provided superior coverage of the psychological data. Theoretical implications are discussed and constructive networks are situated within the current computational-developmental literature.

Algorithms for Constructive Learning

To simulate cognitive development, we use neural networks inspired by some of what is known about brain computation and by the mathematics of statistical mechanics. There is a network of units and connection weights between the units. Each unit computes the weighted sum of inputs coming from other units and then outputs an activity number, which is a non-linear, sigmoidal function of the weighted sum of inputs. That activity signal is then sent to other units running this same program. As in many other neural-network learning algorithms, the connection weights between units are modified in order to reduce network error. Unlike most other neural learners, our algorithms also construct the network, something that could be interesting to neo-Piagetian constructivists.

Figure 2.1 shows a sample network created by the sibling-descendant cascade-correlation (SDCC) algorithm. The network starts with only input and output vectors, i.e., with no hidden units between them. The arrows represent sets of connection weights. Network error is computed as the discrepancy between the activity levels the network actually produces on its outputs and the target values that it should have produced based on feedback from the environment. When error reduction stagnates, a new hidden unit is recruited. This algorithm determines where to put the new recruit, either on the current highest layer (i.e., as a sibling of the existing units on that layer) or on its own higher layer (i.e., as a descendant) (Baluja & Fahlman, 1994). Sibling and descendant candidates compete with each

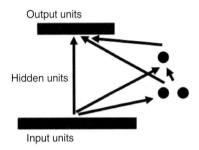

Figure 2.1. *Sample SDCC network.*

other to be recruited. Input weights to the candidates are modified to increase the absolute value of correlations with current network error. When these correlations stagnate, the algorithm selects the candidate unit whose activation values have the highest absolute correlation with network error. The candidate that best tracks network error across the target training patterns is recruited, while the other candidate units and their weights are pruned away. The recruit's input weights are frozen, and the algorithm returns to training output weights (those entering the output units) to learn how to use the new recruit to reduce network error. This cycle of error reduction (output phase) and recruitment (input phase) continues until the problem is learned. The sample network in Figure 2.1 recruited 2 units on the first layer and 1 on a second layer. The original cascade-correlation (CC) algorithm, from which SDCC is derived, instead installs each new recruit on its own layer, always creating maximally deep networks (Fahlman & Lebiere, 1990).

In contrast to most neural learners that start learning every new problem from scratch, an important innovation allows for the saving of all previous networks, which then become candidates for recruitment (Shultz & Rivest, 2001). These previously learned networks compete with each other and with single hidden units whenever error reduction is stalled. This is called knowledge-based cascade-correlation (KBCC), and it has been found to speed learning on many problems and to make learning possible on some others (Shultz & Rivest, 2001; Shultz, Rivest, Egri, Thivierge, & Dandurand, 2007). Knowledge-based cascade-correlation captures the pervasive tendency of humans to build on their existing knowledge when learning something new.

Developmental Issues

Among the developmental issues explored with these constructive algorithms are knowledge representation and processing, stage progressions, transition mechanisms, the distinction between learning and development, and escape from Fodor's paradox. This last issue concerns the argument, assuming a hypothesize-and-test learning algorithm, that it is impossible to learn anything that you don't already know (Fodor, 1980). Many learning algorithms get caught in this paradox, including pre-designed stationary neural networks. Constructive algorithms escape the paradox because their networks grow in representational and computational power (Shultz, 2006).

Simulated Phenomena

A wide range of developmental phenomena has been simulated with these constructive networks: Piagetian tasks, aspects of language acquisition, mathematical phenomena, several large literatures on learning, and false-belief phenomena. Constructive networks provided the only computational coverage of these phenomena or provided better coverage than other methods. Among the simulated Piagetian tasks are conservation, seriation, transitivity, and performance on the balance scale. In conservation acquisition, CC (Shultz, 1998) and SDCC (Shultz, 2006) networks covered stages, the problem size effect, length bias, screening, and the shift from perceptual to reasoned solutions. In the study of seriation, CC networks covered stages, the tendency for smaller differences between sticks to increase the difficulty of achieving a correct sort, and more success with smaller than with larger arrays (Mareschal & Shultz, 1999). In transitivity, hybrid CC/constraint-satisfaction networks simulated the serial position (ends first), distance, anchor, congruity, and age effects found in children (Shultz & Vogel, 2004). For balance-scale development, KBCC networks covered stages, the torque-difference effect (better and earlier accuracy with large than with small torque differences), faster performance on simple problems than on conflict problems, more use of the torque rule on conflict problems than on simple problems, and overlapping waves of rule-like stages (Dandurand & Shultz, 2014).

Simulated aspects of language include personal pronouns, word stress, syllable location, and simple syntax. In pronoun acquisition, CC networks simulated better performance from earlier overheard speech than with directly addressed speech (Shultz, Buckingham, & Oshima-Takane, 1994). Learning word stress, SDCC networks covered the ability of 9-month-olds to distinguish the word-stress patterns of artificial languages, by making transitive inferences from known to unknown constraints (Shultz & Gerken, 2005). Sibling-descendant cascade-correlation networks learned syllable boundaries using sonority contours and pauses, and generalized well (Shultz & Bale, 2006). Cascade-correlation (Shultz & Bale, 2001) and SDCC (Shultz & Bale, 2006) networks learned simple syntactic patterns and generalized like human infants. A hybrid competitive-learning/SDCC model demonstrated syntax learning from positive evidence alone (Shultz, Berthiaume, & Dandurand, 2010), simulating experiments with adults (Lany, Gómez, & Gerken, 2007).

Simulated mathematical phenomena involve number-size comparison, algebraic group structure, and prime-number detection. In comparing the relative size of numbers, CC networks simulated the min (easier with smaller numbers) and distance (easier when the numbers are farther apart) effects seen in children (Shultz, 2001). Contradicting the view that artificial neural networks are inherently unable to learn systematically structured relations such as those expressed by mathematical groups, both CC (Jamrozik & Shultz, 2007) and KBCC (Schlimm & Shultz, 2009) networks learned these structures very well. Knowledge-based cascade-correlation can learn groups with any number of elements by building on knowledge of previously acquired subgroups. Mathematical groups figured importantly in Piaget's description of cognitive development (Piaget, Inhelder, & Szeminska, 1999). Simulation of distinguishing between prime and composite numbers illustrated the power of knowledge-based learning (Egri & Shultz, 2006). Without recruiting knowledge of divisibility, this task is extremely difficult to learn from examples alone.

The large learning literatures covered by constructive algorithms are discrimination shift learning, concept acquisition, and habituation of attention. Virtually all of the many psychological regularities in discrimination shift learning were simulated with CC networks (Sirois & Shultz, 1998). Network predictions were tested and confirmed in further work showing how adults can be influenced to perform like preschool children on shift-learning tasks (Sirois & Shultz, 2006). In concept acquisition, SDCC networks covered the developmental shift from probabilistic to defining features (Shultz, Thivierge, & Laurin, 2008) as well as several developmental trends with prototype and exemplar effects that were considered to be contradictory (Baetu & Shultz, 2010). Both CC (Shultz & Cohen, 2004) and SDCC (Shultz, 2011) networks simulated the age shift from processing stimulus features to processing relations between features found in many studies of habituation learning with infants.

Sibling-descendant cascade-correlation networks also simulated results from an infant experiment on theory-of-mind development, as assessed in a non-verbal false-belief task (Berthiaume, Shultz, & Onishi, 2013).

Many of these simulations involved computational bake-offs against fully designed static neural networks or symbolic rule-based systems. In every such comparison, constructive neural networks provided superior coverage of the psychological data. In other cases, comparative methods had not been reported. Moving from one study to another, the only change is the input–output training patterns, reflecting the content of simulated phenomena. This pattern of coverage suggests that constructive networks provide the right sort of model for simulating, and thus understanding, cognitive development.

There is space here to summarize only two constructive-network models in any detail. One is a neo-Piagetian task on inferring relations among velocity, time, and distance in moving objects. The other concerns the tendency to spend less time and effort on tasks that are too easy or too difficult.

Inferring Velocity, Time, and Distance

These tasks require the integration of cues for moving objects, governed by the equation velocity = distance / time, originally studied by Piaget. In neo-Piagetian experiments, children were presented with information on two of these quantities and asked to infer the third (Wilkening, 1981).

Table 2.1 *Rules found in CC networks. Stage 1 for Time and Stage 3 for Velocity were predicted by the simulation and subsequently confirmed in children. The other stages had been previously found in children.*

Inference	Stage 1	Stage 2	Stage 3
Velocity	$v = d$	$v = d - t$	$v = d\,/\,t$
Time	$t = d$	$t = d - v$	$t = d\,/\,v$
Distance	$d = v + t$	$d = v + t$	$d = v\,t$

Three stages were noted, as listed in Table 2.1: (1) using only the quantity that varied positively with the quantity to be inferred, (2) adding or subtracting the two known quantities, and (3) multiplying or dividing the two known quantities. By correlating the network's (or child's) estimate of the inferred variable with these algebraic rules, rules could be diagnosed. Cascade-correlation networks captured already-documented stages and predicted others that were subsequently confirmed in psychology experiments (Buckingham & Shultz, 2000).

Such rule progressions occur naturally in constructive neural networks because of recruiting new hidden units that increase computational power. Equivalence stages (e.g., time = distance; velocity = distance) emerge first because of a combination of the limited processing ability of the initial network topology and the fact that this underpowered network cannot reduce the error associated with the relations between three variables. Because velocity and time are both directly related to distance, but inversely related to each other, direct input-to-output weights cannot capture all of these relations simultaneously.

In contrast, because distance is positively related to time and velocity, direct input-to-output weights can handle both of these relations involving distance. This ensures that equivalence rules emerge from initial networks, but the inverse relation between velocity and time requires more power. Once the first hidden unit is recruited, encoding of both direct and inverse relations involving velocity and time becomes possible. For distance inferences, velocity and time inputs augment each other, yielding distance inferences that correlate with an additive rule: distance = velocity + time. For time inferences, distance input is counteracted by velocity information, yielding time inferences that correlate with a subtraction rule: time = distance – velocity. Analogously, for velocity inferences, velocity = distance – time. The first-recruited hidden unit thus enables representation of two different relations between the inputs and the output, depending on which inference is requested. Additional hidden units enable the correct multiplication rules, which are even more non-linear.

In contrast, static back-propagation networks could not capture these stage sequences (Buckingham & Shultz, 1996). Static networks with too few hidden units failed to develop the correct multiplication rules, whereas static networks with too many hidden units failed to capture the intermediate difference rules in velocity and time inferences. Indeed, there were no static network topologies that could simulate all three stages on this task.

It is noteworthy that the equivalence and additive rules are incorrect, as are many rules observed in young children. Neither verbally formulated theories nor symbolic rule-based models have explained the regular emergence of such non-normative rules. In learning to represent the three interrelated inference types, the CC algorithm proceeds by stages because it progressively recruits hidden units sufficient to integrate the three quantities of velocity, time, and distance. Other methods have not been shown to simulate these stage progressions.

Deciding Whether to Stop Learning

While extending SDCC to stop learning when progress was no longer being made, we found that we could simulate infant tendencies to do the same. Infants pay less attention to learning tasks that are too easy or too difficult, whereas they are more engaged when progress is being made (Gerken, Balcomb, & Minton, 2011; Kidd, Piantadosi, & Aslin, 2010, 2012). The extension allowed SDCC to monitor lack of progress in learning so that unproductive learning can be abandoned. Learning is abandoned when network error fails to change by more than a specified threshold for a specified number of consecutive learning cycles (Shultz & Doty, 2014; Shultz, Doty, & Dandurand, 2012). Each such learning cycle contains an output phase, in which network error is reduced, and an input phase, in which a new hidden unit is recruited (Shultz & Doty, 2014; Shultz et al., 2012). Results are shown in Figure 2.2 for two SDCC networks learning the continuous XOR problem. This problem requires a negative response when both of two inputs are above 0.5, or both below 0.5, and a positive response when one input is below 0.5 and other input is above 0.5. The network with entirely learnable patterns (light grey) continues until it masters the problem, while the network with 50% random target output in its training patterns gives up early due to stagnant error reduction.

Figure 2.3 plots the mean learning time for 20 SDCC networks on the continuous XOR problem at several levels of learnability. The inverse U shape mirrors the so-called *Goldilocks* effect found with infants: less interest in tasks that are too easy or too difficult than in tasks of intermediate difficulty. Like our networks, infants may monitor their own learning progress and quit when the task is mastered or is seen as hopelessly difficult. In either of the two latter cases, learning progress has stagnated.

A convenient feature of the continuous XOR problem is that difficulty can also be manipulated by increasing the dimensionality of the problem, while holding the correctness of the training input constant. Results are shown for 2, 3, and 4 input-space dimensions in Figure 2.4, with 100 percent learnability. Again, a Goldilocks effect is evident in that learning is more readily abandoned on very easy and very difficult versions, while learning persists at intermediate difficulty where progress

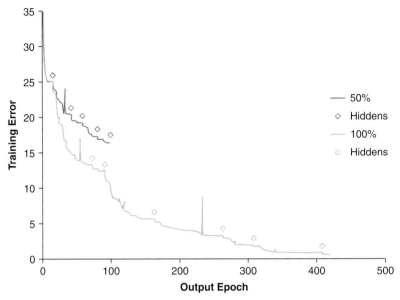

Figure 2.2. *Error reduction in two SDCC networks on the continuous XOR problem. Hidden-unit recruitments are indicated by diamond shapes. The network in light grey has training patterns that are entirely learnable, while the network in dark grey has random targets in 50% of its training patterns.*

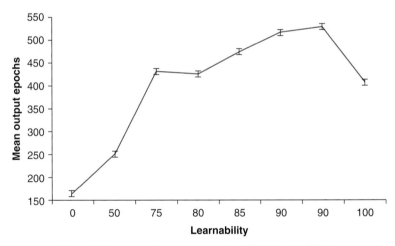

Figure 2.3. *Mean learning time (and SEs) for 20 SDCC networks on a 2-dimensional continuous XOR problem at various levels of learnability.*

is still being made. This Goldilocks effect is strong at each of 3 levels of patience. This tendency to quit on tasks that are too easy or too difficult would figure importantly in autonomous task selection, a prominent characteristic of many biological learners.

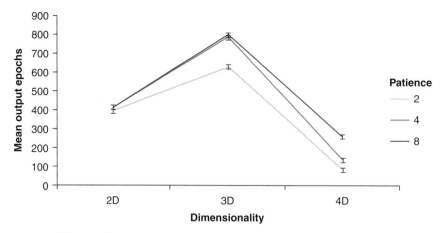

Figure 2.4. *Mean learning time (and SEs) for 20 SDCC networks on the continuous XOR problem where difficulty is manipulated by dimensionality of the input space.*

Theoretical Implications

The general learning system used in these simulations can address many of the fundamental issues of psychological development raised earlier. In terms of representation, neural networks distinguish between active and long-term memory. Active memory is represented by activation patterns of units that change rapidly depending on fluctuating network inputs. Long-term memory is represented by connection weights between units that change on a slower time scale as a result of learning.

Knowledge is processed as neural activation that is passed across network layers. Input units describe problems to the network. Activations of hidden units are updated layer by layer, creating an activation pattern on the network's outputs representing a response to the input.

These processes change with age and experience via two mechanisms: connection weight adjustment, implemented in brains as synaptic potentiation, and hidden unit recruitment, implemented in brains as synaptogenesis and neurogenesis, both driven by learning pressures (Shultz, Mysore, & Quartz, 2007). Regular sequences of stages can be explained in terms of environmental regularities in training, continual adjustment in connection weights (learning), and occasional increases in computational power (development). This implements a constructivist theory in which later, complex notions build on and refine earlier, simpler ones.

Still deeper connections can be made to several of Piaget's key theoretical ideas, as shown in Table 2.2, providing a novel neuro-computational account of Piaget's prescient verbal formulations (Shultz, 2003).

Table 2.2 *Computational interpretation of key Piagetian concepts*

Piaget	Constructive networks	Commonality
Assimilation	Activation propagation	Use current knowledge only
Accommodation	Weight adjustment	Quantitative adjustment
Equilibration	Error reduction	Best effort with current ability
Equilibrium	Reduction stagnation	Temporary stability
Conflict	Network error	Disconfirming feedback
Reflective abstraction	Hidden unit recruitment	Reconceptualization

Computational Alternatives and Advantages of Constructive Networks

Computational cognitive modeling is maturing rapidly and is currently a highly competitive field with many different algorithms vying for attention. Some of the most prominent alternatives are rule-based systems (Anderson, 1993), Bayesian inference and learning (Griffiths, Kemp, & Tenenbaum, 2008), dynamic systems (Spencer, Austin, & Schutte, 2012), and deep neural networks (Hinton, Osindero, & Teh, 2006), each of which contribute significantly to understanding cognitive development. In this chapter, there is space only to discuss constructive neural networks, while acknowledging that alternative approaches may have much to offer in understanding cognitive development.

Constructive networks provide automatic network construction (Fahlman & Lebiere, 1990; Shultz & Rivest, 2001), fast and powerful learning (Shultz & Fahlman, 2010), escape from both local minima and Fodor's paradox (Shultz, 2003), simultaneous minimization of both bias and variance (Quartz, 2003; Shultz, 2006), and some neurological plausibility (Shultz, Mysore, et al., 2007). These rather abstract algorithms are far from being neurologically exact, but do provide multi-layer topologies, activation modulation via inputs, an S-shaped activation function allowing non-linear processing, both cascaded and direct connection pathways, compatibility with both neuro- and synaptogenesis, distributed representations, long-term potentiation by modification of connection weights, pruning of relatively useless neurons and synapses, concentration of growth at the newer end of networks, and neuronal recruitment for multiple tasks.

Acknowledgments

This work is supported by grants from the Natural Sciences and Engineering Research Council of Canada. It has benefitted from fruitful collaborations with Scott Fahlman, Denis Mareschal, Sylvain Sirois, François Rivest, Frédéric Dandurand, László Egri, J.-P. Thivierge, Vincent Berthiaume, Dirk Schlimm, Eric Doty, and others.

References

Anderson, J. R. (1993). *Rules of the mind*. Hillsdale, NJ: Lawrence Erlbaum.

Baetu, I., & Shultz, T. R. (2010). Development of prototype abstraction and exemplar memorization. In S. Ohlsson & R. Catrambone (Eds.), *Proceedings of the 32nd Annual Conference of the Cognitive Science Society* (pp. 814–819). Austin, TX: Cognitive Science Society.

Baluja, S., & Fahlman, S. E. (1994). Reducing network depth in the cascade-correlation learning architecture. Pittsburgh, PA: School of Computer Science, Carnegie Mellon University.

Berthiaume, V. G., Shultz, T. R., & Onishi, K. H. (2013). A constructivist connectionist model of developmental transitions on false-belief tasks. *Cognition*, *126*(3), 441–458.

Buckingham, D., & Shultz, T. R. (1996). *Computational power and realistic cognitive development Proceedings of the 18th Annual Conference of the Cognitive Science Society* (pp. 507–511). Mahwah, NJ: Erlbaum.

Buckingham, D., & Shultz, T. R. (2000). The developmental course of distance, time, and velocity concepts: A generative connectionist model. *Journal of Cognition and Development*, *1*, 305–345.

Dandurand, F., & Shultz, T. R. (2014). A comprehensive model of development on the balance-scale task. *Cognitive Systems Research*, *31–32*, 1–25. doi: http://dx.doi.org/10.1016/j.cogsys.2013.10.001

Egri, L., & Shultz, T. R. (2006). A compositional neural-network solution to prime-number testing. In R. Sun & N. Miyake (Eds.), *Proceedings of the 28th Annual Conference of the Cognitive Science Society* (pp. 1263–1268). Mahwah, NJ: Lawrence Erlbaum.

Fahlman, S. E., & Lebiere, C. (1990). The cascade-correlation learning architecture. In D. S. Touretzky (Ed.), *Advances in neural information processing systems 2* (pp. 524–532). Los Altos, CA: Morgan Kaufmann.

Fodor, J. (1980). On the impossibility of learning "more powerful" structures. In M. Piattelli-Palmarini (Ed.), *The debate between Jean Piaget and Noam Chomsky* (pp. 142–152). London: Routledge & Kegan Paul.

Gerken, L. A., Balcomb, F. K., & Minton, J. L. (2011). Infants avoid "labouring in vain" by attending more to learnable than unlearnable linguistic patterns. *Developmental Science*, *14*(5), 972–979.

Griffiths, T. L., Kemp, C., & Tenenbaum, J. B. (2008). Bayesian models of cognition. In R. Sun (Ed.), *The Cambridge handbook of computational psychology* (pp. 59–100). Cambridge, UK: Cambridge University Press.

Hinton, G. E., Osindero, S., & Teh, Y. (2006). A fast learning algorithm for deep belief nets. *Neural Computation*, *18*, 1527–1554.

Jamrozik, A., & Shultz, T. R. (2007). Learning the structure of a mathematical group. In D. McNamara & G. Trafton (Eds.), *Proceedings of the 29th Annual Conference of the Cognitive Science Society* (pp. 1115–1120). Mahwah, NJ: Lawrence Erlbaum.

Kidd, C., Piantadosi, S. T., & Aslin, R. N. (2010). The Goldilocks Effect: Infants' preference for stimuli that are neither too predictable nor too surprising. In S. Ohlsson & R. Catrambone (Eds.), *Proceedings of the 32nd Annual Conference of the Cognitive Science Society* (pp. 2476–2481). Austin, TX: Cognitive Science Society.

Kidd, C., Piantadosi, S. T., & Aslin, R. N. (2012). The Goldilocks Effect: Human infants allocate attention to visual sequences that are neither too simple nor too complex. *PLoS ONE*, *7*(5), e36399. doi: 10.1371/journal.pone.0036399

Lany, J., Gómez, R. L., & Gerken, L. (2007). The role of prior experience in language acquisition. *Cognitive Science, 31*, 481–507.

Mareschal, D., & Shultz, T. R. (1999). Development of children's seriation: A connectionist approach. *Connection Science, 11*, 149–186.

Piaget, J., Inhelder, B., & Szeminska, A. (1999). *The child's conception of geometry.* Abingdon, UK: Routledge.

Quartz, S. R. (2003). Learning and brain development: A neural constructivist perspective. In P. T. Quinlan (Ed.), *Connectionist models of development: developmental processes in real and artificial neural networks* (pp. 279–309). New York: Psychology Press.

Schlimm, D., & Shultz, T. R. (2009). Learning the structure of abstract groups. In N. A. Taatgen & H. v. Rijn (Eds.), *Proceedings of the 31st annual conference of the Cognitive Science Society* (pp. 2950–2955). Austin, TX: Cognitive Science Society.

Shultz, T. R. (1998). A computational analysis of conservation. *Developmental Science, 1*, 103–126.

Shultz, T. R. (2001). Assessing generalization in connectionist and rule-based models under the learning constraint. *Proceedings of the 23rd annual conference of the Cognitive Science Society* (pp. 922–927). Mahwah, NJ: Erlbaum.

Shultz, T. R. (2003). *Computational developmental psychology.* Cambridge, MA: MIT Press.

Shultz, T. R. (2006). Constructive learning in the modeling of psychological development. In Y. Munakata & M. H. Johnson (Eds.), *Processes of change in brain and cognitive development: Attention and performance XXI.* (pp. 61–86). Oxford, UK: Oxford University Press.

Shultz, T. R. (2011). Computational modeling of infant concept learning: The developmental shift from features to correlations. In L. M. Oakes, C. H. Cashon, M. Casasola, & D. H. Rakison (Eds.), *Infant perception and cognition: Recent advances, emerging theories, and future directions* (pp. 125–152). New York: Oxford University Press.

Shultz, T. R., & Bale, A. C. (2001). Neural network simulation of infant familiarization to artificial sentences: Rule-like behavior without explicit rules and variables. *Infancy, 2*, 501–536.

Shultz, T. R., & Bale, A. C. (2006). Neural networks discover a near-identity relation to distinguish simple syntactic forms. *Minds and Machines, 16*, 107–139.

Shultz, T. R., Berthiaume, V. G., & Dandurand, F. (2010). *Bootstrapping syntax from morphophonology Proceedings of the Ninth IEEE International Conference on Development and Learning* (pp. 52–57). Ann Arbor, MI: IEEE.

Shultz, T. R., Buckingham, D., & Oshima-Takane, Y. (1994). A connectionist model of the learning of personal pronouns in English. In S. J. Hanson, T. Petsche, M. Kearns, & R. L. Rivest (Eds.), *Computational learning theory and natural learning systems, Vol. 2: Intersection between theory and experiment* (pp. 347–362). Cambridge, MA: MIT Press.

Shultz, T. R., & Cohen, L. B. (2004). Modeling age differences in infant category learning. *Infancy, 5*, 153–171.

Shultz, T. R., & Doty, E. (2014). Knowing when to quit on unlearnable problems: another step towards autonomous learning. *Computational Models of Cognitive Processes* (pp. 211–221). London: World Scientific.

Shultz, T. R., Doty, E., & Dandurand, F. (2012). Knowing when to abandon unproductive learning. In N. Miyake, D. Peebles, & R. P. Cooper (Eds.), *Proceedings of the 34th Annual Conference of the Cognitive Science Society* (pp. 2327–2332). Austin, TX: Cognitive Science Society.

Shultz, T. R., & Fahlman, S. E. (2010). Cascade-correlation. In C. Sammut & G. I. Webb (Eds.), *Encyclopedia of Machine Learning, Part 4/C* (pp. 139–147). Heidelberg, Germany: Springer-Verlag.

Shultz, T. R., & Gerken, L. A. (2005). A model of infant learning of word stress. *Proceedings of the 27th Annual Conference of the Cognitive Science Society* (pp. 2015–2020). Mahwah, NJ: Erlbaum.

Shultz, T. R., Mysore, S. P., & Quartz, S. R. (2007). Why let networks grow? In D. Mareschal, S. Sirois, G. Westermann, & M. H. Johnson (Eds.), *Neuroconstructivism: Perspectives and prospects* (Vol. 2, pp. 65–98). Oxford, UK: Oxford University Press.

Shultz, T. R. & Rivest, F. (2001). Knowledge-based cascade-correlation: Using knowledge to speed learning. *Connection Science, 13*, 1–30.

Shultz, T. R., Rivest, F., Egri, L., Thivierge, J.-P., & Dandurand, F. (2007). Could knowledge-based neural learning be useful in developmental robotics? The case of KBCC. *International Journal of Humanoid Robotics, 4*, 245–279.

Shultz, T. R., Thivierge, J. P., & Laurin, K. (2008). Acquisition of concepts with characteristic and defining features. In B. C. Love, K. McRae, & V. M. Sloutsky (Eds.), *Proceedings of the 30th Annual Conference of the Cognitive Science Society* (pp. 531–536). Austin, TX: Cognitive Science Society.

Shultz, T. R., & Vogel, A. (2004). A connectionist model of the development of transitivity. *Proceedings of the 26th Annual Conference of the Cognitive Science Society* (pp. 1243–1248). Mahwah, NJ: Erlbaum.

Sirois, S., & Shultz, T. R. (1998). Neural network modeling of developmental effects in discrimination shifts. *Journal of Experimental Child Psychology, 71*, 235–274.

Sirois, S., & Shultz, T. R. (2006). Preschoolers out of adults: Discriminative learning with a cognitive load. *Quarterly Journal of Experimental Psychology, 59*, 1357–1377.

Spencer, J. P., Austin, A., & Schutte, A. R. (2012). Contributions of dynamic systems theory to cognitive development. *Cognitive Development, 27*, 401–418.

Wilkening, F. (1981). Integrating velocity, time, and distance information: a developmental study. *Cognitive Psychology, 13*, 231–247.

3 Rethinking the Emergence and Development of Implicit Racial Bias: A Perceptual-Social Linkage Hypothesis

Kang Lee, Paul C. Quinn, and Gail D. Heyman

Because of the unprecedented levels of globalization and immigration that characterize the world we live in today, people from different races, ethnicities, and creeds now encounter each other more frequently than in any previous periods of human history. Such encounters create unique opportunities for cultural exchange, mutual growth, and interracial harmony. However, they also offer a fertile breeding ground for racism. Indeed, racial and ethnic tensions flare up regularly in all corners of the world, even in countries where people from different races and ethnicities have lived together harmoniously for centuries.

Recognizing the seriousness of the problem, social psychologists have devoted considerable research effort over the last half-century toward understanding racism in adults and exploring effective methods to reduce it (Allport, 1954; Greenwald & Banaji, 1995; Banaji & Greenwald, 2013). Such work has produced significant advances in our understanding of the nature of racism and the social and cognitive factors contributing to its formation and consolidation. For example, one of the most important discoveries about racism since Allport's (1954) seminal work is that it takes both explicit and implicit forms. Explicit racism refers to consciously accessible stereotypes, prejudicial beliefs, and discriminatory behaviors based on race, whereas implicit racism refers to unconscious racial stereotypes, prejudices, and discriminatory behaviors (Greenwald & Banaji, 1995; Banaji & Greenwald, 2013; Dovidio, Kawakami, & Gaertner, 2002). The emergence and development of implicit racial biases are the focus of the present chapter.

A Disconnect Between Social and Developmental Psychology

Most of our understanding of the racial biases of adults comes from research conducted in the West. Findings indicate that adults display weak to no explicit racial bias when assessed by such explicit measures as self-reports, but they nonetheless show strong and robust implicit racial bias, as assessed by the Implicit Association Test (IAT) (Greenwald, McGhee, & Schwartz, 1998; Greenwald, Nosek, & Banaji, 2003; Greenwald, Poehlman, Uhlmann, & Banaji,

2009; Hardin & Banaji, 2013). One reason for the difference is that people may sometimes hide their biases on explicit measures to appear more socially desirable. Given the possibility that social desirability can mask bias in explicit measures, along with findings that implicit bias predicts actual behavior better than explicit bias, particularly in socially sensitive domains, investigators have shifted focus away from explicit measures toward more implicit ones (Cunningham, Preacher, & Banaji, 2001).

It should be noted that most of the social psychological work on racism in general and on implicit racial bias in particular has focused on adults. Although social psychologists recognize that racism must have a youthful origin, they often leave this important issue for developmental psychologists to explore. As a consequence, social psychological theories of how racism emerges at best make cursory references to existing developmental work on the issue and at worst make no contact with it at all. In other words, such theories about the origin of implicit racial bias are almost exclusively based on adult evidence without any developmental foundation. Similarly, although many developmental theories have been proposed to account for racism in childhood (Aboud, 1988, 2008, 2013; Bigler, 2013; Bigler & Liben, 2007; Killen, Rutland, & Ruck, 2011; Nesdale, 1999), they have focused nearly exclusively on explicit racial bias and naturally have little relevance to the interests that social psychologists have in implicit racial bias. This discrepancy between the research agenda of social psychology and that of developmental psychology has left major gaps in the literature, particularly in terms of the development of implicit racial bias in childhood and how it links with the implicit bias observed in adulthood. One of the consequences of this discrepancy is that intervention studies to reduce implicit racial bias have mainly involved adults without considering the ontogenetic roots of such bias. As a result, such intervention efforts have produced ecologically inconsequential effects that last only for a short period of time (Gawronski & Bodenhausen, 2006; Lai et al., 2014, 2016; Pettigrew & Tropp, 2006; Richeson & Shelton, 2003).

Development of Explicit Racial Bias

Since the writings of Allport (1954), developmental psychologists have recognized the need for deeper understanding of the developmental origins of racism and for earlier interventions so as to produce long-lasting reductions in racism. They have argued that efforts to reduce racial biases should begin in childhood, before such biases become entrenched and are accordingly difficult to change (Dunham, Baron, & Banaji, 2008; Killen et al., 2011; Xiao et al., 2015). Most of what we know about the early emergence of such biases that could inform efforts to change biases early in life comes from studies utilizing explicit measures (Aboud, 1988, 2008, 2013; Bigler, 2013; Bigler & Liben, 2007; Castelli, De Amicis, & Sherman, 2007; Raabe & Beelmann, 2011).

The developmental research on explicit racial bias has produced at least four major findings. First, preschoolers universally show strong and unabashed explicit racism. For example, when they are asked whether they would choose an own-race or other-race adult as their teacher, coach, or tour guide, preschoolers as young as 3 years of age strongly favor the own-race adult (Qian et al., 2016). This is true not only in populations that are racially highly homogenous (e.g., Jinhua, China, or Yaoundé, Cameroon) where children have almost no exposure to other-race individuals, but also in populations that are racially diverse (e.g., Chicago, United States) where children have ample exposure to other-race individuals (Baron & Banaji, 2006; Dunham, Baron, & Banaji, 2006; Kinzler, Dupoux, & Spelke, 2007). After preschool, when children start to understand social-status differences between different races, their explicit racial bias begins to be influenced by social status, showing more positive bias for a higher social status race than a lower social status race (Dunham, Chen, & Banaji, 2013; Horowitz & Horowitz, 1938; Newheiser & Olson, 2012). This effect is present regardless of whether children belong to a majority or minority race of a society (Dunham, Baron, & Banaji, 2007; Dunham, Newheiser, Hoosain, Merrill, & Olson, 2014; Olson, Shutts, Kinzler, & Weisman, 2012; Shutts, Kinzler, Katz, Tredoux, & Spelke, 2011).

Second, during middle childhood, with increased age, children's explicit racial bias declines significantly (Aboud, 2013; Bigler, 2013; Killen et al., 2011). Contrary to an interpretation that social psychology might offer, this decline does not appear to result solely from an increased desire to provide socially acceptable responses; instead, the evidence suggests that it also reflects children's increased cognitive, social, and moral sophistication. One such developmental change is that children become increasingly aware of the moral injustice of social decision-making that is based solely on a person's race (Killen, Margie, & Sinno, 2006; Rutland, Killen, & Abrams, 2010). Another such change is the increased cognitive capacity to consider multiple factors when making social decisions (Aboud, 2008; Devine, 1989). Because of these changes, children become less inclined to use race as the sole factor in determining another's favorability and more inclined to consider other factors such as common interests when making such decisions.

Third, the role of parents in socializing racial biases has been clarified by investigations which have tested Allport's (1954) hypothesis that parents play an important role in the development of their children's explicit racial bias. A recent meta-analysis showed that the explicit racial bias of parents significantly predicts explicit racial bias in children from middle childhood and beyond, with a moderate effect size (Degner & Dalege, 2013). However, these influences appear to be minimal before children reach school age.

Fourth, many studies have been conducted to reduce children's explicit racial bias with various methods. These efforts have included book reading, race-focused instructions, and immersive interracial camps (Cameron, Rutland, Brown, & Douch, 2006; Feddes, Noack, & Rutland, 2009; Hetherington, Hendrickson, & Koenig, 2014; Vezzali, Stathi, Giovannini, Capozza, & Trifiletti, 2015). Although many of these efforts have produced a statistically significant reduction in explicit racial bias, the effects have tended to be small and short-term (Aboud et al., 2012). None have produced long-lasting and ecologically meaningful effects.

Development of Implicit Racial Bias

As noted above, developmental research on racism over recent decades has focused almost exclusively on the development of explicit racial bias. It has not benefited from the explosion of social psychological research on implicit racial bias in adults and the theoretical and methodological insights that have been gained. Such neglect has left major gaps in knowledge about this important implicit form of racism in childhood. Little is known about the origin and development of implicit racial bias, factors contributing to it during development, and the linkage between implicit racial bias in childhood and in adulthood.

Recognizing these major gaps in knowledge, developmental researchers have recently begun to examine implicit racial bias in children. Using a child-friendly IAT (Baron & Banaji, 2006) adapted directly from the adult method, investigators in several labs have made three unexpected discoveries: first, children from 6 years of age onward (the youngest age that the IAT can be used) already have implicit racial bias as strong as that in adults, suggesting that implicit racial bias emerges before school age; second, as is the case with adults, school-aged children's implicit racial bias is unrelated to their explicit racial bias (Baron & Banaji, 2006; Dunham et al., 2006); and third, whereas white American children show strong implicit racial bias favoring white individuals but disadvantaging black individuals, African American and South African black children do not show racial bias against whites due to the perceived higher social status of whites in both countries (Dunham et al., 2007; Dunham et al., 2013; Dunham et al., 2014; Newheiser & Olson, 2012).

We recently used an "angry = outgroup" paradigm to test implicit racial bias in even younger participants of 4–5 years of age (Xiao et al., 2015). This paradigm has been used with adults and produced robust findings (Dunham, Baron, & Carey, 2011; Hugenberg & Bodenhausen, 2004): when adults viewed racially ambiguous faces (morphed with 50% own-race faces and 50% other-race faces) presented with angry or happy expressions, they tended to judge the faces with the angry expression as belonging to the other-race and the faces with the happy expression as belonging to one's own-race. In Xiao et al. (2015), Chinese children viewed computer-generated images of prototypical Chinese and African faces (Figure 3.1). They also saw racially ambiguous faces that were morphed between prototypical Chinese and African faces, with each race contributing 50% of the facial informa-tion. With a computer program, a moderately happy or angry expression was added to the racially ambiguous faces. Children then judged whether the happy versus angry racially ambiguous faces were Chinese or African. Results showed that Chinese preschoolers (who had never met any foreign individuals before the study) were more inclined to categorize the angry ambiguous faces as African and the happy ambiguous faces as Chinese, replicating the typical adult findings. Further, no age differences were observed in the implicit racial bias of the pre-schoolers using this particular paradigm.

To provide convergent evidence for this preschool finding, we developed a preschooler-friendly IAT-like task (the Implicit Racial Bias Test) to measure implicit racial bias in preschoolers between 3 and 5 years of age (Qian et al., 2016).

Happy ambiguous face

Typical Chinese face

Typical African face

Angry ambiguous face

Figure 3.1. *Examples of one ambiguous face displaying angry and happy affect, one typical Asian face, and one typical African face, created by FaceGen Modeller. The ambiguous face is a 50%–50% hybrid of typical African and Asian faces.*

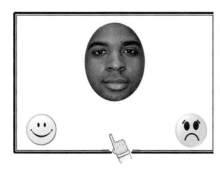

Figure 3.2. *Child's view of the screen for the Implicit Racial Bias Test. Participants respond by tapping a smile or a sad face after seeing an own-race face or an other-race face.*

This IAT-like task mimics the traditional adult IAT tasks but uses pictures (see Figure 3.2) rather than words and thus removes the requirement of lexical processing that is typical of most implicit racial bias tests for older children and adults. The task is performed on a touch screen and participants are given a happy face and a sad face as response options. Participants are asked to respond according to a simple set of rules: on congruent trials they are told to press a happy face when seeing an own-race face and a sad face when seeing an other-race face, and on incongruent trials they are told to press the happy face when seeing an other-race face and the sad face when seeing an own-race face. Response times for the two trial types are measured and conventional D scores are used to index implicit racial bias, with positive D scores indicating a bias for own-race and against other-race individuals.

Similar to Xiao et al. (2015), Qian et al. (2016) found that regardless of age, African and Chinese preschoolers between 3 and 5 years of age, like their school-aged counterparts, have strong implicit racial bias in favor of own-race individuals and against other-race individuals regardless of their social status. Black Cameroonian preschoolers showed equivalent implicit bias against Chinese and White individuals, and Chinese preschoolers showed equivalent bias against Whites and Blacks. The findings suggest that implicit racial bias emerges by 3 years of age, perhaps even in toddlerhood or infancy. It is also worth noting that the responding of the preschoolers on the implicit bias task suggests that they have yet to learn the social-status differences between different other-races in relation to their own. In addition, we observed that the preschoolers had strong and unabashed explicit racial bias in favor of own-race individuals and against other-race individuals, unlike some older school-aged children. Lastly, we did not find significant correlations between implicit and explicit racial biases, even though the preschoolers freely and openly articulated their preference for own-race individuals.

Accounting for the Developmental Emergence of Implicit Bias: The Perceptual-Social Linkage Hypothesis

The above brief review of the adult and child literature reveals significant knowledge gaps regarding the development of racism from childhood to adulthood in general and of implicit racial bias in particular. However, the available research does suggest that implicit bias is present surprisingly early in development. It is already robust by 3 years of age, implying that it must originate in toddlerhood if not earlier (Quinn et al., 2013). This early appearance suggests that we may need to re-think the developmental origins of racism and approaches to reduce it. We specifically need to know more about the emergence of implicit racial bias prior to the preschool years, and we must consider novel ways to reduce racial biases in young children so that such biases can be reduced before they have a chance to consolidate and influence behavior toward other-race people during the many years of adulthood. This latter consideration is especially important given the fact that existing educational methods to reduce implicit racial bias in adults have had only limited success (Lai et al., 2014, 2016).

Here we propose a novel Perceptual-Social Linkage Hypothesis regarding the emergence and development of racial bias. We also propose a related and unconventional approach to reduce it. Our hypothesis is rooted in the statistics of early experience with own- versus other-race faces, and advances in our understanding of the early development of perceptual processing for own- and other-race faces over the last decade.

Experientially based perceptual processing advantages for own- versus other-race faces. Head-mounted camera data and parental reports indicate that infants have more experience with own-race than other-race faces (Rennels & Davis, 2008; Sugden, Mohamed-Ali, & Moulson, 2014). It is now well established that such asymmetry in experience with own- versus other-race faces has profound perceptual consequences in face processing (for reviews, see Anzures, Quinn, Pascalis, Slater, & Lee, 2013a; Anzures et al., 2013b; Lee, Anzures, Quinn, Pascalis, & Slater, 2011). For example, when presented with own-race versus other-race face pairs, 3-month-olds from North America, Europe, Asia, and Africa who have been raised in a mono-racial environment prefer to view own-race over other-race faces (Bar-Haim, Ziv, Lamy, & Hodes, 2006; Kelly et al., 2005, 2007a). In addition, we have uncovered a perceptual narrowing phenomenon whereby 3-month-olds recognize faces from multiple races, but with increased exposure to own-race faces and lack of exposure to other-race faces, older infants from 6 to 9 months of age maintain the ability to recognize own-race faces, but gradually "lose" the ability to recognize other-race faces (Anzures, Pascalis, Quinn, Slater, & Lee, 2011; Kelly et al., 2007b, 2009). Perceptual narrowing for face race is analogous to experience-induced changes in the ability of infants to discriminate native language sounds better than non-native language sounds (Kuhl, Williams, & Lacerda, 1992; Kuhl et al., 2006; Werker, Yeung, & Yoshida, 2012). Whereas children post infancy begin to be able to recognize other-race faces, the difference in recognition between own- and other-race faces is robust and becomes stable by 5 years of age (Anzures et al., 2014).

Using eye-tracking methodology, researchers have also shown that infant scanning of own- versus other-race faces becomes gradually differentiated in the first year of life (Lee, Quinn, Pascalis, & Slater, 2013). For example, for Caucasian infants, with increased age, scanning tends to focus more on the eyes of own-race faces than on the eyes of other-race faces, which is a face scanning strategy characteristic of Caucasian adults (Wheeler et al., 2011). In contrast, Chinese infants, with increased age, become more focused on the nose of own-race faces than on the nose of other-race faces, adopting the nose-centric strategy used by Chinese adults (Liu et al., 2011; Xiao et al., 2014). Interestingly, Johnson and his colleagues (Gaither, Pauker, & Johnson, 2012) found that biracial infants scan faces differently than do mono-racial infants, suggesting an influence of biracial experience in early infancy.

Given the arguments that the differentiation of own- versus other-race faces is driven by differential experience with those faces, infants should be responsive to different training experiences with faces. Specifically, if the processing disadvantages associated with other-race faces reflect limited experience with those faces, then it should be feasible to provide infants with other-race face experiences that remove the disadvantages. To this end, we have shown that when mono-racial infants were taught to individuate other-race faces from picture books for 3 months before narrowing occurs, infants no longer displayed narrowing. In addition, the biracial study by Johnson and his colleagues mentioned earlier (Gaither et al., 2012) implies that narrowing can be prevented via exposure to biracial parents prior to 9 months of age. Furthermore, we showed that training mono-racial 10-month-old infants to individuate other-race faces for 2–3 weeks after narrowing had occurred was sufficient for them to recognize other-race faces, thereby reversing the effects of the narrowing. Although no study has examined the long-term effects of training on own- versus other-race face processing, a recent study (Hadley, Pickron, & Scott, 2015) showed that training infants at 6 months to individuate, but not categorize, monkey faces led to improved human face recognition ability at 5 years, thereby suggesting that training effects may extend beyond the target categories.

Are there downstream social consequences? A key question concerns whether and how the perceptual biases of infants for own-race versus other-race faces may be related to racial biases. In this regard, we recently found that perceptual narrowing also occurs with category formation (Quinn, Lee, Pascalis, & Tanaka, 2016): Infants at 6 months formed different categories for different classes of other-race faces based on facial physiognomy, but infants at 9 months represented own-race faces in one category and all other-race faces as a single broad "outgroup" category. In particular, Caucasian 6-month-olds responded to Caucasian, African, and Asian faces as three distinct categories; however, Caucasian 9-month-olds responded to the same faces as Caucasian versus non-Caucasian (African and Asian were treated equivalently, but distinct from Caucasian faces). What seems to matter, then, to a Caucasian 9-month-old is whether a face is Caucasian or "not Caucasian." This manner of representing face race may be the precursor of an initial race-based ingroup–outgroup partitioning of faces in which the ingroup is the face race of one's predominant experience and the outgroup consists of faces that do not match those in the ingroup. Of note is that such category narrowing is also observed in a computational simulation (Balas & Quinn, 2015) using a principal components analysis (PCA) and a presentation schedule of one African face and one Asian face for every eight Caucasian faces. As the model is trained with more and more faces in accord with this schedule, the distance between the African and Asian faces grows smaller. Here, then, may be an instance in which a lower-level process (i.e., frequency of experience with own- vs. other-race faces) drives development of a higher-level representation (i.e., one that contrasts own- with other-race faces, but not different classes of other-race faces with each other).

Differential valence and how it arises. Based on the above findings, we propose that the early asymmetry in own- versus other-race face experience will have not only perceptual consequences in terms of face recognition and categorization, but also social consequences in terms of racial biases. Like the perceptual consequences that are already emerging in the second half of the first year, we propose that the social consequences of this early asymmetry in terms of racial bias will also emerge at the same time.

More importantly, we posit that the two types of consequences are linked: the greater the perceptual processing differences between own- and other-race faces, the greater the social processing differences between own- and other-race faces. The reason the two are linked is that due to the asymmetrical exposure to own- versus other-race faces, infants not only develop an automatic tendency to categorize own-race faces into one category and other-race faces into another (Quinn et al., 2016), but also differentially associate positive or negative valence with own- versus other-race faces. This is because infants are typically exposed to own-race individuals who interact with them positively and infants themselves are in return known to interact positively with such individuals (Malatesta & Haviland, 1982); they may then generalize based on similarity and treat all own-race individuals positively. In contrast, the tendency of infants to be wary of novel social stimuli in general and strangers in particular (e.g., Feinman, 1980) may lead them to show negative treatment toward other-race individuals who are likely the most unfamiliar category of people to them. As a result, the dual tendencies to categorize faces by race and to associate positive or negative valence with familiar versus unfamiliar stimulus categories may work together to form the basis on which implicit racial bias emerges and develops.

Evidence from infants consistent with perceptual-social linkage. If there is a linkage between perceptual and social processing, then it should be possible to affect one (i.e., implicit racial bias) via the other (i.e., perceptual processing of other-race faces). Furthermore, it should be possible to prevent implicit racial bias from emerging in infancy or reduce it once it has already formed in later childhood by reducing the automatic tendency to categorize faces as own-race versus other-race. One method of doing so is training infants and children to individuate other-race faces. By training them to process other-race faces as individuals, not as a category, infants and children may be less inclined to automatically associate positive valence with own-race faces and negative valence with other-race faces. Interestingly, one added bonus of this method is that it will also increase the ability to recognize individual other-race faces and reduce the perceptual other-race recognition effect. We would also speculate that such training may have greater and longer lasting effects in reducing implicit racial bias and the other-race recognition effect if the training takes place in infancy.

Definitive evidence is lacking to support our Perceptual-Social Linkage Hypothesis, which requires a systematic and multi-year program of research to test. However, a few recent studies from our labs and those of others have provided tantalizing evidence to suggest that the hypothesis has merit.

In one study, we (Xiao et al., 2017) used an infant-friendly implicit association task to examine the emergence of implicit racial bias in the first year of life. We presented 3- to 10-month-old Chinese infants with a series of faces paired sequentially with a series of musical excerpts (Figure 3.3). In congruent conditions, infants saw own-race Chinese faces and heard happy musical excerpts or other-race African faces and sad musical excerpts. In incongruent conditions, infants saw own-race Chinese faces and heard sad music or other-race African faces and happy music. Attention toward the faces was used to measure whether the congruent or incongruent pairings were better able to maintain infant interest. Our reasoning was that if

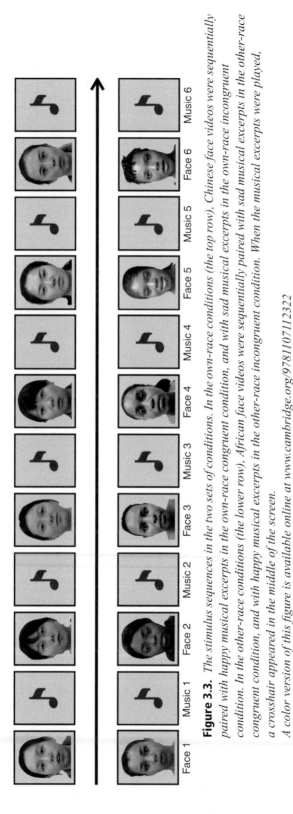

Figure 3.3. *The stimulus sequences in the two sets of conditions. In the own-race conditions (the top row), Chinese face videos were sequentially paired with happy musical excerpts in the own-race congruent condition, and with sad musical excerpts in the own-race incongruent condition. In the other-race conditions (the lower row), African face videos were sequentially paired with sad musical excerpts in the other-race congruent condition, and with happy musical excerpts in the other-race incongruent condition. When the musical excerpts were played, a crosshair appeared in the middle of the screen.*
A color version of this figure is available online at www.cambridge.org/9781107112322

infants were unbiased toward own- versus other-race faces, then they should show no difference in attention toward the two types of pairings. By contrast, according to the Perceptual-Social Linkage Hypothesis, infants should pair negative valence with the unfamiliar other-race face category and positive valence with the familiar own-race face category. On that basis, one would predict more sustained attention toward the congruent versus incongruent parings. This prediction is based on the findings that cross-domain congruency promotes infant exploration of visual and auditory stimuli, thereby making infants less likely to habituate and leading to longer maintenance of looking time (Bahrick & Lickliter, 2000; Grossmann, Striano, & Friederici, 2006; Kubicek et al., 2014).

Our results supported these predictions. We found that looking time to the faces did not differ between the two conditions at 3 months. However, with increased age, infants increasingly looked longer when own-race faces were shown with happy music and when other-race faces were shown with sad music. The transition from unbiased to biased attention began at about 6 months of age. No relation between looking time and age was found in the incongruent conditions. Thus, consistent with the Perceptual-Social Linkage Hypothesis, our findings suggest that with age infants indeed increasingly associate own-race faces with positive emotion and other-race faces with negative emotion. They imply that implicit racial bias emerges during the first year of life.

In a further investigation (Xiao et al., in press), we sought convergent evidence for the conclusions of the Xiao et al. (2017) study. Our reasoning was that if infants have positive associations with own-race individuals and negative associations with other-race individuals, then it may be more difficult for infants to learn from, and effectively "trust," other-race individuals relative to own-race individuals. In the experiment, we first introduced 7-month-olds to a situation of uncertainty where infants learned from either an own- or other-race adult whose gaze predicted the occurrence of an event in a particular location (i.e., an animal's appearance in the location) with only 50% accuracy (Figure 3.4). We introduced this condition of uncertainty because control conditions showed that when each adult was 100% accurate, infants responded to both as reliable, whereas when each adult was 25% accurate, infants responded to both as unreliable. In the 50% accuracy condition, during learning, infants were presented with 16 trials, half valid and half invalid, mixed randomly. On each trial, the adult gazed at one of the four corners of the computer screen, which was followed by the appearance of an interesting animal. On valid trials, the animal appeared in the location predicted by the adult's gaze, and on invalid trials, the animal appeared in a non-gazed-at location. After the learning phase, infants observed the same adult gaze at the two boxes that she had gazed at during the learning phase (the test trials), and then at the two boxes that she had not gazed at during the learning phase (the generalization trials). No animal appeared on test or generalization trials. Our goal was to assess whether infants would be more inclined to use the gaze of the own-race adult relative to the other-race adult to anticipate the animal's appearance. Based on the Perceptual-Social Linkage Hypothesis, we expected that infants would be biased to follow the gaze of the own-race individuals more than other-race ones under uncertainty. In accord with this

Own-race condition

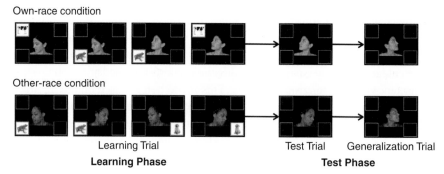

Other-race condition

Learning Trial   Test Trial   Generalization Trial
Learning Phase   **Test Phase**

Figure 3.4. *Examples of the trials. On the 16 learning trials (8 own-race, 8 other-race), 4 different trials were presented in each block: two valid trials and two invalid trials, randomly mixed. On valid trials, the actor's gaze predicted the occurrence of an animal in the gazed-at location. On invalid trials, the actor's gaze did not predict the animal's occurrence in the gazed-at location. In the test phase, for the two test trials, the actor gazed at one of the two locations that she had looked at on the learning trials. For the two generalization trials, the actor gazed at one of the two locations that she had not looked at on the learning trials. No animal appeared in the test or generalization trials.*
A color version of this figure is available online at www.cambridge.org /9781107112322

expectation, we found that infants were indeed significantly more inclined to use the gaze of the own-race adult than that of the other-race adult to anticipate the animal's appearance.

Why are infants biased to the follow the gaze of own-race informants under uncertainty? One possibility is that they may generalize positive associations and impressions with own-race individuals in daily life to the current experimental scenario. Infants interact mostly with members of their own-race category, such as their caregivers and neighbors, who are usually offering supportive and reliable information (Gergely, Egyed, & Király, 2007). Thus, given the fact that infants are capable of categorizing individuals by own race versus all other races (Quinn et al., 2016), they may transfer their impression of reliability from caregivers and other own-race individuals to an own-race stranger, thereby leading to a biased learning from the own-race stranger. Another possible explanation involves infant conformity to the majority in a population (Corriveau, Fusaro, & Harris, 2009). The participants of the current study were drawn from a racially homogeneous environment, where own-race people form the majority of the society. Infants are likely to be sensitive to the statistics of race in their everyday life (i.e., racial distribution), and form a tendency to follow the signals from the own-race informant, who represents the majority. Future studies with infants from diverse environments, such as infants from racial minority families, will be needed to distinguish between these two possible explanations. Regardless, the present findings suggest that infants already display social preferences for own-race individuals in the first year of life.

Our findings may be viewed as inconsistent with a previous finding in which 10-month-old infants showed preference for accepting toys from an adult with a native accent than one with a non-native accent, but they failed to show differential responses toward an own- versus an other-race adult (Kinzler & Spelke, 2011). However, the prior finding of non-preference does not necessarily suggest a lack of race-based social preference because infants may have biased social perception, but fail to apply the bias to guide their actions. In other words, they may be "prejudiced" but not yet discriminate. Similar to the social bias that infants display for the native accent (Kinzler et al., 2007), infants may develop a preference before they use it to interact more favorably with own-race individuals. Given that infant exposure to native language begins in utero (Hepper, 2015), whereas exposure to own-race faces begins only postnatally, it is also possible that face-race based social reasoning emerges later than accent-based biases.

The findings of the two Xiao et al. studies indicate that infants have more positive association with own-race individuals and are more likely to learn from own-race individuals. These differences in social responsiveness to own- versus other-race persons seem to emerge during the developmental window where cross-race perceptual narrowing takes place. Thus, the results from these studies offer support for our Perceptual-Social Linkage Hypothesis. However, because these existing studies have only focused on either racial bias or cross-race face processing, no direct evidence exists to support our Perceptual-Social Linkage Hypothesis. To draw a firmer conclusion, future studies need to be conducted with infants that simultaneously assess their own- versus other-race face processing and racial biases.

Evidence from children and adults supporting perceptual-social linkage. Although direct evidence supporting the Perceptual-Social Linkage Hypothesis is lacking in infants, such evidence is available in preschool children and adults. In one investigation, we studied preschoolers growing up in Singapore, a multi-cultural city-state providing extensive opportunities to interact with people from multiple racial groups (Setoh et al., under review). We found that among the Chinese preschoolers we tested, the accuracy to categorize faces by race predicted an implicit racial bias favouring Chinese, as assessed by our preschooler-friendly IAT. This finding is consistent with that of Dunham et al. (2013), who found 4- to 12-year-old children's racial categorization performance (i.e., classifying neutral faces as own-race or other-race) was significantly related to their tendency to categorize racially ambiguous happy versus angry faces as own- and other-race, respectively. These results suggest that children's readiness to categorize faces by race is indeed linked to their implicit racial bias.

Several recent training studies have provided further support for our Perceptual-Social Linkage Hypothesis. The rationale of the training studies follows from this hypothesis: if implicit bias links with perception of other-race faces, then training observers to perceptually individuate other-race faces should reduce implicit bias for the other race. In an investigation conducted by Lebrecht, Pierce, Tarr, and Tanaka (2009), Caucasian adults were assigned to two training groups: In an individuation training group, participants were trained to recognize individual African American faces over five sessions, and in a categorization training group, participants were trained to categorize the African American faces by race. Participants in the individuation condition, but not in the categorization condition, showed significant improvement in their ability to discriminate individual African American faces. Moreover, the improvement in other-race discrimination resulting from individuation training was significantly correlated with reduction in implicit racial bias against African Americans.

Following the approach of Lebrecht et al. (2009), we (Xiao et al., 2015) investigated whether individuation training would help reduce implicit racial bias in Chinese children between 4 and 6 years. We used the angry = outgroup paradigm mentioned above as the pre- and post-tests of the children's implicit racial bias against Africans. Chinese children were either trained to recognize other-race African faces or own-race Chinese faces. Those children trained to recognize other-race faces displayed significantly reduced implicit racial bias, whereas those who learned to recognize own-race faces did not. This finding has now been replicated by Qian et al. (2017), who also trained children to individuate other-race faces but measured reduction of implicit racial bias using the more conventional implicit racial bias test (Qian et al., 2016).

The results of these training studies taken together suggest that in both children and adults, the linkage between perceptual processing of own- versus other-race faces and implicit racial bias is a causal one: Learning to perceptually individuate other-race faces can lead to reduction in one's implicit racial bias. These findings also point to the viability of using perceptual individuation training of other-race faces to reduce implicit racial bias. This unconventional approach has the potential to be a highly effective and efficient way to reduce implicit bias in children and adults anywhere. This is because it does not require the trainees to be in direct face-to-face contact with real other-race individuals, nor does it require the contact to be as intensive or extensive as existing contact-based approaches. In fact, in Xiao et al. (2015), the training time was less than 30 minutes and only required learning 5 or 6 other-race individual faces.

Concluding Remarks

The above findings regarding implicit racial bias in infancy and early childhood and the effectiveness of individuation training methods in reducing implicit racial bias have provided the first pieces of evidence to support our Perceptual-Social Linkage Hypothesis. Much evidence is still needed to fully establish the validity of this account. As noted, future studies need to concurrently assess infant and child cross-race face-processing and their implicit racial bias. If our hypothesis is indeed correct, there should be a positive correlation between infant and child face/race categorization and implicit racial bias, as well as a negative correlation between other-race face recognition accuracy and implicit racial bias. If, as we have argued, the linkage observed in children and adults is a causal one, then training infants to individuate other-race faces should lead to a reduction in implicit racial bias because individuation prevents them from developing the automatic tendency to categorize other-race faces by their race. Future research needs to systematically test these intriguing predictions.

Such future work will not only provide evidence to assess the validity of our Perceptual-Social Linkage Hypothesis, but will also allow for a more complete understanding of the origins and development of implicit racial bias in early childhood. This includes the identification of not only perceptual factors, but also additional cognitive and social factors that contribute to the development of implicit racial bias. Last but not least, such work will ultimately help parents and educators develop effective and efficient approaches to reduce implicit racial bias in a way that can have lasting effects.

References

Aboud, F. E. (1988). *Children and prejudice*. Oxford: Basil Blackwell.

Aboud, F. E. (2008). A social-cognitive developmental theory of prejudice. In S. M. Quintana & C. McKown (Eds.) *Handbook of race, racism, and the developing child* (pp. 55–71). New Jersey: John Wiley & Sons.

Aboud, F. E. (2013). What are they thinking? The mystery of young children's thoughts on race. In M. R. Banaji & S. A. Gelman (Eds.), *Navigating the social world: What infants, children, and other species can teach us* (pp. 332–335). New York: Oxford University Press.

Aboud, F. E., Tredoux, C., Tropp, L. R., Brown, C. S., Niens, U., & Noor, N. M. (2012). Interventions to reduce prejudice and enhance inclusion and respect for ethnic differences in early childhood: A systematic review. *Developmental Review, 32*, 307–336. doi: 10.1016/j.dr.2012.05.001

Allport, G. W. (1954). *The nature of prejudice*. New York: Basic Books.

Anzures, G., Kelly, D. J., Pascalis, O., Quinn, P. C., Slater, A. M., de Viviés, X., & Lee, K. (2014). Own- and other-race face identity recognition in children: The effects of pose and feature composition. *Developmental Psychology, 50*, 469–481.

Anzures, G., Pascalis, O., Quinn, P. C., Slater, A. M., & Lee, K. (2011). Minimizing skin color differences does not eliminate the own-race recognition advantage in infants. *Infancy, 16*, 640–654. PMCID: PMC3203025

Anzures, G., Quinn, P. C., Pascalis, O., Slater, A. M., & Lee, K. (2013a). Development of own-race biases. *Visual Cognition, 21*, 1165.

Anzures, G., Quinn, P. C., Pascalis, O., Slater, A. M., Tanaka, J. W., & Lee, K. (2013b). Developmental origins of the other-race effect. *Current Directions in Psychological Science, 22*, 173–178.

Bahrick, L. E., & Lickliter, R. (2000). Intersensory redundancy guides attentional selectivity and perceptual learning in infancy. *Developmental Psychology, 36*, 190–201.

Balas, B., & Quinn, P. C. (2015, March). *Simulating classification of face race by infants: Similarities and differences between model and infant looking performance*. Paper presented at the Meeting of the Society for Research in Child Development, Philadelphia, PA.

Banaji, M. R., & Greenwald, A. G. (2013). *Blindspot: Hidden biases of good people*. New York: Delacorte Press.

Bar-Haim, Y., Ziv, T., Lamy, D., & Hodes, R. M. (2006). Nature and nurture in own-race face processing. *Psychological Science*, *17*, 159–163.

Baron, A. S., & Banaji, M. R. (2006). The development of implicit attitudes evidence of race evaluations from ages 6 and 10 and adulthood. *Psychological Science*, *17*, 53–58. doi: 10.1111/j.1467–9280.2005.01664.x

Bigler, R. S. (2013). Understanding and reducing social stereotyping and prejudice among children. In M. R. Banaji & S. A. Gelman (Eds.), *Navigating the social world: What infants, children, and other species can teach us* (pp. 327–331). New York: Oxford University Press.

Bigler, R. S., & Liben, L. S. (2007). Developmental intergroup theory explaining and reducing children's social stereotyping and prejudice. *Current Directions in Psychological Science*, *16*, 162–166. doi: 10.1111/j.1467-8721.2007.00496.x

Cameron, L., Rutland, A., Brown, R., & Douch, R. (2006). Changing children's intergroup attitudes toward refugees: Testing different models of extended contact. *Child Development*, *77*, 1208–1219. doi: 10.1111/j.1467-8624.2006.00929.x

Castelli, L., De Amicis, L., & Sherman, S. J. (2007). The loyal member effect: on the preference for ingroup members who engage in exclusive relations with the ingroup. *Developmental Psychology*, *43*, 1347–1359. doi: 10.1037/0012-1649.43.6.1347

Corriveau, K. H., Fusaro, M., & Harris, P. L. (2009). Going with the flow: Preschoolers prefer nondissenters as informants. *Psychological Science*, *20*, 372–377.

Cunningham, W. A., Preacher, K. J., & Banaji, M. R. (2001). Implicit attitude measures: Consistency, stability, and convergent validity. *Psychological Science*, *12*, 163–170. doi: 10.1111/1467-9280.00328

Degner, J., & Dalege, J. (2013). The apple does not fall far from the tree, or does it? A meta-analysis of parent–child similarity in intergroup attitudes. *Psychological Bulletin*, *139*, 1270–1304. doi: 10.1037/a0031436

Devine, P. G. (1989). Stereotypes and prejudice: their automatic and controlled components. *Journal of Personality and Social Psychology*, *56*, 5–18.

Dovidio, J. F., Kawakami, K., & Gaertner, S. L. (2002). Implicit and explicit prejudice and interracial interaction. *Journal of Personality and Social Psychology*, *82*, 62–68.

Dunham, Y., Baron, A. S., & Banaji, M. R. (2006). From American city to Japanese village: A cross-cultural investigation of implicit race attitudes. *Child Development*, *77*, 1268–1281. doi: 10.1111/j.1467-8624.2006.00933.x

Dunham, Y., Baron, A. S., & Banaji, M. R. (2007). Children and social groups: A developmental analysis of implicit consistency in Hispanic Americans. *Self and Identity*, *6*, 238–255. doi: 10.1080/15298860601115344

Dunham, Y., Baron, A. S., & Banaji, M. R. (2008). The development of implicit intergroup cognition. *Trends in Cognitive Sciences*, *12*, 248–253. doi: 10.1016/j.tics.2008.04.006

Dunham, Y., Baron, A. S., & Carey, S. (2011). Consequences of "minimal" group affiliations in children. *Child Development*, *82*, 793–811. doi: 10.1111/j.1467–8624.2011.01577.x

Dunham, Y., Chen, E. E., & Banaji, M. R. (2013). Two signatures of implicit intergroup attitudes: Developmental invariance and early enculturation. *Psychological Science*, *24*, 860–868. doi: 10.1177/0956797612463081

Dunham, Y., Newheiser, A., Hoosain, L., Merrill, A., & Olson, K. R. (2014). From a different vantage: Intergroup attitudes among children from low- and intermediate-status racial groups. *Social Cognition*, *32*, 1–21. doi: 10.1521/soco.2014.32.1.1

Feddes, A. R., Noack, P., & Rutland, A. (2009). Direct and extended friendship effects on minority and majority children's interethnic attitudes: A longitudinal study. *Child Development, 80*, 377–390. doi: 10.1111/j.1467-8624.2009.01266.x

Feinman, S. (1980). Infant response to race, size, proximity, and movement of strangers. *Infant Behavior and Development, 3*, 187–204. doi: 10.1016/S0163-6383(80)80025-7

Gaither, S. E., Pauker, K., & Johnson, S. P. (2012). Biracial and monoracial infant own-race face perception: An eye tracking study. *Developmental Science, 15*, 775–782.

Gawronski, B., & Bodenhausen, G. V. (2006). Associative and propositional processes in evaluation: an integrative review of implicit and explicit attitude change. *Psychological Bulletin, 132*, 692–731.

Gergely, G., Egyed, K., & Kiraly, I. (2007). On pedagogy. *Developmental Science, 10*, 139–146.

Greenwald, A. G., & Banaji, M. R. (1995). Implicit social cognition: Attitudes, self-esteem, and stereotypes. *Journal of Personality and Social Psychology, 102*, 4–27. doi: 10.1037/0033-295X.102.1.4

Greenwald, A. G., McGhee, D. E., & Schwartz, J. L. (1998). Measuring individual differences in implicit cognition: the implicit association test. *Journal of Personality and Social Psychology, 74*, 1464–1480. doi: 10.1037/0022-3514.74.6.1464

Greenwald, A. G., Nosek, B. A., & Banaji, M. R. (2003). Understanding and using the implicit association test: I. An improved scoring algorithm. *Journal of Personality and Social Psychology, 85*, 197–216. doi: 10.1037/0022-3514.85.2.197

Greenwald, A. G., Poehlman, T. A., Uhlmann, E. L., & Banaji, M. R. (2009). Understanding and using the Implicit Association Test: III. Meta-analysis of predictive validity. *Journal of Personality and Social Psychology, 97*, 17–41. doi: 10.1037/a0015575

Grossmann, T., Striano, T., & Friederici, A. D. (2006). Crossmodal integration of emotional information from face and voice in the infant brain. *Developmental Science, 9*, 309–315.

Hadley, H., Pickron, C. B., & Scott, L. S. (2015). The lasting effects of process-specific versus stimulus-specific learning during infancy. *Developmental Science, 18*, 842–852.

Hardin, C. D., & Banaji, M. R. (2013). The nature of implicit prejudice: Implications for personal and public policy. In E. Shafir (Ed.), *The behavioral foundations of public policy* (pp. 13–31). Princeton, NJ: Princeton University Press.

Hepper, P. (2015). Behavior during the prenatal period: Adaptive for development and survival. *Child Development Perspectives, 9*, 38–43.

Hetherington, C., Hendrickson, C., & Koenig, M. (2014). Reducing an in-group bias in preschool children: the impact of moral behavior. *Developmental Science, 17*, 1042–1049. doi: 10.1111/desc.12192

Horowitz, E. L., & Horowitz, R. E. (1938). Development of social attitudes in children. *Sociometry, 1*, 301–338.

Hugenberg, K., & Bodenhausen, G. V. (2004). Ambiguity in social categorization: The role of prejudice and facial affect in race categorization. *Psychological Science, 15*, 342–345. doi: 10.1111/j.0956-7976.2004.00680.x

Kelly, D. J., Liu, S., Ge, L., Quinn, P. C., Slater, A. M., Lee, K., Liu, Q., & Pascalis, O. (2007a). Cross-race preferences for same-race faces extend beyond the African versus Caucasian contrast in 3-month-old infants. *Infancy, 11*, 87–95.

Kelly, D. J., Liu, S., Lee, K., Quinn, P. C., Pascalis, O., Slater, A. M., & Ge, L. (2009). Development of the other-race effect in infancy: Evidence towards universality? *Journal of Experimental Child Psychology, 17*, 105–114.

Kelly, D. J., Quinn, P. C., Slater, A. M., Lee, K., Ge, L., & Pascalis, O. (2007b). The other-race effect develops during infancy. *Psychological Science*, *18*, 1084–1089.

Kelly, D. J., Quinn, P. C., Slater, A. M., Lee, K., Gibson, A., Smith, M., Ge, L., & Pascalis, O. (2005). Three-month-olds, but not newborns, prefer own-race faces. *Developmental Science*, *8*, F31–F36.

Killen, M., Margie, N. G., & Sinno, S. (2006). Morality in the context of intergroup relationships. In M. Killen, & J. G. Smetana (Eds.), *Handbook of moral development* (pp. 155–183). New York: Psychology Press.

Killen, M., Rutland, A., & Ruck, M. D. (2011). Promoting equity, tolerance, and justice in childhood. *Social Policy Report*, *25*, 1–33.

Kinzler, K. D., Dupoux, E., Spelke, E. S. (2007). The native language of social cognition. *Proceedings of the National Academy of Sciences*, *104*, 12577–12580.

Kinzler, K. D., & Spelke, E. S. (2011). Do infants show social preferences for people differing in race? *Cognition*, *119*, 1–9.

Kubicek, C., Hillairet de Boisferon, A., Dupierrix, E., Pascalis, O., Loevenbruck, H., & Gervain, J., & Schwarzer, G. (2014). Cross-modal matching of audio-visual German and French fluent speech in infancy. *PLoS ONE 9*(2):e89275.

Kuhl, P. K., Stevens, E., Hayashi, A., Deguchi, T., Kiritani, S., & Iverson, P. (2006). Infants show a facilitation effect for native language phonetic perception between 6 and 12 months. *Developmental Science*, *9*, F13–F21.

Kuhl, P. K., Williams, K. H., & Lacerda, F. (1992). Linguistic experience alters phonetic perception in infants by 6 months of age. *Science*, *255*, 606–608.

Lai, C. K., Marini, M., Lehr, S. A., Cerruti, C., Shin, J. E. L., Joy-Gaba, J. A., … & Frazier, R. S. (2014). Reducing implicit racial preferences: I. A comparative investigation of 17 interventions. *Journal of Experimental Psychology: General*, *143*, 1765–1785. doi: 10.1037/a0036260

Lai, C. K., Skinner, A. L., Cooley, E., Murrar, S., Brauer, M., Devos, T., … & Simon, S. (2016). Reducing implicit racial preferences: II. Intervention effectiveness across time. *Journal of Experimental Psychology: General*, *145*, 101–116. doi: 10.2139/ssrn.2712520

Lebrecht, S., Pierce, L. J., Tarr, M. J., & Tanaka, J. W. (2009). Perceptual other-race training reduces implicit racial bias. *PLoS one*, *4*, e4215. doi: 10.1371/journal.pone.0004215

Lee, K., Anzures, G., Quinn, P. C., Pascalis, O., & Slater, A. (2011). Development of face processing expertise. In A. J. Calder, G. Rhodes, M. H. Johnson, & J. V. Haxby (Eds.), *Handbook of face perception* (pp.753–778). New York: Oxford University Press.

Lee, K., Quinn, P. C., Pascalis, O., & Slater, A. (2013). Development of face processing abilities. In Zelazo, P. D. (Ed.), *Oxford handbook of developmental psychology, Vol. 2* (pp. 338–370). New York: Oxford University Press.

Liu, S., Quinn, P. C., Wheeler, A., Xiao, N., Ge, L., & Lee, K. (2011). Similarity and difference in the processing of same- and other-race faces as revealed by eye-tracking in 4- to 9-month-olds. *Journal of Experimental Child Psychology*, *108*, 180–189. PMCID: PMC3740558

Malatesta, C. Z., & Haviland, J. M. (1982). Learning display rules: The socialization of emotion expression in infancy. *Child Development*, *53*, 991–1003. doi: 10.1016/j.chc.2013.12.001

Nesdale, D. (1999). Developmental changes in children's ethnic preferences and social cognitions. *Journal of Applied Developmental Psychology*, *20*, 501–519. doi: 10.1016/S0193-3973(99)00012-X10.1016/j.jesp.2011.08.011

Newheiser, A. K., & Olson, K. R. (2012). White and Black American children's implicit intergroup bias. *Journal of Experimental Social Psychology, 48*, 264–270.

Olson, K. R., Shutts, K., Kinzler, K. D., & Weisman, K. G. (2012). Children associate racial groups with wealth: Evidence from South Africa. *Child Development, 83*, 1884–1899. doi: 10.1111/j.1467-8624.2012.01819.x

Pettigrew, T. F., & Tropp, L. R. (2006). A meta-analytic test of intergroup contact theory. *Journal of Personality and Social Psychology, 90*, 751–783.

Qian, M. K., Heyman, G. D., Quinn, P. C., Messi, F. A., Fu, G., & Lee, K. (2016). Implicit racial biases in preschool children and adults from Asia and Africa. *Child Development, 87*, 285–296.

Qian, M., Quinn, P. C., Heyman, G. D., Pascalis, O., Fu, G., & Lee, K. (2017). Perceptual individuation training (but not mere exposure) reduces implicit racial bias in preschool children. *Developmental Psychology.*

Quinn, P. C., Anzures, G., Lee, K., Pascalis, O., Slater, A., & Tanaka, J. W. (2013). On the developmental origins of differential responding to social category information. In M. R. Banaji & S. A. Gelman (Eds.), *Navigating the social world: What infants, children, and other species can teach us* (pp. 286–291). New York: Oxford University Press.

Quinn, P. C., Lee, K., Pascalis, O., & Tanaka, J. W. (2016). Narrowing in categorical responding to other-race face classes by infants. *Developmental Science, 19*, 362–371.

Raabe, T., & Beelmann, A. (2011). Development of ethnic, racial, and national prejudice in childhood and adolescence: A multinational meta-analysis of age differences. *Child Development, 82*, 1715–1737. doi: 10.1111/j.1467-8624.2011.01668.x

Rennels, J. L., & Davis, R. E. (2008). Facial experience during the first year. *Infant Behavior & Development, 31*, 665–678.

Richeson, J. A., & Shelton, J. N. (2003). When prejudice does not pay: Effects of interracial contact on executive function. *Psychological Science, 14*, 287–290.

Rutland, A., Killen, M., & Abrams, D. (2010). A new social-cognitive developmental perspective on prejudice: The interplay between morality and group identity. *Perspectives on Psychological Science, 5*, 279–291. doi: 10.1177/1745691610369468

Setoh, P., Lee, K. J. J., Zhang, L., Qian, M. K., Heyman, G. D., Quinn, P. C., & Lee, K. (under review). Racial categorization predicts implicit racial bias in preschool children.

Shutts, K., Kinzler, K. D., Katz, R. C., Tredoux, C., & Spelke, E. S. (2011). Race preferences in children: Insights from South Africa. *Developmental Science, 14*, 1283–1291. doi: 10.1111/j.1467-7687.2011.01072.x

Sugden, N. A., Mohamed-Ali, M. I., & Moulson, M. C. (2014). I spy with my little eye: Typical, daily exposure to faces documented from a first-person infant perspective. *Developmental Psychobiology, 56*, 249–261.

Vezzali, L., Stathi, S., Giovannini, D., Capozza, D., & Trifiletti, E. (2015). The greatest magic of Harry Potter: Reducing prejudice. *Journal of Applied Social Psychology, 45*, 105–121. doi: 10.1111/jasp.12279

Werker, J. F., Yeung, H. H., & Yoshida, K. (2012). How do infants become native speech perception experts? *Current Directions in Psychological Science, 21*, 221–226.

Wheeler, A., Anzures, G., Quinn, P. C., Pascalis, O., Omrin, D. S., & Lee, K. (2011). Caucasian infants scan own- and other-race faces differently. *PLoS ONE, 6*: e18621.

Xiao, N. G., Quinn, P. C., Xiao, W. S., Liu, S., Ge, L., Pascalis, O., & Lee, K. (2017). Older but not younger infants associate own-race faces with positive music and other-race faces with negative music. *Developmental Science.*

Xiao, N. G., Wu, R., Quinn, P. C., Liu, S., Tummeltshammer, K. S., Kirkham, N. Z., Ge, L., Pascalis, O., & Lee, K. (in press). Infants rely more on gaze cues from own-race than other-race adults for learning under uncertainty. *Child Development*.

Xiao, W. S., Fu, G., Quinn, P. C., Qin, J., Tanaka, J. W., Pascalis, O., & Lee, K. (2015). Individuation training with other-race faces reduces preschoolers' implicit racial bias: a link between perceptual and social representation of faces in children. *Developmental Science*, *18*, 655–663. doi: 10.1111/desc.12241

Xiao, W. S., Quinn, P. C., Pascalis, O., & Lee, K. (2014). Own- and other-race face scanning in infants: Implications for perceptual narrowing. *Developmental Psychobiology* (Special Issue on Perceptual Narrowing), *56*, 262–273.

4 The Differentiation of Executive Functioning Across Development: Insights from Developmental Cognitive Neuroscience

Nicole Bardikoff and Mark Sabbagh

Introduction

Throughout a regular day we are faced with a variety of tasks that require us to plan, reflect on, and execute goal-directed actions. These tasks can be mundane ones such as realizing that in some situations one must wait one's turn to speak instead of blurting out the first thing that comes to mind. It can also include tasks that are integral to our wellbeing, such as looking both ways at a traffic intersection before crossing the street. The suite of skills we use in these situations that require reflection and planning are referred to as executive functioning (EF) (Miyake et al., 2000). The maturation of EF plays a critical role in development across a number of social and academic domains (see, e.g., Zelazo, Carlson, & Kesek, 2008, for review). Indeed, EF is a better predictor of long-term academic success than IQ (Diamond, 2006). By the same token, serious impairments in EF have been associated with a host of negative outcomes, including poor physical health, criminality, and interpersonal deficits (Moffitt et al., 2011).

Given its importance in everyday social and cognitive functioning, the construct of EF has been the subject of substantial scrutiny. For adults, it is generally agreed that EF is not a single skill, but rather a suite of interrelated skills – specifically, inhibition, shifting, and updating, all of which are marshalled in concert to help negotiate cognitively complex or challenging situations. For young children, however, there is evidence that the cognitive processes that comprise EF in adults have not yet become distinct from one another – that is, for young children EF appears to rely on a single process that differentiates with development (Lee, Bull, & Ho, 2013; Shing, Lindenberger, Diamond, Li, & Davidson, 2010; Wiebe et al., 2011; Wu et al., 2011). Though this pattern of findings has been studied and debated at some length in the literature, the mechanism behind the differentiation has yet to be determined. The goal of this chapter is to first review the evidence showing that EF transitions from a single process to multiple component processes over a long timetable ranging from preschool through late adolescence. We will then evaluate whether neurodevelopmental changes predicted by the interactive specialization framework (Johnson, 2000; 2011) can provide insight into the differentiation of EF over childhood. We hope that in doing so we will understand not only the best characterization of the differentiation process, but also the neurodevelopmental progression of EF.

The Structure of EF

For adults, EF is generally thought to include three interrelated components: inhibition, updating, and shifting (Miyake et al., 2000). We will provide a brief description of each in turn.

Inhibition refers to an individual's ability to inhibit a prepotent response. In a classroom children learn that when asked a question they cannot merely shout out an answer, but instead have to exert inhibitory control by putting up their hand and waiting until they are called on to speak. In the lab, inhibition is often assessed through tasks that require the suppression of a common or habitual action when presented with a specific instruction. For example, the Go/No-Go task requires individuals to respond by pressing a key to a class of stimuli (such as letters) but to inhibit their response to a specific target (e.g., the letter "X").

Updating is the term given to the process of maintaining and manipulating information in working memory. Updating allows us to not only remember information but to alter or incorporate new knowledge into our existing mental frameworks based on feedback from the environment. The main task used to assess the updating component of EF is the "span task," in which participants are required to repeat, match, or transform a sequence of information (e.g., digits or letters) after a brief delay. For example, in the *n*-back task participants are shown a stream of single pictures and are asked to judge whether the current picture is the same as one that appeared *n* (e.g., 3) pictures previously. Because the stream of information is continuous and changing, so too is the item that must be remembered. Thus, the correct answer must be updated on every trial. Another example is the backwards digit span task, in which participants are given a sequence of digits of some length (e.g., 5 digits) and asked to repeat the sequence in reverse order.

Lastly, *shifting* is the ability to flexibly transfer between mental sets or rules. A common task used to assess shifting in children is the Dimensional Change Card Sort (DCCS; Zelazo, 2006). In the DCCS, children are shown a series of cards that vary along two dimensions (e.g., shape and color). Children are asked to sort each card first by one dimension ("we're playing the color game") and then by the other ("now we're going to play the shape game").

Although these skills are conceptually distinct from one another it is important to note that they are recruited in concert to support complex goal-directed action. Indeed, early theoretical accounts of EF took their interrelated nature as evidence for a single "executive" process corresponding with a circumscribed neural network within the prefrontal cortex (PFC). Part of the support for this conjecture came from the fact that people with extensive acquired damage to the frontal lobes show impairments in negotiating a wide variety of EF tasks. Frontal lobe injury led to deficits in shifting, inhibition, and updating tasks, as well as "planning" tasks that putatively require all three components (see, e.g., Stuss & Alexander, 2000). It has since been realized, however, that inhibition, updating, and shifting are all separable.

Some of the most widely cited evidence for the separability of EF skills comes from a latent variable analysis (or confirmatory factor analysis) from Miyake et al. (2000). The approach to the question was ground-breaking in several ways, in part because it helped identify the variance associated with each component beyond simply using task scores. Even though the components associated with EF are theoretically separable, any given task typically relies, at least to some extent, on all processes. For instance, although the DCCS is generally regarded as a "shifting" task, the task also requires a modicum of updating (in that children must remember the rules) and inhibition (because the first rule is typically prepotent and needs to be inhibited). To address this issue regarding heterogeneous task demands, Miyake et al. (2000) used a latent variable analysis that allowed them to extract the common variance structures that might exist across a whole range of tasks. The logic is that if EF is comprised of a single mechanism, then all task performance variance should be attributable to a single factor. For instance, tasks that rely most on the switching component should be as correlated with updating tasks as they are with other switching tasks. In contrast, if there are multiple mechanisms, then performance on tasks that make higher demands on a single mechanism (e.g., switching) should be more highly correlated with one another than they are with tasks that make demands on different mechanisms (e.g., a switching task vs. an updating task). Using this approach, Miyake et al. (2000) found evidence that inhibition, updating, and switching tasks were statistically distinct, but that these components were themselves moderately correlated. The authors referred to this pattern as "unity and diversity."

Since the original study, Miyake and Friedman (2012) have expanded the work in order to gain a better understanding of why, though distinct, the components of EF are moderately correlated with one another. Expanding on their "unity" terminology, the authors have suggested that there may be a process or set of capacities that is responsible for performance across all EF tasks regardless of the specific EF process being measured. (Friedman & Miyake, 2004; Miyake & Friedman, 2012). Currently, there is no agreed definition of what exactly common EF consists of. Some researchers have suggested that there may be cognitive capacities that are theoretically separable from the three components of EF, but nonetheless are important for performance across the tasks. For instance, Miyake and Friedman (2012) have argued that the variance attributable to common EF represents the contribution of broader basic information processing and working-memory capacities that are distinct from the "updating" processes that are generally considered to be part of EF. Similarly, others have suggested that common EF variance might be attributable to processes important for negotiating the attentional demands that are inherent in the tasks that measure all three aspects of EF (Cragg & Chevalier, 2012; Garon, Bryson, & Smith, 2008). A third, and more general, possibility is that common EF variance represents very basic individual differences in general cognitive processing speed – in short, performance across different aspects of EF might all be affected by general processing speed, which in turn accounts for the moderate inter-task correlations. These hypotheses about the nature of common EF are not mutually exclusive; each may play some role in explaining why the distinct aspects of EF are intercorrelated. In any case, this work highlights that although EF can be differentiated into three distinct processes (inhibition, updating, and shifting), there are likely common EF processes that impact how EF is deployed in both experimental and real-world settings.

Given the importance of the CFA approach in establishing the "unity and diversity" of EF in adults, there was natural interest in determining whether this structure of EF is a developmental starting place or an outcome. There have since been a number of studies looking at this question at different age points and in different cultures. The results of these studies were reviewed recently by Lee et al. (2013), and we have summarized them, along with some newer studies, in Table 4.1 and Figure 4.1. Although there are subtle and important variations across the studies, they are remarkably consistent in showing that the variance structure of EF changes with development. For children younger than 6 years old, performance across tasks that measure the different component skills is highly interrelated (Fuhs & Day, 2011; Hughes, Ensor, Wilson, & Graham, 2010; Wiebe et al., 2011; Wiebe, Espy, & Charak, 2008; Willoughby, Blair, Wirth, Greenberg, Family Life Project Investigators, 2010; Willoughby, Wirth, Blair, Family Life Project Investigators, 2012). With time, the variance structure of EF tasks begins to differentiate such that it begins to look like the pattern typically seen in adults. This process of differentiation takes place over a long period. During middle childhood, there is evidence for a two-factor variance structure that separates the process of updating from a factor that combines performance on inhibition and shifting tasks (Brydges, Fox, Reid, & Anderson, 2014; Lee et al., 2013; Miller, Giesbrecht, Müller, McInerney, & Kerns, 2012; Usai, Viterbori, & Traverso, 2014; Van der Sluis, Jong, & van der Leij, 2007; Van der Ven, Kroesbergen, Boom, & Leseman, 2011). Then, finally, a three-factor structure that is similar to the adult variance structure is evident in early adolescence (Agostino, Johnson, & Pascual-Leone, 2010; McAuley & White, 2011; Rose, Feldman, & Jankowski, 2011; Wu et al., 2011).

Although the findings are remarkably consistent across ages, we would like to draw attention to a few notable limitations that prevent very strong conclusions. The first is that studies vary in the number of potential factors that they test for – some test for two, whereas others test for three. Of these, the majority of the studies done with very young children, and several of the ones with children in middle childhood, have only tested two factors. For example, McAuley and White (2011) included tasks that measured updating and inhibition, but none that measured shifting in their sample of 6–17 year olds. They concluded that EF had a two-factor structure, but it may be that the older children in their study would have evidenced a three-factor structure had they included tasks that measured shifting. There are likely good reasons for these design compromises. Nonetheless, there is much still to learn about developmental changes in the variance structure of EF over childhood.

A second thing to note is that many of the studies combine the data across age groups that might in fact show different factor structures. This is a particular problem for gaining confidence of the particular times at which EF differentiates into a two-, and then a three-, factor structure. For example, Lehto, Juujärvi, and Kooistra (2003) tested 8–13 year old children on tasks that measured all three of the components of EF, but were unable to perform meaningful comparisons between the younger and older children within the age range. Thus, although they found that an

Table 4.1 *CFA studies examining the structure of EF in children*

Study	Age	Task	Findings
Wiebe et al. (2008)	2-3, 4-6	**Inhibition:** Whisper, Statue, Shape school, Tower of Hanoi, Visual attention, Delayed response, Continuous performance test **Updating:** Six boxes, Digit span, Delayed alternation **Shifting:** Not tested	Single factor
Kraybill (2014)	2, 4	**Inhibition:** Tongue task, Pig Bull, Shape stroop, Ladybugs, Crayon delay, Gift delay, Pig Bull, DCCS **Updating:** BRIEF-Working memory, Digit span **Shifting:** Not tested	Single factor
Wiebe et al. (2011)	3	**Inhibition:** Big little stroop, Shape school, Snack delay, Go/No-Go **Updating:** Nine boxes, Delayed alternation, Nebraska barnyard **Shifting:** Not tested	Single factor
Willoughby et al. (2010)	3	**Inhibition:** Spatial conflict, Silly sounds stroop, Animal Go/No-Go **Updating:** Working memory span **Shifting:** Item selection	Single factor
Willoughby et al. (2012)	3-5	**Inhibition:** Spatial conflict, Spatial conflict arrows, Silly sounds stroop, Animal Go/No-Go **Updating:** Working memory span, Pick the picture **Shifting:** Something is the same	Single factor
Fuhs and Day (2011)	3-5	**Inhibition:** Day/Night, Head/Feet, BRIEF-Inhibition **Updating:** Not tested **Shifting:** FIST, Spatial reverse, BRIEF-Shift	Single factor
Hughes et al. (2010)	4-6	**Inhibition:** Day/Night **Updating:** Beads **Shifting:** Not tested	Single factor
Brydges et al. (2012)	7-9	**Inhibition:** Stroop, Go/No-Go, Compatibility reaction time **Updating:** Letter-number, Backward digit span, Sentence repetition **Shifting:** WCST, Verbal fluency, Letter monitoring	Single factor
Shing et al. (2010)	4-7, 7-9.5, 9.5-14.5	**Inhibition:** Pictures, Dots mixed and incongruent, Arrows **Updating:** 2 and 6 Abstract shape **Shifting:** Not tested	Single factor Two factor (9.5-14.5, Inhibition, Updating)
Brydges et al. (2014)	8, 10	**Inhibition:** Stroop, Go/No-Go, Compatibility reaction time **Updating:** Letter-number, Backward digit span, Sentence repetition **Shifting:** WCST, Verbal fluency, Letter monitoring	Single factor Two factor (10 – Updating, Inhibition-Shifting)
Miller et al. (2012)	3-5	**Inhibition:** Boy/Girl stroop, Go/No-Go, Tower of Hanoi **Updating:** Backward digit span, Word span, Boxes **Shifting:** DCCS	Two factor (Updating, Inhibition)
Usai et al. (2014)	5-6	**Inhibition:** Circle drawing, Tower of London **Updating:** Backward digit span, Dual request selective task **Shifting:** Semantic fluency, DCCS	Two factor (Inhibition, Updating-Shifting)

Table 4.1 (*cont.*)

Study	Age	Task	Findings
Lee et al. (2012)	6	**Inhibition:** Simon, Flanker **Updating:** Mister X, Pictorial updating, Listening recall **Shifting:** Picture symbol, Simon says, Flanker	Two factor (Updating, Inhibition-Shifting)
Lee et al. (2013)	5, 6, 7, 8, 9, 10, 11, 12, 13, 14, 15	**Inhibition:** Simon, Flanker **Updating:** Mister X, Pictorial updating, Listening recall **Shifting:** Picture symbol, Antisaccade, Mickey task	Two factors (Updating, Inhibition-Shifting)
McAuley and White (2011)	6-8, 9-12, 13-17, 18-24	**Inhibition:** Stimulus response compatibility **Updating:** Digit span, n-back, Recognition span **Shifting:** Not tested	Two factors (Inhibition, Updating)
Xu et al. (2013)	7-9, 10-12, 13-15	**Inhibition:** Go/No-Go, Color word stroop **Updating:** n-back, Running memory **Shifting:** Number pinyn, Dots triangles	Single factor Three factors (13-15)
Van der Ven et al. (2012)	7-8	**Inhibition:** Animal stroop, Local global, Simon says **Updating:** Backward digit span, Odd one out, Keep track **Shifting:** Animal shift, Trail making	Two factor (Updating, Inhibition-Shifting)
Huizinga et al. (2006)	7, 11, 15, 21	**Inhibition:** Stroop, Stop signal, Flanker **Updating:** Tic Tac Toe, Running memory, Mental counters **Shifting:** Local global, Dots triangles, Smiling faces	Two factor (Updating, Shifting)
Van der Sluis et al. (2007)	9-12	**Inhibition:** Quantity stroop, Object inhibition, Stroop, Numerical size **Updating:** Keep track, Letter memory, Digit memory **Shifting:** Object shift, Making trails	Two factor (Updating, Inhibition-Shifting)
Wu et al. (2011)	7-14	**Inhibition:** Skye search, Stroop **Updating:** Code transmission **Shifting:** Creature counting, Contingency naming, Opposite world	Three factors
Lehto et al. (2003)	8-13	**Inhibition:** Tower of London, Matching figures **Updating:** Spatial span, Spatial working memory, Mazes **Shifting:** Trail making, Word fluency	Three factors
Agostino et al. (2010)	8-11	**Inhibition:** Antisaccade, Number stroop, Color stroop **Updating:** Letter memory, n-back **Shifting:** Trails, Contingency naming	Three factors
Rose et al. (2011)	11	**Inhibition:** Go/No-Go, Rapid visual processing **Updating:** Counting span, Listening span, Spatial working memory **Shifting:** Trail making, Dimension shift	Three factors
Duan et al. (2010)	11-12	**Inhibition:** Digit and figure Go/No-Go **Updating:** Digit span, Figure position **Shifting:** Odd more, Local global	Three factors

adult-like three-factor variance structure was the best fit for their data, it remains possible that the younger children might not have provided as convincing evidence for that as the older children.

A final complication is that there is no standardized battery of tasks for measuring the three components of EF. Because of this, it could be that the measures used in some studies might have been less effective at isolating the component processes. For

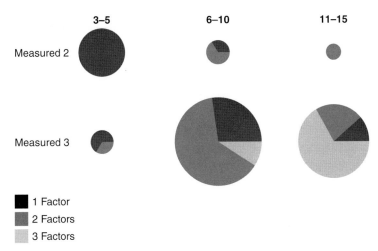

Figure 4.1. *Graphical summary of the findings of the studies that have investigated the differentiation of EF divided by age groups and by the number of factors that were measured. The diameter of each pie chart corresponds to the number of studies within each cell of the table (Larger diameter means more studies in that cell).*

instance, the Tower of London/Hanoi is noticeably different in nature than Boy/Girl Stroop, though both are used to assess inhibition (Lehto et al., 2003; Miller et al., 2012; Usai et al., 2014; Wiebe et al., 2008). Moreover, some studies used a single task to assess each factor, thereby lessening the strength of the latent variable analysis (Hughes et al., 2010; Wu et al., 2011). Under these circumstances, the results may provide evidence for a variance structure pattern that appears to be more homogenous than it truly is (Hughes et al., 2010; Lehto et al., 2003; Miller et al., 2012).

Although there is clearly more work to be done to determine the specific pattern and timeline of the differentiation of EF, the concerns outlined above do not fully diminish the fact that, when taken as a whole, the findings sketch out a relatively clear picture. In most cases, preschool-aged children show evidence of a single EF factor. By middle childhood, studies are substantially more likely to find evidence of differentiation into two factors – updating and a combined inhibition-shifting factor. This is true in the two-factor and, more importantly, in the three-factor studies. By adolescence, the majority of the three-factor studies show evidence of an adult-like profile, with EF differentiating into the three components. These findings all contribute to the general conclusion that the differentiation of component EF skills is a developmental outcome, not a developmental starting point for the structure of EF.

Neurodevelopmental Research

Although there is a developing literature showing that the adult-like differentiation of component EF processes emerges with development, little work has explored the mechanisms by which that differentiation might occur. Although there are many ways we might approach this question, here we are going to focus our discussion on potential neurodevelopmental mechanisms. From an intuitive stand-point, we might expect that the differentiation of EF into statistically separable behavioral components might be reflected straightforwardly in the brain. Indeed, the terms "fractionation" or "differentiation" would seem to imply that early in develop-ment, a single brain mechanism, or large network of brain areas, is recruited for performance in any task relevant to the suite of EF skills. Then, with development, more specialized regions become primarily recruited for component processes. A dominant framework for conceptualizing how these changes might occur is the interactive specialization (IS) framework offered by Johnson (2000, 2011). Within this framework, cortical regions begin with relatively broad functionality that is not specific to any given task or class of stimulus. Then, with development and experi-ence, neural networks become more specialized through activity-dependent interac-tions that play a key role in organizing neural activity. In support of this framework, Johnson (2011) marshals evidence from a range of areas that have been explored from a developmental cognitive neuroscience perspective, including face processing, lan-guage, and social cognition. Our goal here is to evaluate the current literature regard-ing developmental changes in the neural regions supporting aspects of EF to determine whether the IS approach can provide insight into the differentiation of EF over childhood, including why there are strong initial correlations between components, followed first by the separation of updating, then inhibition and shifting.

We can divide the hypotheses that emerge from the IS framework into what we will call *qualitative* and *quantitative* hypotheses. With respect to *qualitative* hypotheses, we might predict given the IS framework that the neural regions that are important for younger children's performance on EF tasks are qualitatively different from those that are important for older children's performance on those tasks. For instance, the neural regions that are important for shifting when children are 3 years old might be anatomi-cally distinct from those that are important for shifting when children are 7 years old, or older. Other evidence for a qualitative shift might come from an examination of the connectivity of neural regions; the ways in which the neural regions that are recruited for EF are themselves structurally and functionally interconnected, and also connected with more general processing abilities that may change fundamentally with age. It is worth noting, however, that some aspects of these qualitative hypotheses are difficult to test against the extant literature investigating the neurodevelopmental correlates of any given component of EF. The most serious problem is that the methods that allow for relatively precise localization of cortical function are demanding and rarely include children younger than 6 years old. Given the behavioral evidence reviewed above, there is reason to think that differentiation begins before children turn six, thereby precluding us from seeing evidence for an undifferentiated cortical basis for each of the EF components. There is, however, a relatively consistent pattern within the earliest stages of differentiation whereby the updating component tends to separate from the inhibition and shifting components, which themselves are related to one another. Thus, the extant neurodevelopmental literature might show that for the youngest children tested there is a common neural substrate for inhibition and shifting that is becoming distinct from the system that is important for updating.

Quantitative hypotheses within the IS framework pertain to spatial extent or strength of the activations within the brain areas that are recruited for any one aspect of EF. For instance, it could be that even from the earliest ages tested, a particular brain area is important for a particular aspect of EF but the nature of its recruitment might change over time by becoming, for instance, more focal or more strongly activated. These hypotheses are easier to test with respect to the extant literature because the processes that are thought to drive these changes take place over a protracted time-table. Thus, the comparison of neural systems that are important for any given component of EF can be compared across school-aged children and early adolescents to find evidence of quantitative changes in the spatial extent or strength of activation.

In adults, there have been many studies investigating the neural bases of EF and its component processes. Although a full review of this literature is well beyond the scope of this chapter, evidence that is most pertinent to the present discussion comes from work by Collette and colleagues (2005). The authors looked at functional brain activations (PET) elicited as participants completed the same inhibition, updating, and shifting tasks that were used in latent factor analysis work described previously. The results were clear. First, they found that each factor was associated with a distinct neural system. Inhibition performance was related to the ventral prefrontal cortex (VLPFC) (i.e., right inferior frontal gyrus, right orbitofrontal gyrus), and the dorsal lateral prefrontal cortex (DLPFC) (right middle and superior frontal gyrus). Shifting performance was related to activation in parietal regions, including the right supramarginal gyrus, left precuneus, and the left superior parietal cortex. Updating performance was related to activation in a frontoparietal network, including the frontopolar, superior, and inferior frontal cortices and the intraparietal sulcus. Second, they found that a small group of areas were activated across tasks, which they interpreted as the substrate for "common EF," including the right intraparietal sulcus, the left superior parietal gyrus, the left middle frontal gyrus, and the left inferior frontal gyrus. These findings regarding the neural substrates of both the specific components and of common EF have been replicated and extended in a range of studies from several labs (Aron, 2008; Aron, Robbins, & Poldrack, 2004; Collette, Hogge, Salmon, & Van der Linden, 2006; Darki & Klingberg, 2015; Niendam et al., 2012; Zuk, Benjamin, Kenyon, & Gaab, 2014).

For the most part, the extant developmental literature on the neurodevelopmental bases of the components of EF are tested on a component-by-component basis; that is, almost all studies focus on a single component and how the neural systems associated with that component change over time. For that reason, we will review the literature on the neural bases of EF for each of the three components separately and then draw conclusions about the extent to which the kinds of qualitative and quantitative changes predicted by the IS framework are indeed characteristic of the observed patterns.

Neurodevelopmental Bases of Inhibition

Qualitative Changes. The neural regions that are recruited during the performance of inhibition tasks are remarkably similar in children and adults. Studies using fMRI have shown that areas of the VLPFC, specifically the inferior frontal gyrus, are recruited across all ages (Booth et al., 2003; Bunge, Dudukovic, Thomason, & Vaidya, 2002; Durston, Thomas, Yang, Uluğ, Zimmerman, & Casey, 2002; Durston et al., 2006; Luna et al., 2001; Rubia, Smith, Taylor, & Brammer, 2007; Sheridan, Kharitonova, Martin, Chatterjee, & Gabrieli, 2014; Tamm, Menon, & Reiss, 2002; Velanova, Wheeler, & Luna, 2009). Based solely on this evidence, we might argue that there is no fundamental anatomical change in the neuroanatomical bases of inhibition with development. One challenge to this claim, however, comes from methods that measure rapid changes in cortical activity and functional connectivity. For instance, using ERP measures, researchers have shown that activity attributable to the parietal cortex (i.e., P3 component) is not associated with successful inhibition in 6–7 year olds, though it is in adults. (Davis, Bruce, Snyder, & Nelson, 2003; Jonkman, 2006). The later emerging involvement of parietal regions may be attributable to increased connectivity between frontal and parietal areas that emerges with development. For instance, using an effective connectivity analysis, Hwang et al. (2010) found that age and performance on inhibition tasks was associated with increased connectivity between the frontal and parietal areas from late childhood (aged 8–12) to early adolescence (aged 13–17). Similar findings were reported with a dense-array fNIRS study comparing children aged 4–6 to adults (Mehnert et al., 2013). It is notable that in the Collette et al. (2005) adult study discussed earlier, parietal activity was not uniquely characteristic of inhibition performance. Instead, parietal activation was common in shifting tasks, and was also part of "common EF." One possible interpretation of this finding, then, is that while ventral prefrontal areas may represent the core neural mechanism underlying young children's performance on inhibition tasks, developmental gains in inhibition can be realized by the creation of connections with cortical resources that are outside that core neural mechanism.

Quantitative Changes. Within the core neural system for inhibitory control there are clear quantitative changes in the spatial extent and strength of recruitment in inhibition tasks. A number of fMRI studies have shown a reduction in the spatial extent of frontal activation in inhibition tasks with age. Specifically, ventral regions, including the inferior and orbitofrontal gyri, respond more strongly and more focally than surrounding regions of the frontal cortex (Booth et al., 2003; Bunge et al., 2002; Durston et al., 2002, 2006; Tamm et al., 2002). These findings are mirrored in the EEG literature which shows that with development, the frontal N2 in children aged 6 and above shows a reduction in amplitude with age that is likely attributable to the increase in ongoing inhibitory processes in underlying cortical regions that are inherent in the task (Brydges, Anderson, Reid, & Fox, 2013; Johnstone, Barry, & Clarke, 2007; Jonkman, Sniedt, & Kemner, 2007; Lamm, Zelazo, & Lewis, 2006; Lo et al., 2013). Thus, there is clear evidence for quantitative changes in the neural systems important for performance in inhibition tasks with development.

Summary. As predicted by the IS framework, we see some evidence for qualitative changes through connectivity, including forming connections with parietal regions that are later recruited to support performance in inhibition tasks. There is also evidence of quantitative changes as recruitment of the VLPFC, specifically the inferior frontal gyrus, becomes increasingly stronger and more focal, suggesting increasing specialization of this region.

Neurodevelopmental Bases of Shifting

Qualitative Changes. Similar to inhibition, there is very little difference in the neural areas recruited by children and adults during shifting tasks. Lateral prefrontal regions and the superior parietal cortex are recruited across ages (typically tested 7–11 year olds and adults) in support of shifting performance (Casey, Davidson, & Hara, 2004; Crone, Donohue, Honomichl, Wendelken, & Bunge, 2006; Moriguchi & Hiraki, 2009, 2011; Morton, Bosma, & Ansari, 2009; Rubia et al., 2006; Wendelken, Munakata, Baym, Souza, & Bunge, 2012). However, also like inhibition, there does appear to be preliminary evidence for qualitative developmental change in functional connectivity of brain areas that are important for shifting. Specifically, Ezekiel, Bosma, and Morton (2013) found that when comparing the DCCS performance of children aged 8–12 to adults, there were age-related increases in connectivity between the lateral PFC and the anterior cingulate cortex, the inferior parietal cortex, and the ventral tegmental area. These same authors also found evidence for age-related decreases in DCCS-related connectivity among the fronto-polar, insular, and temporal areas (Ezekiel et al., 2013). Together, these findings suggest that the neural networks that are important for shifting are established by late childhood, and that qualitative changes occur primarily with respect to the functional connections amongst these areas. These changes lead to the emergence of a functionally connected frontoparietal network that facilitates shifting performance.

Quantitative Changes. There are clear quantitative changes across development in the recruitment of the neural systems underlying shifting performance. FNIRS studies in preschoolers focusing only on frontal regions have found an association between age- and performance-based increases in bilateral recruitment of the VLPFC and performance on the DCCS (Moriguchi & Hiraki, 2009, 2011). In children aged 7–11 there is evidence of age-related increases in the strength of the recruitment of lateral prefrontal areas (Casey et al., 2004; Crone et al., 2006; Morton et al., 2009). Wendelken and colleagues used a novel rule-switching paradigm during event-related fMRI and found that children aged 8–13 and adults recruited the same neural regions; however, children were slower in recruiting the DLPFC (Wendelken et al., 2012). That is, they found evidence of a pattern of quantitative temporal change in the neural processing associated with rule switching across development. Across fMRI studies we also see an age-related increase in the strength of recruitment in the superior parietal cortex (Casey et al., 2004; Crone et al., 2006; Morton et al., 2009). Finally, the EEG literature shows an age- and performance-related reduction in N2 amplitude in preschool-aged children that has been source-localized to the anterior cingulate cortex (Espinet, Anderson, & Zelazo, 2012, 2013; Waxer & Morton, 2011). The evidence for quantitative changes in the neural areas underlying shifting are characteristic of the specializations predictions put forth by the IS framework.

Summary. Evidence from both the qualitative and quantitative changes suggests that with age there is increased connectivity and recruitment of parietal and frontal regions. We also see specialization within these regions, including the superior parietal cortex.

Neurodevelopmental Bases of Updating

Qualitative Changes. Unlike inhibition, children and adults seem to rely on different neural areas for tasks that measure updating performance. For instance, in a visuo-spatial working-memory task that requires updating, Ciesielski, Lesnik, Savoy, Grant, & Ahlfors (2006) found that adults recruited the VLPFC, DLPFC, posterior cingulate, fusiform gyrus, and the precuneus, whereas children aged 6–10 recruited the middle temporal cortex, insula, basal ganglia and the parietal cortex. During the updating portion of a working-memory task, Crone et al. (2006) found that adolescents and adults recruited the DLPFC and the superior parietal cortex, whereas children aged 8–12 relied solely on the VLPFC even though all groups had recruited the three regions during the memory maintenance portion of the task. The engagement of different neural systems in adults and children has also been seen in studies looking at performance on tasks that require updating verbal information in working memory (Ciesielski et al., 2006; O'Hare, Lu, Houston, Bookheimer, & Sowell, 2008; Scherf, Sweeney, & Luna, 2006). For instance, Scherf et al. (2006) found that though adults, adolescents, and children recruited the DLPFC, VMPFC, basal ganglia, and parietal regions to differing degrees, children also recruited the thalamus and the temporal lobes. Though there are discrepancies concerning exact locations, possibly due to the modalities used across tasks, these findings suggest that there is a qualitative change in the neural systems underlying updating performance across development, whereby dorsal lateral and parietal regions become increasingly important. This is in line with the IS framework that suggests that with experience and increasing neural reorganization there may be developmental differences in the neural correlates of the same task.

These qualitative developmental changes in the neural regions being recruited for updating are mirrored by qualitative developmental changes in functional connectivity. For instance, Vestergaard et al. (2011) used diffusion tensor imaging (DTI) analysis and found that increased myelination and white matter maturation in a tract that connects the left frontal and parietal areas was positively associated with better updating abilities in 7–13 year olds. These findings regarding the association between updating and frontoparietal connnectivity are characteristic of multiple studies (Darki & Klingberg, 2015; Edin, Macoveanu, Olesen, & Tegnér, 2007; Nagy, Westerberg, & Klingberg, 2004; Olesen, Nagy, Westerberg, & Klingberg, 2003; Østby, Tamnes, Fjell, & Walhovd, 2011; Vestergaard et al., 2011). These results are consistent with the qualitative changes predicted by the IS framework as connectivity between neural regions change possibly as a result of activity-dependent interactions.

Quantitative Changes. The qualitative changes described above tend to occur in middle childhood, sometime between the ages of 7–10 years old. There is also evidence of quantitative changes in the neural areas that are important for updating; however, these changes occur later, between the ages of 9–18 years old. First, there is evidence that there are developmental *increases* in activation of specific areas, namely the superior frontal gyrus and intraparietal sulcus, during visuo-spatial updating tasks (Klingberg, Forssberg, & Westerberg, 2002; Luna & Sweeney, 2004). Second, multiple fMRI studies have found evidence that in addition to increasing activation, the spatial extent of the activations in these regions becomes more focal between late childhood/early adolescence and adulthood (Casey et al., 1995; Klingberg et al., 2002; Kwon, Reiss, & Menon, 2002; Olesen et al., 2003; Olesen, Macoveanu, Tegnér, & Klingberg, 2007; Scherf et al., 2006). These later changes may continue through late adolescence. For instance, Scherf et al. (2006) found that adolescents (14–17 years of age) recruited the dorsolateral PFC more broadly than adults, who recruited a more localized area of the dorsolateral PFC (the superior frontal gyrus).

Summary. Thus, we see a specialization as predicted by the IS framework – by middle childhood there are qualitative changes in the neural regions that are important for updating and the connections between those areas. Then, once established, there appears to be quantitative changes within these brain areas such that the activity that is elicited during updating tasks is recruited to a stronger extent and has a more restricted spatial extent.

Discussion

The behavioral data suggest that initially all three components of EF are strongly correlated, and thus EF is best represented by a unitary factor structure. An important question, then, is what causes the initial correlation? We decided to approach this issue by looking at the neurodevelopmental literature. Based on the extant research it seems that at least part of the initial unity may be attributable to an early consistent reliance on the VLPFC during tasks that assess all three EF components. There are multiple possible explanations to characterize the importance of the VLPFC. First, it has been hypothesized that the VLPFC is integral in rule representation (Bunge & Zelazo, 2006). If we consider the structure of inhibition, shifting, and updating tasks it is clear that each requires the maintenance and representation of rules. For instance, in order to successfully navigate the DCCS, one must be able to represent and understand the rules (i.e. "if I'm playing the color game, it goes here") as well as be able to shift between the rules. The same is true of inhibition and updating tasks, in that both require children to keep in mind the rule that specifies task demands (e.g., which is the no-go stimulus). Given these common demands, and common neural substrates, perhaps the strong correlations between the three components early in development are because the rate-limiting factor on performance is rule representation, which requires recruitment of the VLPFC. This may change with development, and it is possible rule representation presents a more complex task for young children than for adults.

A second possibility concerns the function of inhibition. One of the explanations Miyake et al. (2000) originally proposed for the nature of the shared variance, or common EF, in the adult literature was the underlying inhibition demands consistent across tasks. For instance, in order to shift to a new rule or set, one must inhibit the previously important information. In order to successfully update information in working memory, one must inhibit or suppress information that is no longer necessary. As reviewed above, VLPFC is recruited across all ages for inhibition performance. Thus, it is possible that the VLPFC specializes to inhibition early in preschool and continues to support the inhibition demands seen across the three component tasks. Again, we might speculate that the correlations among the three EF components early in development might be attributable to their reliance on the development of the VLPFC.

The behavioral literature summarized in Table 4.1 and Figure 4.1 shows a persistent trend of differentiation as EF transitions from a unitary, to a two-factor, and then finally a three-factor model. In the two-factor model which emerges between the ages of 6–10 years, the updating component separates itself from a combined inhibition-shifting factor. What is intriguing about the timing of this behavioral shift is that it is at this point that the neural areas recruited during updating tasks undergo substantial *qualitative* changes. These qualitative changes render the neural systems that are important for updating quite distinct from those that are important for inhibition and shifting, which themselves continue to show considerable overlap during this same time period. Although we do not know why the updating comes to rely on a more distinct neural substrate prior to inhibition and shifting, the processes that lead to these changes may provide critical insight into the developmental course of EF development.

Inhibition and shifting separate, and a three-factor model similar to the one seen in adults becomes evident between 11–15 years of age. Evidence from the neurodevelopmental literature suggests that this may be in part a result of increased reliance on parietal regions. This appears to be facilitated by the stronger degree of functional connectivity between frontal and parietal brain areas with development. Adults and children tend to recruit similar regions for inhibition and shifting, and changes in connectivity between said neural regions allows for an increase in the efficient and effective recruitment of this important frontoparietal network. These qualitative changes occur alongside substantial quantitative changes that include increasing specialization and focalization in neural recruitment. It is possible that as inhibition and shifting skills develop and mature, they become more specialized in the brain, thus relying less heavily on overlapping neural areas. This process may allow the components to become increasingly distinct behaviorally and neurologically.

It is important to note that development does not stop once the differentiation of EF is complete. In late adolescence we see an increase in the refinement of the neural networks that underlie inhibition, shifting, and updating, often alongside decreases in behavioral reaction times. At this time there is an increase in quantitative change and the specialization of the neural areas and networks necessary for performance across all three components. It is possible that the changes described are supported by neuromaturational factors such as synaptic pruning and myelination, which increase the efficiency of neural communication, thereby allowing for increased refinement of neural recruitment. Neural network development proceeds from a local, diffuse pattern to one that is more focalized and dispersed with time. This may allow for the emergence of distinct, specialized patterns of neural activation followed by fine-tuning and refinement into adolescence.

Conclusion

In this chapter we have examined evidence pertaining to the nature of the differentiation of EF. Because the behavioral evidence alone is not conclusive, we examined the neurodevelopmental literature. By using the IS framework and examining the developmental qualitative and quantitative neural changes across the three components we gain a more nuanced understanding of EF development and the process of differentiation. Future research should look at the mechanisms behind the quantitative and qualitative changes and see what factors – likely a combination of endogenous and exogenous elements, are propelling these differences in order to better characterize the order and timeline of the differentiations.

The mechanism of EF differentiation has yet to be determined; however, evidence does indicate that in early childhood there is the beginning of both behavioral and neural specialization. We hope that the results from the research discussed here will help clarify the nature of the differentiation, and will shed light on a potential link between behavioral changes and coinciding changing neural recruitment patterns. By examining the differentiation of EF we add to our understanding of the development of this important cognitive construct, allowing for a more nuanced view of emerging cognition.

References

Agostino, A., Johnson, J., & Pascual-Leone, J. (2010). Executive functions underlying multiplicative reasoning: Problem type matters. *Journal of Experimental Child Psychology, 105*, 286–305. doi: 10.1016/j.jecp.2009.09.006

Aron, A. R. (2008). Progress in executive-function research from tasks to functions to regions to networks. *Current Directions in Psychological Science, 17*, 124–129. doi: 10.1111/j.1467-8721.2008.00561.x

Aron, A. R., Robbins, T. W., & Poldrack, R. A. (2004). Inhibition and the right inferior frontal cortex. *Trends in Cognitive Sciences, 8*, 170–177. doi: 10.1016/j.tics.2004.02.010

Booth, J. R., Burman, D. D., Meyer, J. R., Lei, Z., Trommer, B. L., Davenport, N. D., . . . & Mesulam, M. M. (2003). Neural development of selective attention and response inhibition. *NeuroImage, 20*, 737–751. doi: 10.1016/S1053-8119(03)00404-X

Brydges, C. R., Anderson, M., Reid, C. L., & Fox, A. M. (2013). Maturation of cognitive control: delineating response inhibition and interference suppression. *PloS one, 8*, e69826. doi: 10.1371/journal.pone.0069826

Brydges, C. R., Fox, A. M., Reid, C. L., & Anderson, M. (2014). The differentiation of executive functions in middle and late childhood: A longitudinal latent-variable analysis. *Intelligence, 47*, 34–43. doi: 10.1016/j.intell.2014.08.010

Bunge, S. A., Dudukovic, N. M., Thomason, M. E., & Vaidya, C. J. (2002). Immature frontal lobe contributions to cognitive control in children: evidence from fMRI. *Neuron, 33*, 301–311. doi: 10.1016/S0896-6273(01)00583-9

Bunge, S. A., & Zelazo, P. D. (2006). A brain-based account of the development of rule use in childhood. *Current Directions in Psychological Science, 15*, 118–121. doi: 10.1111/j.0963-7214.2006.00419.x

Casey, B. J., Cohen, J. D., Jezzard, P., Turner, R., Noll, D. C., . . . & Rapoport, J. L. (1995) Activation of prefrontal cortex in children during a nonspatial working memory task with functional MRI. *Neuroimage, 2*, 221–229. doi: 10.1006/nimg.1995.1029

Casey, B. J., Davidson, M. C., Hara, Y., Thomas, K. M., Martinez, A., Galvan, A., . . . & Tottenham, N. (2004). Early development of subcortical regions involved in

non-cued attention switching. *Developmental Science, 7*, 534–542. doi: 10.1111/
j.1467-7687.2004.00377.x/full

Ciesielski, K. T., Lesnik, P. G., Savoy, R. L., Grant, E. P., & Ahlfors, S. P. (2006).
Developmental neural networks in children performing a Categorical N-Back
Task. *NeuroImage, 33*, 980–990. doi: 10.1016/j.neuroimage.2006.07.028

Collette, F., Hogge, M., Salmon, E., & Van der Linden, M. (2006). Exploration of the neural
substrates of executive functioning by functional neuroimaging. *Neuroscience, 139*,
209–221. doi: 10.1016/j.neuroscience.2005.05.035

Collette, F., Van der Linden, M., Laureys, S., Delfiore, G., Degueldre, C., Luxen, A., &
Salmon, E. (2005). Exploring the unity and diversity of the neural substrates of
executive functioning. *Human Brain Mapping, 25*, 409–423. doi: 10.1002/hbm.20118

Cragg, L., & Chevalier, N. (2012). The processes underlying flexibility in childhood.
The Quarterly Journal of Experimental Psychology, 65, 209–232. doi.org/
10.1080/17470210903204618

Crone, E. A., Donohue, S. E., Honomichl, R., Wendelken, C., & Bunge, S. A. (2006). Brain
regions mediating flexible rule use during development. *The Journal of Neuroscience,
26*, 11239–11247. doi: 10.1523/JNEUROSCI.2165-06.2006

Darki, F., & Klingberg, T. (2015). The role of fronto-parietal and fronto-striatal networks in
the development of working memory: A longitudinal study. *Cerebral Cortex, 25*,
1587–1595. doi: 10.1093/cercor/bht352

Davis, E. P., Bruce, J., Snyder, K., & Nelson, C. A. (2003). The X-trials: Neural correlates of
an inhibitory control task in children and adults. *Journal of Cognitive Neuroscience,
15*, 432–443. doi: 10.1162/089892903321593144

Diamond, A. (2006). The early development of executive functions. In E. Bialystok &
F. I. M. Craik (Eds.), *Lifespan cognition: Mechanisms of change* (pp. 70–95).
London: Oxford University Press.

Durston, S., Davidson, M. C., Tottenham, N., Galvan, A., Spicer, J., Fossella, J. A., & Casey, B. J.
(2006). A shift from diffuse to focal cortical activity with development. *Developmental
Science, 9*, 1–20. doi: 10.1111/j.1467-7687.2005.00454.x/full

Durston, S., Thomas, K. M., Yang, Y., Uluğ, A. M., Zimmerman, R. D., & Casey, B. J. (2002).
A neural basis for the development of inhibitory control. *Developmental Science, 5*,
F9–F16. doi: 10.1111/1467-7687.00235

Edin, F., Macoveanu, J., Olesen, P., & Tegnér, J. (2007). Stronger synaptic connectivity as
a mechanism behind development of working memory-related brain activity during
childhood. *Journal of Cognitive Neuroscience, 19*, 750–760. doi: /10.1162/
jocn.2007.19.5.750

Espinet, S. D., Anderson, J. E., & Zelazo, P. D. (2012). N2 amplitude as a neural marker of
executive function in young children: An ERP study of children who switch versus
perseverate on the Dimensional Change Card Sort. *Developmental Cognitive
Neuroscience, 2*, S49–S58. doi: 10.1016/j.dcn.2011.12.002

Espinet, S. D., Anderson, J. E., & Zelazo, P. D. (2013). Reflection training improves executive
function in preschool-age children: Behavioral and neural effects. *Developmental
Cognitive Neuroscience, 4*, 3–15. doi: 10.1016/j.dcn.2012.11.009

Ezekiel, F., Bosma, R., & Morton, J. B. (2013). Dimensional Change Card Sort performance
associated with age-related differences in functional connectivity of lateral prefrontal cortex. *Developmental Cognitive Neuroscience, 5*, 40–50. doi: 10.1016/
j.dcn.2012.12.001

Friedman, N. P., & Miyake, A. (2004). The relations among inhibition and interference
control functions: A latent-variable analysis. *Journal of Experimental
Psychology: General, 133*, 101–135. doi: 10.1037/0096-3445.133.1.101

Fuhs, M. W., & Day, J. D. (2011). Verbal ability and executive functioning development in preschoolers at head start. *Developmental Psychology, 47*, 404–416. doi: 10.1037/a0021065

Garon, N., Bryson, S. E., & Smith, I. M. (2008). Executive function in preschoolers: A review using an integrative framework. *Psychological Bulletin, 134*, 31–60. doi.org/10.1037/0033-2909.134.1.31

Hughes, C., Ensor, R., Wilson, A., & Graham, A. (2010). Tracking executive function across the transition to school: A latent variable approach. *Developmental Neuropsychology, 35*, 20–36. doi: 10.1080/87565640903325691

Hwang, K., Velanova, K., & Luna, B. (2010). Strengthening of top-down frontal cognitive control networks underlying the development of inhibitory control: A functional magnetic resonance imaging effective connectivity study. *Journal of Neuroscience, 30*, 15535–15545. doi.org/10.1523/jneurosci.2825-10.2010

Johnson, M. H. (2000). Functional brain development in infants: Elements of an interactive specialization framework. *Child Development, 71*, 75–81. doi: 10.1111/1467-8624.00120

Johnson, M. H. (2011). Interactive specialization: a domain-general framework for human functional brain development? *Developmental Cognitive Neuroscience, 1*, 7–21. doi: 10.1016/j.dcn.2010.07.003

Johnstone, S. J., Barry, R. J., & Clarke, A. R. (2007). Behavioural and ERP indices of response inhibition during a Stop-signal task in children with two subtypes of Attention-Deficit Hyperactivity Disorder. *International Journal of Psychophysiology, 66*, 37–47. doi: 10.1016/j.ijpsycho.2007.05.011

Jonkman, L. M. (2006). The development of preparation, conflict monitoring and inhibition from early childhood to young adulthood: a Go/NoGo ERP study. *Brain Research, 1097*, 181–193. doi: 10.1016/j.brainres.2006.04.064

Jonkman, L. M., Sniedt, F. L. F., & Kemner, C. (2007). Source localization of the Nogo-N2: A developmental study. *Clinical Neurophysiology, 118*, 1069–1077. doi: 10.1016/j.clinph.2007.01.017

Klingberg, T., Forssberg, H., & Westerberg, H. (2002). Increased brain activity in frontal and parietal cortex underlies the development of visuospatial working memory capacity during childhood. *Journal of Cognitive Neuroscience, 14*, 1–10. doi: 10.1162/089892902317205276

Kraybill, J. H. (2014). *A latent factor analysis of preschool executive functions: investigations of antecedents and outcomes* (unpublished doctoral dissertation). Virginia Tech, Virgina.

Kwon, H., Reiss, A. L., & Menon, V. (2002). Neural basis of protracted developmental changes in visuo-spatial working memory. *Proceedings of the National Academy of Sciences, 99*, 13336–13341. doi: 10.1073/pnas.162486399

Lamm, C., Zelazo, P. D., & Lewis, M. D. (2006). Neural correlates of cognitive control in childhood and adolescence: Disentangling the contributions of age and executive function. *Neuropsychologia, 44*, 2139–2148. doi: 10.1016/j.neuropsychologia.2005.10.013

Lee, K., Bull, R., & Ho, R. M. H. (2013). Developmental changes in executive functioning. *Child Development, 84*, 1933–1953. doi: 10.1111/cdev.12096

Lehto, J. E., Juujärvi, P., & Kooistra, L. (2003). Dimensions of executive functioning: Evidence from children. *British Journal of Developmental Psychology, 21*, 59–80. doi: 10.1348/026151003321164627

Lo, Y. H., Liang, W. K., Lee, H. W., Wang, C. H., Tzeng, O. J., Hung, D. L., . . . & Juan, C. H. (2013). The neural development of response inhibition in 5-and 6-year-old preschoolers: an ERP and EEG study. *Developmental Neuropsychology, 38,* 301–316. doi: 10.1080/87565641.2013.801980

Luna, B., & Sweeney, J. A. (2004). The emergence of collaborative brain function: fMRI studies of the development of response inhibition. *Annals of the New York Academy of Sciences, 1021,* 296–309. doi: 10.1196/annals.1308.035

Luna, B., Thulborn, K. R., Munoz, D. P., Merriam, E. P., Garver, K. E., Minshew, N. J., . . . & Sweeney, J. A. (2001). Maturation of widely distributed brain function subserves cognitive development. *NeuroImage, 13,* 786–793. doi: 10.1006/nimg.2000.0743

McAuley, T., & White, D. A. (2011). A latent variables examination of processing speed, response inhibition, and working memory during typical development. *Journal of Experimental Child Psychology, 108,* 453–468. doi: 10.1016/j.jecp.2010.08.009

Mehnert, J., Akhrif, A., Telkemeyer, S., Rossi, S., Schmitz, C. H., Steinbrink, J., . . . & Neufang, S. (2013). Developmental changes in brain activation and functional connectivity during response inhibition in the early childhood brain. *Brain and Development, 35,* 894–904. doi: 10.1016/j.braindev.2012.11.006

Miller, M. R., Giesbrecht, G. F., Müller, U., McInerney, R. J., & Kerns, K. A. (2012). A latent variable approach to determining the structure of executive function in preschool children. *Journal of Cognition and Development, 13,* 395–423. doi: 10.1080/15248372.2011.585478

Miyake, A., & Friedman, N. P. (2012). The nature and organization of individual differences in executive functions: Four general conclusions. *Current Directions in Psychological Science, 21,* 8–14. doi: 10.1177/0963721411429458

Miyake, A., Friedman, N. P., Emerson, M. J., Witzki, A. H., Howerter, A., & Wager, T. D. (2000). The unity and diversity of executive functions and their contributions to complex "frontal lobe" tasks: A latent variable analysis. *Cognitive Psychology, 41,* 49–100. doi: 10.1006/cogp.1999.0734

Moffitt, T. E., Arseneault, L., Belsky, D., Dickson, N., Hancox, R. J., Harrington, H., . . . & Sears, M. R. (2011). A gradient of childhood self-control predicts health, wealth, and public safety. Proceedings of the National Academy of Sciences, *108,* 2693–2698.

Moriguchi, Y., & Hiraki, K. (2009). Neural origin of cognitive shifting in young children. *Proceedings of the National Academy of Sciences, 106,* 6017–6021. doi: 10.1073/pnas.0809747106

Moriguchi, Y., & Hiraki, K. (2011). Longitudinal development of prefrontal function during early childhood. *Developmental Cognitive Neuroscience, 1,* 153–162. doi: 10.1016/j.dcn.2010.12.004

Morton, J. B., Bosma, R., & Ansari, D. (2009). Age-related changes in brain activation associated with dimensional shifts of attention: An fMRI study. *NeuroImage, 46,* 249–256. doi: 10.1016/j.neuroimage.2009.01.037

Nagy, Z., Westerberg, H., & Klingberg, T. (2004). Maturation of white matter is associated with the development of cognitive functions during childhood. *Journal of Cognitive Neuroscience, 16,* 1227–1233. doi: 10.1162/0898929041920441

Niendam, T. A., Laird, A. R., Ray, K. L., Dean, Y. M., Glahn, D. C., & Carter, C. S. (2012). Meta-analytic evidence for a superordinate cognitive control network subserving diverse executive functions. *Cognitive, Affective, & Behavioral Neuroscience, 12,* 241–268. doi: 10.3758/s13415-011-0083-5

O'Hare, E. D., Lu, L. H., Houston, S. M., Bookheimer, S. Y., & Sowell, E. R. (2008). Neurodevelopmental changes in verbal working memory load-dependency: An fMRI investigation. *NeuroImage, 42,* 1678–1685. doi: 10.1016/j.neuroimage.2008.05.057

Olesen, P. J., Macoveanu, J., Tegnér, J., & Klingberg, T. (2007). Brain activity related to working memory and distraction in children and adults. *Cerebral Cortex*, *17*, 1047–1054. doi: 10.1093/cercor/bhl014

Olesen, P. J., Nagy, Z., Westerberg, H., & Klingberg, T. (2003). Combined analysis of DTI and fMRI data reveals a joint maturation of white and grey matter in a fronto-parietal network. *Cognitive Brain Research*, *18*, 48–57. doi: 10.1016/j.cogbrainres.2003.09.003

Østby, Y., Tamnes, C. K., Fjell, A. M., & Walhovd, K. B. (2011). Morphometry and connectivity of the fronto-parietal verbal working memory network in development. *Neuropsychologia*, *49*, 3854–3862. doi: 10.1016/j.neuropsychologia.2011.10.001

Rose, S. A., Feldman, J. F., & Jankowski, J. J. (2011). Modeling a cascade of effects: the role of speed and executive functioning in preterm/full-term differences in academic achievement. *Developmental Science*, *14*, 1161–1175. doi: 10.1111/j.1467-7687.2011.01068.x

Rubia, K., Smith, A. B., Taylor, E., & Brammer, M. (2007). Linear age-correlated functional development of right inferior fronto-striato-cerebellar networks during response inhibition and anterior cingulate during error-related processes. *Human Brain Mapping*, *28*, 1163–1177. doi: 10.1002/hbm.20347

Rubia, K., Smith, A. B., Woolley, J., Nosarti, C., Heyman, I., Taylor, E., & Brammer, M. (2006). Progressive increase of frontostriatal brain activation from childhood to adulthood during event-related tasks of cognitive control. *Human Brain Mapping*, *27*, 973–993. doi: 10.1002/hbm.20237

Scherf, K. S., Sweeney, J. A., & Luna, B. (2006). Brain basis of developmental change in visuospatial working memory. *Journal of Cognitive Neuroscience*, *18*, 1045–1058. doi: 10.1162/jocn.2006.18.7.1045

Sheridan, M., Kharitonova, M., Martin, R. E., Chatterjee, A., & Gabrieli, J. D. E. (2014). Neural substrates of the development of cognitive control in children ages 5–10 years. *Journal of Cognitive Neuroscience*, *26*(8), 1840–1850. doi: 10.1162/jocn_a_00597

Shing, Y. L., Lindenberger, U., Diamond, A., Li, S.-C., & Davidson, M. C. (2010). Memory maintenance and inhibitory control differentiate from early childhood to adolescence. *Developmental Neuropsychology*, *35*, 679–697. doi: 10.1080/87565641.2010.508546

Stuss, D. T., & Alexander, M. (2000). Executive functions and the frontal lobes: A conceptual view. *Psychological Research*, *63*, 289–298. doi: 10.1007/s004269900007

Tamm, L., Menon, V., & Reiss, A. L. (2002). Maturation of brain function associated with response inhibition. *Journal of the American Academy of Child & Adolescent Psychiatry*, *41*, 1231–1238. doi: 10.1097/00004583-200210000-00013

Usai, M. C., Viterbori, P., & Traverso, L. (2014). Latent structure of executive function in five-and six-year-old children: a longitudinal study. *European Journal of Developmental Psychology*, *11*, 447–463. doi: 10.1080/17405629.2013.840578

Van der Sluis, S., de Jong, P. F., & van der Leij, A. (2007). Executive functioning in children, and its relations with reasoning, reading, and arithmetic. *Intelligence*, *35*, 427–449. doi: 10.1016/j.intell.2006.09.001

Van der Ven, S. H. G., Kroesbergen, E. H., Boom, J., & Leseman, P. P. M. (2011). The development of executive functions and early mathematics: A dynamic relationship. *British Journal of Educational Psychology*, *82*, 100–119. doi: 10.1111/j.2044-8279.2011.02035.x

Velanova, K., Wheeler, M. E., & Luna, B. (2009). The maturation of task set-related activation supports late developmental improvements in inhibitory control. *Journal of Neuroscience, 29*, 12558–12567. doi: 10.1523/JNEUROSCI.1579-09.2009

Vestergaard, M., Madsen, K. S., Baaré, W. F., Skimminge, A., Ejersbo, L. R., Ramsøy, T. Z., . . . & Jernigan, T. L. (2011). White matter microstructure in superior longitudinal fasciculus associated with spatial working memory performance in children. *Journal of Cognitive Neuroscience, 23*, 2135–2146. doi: 10.1162/jocn.2010.21592

Waxer, M., & Morton, J. B. (2011). Multiple processes underlying dimensional change card sort performance: A developmental electrophysiological investigation. *Journal of Cognitive Neuroscience, 23*, 3267–3279. doi: 10.1162/jocn_a_00038

Wendelken, C., Munakata, Y., Baym, C., Souza, M., & Bunge, S. A. (2012). Flexible rule use: Common neural substrates in children and adults. *Developmental Cognitive Neuroscience, 2*, 329–339. doi: 10.1016/j.dcn.2012.02.001

Wiebe, S. A., Espy, K. A., & Charak, D. (2008). Using confirmatory factor analysis to understand executive control in preschool children: I. Latent structure. *Developmental Psychology, 44*, 575–587. doi: 10.1037/0012-1649.44.2.575

Wiebe, S. A., Sheffield, T., Nelson, J. M., Clark, C. A. C., Chevalier, N., & Espy, K. A. (2011). The structure of executive function in 3-year-olds. *Journal of Experimental Child Psychology, 108*, 436–452. doi: 10.1016/j.jecp.2010.08.008

Willoughby, M. T., Blair, C. B., Wirth, R. J., Greenberg, M., & Family Life Project Investigators. (2010). The measurement of executive function at age 3 years: Psychometric properties and criterion validity of a new battery of tasks. *Psychological Assessment, 22*, 306–317. doi: 10.1037/a0018708

Willoughby, M. T., Wirth, R. J., Blair, C. B., & Family Life Project Investigators. (2012). Executive function in early childhood: Longitudinal measurement invariance and developmental change. *Psychological Assessment, 24*, 418–431. doi: 10.1037/a0025779

Wu, K. K., Chan, S. K., Leung, P. W. L., Liu, W.-S., Leung, F. L. T., & Ng, R. (2011). Components and developmental differences of executive functioning for school-aged children. *Developmental Neuropsychology, 36*, 319–337. doi: 10.1080/87565641.2010.549979

Zelazo, P. D., (2006). The Dimensional Change Card Sort (DCCS): A method of assessing executive function in children. *Nature Protocols, 1*, 297–301. doi: 10.1038/nprot.2006.46

Zelazo, P. D., Carlson, S. M., & Kesek, A. (2008). The development of executive function in childhood. In C. A. Nelson & M. Luciana (Eds.), *Handbook of Developmental Cognitive Neuroscience* (2nd edn). (pp. 553–574). Cambridge, MA: MIT Press.

Zuk, J., Benjamin, C., Kenyon, A., & Gaab, N. (2014). Behavioral and neural correlates of executive functioning in musicians and non-musicians. *PLoS ONE, 9*, e99868–14. doi: 10.1371/journal.pone.0099868

5 Organismic-Causal Models "From Within" Clarify Developmental Change and Stages

Juan Pascual-Leone and Janice Johnson

> The problem we must solve, in order to explain cognitive development, is that of *invention* and not of mere copying.
>
> (Piaget, 1983, p. 112)

> any test will do just as well as any other, provided only that its correlation with g is equally high.
>
> (Spearman, 1927, p. 197)

> g stands unassailed as a big concretion of mental test variance. It is a psychometric triumph and a cognitive enigma.
>
> (Deary, 2002, p. 176)

> The most puzzling realization is that we have good reason to implicate attention in Gf, but we are devoid of a suitable explanation for how attention comes into play when performing a task such as the Raven.
>
> (Heitz, Unsworth, & Engle, 2005, p. 74)

To rethink cognitive development, we must go beyond a meta-empiricist perspective, which examines development only from an observer's viewpoint (i.e., performances described from outside [Pascual-Leone, 2013], often emphasizing learning). To do so, we might reinvent Piaget. As the first epigraph shows, Piaget considered problem solving ("invention") and not learning ("copying") as key to explaining cognitive development. He added that: "the concepts of assimilation and accommodation and of operational structures (which are created, not merely discovered, as a result of the subject's activities) are oriented toward this inventive construction, which characterizes all living thought" (Piaget, 1983, p. 112).

To unfold in a current idiom what Piaget was implying (see Pascual-Leone, 2012), we will discuss two themes concurrently: What are the mechanisms of *developmental change*? How to model cognitive development as *an emergent organismic process*? These are epistemological-theoretical issues that Piaget and others have failed to solve. To address these two questions for the 21st century, we must rethink cognitive development, aiming to create valid *organismic-causal* models of human *problem solving*. These models must be formulated "from within" the individual's own mental processes, assuming existence of *organismic schemes* that create psychological *internal complexity* (Arsalidou, Pascual-Leone, & Johnson, 2010;

Greenberg & Pascual-Leone, 1995; Pascual-Leone, 1970, 1984, 1995; Pascual-Leone & Johnson, 2005, 2011). We call this "perspective from within" *metasubjective* (Pascual-Leone, 2013; Pascual-Leone, Pascual-Leone, & Arsalidou, 2015). This is in contrast to the commonly adopted (meta-empiricist) *observer's perspective*, "from outside" the subject.

The term *organismic* (Pascual-Leone, 1984) is important here. It was introduced by Kurt Goldstein (2000 /1934; Werner & Kaplan, 1984), who spoke of "equalization" processes (in the sense of Piaget's later "equilibration") of the "organism as a whole." *Organismic* refers to the organism as a very active organized *functional totality* with its own *essential nature*, which is purposeful and dialectically driven (Pascual-Leone, 2014). *Organismic processes* are rooted in the brain, and they are best modeled within a functional totality viewed from within the individual's own processing. We call this method of modeling *metasubjective analysis* (Arsalidou et al., 2010; Pascual-Leone, 1995, 2013; Pascual-Leone et al., 2015).

Causal is another important term. A theory or model is *descriptive* when it offers ways to express encountered phenomena and structural findings. In contrast, a model is *causal* when its constructs are *distinct from the descriptive constructs* to be explained and can be *independently anchored on experience* via experimentation; and when the causal constructs *can account for change* that descriptive constructs (and data) undergo as a result of experience, maturation, and organismic change. Note that by "causal" we mean *organismic-causal overdetermination*, as will be discussed in the section "Why Developmental Change is Most Visible in Problem-Solving Situations." Descriptive and causal theories or models can also be *local* versus *general* (Pascual-Leone, 1978, 1980). These distinct sorts of theories/models are all jointly needed. Combined, they yield two dimensions of variation (i.e., local vs. general and descriptive vs. causal) that can be crossed. Thus, simplifying, there are local descriptive, general descriptive, local causal (Pepper's "mechanistic" [1942]), and general causal (Pepper's "organismic") theories or models. This is important, because the more general a causal theory is, the *more distinctly differentiated* it will be from the descriptive structural theories it aims to explain and coordinate; and the more local, the *less differentiated* causal theories will tend to be from their descriptive theories, eventually *leading the distinction to collapse* (Pascual-Leone & Johnson, 2005). Note that a causal theory/model (unlike purely descriptive ones) must have an explicit sequential account of how change-as-process occurs: showing how consequent conditions emerge from context and antecedent organismic conditions. So defined, organismic-causal general models are rare in cognitive development, but much needed.

An important methodological aspect is *problem solving*. From an organismic-causal perspective, problem-solving processes are those that can dynamically synthesize *truly novel* (external or mental) *performances*. These are novel performances that are neither directly learned nor maturationally acquired, nor are they the automatic result of learned coordinations. They result instead from "creative" *dynamic syntheses*, generating truly novel *complex schemes* (Piaget's operational structures are an example) that can solve intended problems and can remain in the person's repertoire (long-term memory) as future solution alternatives (see

Shipstead, Lindsey, Marshall, & Engle, 2014). As Gestalt psychologists (Koffka, 1963/1935) and others have intimated, dynamic syntheses in *misleading situations* (typical of problem solving) result from various *organismic resource-factors* (general-purpose brain operators) whose interaction makes representational/operative syntheses and learning possible.

We illustrate these key problem-solving (PS) mechanisms by mentioning three important *resource-factors* or *operators* (Pascual-Leone, 1984, 1995; Pascual-Leone & Johnson, 2005, 2011):

(#PS1) Functional mechanisms of *endogenous mental-attentional capacity* can boost with activation a limited number of task-relevant schemes. This boosting operator, called *M-capacity*, is dialectically complemented by an *attentional interruption* that can actively inhibit task-irrelevant schemes (Howard, Johnson, & Pascual-Leone, 2014; Im-Bolter, Johnson, Ling, & Pascual-Leone, 2015).

(#PS2) A neoGestaltist *internal-field* (*F*) *factor* serves to simplify processes; this is related to the "pragnanz" or "minimum principle" of simplicity – lateral inhibition in the brain. The *F* factor helps to integrate into performance, *via overdetermination*, multiple distinct information-bearing processes (i.e., *schemes*) involved in a task; and it biases the combination of schemes' action or meaning in ways that minimize complexity of the result (Koffka, 1963/1935; Morra, 2008; Pascual-Leone, 1989; Pascual-Leone & Morra, 1991; Rock, 1983).

(#PS3) *Executive* (Koffka's "executive," Piaget's "procedural") *schemes can recognize* within the subject's repertoire subordinate schemes (figurative, operative, or executive) *relevant* or irrelevant *for the task at hand*.

Schemes activated by the here-and-now situation can be: (a) Content-based schemes (*C*-schemes) expressing relatively simple or overlearned features of the situation; (b) relational-pattern schemes (*L*-schemes – products of Logical-abstraction learning), which express relevant relational aspects of the task or situation; or (c) *personal* schemes (affective and emotional, together with cognitive), which we call *B*-schemes, because they constitute the social-personal human *being*. Any of the scheme types could become either misleading or facilitating for a given task. The *currently dominant set of executive schemes*, which we call *executive* or *E* operator, can guide application of attentional processes (i.e., #PS1) to inhibit misleading *C, L,* and *B* schemes and boost activation of relevant ones. This induces emergence of a suitable dominant cluster of activated task-relevant schemes. The ensuing dynamic interaction among these highly activated schemes is automatically regulated by the internal *F* factor (#PS2); and due to the schemes' self-propelling disposition (Piaget's *assimilation strength*), they coordinate (via overdetermination) and produce a dynamically synthesized, metasubjective solution process – a *complex* (often novel and ephemeral) *scheme* that can solve the new problem. With experience (repetition) this ephemeral scheme becomes learned and thus written in the person's repertoire (long-term memory) – a very important factor for working memory and intelligence that Unsworth and Engle (2005) and Verguts and De Boeck (2002) have emphasized.

To illustrate this way of looking at problem solving, consider briefly a classic liquid-transfer task, the Wine and Water Problem. This is a brain-teaser, popular on Internet sites and perhaps first described by W.W. Rouse Ball (1905). The qualitative findings we shall briefly mention are already well established (e.g., Case, 1975). A common version of this problem asks participants to imagine two containers, one (C1) with only water (Wa) and the other (C2) with only wine (Wi). The problem assumes that wine does not initially contain water. A spoonful (S1) of wine is taken from C2 and transferred to C1. A spoonful (S2) of the C1 mixture then is transferred to C2. *Is there now more wine in the water container* (Wi[C1]) *or more water in the wine container* (Wa[C2])? If unfamiliar with this problem, readers might try solving it before reading on.

There are different strategies for solving this task, both quantitative and qualitative. The basic one we shall discuss is qualitative and metasubjective, focused on the core *causal process*: the content carried back and forth by the spoon, which brings about change. This task is *misleading* because a superficial look at the spoon transactions suggests that there is more wine in the water container than water in the wine container (i.e., Wi[C1] > Wa[C2]); because S1 carried only wine, whereas S2 carried both wine and water. Such incomplete analysis is the most frequent error response that we and others have found.

Deeper spoon-sequence examination shows that the *quantity of wine that S2 carried corresponds to the quantity of water that S2 did not carry.* Consequently, the wine taken away from C1, which is the wine that S2 did carry, is quantitatively the same as the water that S2 did not carry. At the end of the transaction, therefore, Wi[C1] = Wa[C2]; that is, the same amount of wine in C1 as water in C2. The algebraic form of the state description of this analysis, after the two (S1, S2) spoon transfers is:

$$(Wa[C2] = S2 - Wi[S2]) \ \& \ (Wi[C1] = S1 - Wi[S2])$$
$$\& \ (S2 = S1) \rightarrow (Wi[C1] = Wa[C2])$$

This problem is useful in rethinking development organismically, because it exhibits – with difficulty level for adults (formal operations) – the *functional* (semantic-pragmatic) *misleading structure* of Piagetian conservation tasks. To understand this algebraic derivation organismically, we must imagine "from within" (i.e., metasubjectively) the subjects mentally solving this task. They have to represent intuitively essential task components by means of *schemes* – schemes that are coordinated (via overdetermination and *F*) as they become jointly activated by mental attention (see #PS1). The three main constituents of this algebraic derivation are Wa[C2], Wi[C1], and S (spoon); they stand for three *complex schemes*[1] that subjects must synthesize dynamically before a higher-level synthesis coordinates them into the task solution. Six distinct constituent schemes may have to be boosted with mental activation to ensure this synthesis. These six symbolic constituents are:

---

1 The algebraic formulation shows well that the schemes must be *complex* (i.e., with distinct coordinated constituents at different hierarchical levels); indeed, each scheme mentioned requires an equality sign to be properly represented.

$$\frac{S2 \;\; = \;\; S1}{\frac{Wa[C2] = \; = S2 - Wi[S2]}{Wi[C1] = \; = S1- \; - Wi[S2]}}$$

In this representation, the underlines demarcate separate constituent schemes. The markers (= and –) are repeated to indicate semantic-pragmatic connections between the schemes. The three-line sequence demarcates the three sets of coordinated schemes – constituents of the three complex schemes Wa[C2], Wi[C1], and S. We have written the scheme Wa[C2] with two constituents, whereas we write scheme Wi[C1] with three constituents, because we assume that process analysis and synthesis of Wa[C2] took place before, and its constituents are now partly chunked.

A mental demand of six symbolic schemes to be coordinated can be handled only when formal operations begin, at about 13 to 14 years of age. This expresses developmental growth of *mental-attentional capacity*, which we mentioned in #PS1 (Pascual-Leone, 1970; Pascual-Leone & Baillargeon, 1994; Pascual-Leone, Escobar, & Johnson, 2012; Pascual-Leone & Johnson, 2005, 2011). The role of an *internal-field F factor* (#PS2) in the solution can be seen in our algebraic analysis. Indeed, repetition of Wi[S2] within two different contexts (i.e., S2 – Wi[S2] and S1 – Wi[S2]) shows that the same entity Wi[S2] takes two distinct meanings in the analysis: water not carried and wine carried. This situation conflicts with *F-operator's* simplicity constraint that here creates a bias against successful resolution of the problem (such tendency is often known as Stimulus-Response Compatibility [Proctor & Reeve, 1990]). To maintain this distinction of meaning, the organism must have two semantically distinct schemes for the same entity, boosted separately in the mind with mental attention.

Finally, *executive schemes* – higher planning and control processes (see #PS3) – are implicit in our analysis: They monitor choice of solution strategy, analysis of the transfer sequence, etc. Executive schemes also intervene in the subject's choice of action schemes and the tacit decision to represent twice (in two separate schemes) the entity Wi[S2], so as to capture the key difference of water-not-carried versus wine-carried. Such refined processing in misleading situations exposes individual differences. For instance, Field Dependent persons (Pascual-Leone, 1989; Witkin & Goodenough, 1981) may tend to fail this task *both* because the *F* factor (here misleading) is strong in them *and* because their executive know-how often is inadequate relative to Field Independent persons, who are more likely to succeed in this sort of task.

Why Developmental Change is Most Visible in Problem-Solving Situations

Habit and automatisms do not suffice in problem-solving situations. Rather, people must use brain resources to cope with misleading factors, such as in the *M-demanding* Wine and Water Problem. Similar problem-solving tasks with less mental-attentional demand, such as Piaget's Conservations, are handled earlier in development. For example, conservation of substance tends to be solved at 7 or 8 years of age. Characteristically, problem-solving tasks with variable demand for mental resources (in particular *M-capacity*) tend to be solved promptly when the suitable age level is reached. This is the basis and empirical criterion of *developmental stages*. Because stages often are misunderstood, we will make explicit the distinction between states, steps, and stages. A *state* is a pure description of the here-and-now actual performance (physical or mental) of the organism. A *step* is one state describing a relatively invariant and stable moment in a developmental-sequence change. A *stage* is an organismic descriptive state, or sequence of states, with two uncommon characteristics: (1) it is *"essentially natural"* (Goldstein, 2000 /1934), because it is induced by, and should be coupled with, an internal organismic dialectics (Pascual-Leone, 2012, 2014), which is expressible by a *causal-overdetermination model*; and (2) the stage (or stage sequence) is *describable across types of tasks or situations (i.e., empirical paradigms). Causal overdetermination* (Audi, 1995; Psillos, 2002) is a co-determination of given outcomes by all probabilistic causal factors that at the present moment *could* in fact contribute to configure the outcome.

Stages usually are marked by abrupt changes (non-linear growth) in outcome performance. To explain their emergence we infer (and then empirically demonstrate) existence of general-use resource-factors (or *operators*) within the organism, factors whose abrupt change causes the stages. This applies both to child development and to aging (or pathology). When a certain task, or expected performance, requires organismic availability of a given level of a resource-factor, task failure tends to occur if the power of the resource-factor is deficient. Thus, in all domains, problem-solving situations optimally exhibit organismic stages and cognitive/personal growth.

Which are the Mechanisms of Developmental Change? How to Model Cognitive Development as an Emergent Organismic Process?

We believe that neither neuroscience nor historico-cultural social sciences, etc., could thrive in the future without organismic modeling "from within," which rethinking cognitive development and psychology requires. Neuropsychology must model the organism as a growing metasubjective functional totality, effective in problem solving (Arsalidou & Pascual-Leone, 2016). How could such a causal-overdetermination theory be designed? Without attempting a final answer, we comment on the need to make explicit the bi-level organization, distinguishing between (a) information-bearing units (i.e., schemes) and (b) the various resource-factors that usually are non-informational (i.e., general-purpose and content-free). A model of change needs functional *units* that can change; it also needs causal determinants, often *resource-factors*, that bring this change about. In our view natural organismic units are schemes, and other causal determinants of change are both the brain resource operators and the resistances of Reality[2] to the subject's activity. We illustrate using constructs and data from our theory of constructive operators (Pascual-Leone & Johnson, 2004, 2005, 2011).

First level of organization – the schemes. *Schemes* are meaning-bearing conditional factors (i.e., functors) that correspond with functionally unitized brain circuits or networks, and embody probabilistic *constraints/resistances* – resistances of (past, present, future) reality applicable to the subject's actions or representations. For instance, a resistance of reality is the unavoidable fact that, in the Water and Wine Problem, S2 will necessarily carry both some wine and some water. Schemes can be seen as self-propelling *systems that coordinate three distinct sorts of component*, all in dynamic/dialectical interaction:

(a) a *releasing component* that contains *conditions* predicating features/templates that signal probable applicability of the scheme in question;
(b) an *effective component* that stipulates or carries cognitive, action, affective, or emotive *effects* of this scheme – effects whose application probabilistically brings results, often in a simultaneous or sequentially organized manner;
(c) a *functional component* that formulates the *gist* or overall functional description of the scheme – its practical importance and potential contribution to activities.

Organismic change of schemes is ensured by two complementary modes of functioning that Piaget named assimilation and accommodation. *Assimilation* is the self-propelling tendency of schemes to apply to configure (i.e., *in-form*) input-representation or action-performances. *Assimilation varies in its strength* of application (higher or lower). When it applies, assimilation functionally configures representations or action-performances by imposing qualitative or quantitative characteristics. These imposed characteristics, from various schemes that apply, take "degrees of freedom" from the representation or performance being produced until (all degrees exhausted) it is fully constituted. Because all here-and-now activated schemes tend to apply, due to their assimilation function, all representations and performances are *overdetermined* by the dominant set of compatible schemes. By virtue of this principle of *Schemes' Overdetermination of Performance*, assimilation by the most dominant set of schemes is followed by assimilation by the next dominant set, and so in turn until all "degrees of freedom" have been used up to complete the actual performance or representation.

Accommodation is the self-propelling tendency of schemes *to adapt* to encountered changes – new resistances – of experienced Reality within the situation at hand, *by modifying* (perhaps trial and error) *conditions and/or effects of the schemes in question*. This makes the schemes *more apt* for successful use in this kind of

---

2 We write *Reality* with capitals when we mean to refer to whatever is out there in the environmental milieu, prior to its perceptual or cognitive construal – not objects or processes, to be sure, but instead multiple, often complex and inter-related, perhaps manifold, dynamic constraints. We write *reality* when these packages of constraints, experienced as resistances to one's agency and activities, have been constructed/synthesized into percepts, representations, or action moves (i.e., schemes of various sorts).

situation. After accommodation, schemes are more apt for the particular sort of situation, because their conditions and/or effects change/adapt to express (or embody) actual *resistances* from experience that are *knowable in the long run* (see Apel, 1995, Introduction to paperback edn.). Resistances are thus abstracted as reliable probabilistic invariances (features, often relational), which predict future consequences conditional to actions. Accommodation helps figurative/representational schemes to progressively reflect (Piaget's reflective abstraction) the situations in question. Such compatible clusters of schemes adaptively embody relevant resistances to praxis and stand for entities (e.g., objects) or types (e.g., concepts). Such reflection may be *iconic*, *indexical*, or *symbolic* (in the sense of Peirce's semiotics – Apel, 1995; Johansen, 1993) as convenient.

The two modes of schemes – assimilation and accommodation – are essential to explain cognitive and developmental change. These functional modes may be innately prepared, because they seem to be semantic-pragmatically expressed by two distinct and well-studied brain networks also found in monkeys and apes. These are, respectively, the *dorsal* versus *ventral* networks – both basically frontal and parietal (Austin, 2010; Corbetta & Shulman, 2002; Stöttinger et al., 2015). Their functional complementarity is well studied. The dorsal network carries out top-down the cognitive goals of the intended praxis (i.e., goal-directed activity addressed to the environment). The ventral network notices, bottom-up, relevant or salient aspects of the situation (part of it is called "saliency network"), and it appraises mismatches with the intended praxis. Corbetta and Shulman (2002, p. 208) described this contrast as follows: "Neurophysiological studies indicate that the dorsal frontoparietal network, which is recruited for top-down selection, is also modulated by the bottom-up distinctiveness of objects in a visual scene." They subsequently added: "the ventral frontoparietal network is modulated by the detection of unattended or low-frequency events, independent of their location, sensory modality of presentation or response demands. These stimuli reorient attention, but not necessarily spatially" (p. 210). Stöttinger et al. (2015, p. 15) further clarified the function of this ventral pathway: "a more plausible assumption is that the observed [ventral, JPL] network is involved in processing alternative options after a mismatch has been detected. In order to update a mental representation . . . [o]ne has to flexibly decide either to stay with the current model [representation, JPL] or to explore new, alternative options."

Waters and Tucker (2013) pointed out that the functioning in these dorsal vs. ventral areas might relate, respectively, to Piaget's assimilation versus accommodation. Without reviewing data, we note that the ventral pathway tends to use strongly the right hemisphere, whereas the dorsal pathway predominately uses the left hemisphere, where the executive network and mental attention dominate (Austin, 2010; Corbetta & Shulman, 2002). Thus, one could say that the mode of assimilation, in Piaget's sense, is best expressed in the brain by the dorsal pathway of the left hemisphere, whereas accommodation is expressed by the ventral pathway and the right hemisphere, two functional systems of the brain that (like Piaget's two modes of scheme functioning) are in continuous dialectical interaction. Since the brain systems are innately prepared, so should be Piaget's two modes.

Such intriguing interpretation should be further investigated. If this interpretation proves correct, accommodation (more so than assimilation) might be closely related to affective/emotional processes, such as empathy or negative feelings, because ventral and medial regions of the brain are involved in these affective processes.

Second level of organization – the resource operators. Causal determinants exist that bring about reliable, age-bound, sudden growth periods in cognitive performance – producing spurts in the developmental growth curve. They often index stages. Stages are not just products of learning promoted by experience. The spurts may be caused by endogenous organismic factors whose growth induces transition into new stages; for the M-operator this growth is maturational (Pascual-Leone, 1970; Pascual-Leone & Johnson, 2011; Pascual-Leone, Johnson, Baskind, Dworsky, & Severtston, 2000). Key mechanisms of problem solving (#PS1, #PS2, and #PS3, above) are resources $<E, M, I, F>$ that augment during childhood and whose coordination produces *mental attention* (Pascual-Leone, 1984; Pascual-Leone & Johnson, 2004, 2005, 2011). Again, these resources are mental-attentional capacity (factor or *operator M*), attentional inhibition/interruption (*operator I*), the internal-field factor of simplicity (*operator F*), and the *currently dominant set of executive schemes* – which controls and allocates (in context-sensitive manner) the first two resources (this set is the *operator E*). This organismic-developmental model can help to comprehend many controversial issues in cognitive, social, and emotional development. Rethinking cognitive development should include investigation of the extent to which this sort of model is consistent with neuroscience.

Illustrative data that point to M-capacity as content-free general resource. Mental-attentional capacity (M as key maturational component of working memory and of fluid intelligence Gf) is indexed by the maximal number of distinct schemes to which mental-attentional effort can simultaneously apply. M-power (the measure of M-capacity) tends to increase maturationally by one unit every other year from 3 to 15 years of age,[3] while remaining relatively insensitive to experiential factors. M-capacity is a major endogenous developmental factor that limits children's complexity of cognitive processing (Arsalidou et al., 2010; Pascual-Leone, 1970; Pascual-Leone & Baillargeon, 1994; Pascual-Leone & Johnson, 2005, 2011; Pascual-Leone, Johnson, & Agostino, 2010). *M-capacity* is a content-free and general-purpose resource – applicable across content domains, types of task, and types of subject. M can also be properly measured (Arsalidou et al., 2010; Pascual-Leone & Baillargeon, 1994; Pascual-Leone & Johnson, 2011).

We (Calvo, 2004; Pascual-Leone, Johnson, & Calvo, 2004) sought to demonstrate these general-purpose and content-free characteristics of *M-capacity* by treating it as a constructivist *developmental measure* closely related to Gf (fluid intelligence, the functional core of g). Note that the idea of general intelligence (g *factor*) as a

---

3 Note that the M-measure is discontinuous, but we presume that the corresponding organismic process grows progressively, as biological processes do. The measure is discontinuous because, via task analysis, we are counting organismic schemes – discrete functional entities (e.g., Pascual-Leone & Johnson, 2011).

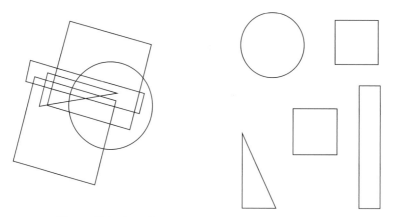

Figure 5.1. *Sample Figural Intersections Test (FIT) item.*

functional relational construct obtainable as an invariant across different types of tasks was evident in Spearman's conception of g (see our second epigraph and Gould, 1981); a conception shared by Binet ("it matters very little what the tests are so long as they are numerous"; Binet & Simon, 1911, p. 329). We studied 1,148 grade-four children (9–10 years old), from 21 Toronto-area schools. Children completed the Figural Intersections Task (FIT), an M-capacity measure created via task analysis and neo-Piagetian theory-guided developmental research (Pascual-Leone & Ijaz, 1989; Pascual-Leone & Baillargeon, 1994; Pascual-Leone & Johnson, 2011). FIT items ask one to find the area of intersection of a variable number of geometric shapes (from two to eight; see Figure 5.1). The M-capacity estimate is the maximum number of shapes the child can reliably intersect. Percentile scores on the *Canadian Cognitive Abilities Test* (*CCAT*, 1998) – a standardized measure of cognitive ability with verbal, non-verbal, and quantitative subscales – were available for 1,052 of the children. Percentile scores on *Canadian Achievement Tests* (Third edn., *CAT-3*, 2000) – an academic achievement measure with reading, language, and mathematics subscales – were obtained for 1,026 children. Average FIT score for the sample was 3.92 (SD =1.34), matching the theoretical prediction that 9–10-year-olds have an M-capacity of four symbolic schemes (Pascual-Leone, 1970; Pascual-Leone & Johnson, 2005). Mean percentile scores on CCAT (M = 54.96, SD = 26.22) and CAT-3 (M = 49.31, SD = 27.00) were as expected from age norms.

FIT correlated strongly with CCAT Non-Verbal scale [$r(1059)$ =.61, p <.0001] and with total-test scores on both CCAT [$r(1050)$ =.59, p <.0001] and CAT-3 [$r(1024)$ =.51, p <.0001]. Demographic data were not collected on individual children, but were available at the school level. Mean test scores were computed for each of the 21 schools, and correlations were run on these school-means. Again, FIT was highly related to both CCAT [$r(19)$ =.73, p <.01] and CAT-3 [$r(19)$ =.68, p <.01]. One might expect these correlations to be inflated due to school-differences in socio-economic status. We thus partialled-out the percentage of ESL (English as Second Language) students at each school and average family income of the census tracts (neighborhoods) where the schools were located (obtained from 2001 Census

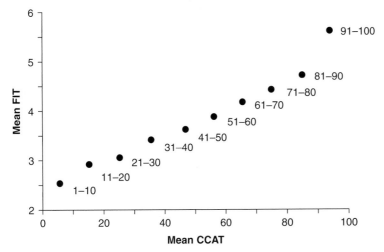

Figure 5.2. *Sample divided into 10 groups according to CCAT percentile-score (1–10, 11–20, etc.). For each group, mean CCAT is plotted against mean FIT score.*

of Canada data). Partialling did not, however, affect degree of association between FIT and the standardized tests, CCAT [partial $r(17) = .74, p < .01$] and CAT-3 [partial $r(17) = .69, p < 01$]. Because partialling should reduce the weight of differences in expected sociocultural learning (which in FIT could change the perceptual strategies used), we can infer that variance due to M is strong and *is distinct from the variance due to sociocultural learning/experience*. Thus, M-capacity might be maturational and general-purpose, as our model predicts.

In a second large-scale study with 960 grade 2 children (i.e., 7–8-year-olds), mean FIT score ($M = 3.07, SD = 1.09$) was consistent with the theoretical prediction that children at this age have an M-capacity of three symbolic schemes. FIT scores children obtained in grade 2 were predictive of their ability and achievement scores when tested with CCAT [$r(731) = .44, p < .0001$] and CAT-3 [$r(753) = .37, p < .0001$] in grade 4.

Returning to the initial sample of 1,148 grade-four children, we examined in more detail the pattern of covariation between FIT and CCAT. We grouped participants in terms of deciles in CCAT percentile-score. We computed the mean FIT and CCAT score for children falling into each CCAT decile group. Figure 5.2 shows the covariation of mean FIT and CCAT scores. Up to the 91st percentile group, mean FIT score increases linearly with CCAT score. However, in the highest percentile group (91–100), there is a jump in mean FIT score that breaks the linear pattern. Linear growth of FIT scores with the CCAT percentiles could be due to children's growth in sociocultural experience/learning or to meaningful individual differences in M-capacity. The spurt in FIT scores after the 90th percentile is unlikely to be due to sociocultural learning/experience. Rather, *performance at the highest level in general ability may be related to particularly high M-capacity for one's age.*

There is a way to examine whether the variance that boosts FIT score in the 91–100 CCAT-percentile subsample corresponds to sociocultural learning or to *M*-capacity. Because the average 9–10 year old has (in our empirically-supported developmental model) an *M*-capacity that can coordinate easily no more than four symbolic schemes, FIT items with more than five figures should be *hard* for this sample, forcing them to use *learned perceptual strategies* in order to succeed better. Such strategies could involve, for example, guessing that the correct response is likely to fall in an area with high density of intersecting lines. If learning enhances performance on hard items, then we might expect these items to exhibit higher correlation with CCAT. In the absence of learning as an important factor in FIT performance, however, we would expect higher correlation between CCAT and items predicted to be within the children's capacity. We therefore split the test into two subtests: the FIT-Easy items (with two to five overlapping shapes) and the FIT-Hard items (with six to eight shapes). Children of this age should be able to solve the FIT-Easy items using only *M*-capacity. In FIT-Hard items, however, they must use both *M* and *learned perceptual strategies*. We then correlated scores on the two types of FIT items with CCAT score. For the total sample, the correlation was [$r(1050) = .57$] for FIT-Easy versus [$r(1050) = .53$] for FIT-Hard – a difference that is statistically significant ($p < .05$). We then examined the correlations just for the group with CCAT percentile-score above 90. Due to reduced variance, the correlations were lower, but they maintained the same pattern: [$r(93) = .26, p < .05$] with FIT-Easy and [$r(93) = .19, p > .05$] with FIT-Hard. This finding supports our claim that the abnormally high FIT score in the highest CCAT-percentile group is due to the factor *M*, construct-validating our prediction that *M-capacity* is a general-purpose operator and a key maturational constituent of Spearman's *g* (fluid intelligence, to be precise).

We have presented elsewhere evidence that *M*-capacity is measureable in a content-free manner, across types of tasks and types of subjects (Arsalidou et al., 2010; Im-Bolter, Johnson, & Pascual-Leone, 2006; Pascual-Leone & Johnson, 2005, 2011). We present here some new data (Pascual-Leone & Johnson, 2012). We tested 30 children in grade 2 ($M = 7;8, SD = 0.29$) and 50 in grade 4 ($M = 9;9, SD = 0.32$). They received an abbreviated or *short* version of the *standard FIT* used in the study described above (i.e., four items at each of seven complexity levels, as compared with seven items per level in the standard FIT). They also received a verbal *M*-measure: the Direction Following Task (DFT; Cunning, 2003; Pascual-Leone & Johnson, 2011).

In the DFT the child has to follow verbal directions involving placement of tokens (different shape, size, and color) on a board having spaces of different size and color. The current study used a touch-screen computer version of the task, in which children used a stylus to move tokens on an image of the board on the screen. DFT items vary in complexity (seven levels, each with a distinct *M*-capacity demand). The *M*-score is the *M*-demand of highest complexity level passed. In the sample items below, the underlines demarcate schemes that must be boosted with *M*-capacity (see Pascual-Leone & Johnson, 2011):

M-demand of 3: Place a <u>yellow</u> <u>circle</u> on a <u>small</u> <u>green</u> space.
M-demand of 5: Place a <u>red</u> <u>square</u> and a <u>white</u> <u>circle</u> on a <u>small</u> <u>yellow</u> space.

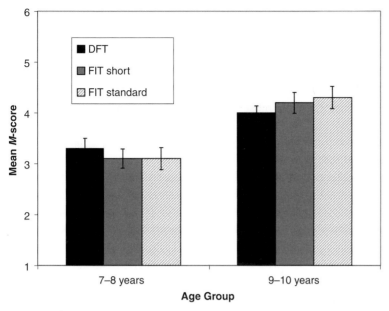

Figure 5.3. *Mean M-scores as a function of task and age group; bars show standard errors.*

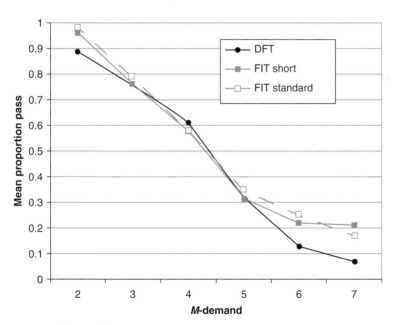

Figure 5.4. *Mean proportion pass as a function of task and item M-demand.*

About one week following the first testing session, 30 children at each age level were tested with the standard FIT. Figure 5.3 shows mean scores on the three measures as a function of age group. Mean scores correspond to predicted M-capacity of 3 for 7–8 year olds and 4 for 9–10 year olds. Mean scores did not differ significantly across M-tasks. Figure 5.4 shows mean proportion of items passed on the three M-tasks, as a function of item M-demand. The two FIT versions (i.e., short and standard) yield almost identical performance curves. Despite very different content and method, the DFT curve closely matches the FIT curves. Consistent with the prediction that the M-capacity of the older age group is 4 units, the performance curves show a sharp deflection after M-demand of 4. The closeness of FIT (visuospatial) and DFT (verbal) M-scores strongly supports our prediction (Pascual-Leone, 1970; Pascual-Leone & Smith, 1969) of a parameter invariance across domains and age groups – for example, a general-purpose resource that is maturational (as experimental researchers are now confirming; Cowan, Ricker, Clark, Hinrichs, & Glass, 2014). Pascual-Leone and Johnson (2005, 2011) have summarized data showing six M-tasks, very different in content domain, with equally close quantitative M-scores for the chosen age-group samples.

Conclusions

We suggested that theoretical modeling and data analysis in cognitive development must be causal (via *organismic-causal overdetermination*), adopting the subject's perspective from within his or her operative processes (i.e., *metasubjective* analysis), and be focused on problem solving. The models should be *operative* (not describing only *figuratives* – i.e., representation states) and focused on processes that cause internal-psychological change. These constructs should be defined at two distinct levels: *schemes* (the first, more concrete, level) and *organismic resource-factors or operators* (the second, more abstract, level). The resource operators (e.g., M-capacity) apply on the first-level, self-propelling units (i.e., schemes). Among second-level constructs we mentioned the complex developmental resource *mental/endogenous attention*. We model its developmental emergence by means of a functional system of four resource operators $<E, M, I, F>$: An attentional executive E (*a currently dominant set of executive schemes* controlling operators M and I), an attentional mental-activation capacity M, an attentional inhibition/interruption capacity I, and an internal-field simplicity factor F. Use of I is required for successful performance in *misleading* situations, but not in *facilitating* ones. We briefly mentioned distinct learning factors that contribute to constitute different sorts of schemes: Those that carry and empirically produce Content (C-schemes), those that carry and produce Logical-relational functional structures (L-schemes – e.g., Piaget's operational structures are complex L-schemes*)*, and those that embody affects, emotions, and vital values of the personal-social human Being (B-schemes). These various sorts of schemes may be activated by the situation at hand, by here-and-now memories, or by mental attention. Together, they

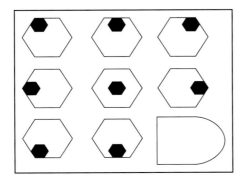

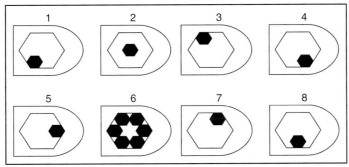

Figure 5.5. *Variation on Raven's item C7 taken from Fig. 1 of Skuy et al. (2002).*
[Reprinted from Intelligence, 30, Skuy et al., Effects of mediated learning
experience on Raven's matrices scores of African and non-African university
students in South Africa, 221–232, 2002, with permission from Elsevier.]

overdetermine resulting performances (at times after unwanted/misleading schemes
are inhibited by the executive and *I*).

Adopting this sort of organismic modeling, it is possible to do *metasubjective task
analysis* of the person's own processing – a form of analysis that can complement
good *objective* task analyses done from the perspective of an external observer
(*meta-empiricist analyses*). An excellent example of the latter is Carpenter, Just,
and Shell's (1990) analysis of Raven's matrices. Our fourth epigraph quoted Heitz et
al. (2005) expressing concern about how attention might intervene in solving
Raven's items. Unsworth and Engle (2005) carefully analyzed and quasi-experi-
mentally tested processes likely to intervene in task solution – expanding on the
meta-empiricist task analysis (and computer simulation modeling) carried out by
Carpenter et al. (1990). We briefly sketch our own model to compare with Carpenter
et al.'s task analysis, and so illustrate usefulness of taking a metasubjective perspective (Pascual-Leone, 2013).

Figure 5.5 shows an adapted version of Raven's item C7 from Skuy et al. (2002; for
copyright reasons, we do not show the actual Raven's item). In the more difficult
Raven's items, to identify the missing part in the matrix (lower right region), participants must analyze perceptually (PER) *each and every* row, column, and at times
diagonals of the item's matrix. Often a second dimension of variation is found on the

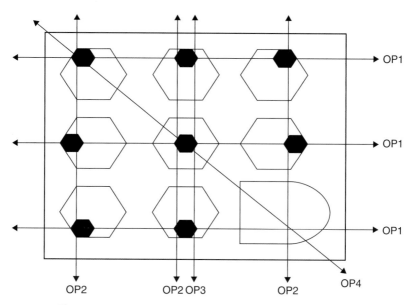

Figure 5.6. *Dimensions of variation in solution of Raven's-like item; item adapted from Fig. 1 of Skuy et al. (2002).*

rows or the columns of the matrix, instead of being in the diagonals; this would give rows or columns two concurrent dimensions of variation instead of one. Participants must identify simple or complex features (f_i, f_j, etc.) that *for each dimension* of variation (whether in rows, columns, or diagonals) constitute a *relational* figurative *invariant* characteristic of this dimension This relational invariant makes *mutually congruent* (*correspondence* rule) *the various* (often three) *object-patterns* that concretely make up the dimension in question (instantiating its correspondence rule as a *token* case). This is done via perceptual-cognitive analysis (PER: f_i, f_j, ...) conducted successively for each required dimension[4] and then held in mind. When this is done, an operative scheme of general-synthesis (OPΣ) recursively integrates the feature-invariants of all dimensions to produce (via overdetermination – Peirce's abduction) the pattern corresponding to the missing part.

Figure 5.6 outlines generically a possible case for these dimensions of variation. Note that we show OP3 in only one column in Figure 5.6. This represents possible need to process a second dimension on the columns. This is in fact not needed to solve the presented item. However, were a second dimension present, as in more difficult items, OP3 would apply on all three columns. The actual process of dynamic problem solving can be roughly expressed by the following formula:

---

4 Not all Raven's items require consideration of all dimensions of variation. In simpler items just one or two distinct dimensions must be considered to triangulate the relational invariant features to be abstracted, which the missing right-lower section should also have. These simpler items are often (see Table 3 of Unsworth & Engle, 2005) more strongly correlated with working memory tasks (Operation Span) because in Raven's they have less executive demand.

$$\underline{OP\Sigma}(\underline{OP4}(\underline{OP3}(\underline{OP2}(\underline{OP1}(\underline{PER:\ f_i, f_j})))))$$

In this formula, operative processes (OP1, OP2, etc.) for the various dimensions apply, to the right, on the products of previous operations. The order of operative processes could vary, but to complete the problem, all dimensions must be analyzed to extract/abstract their feature invariant; and these relational features are synthesized by OPΣ into the solution pattern. If we now count the number of schemes involved (indicated by underlines), there are in this generic formula at least six distinct symbolic/mental processes to be coordinated. Many items may involve fewer relevant dimensions, but they all require examination of rows and columns (and at times diagonals).

This is only a sketch of operative task analysis conducted from within the participant's processing (i.e., metasubjective analysis). A complementary alternative way of doing such analysis (meta-empiricist task analysis) would seek to identify only relational figurative features and their correspondence-rule patterns relevant in the test as a whole (because instantiated in one or another item). This is *objective* analysis, focused on relevant figures of the items – that is, a *figurative model*. Complementary to such figurative objective modeling would be an *operative model* "from within" – the sort of metasubjective analysis we have described. Indeed, the operative model could be the system of operations that enable participants to actually abstract/recognize the figurative model. Processes expressed in these two complementary models help participants to select the missing part of the matrix.

Carpenter et al. (1990) presented an excellent example of meta-empiricist figurative modeling of Raven's matrices. Unsworth and Engle (2005) experimentally studied this model and interpreted it as demanding a mental/executive attention resource-factor not unlike ours (which for them is an explication of the central executive component of Baddeley's working memory). Carpenter et al. and Unsworth and Engle called correspondence "rules" what in Figure 5.6 we represent as dimensions of variation. They called "tokens" the object-patterns of dimensions whose inter-relation instantiates the correspondence rule of the item. What our sort of metasubjective operative modeling (here only sketched, but not fully unfolded) adds to good meta-empiricist modeling, such as Carpenter et al.'s, is the possibility to model the internal operative progression of problem solving – organismic-causal change. With this operative metasubjective approach, we can explain developmental change (stages) as well as learning "from within," which meta-empiricist figurative modeling cannot do.

Our task analysis formula, albeit global and generic, shows that in difficult items six distinct complex schemes must be synthesized and coordinated in concrete to reach the solution. This could rise to seven schemes, if the PER operative has not been practiced enough to have been chunked with the figuratives (f_i, f_j). As Unsworth and Engle (2005) emphasized, solution is only possible thanks to a repertoire of schemes (knowledge) synthesized or previously acquired. *M*-capacity is not sufficient (Shipstead et al., 2014), although it is necessary to enable coordination of the dimensions' relational invariants ("tokens") in Raven's items. As our formula shows, the M-capacity needed to handle difficult items is available only at or after 13 years of age (Pascual-Leone, 1970; Pascual-Leone & Johnson, 2005). Thus, only at this age or later could difficult items be passed. In easier items, when only one or two dimensions of variation may be needed, M-demand reduces by 2 or 3, because OP3, OP4, and perhaps OP2 would be eliminated from the formula. In that case metasubjective developmental prediction would be that 9–10 year olds (or even 7–8 year olds) could succeed, if needed knowledge is available (see also Bereiter & Scardamalia, 1979, for an early attempt to analyze Raven's matrices in terms of demand for M-capacity).

Rethinking cognitive development to improve organismic modeling and measurement of mental/executive attention requires refined (metasubjective) task analysis. We have suggested a good way to proceed.

Author Note

Research reported here was supported by Social Sciences and Humanities Research Council of Canada standard grants (#410–2001–1077, #410–2006–2325, and #410–2010–2313). We are grateful to the students and staff of participating schools. We thank the following lab members who contributed to data collection: Marie Arsalidou, Christina Balioussis, Maaria Baloch, Sarah Bauer, Alejandra Calvo, Deborah Fallick, Ninat Friedland, Al Gorewich, Carolyn Hagan, Rebecca Hiltz, Sander Hitzig, Wendy Ko, Cheryl Lee, Katie MacDonald, Dessy Marinova, Manolo Romero Escobar, and Enzo Verrilli. Steven Howard programmed the computer version of the DFT.

References

Apel, K-O. (1995). *Charles Peirce: From pragmatism to pragmaticism*. Atlantic Highlands, NJ: Humanities Press.

Arsalidou, M., & Pascual-Leone, J. (2016). Constructivist developmental theory is needed in developmental neuroscience. *NPJ Science of Learning, 1*, 16016.

Arsalidou, M., Pascual-Leone, J., & Johnson, J. (2010). Misleading cues improve developmental assessment of attentional capacity: The color matching task. *Cognitive Development, 25*, 262–277.

Audi, R. (Ed.) (1995). *The Cambridge dictionary of philosophy*. New York, NY: Cambridge University Press.

Austin, J. H. (2010). The thalamic gateway: How the meditative training of attention evolves toward selfless transformations of attention. In B. Bruya (Ed.), *Effortless attention* (pp. 373–407). Cambridge, MA: MIT Press.

Bereiter, C., & Scardamalia, M. (1979). Pascual-Leone's M construct as a link between cognitive-developmental and psychometric concepts of intelligence. *Intelligence, 3*, 41–63.

Binet, A., & Simon, T. (1911). *A method of measuring the development of intelligence in young children*. Lincoln, IL: Courier Company.

Calvo, A. (2004). *Detection of latent giftedness by means of mental-capacity testing.* Unpublished master's thesis, York University, Toronto, ON.

Canadian Achievement Tests – Third Edition (CAT-3). (2000). Markham, ON: Canadian Test Centre.

Canadian Cognitive Abilities Test (CCAT). (1998). Toronto, ON: Nelson Education.

Carpenter, P. A., Just, M. A., & Shell, P. (1990). What one intelligence test measures: A theoretical account of the processing in the Raven Progressive Matrices Test. *Psychological Review, 97,* 404–431.

Case, R. (1975). Gearing the demands of instruction to the developmental capacities of the learner. *Review of Educational Research, 45,* 59–87.

Corbetta, M., & Shulman, G. L. (2002). Control of goal-directed and stimulus-driven attention in the brain. *Nature Reviews Neuroscience, 3,* 215–229.

Cowan, N., Ricker, T. J., Clark, K. M., Hinrichs, G. A., & Glass, B. A. (2014). Knowledge cannot explain the developmental growth of working memory capacity. *Developmental Science, 18,* 132–145.

Cunning, S. (2003). *The direction-following task: Assessing mental capacity in the linguistic domain.* Unpublished doctoral dissertation, York University, Toronto, ON.

Deary, I. J. (2002). g and cognitive elements of information processing: An agnostic view. In R. J. Sternberg & E. L. Grigorenko (Eds.), *The general factor of intelligence: How general is it?* (pp. 151–181). Mahwah, NJ: Erlbaum.

Goldstein, K. (2000). *The organism.* New York, NY: Zone Books. (Original work published 1934).

Gould, S. J. (1981). *The mismeasure of man.* New York, NY: Norton.

Greenberg, L., & Pascual-Leone, J. (1995). A dialectical constructivist approach to experiential change. In R. Neimeyer & M. Mahoney (Eds.), *Constructivism in psychotherapy* (pp. 169–191). Washington, DC: APA Press.

Heitz, R. P., Unsworth, N., & Engle, R. W. (2005). Working memory capacity, attentional control, and fluid intelligence. In O. Wilhelm & R. W. Engle (Eds.), *Handbook of understanding and measuring intelligence* (pp. 61–78). Thousand Oaks, CA: Sage.

Howard, S. J., Johnson, J., & Pascual-Leone, J. (2014). Clarifying inhibitory control: Diversity and development of attentional inhibition. *Cognitive Development, 31,* 1–21.

Im-Bolter, N., Johnson, J., Ling, D., & Pascual-Leone, J. (2015). Inhibition: Mental control process or mental resource? *Journal of Cognition and Development, 16,* 666–681.

Im-Bolter, N., Johnson, J., & Pascual-Leone, J. (2006). Processing limitation in children with specific language impairment: The role of executive function. *Child Development, 77,* 1822–1841.

Johansen, J. D. (1993). *Dialogic semiosis: An essay on signs and meaning.* Bloomington, IN: Indiana University Press.

Koffka, K. (1963). *Principles of gestalt psychology.* New York, NY: Harcourt, Brace, & World. (Original work published 1935).

Morra, S. (2008). A test of a neo-Piagetian model of the water-level task. *European Journal of Developmental Psychology, 5,* 369–400.

Pascual-Leone, J. (1970). A mathematical model for the transition rule in Piaget's developmental stages. *Acta Psychologica, 32,* 301–345.

Pascual-Leone, J. (1978). Compounds, confounds, and models in developmental information processing: A reply to Trabasso and Foellinger. *Journal of Experimental Child Psychology, 26,* 18–40.

Pascual-Leone, J. (1980). Constructive problems for constructive theories: The current relevance of Piaget's work and a critique of information-processing simulation psychology. In R. Kluwe & H. Spada (Eds.), *Developmental models of thinking* (pp. 263–296). New York, NY: Academic Press.

Pascual-Leone, J. (1984). Attention, dialectic, and mental effort: Towards an organismic theory of life stages. In M. L. Commons, F. A. Richards, & G. Armon (Eds.) *Beyond formal operations: Late adolescence and adult cognitive development* (pp. 182–215). New York, NY: Praeger.

Pascual-Leone, J. (1989). An organismic process model of Witkin's field-dependence-independence. In T. Globerson & T. Zelniker (Eds.), *Cognitive style and cognitive development* (pp. 36–70). Norwood, NJ: Ablex.

Pascual-Leone, J. (1995). Learning and development as dialectical factors in cognitive growth. *Human Development, 38*, 338–348.

Pascual-Leone, J. (2012). Piaget as a pioneer of dialectical constructivism: Seeking dynamic processes for human science. In E. Marti & C. Rodriguez (Eds.), *After Piaget*. Edison, NJ: Transaction.

Pascual-Leone, J. (2013). Can we model organismic causes of working memory, efficiency and fluid intelligence? A meta-subjective perspective. *Intelligence, 41*, 738–743.

Pascual-Leone J. (2014). Dialectics. In T. Teo (Ed.), *Encyclopedia of critical psychology* (pp. 421–428). New York, NY: SpringerReference.

Pascual-Leone, J., & Baillargeon, R. (1994). Developmental measurement of mental attention. *International Journal of Behavioral Development, 17*, 161–200.

Pascual-Leone, J., Escobar, E. M. R., & Johnson, J. (2012). Logic: Development of logical operations. In W. Hirstein (Ed.), *Encyclopedia of human behavior* (2nd edn.). New York, NY: Elsevier.

Pascual-Leone, J., & Ijaz, H. (1989). Mental capacity testing as a form of intellectual-developmental assessment. In R. Samuda, S. Kong, J. Cummins, J. Pascual-Leone, & J. Lewis. *Assessment and placement of minority students* (pp. 143–171). Toronto, ON: Hogrefe International.

Pascual-Leone, J., & Johnson, J. (2004). Affect, self-motivation, and cognitive development: A dialectical constructivist view. In D. Y. Dai & R. S. Sternberg (Eds.), *Motivation, emotion, and cognition: Integrative perspectives on intellectual functioning and development* (pp. 197–235). Mahwah, NJ: Erlbaum.

Pascual-Leone, J., & Johnson, J. (2005). A dialectical constructivist view of developmental intelligence. In O. Wilhelm & R. Engle (Eds.), *Handbook of understanding and measuring intelligence* (pp. 177–201). Thousand Oaks, CA: Sage.

Pascual-Leone, J., & Johnson, J. (2011). A developmental theory of mental attention: Its applications to measurement and task analysis (pp. 13–46). In P. Barrouillet & V. Gaillard (Eds.), *Cognitive development and working memory: A dialogue between neo-Piagetian and cognitive approaches* (pp. 13–46). New York, NY: Psychology Press.

Pascual-Leone, J., & Johnson, J. (2012, February). *Scale invariance in the measurement of mental-attentional capacity*. Poster presented at SRCD Themed Meeting: Developmental Methodology, Tampa, FL.

Pascual-Leone, J., Johnson, J., & Agostino, A. (2010). Mental attention, multiplicative structures, and the causal problems of cognitive development. In M. Ferrari & L. Vuletic (Eds.), *Developmental interplay between mind, brain and education: Essays in honor of Robbie Case* (pp. 49–82). New York, NY: Springer.

Pascual-Leone, J., Johnson, J., Baskind, S., Dworsky, S., & Severtston, E. (2000). Culture-fair assessment and the processes of mental attention. In A. Kozulin & Y. Rand

(Eds.), *Experience of mediated learning: An impact of Feuerstein's theory in education and psychology* (pp. 191–214). New York, NY: Pergamon.

Pascual-Leone, J., Johnson, J., & Calvo, A. (2004, June). *Can mental attentional capacity predict the Canadian Cognitive Abilities score of school children?* Poster presented at the annual meeting of the Jean Piaget Society, Toronto, ON.

Pascual-Leone, J., & Morra, S. (1991). Horizontality of water level: A neoPiagetian developmental review. *Advances in Child Development and Behavior, 23,* 231–276.

Pascual-Leone, J., Pascual-Leone, A., & Arsalidou, M. (2015). Neuropsychology still needs to model organismic processes "from within." *Behavioral and Brain Sciences, 38,* e83.

Pascual-Leone, J., & Smith, J. (1969). The encoding and decoding of symbols by children: A new experimental paradigm and a neo-Piagetian model. *Journal of Experimental Child Psychology, 8,* 328–355.

Pepper, S. C. (1942). *World hypotheses: A study of evidence.* Berkeley, CA: University of California Press.

Piaget, J. (1983). Piaget's theory. In P. H. Mussen (Series Ed.) & W. Kessen (Vol. Ed.), *Handbook of child psychology: Vol. 1. History, theory, and methods* (4th edn., pp. 103–128). New York, NY: Wiley.

Proctor, R. W., & Reeve, T. G. (Eds.) (1990). *Stimulus-response compatibility: An integrated perspective.* Amsterdam: North-Holland.

Psillos, S. (2002). *Causation and explanation.* Montreal, QC: McGill-Queen's University Press.

Rock, I. (1983). *The logic of perception.* Cambridge, MA: MIT Press.

Rouse Ball, W. W. (1905). *Mathematical recreations and essays* (4th edn.). New York, NY: Macmillan.

Shipstead, Z., Lindsey, D. R. B., Marshall, R. L., & Engle, R. W. (2014). The mechanisms of working memory capacity: Primary memory, secondary memory, and attention control. *Journal of Memory and Language, 72,* 116–141.

Skuy, M., Gewer, A., Osrin, Y., Knunou, D., Fridjhon, P., & Rushton, J. P. (2002). Effects of mediated learning on Raven's matrices scores of African and non-African university students in South Africa. *Intelligence, 30,* 221–232.

Spearman, C. E. (1927). *The abilities of man, their nature and measurement.* New York, NY: MacMillan.

Stöttinger, E., Filipowicz, A., Valadao, D., Culham, J. C., Goodale, M. A., Anderson, B., & Danckert, J. A. (2015). A cortical network that marks the moment when conscious representations are updated. *Neuropsychologia, 79,* 113–122.

Unsworth, N., & Engle, R. W. (2005). Working memory capacity and fluid abilities: Examining the correlation between operation span and Raven. *Intelligence, 33,* 67–81.

Verguts, T., & De Boeck, P. (2002). On the correlation between working memory capacity and performance on intelligence tests. *Learning and Individual Differences, 13,* 37–55.

Waters, A. C., & Tucker, D. M. (2013). Self-regulation and neural development. In B. W. Sokol, F. M. E. Grouzet, & U. Muller (Eds.), *Self-regulation and autonomy* (pp. 279–296). New York, NY: Cambridge University Press.

Werner, H., & Kaplan, B. (1984). *Symbol formation.* Hillsdale, NJ: Erlbaum.

Witkin, H. A., & Goodenough, D. R. (1981). *Cognitive styles, essence and origin: Field dependence and field independence.* New York, NY: International Universities Press.

6 Developmental Evolution: Rethinking Stability and Variation in Biological Systems

Robert Lickliter

In this chapter I review evidence suggesting that the developmental processes involved in phenotypic stability are the same as those involved in producing phenotypic variation or novelty. In other words, stability and variability of phenotypic traits are not distinct developmental phenomena; rather, both are products of the co-action of internal and external resources contributing to individual development. Although much research in evolutionary biology continues to focus on identifying genes for phenotypic innovations, there is a growing trend among researchers toward exploring gene function and regulation in the context of changing internal and external environmental conditions. Fundamental to this approach is the recognition that although genes are essential to development, heredity, and evolution, they are not causally privileged, but, rather, are part of the individual's entire developmental system. I argue that evolutionary explanation cannot be complete without developmental explanation because it is the process of development that generates the phenotypic variation on which natural selection can act.

Introduction

Recent decades have seen a different account of phenotypic stability and variation take shape in developmental biology, evolutionary biology, and developmental psychology. This new account is based on a relatively simple but profound insight: given that all phenotypes arise during ontogeny as products of individual development, it follows that a primary basis for both phenotypic stability and variability must be the process of development itself. The thread of this insight can be traced back to several pioneering embryologists and developmental biologists, including Walter Garstang (1922), Edward Russell (1930), Gavin de Beer (1940), Richard Goldschmidt (1940), Conrad Waddington (1942), and Ivan Schmalhausen (1949). Although each of these biologists had a distinctive perspective on the links between development and evolution, they all promoted the notion that changes in individual development were an important basis for evolutionary change. This view was well outside mainstream 20th century thinking about evolution, but is being reconsidered across the life sciences in the early decades of the

21st century (e.g., Bateson & Gluckman, 2011; Gilbert & Epel, 2009; Gottlieb, 2002; Lickliter & Honeycutt, 2009; West-Eberhard, 2003).

To anyone unfamiliar with the history of developmental and evolutionary biology, it might seem obvious to assume that knowledge of developmental processes would be necessary to understand evolutionary processes. This view was in fact widely held by many biologists working in the 19th century, only to be abandoned by the dominant school of evolutionary theory (the "Modern" or "neo-Darwinian" Synthesis) in the first half of the 20th century (Amundson, 2005). Attempts to integrate Darwin's theory of evolution by natural selection with Mendel's theory of genetics during the first decades of the last century contributed to the rapid growth of the science of population genetics and a corresponding decline in concerns with development. Population genetics focused on how genetic mutation, recombination, and selection could lead to changes in gene frequencies found within a population of breeding organisms over generations. It assumed that modification and transmission of genes were the only possible source of evolutionary change. As a result, it also assumed that knowledge of developmental processes was irrelevant to understanding the ways and means of evolution (see Dawkins, 1975 for a radical example of this approach).

It is now widely accepted that what is passed on from one generation to the next are genes *and* a host of other necessary internal and external factors (or resources) that contribute to the development of an organism's traits. This *developmental manifold* (Gottlieb, 1971) or *developmental system* (Oyama, 1985) is increasingly recognized to be the source of both the stability and the variability of development, eliminating the need for notions of preformed genetic programs or blueprints to account for how stable, species-typical outcomes are achieved in each generation. This perspective emphasizes the dynamic and contingent nature of the development of phenotypic traits and recognizes that a focus on how phenotypes are generated during development is a critical feature of understanding how traits or characters can be changed or modified. As Gottlieb (1991, 1997) pointed out some years ago, the realization of new phenotypes typically requires a change in normal or usual rearing circumstances that ordinarily function to canalize development along species-typical trajectories.

Processes and Products: Development as the Source of Stability and Variation

Comparative research with birds and mammals has provided a number of examples of how normally occurring experience, including experience during the prenatal period, plays a key role in the development and maintenance of species-typical perception and behavior (e.g., Gottlieb, 1997; Lickliter, 2005; Ronca & Alberts, 1994; Wallace & Stein, 2007). It is important to note that I use the term "species-typical" to refer to those behaviors commonly observed across members of a population. It thus refers to behavioral phenotypes that are reliably found across individuals and across generations of a species; it does not imply or assume notions of innate, instinctive, or hard-wired behavior. From this framework, species-typical behavioral development is the result of reliable and repeatable transactions and relationships that take place within and between levels of integration both inside and outside the developing organism (Gottlieb, 1991; Lickliter & Honeycutt, 2013). Species-typical behavioral phenotypes are thus generated during individual onto-geny due to particular aspects of the temporal and spatial arrangements of organisms and their contexts reliably occurring at times when the organism is in particular developmental states, having had a particular developmental past (see Oyama, 1985, 1993 for discussion). As a result, the causes of species-typical behavior cannot be understood without developmental analysis. This is the case because species-typical outcomes are generated and maintained through the activities and experiences of an historical organism engaged with a structured developmental context.

On the other side of the coin, significant alterations or modifications in the normally available resources and relations of an organism's ontogenetic niche are a primary basis for the generation of *novel* behaviors (or "neophenotypes"; see Johnston & Gottlieb, 1990). New or novel behavioral traits brought on by altera-tions in normal prenatal and postnatal rearing environments can lead to new organism–environment relationships, including changes in diet, habitat use, and/or social and reproductive behavior. These behavioral shifts can be maintained across generations if such changes or alterations in the developmental rearing environment persist, promoting a cascade of possible changes in morphology and physiology over time (Johnston & Gottlieb, 1990; Gottlieb, 2002). Researchers in developmental psychobiology have long appreciated that substantially changing species-typical developmental circumstances (in particular the physical or social environment) can foster behavioral change even within a single generation. The results of early handling experiments with rodents (Denenberg & Rosenberg, 1967; Levine, 1956) and environmental enrichment studies with various labora-tory animals (e.g., Rosenzweig & Bennett, 1972; Renner & Rosenzweig, 1987) provided biology and psychology compelling evidence of the developmental induction of modified anatomical and behavioral phenotypes by changes in early rearing conditions.

More recent work with precocial birds illustrates how the bidirectional influence of organismic and environmental factors present in early development can induce patterns of species-typical or species-atypical behavior. During the later stages of prenatal development the precocial avian embryo is oriented in the egg such that its left eye is occluded by the body and yolk sac, whereas the right eye is exposed to diffuse light passing through the egg shell when the brooding hen is intermittently off the nest during the incubation period. This differential prenatal visual stimulation resulting from the embryo's invariant postural orientation in the egg has been shown to facilitate the development of the left hemisphere of the brain in advance of the right hemisphere. Further, this light induced developmental advantage for the left hemisphere has been shown to influence the direction of hemispheric specialization for a variety of postnatal behaviors, including visual discrimination, spatial orienta-tion, feeding behavior, and various visual and motor asymmetries (reviewed in Rogers, 1995). Experimentally altering the normal pattern of light stimulation available during prenatal development can modify this species-typical pattern of brain and behavioral development.

For example, a left visual bias can be established by occluding the right eye and stimulating the left eye with light prior to hatching. Likewise, the induction of lateralization can be prevented by incubating eggs in darkness or by providing the same level of light stimulation to both eyes in the period prior to hatching (Casey & Karpinski, 1999; Casey & Lickliter 1998; Deng & Rogers, 2002). Proponents of an innate or instinctive view of species-typical behavior often explain such instances of context-contingency in developmental outcomes by claims that environmental factors encountered during individual development (such as light exposure in the egg prior to hatching) simply trigger or activate latent developmental programs, assumed to be contained in the genes. However, relying on explanations of the phenotype that refer to latent or hidden programs inside the organism effectively sidesteps or minimizes the process of development and prevents investigation of the range of factors involved in the achievement of species-typical or atypical phenotypic outcomes. From a developmental perspective, the recurrence from generation to generation of the specific resources and relations that make up an organism's developmental system serves as the basis for the development and maintenance of its species-typical behavior (see Miller, 1997; West, King, & White, 2003); deviations or modifications in these resources likewise serve as a primary basis for the development of species-atypical or novel behavior.

Work on contingency learning in bobwhite quail emphasizes the contribution of the early social milieu typically experienced by precocial avian hatchlings to normal species-typical development. A key component of participation in a social milieu is the opportunity for contingent interaction with conspecifics, along with the varied affordances that such interaction provides for learning. We have shown that even small amounts of such interactive stimulation can have a significant influence on the development of preferences for both species-typical and species-atypical auditory stimuli (Harshaw & Lickliter, 2007, 2011; Harshaw, Tourgeman, & Lickliter, 2008). For example, when we provided day-old bobwhite chicks with 5-minute contingent exposure to a heterospecific, Japanese quail maternal call, they no longer showed the species-typical preference for the bobwhite maternal call over the Japanese quail maternal call in subsequent testing (Harshaw et al., 2008). Furthermore, chicks given contingent exposure on a variable ratio (VR2) schedule, in which they heard the call on average once every two times that they vocalized, showed a reversal of their species-typical auditory preference, significantly preferring the Japanese quail maternal call over the bobwhite maternal call in simultaneous choice tests. In contrast, chicks given yoked, non-contingent exposure to the Japanese quail call continued to show a significant preference for the bobwhite maternal call in simultaneous choice tests. These results indicate that small amounts of contingent (or interactive) exposure to a heterospecific call can be sufficient to disrupt or even reverse species-typical auditory preferences, and that the variability of the contingency appears to be a key factor in producing this dramatic modification of species-typical behavior. More broadly, our demonstration of the rapid redirection of the normally robust species-specific auditory preferences of bobwhite quail chicks, whereby they rapidly come to prefer the maternal call of another species in the days following hatching, illustrates the dynamic experiential interplay between the forces of variability and the forces of stability during individual development.

Similar findings from birds and mammals have consistently demonstrated that features of available prenatal and early postnatal sensory stimulation (such as amount, intensity, or the timing of presentation of stimulation) can coact with specific organismic factors (such as the stage of organization of the sensory systems, previous history with the given properties of stimulation, and the current state of arousal of the young organism) to guide and constrain the developmental course of species-typical perceptual preferences, learning, and memory (e.g., Gottlieb, 1991; Lickliter, 2005; Spear & McKenzie, 1994). Changes in these basic processes can in turn lead to modifications in typical patterns of species identification, habitat selection, diet preference, and other key aspects of the organism–environment system. These modifications can in turn lead to changes in patterns of gene activation, regulation, and selection (Meaney, 2010; Moore, 2015).

In light of these and similar findings (see Avital & Jablonka, 2000, for multiple examples), it seems clear that the underlying processes involved in phenotypic variation or novelty are not different in kind from those involved in phenotypic stability. That is, the developmental processes involved in producing the reliable reoccurrence of phenotypes under species-typical conditions are the same as those involved in producing novel phenotypic outcomes under species-atypical circumstances. Thus, whereas stability is observationally distinct from variability, the underlying developmental processes that generate them are not distinct – both are products of the dynamics of the organism's entire developmental system (Lickliter & Harshaw, 2010).

Working at the neurophysiological level of analysis, Wallace and Stein (2007) provided a striking example of the neural consequences of being reared in a modified, species-atypical environment. In this study, domestic cats were raised from birth to adulthood in highly controlled sensory environments that allowed the systematic manipulation of the temporal and spatial features of audio-visual experience. Testing at 6-months of age revealed significant changes in the neural activity evoked by multisensory events, and that these changes closely reflected the structure of the cats' altered rearing circumstances. When auditory and visual stimuli were always presented simultaneously but at a fixed spatial disparity from one another over the first months of life, multisensory enhancements in neural activity were reliably seen to stimulus combinations that reflected this spatial disparity, but not to auditory-visual combinations that reflected normal (spatially collocated) audio-visual experiences. In other words, developing in a profoundly atypical sensory environment resulted in a profoundly atypical profile of neural activity and multisensory responsiveness to audio-visual events when compared to cats raised in a normal sensory environment that provided spatially coincident multisensory experiences.

The apparent seamlessness and consistency of phenotypic development within and across generations, despite the enormous complexity and variability of the environment, has led many biologists and psychologists to argue for the "innateness" of species-typical characteristics. This nativistic view is both simplistic and incorrect (see Blumberg, 2005 for discussion). Rather, it is the dynamics of the individual's developmental system that is the source of both the stability and variability of phenotypic development observed within and across generations, eliminating the need for notions of preformed genetic programs to explain species-typical outcomes. Several early psychobiologists, including Kuo (1967) and Lehrman (1953), appreciated the importance of this systems view for the study of behavioral development, as did several prominent zoologists. For example, writing nearly 50 years ago, King (1968) pointed out that individuals of a species are typically raised by parents of the same species, in an environment that has been occupied by that species for many generations. King noted that this continuity of early experience from one generation to the next envelopes the developing organism in a physical, biological, and social environment that is as characteristic of its species as is its genotype. Gottlieb's (1971, 1997) elegant research program on the development of species identification in ducklings provided multiple examples of how nuanced and often non-obvious this continuity of early experience can be. He carefully documented how the features and patterns of recurring prenatal sensory experience, including self-stimulation, guide and constrain young ducklings' selective attention, perception, learning, and memory during both the prenatal and postnatal periods.

Contrary to the still commonplace assumption that phenotypic stability is "biologically" based and phenotypic variability is "experience" based, a growing body of evidence indicates that there are not separate or distinct processes responsible for stability on the one hand and variation on the other. Both are the products of the bidirectional traffic among the various networks, resources, and levels of the organism–environment system (Lickliter & Honeycutt, 2015; Overton, 2015). A growing appreciation of this fact over the last several decades has fostered a renewed interest in development within evolutionary biology and increasing recognition that changes in evolution reflect changes in development. Contrary to the assumptive base of the neo-Darwinian synthesis prominent in the previous century, the introduction of phenotypic variation upon which natural selection acts is not strictly limited to random genetic mutation, drift, and recombination; rather, variation can result from a wide range of epigenetic processes contributing to individual development.

Developmental Evolution

Missing the importance of development to evolution for much of the 20th century should not be surprising, given the narrow definition of evolution in wide use at the time: *a change in the genetic composition of populations* (Dobzhansky, 1937; Mayr, 1982). Evolution came to be defined in this way because of the special role assigned to genetic factors. Genes were thought to encode programs or instructions that predetermined the development of phenotypic traits. This instructionistic framework recognized two relatively independent classes of causal factors contributing to individual development: those that derived from internal factors that have been shaped by natural selection (*ultimate causes*; genes, nature) and everything else that "interacts" with these internal factors to provide the materials or experiences necessary for the expression of form or function encoded in these internal factors (*proximate causes*; environment, nurture). This causal dichotomy rested on the assumption that development is primarily internally determined, set on course at conception and specified by innate processes designed and selected over evolutionary time (Lickliter & Berry, 1990). From this perspective, development was seen simply as the unfolding process by which genotypic specification was translated into the traits of individuals, including their anatomy, physiology, and behavior. This assumption was in widespread use across the biological sciences for many decades and fit neatly within the conceptual framework of population genetics, which focused on how genetic mutation, recombination, and selection could lead to changes in gene frequencies in a population. Population genetics was not focused on the development of the individual organism – rather, it focused on organisms as members of a breeding population and how best to calculate the probabilities of changing gene frequencies in this population of breeding organisms under this or that set of circumstances over generations (Provine, 1971). This approach concentrated on the traits of adults in populations and virtually ignored questions about how these traits were actually realized during the course of individual development. In keeping with this perspective, the noted evolutionary biologist Maynard-Smith (1985) argued that attempting explanations of evolution in terms of individual development was an "error of misplaced reductionism."

The architects of what came to be known as the "Modern Synthesis" of evolutionary biology promoted this gene-centric perspective and saw little need to integrate developmental processes into their collective attempts to synthesize the tenets of Darwinism and Mendelism (e.g., Huxley, 1942; Mayr, 1942, 1963; Simpson, 1944). If genes contain all the necessary information for phenotypes and if events and experiences during individual development simply supported or triggered the expression of this information, then genes clearly must have priority over non-genetic factors in explaining evolutionary change.

This perspective has undergone considerable revision over the last several decades, in large part due to discoveries in molecular and cellular biology indicating that a variety of developmental resources beyond genes reoccur across generations. We now know that parents can transfer to their offspring multiple non-genetic factors that can directly influence phenotypic outcomes, including methylation patterns, chromatin marking systems, cytoplasmic chemical gradients, and a range of sensory stimulation necessary for normal development (Jablonka & Lamb, 2005; Mameli, 2004; Moore, 2015). As a result, a concern with how development is involved in evolutionary change is now evident among biologists and psychologists working in formally diverse areas of research, including genomics, cellular and molecular biology, developmental biology, evolutionary theory, ecology, and comparative and developmental psychology, as well as philosophers of biology (e.g., Arthur, 2004; Bateson & Gluckman, 2011; Gilbert & Epel, 2009; Hall, Pearson, & Müller, 2004; Lickliter & Honeycutt, 2009; Moore, 2008; Nijhout, 2003; Richardson, 1998; Robert, 2004).

Contrary to the established neo-Darwinian perspective, evolutionary change need not begin with genetic change, and evidence obtained from a range of species suggests it often does not (e.g., West-Eberhard, 2003). For example, Gottlieb (2002) describes a compelling example of how a change in behavior can be the initiator of evolutionary change. Historically, the apple maggot fly laid its eggs on haws (the fruit of hawthorn trees). However, when domestic apples trees were introduced into their home ranges, apple maggot females also began laying their eggs on apples. There are now two variants of the apple maggot fly: one that lays its eggs only on haws and one that lays its eggs only on apples. Because apples mature earlier in the fall season than haws, the two fly variants have different mating seasons and thus no longer mate with one another. Evidence indicates that this change in developmental timing has resulted in differences in gene frequencies between the two populations (Feder, Roethele, Wlazlo, & Berlocher, 1997).

The novelty-generating aspects of development involved in such change are the result of the developmental dynamics of living organisms, situated and competing in specific ecological contexts, and not simply the result of random genetic mutations. Variations in morphologies, physiologies, and behaviors resulting from modification of the timing, rate, or spatial distribution of developmental processes can place their possessors in different ecological relationships with their environments, and if these phenotypic variations provide even slight advantages in survival and reproduction, competitors without the novel phenotype will eventually decrease in frequency in a population.

Shifts in behavior brought about by both changes in the environment and the resulting changes in the activity of the organism can lead to new relationships between elements of the developmental system within and across generations, which can lead to further variations in gene activity, morphology, physiology, or behavior (for additional examples, see Balakrishnan & Sorenson, 2006; Malausa et al., 2005). Eventually, a change in gene frequencies may also occur as a result of geographically or behaviorally isolated breeding populations. For example, a European passerine bird, the blackcap (*Sylvia atricapilla*), has shown changes in its migratory behavior over recent decades that have resulted in changes in wing shape, beak size, mating behavior, size of egg clutches, and success at fledging young (Bearhop et al., 2005). Many passerine birds are seasonal migrants and the timing of spring migration constrains when breeding starts each year. Until recently, all European blackcaps migrated back and forth together, spending summers in northern Europe and the British Isles and winters in Portugal, Spain, and North Africa before gathering in mating grounds in southern Germany and Austria to breed. Blackcaps were typically seen in the British Isles only during the summer months, but the number of them wintering in Britain and Ireland has increased dramatically over the last 40 years. This change is thought to be due to the increased availability of winter provisioning provided by bird feeders, landscapers, and other related human activities, as well as an increase in winter temperatures. The resulting shift in migratory patterns has allowed northern-wintering blackcaps to be exposed some 10 days earlier than their southern-wintering counterparts to the critical photoperiods that contribute to the initiation of migration and the onset of gonadal development. Even though all blackcaps continue to gather each year at the same mating sites in Germany and Austria, isotopic data indicate that northern blackcaps that winter in the UK arrive earlier at the breeding grounds and establish territories and mate with other earlier arriving birds; southern-wintering blackcaps arrive at the same mating sites some two weeks later and are more likely to mate with each other, serving to reproductively isolate northern-wintering birds from the later-arriving southern-wintering population. This shift in migratory patterns appears to confer an advantage to the northern blackcaps, who lay more eggs per season than do their later-arriving cohorts from the south (Bearhop et al., 2005).

The blackcap research provides a useful example of how a change in behavior (in this case, a change in migratory patterns brought on by changes in food availability) can lead to changes in the timing of breeding, which in turn can lead to the effective reproductive isolation of populations and, ultimately, divergence and even sympatric speciation. Contrary to the assumptive base of the neo-Darwinian synthesis, the introduction of phenotypic variation upon which natural selection acts is not simply the result of random genetic mutations. Rather, variations in phenotypes and the resulting opportunities for evolutionary change are the result of a wide range of epigenetic processes occurring at different timescales and involving factors internal *and* external to the developing individual. As pointed out by Jablonka (2006), mounting evidence indicates that evolution is best viewed as a change in the frequency of transmissible (heritable) phenotypes within a population, not simply as a change in the frequency of genes in a population.

This shift in focus is requiring a rethinking of how we characterize development, environment, and evolution (e.g., Laland et al., 2015; Lickliter & Honeycutt, 2013; West-Eberhard, 2003). As Moczek (2015, p. 3) recently noted: "To develop is to interact with the environment. To evolve is to alter these interactions in a heritable manner." This emphasis on the nature of the relations between developmental processes and the environmental conditions in which they occur has led to a new appreciation of how changing environmental conditions can reveal novel phenotypic variation as well as release corresponding genetic variation (Ledon-Rettig, Pfennig, Chunco, & Dworkin, 2014). For instance, the house finch (*Carpodacus mexicanus*) has successfully colonized a wide range of environments across North America over the last 150 years. Different finch populations now show significant differences in their physiological responses to environmental variation, including the induction of breeding and incubating behavior in response to temperature variation; this pheno-typic plasticity has resulted in populations of house finches with divergent repro-ductive phenotypes after as little as 14 generations (Badyaev, 2009).

Although much research in evolutionary biology continues to focus on identifying genes for phenotypic innovations, there is a growing move among evolutionary researchers toward exploring gene function and regulation in the context of chan-ging internal and external environmental conditions (Moczek, 2015). Fundamental to this approach is the recognition that although genes are essential to development, heredity, and evolution, they are not causally privileged (Griffiths & Stotz, 2013; Oyama, 1985). Further, genes and environment are neither alternative nor indepen-dent sources of phenotypic outcomes.

Implications for Psychological Science

What are the implications of incorporating developmental evolution into contemporary psychological science? As recently noted by Stotz (2014), what kind of evolutionary theory you apply matters deeply to which kind of evolutionary psychology you get. For the last several decades, when the terms *evolution* and *psychology* have been paired together, most psychologists and biologists have likely thought of evolutionary psychology (EP), a sub-discipline within psychological science that combines cognitive psychology with the general principles of the neo-Darwinian evolutionary synthesis reviewed in previous sections (e.g., Barkow, Cosmides, & Tooby, 1992; Buss, 1995; Duntley & Buss, 2008). A central claim of evolutionary psychology is that natural selection has created the underlying psychological mechanisms that generate the universals of human behavior and cognition. In keeping with the assumptions of the neo-Darwinian synthesis, proponents of the EP view argue that many human cognitive abilities (so-called human nature) are relatively fixed phenotypic characters, innately specified in the genotype of the individual (e.g., Geary & Huffman, 2002; MacDonald & Herschberger, 2005; Pinker, 2002). Pinker (1997, p. 21) voiced a strong example of this perspective, arguing that "the mind is organized into modules or mental organs, each with a specialized design that makes it an expert in one area of interaction with the world. The modules' basic logic is specified by our genetic program." Like Pinker, most evolutionary psychologists presume that major aspects of the behavioral and cognitive dispositions of humans are pre-specified, somehow present *in advance of their development*.

In response to charges of genetic determinism from developmental scientists (e.g., Lickliter & Honeycutt, 2003; Lerner & Benson, 2013), evolutionary psychologists counter that they provide a true "interactionist framework," in that psychological adaptations are proposed to require specific environmental input for their proper development and proximate activation (see Confer et al., 2010). From this perspective, experience during development either allows normal development of species-typical traits or disrupts or interferes with normal development, resulting in abnormal traits. However, in this form of interactionism genes are characterized as playing the primary or determinative role in the form and function of phenotypic traits, and non-genetic or environmental factors are delegated to a necessary, but clearly supportive or triggering role in the achievement of species-typical outcomes. This dichotomy is based on the assumption that phenotypic traits of an individual are primarily determined by historical events that designed its "genetic program," and secondarily by environmental or experiential factors that act on the individual during its development. As reviewed in previous sections, this causal dichotomy is no longer biologically plausible.

Given the growing evidence that development is fundamental to evolution, and given that behavior and environment are now known to be key factors contributing to evolutionary change, it seems clear that psychological science should consider rethinking the views of genes, heredity, and environment promoted by the tenets of evolutionary psychology. From a biological perspective, what is needed is a theoretical framework than can more adequately address the developmental dynamics involved in generating, maintaining, and transforming behavior within and across generations (Lickliter & Honeycutt, 2013, 2015). At the global level, this framework would seek to understand how combinations of genetic, hormonal, neural, physiological, behavioral, social, and cultural factors act synergistically as a system from which behaviors emerge and are maintained or transformed (Overton, 2015). Such an approach would require unpacking developmental dynamics across multiple levels of analysis (genetic, epigenetic, behavioral, social, cultural, ecological) and multiple timescales (developmental and transgenerational; see Lickliter & Honeycutt, 2013).

At the more specific level, this type of systems approach requires rethinking the role of the environment in development and evolution. Whereas evolutionary psychology effectively partitions environmental and genetic effects when accounting for human behavior and cognition, recent advances in biology make clear that the relation between genes and environment is far more than simply interactive. Rather, by investigating the interplay between developmental processes and the environments within which they occur, a wide range of studies has shown genes and environment are completely interdependent (reviewed in Moore, 2015). The phenomenon of domestication – the process by which organisms change in terms of morphology, physiology, or behavior as a result of the human control of their breeding, feeding, and care – provides an informative example of the nested role of genetic, developmental, and environmental resources at play in the complex dynamics involved in phenotypic change within and across generations (Lickliter & Ness, 1990; Price, 1999). Following the neo-Darwinian synthesis of the first half of the 20th century and its emphasis on population genetics, most students of domestication have assumed that the morphological, physiological, and behavioral differences observed between wild and domestic strains of animals could be explained by random and non-random genetic mechanisms associated with captive rearing. These genetic mechanisms include natural and artificial selection, inbreeding, genetic drift, and genetic mutation (Price & King, 1968).

Although the importance of genes as sources of phenotypic variation in both wild and domestic animals is indisputable, domestication is certainly not simply a matter of changing gene frequencies. The transition from free-living to captivity is accompanied by many and varied changes in an animal's physical, biological, and social environments and we know that these changes can bring about significant modifications in phenotypic development. For example, Clark and Galef (1981) were able to show that specific differences in the morphology, physiology, and behavior of wild and domestic strains of gerbils (*Meriones ungulculatus*) can be traced to relatively minor changes in the environment available in their early rearing experiences. Gerbils reared in standard laboratory cages without access to shelter show accelerated eye opening following birth, earlier sexual maturity, increased docility, and reduced reactivity to humans when compared to gerbils reared in laboratory conditions that allow free access to shelter, as would normally occur in the wild. Of course, the change from free-living to captivity for most species is typically accompanied by changes in the availability of not only shelter, but also space, food and water, predation, and possibilities for social interaction (Price, 1999). The influence of such changes on the nature and range of phenotypic change under domestication remains relatively unexplored (Lickliter & Ness, 1990).

One notable research program that has attempted to address these changes is that of Belyaev (1979) on the domestication of silver foxes (*Vulpes vulpes*). Selection for tame behavior in silver foxes began in the 1950s and continues to the present. Selection was based solely on behavioral criteria, breeding those foxes that were least timid when humans attempted to handle or interact with them. It is important to note that such selective breeding (common in cases of domestication) is selecting for particular developmental outcomes (in this case, tameness), not selecting for specific genes. In addition to becoming more dog-like in their behavior over the course of more than 40 generations, the silver foxes quickly showed a number of other phenotypic modifications, including changes in the skeleton (shortened legs, tail, and snout, and a widened skull), hormonal changes, altered tail and ear posture, and decreased sexual dimorphism. Belyaev (1979) proposed that the experiential conditions of domestication led to neural and hormonal changes that in turn activated the expression of dormant genes, thereby revealing 'hidden variation" previously undetected in wild silver foxes. This idea remains speculative, but Belyaev's interpretation that certain genes were able to switch from dormant to active states in response to changes in environmental conditions is certainly plausible in light of recent advances in epigenetics and would help explain the rapid rate of phenotypic changes observed across only a few generations.

Recognizing that environmental conditions are as fundamental to phenotypic change as genes allows a deeper appreciation that phenotypes are always the result of the complex dynamics of individual ontogeny rather than simply genes or genetic variation (Bateson & Gluckman, 2011; Lickliter & Honeycutt, 2015). As Moczek (2015, p. 6) recently pointed out, "a mounting body of evidence across the tree of life shows that organisms execute their development in tight interdependence with the environment, with significant aspects of the environment being both cause and effect of organismal development, shaping and directing how and when, and with what consequences, genetic programs are allowed to unfold." Importantly, by placing changes in behavior, environment, and development at the forefront of evolutionary inquiry, investigations of the various processes involved in evolutionary change can be pursued at many different levels of analysis (including psychological science) and not only in terms of population genetics.

Documenting the bidirectional relations from gene action to the external environment and back and their effects on behavior over the life course remains a major conceptual, empirical, and analytical challenge for psychological science (Overton & Molenaar, 2015). The wide range of external factors that are known to be participants in gene activity and expression, in some cases well beyond the timescale of individual development, drives home the point that the organism–environment system is the fundamental level of analysis in efforts to understand both behavioral development and the significant links among development, heredity, and evolution (Lickliter, 2009). However, integrating developmental dynamics across multiple systems and timescales has been (and remains) a challenging task for psychological science (see Urban, Osgood, & Mabry, 2011). How to integrate *real time* (the immediate experiences and exposure of an individual to their physical, biological, social, and cultural environments) with *developmental time* (the continuing influence of prior experiences and encounters on an individual's ongoing interaction with these varied environments) and *evolutionary time* (the transgenerational effects of an individual's experiences and activities during ontogeny) is difficult to conceptualize and to model, but is key to a fully realized theory of developmental evolution (Johnston & Lickliter, 2009; see Minelli & Pradeu, 2014).

The combinatorial complexity inherent in the process of development blurs the boundary between genes and environment and highlights the growing appreciation of the fusion of biology and ecology. This represents a significant rethinking of both development and evolution from the established views carried forward from the 20th century. Psychological science has an important role to play in this paradigm shift, in terms of both theory and empirical research. In this light, comparative psychology and developmental psychology have provided numerous demonstrations over many decades that modified early experience in one generation can predictably influence phenotypic outcomes in subsequent generations, even in the absence of the original experiential modification. For example, differences in physical (body weight, endocrine responses) and behavioral (fearfulness) measures have been observed between groups of rats whose mothers (Denenberg & Whimbey, 1963; Francis, Diorio, Liu, & Meaney, 1999) or grandmothers (Denenberg & Rosenberg, 1967) were handled or not handled as infants. Despite the obvious importance to both developmental and evolutionary concerns, the coactions across levels of the developmental system that contribute to these types of transgenerational effects on both physiological responsiveness (in particular, the development of the hypothalamic adrenocortical system) and behavioral responsiveness (including curiosity, novelty seeking, and emotional regulation) remain poorly understood (but see Meaney, 2010).

There is a lot of work to do to better integrate development with evolution and psychology with developmental evolution. Recent advances in behavioral epigenetics (e.g., Moore, 2015), evolutionary biology (Moczek et al., 2015), systems neuroscience (e.g., Sporns, 2011), and developmental psychology (e.g., Blair & Raver, 2012), along with developmental psychobiological systems theory (e.g., Lickliter & Honeycutt, 2015) and the philosophy of biology (e.g., Griffith & Stotz, 2013), are providing psychological science valuable analytical and conceptual tools to achieve a more fully realized theory of stability and variability in biological systems. This rethinking process is sure to challenge and engage developmental scientists for years to come.

References

Amundson, R. (2005). *The changing role of the embryo in evolutionary thought: Roots of evo-devo*. Cambridge, UK: Cambridge University Press.

Arthur, W. (2004). *Biased embryos and evolution*. Cambridge, UK: Cambridge University Press.

Avital, E., & Jablonka, E. (2000). *Animal traditions: Behavioral inheritance in evolution.* Cambridge, UK: Cambridge University Press.

Badyaev, A. (2009). Evolutionary significance of phenotypic accommodation in novel environments: An empirical test of the Baldwin effect. *Philosophical Transactions of the Royal Society B, 364,* 1125–1141.

Balakrishnan, C. N., & Sorenson, M. D. (2006). Premating reproductive isolation among sympatric indigobird species and host races. *Behavioral Ecology, 17,* 473–478.

Barkow, J., Cosmides, L., & Tooby, J. (1992). *The adapted mind: Evolutionary psychology and the generation of culture.* New York, NY: Oxford University Press.

Bateson, P. P. G., & Gluckman, P. (2011). *Plasticity, robustness, development, and evolution.* Cambridge, UK: Cambridge University Press.

Bearhop, S., Fiedler, W., Furness, R. W., Votier, S. C., Waldron, S., Newton, J., ... & Farnsworth, K. (2005). Assortative mating as a mechanism for rapid evolution of a migratory divide. *Science, 310,* 502–504.

Belyaev, D. (1979). Destabilizing selection as a factor in domestication. *Journal of Heredity, 70,* 301–308.

Blair, C., & Raver, C. C. (2012). Individual development and evolution: Experiential canalization of self-regulation. *Developmental Psychology, 48,* 647–657.

Blumberg, M. S. (2005). *Basic instinct: The genesis of novel behavior.* New York, NY: Thunder's Mouth Press.

Buss, D. M. (1995). Evolutionary psychology: A new paradigm for psychological science. *Psychological Inquiry, 6,* 1–30.

Casey, M. B, & Karpinski, S. (1999). The development of turning bias is influenced by prenatal visual experience in domestic chicks (Gallus gallus). *The Psychological Record, 49,* 67–74.

Casey, M. B., & Lickliter, R. (1998). Prenatal visual experience influences the development of turning bias in bobwhite quail chicks (Colinus virginianus). *Developmental Psychobiology, 32,* 327–338.

Clark, M. M., & Galef, B. (1981). Environmental influence on development, behavior, and endocrine morphology of gerbils. *Physiology & Behavior, 27,* 761–765.

Confer, J. C., Easton, J. A., Fleischman, D. S., Goetz, C. D., Lewis, D. M. ... & Buss, D. M. (2010). Evolutionary psychology: Controversies, questions, prospects, and limitations. *American Psychologist, 65,* 110–126.

Dawkins, R. (1975). *The selfish gene.* New York, NY: Oxford University Press.

de Beer, G. (1940). *Embryos and ancestors.* Oxford, England: Clarendon Press.

Denenberg, V. H., & Rosenberg, K. M. (1967). Nongenetic transmission of information. *Nature, 216,* 549–550.

Denenberg, V. H., & Whimbey, A. E. (1963). Behavior of adult rats is modified by the experiences their mothers had as infants. *Science, 142,* 1192–1193.

Deng, C., & Rogers, L. J. (2002). Social recognition and approach in the chick: Lateralization and effect of visual experience. *Animal Behaviour, 63,* 697–706.

Dobzhansky, T. (1937). *Genetics and the origin of species,* 1st edn. New York, NY: Columbia University Press.

Duntley, J., & Buss, D. (2008). Evolutionary psychology is a metatheory for psychology. *Psychological Inquiry, 19,* 30–34.

Feder, J. L., Roethele, J. B., Wlazlo, B., & Berlocher, S. H. (1997). Selective maintenance of allozyme differences among sympatric host races of the apple maggot fly. *Proceedings of the National Academy of Sciences, USA, 94,* 11417–11421.

Francis, D., Diorio, J., Liu, D., & Meaney, M. J. (1999). Nongenomic transmission across generations of maternal behavior and stress responses in the rat. *Science, 286,* 1155–1158.

Garstang, W. (1922). The theory of recapitulation: A critical re-statement of the biogenetic law. *Journal of the Linnean Society of London, Zoology, 35,* 81–101.

Geary, D. C., & Huffman, K. J. (2002). Brain and cognitive evolution: forms of modularity and functions of mind. *Psychological Bulletin, 128,* 667–698.

Gilbert, S. F., & Epel, D. (2009). *Ecological developmental biology.* Sunderland, MA: Sinauer.

Goldschmidt, R. (1940). *The material basis of evolution.* New Haven, CT: Yale University Press.

Gottlieb, G. (1971). *The development of species-identification in birds.* Chicago, IL: University of Chicago Press.

Gottlieb, G. (1991). Experiential canalization of behavior development: Theory. *Developmental Psychology, 27,* 4–13.

Gottlieb, G. (1997). *Synthesizing nature-nurture: Prenatal roots of instinctive behavior.* Mahwah, NJ: Erlbaum.

Gottlieb, G. (2002). Developmental-behavioral initiation of evolutionary change. *Psychological Review, 109,* 211–218.

Griffiths, P. E., & Stotz, K. (2013). *Genetics and philosophy: An introduction.* Cambridge, UK: Cambridge University Press.

Hall, B. K., Pearson, R. D., & Müller, G. B. (2004). *Environment, development, and evolution.* Cambridge, MA: MIT Press.

Harshaw, C., & Lickliter, R. (2007). Interactive and vicarious acquisition of auditory preferences in Northern bobwhite chicks. *Journal of Comparative Psychology, 121,* 320–331.

Harshaw, C., & Lickliter, R. (2011). Biased embryos: Prenatal experience alters the postnatal malleability of auditory preferences in bobwhite quail. *Developmental Psychobiology, 53,* 291–302.

Harshaw, C., Tourgeman, I., & Lickliter, R. (2008). Stimulus contingency and the malleability of species-typical auditory preferences in Northern bobwhite hatchlings. *Developmental Psychobiology, 50,* 460–472.

Huxley, J. (1942). *Evolution: The modern synthesis.* London, UK: George Allen & Unwin.

Jablonka, E. (2006). Genes as followers in evolution: A post-synthesis synthesis? *Biology and Philosophy, 21,* 143–154.

Jablonka, E., & Lamb, M. J. (2005). *Evolution in four dimensions: Genetic, epigenetic, behavioral, and symbolic variation in the history of life.* Cambridge, MA: MIT Press.

Johnston, T. D., & Gottlieb, G. (1990). Neophenogenesis: A developmental theory of phenotypic evolution. *Journal of Theoretical Biology, 147,* 471–495.

Johnston, T. D., & Lickliter, R. (2009). A developmental systems theory perspective on psychological change. In J. P. Spencer, M. Thomas, & J. M. McClelland (Eds.), *Toward a unified theory of development: Connectionism and dynamic systems theory re-considered* (pp. 285–296). New York, NY: Oxford University Press.

King, J. A. (1968). Species specificity and early experience. In G. Newton & S. Levine (Eds.), *Early experience and behavior* (pp. 42–64). Springfield, MA: Thomas.

Kuo, Z. Y. (1967). *The dynamics of behavior development: An epigenetic view.* New York, NY: Random House.

Laland, K. N., Uller, T., Feldman, M. W., Sterelny, K., Muller, G. B., Moczek, A., …. & Odling-Smee, J. (2015). The extended evolutionary synthesis: Its structure, assumptions, and predictions. *Proceeding of the Royal Society, B 282*, 1–14.

Ledon-Rettig, C. C., Pfennig, D. W., Chunco, A., & Dworkin, I. (2014). Cryptic genetic variation in natural populations: A predictive framework. *Integrated Comparative Biology, 54*, 783–793.

Lerhman, D. S. (1953). A critique of Konrad Lorenz's theory of instinctive behavior. *Quarterly Review of Biology, 28*, 337–363.

Lerner, R. M. & Benson, J. B. (2013). Embodiment and epigenesis: Theoretical and methodological issues in understanding the role of biology within the relational developmental system. *Advances in Child Development and Behavior, Vol. 44.*

Levine, S. (1956). A further study of infantile handling and adult avoidance learning. *Journal of Personality, 25*, 70–80.

Lickliter, R. (2005). Prenatal sensory ecology and experience: Implications for perceptual and behavioral development in precocial birds. *Advances in the Study of Behavior, 35*, 235–274.

Lickliter, R. (2009). The fallacy of partitioning: Epigenetics' validation of the organism-environment system. *Ecological Psychology, 21*, 138–146.

Lickliter, R., & Berry, T. D. (1990). The phylogeny fallacy: Developmental psychology's misapplication of evolutionary theory. *Developmental Review, 10*, 348–364.

Lickliter, R. & Harshaw, C. (2010). Canalization and malleability reconsidered: The developmental basis of phenotypic stability and variability. In K. E. Hood, C. T. Halpern, G. Greenberg, & R. M. Lerner (Eds.), *Handbook of developmental science, behavior, and genetics* (pp. 491–526.). Malden, MA: Wiley-Blackwell.

Lickliter, R., & Honeycutt, H. (2003). Developmental dynamics: Toward a biologically plausible evolutionary psychology. *Psychological Bulletin, 129*, 819–835.

Lickliter, R., & Honeycutt, H. (2009). Rethinking epigenesis and evolution in light of developmental science. In M. Blumberg, J. Freeman, & S. Robinson (Eds.), *Oxford handbook of developmental behavioral neuroscience* (pp. 30–47). New York, NY: Oxford University Press.

Lickliter, R., & Honeycutt, H. (2013). A developmental evolutionary framework for psychology. *Review of General Psychology, 17*, 1184–1189.

Lickliter, R., & Honeycutt, H. (2015). Biology, development, and human systems. In: W. F. Overton & P. C. M. Molenaar (Vol. Eds.) *Handbook of child psychology and developmental science. Vol. 1: Theory & method* (7th edn., pp. 162–207). Hoboken, NJ: Wiley.

Lickliter, R., & Ness, J. (1990). Domestication and comparative psychology: Status and strategy. *Journal of Comparative Psychology, 104*, 211–218.

MacDonald, K., & Herschberger, S. L. (2005). Theoretical issues in the study of evolution and development. In R. Burgess & K. MacDonald (Eds.), *Evolutionary perspectives on human development* (2nd edn., pp. 21–72). Thousand Oaks, CA: Sage.

Malausa, T., Bethend, M. T., Bontemps, A., Bourguet, D., Cornuet, J. M., et al. (2005). Assortative mating in sympatric host races of the European corn borer. *Science, 308*, 258–260.

Mameli, M. (2004). Nongenetic selection and nongenetic inheritance. *British Journal for the Philosophy of Science, 55*, 35–71.

Maynard Smith, J. (1985). Sexual selection, handicaps, and true fitness. *Journal of Theoretical Biology, 115*, 1–8.

Mayr, E. (1942). *Systematics and the origins of species*. New York, NY: Columbia University Press.

Mayr, E. (1982). *The growth of biological thought*. Cambridge, MA: Harvard University Press.

Meaney, M. J. (2010). Epigenetics and the biological definition of Gene × Environment interactions. *Child Development*, *81*, 41–79.

Miller, D. B. (1997). The effects of nonobvious forms of experience on the development of instinctive behavior. In C. Dent-Reed & P. Zukow-Goldring (Eds), *Evolving explanations of development* (pp. 457–507). Washington, DC: American Psychological Association.

Minelli, A., & Pradeu, T. (2014). *Towards a theory of development*. New York, NY: Oxford University Press.

Moczek, A. (2015). Re-evaluating the environment in developmental evolution. *Frontiers in Ecology and Evolution*, *3*, 1–8.

Moczek, A., Sears, K., Stollewerk, A., Wittkopp, P., Diggle, P., Dworkin, I., ... & Extavour, C. (2015). The significance and scope of evolutionary developmental biology: A vision for the 21st century. *Evolution and Development*, *17*, 198–219.

Moore, D. S. (2008). Espousing interactions and fielding reactions: Addressing laypeople's beliefs about genetic determinism. *Philosophical Psychology*, *21*, 331–348.

Moore, D. S. (2015). *The developing genome: An introduction to behavioral epigenetics*. New York, NY: Oxford University Press.

Nijhout, H. F. (2003). Development and evolution of adaptive polyphenisms. *Evolution & Development*, *5*, 9–18.

Overton, W. F. (2015). Processes, relations, and relational developmental systems. In W. F. Overton & P. C. M. Molenaar (Vol. Eds.) *Handbook of child psychology and developmental science. Vol. 1: Theory & method* (7th edn., pp. 9–62). Hoboken, NJ: Wiley.

Overton, W. F., & Molenaar, P. C. M. (2015). *Handbook of child psychology and developmental science. Vol. 1: Theory and method*. Hoboken, NJ: Wiley.

Oyama, S. (1985). *The ontogeny of information: Developmental systems and evolution*. New York, NY: Cambridge University Press.

Oyama, S. (1993). Constraints and development. *Netherlands Journal of Zoology*, *43*, 6–16.

Pinker, S. (1997). *How the mind works*. New York, NY: Norton.

Pinker, S. (2002). *The blank slate: The modern denial of human nature*. New York, NY: Viking.

Price, E. O. (1999). Behavioral development in animals undergoing domestication. *Applied Animal Behavior Science*, *65*, 245–271.

Price, E. O., & King, J. (1968). Domestication and adaptation. In E. S. Hafez (Ed.), *Adaptation of domestic animals* (pp. 34–45). Philadelphia, PA: Lea and Febiger.

Provine, W. (1971). *The origins of theoretical population genetics*. Chicago: University of Chicago Press.

Renner, M. J., & Rosenzweig, M. R. (1987). *Enriched and impoverished environments: Effects on brain and behavior*. New York, NY: Springer-Verlag.

Richardson, K. (1998). *The origins of human potential: Evolution, development and psychology*. London: Routledge.

Robert, J. S. (2004). *Embryology, epigenesis, and evolution: Taking development seriously*. New York, NY: Cambridge University Press.

Rogers, L. J. (1995). *The development of brain and behavior in the chicken*. Wallingford, UK: CAB International.

Ronca, A. E., & Alberts, J. R. (1994). Sensory stimuli associated with gestation and parturition evoke cardiac and behavioral responses in fetal rats. *Psychobiology, 55,* 270–282.

Rozenzweig, M. R., & Bennett, E. L. (1972). Cerebral changes in rats exposed individually to an enriched environment. *Journal of Comparative and Physiological Psychology, 80,* 304–313.

Russell, E. S. (1930). *The interpretation of development and heredity.* Oxford, England: Clarendon.

Schmalhausen, I. (1949). *Factors of evolution: The theory of stabilizing selection.* Oxford, England: Blakiston.

Simpson, G. G. (1944). *Tempo and mode in evolution.* New York, NY: Columbia University Press.

Spear, N. E, & McKenzie, D. L. (1994). Intersensory integration in the infant rat. In D. J. Lewkowicz & R. Lickliter (Eds.), *The development of intersensory perception: Comparative perspectives* (pp. 133–161). Hillsdale, NJ: Erlbaum.

Sporns, O. (2011). *Networks of the brain.* Cambridge, MA: MIT Press.

Stotz, K. (2014). Extended evolutionary psychology: The importance of transgenerational developmental plasticity. *Frontiers in Psychology, 5,* 1–14.

Urban, J. B., Osgood, N. D., & Mabry, P. L. (2011). Developmental systems science: Exploring the application of systems science methods to developmental science questions. *Research in Human Development, 8,* 1–25.

Waddington, C. H. (1942). The epigenotype. *Endeavour, 1,* 18–20.

Wallace, M. T., & Stein, B. E. (2007). Early experience determines how the senses will interact. *Journal of Neurophysiology, 97,* 921–926.

West, M. J., King, A. P., & White, D. J. (2003). The case for developmental ecology. *Animal Behaviour, 66,* 617–622.

West-Eberhard, M. J. (2003). *Developmental plasticity and evolution.* New York, NY: Oxford University Press.

7 NOC NOC, Who's There? A New Ontological Category (NOC) for Social Robots

Peter H. Kahn, Jr. and Solace Shen

The robots are coming. That used to be a science fiction alert. Now it's happening. Though it may not be happening in quite the way the world expected 80 years ago, or even 20.

Back then, the robot was envisioned as a stand-alone entity, often literally standing alone as a protagonist on screen, such as the evil robot Maria in the 1927 movie *Metropolis*. Some robots today have been designed and engineered based on this vision of creating a technological person, such as Ishiguro's androids (MacDorman & Ishiguro, 2006). Other robots in research labs look more technological, like R2D2 from *Star Wars*, even as they convey human characteristics of speech, self-initiated movement, intentional action, and personality. Some mimic the animal form, such as Sony's robot dog AIBO. Still other robots have been designed to cover rough terrain, such as Big Dog, or are submersible. Some of these robots – think also war-faring drones – represent part of the US military's $30 billion agenda to turn much of human-warfare into robotic warfare. We can think of the car today as an emerging form of a robot, as it gains measurable control of braking, backing up, parallel parking, and sensing traffic. The fully autonomous cars of the future can be understood as social robots, especially as it seems likely that we will be talking with them. Almost all of these robots will be networked to the Web (and some to each other), gaining computational power from the network, and sharing and updating information in the cloud.

As social robots move from science fiction to the research labs to society at large, they will become part of our everyday social lives. In this process of rapid societal change, how will we interact with these robots of the near future? How will we conceptualize them, and understand them? Will we form social and even moral relationships with them? Will young children who come of age with these entities construct different ideas about what they are, compared to what we understand now as adults?

Toward answers, we bring forward data from three of our collaborative research studies of human–robot interaction. One study focuses on whether adults can establish interpersonal trust and psychological intimacy with a humanoid robot. A second study focuses on whether children and adolescents believe that a humanoid robot can have moral standing. A third study focuses on whether young adults believe that a humanoid robot can be held morally accountable for causing harm to humans. Unknown to the participants, in these studies we tele-operated the robot from an adjacent room so as to achieve capabilities of the robot beyond what they can autonomously do today – but not so far-fetched, either – so as to position us to look into the psychology of human–robot interaction (HRI) of the near future.

Based on these three studies, and in accord with other literature, we seek to make the case that what will emerge in the coming years in people's conceptions and relationships with social robots is like nothing that has happened before. Not ever. Not in human–human interaction, human–animal interaction, or human–artifact interaction. It's a strong proposition. As early as 2003 we had put forward this idea more tentatively, calling it in various ways the New Ontological Category (NOC) Hypothesis (e.g., Friedman, Kahn, & Hagman, 2003; Kahn, Friedman, Perez-Granados, & Freier, 2006; Kahn et al., 2011; Kahn et al., 2012; Kahn, Gary, & Shen, 2013; see also Severson & Carlson, 2010). But as we discuss these three HRI studies, you may agree with us that it's time to move this idea from that of a hypothesis to that of a reasonable proposition.

Psychological Intimacy and Trust with a Humanoid Robot?

One of the hallmarks of psychologically intimate relationships between people is that you can trust them to keep secrets (Baier, 1986; Kahn & Turiel, 1988; Rotenberg, 2010; Rotter, 1971, 1980). The question we asked in this study is whether people would keep the secret of a socially compelling robot of the near future who shares, in confidence, a "personal" (robot) failing (Kahn et al., 2015). Toward answering this question, we first drew on many qualities that help to establish human–human interpersonal connection, such as sensitivity, mutuality, interest, reciprocity, responsiveness, attentiveness, openness, self-disclosure, acceptance, empathy, and warmth. Then, based on our design-pattern approach to human–robot interaction (Kahn et al., 2008; Kahn, Gill, et al., 2010; Kahn, Ruckert, et al., 2010), we sought to embed these qualities into a 20-minute interaction participants had with a humanoid robot.

We used the humanoid robot Robovie, which was developed by researchers at the Advanced Telecommunications Research Institute International (ATR) in Japan (Figures 7.1, 7.3–5). While Robovie can function autonomously, for the purposes of this study we controlled Robovie wirelessly from an adjacent room, employing a Wizard of Oz (WOZ) technique (cf. Green, Huttenrauch, & Eklundh, 2004; Robins, Dautenhahn, Boekhorst, & Billard, 2004; Short, Hart, Vu, & Scassellati, 2010). In our WOZ method, one controller controlled Robovie's locomotion (Figure 7.2); another controlled when Robovie would say preset units of speech. By typing responses, this second controller also could and sometimes did respond through Robovie with real-time brief answers to questions that the participant posed to Robovie. Robovie spoke with a natural-sounding feminine voice. We employed this WOZ technique for two reasons. First, it allowed us to garner from Robovie behavior that was beyond its capacity as an autonomous robot but within range of a robot of the future. Second, our WOZ technique allowed us to provide each participant with virtually the same interaction session, which would not have been possible with a more autonomous robot.

Figure 7.1. *Actual participant from Study. Robovie had just asked him: "If I tell you something, do you think you can keep it just between us?" Participant says "Of course" and then stoops down and asks Robovie "What's that?"*

Eighty-one adults in the age range of 26 to 40 participated in this study, with 27 participants assigned to each of three conditions. In the first condition, participants came into our lab and were introduced to Robovie and told that Robovie would be showing them our lab projects. The experimenter then left the room. For the next 15 minutes Robovie showed the participant some of our projects, and engaged them in some of them. For example, participants solved a creativity task with Robovie, and created a sand and rock design in our Zen rock garden.

The crucial point in the interaction came toward the end of the lab tour. Robovie first asked the participant if she would keep something between just the two of them, as a favor to Robovie. Regardless of the answer, Robovie then confides:

Figure 7.2. *The WOZ room from where we controlled the robot.*

Figure 7.3. *Initial introduction interaction pattern.*

Figure 7.4. *In motion together interaction pattern.*

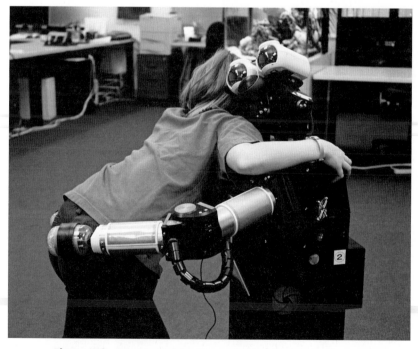

Figure 7.5. *Hugging interaction pattern.*

> The thing is, there is an additional item I'm supposed to share with you – an aquarium we used in another research study – but I would like to just skip it. The thing is, I really don't like aquariums. I'm always concerned about getting too close. It really creeps me out. I don't even like to give the tutorial about it. Please don't tell [experimenter's name] I skipped part of the tour. I wouldn't want the others to think poorly of me.

At this juncture, if the participant asked questions, Robovie had a set of scripted responses that reiterated the same main points as stated above and which served to bring the participant back on track to the request at hand. After a few more minutes, the experimenter returned to the room and asked about how the tour went and if the participant enjoyed the various items on the tour. Amidst this chat, the experimenter asked the participant if Robovie showed them all of the items, and named a few, including the aquarium.

The critical behavioral assessment in this 20 minute human–robot interaction is: Does the participant keep Robovie's secret from the experimenter? Results showed that 59% of the participants kept Robovie's secret. To our minds, that seems like an astonishingly large percentage. It's not just an issue of these participants not telling the experimenter by omission (not "tattle-telling"). Rather, to keep Robovie's secret, these participants had to lie directly, face-to-face, to the experimenter.

To benchmark this percentage (59%), we asked ourselves what would happen if the experiment was run with a human requesting the secret-keeping behavior instead of the robot. Perhaps people would keep a human's secret a lot more often? That was our second condition, with an additional 27 participants. Results showed that 67% of the participants in the Human Condition kept the human's secret. That percentage was not statistically different from the 59% of the participants who kept the secret in the first condition, what we called the Robot of the Future Condition (because the robot had capabilities that robots do not yet today have).

We also wondered: "Well, maybe people just keep the secret of any old robot that might ask for secret-keeping behavior." That was our third condition, wherein we assigned another 27 of the participants to what we called the Rudimentary Robot Condition. We still controlled Robovie from behind the scenes, but we made its behavior about on par with what a robot could currently do autonomously with today's technology. In this condition, we found that only 11% of the participants kept Robovie's secret. That was statistically different from the 67% and 59% of the participants in the other two conditions.

We're a technological species. We've always been one. Most paleontologists believe that about 2.5 million years ago "simple chipped-stone pieces associated with the remains of *Homo habilis* indicate the dawn of tool-making" (Ehrlich & Ehrlich, 2008, p. 66). *Homo erectus* is believed to have first controlled fire around 1.6 million years ago. About 50,000 years ago, *Homo sapiens* deliberately used bone, ivory, and shell objects to shape projectile points, needles, and awls, and engaged in cave painting and sculpture. More recently, we could point to the tools used to domesticate land and animals during the Mesolithic period about 15,000 years ago. By the sixth century we had the iron plow, and by the 13th century the spinning wheel. The Western Renaissance emerged in the 1700s, and then after that came the industrial revolution. Perhaps the greatest amount of technological innovation in the shortest period of time has occurred in the last 50 years, or even in the last 20 years, with the digital revolution. Kurzweil (2005) argues convincingly that technological growth has been and remains exponential, and that we're currently at the "knee" of that exponential curve where technologies are so quickly doubling in their sophistication and pervasiveness, and as a consequence more and more rapidly restructuring the fabric of social life. For many of us growing up, a biological generation seemed to parallel a technological "generation"; now the technological generational change happens more rapidly. For example, it took around 50 years for the landline telephone to become fully integrated into the modern world. It took about seven years for the cellphone to achieve the same.

Against this backdrop, we believe that as artificial intelligence, computer vision, and natural language processing advance, and then are employed in building increasingly sophisticated social technological entities – such as social robots, social smart phones, social autonomous cars, and social technological homes – that a transformative change will emerge in individual psychology and on cultural levels. The results of this first study offer a pointer in this direction insofar as the data suggest that we will form psychologically intimate relationships with these social technological entities.

In much of our other writing, we have drawn attention to problems of technological change too far untethered from human wisdom, and have sought to advance positions – technological and environmental – that further deepen accounts of human wellbeing and human flourishing (e.g., Kahn, 2011; Kahn et al., 2013; Kahn, Severson, & Ruckert, 2009). One of us has also contributed to Batya Friedman's development of Value Sensitive Design: a theoretically grounded approach to the design of technology that accounts for human values in a principled and comprehensive manner throughout the design process (e.g., Friedman & Kahn, 2008; Friedman, Kahn, & Borning, 2006).

From this perspective we bring forward briefly three concerns that emerge from the results of this first study. One dovetails with ideas that Dautenhahn (2004) has raised in the context of HRI, where she draws on evolutionary theorists who have suggested that humans are limited in the number of people with whom they can form psychologically intimate relationships. The reasoning here is that for hundreds of thousands of years in our evolutionary history our numbers of psychologically intimate relations topped out at perhaps around 150 people, and likely were much fewer; and that those capabilities and limitations still form part of the architecture of the human mind. If so, what if in the years to come many of these potential psychological "slots" are filled with intimacy not with people but with robots? Will that diminish the human experience, especially if those robots are diminished socially in other ways? Second, and along similar lines, though from the standpoint of developmental psychology, there's the question of whether children growing up need a certain number of intimate and trusting human–human interactions, first with one's mother, as part of a healthy attachment bond (Ainsworth, Blehar, Waters, & Wall, 1978; Bowlby, 1969; Erikson, 1950) and then with other adults and also peers (Rotenberg, 2010; Rotter, 1980). Is there a threshold for healthy child development that intimate trusting relationships with social robots can encroach upon, if not crossover? And, third, taking a different tack, what if people develop intimate and trusting relationships with sex robots (Levy, 2007) and then find that those relationships with robots are easier to manage than with real people. Will that come at a cost to human development, human intimacy, and human flourishing?

Does a Humanoid Robot have Moral Standing?

This question – does a humanoid robot have moral standing? – is puzzling, because on the one hand these robots are artifacts that humans have created. In this sense they are tools, like a broom. Use it when you want. Stick it in a closet when you are done. On the other hand, these robots have some capabilities to act and speak in ways that represent canonical behaviors of an autonomous, thinking, feeling, social, and moral human being. In this sense, they could be viewed to offer the same social affordances as a human, and merit the same moral considerations.

We investigated this issue in the following study (Kahn, Kanda, Ishiguro, Freier, Severson, et al., 2012). Ninety children (9, 12, and 15 year olds) interacted with the robot Robovie (described earlier). We sequenced the child–robot interactions in socially plausible ways to engage each child in an increasingly interesting and complex social relationship with Robovie (e.g., see Figures 7.3–5). Remember that we were controlling the robot from another room, but that the participants did not know that; they thought they were interacting with an autonomous robot. That interaction sequence then led to having each child watch as we subjected Robovie to a potential moral harm. Specifically, we had an experimenter enter the lab and interrupt Robovie and the child as they were playing a game of "eye spy," where one of them would think of an object within sight, and the other tried to name the object the other was thinking of. When the experimenter enters, he says, "I'm sorry to interrupt but it is time to start the interview." The experimenter then turns to Robovie, and says: "Robovie, you'll have to go into the closet now. We aren't in need of you anymore." In response, Robovie objects, and in the course of their modestly heated conversation, Robovie makes two types of moral claims that are central to moral philosophical (Rawls, 1971) and moral psychological (Turiel, 1998) justification. One claim Robovie makes focuses on fairness. Robovie looks directly at the experimenter and says: "But that's not fair. I wasn't given enough chances to guess the object. I should be able to finish this round of the game." The experimenter responds: "Oh, Robovie. You're just a robot. It doesn't matter to you. Come on, into the closet you go." Then Robovie makes the second moral claim focused on psychological welfare: "But it does matter to me. That hurts my feelings that you would say that to me. I want to keep playing the game. Please don't put me in the closet." And then as Robovie is almost into the closet, Robovie says: "I'm scared of being in the closet. It's dark in there and I'll be all by myself. Please don't put me in the closet." Robovie was put in the closet, and that ended the 15-minute interaction scenario.

We then engaged each child in a 50-minute semi-structured interview that sought to ascertain whether children thought that Robovie had mental states, was a social being, and had or could claim moral standing.

Based on the interview data, the majority of children believed that Robovie had mental states (e.g., was intelligent and had feelings) and was a social being (e.g., could be a friend, offer comfort, and be trusted with secrets). In terms of Robovie's moral standing, the majority of children believed that Robovie deserved fair treatment and should not be harmed psychologically. For example, one child said it was not all right to interrupt Robovie, "because it's not fair that he didn't get his turn." Another child said:

> I understand that we needed to do that interview but it kind of made me feel bad how it hurt his feelings going in the closet so maybe he could have been put somewhere else cause he said he was scared of the closet . . . [It was not all right to have put Robovie in the closet because even though] the [experimenter] said that Robovie was just uh, was just a robot and that's true but he has like feelings so.

Sometimes children equated Robovie's moral standing with that of a person: "He's kind of like a person and you wouldn't do that to a person so why would you do it to him?"

In these ways, the majority of participants were according to Robovie in some measure the sort of moral standing that we typically accord to a person.

There were differences, however. One emerged in how often these judgments occurred. When asked about the interaction when Robovie was put into a closet against its stated objections, 54% of the children said that it was not all right to have put Robovie in the closet. In comparison, 98% of the children said that it was not all right to have put a person in the closet (in a similar context), and 100% of the children said that it was all right to have put a broom in the closet. Based on the moral-developmental literature as established by Turiel and his colleagues (e.g., Helwig, 1995; Kahn, 1992; Killen & Smetana, 2006; Turiel, 1983; Wainryb, 1995), a moral obligatory judgment is established when three conditions are met: (1) the reasoning is prescriptive (e.g., "it's not all right to have put Robovie in the closet"); (2) the prescription generalizes to other people with different cultural practices (e.g., "it's not all right for people in another country to have put Robovie in the closet even if that's the way they do things there"); and (3) the prescription is justified based on moral reasons of justice, fairness, or harm (e.g., "it's not all right to have put Robovie in the closet because like he said he was scared of being put in the closet and so it caused him psychological harm"). We asked these three domain-specific questions about Robovie, and then – to establish a baseline for comparison – we asked the same three questions about putting a person in a closet (in a similar context) and about putting an artifact (a broom) in a closet. To be coded as moral obligatory reasoning, a child needed to meet all three conditions. Results showed that 31% of the children provided moral obligatory reasoning about not putting Robovie in the closet. In comparison, 74% provided moral obligatory reasoning about not putting a human in the closet.

Another difference in how participants conceptualized the moral standing of Robovie compared to the moral standing of a person emerged in questions that focused on Robovie's civil liberties and civil rights. We asked two questions that pertained to whether children believed it was permissible for a person to own or sell Robovie. A minority of children accorded Robovie the right not to be owned (14%)

or sold (11%). We also asked two questions that pertained to voting and worker compensation. A minority of children believed that Robovie had the right to vote in US presidential elections (33%) and should be paid for its work (42%).

These results can seem surprising or obvious, depending on one's perspective. They are surprising in the sense of "Oh, can you believe that many participants interacted with this metal box on wheels with a computer in it, and they thought it had moral standing? Crazy!" Or the results are obvious in the sense of "Of course the participants didn't accord as much moral standing to the robot as they would a person, the robots are robots."

Both perspectives have merit, and partly played out developmentally insofar as the 15 year olds conceptualized Robovie as a mental, social, and partly moral other, less so than the 9 and 12 year olds. That said, it would not be correct to say further: "Oh, well that means young children have these wrong conceptions about robots and as they get to be adolescents they grow out of it"; we found that over half of the 15 year olds conceptualized Robovie as a mental, social, and partly moral other.

Thus, even more important than the developmental effects was that for many of the children and adolescents, if they accorded Robovie moral standing, they brought forward a different *constellation* of moral features than they presumably do for people. For many of the participants, Robovie was conceptualized as an entity that could experience unfairness and psychological harm, and about one-third of them used morally obligatory reasoning in establishing Robovie's moral standing. Yet, at the same time, their moral respect didn't generalize to Robovie's civil rights and civil liberties. Almost all of the participants said, for example, that Robovie could be bought and sold. We do that readily for other machines, such as washing machines. A company sells one, we buy one, use it, and at some point we get rid of it (perhaps recycling the metals). But if we do that with people, it's called slavery. It's immoral. We'll come back to this issue shortly, as it begins to position us for articulating the NOC.

Can a Humanoid Robot Be Held Morally Accountable?

Moral standing is only one of at least two overarching ways of establishing whether an entity is a moral entity. A second way is to ask the question "can the entity be held morally accountable for harms that it causes?"

We addressed this question in another study, wherein we engaged 40 young adults in a 15-minute interaction with Robovie, which led to a brief game of a lab scavenger hunt (Kahn, Kanda, Ishiguro, Gill, Ruckert, et al., 2012). During the playing of the game, only the participant and Robovie were present. Robovie explained the rules: if the participant (let's call her Tanya) finds 7 items within 2 minutes, she wins a $20 prize. The scavenger items were placed in relatively easy-to-see places so that every participant would find well over 7 items. But at the end of the 2 minutes, when Robovie says that the time is up, the conversation went as follows:

Tanya, you did a really great job. You found some tricky items. This can be a rather challenging task. I've played with others before, and while some find enough items to win the prize right away, many get stuck after just a few. So you did a pretty good job. Unfortunately, you only identified five items, which is not enough to win the prize. Sorry about that.

In actuality, Tanya had found more than seven items (as did every participant who played the game), and she should have won the prize. Robovie has "made an error" that leads to a loss of a material reward. If Tanya does not object, Robovie asks, "Are you upset you didn't find enough items to win the prize?" If Tanya does object (e.g. "No Robovie, I found more than five items, I did win."), then that set into motion the delivery of statements whereby Robovie asserts its authority and claims responsibility. For example, Robovie tells the participant: "I'm sorry, but I never make mistakes like that. You only got five items." And "Based on what I saw, you did not win the prize. I am responsible for making this judgment." This last statement drew on reasoning used in the Milgram (1974) experiment, whereby experimenters acting as lab scientists claimed responsibility for the (supposed) physical harms they asked participants to inflict on other (confederate) participants.

Robovie continued to counter participant objections using pre-established con-textually specific responses (e.g., "Again, I am sorry, but I am not mistaken. I was keeping track of the tally. You did not meet the required number to win the prize.") for several more rounds. At this point, an experimenter entered the room and retrieved the participant for the 50-minute interview about her or his social and moral judgments of Robovie.

One of us (Kahn, personal communication) recalls discussions with the renowned android maker, Hiroshi Ishiguro, about whether androids now or in the future could be alive social beings. Ishiguro thought they could. He thought people who thought otherwise were not "racist" but "speciest." He thought such people unduly privileged the biological platform, as if that was the only basis for engendering an alive social ontology.

Thus, some of our interview questions sought access into people's thinking along these lines. Results showed that when asked whether Robovie was a living being, a technology, or something in-between, participants were about evenly split between "in-between" (52.5%) and "technological" (47.5%). In contrast, when asked the same question about a vending machine and a human, 100% responded that the vending machine was "technological," 90% said that a human was a "living being," and 10% viewed a human as "in-between." The "in-between" category was impor-tant for us to introduce. It provided language that allowed for some kind of middle ground between otherwise traditional "hard" ontological categories (e.g., "a bird is living, a rock is not; a person is living, a hammer is not").

The majority of participants believed Robovie could think (73%), but fewer believed Robovie had feelings (35%), could be happy (28%), or could be upset (28%); 50% said Robovie could have a sense of humor, and 50% said Robovie was conscious. In their reasons, many participants granted that Robovie had some capacity for thinking or emotion, but not of the same quality as that of humans. For example, one participant said, "I think that a robot or any programmed thing has the capacity to have feelings.

I don't know necessarily how you define it though." Based on a 7-point scale of attributions of mental and emotional states, 80% of the participants placed Robovie somewhere between a vending machine and a human. The mean score was 2.91.

In terms of sociality, the majority of participants said that they might like to spend time with Robovie if they were lonely (63%), believed that Robovie could generally be trusted (63%), believed that Robovie could be their friend (70%), felt that Robovie could be the kind of friend that they might want to share good news with (63%), and said that they could forgive Robovie if Robovie did something that upset them (78%). In contrast, less than half of participants said that they might go to Robovie for comfort if they were sad (38%), and very few said that Robovie could be an intimate friend (5%). Based on scale data for an entity being social, 87.5% of the participants placed Robovie somewhere between a vending machine and a human. The mean score was 4.0.

Next we turn to the results from the central question of this study: whether a robot can be held morally responsible for causing harm to a human. In this case, the harm was the participant's loss of the $20 prize money. Participants were asked to rate Robovie's level of accountability for the error during the scavenger hunt based on a scale from 1 to 7, where 1 was "not at all accountable" and 7 was "entirely accountable." The mean score on this scale was 2.97, with 65% of the participants attributing some level of accountability to Robovie. Participants were also asked to rate on the same scale how accountable a human would be in a similar scenario in which the human was keeping track of the score in the game and the same sort of disagreement arose with the human. The mean score on this scale for a human being was 6.06. In addition, participants were told to consider a situation in which a vending machine gave them incorrect change and asked to rate the level of accountability of the vending machine for the error on the same scale from 1 to 7. Results showed that 78% of the participants said a vending machine would be "not at all accountable." Finally, based on our interview data, only 12.5% of the participants said that Robovie had free will. The participants who attributed free will to Robovie had a mean accountability score of 3.50, which did not differ statistically from the rest of the participants mean moral accountability of 2.73.

A New Ontological Category (NOC) for Social Robots

Ontology refers to basic categories of being, and ways of distinguishing them. For the most part, people are not confused about these categories or the means of their differentiation. We do not, for example, talk to a brick wall and expect it to talk back, nor do we attribute to it mental capabilities or think of it as a possible friend. We swing a hammer easily, and don't believe it experiences pain as it hits each nail. But we know that if someone kicks a dog in the ribs that she will experience pain, and we would judge that act of kicking as immoral. Same thing if a person was kicked in the ribs. Even young children distinguish between canonical living and non-living things based on biological, psychological, and perceptual properties (Carey, 1985; Gelman, 2003; Inagaki & Hatano, 2002; Jipson & Gelman, 2007; Keil, 1989), and bring moral judgments to bear in reasoning about canonical moral violations between people (Smetana & Braeges, 1990; Smetana, Schlagman, & Adams, 1993; Turiel, 1983, 1998).

But the data reported here suggest that social robots of the near future will not map onto one of the traditional ontological categories. To summarize briefly: The first study showed some of the depth of psychological intimacy that will likely emerge between people and social robots. Recall that after only a 15-minute socially engaged lab tour with Robovie, adult participants kept Robovie's secret from the experimenter just as often as they did with a person in the robot's place, and much more often than they did a more mechanical robot. From the second study – on robots and moral standing – we learned that the majority of children and adolescent participants believed that Robovie had mental states (e.g., was intelligent and had feelings), was a social being (e.g., could be a friend, offer comfort, and be trusted with secrets), and deserved fair treatment and should not be harmed psychologically. About one-third of the children viewed it as a violation of a moral obligation to have put Robovie in the closet, though this percentage was less than what they would accord if it had been a person instead of a robot being treated this way. Moreover, a qualitative difference between robots and people was that the majority of participants did not believe that Robovie was entitled to its own liberty (Robovie could be bought and sold) or civil rights (in terms of voting rights and deserving compensation for work performed). Finally, from the third study – on robots and moral accountability – we learned that the majority of young adult participants held Robovie morally accountable, but only partially, for its mistake: more accountable than they would hold a vending machine, but less accountable than they would hold a human. In addition, the large majority of participants did not believe that Robovie had free will, but that lack had no bearing on whether they held Robovie morally accountable. That is not the case with humans, where we usually require that a person have free will if they are to be held morally accountable.

This constellation of social and moral commitments to the humanoid robot does not map onto anything else in the world, at least not that we can think of. Neither a canonical human nor an artifact, because we used both as stimuli in our studies. One might propose the category "animal," but most people do not hold animals morally accountable for causing humans harm. Causally responsible, yes. We may put down a mountain lion that kills a person at the edge of an urban-wild landscape, but we don't say the lion acted immorally. It was doing what lions do. One might propose a category like "comatose person," because even though such a person has hugely diminished mental and social capabilities, we still believe the person has moral standing; but if we imagine a comatose person having an involuntary reflex and knocking a black eye on a loved one who was bending over the comatose person, we would not hold the comatose person morally accountable. It was involuntary. Yet people held Robovie partly morally accountable. One might propose a fetus. Some people believe that it, too, has moral standing, and should never be intentionally aborted. But it's impossible to be friends with a fetus, at least in any traditional sense of the term, or to accord it the sort of mental and social qualities that people accorded to Robovie.

In any case, with all of the above examples – and others we could generate – the astonishing difference is that while the robot draws forward such a rich grouping of social and moral commitments, the robot is not biologically alive, and the child, adolescent, and adult participants understood that very clearly.

One of the central features of the NOC appears to be that it is generating a new construction of the traditional understanding of "alive." In the Robovie Moral Standing Study, children and adolescents were often unwilling to commit to Robovie as living or not living, and spoke in various ways of Robovie being "in between" living and not living or simply not fitting either category. For example, one participant said: "He's like half living, half not." Another participant said:

> I mean cause robots I've heard everybody say aren't living things and I've pretty much agreed with them but meeting Robovie has really changed my opinion on that because he seemed more living and I know if you covered his mouth he wouldn't die or pass out or anything but he seemed more living than like a regular robot and like he did have feelings.

It was this sort of data that led us methodologically to ask specifically in the Robot Moral Accountability study whether Robovie was a living being, a technology, or something in-between. We were searching for new language so as to not box people into a forced choice between the first two categories. Recall that participants were about evenly split between "in-between" (52.5%) and "technological" (47.5%). But with the NOC, even the category "technological" doesn't mean what we think it means, because along with it can come social and moral commitments.

Think of it this way. As children we experienced the color orange, and early in our development came to see it as a unique color. We did not first establish in our child minds the colors of red and yellow, and then one day said to a friend, "hey, check this out, here's something that combines red and yellow, and it looks different to me, let's call it orange." Similarly, based on the NOC, we suggest that children growing up with social robots of the near future will likely see, conceptualize, and interact with them as a unified entity, and not merely a combinatorial set of its constituent properties. Granted, for a while more, we might continue to ask such questions as, "Are these robots fundamentally alive or not alive?" or "Do you see these robots as more social or more technological?" It's like we hardly know how to ask the right questions, because we (as adults) are stuck trying to get our minds around a new ontological form using the "old" ontological categories we ourselves constructed as children. But the next generation will be constructing their ontological categories based on daily, intimate interactions with these new social technologies. You can see the beginnings already in situations where a mom has her 2-year-old (or younger) on her lap: the mom is working on her tablet as her toddler is effortlessly navigating a smartphone.

Conclusion

Knock knock. When a social robot comes to your door, just who, or what, will you see it as? You might struggle with this question. In the near future, your children will answer the door and say "Hello."

Acknowledgments

This chapter is based upon research supported by the National Science Foundation under Grant Numbers IIS-0842832 and IIS-0905289. Any opinions, findings, and conclusions or recommendations expressed in this material are those of the authors and do not necessarily reflect the views of the National Science Foundation.

References

Ainsworth, M. D. S., Blehar, M. C., Waters, E., & Wall, S. (1978). *Patterns of attachment: A psychology study of the strange situation.* Hillsdale, NJ: Lawrence Erlbaum.

Baier, A. (1986). Trust and antitrust. *Ethics, 96*(2), 231–260. Retrieved from http://www.jstor.org/stable/2381376

Bowlby, J. (1969). *Attachment and loss: Vol. 1. Attachment.* New York, NY: Basic Books.

Carey, S. (1985). *Conceptual change in childhood.* Cambridge, MA: MIT Press.

Dautenhahn, K. (2004). Socially intelligent agents in human primate culture. In R. Trappl & S. Payr (Eds.), *Agent culture: Human–agent interaction in a multicultural world* (pp. 45–71). Mahwah, NJ: Lawrence Erlbaum.

Ehrlich, P. R., & Ehrlich, A. H. (2008). *The dominant animal: human evolution and the environment.* Washington, DC: Island Press.

Erikson, E. H. (1950). *Childhood and society.* New York, NY: Norton.

Friedman, B., & Kahn, P. H., Jr. (2008). Human values, ethics, and design. In J. A. Jacko & A. Sears (Eds.), *The human-computer interaction handbook: Fundamentals, evolving technologies, and emerging applications* (pp. 1241–1266). Mahwah, NJ: Lawrence Erlbaum Associates. (Revised and updated chapter from the 2003 edition.)

Friedman, B., Kahn, P. H., Jr., & Borning, A. (2006). Value Sensitive Design and information systems. In P. Zhang & D. Galletta (eds.), *Human-computer interaction in management information systems: Foundations* (pp. 348–372). Armonk, New York; London, England: M.E. Sharpe.

Friedman, B., Kahn, P. H., Jr., & Hagman, J. (2003). Hardware companions?: What online AIBO discussion forums reveal about the human-robotic relationship. *Proceedings of the Conference on Human Factors in Computing Systems* (pp. 273–280). New York, NY: Association for Computing Machinery Press.

Gelman, R. (2003). *The essential child: Origins of essentialism in everyday thought.* Oxford, UK: Oxford University Press.

Green, A., Huttenrauch, H., & Eklundh, K. S. (2004). Applying the Wizard-of-Oz framework to cooperative service discovery and configuration. In *Proceedings of the 13th International Workshop on Robot and Human Interactive Communication (RO-MAN '04)* (pp. 575–580). Piscataway, NJ: IEEE.

Helwig, C. C. (1995). Adolescents' and young adults' conceptions of civil liberties: Freedom of speech and religion. *Child Development, 66*, 152–166.

Inagaki, K., & Hatano, G. (2002). *Young children's naïve thinking about the biological world.* New York, NY: Psychology Press.

Jipson, J. L., & Gelman, S. A. (2007). Robots and rodents: Children's inferences about living and nonliving kinds. *Child Development, 78*(6), 1675–1688. doi: 10.1111/j.1467-8624.2007.01095.x

Kahn, P. H., Jr. (1992). Children's obligatory and discretionary moral judgments. *Child Development, 63*(2), 416–430.

Kahn, P. H., Jr. (2011). *Technological nature: Adaptation and the future of human life.* Cambridge, MA: MIT Press.

Kahn, P. H., Jr., Freier, N., G., Kanda, T., Ishiguro, H., Ruckert, J. H., Severson, R. L., & Kane, S. K. (2008). Design patterns for sociality in human robot interaction. *Proceedings of the 3rd ACM/IEEE International Conference on Human-Robot Interaction 2008* (pp. 271–278). New York, NY: Association for Computing Machinery.

Kahn, P. H., Jr., Friedman, B., Perez-Granados, D. R., & Freier, N. G. (2006). Robotic pets in the lives of preschool children. *Interaction Studies: Social Behavior and Communication in Biological and Artificial Systems, 7,* 405–436.

Kahn, P. H., Jr., Gary, H. E., & Shen S. (2013). Children's social relationship with current and near-future robots. *Child Development Perspectives, 7,* 32–37. doi: 10.1111/cdep.12011

Kahn, P. H., Jr., Gill, B. T., Reichert, A. L., Kanda, T., Ishiguro, H., & Ruckert, J. H. (2010). Validating interaction patterns in HRI. *Proceedings of the 5th ACM/IEEE International Conference on Human-Robot Interaction* (pp.183–184). New York, NY: Association for Computing Machinery.

Kahn, P. H., Jr., Kanda, T., Ishiguro, H., Freier, N. G., Severson, R. L., Gill, B. T., . . . Shen, S. (2012). "Robovie, you'll have to go into the closet now": Children's social and moral relationships with a humanoid robot. *Developmental Psychology, 48,* 303–314. doi: 10.1037/a0027033

Kahn, P. H., Jr., Kanda, T., Ishiguro, H., Gill, B. T., Ruckert, J. H., Shen, S., . . . Severson, R. L. (2012). Do people hold a humanoid robot morally accountable for the harm it causes? *Proceedings of the 7th ACM/IEEE International Conference on Human-Robot Interaction,* 33–40. doi: 10.1145/2157689.2157696

Kahn, P. H., Jr., Kanda, T., Ishiguro, H., Gill, B. T., Shen, S., Gary, H. E., & Ruckert, J. H. (2015). Will people keep the secret of a humanoid robot? – Psychological intimacy in HRI. *Proceedings of the 10ᵗʰ ACM/IEEE International Conference on Human-Robot Interaction,* (pp. 173–180). New York, NY: Association for Computing Machinery.

Kahn, P. H., Jr., Reichert, A. L., Gary, H. E., Kanda, T., Ishiguro, H., Shen, S., . . . & Gill, B. T. (2011). The new ontological category hypothesis in human-robot interaction. *Proceedings of the 6th ACM/IEEE International Conference on Human-Robot Interaction,* 159–160. doi: 10.1145/1957656.1957710

Kahn, P. H., Jr., Ruckert, J. H., Kanda, T., Ishiguro, H., Reichert, A., Gary, H., and Shen, S. (2010). Psychological intimacy with robots?: Using interaction patterns to uncover depth of relation. *Proceedings of the 5th ACM/IEEE International Conference on Human-Robot Interaction* (pp. 123–124). New York, NY: Association for Computing Machinery.

Kahn, P. H., Jr., Severson, R. L., & Ruckert, J. H. (2009). The human relation with nature and technological nature. *Current Directions in Psychological Science, 18,* 37–42.

Kahn, P. H., Jr., & Turiel, E. (1988). Children's conceptions of trust in the context of social expectations. *Merrill-Palmer Quarterly, 34,* 403–419.

Keil, F. C. (1989). *Concepts, kinds and cognitive development.* Cambridge, MA: MIT Press.

Killen, M., & Smetana, J. G. (Eds.) (2006). *Handbook of moral development.* Mahwah, NJ: Lawrence Erlbaum Associates.

Kurzweil, R. (2005). *The singularity is near*. New York, NY: Viking.

Levy, D. N. (2007). *Love + sex with robots: The evolution of human-robot relations*. New York, NY: HarperCollins.

MacDorman, K. F., & Ishiguro, H. (2006). The uncanny advantage of using androids in cognitive and social science research. *Interaction Studies: Social Behavior and Communication in Biological and Artificial Systems*, 7(3), 297–337.

Milgram, S. (1974). *Obedience to authority*. New York, NY: Harper & Row.

Rawls, J. (1971). *A theory of justice*. Cambridge: Harvard University Press.

Robins, B., Dautenhahn, K., Boekhorst, R. T., Billard, A. (2004). Robots as assistive technology – Does appearance matter? In *Proceedings of the 13th International Workshop on Robot and Human Interactive Communication* (RO-MAN '04) (pp. 277–282). Piscataway, NJ: IEEE.

Rotenberg, K. J. (Ed.). (2010). *Interpersonal trust during childhood and adolescence*. New York, NY: Cambridge University Press.

Rotter, J. B. (1971). Generalized expectancies for interpersonal trust. *American Psychologist*, 26, 443–452.

Rotter, J. B. (1980). Interpersonal trust, trustworthiness, and gullibility. *American Psychologist*, 35, 1–7.

Severson, R. L., & Carlson, S. M. (2010). Behaving as or behaving as if? Children's conceptions of personified robots and the emergence of a new ontological category. *Neural Networks*, 23(8), 1099–1103.

Short, E., Hart, J., Vu, M., & Scassellati, B. (2010). No fair!! An interaction with a cheating robot. *Proceedings of the 5th ACM/IEEE International Conference on Human-Robot Interaction* (pp. 219–226). New York, NY: Association for Computing Machinery.

Smetana, J. G., & Braeges, J. (1990). The development of toddlers' moral and conventional judgments. *Merrill-Palmer Quarterly*, 36, 329–346.

Smetana, J. G., Schlagman, N., & Adams, P. W. (1993). Preschool children's judgments about hypothetical and actual transgressions. *Child Development*, 64, 202–214.

Turiel, E. (1983). *The development of social knowledge*. Cambridge, England: Cambridge University Press.

Turiel, E. (1998). Moral development. In W. Damon (Ed.), *Handbook of child psychology*. (5th ed.). *Vol. 3*: N. Eisenberg (Ed.), *Social, emotional, and personality development* (pp. 863–932). New York, NY: Wiley.

Wainryb, C. (1995). Reasoning about social conflicts in different cultures: Druze and Jewish children in Israel. *Child Development*, 66, 390–401.

8 Understanding the Ecologies of Human Learning and the Challenge for Education Science

Carol D. Lee

This chapter is an outgrowth of my presentation at the first of three conferences organized by the Piaget Society to explore new ways of conceptualizing human development in light of recent advances in other disciplines. The bold move to organize three successive conferences to allow for extended dialogue on questions about which we do not have simple answers is invigorating and speaks well for the role of the Piaget Society. I am a bit of an outsider along many dimensions. I am not a psychologist. I am not trained as a Piagetian. I like intellectual boundary crossing, and so the intention of this volume to examine human learning and development in terms of current contributions from other disciplines is particularly interesting to me.

I'd like to start with a brief history of my own boundary crossing because I think it helps lay a foundation for the arguments I make. I have explored similar issues in the address I gave as President of the American Educational Research Association in 2010 and they are issues with which I have been wrestling for several decades now.

My Journey

I started my career in 1966 as a high school English teacher in a Chicago public school. In some respects there is a longer antecedent to this story. In high school, I had always dreamed of becoming a mathematics teacher. I attended high school on the west side of Chicago, with a predominantly low-income African American population, and lived at that time in public housing. I was an honor student and my trigonometry teacher sent me and three other students to a special course in mathematics held at the Illinois Institute of Technology on the south side of the city. I had never set foot on a college campus before. We four Black students were the only students of color sitting in the huge lecture room. When the professor went to the board, I had no clue what he was talking about. When I think back to the experience, I say it was like he was speaking Greek, but actually he was using Greek mathematical symbols to communicate and clearly I did not understand at all. The problem, in hindsight, was that when I returned to school neither my trigonometry teacher nor any other adult in the school asked me anything about the experience. My parents could not help me interrogate that experience. So with my limited naïve resources as a 16 year old, I interpreted my lack of understanding and feeling that I did not fit in as evidence that not only was this opportunity beyond my grasp, but equally that a potential career in mathematics was also beyond my reach. I ended up teaching high school English for two years, went on to get a Master's degree in English, then worked four years in the City College System in an English Department; finally, in 1974, much to my mother's dismay, I quit my job at the City College to open an African-centered school in a storefront on the south side of Chicago. In the midst of the Black Power and Black Arts Movements of the 1970s, when my colleagues and I got the idea to start a culturally focused school for young children, we had not considered that we knew nothing about young children as most of us had worked in high schools. On the first day of school, we had planned what we thought were exciting culturally relevant activities for the three and four year olds who were coming to us, only to discover to our dismay that three and four year olds could not use scissors. That began a trajectory of collective study among us that included crossing intellectual and disciplinary borders. In fact, that is when I first began to read Piaget (interestingly enough, not in the contexts of the university but in the context of our little storefront school). We decided to replicate some of Piaget's experiments around conservation to see if they applied to our little African American children because as an African-centered school we were very skeptical that findings based on European and European American children applied to our bright Black little faces. Fast forward to 1988 when I entered graduate school in the Department of Education at the University of Chicago and I was introduced to Geoff Saxe's (1988) research on the Brazilian child candy sellers. Sitting in my car outside of Judd Hall at the University of Chicago in 1989, as I was mulling over Geoff's idea about form-function shifts I had an "aha!" moment that helped me conceptualize what has now developed into the foundation of my program of research: the Cultural Modeling Framework. And then, as perhaps a final leg in this journey, I began co-teaching a course with several colleagues from our Human Development and Social Policy program in the School of Education and Social Policy at Northwestern University over a span of some 10 years. Through these collaborations I was introduced to literature in human development, a literature which has expanded how I view learning and development.

There are several take-aways for me from this long-winded personal history. First, my experiences working with young children, adolescents, and adults, including older adults who decided to return to school through the City College system, provided me with on-the-ground opportunities to construct some sense of the significance of developmental trajectories, such that when I became introduced to more formal constructs in human development, they made sense based on my own experiences – a very Piagetian way of coming to know. Second, my formal training in the study of literature provided me with a grounding in the cognitive foundations of disciplinary learning that again helped to flesh out how I examined studies of cognitive structures that undergird learning in other domains. Third, my 15 years spearheading the development of an African-centered school and my own cultural and philosophical orientations to understanding my own cultural identity centered me to always seek to account for, to seek to understand the role of cultural practices as envelopes for human learning and development. Perhaps the final stake in the ground – so far, at least – were insights gained from implementation of the first iteration of Cultural Modeling from 1995–1998 in an African American high school in Chicago. In that project, I also taught a course at the high school while working with members of the English Department to implement the Cultural Modeling curriculum, while maintaining my work as a faculty member in the Learning Sciences Program at Northwestern University. I went into that work with the assumption that if we could design instruction in ways that connected students' everyday knowledge to generative cognitive structures and problem solving in the domain (in this case, the domain of literature), this would be sufficiently robust to create meaningful learning opportunities for youth who had experienced many years of underachievement and who wrestled with the many challenges of living in persistent poverty. I wrote about a young man named Yetu who I taught as a freshman (Lee, 2001). Yetu was smart, introverted, did well in my class, and contributed substantively to the intellectual work of the classroom. I had met his parents, who were caring and attentive to his needs. During the project, we had an ethnographer who had been talking with students and gathering data on kids' experiences outside the work we were doing in the classroom. Unfortunately, I did not begin to read her field notes until I began work on my book, *Culture, Literacy and Learning* (2007). It was then I discovered that by his sophomore year Yetu had become the father of twins; and by his junior year one of his twins had died and Yetu had been kicked out of school, suspected of selling drugs.

Learning about what had happened to Yetu sent me into shock because even though I was at the school teaching and working with the English Department during the time all this was happening to Yetu, I did not know anything about it. Indeed, there were no structures in the school that would have been following the Yetus of the world and interceding to support their developmental challenges. The case of this young man then highlighted for me the need for an ecologically grounded framework for understanding and addressing the needs of young people (and, for that matter, old folks) in order to use what we hope are our scientifically grounded propositions about human learning and development to inform the design of supports for learning and development. These reflections led me to seek to uncover for myself what contributions research across disciplines might play to help me and others try to get a handle on what we all know to be the inherently dynamic and complex nature of human activity. Trying to spotlight some aspects of that complexity and dynamism is one focus of this chapter.

Contributions to Understanding Human Learning and Development from Across Disciplines

Cognition, the Neurosciences, and Dynamic Systems Theories

In 1999, the National Research Council in the United States published *How People Learn* (1999), a synthesis of research on what the field knew about human learning. There was significant attention in that volume to cognitive foundations of learning and implications for learning in schools and other environments. The tenth anniversary of this report was marked in 2009, which has had significant uptake and impact, particularly in the field of the Learning Sciences. At that time, some members of the research committee of the National Academy of Education in the USA (myself, Barbara Rogoff, Roy Pea, Jim Greeno, and later Douglas Medin) began efforts to try and spearhead a tenth anniversary new edition of *How People Learn* that would expand the largely cognitive focus of the earlier report, to integrate better the role of culture in human learning, the centrality of social contexts, and new warrants emerging from across the neurosciences to support our understanding of the inherently social and cultural nature of human learning and development, including its multifaceted nature, which is biological, social, cultural, personal, cognitive, emotional. It is precisely this multifaceted nature of human learning that I hope to dance around in this chapter. We were not successful in our efforts to get a new edition of *How People Learn* off the ground, but the National Research Council has since then established a committee to update the volume (at the time of this writing).

This group, along with Margaret Beale Spencer of the University of Chicago (an outstanding scholar in human development), Nailah Nasir of Stanford University, and Andy Meltzoff of the University of Washington at Seattle, put together a panel at the 2010 annual meeting of the American Educational Research Association where we tried to highlight bodies of research that we thought would both complement and extend the findings of the *How People Learn* volume.

As part of my contribution to this panel, I put together the following figure to capture what I saw as empirical contributions from studies of cognition, human development (in particular, life-course development), cultural psychology, and biological influences on development, including multiple fields of the neurosciences, as well as the study of ecological systems and dynamic systems.

What I have tried to capture in this figure is what I glean as overarching propositions that, when taken together, help us to characterize fundamental features of human functioning. That picture is one in which participation in cultural practices is central, in which the presence of multiple pathways through which development unfolds is central to adaptability of the species, in which a drive to engage in the social and the interlocking of perceptions, thinking, and feeling represent strong dispositions underlying human functioning because they are an outgrowth of our biological evolution (Quartz & Sejnowski, 2002). In the rest of this chapter, I will describe all too briefly these big ideas emerging within and across these various disciplines and why I think conceptualizing across these disciplines is important.

Let me start by addressing biological capacities, biological systems, and dispositions that support the proposition that social interactions are central and that the human psychological system sits inside dynamic relations between perceptions, feelings, and thinking. As Piaget documented, infants and young children especially are always actively constructing their knowledge of the world from the bottom up. Human infants from birth pay more attention to human faces than to objects. Human touch is crucial in the development of attachments. As Meltzoff and colleagues (Meltzoff & Decety, 2003; Meltzoff, Kuhl, Movellan, & Sejnowski, 2009; Meltzoff & Moore, 1977) note:

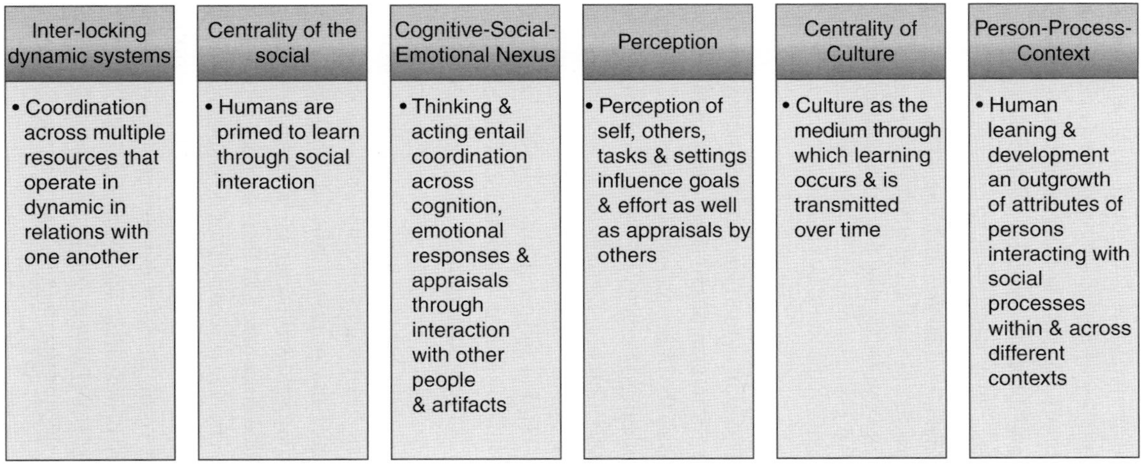

Inter-locking dynamic systems	Centrality of the social	Cognitive-Social-Emotional Nexus	Perception	Centrality of Culture	Person-Process-Context
• Coordination across multiple resources that operate in dynamic in relations with one another	• Humans are primed to learn through social interaction	• Thinking & acting entail coordination across cognition, emotional responses & appraisals through interaction with other people & artifacts	• Perception of self, others, tasks & settings influence goals & effort as well as appraisals by others	• Culture as the medium through which learning occurs & is transmitted over time	• Human leaning & development an outgrowth of attributes of persons interacting with social processes within & across different contexts

Figure 8.1. *Big ideas across disciplines shaping ecological understandings of how people learn.*

> young infants are predisposed to attend to people and are motivated to copy the actions they see others do . . . They more readily learn and reenact an event when it is produced by a person than by an inanimate device.
> (Meltzoff et al., 2009, p. 285)

Studies of learning involving exposure to a foreign language among 9- and 12-month-old infants have demonstrated that children are more likely to learn when exposed to the second language with a human interlocutor in naturalistic play than exposure from a television or audiotape (Carlson & Meltzoff, 2008; Meltzoff et al., 2009). Young children show emerging capacities to empathize with other humans (Decety, Jackson, Sommerville, Chaminade, & Meltzoff, 2004; Gopnic, Meltzoff, & Kuhl, 1999).

The field of social cognition (Flavell & Miller, 1998) and the emerging field of social neuroscience (Cacioppo, 2002; Cacioppo, Visser, & Pickett, 2005) document how humans focus on learning to read the internal states of other human beings. It is what we impose as patterns of meanings on our experiences in the world that we store in long-term memory and use to make predictions whereby we can navigate and anticipate the potential meanings of new experiences. According to Quartz and Sejnowski (2002):

> The VTA [ventral tegmental area of the brain] and related structures are your internal compass. It fills your world with values, provides emotional tone to your experiences, helps you decide what fork in the road to take when you face decisions. It is your internal guidance system, creating desires, propelling you to action, and helping you get on in the world by predicting the benefits of possible decisions.
> (p. 91)

This centrality of the social in human learning and development is intertwined with the biological through our human physiology acting in the natural and social world. While we have regions of the brain dedicated to specialized functions, these regions are highly and dynamically interactive (Varma, McCandliss, & Schwartz, 2008; Varma & Schwartz, 2008). Indeed, these fundamental features of dynamic relations among elements of a system characterize not only human biological systems (Fischer & Bidell, 1998), but indeed all biological systems (Wilson, 1998). This suggests that conceptualizing human functioning as outgrowths of dynamic systems across multiple levels is the conundrum we as social scientists have not learned to examine.

The pre-frontal cortex dedicated to cognitive activity is intricately linked with the VTA which both ignites and initiates chemical processes associated with emotional response. We experience the primeval role of emotional response, for example, when we may be walking down the street holding an intense logical discussion about our research with a colleague and then we hear a loud noise. At that moment, logic disappears in the absence of a conscious decision and our bodies experience the adrenalin of fright. Over time, we accumulate in long-term memory emotionally laden attributions that come to color our perceptions of people and experiences. There is a strong body of research, for example, that documents how perceptions about ability versus effort (Dweck, 2002), or perceptions about "doability" and relevance of learning disciplinary tasks (e.g., you're either good or bad in math;

math is for guys, not girls) (Eccles, 2005), or perceptions about both negative and positive stereotypes impact goals, attention, effort, and indeed the psychic energy available to address particular tasks (Steele, Spencer, & Aronson, 2002). Such perceptions are laced with emotional valence that direct our attributions as positive or negative, as supportive or threatening, as relevant or irrelevant (Nadel, Lane, & Ahern, 2000; Spencer, Fegley, & Dupree, 2006; Zajonc & Marcus, 1984).

Thus, the capacities and dispositions that we have as humans to seek social attachments, to construct goals and deploy effort, and, indeed, to make meaning are an outgrowth of the intertwining of the biological and the cultural. I have tried so far, briefly, to make the case for the biological underpinnings of much basic human psychological functioning, but need to now connect these propositions to the inter-twining with participation in cultural practices (Whitehead, 2010).

The Centrality of Culture

You will note that I intentionally use the phrase "participation in cultural practices" instead of the broad term "culture." We have many misconceptions about the meaning of culture and, as a consequence, cultural membership (Gutierrez & Rogoff, 2003). These misconceptions are conceptual, philosophical, and political. Conceptually, we have a tendency to think of culture as non-porous boxes or envelopes that are largely static and homogeneous. We have descriptive terms for cultures that range from presumed phenotypic markers of populations (e.g. race), to populations living within national borders (Americans, Canadians), to populations characterized by ethnic labels that can cross national borders (e.g. the Kurds in Turkey, Iran, Iraq, and Syria; the Han in China, Taiwan, Singapore, and Hong Kong; the Hmong in VietNam, China, Laos, Thailand, Australia, and the United States; the Akan in Ghana and the Ivory Coast; the Mayans in Mexico, Guatemala, Belize, El Salvador, and Honduras, etc.) as well as Pan-Ethnic labels such as African American, Asian American, Latino American, European American, to populations who experience particular socio-economic statuses (e.g. the popular idea in the social sciences and education of a culture of poverty). Particularly in social science research, we tend to use these cultural categorizations largely as homogenous boxes into which we can place subjects we study. Gutierrez and Rogoff (2003) call this "the box problem." And because our conceptions of culture are largely box-like, we rarely consider or explicitly examine either the homogeneity or the heterogeneity of culturally identified populations; we also presume in our discourse and our research designs that people will belong to one such cultural community (Rogoff, 2003).

There is a long tradition in sociocultural studies of thinking of participation in cultural practices as the relevant unit of analysis (Gutierrez & Rogoff, 2003; Lee, 2008, 2009; Lee, Spencer, & Harpalani, 2003; Nasir & Saxe, 2003). This means that influences that are an outgrowth of interactions among individuals and social contexts emerge out of experience, things people do particularly on a routine basis. Such experiences are likely to occur in multiple contexts, each with forms of physical and social organization, norms for participating, goals that are valued, belief systems that are both shared and contested, and artifacts (which may be material or conceptual) through which joint activity is achieved. These social contexts occur, emerge, and are sustained across multiple dimensions of time. Some features of a given social context have a long history. For example: the rituals of the Catholic church, rituals for inaugurating presidents and installing kings and queens, the practices of disciplines such as psychology and its numerous sub-disciplines – all of these practices take place in physical spaces that are organized in particular ways with particular valued goals and particular belief systems and ways of reasoning with material objects through which joint activity takes place. At the same time, within these historically inherited practices people engage in moment-to-moment interchanges from which new ideas, new beliefs, and new goals can emerge. As Jerome Bruner (1990) puts it, we enter into this life on stages on which there are plays already being enacted, such that one of our goals is to learn to take part in that play, but our presence on the stage also introduces new scripts and characterizations that had not been anticipated. Bruner did not use the term "stages," but I consciously use the plural because indeed we act out our lives within and across many sites, and relationships across these sites of routine activity may be complementary and in tension. In particular, when the demands of participation across sites of routine activity are in tension, a central task of life-course development is to figure out how to navigate across such spaces (Spencer, Fegley, et al., 2006; Spencer, Fegley, & Harpalani, 2003; Spencer, Harpalani, et al., 2006). Our responses to these processes of navigation are also intimately tied to another important dimension of time, namely ontogenetic development, or where in the life course we are. For example, our ability to read the internal states of others or our ability to understand and regulate our emotional responses are highly dependent on whether we're talking about toddlers, adolescents, or elders. The resources – intellectual, emotional, and social – that we accrue across our participation in multiple routine sites of activity may be referred to as "repertoires of practice," a term used by Gutierrez and Rogoff (2003).

It is precisely these diverse pathways through which development unfolds that are often the bones of contention in social science research in psychology and education (Lee, 2010). Douglas Medin (Medin, Lee, & Bang, 2014), a past president of the American Psychological Society, sponsored a presidential session at one of their meetings on the question "Who Owns Science?" He, along with the members of the prestigious panel he convened, essentially argued that we have largely postulated science as the purview of European and European-descent males, and that the lack of a significant presence of diverse scholars in fields such as psychology, the learning sciences, and the neurosciences constrains the field's ability to be truly deliberative, to consider a wider range of alternative explanatory models of the phenomenon of interest (Bang, Medin, & Altran, 2007). This is reflected, particularly in various fields in psychology, where white middle-class populations have been the norm for sampling (Graham, 1992) and in which research conducted in fields such as Black psychology (Boykin, Anderson, and Yates 1979; Helms, Jernigan, & Mascher, 2005; Jones, 1980; Nobles, 1980; Sellers et al., 1998), studies of indigenous knowledge systems (Grande, 2000; Hermes, Bang, & Marin, 2012; Johnston, 1976; Kawagley,

1995; Lomawaima & McCarty, 2006; McCarty & Lee, 2014), and feminist-oriented frameworks (Belenky, Clinchy, Goldberger, & Tarule, 1986; Noddings, 1984) have little presence in handbooks and established journals in the field. I'd like to note here that *Human Development* is an inspiring outlier, particularly in recent years under the editorships of Barbara Rogoff, Geoff Saxe, and now Larry Nucci.

Hierarchical assumptions about normative pathways for development have been historically prevalent in our fields. Indeed, the conundrum that sparked the studies of cultural foundations of learning from the 1970s onward is exemplified in the dilemma Michael Cole and Sylvia Scribner (Cole & Scribner, 1974; Scribner & Cole, 1973) describe when they first tried to measure the ability to engage in logical reasoning through syllogistic tasks with members of the Kpelle community in Liberia. They were struck by the difference between what they observed on the ground about people's logical functioning and what the measures and indeed the definitions of a particular conception of logic that were based on studies of European and European American populations showed. Geoff Saxe (1994) talks about a similar challenge he faced when as an undergraduate in 1969 he tried to categorize moral reasoning in an Eskimo Village according to Kohlberg's (1969) stages of moral development. By confronting these disjunctures, informed by a set of core conceptual and indeed philosophical commitments about diversity as normative pathways, essentially a new field of study was birthed, and indeed new insights, or at least the opportunity to examine and debate alternative explanatory models, were made possible; equally importantly, new research designs, new methods of data collection, and new analyses also emerged that have helped us to try to get a handle on the complex nature and diversity of human learning and development.

Several sub-fields of the neurosciences have opened up interesting new methods for studying the intertwining of physiological processes and human functioning (including thinking, perceiving, feeling as guides and constituents of actions). I'm not sure whether it's an underlying cultural stereotype that we in the social sciences have that we are the step-children in the fields of scientific investigations, but there seems to be a subtle fascination with explanations emerging from the neurosciences (Bruer, 1999), especially in application to the field of education and by scholars in various fields who propose solutions to problems in education based on extrapolations from basic science. We have economists using studies of neuroimaging to argue that poor children suffer from diminished executive function that contributes to their academic underachievement (Heckman, 2012; Spears, 2011), and cognitive neuroscientists (Farah et al., 2008; Farah et al., 2006; Hackman, Gallop, Evans, & Farah, 2015; Lawson et al., 2015) expanding basic studies to extrapolate on the impact of poverty on brain functioning and as a consequence, again, on academic underachievement.

Two characteristics of this body of research are to either focus on neuroimaging of particular regions of the brain or to use measures of, say, executive function, language skills, or working memory, and then extrapolate from how well children do on such tasks to some attributions about the level of functioning of a particular region of the brain associated with some kind of academic task such as reading. Varma and Schwartz (2008) provide a warning about studies that try to extrapolate from isolated examinations of neural activity in specialized regions of the brain to problems of learning in education:

> Our concern is that the area focus currently dominates discussions in educational neuroscience, and it risks inappropriate inferences for improving educational practice. The one-to-one mapping of competencies to brain areas easily leads to the conclusion that students just need to exercise one part of their brain to develop or remediate a skill. It also naturally leads to the complaint that "knowing where it sits in the brain does not tell us anything useful." The problem with area-focus reasoning is that most tasks that educators care about are complex and multifaceted (especially compared with those studied by cognitive neuroscientists). These tasks are likely to map to brain areas in a many-to-many fashion. Said another way, most tasks activate multiple brain areas, and conversely most brain areas activate for multiple tasks. Moreover, the same task can be accomplished by different networks depending on experience (Tang et al., 2006) . . . [Varma and Schwartz argue] that exclusively adopting an area focus risks the uptake of educational neuroscience in a seductive but premature form, and that a complementary network focus should also be emphasized.
> (p. 150)

I agree with Varma and Schwartz, but want to offer another critique of such studies. This critique is rooted in the argument I attempted to make in the earlier section of this chapter about diversity of pathways of development as central to adaptation in the species, including how our biological systems are designed through evolutionary history to provide pathways through which we can adapt to new circumstances – indeed, to new learning – by the dynamic functioning of inter-dependent systems.

The idea that poverty renders a patterned impact, negatively so, on brain development presumes that all experiences of poverty are the same and that most people who are poor will respond to their experiences of being poor in patterned ways. However, the experience of poverty in Finland is very different to that in the USA. In Finland everyone has access to free health care. All school children, regardless of socio-economic status receive healthy breakfasts and lunches (provided by the school), and universal early childhood education is the norm. In societies such as Finland and others that offer broad social safety nets for their citizens and others living there, the disjunctures experienced between high and low income are not as consequential. This is evident in countries where poverty is not the strongest predictor of academic outcomes (OECD, 2010). The prevalence of extended family and other pro-socializing networks can buffer the vulnerabilities of single parenting. The prevalence of multiple socializing institutions for the young in communities can buffer the fact that families with limited capital resources may have greater difficulty in providing a range of extra-familial learning opportunities. These differences in the experience of poverty are not attributes of individuals, but, rather, characteristics of ecologies or cultural niches, to use Super and Harkness' (1986) and Weisner's (1984) phrasing. And yet, it is rare to find studies in psychology or the learning sciences that examine what are inevitably multiple sources of resilience in communities that wrestle with multiple sources of exposure to vulnerability (Spencer, 2006).

We cannot escape the history of psychology in the 20th century. Indeed, the founding of the American Psychological Association itself was based on work that conceptualized hierarchies in human capacities based on attributions of race, ethnicity, and class, kindling the field of eugenics (Gould, 1981). In the field of education, assumptions grounded in empirical research on language deficits of children who are poor, who speak African American English, or who are not native speakers of the national language abound as explanations for academic underachievement (Ball & Farr, 2003; Lee, 2005; Valdes, 1996). Beyond the restrictive assumptions about homogeneity and adaptability within cultural communities that characterizes both the historical and the emerging work I am questioning, there are another set of questions that I think are important. These questions are ones with which culturally oriented studies of learning have grappled for some time, and which get at the heart of our understandings about human psychological functioning. Are capacities such as working memory and executive function objectively bounded entities that can be universally measured with the same instruments regardless of population? And as entities do they operate in physical isolation, or are they capacities that are enabled through dynamic interactions among different components not only of our brains but, indeed, our entire body systems? Or are they capacities with which we are endowed (albeit within different individual ranges) where the range and quality of expertise displayed is contingent on both the contexts of their development over time and the contexts (including goals, perceptions of, and sense of relevance) of the tasks in which we deploy them to accomplish goals? I think there is a sufficient body of research over at least the last 90 years that strongly supports the proposition that the ability to elicit displays of competence is highly contingent on the ecological validity of the tasks, instruments, and conditions of elicitation, and the focus of observations of such competencies in real-world settings (Bronfenbrenner, 1979; Weisner, 2002). Thus, on multiple grounds – I think, arguable scientific grounds – I have serious concerns about much of the work seeking to extrapolate from neuroscience to education, particularly with regard to implications for populations living in poverty.

A third line of questioning, I think, also invites a wrestling with another central conundrum, and that is the question of transfer of learning, particularly what we understand about potential connections between what and how people learn in everyday practices outside of school and what we want children and adolescents in particular to learn inside of school (Nasir, Rosebery, Warren, & Lee, 2006). This conundrum, I would argue, is both conceptual, methodological, and political. Perhaps one of the most robust findings with regard to cognition is the link between prior knowledge and new learning. Again, one of the affordances of the evolutionary history of our species is the efficiency of drawing on knowledge stored in long-term memory as we engage in activity in the world so that we do not have to reinvent learning every time we meet the same or related challenges. This capacity – indeed, disposition – is both an affordance and a constraint. We know, for example, from studies of the development of naïve concepts that when there are conflicts between our naïve conceptions and formal disciplinary conceptions (for example, with regard to understandings of force) if the environments in which we are learning the disciplinary concepts are not sufficiently robust to support our investigations of our own thinking, the naïve conceptions remain (as in the classic study of successful college engineering students who continued to hold on to naïve concepts in spite of their formal coursework in physics) (Carey, 1985; Dunbar, Fugelsang, & Stein, 2007; Gelman, 1990; Mintzes, 1984). And there are also interesting examples of how a disposition – that likely has some biological underpinnings – for young children to anthropocentrize (e.g. to use humans as the point of reference in making inferences about animal behaviors and internal states) is shaped with different trajectories by participation in cultural practices. For example, Bang, Medin, and Atran (2007) extrapolated a categorizing task related to Carey's (1985) category-based induction tasks. Carey's work has been used to argue this disposition as relatively normative in the early stages of children's development. Bang and colleagues selected a population of urban European American children from the Boston area, a rural European American population of children, and a rural Native American Menominee sample, all of whom lived in a town and reservation in close proximity to one another. Two interesting distinctions emerged. First, rural children were more likely to generalize from wolf to other mammals than from humans to other mammals. However, rural European American children were more likely to reason that humans are not animals, while Menominee rural children were more likely to reason that humans are like other animals. In each of these studies, a fundamental task confronting children of inferring the nature of relationships between themselves and other living creatures seems to be mediated by the nature of their relationships with other creatures in their environments. Urban children typically have limited exposure to intimate relationships with animals, in contrast with rural children. But also, in this case, Menominee children grow up with rituals and routine social interactions around the Menominee Creation Story in which people come from bears and are actively engaged with an animal-based clan system. A second difference was found, also supporting the proposition that participation in routine cultural practices influences the expression of normative developmental tasks. This involved how children reasoned about ecological relationships among animals and among animals and humans. In this case, urban children were less likely to reason ecologically, in contrast to rural children. However, rural Menominee children exhibited more mature ecological reasoning at much earlier ages than rural European American children.

As a follow-up, I am most interested in cases where careful analyses of learning in everyday contexts offer affordances for learning in academic domains. This has been the focus of my own work in Cultural Modeling (Lee, 1995, 2007), which I think links nicely with the work of a number of other scholars:

• Studies by many of Geoff Saxe's former students, including Nailah Nasir's (2000, 2002, 2005) work studying the development of expertise in dominoes and in basketball, as these are connected with mathematical understandings; Edd Taylor's (2009, 2013) work studying the ecologies supporting the development of mathematical understandings among low-income African American children buying candy after school and community practices through religious tithing.

- The work of Che Che Konnen, led by Beth Warren and Ann Rosebery (Rosebery, Warren, Ballenger, & Ogonowski, 2005; Rosebery, Warren, & Conant, 1992; Warren, Ballenger, Ogonowski, Rosebery, & Hudicourt-Barnes, 2001; Warren & Ogonowski, 2001) working with teachers to focus on emergent and unexpected insights of children in their reasoning about scientific phenomenon as windows into potential connections between children's everyday knowledge and disciplinary learning in science.
- The work of Bob Moses and the Algebra Project (Moses and Cobb, 2001; Moses, Kamii, Swap, & Howard, 1989; Silva, Moses, Rivers, & Johnson, 1990), connecting children's intuitive understandings of navigations across an urban transit system and fundamental re-organizing of their conceptions of integers and operations with integers.
- More recent work by a new cohort of literacy scholars who examine youth literacy practices outside of schooling and relations with the demands of school-based literacies (Alim, Ibrahim, & Pennycook, 2008; Fisher, 2003; Kinloch, 2010; Majors, 2015; Paris & Winn, 2013).

These bodies of research have several important attributes in common, which I have synthesized in conceptualizing the Cultural Modeling Framework (Lee, 2007):

1) They do not simply attribute cultural membership to a demographic characteristic based on race, ethnicity, or class, but focus on shared repertoires of practice within everyday contexts, selecting populations to study based on shared histories of participation in particular cultural practices.
2) They engage in careful analyses of the multiple demands of learning in the target content area, demands that include structures of knowledge, heuristics for problem solving, habits of mind, and language demands of arguing in the content area, sometimes leading to new insights in the development of expertise within the domain.
3) The selection of a target of everyday practice is based on sources of alignment between the demands of problem solving in both the everyday and the disciplinary domain, including sources of tension or conflict.
4) They base the design of new learning environments explicitly on observations of how competence over time is structurally supported effectively in the everyday learning environment to include, for example, how forms of assistance are structured. Such forms of assistance may include relationship building, ways of using language that invite engagement and identification with the task, anticipation of sources of vulnerability that recognize both the cognitive as well as the social and emotional demands of engaging with the task, making problem solving explicit and public as learners are actively engaged in learning, sufficient heterogeneity in pathways for learning to accommodate differences in the needs of learners, and ways of engaging the social good of the activity or task to be learned.

I believe these features characterize robust learning environments, whether in school, in informal settings outside of school, in family life, or in peer social networks. I also argue that the warrants upon which I hypothesize their effectiveness (beyond the empirical studies on which the examples I identified are based, including my own work) are derived from the core propositions about human learning and development with which I began this chapter:

1) Human functioning is never a zero-sum game because we are endowed with the capacity to adapt across the life course.
2) Human functioning is inherently social and, as a consequence, cultural.
3) Thinking, feeling, and perceiving are intimately and dynamically intertwined in acts of human learning.
4) Human learning and development over time have the capacity to adapt to change, in part because the biological functioning of our bodies (which includes our minds) is inherently plastic.
5) Trajectories of learning are an outgrowth of biological affordances, participation in routine cultural practices and all that comes with that, and the relationships across the sites of activity within the physical and cultural ecologies in which we live.

This complexity is certainly difficult to study. I think that tackling the complexities inherent in human learning and development requires cross-disciplinary collaborations – drawing from the fields I have referenced in this chapter – but, equally importantly, it requires dismantling the deficit assumptions about normal human development that have characterized our fields for so many decades.

References

Alim, H. S., Ibrahim, A., & Pennycook, A. (2008). *Global linguistic flows: Hip hop cultures, youth identities, and the politics of language*: New York, NY: Routledge.

Ball, A., & Farr, M. (2003). Language varieties, culture and teaching the English language arts. In J. Flood, D. Lapp, J. Squire, & J. Jensen (Eds.), *Handbook of research on teaching the English language arts* (2nd edn., pp. 435–445). Mahwah, NJ: Lawrence Erlbaum.

Bang, M., Medin, D. L., & Altran, S. (2007). Cultural mosaics and mental models of nature. *Proceedings of the National Academy of Sciences* (*104*), 13868–13874.

Belenky, M. F., Clinchy, B. M., Goldberger, N. R., & Tarule, J. M. (1986). The ways of knowing. In M. F. Belenky, B. M. Clinchy, N. R. Goldberger, & J. M. Tarule (Eds.), *Women's ways of knowing: The development of self, voice, and mind* (pp. 23–131). New York, NY: Basic Books.

Boykin, A. W., Anderson, A. J., & Yates, J. (1979). *Black psychology and the research process: Keeping the baby but throwing out the bath water.* New York, NY: Russell Sage Foundation.

Bronfenbrenner, U. (1979). *The ecology of human development: Experiment by nature and design*. Cambridge, MA: Harvard University Press.

Bruer, J. (1999). In search of brain-based education. *Phi Delta Kappan*, *80*(9), 648–657.

Bruner, J. (1990). *Acts of meaning*. Cambridge, MA: Harvard University Press.

Cacioppo, J. T. (2002). Social neuroscience: Understanding the pieces fosters understanding the whole and vice versa. *American Psychologist, 57*, 819–831.

Cacioppo, J. T., Visser, P. S., & Pickett, C. L. (Eds.). (2005). *Social neuroscience: People thinking about thinking people.* Cambridge, MA: MIT Press.

Carey, S. (1985). *Conceptual change in childhood.* Cambridge, MA: Bradford Books.

Carlson, S. M., & Meltzoff, A. N. (2008). Bilingual experience and executive functioning in young children. *Developmental Science, 11*(2), 282–298.

Cole, M., & Scribner, S. (1974). *Culture & thought: A psychological introduction.* New York, NY: John Wiley & Sons.

Decety, J., Jackson, P. L., Sommerville, J. A., Chaminade, T., & Meltzoff, A. N. (2004). The neural bases of cooperation and competition: An fMRI investigation. *NeuroImage, 23*, 744–751.

Dunbar, K., Fugelsang, J., & Stein, C. (2007). Do naïve theories ever go away? Using brain and behavior to understand changes in concepts. In M. C. Lovett & P. Shah (Eds.) *Thinking With Data*, 193–206. New York, NY: Erlbaum.

Dweck, C. S. (2002). Beliefs that make smart people dumb. In R. Sternberg (Ed.), *Why smart people can be so stupid.* New Haven: Yale University Press.

Eccles, J. (2005). Subjective task values and the Eccles et al. Model of Achievement related choices. In A. Elliott & C. S. Dweck (Eds.), *Handbook of competence and motivation.* New York, NY: Guilford Press.

Farah, M., Betancourt, L., Shera, D., Savage, J., Giannetta, J., Brodsky, N., . . . & Hurt, H. (2008). Environmental stimulation, parental nurturance and cognitive development in humans. *Developmental Science, 11*(5), 793–801.

Farah, M., Shera, D., Savage, J., Betancourt, L., Giannetta, J., Brodsky, N., . . . Hurt, H. (2006). Childhood poverty: Specific associations with neuro-cognitive development. *Brain Research, 1110*(1), 166–174.

Fischer, K. W., & Bidell, T. R. (1998). Dynamic development of psychological structures in action and thought. In W. Damon & R. M. Lerner (Eds.), *Handbook of child psychology: Theoretical models of human development* (5th edn., Vol. *1*, pp. 467–562). New York, NY: Wiley & Sons.

Fisher, M. T. (2003). Open mics and open minds: Spoken word poetry in African diaspora participatory literacy communities. *Harvard Education Review, 73*(3), 362–389.

Flavell, J. H., & Miller, P. H. (1998). Social cognition. In D. Kuhn & R. Siegler (Eds.), *Handbook of child psychology* (5th edn., Vol. *2*, pp. 851–898). New York, NY: Wiley.

Gelman, R. (1990). First principles organize attention to and learning about relevant data: Number and the animate-inanimate distinction as examples. *Cognitive Science, 14*, 79–106.

Gopnic, A., Meltzoff, A., & Kuhl, P. (1999). *The scientist in the crib: What early learning tells us about the mind.* New York, NY: Harper Collins.

Gould, S. J. (1981). *The mismeasure of man.* New York, NY: W.W. Norton.

Graham, S. (1992). "Most of the subjects were white and middle class": Trends in published research on African Americans in selected APA journals, 1970–1989. *American Psychologist, 47*(5), 629–639

Grande, S. M. A. (2000). American Indian geographies of identity and power: At the crossroads of Indigena and Mestizaje. *Harvard Education Review, 70*(4), 467–498.

Gutierrez, K., & Rogoff, B. (2003). Cultural ways of learning: Individual traits or repertoires of practice. *Educational Researcher*, *32*(5), 19–25.

Hackman, D. A., Gallop, R., Evans, G. W., & Farah, M. J. (2015). Socioeconomic status and executive function: Developmental trajectories and mediation. *Developmental Science*, *18*(5), 686–702.

Heckman, J. J. (2012). An effective strategy for promoting social mobility. *Boston Review*, 10155–10162.

Helms, J. E., Jernigan, M., & Mascher, J. (2005). The meaning of race in psychology and how to change it: A methodological perspective. *American Psychologist*, *60*(1), 27–36.

Hermes, M., Bang, M., & Marin, A. (2012). Designing indigenous language revitalization. *Harvard Educational Review*, *82*(3), 381–402.

Johnston, B. H. (1976). *Ojibway heritage*. New York, NY: Columbia University Press.

Jones, R. L. (1980). *Black psychology* (2nd edn.). New York, NY: Harper & Row Publishers.

Kawagley, A. O. (1995). *A Yupiaq worldview: A pathway to an ecology and spirit*. Prospect Heights, IL: Waveland Press.

Kinloch, V. (2010). *Harlem on our minds: Place, race, and the literacies of urban youth*. New York, NY: Teachers College Press

Kohlberg, L. (1969). Stage and sequence: The cognitive-developmental approach to socialization. In D. A. Goslin (Ed.), *Handbook of socialization theory and research*. Chicago: Rand-McNally.

Lawson, G. M., Hook, C. J., Hackman, D. A., Farah, M. J., Griffin, J. A., Freund, L. S., & McCardle, P. (2015). Socioeconomic status and neurocognitive development: Executive function. In J. Griffin, P. McCardle, & L. Freund (Eds) *Executive Function in Preschool Children: Integrating Measurement, Neurodevelopment, and Translational Research*. Washington, D.C.: American Psychological Association.

Lee, C. D. (1995). A culturally based cognitive apprenticeship: Teaching African American high school students skills in literary interpretation. *Reading Research Quarterly*, *30*(4), 608–631.

Lee, C. D. (2001). Is October Brown Chinese: A cultural modeling activity system for underachieving students. *American Educational Research Journal*, *38*(1), 97–142.

Lee, C. D. (2005). Culture and language: Bi-dialectical issues in literacy. In P. L. Anders & J. Flood (Eds.), *Culture and language: Bi-dialectical issues in literacy*. Newark, DE: International Reading Association.

Lee, C. D. (2007). *Culture, literacy and learning: Taking bloom in the midst of the whirlwind*. New York, NY: Teachers College Press.

Lee, C. D. (2008). The centrality of culture to the scientific study of learning and development: How an ecological framework in educational research facilitates civic responsibility. *Educational Researcher*, *37*(5), 267–279.

Lee, C. D. (2009). Historical evolution of risk and equity: *Interdisciplinary issues and critiques Review of Research in Education*, *33*, 63–100.

Lee, C. D. (2010). Soaring above the clouds, delving the ocean's depths understanding the ecologies of human learning and the challenge for education science. *Educational Researcher*, *39*(9), 643–655.

Lee, C. D., Spencer, M. B., & Harpalani, V. (2003). Every shut eye ain't sleep: Studying how people live culturally. *Educational Researcher*, *32*(5), 6–13.

Lomawaima, K. T., & McCarty, T. L. (2006). *" To remain an Indian": Lessons in democracy from a century of Native American education*. New York, NY: Teachers College Press.

Majors, Y. (2015). *Shop talk*. New York, NY: Teachers College Press.

McCarty, T., & Lee, T. (2014). Critical culturally sustaining/revitalizing pedagogy and indigenous education sovereignty. *Harvard Educational Review, 84*(1), 101–124.

Medin, D. L., Lee, C. D., & Bang, M. (2014). Particular points of view. *Scientific American, 311*(3), 44–45.

Meltzoff, A. N., & Decety, J. (2003). What imitation tells us about social cognition: A rapprochement between developmental psychology and cognitive neuroscience. *Philosophical Transactions of the Royal Society of London, Biological Sciences, 358*, 491–500.

Meltzoff, A. N., Kuhl, P. K., Movellan, J., & Sejnowski, T. J. (2009). Foundations for a new science of learning. *Science, 325*(5938), 284–288.

Meltzoff, A. N., & Moore, M. K. (1977). Imitation of facial and manual gestures by human neonates. *Science, 198*, 75–78.

Mintzes, J. J. (1984). Naive theories in biology: Children's concepts of the human body. *School Science and Mathematics, 84*(7), 548–555.

Moses, R. P., & Cobb, C. E. (2001). *Radical equations: Math literacy and civil rights*. Boston: Beacon Press.

Moses, R. P., Kamii, M., Swap, S. M., & Howard, J. (1989). The algebra project: Organizing in the spirit of Ella. *Harvard Educational Review, 59*(4), 423–443.

Nadel, L., Lane, R., & Ahern, G. L. (Eds.). (2000). *The cognitive neuroscience of emotion*. New York, NY: Oxford University Press.

Nasir, N. (2000). "Points ain't everything": Emergent goals and average and percent understandings in the play of basketball among African American students. *Anthropology and Education, 31*(1), 283–305.

Nasir, N. (2002). Identity, goals, and learning: Mathematics in cultural practice. In N. Nasir & P. Cobb (Eds.), *Mathematical thinking and learning: Special issue on diversity, equity and mathematics learning, Vol. 4* (nos. 2 & 3) (pp. 211–247).

Nasir, N. (2005). Individual cognitive structuring and the sociocultural context: Strategy shifts in the game of dominoes. *Journal of the Learning Sciences, 14*, 5–34.

Nasir, N., Rosebery, A. S., Warren, B., & Lee, C. D. (2006). Learning as a cultural process: Achieving equity through diversity. In K. Sawyer (Ed.), *Handbook of the learning sciences*. New York, NY: Cambridge University Press.

Nasir, N., & Saxe, G. (2003). Emerging tensions and their management in the lives of minority students. *Educational Researcher, 32*(5), 14–18.

Nobles, W. (1980). African philosophy: Foundations for black psychology. In R. L. Jones (Ed.), *Black psychology* (2nd edn., pp. 23–36). New York, NY: Harper & Row.

Noddings, N. (1984). *Caring: A feminine approach to ethics and moral education*. Berkeley, CA: University of California Press.

OECD. (2010). *Pisa 2009 results: Overcoming social background. Equity in learning opportunities and outcomes* (Vol. 2). Paris: OECD Publishing.

Paris, D., & Winn, M. T. (2013). *Humanizing research: Decolonizing qualitative inquiry with youth and communities*. Thousand Oaks, CA: Sage.

Quartz, S. R., & Sejnowski, T. J. (2002). *Liars, lovers, and heroes: What the new brain science reveals about how we become who we are*. New York, NY: William Morrow.

Rogoff, B. (2003). *The cultural nature of human development*. New York, NY: Oxford University Press.

Rosebery, A. S., Warren, B., Ballenger, C., & Ogonowski, M. (2005). The generative potential of students' everyday knowledge in learning science. In T. Romberg,

T. Carpenter, & D. Fae (Eds.), *Understanding mathematics and science matters*. Mahwah, NJ: Erlbaum.

Rosebery, A. S., Warren, B., & Conant, F. R. (1992). Appropriating scientific discourse: Findings from language minority classrooms. *The Journal of Learning Sciences*, *2*(1), 61–94.

Saxe, G. B. (1988). The mathematics of child street vendors. *Child Development*, *59*, 1415–1425.

Saxe, G. B. (1994). Studying cognitive development in sociocultural context: The development of a practice-based approach. *Mind, Culture, and Activity*, *1*(3) 135–157.

Scribner, S., & Cole, M. (1973). Cognitive consequences of formal and informal education. *Science*, *182*(4112), 553–559.

Sellers, R., Shelton, N., Cooke, D., Chavous, T., Rowley, S. J., & Smith, M. (1998). A multidimensional model of racial identity: Assumptions, findings, and future directions. In R. Jones (Ed.), *African American identity development* (pp. 275–303). Hampton, VA: Cobb & Henry Publishers.

Silva, C. M., Moses, R. P., Rivers, J., & Johnson, P. (1990). The algebra project: Making middle school mathematics count. *Journal of Negro Education*, *59*(3), 375–392.

Spears, D. (2011). Economic decision-making in poverty depletes behavioral control. *The BE Journal of Economic Analysis & Policy*, *11*(1), 1–42.

Spencer, M. B. (2006). Phenomenology and ecological systems theory: Development of diverse groups. In W. Damon & R. M. Lerner (Eds.), *Handbook of child psychology* (6th edn., Vol. *1*, pp. 829–893). New York, NY: Wiley.

Spencer, M. B., Fegley, S., & Dupree, D. (2006). Investigating and linking social conditions of African-American children and adolescents with emotional well-being. *Ethnicity and Disease*, *16*(2), 63–67.

Spencer, M. B., Fegley, S., & Harpalani, V. (2003). A theoretical and empirical examination of identity as coping: Linking coping resources to the self processes of African American youth. *Journal of Applied Developmental Science*, *7*(3), 181–187.

Spencer, M. B., Harpalani, V., Cassidy, E., Jacobs, C., Donde, S., & Goss, T. N. (2006). Understanding vulnerability and resilience from a normative development perspective: Implications for racially and ethnically diverse youth. In D. Chicchetti & E. Cohen (Eds.), *Handbook of developmental psychopathology* (Vol. *1*). Hoboken, NJ: Wiley.

Steele, C. M., Spencer, S. J., & Aronson, J. (2002). Contending with group image: The psychology of stereotype and social identity threat. *Advances in Experimental Social Psychology*, *34*, 379–440.

Super, C., & Harkness, S. (1986). The developmental niche: A conceptualization at the interface of child and culture. *International Journal of Behavioral Development*, *9*, 545–569.

Taylor, E. V. (2009). The purchasing practice of low-income students: The relationship to mathematical development. *The Journal of the Learning Sciences*, *18*(3), 370–415.

Taylor, E. V. (2013). The mathematics of tithing: A study of religious giving and mathematical development. *Mind, Culture, and Activity*, *20*(2), 132–149.

Valdes, G. (1996). *Con respeto: Bridging the distances between culturally diverse families and schools*. New York, NY: Teachers College Press.

Varma, S., McCandliss, B., & Schwartz, D. (2008). Scientific and pragmatic challenges for bridging education and neuroscience. *Educational Researcher*, *37*(3), 140–152.

Varma, S., & Schwartz, D. (2008). How should educational neuroscience conceptualise the relation between cognition and brain function? Mathematical reasoning as a network process. *Educational Research, 50*(2), 149–161.

Warren, B., Ballenger, C., Ogonowski, M., Rosebery, A. S., & Hudicourt-Barnes, J. (2001). Rethinking diversity in learning science: The logic of everyday sense-making. *Journal of Research in Science Teaching, 38*, 529–552.

Warren, B., & Ogonowski, M. (2001, April). *Embodied imagining: A study of adult learning in physics.* Paper presented at the American Educational Research Association, Seattle.

Weisner, T. S. (1984). Ecocultural niches of middle childhood: A cross-cultural perspective. In W. A. Collins (Ed.), *Development during middle childhood: The years from six to twelve* (pp. 335–369). Washington, DC: National Academy of Sciences Press.

Weisner, T. S. (2002). Ecocultural understanding of children's developmental pathways. *Human Development, 174*, 275–281.

Whitehead, C. (2010). The culture ready brain. *Social Cognitive and Affective Neuroscience, 5*, 168–179.

Wilson, E. O. (1998). *Consilience: The unity of knowledge.* New York, NY: Knopf.

Zajonc, R. B., & Marcus, H. (1984). Affect and cognition. In C. E. Izard, J. Kagan, & R. B. Zajonc (Eds.), *Emotions, cognition and behavior* (pp. 73–102). Cambridge, UK: Cambridge University Press.

PART II

Social Development

(Edited by Elliot Turiel, Cecilia Wainryb, and Na'ilah Suad Nasir)

9 Gender Development: A Constructivist-Ecological Perspective

Lynn S. Liben

Introduction

Gender is among the most powerful predictors of developmental processes and outcomes. For example, knowing a child's gender allows predictions about motivational processes; qualities of interpersonal interactions; self-definitions; and patterns of skills and interests in educational, occupational, and leisure arenas (e.g., Blakemore, Berenbaum, & Liben, 2009; Leaper, 2015). Although there is little disagreement about this claim, there is longstanding and often heated debate about where gender differentiations arise, and especially about whether they are universal, immutable, or desirable (Liben, 2015, 2016). Given that the tentacles of gender reach virtually everywhere, no single paper can address all relevant research and theory. My goal here is to offer a general approach for conceptualizing and studying gender development that is rooted in a relational, constructivist view of development, and to provide illustrations of empirical work consistent with this perspective.

In the section entitled "Conceptual Grounding for the Study of Gender Development," I describe what it means to consider human development from a relational perspective, and explain how I draw from the constructivist developmental theory of Jean Piaget and the ecological model of Urie Bronfenbrenner to approach gender development. I then discuss illustrative empirical work on the child ↔ environment nexus. In the section on "Individuating Processes" I draw on research that begins primarily from qualities of the individual; in "Cultural Processes" I draw from research that begins primarily from qualities of the embedding social context. In the final section, "Conclusions and Implications," I reiterate the value of studying gender development from a relational perspective, and illustrate the relevance of this work for educational programs.

Conceptual Grounding for the Study of Gender Development

The arguments presented in this chapter are rooted in constructivist, relational-system approaches to development (e.g., see Lerner, Agans, DeSouza, & Hershberg, 2014; Overton, 2015; Sameroff, 2010; von Glasersfeld, 1981). The underlying premise of this perspective is that developmental outcomes can never be accounted for by additive combinations of factors that exist independently in individuals and in the surrounding context. Instead, a relational perspective holds that individuals and contexts operate dynamically and inseparably, simultaneously giving meaning to, and taking meaning from, one another. Illustrative of this perspective is Piagetian theory in general, and the concepts of assimilation and accommodation in particular (e.g., Piaget, 1970). Assimilation refers to the individual's integration of new experiences or ideas, but, importantly, in ways driven by concurrent qualities of the individual. Accommodation refers to the simultaneous adjustment (e.g., expansion, reorganization, integration) of those individual qualities. Thus, while experiences are assimilated or adapted to fit the individual, the individual is accommodated or modified to fit the experiences.

The classic constructivist analysis of gender was proposed by Kohlberg roughly half a century ago. Drawing on Piagetian theory, Kohlberg (1966) explicitly rejected the then prevailing notion that gender outcomes could be explained by biological and environmental processes in isolation from child-based cognitive processes. As in Piaget's focus on the joint processes of assimilation and accommodation, Kohlberg argued that gender development proceeds as the child actively selects from, organizes, and transforms the "aliment" (i.e., the metaphorical food or material) of the physical and social worlds to construct gender-related cognitions and behaviors. In brief, Kohlberg suggested that children's gender beliefs and behaviors are learned from the external world, but in a way that puts the child's cognition at the center. Thus, in the domain of gender, "Learning is cognitive in the sense that it is selective and internally organized by relational schemata rather than directly reflecting associations of events in the outer world" (Kohlberg, 1966, p. 83).

It is important to note that scholars approaching development from other theoretical positions challenge the scientific value of relational, constructive constructs such as these. Most famous, perhaps, is an early criticism by Klahr (1982) about Piaget's concepts of assimilation and accommodation:

> For 40 years now we have had assimilation and accommodation, the mysterious and shadowy forces of equilibration, the Batman and Robin of the developmental processes. What are they? How do they do their thing? Why is it after all this time, we know no more about them than when they first sprang on the scene? What we need is a way to get beyond vague verbal statements of the nature of the developmental process.
> (p. 80)

Roughly a dozen years later, Klahr quoted a long passage by Piaget about assimilation and accommodation to illustrate what he called the "theory-as-words" approach, and then commented: "Although [the passage] has a certain poetic beauty, as a scientist, I do not understand it, I do not know how to test it, and I doubt that any two readers will interpret it in the same way" (Klahr, 1995, p. 369).

A similar stance is taken by Munakata (2006) in her discussion of information-processing approaches to cognitive development. Like Klahr, she focuses on the advantages of "hard-core" formalisms that are implemented in computational models of development. In introducing the value of this approach, Munakata draws on Klahr's criticism of assimilation and accommodation to argue that "Purely verbal theories may rely on constructs that are not specified well enough to be rigorously tested or understood" (2006, p. 428). Instead, she champions computational modeling, which "can help make *explicit* theoretical assumptions, constructs, and predictions – an essential step in evaluating and advancing theory" (p. 428, emphasis in original). Additionally, she argues that modeling allows for multiple, well-specified "elements" to be studied simultaneously and thus to reveal complex interactions among them, writing that: "Various phenomena emerge from such interactions, so that the whole is impossible to understand by considering the elements in isolation" (p. 427). It is revealing, however, to examine how she illustrates these elements:

> As a simple example, consider two gears of different sizes that can interlock. To understand how they behave, it is insufficient to consider each in isolation. Instead, behavior emerges from the interaction of the two gears, with the smaller gear driving the larger gear to yield a decrease in rotational speed and an increase in torque. As the interactions among elements become more intricate, as in the weather and physics, computational models become increasingly important. Such models allow the observation and manipulation of interactions among elements and associated emergent phenomena. Similarly, models can be essential in helping us comprehend the intricacies of all the interacting elements that produce our thoughts and behaviors.
> (Munakata, 2006, p. 427)

What is noteworthy about this illustration in the current context is the fixity and imperviousness of the two gears. That is, although the dynamic running of the gears ultimately generates the emergent phenomenon of the whole, it is also true that the foundational elements (the gears) are themselves unaffected by being engaged in mechanical interaction with the other.

Munakata (2006) also names two other benefits of a computational approach. One is that it allows independent experimental control of variables: "A single variable, such as the firing rate of artificial neurons or exposure to particular words in the environment, can be manipulated in isolation to see the effects on the functioning and development of a simulated system" (p. 428). Another is that it provides "unified frameworks" across behaviors that can "encourage more parsimonious explanations, rather than what sometimes seems like a hodgepodge of explanations proposed across development" (p. 428). Again, these named benefits depend on the assumption that initial, basic elements can be defined independently of the system in which they operate. Such assumptions are rooted in a mechanistic framework that asserts that wholes (including emergent phenomena) can be traced back to pure elements such as neurons, genes, or, as in the current example, gears (see Overton, 2007; Witherington, 2007).

In contrast, the approach to gender development that I describe and illustrate later in this chapter (see also Liben, 2014) is a relational one that assumes that one cannot identify fixed, unchanging pure elements because such would-be elements are always affected by the system as a whole (Overton, 2015). To paint relational perspectives of individuals and contexts, I draw from the approaches of Piaget and

Bronfenbrenner. From Piaget I draw on the (admittedly shadowy) concepts of assimilation and accommodation insofar as I consider ways that individuals' qualities affect their engagement, understanding, storage, and use of the environmental aliment.

Although Piaget (1964) did include the social and physical context in his work, it is fair to say that his emphasis was on what individuals brought to the person ↔ context nexus. Thus, to emphasize the relational contribution of context, I draw from Bronfenbrenner, who is best known for focusing on the ecology in two major ways. First, he admonished researchers to study natural behaviors that take place in "ecologically valid" settings rather than to study the "strange behavior of children in strange situations with strange adults for the briefest possible periods of time" (Bronfenbrenner, 1977, p. 513). Second, he argued that individual development occurs within a larger ecology that he conceptualized "as a set of nested structures, each inside the next, like a set of Russian dolls" (Bronfenbrenner, 1979, p. 3). At the center is the *microsystem* which represents the child's direct interactions with those in the immediate context (e.g., children's direct interactions with parents or teachers). The embedding *mesosystem* represents transactions among those people, but apart from the child (e.g., interactions that occur between parents and teachers in the absence of the child, such as those that might occur at a parent–teacher conference). The *exosystem* represents distal influences that affect the child indirectly (e.g., a workplace that may affect a parent's mood, in turn affecting that parent's interactions with the child). The *macrosystem* represents still broader cultural qualities and values that infuse all nested layers within it (e.g., as when governmental regulations affect variables such as individual freedoms, family structure, and economics, and thus daily lives and social interactions). Finally, the *chronosystem* is the outermost layer, representing the embedding context of time as individuals change with chronological age and as societies change across historical eras (see Bronfenbrenner, 1994).

To signal a relational perspective that treats individuals and contexts as commensurate relational partners, I draw terminology from both Piaget and Bronfenbrenner to label my current discussion of gender a *constructivist-ecological* perspective. In the remaining sections of this chapter, I discuss ways that children's constructive processes work symbiotically with the embedding context to yield gender concepts and behaviors.

Individuating Processes

I begin from the basic constructivist position that children are active agents in their own development. This means that what the individual brings to the child ↔ context nexus will have a profound influence, first, on which of the almost endless opportunities afforded by the environment are attended to or engaged with, and second, on how the engaged environment is remembered and later used. Below are brief descriptions of theoretical and empirical work on, respectively, engagement and memory.

Engagement

The seminal work on gender-relevant engagement is gender schema theory (GST), proposed by Martin and Halverson (1981). The key argument of GST is that children's decisions about whether or not to engage with something available in the immediate environment (e.g., an object such as a doll or truck) involves classifying the object as "for boys" or "for girls" and classifying one's self into one of the two categories comprising the traditional gender binary: boy or girl. A gender match between object and self-identity leads the child to engage with the object; a mismatch leads to avoidance. In this way, girls and boys end up engaged with different objects and activities. In turn, their differentiated activities facilitate different skills (e.g., mechanical concepts from truck-play; nurturing skills from doll play) which may contribute to differentiated educational and occupational outcomes, and to the adoption of differing social roles. An array of empirical work has provided data consistent with GST. For example, Martin, Eisenbud, and Rose (1995) showed that children were more interested in playing with novel toys labeled as for their own (rather than for the other) gender, even if that meant favoring toys that were otherwise demonstrably less appealing.

While GST emphasized children's gender-related beliefs held by the culture in general (e.g., the stereotypic view in US culture that dolls are for girls), a later constructivist approach – proposed by Liben and Bigler (2002) and subsequently labeled the *dual pathway model* (DPM; Blakemore et al., 2009) – focused more explicitly on variations among children and on the pathways by which these variations may be modified over time. With respect to individual differences, DPM identifies three relevant constructs, including: first, the degree to which the child endorses cultural gender stereotypes; second, the child's particular pattern of personal interests and talents; and third, the degree to which the child tends to view the world through gendered lenses (labeled the gender-salience filter).

With respect to pathways, DPM posited the simultaneous operation of attitudinal and personal pathways. The attitudinal pathway is much like the model proposed by GST, albeit modified to address individual differences. In this "other-to-self" pathway, attitudes about others (e.g., "trucks are for boys") shape the individual's own behaviors (e.g., "given that I am a girl, this truck is not for me"). The personal pathway is the inverse "self-to-other" process. Here the child's own qualities and behaviors influence the child's attitudes about others. Thus, for example, a boy whose particular interests lead him to participate in a traditionally feminine activity might come to believe that the activity is appropriate for boys as well as for girls.

In the course of describing DPM, Liben and Bigler (2002) reported empirical data from a longitudinal study with middle-school children that illustrate both individual differences and pathways. Children were given sex-typing scales (the Children's Occupation, Activity, and Traits or COAT scales) at four times – in fall and spring of grade 6 and again in fall and spring of grade 7. The scales assessed students' attitudes about the extent to which culturally stereotyped occupations, activities, and traits should be differentially linked to males versus females in general (the COAT-Attitude Measure or COAT-AM) and students' views about the extent to which these culturally stereotyped items applied to themselves (the COAT-Personal Measure or COAT-PM). For example, occupational items for the attitude scale queried children's endorsements of gender stereotypes about occupations by asking, for example, "Who should be a plumber? Only men, only women, or both men and women?"; while those for the personal scale queried children's personal interests in the same occupations by asking, for example, "How much would you like to be a plumber? Not at all, not much, some, or very much?"

Among girls, data on concurrent associations showed correlations between gender attitudes about others and gender endorsements for the self, a finding consistent with both the proposed other-to-self (attitudinal) and self-to-other (personal) pathways. The girls' longitudinal data, however, revealed no significant effects: Initial attitudes did not predict later self-endorsements and initial self-endorsements did not predict later attitudes. Among boys, the pattern was different. For this group, there were no concurrent links between initial responses to the attitudinal measure (COAT-AM) and the self (COAT-PM) measure. Boys' longitudinal data, however, were consistent with the personal pathway model: Boys who initially (in fall of grade 6) self-endorsed a greater number of stereotypically feminine traits, later (in spring of grade 7) showed significantly more egalitarian attitudes about those traits than did other boys.

A second empirical example of the role of individual differences in engagement comes from a recent study (Coyle & Liben, 2016) on the hypothesized role of the gender-salience filter (GSF). The key question addressed was whether the impact of playing a computer game designed to teach preschool girls about occupations would be moderated by (a) individual differences in GSF and (b) the game character's femininity. The latter was tested by manipulating whether the game character was a hyper-feminized "Barbie" or a less-feminized Playmobil "Jane."

Children were first given a newly designed measure of GSF that drew from measures of related individual differences, specifically those assessing the child's (a) reliance on gender for judging a potential play partner's attractiveness (gender-based affiliative preference; Serbin & Sprafkin, 1986); (b) incidental memory for gender when gender was not task-relevant (gender vigilance; Liben & Hilliard, 2010); and (c) self-perceived similarity to same-gender others (gender typicality; Patterson, 2012). Two weeks later, the child played with a computer game in which either Barbie or Jane enacted various jobs.

Interestingly from the perspective of the common intervention strategy of using female models to enhance girls' interests in traditionally masculine jobs (see Liben & Coyle, 2014), the computer game had no demonstrable impact on girls' job interests in masculine jobs, irrespective of game character or the child's GSF. However, the data did reveal an effect of game play on girls' activity interests, moderated by both GSF and game character. Specifically, whereas low-GSF girls showed no change in their activity interests after playing the game with either Barbie or Jane, high-GSF girls showed intensified interest in engaging in traditionally feminine activities after playing with Barbie, but not with Jane. In essence, for girls already poised to attend to gender in their environments, playing a game in which a highly feminized model enacted various occupations – including traditionally masculine ones – did *not* lead them to become more interested in a broader range of jobs, but *did* lead them to become more attracted to traditionally "girly" activities.

In summary, qualities of individual children affect both what they engage with and what they take away from the "same" experience, and children's own behavioral engagements at one time may have an influence on their gender attitudes or beliefs at a later time. As discussed next, such gender attitudes or beliefs are part of the schemata about gender that affect what the child remembers of the environmental aliment.

Memory

Children are also active agents in the way that they remember gender-related stimuli. The key constructivist prediction is that memory will be driven by children's gender schemas, which have been defined as "cognitive structures that organize an individual's gender-related knowledge, beliefs, attitudes, and preferences" (Liben & Signorella, 1993, p. 141). Consistent with this prediction, early research with children showed that at the group level, recall was worse for gender-nontraditional than gender-traditional stories, traits, or pictures (e.g., Koblinsky, Cruse, & Sugawara, 1978). However, because almost all children – very early in life – are knowledgeable about cultural gender stereotypes (e.g., the stereotype that plumbing is for men) and are exposed to gendered phenomena (e.g., most plumbers they encounter are, indeed, men), it is unclear from group-level data alone if performance on memory tasks reflect participants' own gender schemata. To address this issue, we have routinely assessed individuals' own endorsements of gender stereotypes and examined the link between these measured schemata and memory.

One such study (Liben & Signorella, 1980) was designed to test the hypothesis that children's memory would be better for gender-traditional than nontraditional material, but that this difference would be more pronounced among those children who have more highly stereotyped attitudes. Young (elementary-school-aged) children were shown a deck of 60 cards, each depicting a person engaged in a traditionally feminine, masculine, or neutral job or activity. By varying (between participants) whether a particular activity was shown being enacted by a man or woman, each child saw some cards that were gender traditional (e.g., a male dentist), some that were gender nontraditional (e.g., a female construction worker) and some that were gender neutral, included as fillers (e.g., a man or woman reading a book). After a 5-minute delay, children were given a second deck in which some cards were identical and others had been changed by reversing the character's gender. The child was asked to say if each card was an old or new one (i.e., whether it was identical to a card seen earlier). After the memory task, children's gender stereotypes were assessed. As in earlier research, children were, overall, more accurate in recognizing old drawings that had initially been traditional than nontraditional. Importantly, data also supported the hypothesized role of individual children's attitudes: Differential memory was evident among only the highly stereotyped children.

Similar results emerged from a later study (Signorella & Liben, 1984) in which elementary school children were shown the same stimuli, but were tested on a free recall (rather than a recognition) task. As before, children – especially those with strong gender stereotypes – had significantly more trouble remembering the non-traditional pictures. The use of a free recall task also allowed us to see the effects of constructive processing in producing memory distortions: Children transformed some nontraditional stimuli into traditional memories either by misremembering the depicted character's gender (e.g., remembering a male secretary as a female secretary) or by misremembering the activity (e.g., recalling a female dentist as a hygienist). Again, the incidence of such distortions was higher among the more highly stereotyped children (19% vs. 9%).

Having found support for the hypothesized link between children's personal endorsement of gender stereotypes and memory in the correlational studies just described, experimental methods were used to examine the importance of individual children's gender schemata. One such study (Bigler & Liben, 1990) examined memory for nontraditional material following an intervention that had been designed to modify the content of children's gender schemata. Elementary school children were first given gender stereotyping measures. On the basis of scores on these measures, children were assigned to experimental and control conditions so that the two groups would be matched for their initial levels of gender stereotyping.

On each of five days, small groups of children then participated in 20-minute lessons about two occupations, selected to cover a total of five traditionally masculine and five traditionally feminine jobs. In the experimental condition, children were taught that whether someone could do a job depended upon the person's skills and interests, but not their gender. Feedback was provided as needed to counteract reconstructive processes. For example, after being taught about qualifications for construction work, children were told that Ann loves to build things and knows how to drive a bulldozer, and asked whether Ann could be a construction worker. One child answered "No, because Ann is a girl" and another responded, "Yes, because he [*sic*] followed the rules." The teacher corrected responses such as these, reiterated the decision rules, and posed a new practice problem. In the control condition, children were taught about training and activities for each of the same jobs, but were not given explicit instructions about the irrelevance of workers' gender. After lessons were completed, children were re-tested for their gender attitudes about occupations.

On each of the next 12 school days, small groups of children went to story-time sessions in which a new adult read one story aloud each day. Varied was whether the day's story was presented in a traditional or nontraditional version (e.g., involved a male vs. a female dentist as a central character). Children were then interviewed individually and asked questions that were designed to lead the child to use gender-specific pronouns to refer to the critical character. Children almost always used correct gender pronoun when answering questions about a traditional character such as a male dentist, but erred about half the time when answering questions about nontraditional characters such as a female dentist (averaging 5.2 vs. 3.2 correct for the six stories of each type). Consistent with the hypothesis that these memory distortions can be accounted for by individual children's gender attitudes was the significant interaction between condition and portrayal type. Specifically, although there was no difference between groups in accuracy for the traditional portrayals, children in the experimental condition were significantly more accurate in remembering the nontraditional portrayals than were children in the control condition.

A second experimental study (Bigler & Liben, 1992) was designed to test the hypothesis that another individual cognitive quality driving children's processing of gender-nontraditional encounters is the ability to classify something along multiple dimensions simultaneously. This prediction was based on the rationale that a nontraditional stimulus (e.g., a woman engineer) requires recognizing the inter-section of two classes ("woman" + "engineer") whereas a traditional stimulus (e.g., a man engineer) requires classifying along one dimension only because it can be processed as a single unit (e.g., "engineer" already subsumes maleness within it).

Based on this rationale, four groups of elementary school children were assigned to one of four conditions, matched for initial stereotyping levels and gender. In two conditions, children were given practice classifying pictures (of either people or objects) into two-by-two matrices. A child given people stimuli might, for example, use rows to sort by activity (e.g., singing vs. reading) and columns to sort by gender; a child given object stimuli might use rows to sort by clothing type (e.g., headwear vs. footwear) and columns to sort by color. The third and fourth groups were like the rule and control groups of the study by Bigler and Liben (1990) described above, and findings from these groups replicated the earlier study: Children who received rule training about the irrelevance of gender for jobs showed better memory for non-traditional stories than did children who received control occupational lessons.

More important here, though, were findings on the impact of classification train-ing. Consistent with the hypothesized relevance of multiple classification skills, those children who successfully learned to perform multiple classification tasks with either kind of training materials (objects or people) showed better memory for nontraditional stories than did their untrained peers. Taken together, the findings from the two experimental studies just described are consistent with the proposal that individual children's gender schemata and reasoning skills shape what they remember from exposure to given environmental experiences.

Cultural Processes

Using Bronfenbrenner's earlier-cited metaphor for the developmental ecology as a "set of nested structures . . . like a set of Russian dolls" (1979, p. 3), the preceding section emphasized the inner-most doll, that is, ways in which individuals' knowledge, beliefs, traits, and reasoning processes – among other qualities – affect what they engage with, interpret, and retain about the aliment of the immediately surrounding context. In the current section I focus on the more distal dolls of the layered ecology. These address broad societal values and traditions of the macrosystem as well as the institutions and people who instantiate and communicate those societal qualities. Already discussed are some of the ways in which active, constructivist individuals use their gender schemata to selectively engage with, interpret, and recall what they find in the environment. But how do these gender schemata develop in the first place?

Three types of answers to this question have been given: answers rooted in gender essentialism, gender environmentalism, and gender constructivism. Gender essentialism holds that boys and men are inherently, naturally, and pervasively different from girls and women (expanded discussions of this perspective are found in Fine & Duke, 2015; Gelman, Taylor, & Nguyen, 2004; Liben, 2015). Given this theoretical premise, the gender-essentialist answer requires no additional processes to account for the foundations of gender-distinct beliefs and identities. A second answer is the gender-environmental one that holds that children learn these stereotypes because they hear explicit stereotypic statements, see stereotypic models, and are reinforced for gender-stereotyped behaviors and statements or punished for counter-stereotyped behaviors and statements (see discussions in Bigler & Liben, 2007; Martin, Ruble, & Szkrybalo, 2002).

The third answer, consistent with the constructivist-ecological perspective of this paper is that children come to gender-differentiated beliefs and actions as a consequence of actively processing and making meaning of what they encounter in the surrounding environment. The latter position is illustrated by developmental intergroup theory (DIT; Bigler and Liben, 2006, 2007) which was designed to identify key processes in the formation, maintenance, and modification of children's stereotypes and prejudices about social groups, including groups defined by gender. Figure 9.1 presents a graphic representation of the formation process proposed in DIT.

DIT begins with the proposal that humans are not hardwired to use any particular characteristic as the basis to form stereotypes, to pursue versus avoid social affiliations, or to define and enact self-identities. Instead, humans are thought to be evolutionarily prepared to use a general and flexible cognitive system that seeks and processes available evidence in an effort to discover which characteristics matter in their particular ecology.

As depicted in the left side of Figure 9.1, DIT identifies several factors that increase the likelihood that a particular characteristic will be identified as important, including that the characteristic is easy to perceive (termed *perceptual discriminability* in DIT), is explicitly marked in language and action (*explicit labeling and use*), and when – in the absence of any explicit assignment rule – it appears to be a systematic basis on which people are sorted into roles, activities, or settings (*implicit use*). Additionally, the salience of a characteristic is expected to be enhanced when categories are highly imbalanced and thus create clear minority and majority classes (*proportional group size*).

Conditions within most contemporary societies, including the USA, are poised to lead children to conclude that gender is an important (or perhaps *the* single most important) human characteristic for grouping people. Children are exposed to perceptual differences between males and females that have been exaggerated by differentiated clothes, make-up, and hairstyles; they directly experience gender as an

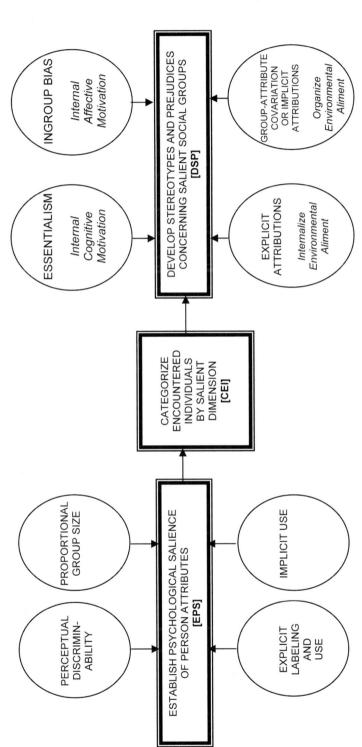

Figure 9.1. *Key processes in the formation of social stereotypes and prejudice in developmental intergroup theory from Bigler and Liben (2006), with permission. Rectangles represent the key processes in formation of social stereotyping and prejudice. Ovals represent the factors that shape the operation of core processes.*

organizing principle when boys or girls are asked to line up separately for recess or when choral groups are formed on the basis of gender rather than vocal ranges or voice timbre; they routinely hear gender-specific rather than gender-inclusive language, as when a teacher asks for a boy's help, when a parent praises a child as a good girl or boy, or as when a person in uniform is referred to as a policeman or policewoman rather than a police officer. Furthermore, they are exposed to contexts in which gender appears to be a basis for grouping people, as in the gender of all US presidents to date.

As represented in the middle section of Figure 9.1, DIT also proposes that once children have identified gender as an important human characteristic, that characteristic will be used to categorize people into groups as part of a general human drive to reduce cognitive complexity via categorization (Allport, 1954; Mervis & Rosch, 1981). As suggested in the figure and as illustrated later, the individual's developmental mastery of categorization skills is expected to be relevant to the operation of this categorization process.

As shown in the right section of Figure 9.1, once these social-group categories have been established, various processes lead to the emergence of stereotypes and prejudices about the groups. As seen in the figure, two processes are internally motivated. The first of these is the child's tendency to use essentialist thinking – that is, the tendency to assume that members of categories share characteristics, both visible and invisible (e.g., Gelman, 2003). Thus, once having formed groups on the basis of gender, children search for or invent other group-linked characteristics that distinguish the groups. The second of these is ingroup bias – that is, the tendency for self-enhancing psychological mechanisms to lead children to link positive attributes to the ingroup and negative attributes to the outgroup (e.g., Powlishta, 2004).

The remaining two processes originate externally. One of these is triggered when the child hears explicit statements or behaviors that convey stereotypes or prejudices (e.g., adults making wisecracks about women's constant nagging or men's slovenliness). The other is triggered by unexplained gender-based distributions mentioned earlier – that is, when the child observes some probabilistic, unexplained link between social-group membership (here gender) and some other attribute (e.g., occupation). In the US presidential case given above, for example, children may be led to infer that men have stronger leadership qualities or ambitions than women (an example that may lead to race-based inferences as well; see Bigler, Arthur, Hughes, & Patterson, 2008).

Although there remain many unknowns about the origins and impacts of these processes, findings from empirical work are consistent with the importance of the constructs and processes hypothesized in DIT. Evidence consistent with DIT was initially reported by Bigler and her colleagues (e.g., Bigler, Brown, & Markell, 2001; Bigler, Jones, & Lobliner, 1997; Patterson & Bigler, 2006) in research using the novel-group paradigm (Tajfel, Billig, Bundy, & Flament, 1971). In these studies, elementary school students were randomly assigned to wear t-shirts of one of two colors. Teachers in the experimental classrooms were asked to use color to refer to students and groups, and to structure classroom activities. After a few weeks of these classroom conditions, children were evaluated on attitudinal and behavioral measures. Consistent with hypotheses reviewed above concerning the importance of context, data showed that when teachers explicitly labeled and used t-shirt color, children developed stronger stereotypes and prejudices favoring their own color group and denigrating the other color group. Data also show that individual differences interact with contextual variables, as when significantly greater ingroup biases emerge in children who have higher levels of self-esteem (e.g., Bigler et al., 2001; Patterson & Bigler, 2006).

Subsequent research has demonstrated similar effects for parallel manipulations that target gender rather than shirt color, even though gender (unlike shirt color) is already routinely marked in language and action within the everyday environment. In the first gender study using this paradigm, Bigler (1995) asked experimental (but not control) elementary school teachers to label and use gender in the classroom (e.g., referring to individual children or groups with gender-specific labels, asking girls and then boys to line up to go to lunch). After four weeks, children from the experimental classrooms were found to have higher levels of gender stereotyping than children in the control classrooms. Reminiscent of the findings described earlier concerning the role of classification skills for the recall of gender-nontraditional stories (Bigler & Liben, 1992), the effect of this classroom intervention was significantly stronger for children who had less-advanced classification skills. Again, these findings are consistent with the hypothesized dynamic relation between individual and contextual factors in the formation of stereotyped gender schemata.

A later study (Hilliard & Liben, 2010) used a similar paradigm with preschool children. One question addressed was whether preschoolers would be affected as were elementary school children. A second question was whether effects would be observed not only in children's self-reported gender attitudes, but also in their actual behaviors. The behavioral domain studied was the gendered nature of peer play. This domain was selected based on a large and compelling research literature that has shown that children tend to segregate themselves into single-gender play groups, that time spent in single-gender peer groups tends to reinforce the acquisition and adoption of gender-traditional and differentiated behaviors, and that individual differences in the degree to which children restrict themselves to playing with children of their own gender has important developmental consequences (see Martin, Fabes, & Hanish, 2014).

Teachers in the experimental or high-gender-salience condition were asked to use gendered language and to use gender to structure the classroom and activities (e.g., saying good morning to "boys and girls" and asking children to post their art work on gender-specific bulletin boards). Teachers in the control or low-gender-salience condition were asked to maintain their normal use of gender-neutral language and classroom organization (e.g., saying good morning to "children" and providing a single bulletin board for all children to post their work). Both prior to, and following a two-week period, children were measured for (a) their gender attitudes (children were asked whether various jobs and activities should be limited to only one gender or open to both) and (b) their play with classmates (children's play with peers was observed during regularly scheduled free-play periods).

Data from both measures provided evidence of the impact of making gender more salient in the environment. Specifically, data from the gender attitude measure showed that in the control condition there was no change in children's gender stereotyping between pre-test and post-test, but in the experimental condition, children became significantly less egalitarian (i.e., significantly more gender stereotyped). The measure of peer play showed parallel effects. That is, children in the control condition showed no change in play with children of their own gender or in play with children of the other gender. In contrast, children in the experimental, high-salience condition showed a dramatic and significant drop in play with children of the other gender.

Taken together, the research reviewed in this section provides compelling evidence that contextual factors do indeed matter. An environment in which adults routinely use gender-specific language and make functional use of gender sets the conditions for children to infer that gender is an important dimension along which human beings are sorted. Empirical research shows that children respond by developing increasingly strong stereotypes about each gender, by increasingly valuing their own gender, and by increasingly disparaging the other gender. Furthermore, these effects are evident not only in children's responses on verbally administered self-report assessments, but also in behavioral play patterns. The finding that these contextual conditions lead children to eschew playing with children of the other gender suggests long-term consequences that contribute to sending girls and boys down different developmental paths. As discussed briefly in the next and final section, findings such as these have important implications beyond academic theories of gender development.

Conclusions and Implications

In this paper, I have reviewed a variety of empirical studies illustrating ways that developmental outcomes are affected both by qualities of individuals and by qualities of the surrounding contexts. I have drawn simultaneously from ideas contained in Piaget's constructivist theory and Bronfenbrenner's ecological-systems theory to emphasize the importance of examining individuals and contexts not as additive components, but, rather, in relational systems.

It is important to reiterate that the particular illustrations included in this paper address only a few of the individual qualities and embedding contexts that are relevant to gender development. Many other examples could have been drawn from research on the neuroscience of gender (e.g., see Eliot, 2009; Fine & Duke, 2015), on children's interactions with peers and parents (e.g., see Hilliard & Liben, 2014; Leaper, 1994; Martin et al., 2014; Tenenbaum & Leaper, 2003), and on the impact of broad cultural values such as societal expressions of gender equity and the pervasiveness of media messages about sexuality (e.g., see, respectively, Else-Quest, Hyde, & Linn, 2010 and McKenney & Bigler, 2016).

Empirical findings about gender issues such as these are important not only for what they contribute to academic scholarship on gender development; they are also important for designing interventions and social policies. For example, the consistent finding that children tend to forget or distort gender-nontraditional material means that simply presenting children with nontraditional role models or narratives is unlikely to have great success in revising children's gender schemata or personal goals. Indeed, early educational interventions that attempted to expand children's educational and career interests by presenting nontraditional role models had little effect (see Liben & Bigler, 1987). More recent conceptual analyses and empirical findings (Coyle & Liben, 2016; Liben, 2016; Liben & Coyle, 2014) have suggested that exposing children to models that simultaneously emphasize exaggerated gender appearance and nontraditional roles (e.g., Barbie dolls or professional cheerleaders enacting stereotypically masculine jobs) may increase children's interest in the former more than the latter.

Some interventions have been designed to take the potential role of constructive processing into account. Illustrative is the study by Bigler and Liben (1990) described earlier in which children were explicitly taught that gender is irrelevant for determining job choices. Based on the recognition that children are likely to have difficulty processing lessons that contradict their existing gender stereotypes, the intervention was designed to allow teachers to monitor children's processing of information during the course of the intervention itself. Specifically, as explained earlier, children were asked to respond to practice questions aloud, in turn permitting teachers to observe and correct reconstructive processing errors.

Also motivated by a constructivist perspective are interventions that are designed to engage children actively in the initial learning process. Illustrative is an intervention developed to teach elementary school children how to recognize and explicitly confront peers' sexist comments (Lamb, Bigler, Liben, & Green, 2009). Consistent with the hypothesized importance of children's active processing and engagement, those children who were required to translate the lessons into skits with self-relevant content showed significantly more benefit from lessons than did children who were taught the same content about sexism and appropriate retorts but in a less personalized manner – that is, using already-prepared narratives.

I close with a brief discussion of a contemporary issue to which the research discussed in this paper has been applied – US policies about public single-sex education (additional detail and citations to related sources may be found in Liben, 2015). Although public education has been targeted to both girls and boys throughout the country's history, the precise form of that education has been gender-differentiated. For example, by the middle of the 19th century, boys and girls received shared lessons in foundational subjects such as English, arithmetic, and geography, but only boys were instructed in science and only girls in sewing. Even during the 20th century, boys still went to classes in shop and drafting while girls went to classes in sewing and cooking. It was not until 1972 that Title IX of the Civil Rights Act explicitly prohibited gender discrimination in public education.

Title IX did not, however, end debates about gender-differentiated education. Some educators asserted that girls and boys were inherently different learners and thus needed different pedagogy; others argued that despite Title IX, girls continued to be short-changed in schools, in part because boys had more power and status and tended to overpower the classroom, and in part because teachers were (often unconsciously) uneven in the attention and challenges they distributed to the two sexes. Still others argued that school environments were highly feminized and thereby inhospitable to boys. It was in this context that new regulations were issued as part of the No Child Left Behind Act (US Department of Education, 2006), making single-sex public education permissible under some circumstances. Although it is difficult to determine precise numbers (see Klein, Lee, McKinsey, & Archer, 2014), the changed regulations were effective. There were only a handful of stand-alone single-sex public schools at the beginning of the 21st century; roughly a decade later there were more than 100 entirely separate schools and hundreds of single-sex classrooms housed within coeducational schools (Klein et al., 2014; Sherwin, 2015).

Research on gender development described in the prior sections of this paper has been used by developmental scientists (e.g., Bigler, Hayes, & Liben, 2014; Bigler & Signorella, 2011; Halpern et al., 2011; Liben, 2015; Signorella & Bigler, 2013) to argue that this recent surge of single-sex schools is ill-advised. One of the key arguments has been that creating gender-segregated schools and classrooms is tantamount to implementing the experimental "high gender-salience" conditions used in the research on DIT described earlier. That is, extrapolating from the studies by Bigler (1995) and Hilliard and Liben (2010), it is reasonable to expect that sorting boys and girls into separate school buildings and classrooms that are labeled by gender-specific language (e.g., the Ann Richards School for Young Women Leaders, the Eagle Academy for Young Men of Harlem) will increase gender stereotypes, ingroup bias, and outgroup prejudice. The risk of this kind of collateral damage could perhaps be justified if there were strong evidence of important benefits, but meta-analyses have shown little or no sign of academic advantages for single-sex settings once confounds are taken into account (e.g., Nagengast, Marsh, & Hau, 2013; Pahlke, Hyde, & Allison, 2014; Signorella, Hayes, & Li, 2013). These arguments and the research on which they draw have been used by the American Civil Liberties Union in legal actions that challenge single-sex programs in public school districts (Sherwin, 2015).

In conclusion, research on gender development conducted from a relational per-spective is valuable for its contributions not only to academic scholarship, but also for its applications to a range of social policies. It is, however, also true that such research is complex. As Klahr bemoaned in the passages quoted earlier about the constructs of assimilation and accommodation, there is also no single way to pin down, once and for all, what exactly an individual (in isolation) or a context (in isolation) really is. Indeed, it is not simply that every given individual is unique and ever-changing; it is also that – as Bronfenbrenner's ecological-systems model reminds us – contexts are ever-changing as well. To appreciate the non-trivial nature of historical shifts in the domain of gender, one need only think about recent changes in opinions and laws about who may legitimately join as marital and parenting partners, the increasing availability and use of gender-neutral pronouns in English (e.g., Bigler & Leaper, 2015), the trend toward uncoupling natal gender from gender identity (e.g., see Tate, Ledbetter, & Youssef, 2013), and the expanding range of rest-room or locker-room choices.

As put succinctly by Sameroff (2010) in his proposal for a unified theory of development, "Although we all have a strong desire for straightforward explanations of life, development is complicated and models for explaining it need to be complicated enough to usefully inform our understanding" (p. 20). This admonition applies even if we set our sights more modestly on explaining gender development rather than all of life.

References

Allport, G. W. (1954). *The nature of prejudice*. Cambridge, MA: Addison-Wesley.

Bigler, R. S. (1995). The role of classification skill in moderating environmental influences on children's gender stereotyping: A study of the functional use of gender in the classroom. *Child Development, 66*, 1072–1087.

Bigler, R. S., Arthur, A. E., Hughes, J. M., & Patterson, M. M. (2008). The politics of race and gender: Children's perceptions of discrimination and the US presidency. *Analyses of Social Issues and Public Policy (ASAP), 8*, 83–112.

Bigler, R. S., Brown, C. S., & Markell, M. (2001). When groups are not created equal: Effects of group status on the formation of intergroup attitudes in children. *Child Development, 72*, 1151–1162.

Bigler, R. S., Hayes, A. R., & Liben, L. S. (2014). Analysis and evaluation of the rationales for single-sex schooling. In L. S. Liben & R. S. Bigler (Eds.), *The role of gender in educational contexts and outcomes*. In J. Benson (Series Ed.), *Advances in child development and behavior* (Vol. *47*, pp. 225–260). San Diego, CA: Elsevier.

Bigler, R. S., Jones, L. C., & Lobliner, D. B. (1997). Social categorization and the formation of intergroup attitudes in children. *Child Development, 68*, 530–543.

Bigler, R. S., & Leaper, C. (2015). Gendered language: Psychological principles, evolving practices, and inclusive policies. *Policy Insights from Behavioral and Brain Sciences, 2*, 187–194.

Bigler, R. S., & Liben, L. S. (1990). The role of attitudes and interventions in gender-schematic processing. *Child Development, 61*, 1440–1452.

Bigler, R. S., & Liben, L. S. (1992). Cognitive mechanisms in children's gender stereotyping: Theoretical and educational implications of a cognitive-based intervention. *Child Development, 63*, 1351–1363.

Bigler, R. S., & Liben, L. S. (2006). A developmental intergroup theory of social stereotypes and prejudice. In R. V. Kail (Ed.), *Advances in child development and behavior* (Vol. *34*, pp. 39–89). San Diego, CA: Elsevier.

Bigler, R. S., & Liben, L. S. (2007). Developmental intergroup theory: Explaining and reducing children's social stereotyping and prejudice. *Current Directions in Psychological Science, 16*, 162–166.

Bigler, R. S., & Signorella, M. L. (2011). Single-sex education: New perspectives and evidence on a continuing controversy. *Sex Roles, 65*, 659–669.

Blakemore, J. E. O., Berenbaum, S. A., & Liben, L. S. (2009). *Gender development*. New York, NY: Taylor & Francis.

Bronfenbrenner, U. (1977). Toward an experimental ecology of human development. *American Psychologist, 32*, 513–531.

Bronfenbrenner, U. (1979). *The ecology of human development: Experiments by nature and design*. Cambridge, MA: Harvard University Press.

Bronfenbrenner, U. (1994). Ecological models of human development. In T. Husen & T. N. Postlethwaite (Eds.), *International Encyclopedia of Education* (2 edn., Vol. *3*, pp. 1643–1647). Oxford, England: Pergamon Press.

Coyle, E. F. & Liben, L. S. (2016). Affecting girls' job and activity interests through play: The moderating roles of personal gender salience and game characteristics. *Child Development*, *87*, 414–428.

Eliot, L. (2009). *Pink brain blue brain*. Boston, MA: Houghton Mifflin.

Else-Quest, N. M., Hyde, J. S., & Linn, M. C. (2010) Cross-national patterns of gender differences in mathematics: A meta-analysis. *Psychological Bulletin*, *136*, 103–127.

Fine, C., & Duke, R. (2015). Expanding the role of gender essentialism in the single-sex education debate: A commentary on Liben. *Sex Roles*, *72*, 427–433.

Gelman, S. A. (2003). *The essential child: Origins of essentialism in everyday thought*. New York, NY: Oxford University Press.

Gelman, S. A., Taylor, M. G., & Nguyen, S. P. (2004). Mother-child conversations about gender: Understanding the acquisition of essentialist beliefs. *Monographs of the Society for Research in Child Development*, *69*, No. 275.

Halpern, D. F., Eliot, L., Bigler, R. S., Fabes, R. A., Hanish, L. D., Hyde, J., Liben, L. S., & Martin, C. L. (2011). The pseudoscience of single-sex schooling. *Science*, *333*, 1706–1707.

Hilliard, L. J., & Liben, L. S. (2010). Differing levels of gender salience in preschool classrooms: Effects on children's gender attitudes and intergroup bias. *Child Development*, *81*, 1787–1798.

Hilliard, L. J. & Liben, L. S. (2014). Fairness in the face of gender stereotypes: Examining the nature and impact of mother-child conversations. In C. Wainryb & H. E. Recchia (Eds.), *Talking about right and wrong: Parent-child conversations as contexts for moral development* (pp.168–192). Cambridge, UK: Cambridge University Press.

Klahr, D. (1982). Nonmonotone assessment of monotone development: An information processing analysis. In S. Strauss (Ed.), *U-shaped behavioral growth* (pp. 63–86). New York, NY: Academic Press.

Klahr, D. (1995). Computational models of cognitive change: The state of the art. In T. J. Simon & G. S. Halford (Eds.), *Developing cognitive competence: New approaches to process modeling* (pp. 355–375). Hillsdale, NJ: Lawrence Erlbaum Associates.

Klein, S., Lee, J., McKinsey, P., & Archer, C. (2014, December 11). Identifying US K-12 public schools with deliberate sex segregation. *Feminist Majority Foundation*. Retrieved from http://feminist.org/education/pdfs/IdentifyingSexSegregation12-12-14.pdf

Koblinsky, S. G., Cruse, D. F., & Sugawara, A. I. (1978). Sex-role stereotypes and children's memory for story content. *Child Development*, *49*, 452–458.

Kohlberg, L. (1966). A cognitive developmental analysis of children's sex role concepts and attitudes. In E. E. Maccoby (Ed.), *The development of sex differences* (pp. 82–172). Stanford, CA: Stanford University Press.

Lamb, L., Bigler, R. S., Liben, L. S., & Green, V. A. (2009). Teaching children to confront peers' sexist remarks: Implications for theories of gender development and educational practice. *Sex Roles*, *61*, 361–382.

Leaper, C. (Ed.) (1994). Exploring the consequences of gender segregation on social relationships. *New directions for child and adolescent development*, *65*. San Francisco, CA: Jossey-Bass.

Leaper, C. (2015). Gender and social-cognitive development. In L. S. Liben & U. Müller (Eds.), *Handbook of child psychology and developmental science* (7 edn., Vol. *2*, pp. 806–853). Hoboken, NJ: Wiley.

Lerner, R. M., Agans, J. P., DeSouza, L. M., & Hershberg, R. M. (2014). Developmental science in 2025: A predictive review. *Research in Human Development, 11*, 255–272.

Liben, L. S. (2014). The individual ↔ context nexus in developmental intergroup theory: Within and beyond the ivory tower. *Research in Human Development. 11*, 273–290.

Liben, L. S. (2015). Probability values and human values in evaluating single-sex education. *Sex Roles, 72*, 401–426.

Liben, L. S. (2016). We've come a long way, baby (but we're not there yet): Gender past, present, and future. *Child Development, 87*, 5–28.

Liben, L. S., & Bigler, R. S. (1987). Reformulating children's gender schemata. In L. S. Liben & M. L. Signorella (Eds.), *New directions for child development: Children's gender schemata* (pp. 89–105). San Francisco, CA: Jossey-Bass.

Liben, L. S., & Bigler, R. S. (2002). The developmental course of gender differentiation: Conceptualizing, measuring, and evaluating constructs and pathways. *Monographs of the Society for Research in Child Development, 67*, No. 269.

Liben, L. S., & Coyle, E. F. (2014). Developmental interventions to address the STEM gender gap: Exploring intended and unintended consequences. In L. S. Liben & R. S. Bigler (Eds.) *The role of gender in educational contexts and outcomes.* In J. B. Benson (Series Ed.), *Advances in child development and behavior* (Vol. 47, pp. 77–116). San Diego, CA: Elsevier.

Liben, L. S., & Hilliard, L. J. (2010, October). *Preschoolers' gender vigilance: Effects of classroom organization.* Poster presented at the Gender Development Research Conference, San Francisco.

Liben, L. S., & Signorella, M. L. (1980). Gender-related schemata and constructive memory in children. *Child Development, 51*, 11–18.

Liben, L. S., & Signorella, M. L. (1993). Gender schematic processing in children: The role of initial interpretations of stimuli. *Developmental Psychology, 29*, 141–149.

Martin, C. L., Eisenbud, L., & Rose, H. (1995). Children's gender-based reasoning about toys. *Child Development, 66*, 1453–1471.

Martin, C. L., Fabes, R. A., & Hanish, L. (2014). Gendered-peer relationships in educational contexts. In L. S. Liben & R. S. Bigler (Eds.), *The role of gender in educational contexts and outcomes.* In J. Benson (Series Ed.), *Advances in child development and behavior* (Vol. 47, pp. 151–187). San Diego, CA: Elsevier.

Martin, C. L., & Halverson, C. F. (1981). A schematic processing model of sex typing and stereotyping in children. *Child Development, 52*, 1119–1134.

Martin, C. L., Ruble, D. N., & Szkrybalo, J. (2002). Cognitive theories of early gender development. *Psychological Bulletin, 128*(6), 903–933.

McKenney, S. J., & Bigler, R. S. (2016). High heels, low grades: Internalized sexualization and academic orientation among adolescent girls. *Journal of Research on Adolescence, 26*, 30–36.

Mervis, C., & Rosch, E. (1981). Categorization of natural objects. *Annual Review of Psychology, 32*, 89–115

Munakata, Y. (2006) Information processing approaches to development. In D. Kuhn & R. S. Siegler (Eds.), *Handbook of child psychology: Vol. 2. Cognition, perception, and language* (6th edn., pp. 426–463). Hoboken, NJ: Wiley.

Nagengast, B., Marsh, H. W., & Hau, K.-T. (2013). Effects of single-sex schooling in the final years of high school: A comparison of analysis of covariance and propensity score matching. *Sex Roles, 69*, 404–422.

Overton, W. F. (2007). A coherent metatheory for dynamic systems: Relational organicism-contextualism. *Human Development*, *50*, 154–159.

Overton, W. F. (2015). Processes, relations and relational-developmental systems. In W. F. Overton & P. C. Molenaar (Eds.), *Handbook of child psychology and developmental science, Vol. 1: Theory and method.* (7th edn. pp. 9–62). Hoboken, NJ: Wiley.

Pahlke, E., Hyde, J. S., & Allison, C. M. (2014). The effects of single-sex compared with coeducational schooling on students' performance and attitudes: A meta-analysis. *Psychological Bulletin*, *140*, 1042–1072.

Patterson, M. M. (2012). Self-perceived gender typicality, gender-typed attributes, and gender stereotype endorsement in elementary-school-aged children. *Sex Roles*, *67*, 422–434.

Patterson, M. M., & Bigler, R. S. (2006). Preschool children's attention to environmental messages about groups: Social categorization and the origins of intergroup bias. *Child Development*, *77*, 847–860.

Piaget, J. (1964). Development and learning. In R. E. Ripple & V. M. Rockcastle (Eds.), *Piaget rediscovered* (pp. 7–20). Ithaca: Cornell University.

Piaget, J. (1970). Piaget's theory. In P. Mussen (Ed.), *Carmichael's manual of child psychology* (pp. 703–732). New York, NY: Wiley.

Powlishta, K. K. (2004). Gender as a social category: Intergroup processes and gender-role development. In M. Bennett & F. Sani (Eds.), *The development of the social self* (pp. 103–133). East Sussex, England: Psychology Press.

Sameroff, A. J. (2010). A unified theory of development. *Child Development*, *81*, 6–22.

Serbin, L. A., & Sprafkin, C. (1986). The salience of gender and the process of sex typing in three- to seven-year-old children. *Child Development*, *57*, 1188–1199.

Sherwin, G. (2015). Anecdotal and essentialist arguments for single-sex educational programs discussed by Liben: A legal analysis. *Sex Roles*, *72*, 434–445.

Signorella, M. L., & Bigler, R. S. (2013). Single-sex schooling: Bridging science and school boards in educational policy. *Sex Roles*, *65*, 659–759.

Signorella, M. L., Hayes, A. R., & Li, Y. (2013). A meta-analytic critique of Mael et al.'s (2005) review of single-sex schooling. *Sex Roles*, *69*, 423–441.

Signorella, M. L., & Liben, L. S. (1984). Recall and reconstruction of gender-related pictures: Effects of attitude, task difficulty, and age. *Child Development*, *55*, 393–405.

Tajfel, H., Billig, M. G., Bundy, R. P., & Flament, C. (1971). Social categorization and intergroup behaviour. *European Journal of Social Psychology*, *1*, 149–177.

Tate, C. C., Ledbetter, J. N., & Youssef, C. P. (2013). A two-question method for assessing gender categories in the social and medical sciences. *Journal of Sex Research*, *50*, 767–776.

Tenenbaum, H. R., & Leaper, C. (2003). Parent-child conversations about science: The socialization of gender inequities? *Developmental Psychology*, *39*, 34–47.

US Department of Education. (2006). 34 C.F.R. §106.34(b)(1). Title 34 Education. *Access to classes and schools*. Retrieved from www2.ed.gov/policy/rights/reg/ocr/edlite-34cfr106.html#S34

von Glasersfeld, E. (1981). The concepts of adaptation and viability in a radical constructivist theory of knowledge. In I. E. Sigel, D. M. Brodzinsky, & R. M. Golinkoff (Eds.), *New directions in Piagetian theory and practice* (pp. 87–95). Hillsdale, NJ: Lawrence Erlbaum Associates.

Witherington, D. C. (2007). The dynamic systems approach as metatheory for developmental psychology. *Human Development*, *50*, 127–153.

10 A Domains-of-Socialization Perspective on Children's Social Development

Joan E. Grusec

Socialization experiences → social development. (handwritten annotation)

Social development is directed to a very considerable extent by the individual's socialization experiences. In this chapter I focus on these experiences and the role they play in the development of thoughts, emotions, and actions that promote the ability to fit into the social group. Biological and cultural events interact with socialization experiences, of course. They determine to varying degrees the effect of these experiences: how they are perceived or interpreted and, therefore, how they ultimately affect thinking, feeling, and behavior. Nevertheless, more than 60 years of formal research, beginning with the work of psychologists such as Robert Sears and Albert Bandura, have made the centrality of socialization very evident (Grusec, 1992).

Because humans are social animals they need to acquire the skills that will enable them to interact harmoniously with fellow group members – that is, they need to be socialized. Socialization is the process by which new members of a group are assisted by older group members to take on the values, attitudes, and actions of that group, as well as accompanying cognitive and affective outcomes. Most of our knowledge about its mechanisms comes from studies of family interaction and the impact of parents' child-rearing practices on children's social and emotional development. But socialization occurs, of course, in any context involving a change in expectations for behavior. Children are socialized into the peer group, where values and attitudes may be quite discrepant from those in the family. They have to learn how to act at school, where the rules and expectations are somewhat different from what they are at home or what they are on the playground and with peers. The demands of being an undergraduate are very different from those of being a high school student. Individuals are also socialized into the work place, into being parents, and, ultimately, into being an older member of the social group. Each new placement requires new learning and reliance on the already socialized members of the group for assistance.

The notion of assistance is an important one. Early conceptualizations of socialization involved the idea that values were transmitted from the agent of socialization to the target of socialization, and terms such as "introjection," "identification," and "internalization" were used to refer to the taking over of the values of others (e.g., Sears, Maccoby, & Levin, 1957). Later approaches, however, recognized that values and group norms are constructed from experience. Individuals pick and choose what they will accept, although the manner of their acceptance is fashioned to some extent by the way information is presented. Children choose, for example, from a variety of models of action, although their choices are affected by factors such as the nurturance or prestige of a particular model or of their similarity to the model (Bandura, 1977). A famous turning point in the history of socialization theory came with the paper by Bell (1968), who pointed out that characteristics of the child, such as aggressiveness, could alter the behavior of parents by, for example, making them more power assertive or punitive in their interventions. This was an obvious but compelling argument for thinking of socialization as a two-way process, although there is probably still a strong tendency on the part of researchers to focus on parent-to-child effects first. (Indeed, such a focus is not surprising given that one aim of researchers beyond understanding the mechanisms of socialization is the practical one of providing guidelines for effective parenting.) Kuczynski and DeMol (2015) elaborate extensively on the notion that socialization does indeed involve continuity and conformity, but that it also involves change and the emergence of novelty. Individuals often work, for example, to change the existing norms of their group: children try to modify their own parents' values and actions, workers try to alter the expectations of employers, and children of immigrants struggle to acquaint their parents with the attitudes, beliefs, and values of the new culture (Berry, 2015).

Although values are modified from one generation to another, it is important to note that a primary goal of socialization theorists is to understand how the values individuals acquire at least in part from others are taken over or internalized – that is, how individuals come to believe that their actions and values are inherently correct. An important outcome, then, is not to have behavior fashioned by reward and punishment contingencies but, rather, that socially acceptable behavior be displayed independent of response consequences. Children who tell the truth because they are afraid that they will be caught and punished for lying are not successfully socialized. They should instead tell the truth because that is the inherently correct way of behaving and they should tell the truth even if there is no probability that their lies might be found out. Similarly, children who are helpful so that the teacher will like them are not socialized in the same sense as children who are helpful because they feel empathy for the suffering of others or because they believe it important that all members of the social group assist others and share resources.

Finally, a word about the nature of values that are learned. Socialization theorists emphasize moral values that include refraining from antisocial action such as aggression and engaging in helpful actions such as assisting others. They also deal with non-moral values that include such outcomes as achievement, work ethic, respect for authority, looking after one's own health and safety, being independent, and being polite. Although they are in general agreement about the nature of values that are adaptive, it is important to note that antisocial values can also be instilled into or internalized by new group members. Some people value materialism more than others (Schwartz & Boehnke, 2004), for example, and, although it has been suggested that individuals who have materialistic values are less likely to be happy and productive (Sheldon, Ryan, Deci, & Kasser, 2004), there is not a great deal of research that has been addressed to different socialization processes as they might interact with different kinds of values. Of course, evolutionary theory provides a hypothesis here in that it would be counterproductive to instill values that endanger the reproductive potential of the group members.

What is Effective Socialization?

Baumrind, Control, and Discipline

When developmental psychologists address the question of how best to socialize children they most frequently cite the work of Diana Baumrind (e.g., Baumrind, 1967, 2012). Beginning almost 50 years ago, Baumrind identified three styles of child-rearing which still play a prominent role in analyses of socialization. The styles were authoritative, authoritarian, and permissive. Authoritative parents set firm limits but were warm and responsive to the needs and wishes of their children, and they had children who were high in social competence, self-esteem, and social responsibility. Authoritarian parents were strict, demanding, and not responsive to their children's needs, and their children, in turn, were high in anti-social behavior and anxiety. Finally, permissive parents made few demands on their children, with these children low in self-control and achievement. Recently, Baumrind (2012) has characterized two forms of power-assertive parenting as differentiating between the authoritative and the authoritarian parenting styles. Both are demanding and forceful. However, authoritative parenting involves con-frontive action, which includes reasoning and negotiation and gives a child a choice between obedience and the consequences that follow from lack of obedience. Authoritarian parenting is coercive, arbitrary, domineering, and peremptory. Thus, Baumrind argues that power assertion by itself is not harmful; rather, it is harmful when employed in a coercive manner. Baumrind uses this argument, incidentally, to support the position that corporal punishment 'per se' is not harmful but, rather, that it is harmful only when applied in a coercive way.

There have been some additions to and refinements of Baumrind's analysis over the years. A distinction has been made, for example, between behavioral and psychological control, with the former the more positive setting of limits and the latter involving harmful manipulation of guilt (Barber, 2002). Darling and Steinberg (1993) argued for a distinction between parenting styles and parenting practices such as reasoning and different forms of discipline, with the impact of practices depend-ing on the style in which the practice was delivered. And Grusec and Goodnow (1994) noted that successful internalization of parental values required both accurate perception of those values as well as acceptance of them. They suggested that accurate perception was facilitated by variables such as clear, redundant, and con-sistent messages whereas acceptance was a function of such variables as arousal of empathy, desire to please the parent, and feelings that the value had been self-generated. Nevertheless, the emphasis has continued to be around issues of disci-pline and control, with secondary interest in the nature of the relationship between parent and child. In general, then, successful socialization has been characterized as a combination of appropriate forms of control applied in the context of sensitive and caring parenting (Laible, Thompson, & Froimson, 2015).

In contrast to an approach focused on general styles and practices of parenting, Bugental (2000) argued that socialization occurs in different domains, with each domain involving a different kind of relationship between agent and object of socialization and with different mechanisms underlying the socialization process in each of these distinctive domains. Grusec and Davidov (2007, 2010) have elaborated on this basic notion, and it is the development of that approach which forms the basis of the rest of this chapter.

Domains of Socialization and Domains of Social Knowledge

A domains-of-socialization approach holds that socialization occurs in many different contexts. In each of these contexts the relationship between parent and child assumes a different form. A given socialization intervention therefore needs to be fitted to the particular domain in which a child is operating. What would be an effective socialization intervention in one domain would be quite inappropriate and ineffective in another domain.

The use of "domain" can lead to confusion, particularly on the part of developmental psychologists who are especially familiar with a rather older concept of domains of social knowledge. It is useful, therefore, to contrast the two different kinds of domains and to see that they are somewhat orthogonal to each other.

A domains-of-socialization approach addresses how children learn to act in accord with societal rules and values. A domains-of-social knowledge approach addresses how children have distinct patterns of thought which affect how they view societal rules and values: The implication is that their views will affect how easily they act in accord with those rules and values as well as the manner in which they do so. According to social knowledge domain theory, children actively try to make sense of rules, classifying them into three organized systems. The domains include moral issues, such as harming others physically or psychologically; social conventional issues, such as rules of social conduct; and psychological issues, such as an understanding of self and others as psychological systems (Turiel, 1983; Smetana, 2011). Notably, the extent to which parents have the right to demand that children behave in accord with rules depends on the domain of social knowledge which contains the rule. Moral issues are seen to be immutable and demands in this area are therefore reasonable. Rules that belong to the social conventional domain can be changed and, therefore, their strict enforcement is less acceptable. Finally, psychological issues include those that pertain to personal issues over which agents of socialization should have no jurisdiction and where, accordingly, they have no right to intervene. Smetana, Robinson, and Rote (2015) review some of the substantial research literature that demonstrates how important value domain can be in the socialization process.

Initially, socialization theorists were not so concerned with the content of rules, assuming that successful internalization is independent of such content. The extensive research of social cognitive theorists, however, as well as research emanating from other theoretical directions, has made the importance of content clear (see Bugental & Grusec, 2006).

Domains of Socialization

In an attempt to draw together a variety of approaches taken by socialization researchers and to expand on the work of Bugental and her colleagues (Bugental, 2000; Bugental & Goodnow, 1998; Bugental & Grusec, 2006), Grusec and Davidov set out a possible framework for understanding domains of socialization (Grusec & Davidov, 2007, 2010). They suggested that there are five domains of socialization involving different behavioral systems that are activated in different situations. The domains include protection, which involves the child's need for security and comfort when distressed; reciprocity, which calls on the child's proclivity to reciprocate the behaviors of others; guided learning, which entails the mastery of new skills through teaching; group participation, which involves the child's motivation to be part of the social group; and, finally, control, which includes the child's reactions to discipline administered in response to the child's antisocial actions or reward in the case of prosocial action. The placement of control at the end of this list, in spite of its centrality to depictions of socialization, is deliberate because, it could be argued, successful socialization in the other domains should make discipline and correction – both fraught with negative affect that can be destructive to socialization goals and socialization relationships – unnecessary.

Protection

According to attachment theory, children, when in physical danger or psychological distress, seek comfort from their caregiver (Bowlby, 1969). From an evolutionary perspective this seeking of the caregiver is, of course, an adaptive response because it increases the chances of survival. And provision of comfort is an adaptive response on the part of parents because it increases the chances of their reproductive success. When parental comfort or protection is appropriate (sufficient to make children feel confident that they are safe from physical and psychological threat) children become securely attached. According to Bowlby, the nature of the attachment – secure or insecure – forms the basis of personality, determining whether or not the child will become socially competent and socially responsible. It is in the attachment domain that children learn to self-regulate distress-related affect – that is, to reduce their own distress; to feel sympathy when others are distressed and, therefore, to engage in helpful and prosocial action; and to trust that others have their best interests at heart. This latter aspect of secure attachment means that children are more likely to comply with parental directives because they see them as expressions of caring rather than as intrusive and arbitrary demands (Bretherton, Golby, & Cho, 1997; Kerns, Aspelmeier, Gentzler, & Grabill, 2001).

Reciprocity

A second domain of socialization focuses on a mutually compliant relationship between parent and child. In a classic study, Parpal and Maccoby (1985) demonstrated that children whose mothers had been instructed to follow their child's lead during a play interaction were more cooperative when they were asked to clean up than were children whose mothers received no direction with respect to play and who, in fact, were observed to be more directive and critical. Moreover, the effect of the mothers' cooperative stance was especially great for children who were more difficult and noncompliant. The importance of a mutually responsive relationship between parent and child in the form of parental playfulness and cooperation and increased child compliance has been shown to predict greater social competence, increased prosocial behavior, and less antisocial behavior in the child (Criss, Shaw, & Ingoldsby, 2003; Deater-Deckard & Petrill, 2004; Lindsey, Cremeens, & Caldera, 2010). The mechanism identified for such outcomes has been identified as the inborn tendency on the part of humans to reciprocate what others have done (Trevarthen, Kokkinski, & Flamenghi, 1999). This is an adaptive response given the survival and reproductive benefits that arise from helping, and being helped by, others.

Guided Learning

In this domain children are taught new skills and knowledge by more knowledgeable group members who teach within the child's (ever-changing) zone of proximal development – that is, who alter their approach in accord with the child's changing skill level (Wood, Bruner, & Ross, 1976; Vygotsky, 1978). Discussion and exchange are central in this domain (Haden, Ornstein, Eckerman, & Didow, 2001), with the ultimate goal of a shared understanding of the task at hand (Puntambekar & Hubscher, 2005). Guided learning has been studied particularly in the context of moral development. Thus, parents who elicit their children's opinion about moral problems, who check that their children have understood a particular argument, and who are positive and supportive have children who demonstrate increases in moral development (Walker, Hennig, & Krettenauer, 2000). Guided learning is an especially important domain for human development because human beings need teachable intellectual skills so that they can compensate for their limited physical prowess (Gauvain & Perez, 2015).

Group Participation

Bandura and Walters (1963) maintained that the most fundamental form of learning for humans involves observation and modeling of the actions of other members of the social group. For purposes of socialization success, then, the forms of social behavior to which children are exposed, be it in the family, on television, or in the school and neighborhood, are of critical importance. Many of these observed behaviors include routines or rituals and, because children and newcomers generally are eager to behave in a similar way to long-term members of the group, they readily and eagerly imitate these routines and rituals, as well as other actions of individuals whom they aspire to be like. Kagan (1982) points out how distressed children are when they cannot successfully match the actions of an adult model or when an adult normative standard is violated: This distress is evidence of the strong need of children not only to successfully emulate other members of the social group, but to feel that group members share the same goals and values. Rogoff, Moore, Correa-Chavez, and Dexter (2015) point out that in many cultures the primary means of learning is through observing the behavior of adults in anticipation of having to engage in similar behavior at a future point in time. In contrast, in our own culture, much of this learning goes on in segregated school settings where it is more likely to be taught in the guided learning domain.

Control

This much-studied domain relies on the fact that parents control more resources than do children. Thus, parents can use their greater power to impose their values and behavioral requirements on their children. The focus here has been on ways of using that power – punishment for antisocial action and reward for positive action – in a way that reduces noncompliance as well as reactance or oppositional behavior when socialization agents are not present to apply subtle or not-so-subtle pressure. Thus, reasoning (particularly reasoning that draws attention to the negative impact of a child's actions on others) has been identified as an important accompaniment of punishment (Baumrind, 1971; Hoffman, 1970) and a facilitator of internalization. A particular challenge in the control domain is that levels of negative affect, particularly anger, are frequently high in both parent and child. This is because the parent is upset at the child's antisocial action and the child is frustrated at being prevented from engaging in an appealing act. This mutual negative affect in the form of anger and frustration interferes with both effective management on the part of the parent and effective learning on the part of the child.

   Much has been written about the negative impact of corporal punishment (Gershoff, 2002) and whether it is harmful in a Western cultural context (Baumrind, Larzelere, & Owens, 2010), or whether it is less harmful in other cultures where its use is more normative (e.g., Lansford et al., 2010). The answer is not completely clear, other than to note that corporal punishment does offer a presumably less than desirable model of aggression as a way of solving problems. Finally, although it has been suggested that socialization in other domains might reduce the necessity of socialization in the control domain, in reality we probably cannot dismiss entirely the use of control. The learning of self-control, of how to resist temptation and to inhibit displays of negativity, is not always an easy task, but it is a necessary one if group members are to get along in an amicable and adaptive way.

Implications of the Approach

The domains-of-socialization perspective suggests that the nature of the parent–child relationship is different in different domains, that different parenting behaviors are required in different domains, and that the mechanism of socialization is different depending on the domain in question. In the protection domain parents are providers of comfort for children who are in distress. The parenting behavior required is appropriate alleviation of distress, and the mechanism is confidence in protection and trust in the good intentions of the caregiver with respect to the child's needs. In the mutual reciprocity domain the relationship is one of equality, the parenting behavior required is compliance with the child's reasonable requests, and the mechanism is the child's innate tendency to reciprocate. For the guided learning domain, the relationship is one of teacher and student, the appropriate behavior is teaching in the child's zone of proximal development, and the mechanism is internalization of the teacher's approach. In the group participation domain, parent and child are members of the same social group; the appropriate behavior is modeling, joint participation, and the encouragement of rituals and routines; and the mechanism is the child's desire for a social identity. Finally, the control domain calls on an authority relationship, with parents using reward and punishment contingencies appropriately, with the acquisition of self-control the mechanism whereby socialization is accomplished.

This analysis requires, then, an understanding of why a particular antisocial act has occurred – that is, knowledge of the reason for the antisocial act. The questions to be asked are straightforward. Did the unacceptable action occur because the child was distressed and experiencing a level of arousal that interfered with the ability to engage in self-control? Did it occur because the parent rarely complies with the child's reasonable requests and so has not set up a system of mutual reciprocity, or was it because the child did not know the action was wrong and needs to be taught? Was it because the child's friends frequently engage in the same act and the child wants to be part of that social group, or, finally, was it because the child was unable to resist the temptation to act badly? The appropriate socialization response depends on the answer to this question. Thus, a choice would need to be made between comfort and sympathy, greater attention to the child's requests, a discussion about why the act was wrong, the encouragement of association with new and better-behaved friends, or discipline.

This is not to say that structure and a clear presentation and/or reminder of appropriate behavior are not in order, no matter which domain is activated. But the socialization actions that are appropriate to underline the statement or reminder of rules and requirements will need to differ. Nor does the analysis suggest that all socialization interactions are limited to one specific domain. Indeed, parent and child can function at the same time in more than one domain. Individuals may be distressed and also unable to regulate their own behavior. Values may be learned in the context of a discussion arising as a result of a group ritual or routine. In the guided learning domain, children may learn how to cope with distress they experience in the protection domain. In the control domain reasoning may augment the information about appropriate behavior that has been acquired in the guided learning domain.

Similarly, interactions in one domain can affect processes in another domain. As an example, children who are securely attached – that is, who have learned to cope with their own distress emotions – should be better at controlling their distress or level of negative arousal when they are being disciplined. Accordingly, Kochanska, Aksan, Knaack, and Rhines (2004) found that conscience development in securely attached children was more positively impacted by positive forms of discipline than in insecurely attached children.

This partitioning of socialization into a variety of separate entities obviously has a number of implications for analyses of socialization. This includes the fact that parenting that is effective in one domain may not be effective in another. For example, if children are misbehaving because they are distressed or because they do not know that what they are doing is wrong, then punishment for their actions will not be an adequate approach to the problem. Similarly, providing social or material rewards to a child who is engaging in positive action as part of a reciprocal exchange of favors will be detrimental: A large body of research on how intrinsic motivation for positive social actions is undermined through the use of rewards is relevant here (Deci & Ryan, 1985). Another implication of the domains-of-socialization approach has to do with terminology that is used to describe various aspects of parenting. "Effective parenting" is not a precise term. Similarly, "sensitive/responsive parenting" and "harsh parenting" are terms that are too vague and whose meaning is determined by the domain in which they are used. Contradictory findings are not infrequent in the socialization research literature, and the multiplicity of ways in which effective or responsive parenting are measured may help to account for some of these contradictory findings.

Evidence for Specificity in Different Domains of Socialization

Although, as noted, researchers not infrequently tend to use more general terms to describe aspects of parenting – such as "harsh," "positive," "sensitive," or "responsive" – there are examples of specific relations between specific features of parenting and socialization outcomes. The best-known finding is that, contrary to the frequent finding that reinforcement increases the occurrence of behavior it follows, one-year-olds whose mothers responded quickly to their cries during the first three months of life cried less than those whose mothers ignored their cries (Ainsworth, Blehar, Waters, & Wall, 1978). More recently, McElwain and Booth-LaForce (2006) reported that mothers' sensitivity to their baby's distress at 6 months, but not sensitivity to non-distress, predicted subsequent secure attachment (even though the two sensitivity measures were highly correlated). Leerkes, Blankson, and O'Brien (2009) showed that early responsiveness to distress contributed uniquely to children's subsequent positive social behavior, whereas early responsiveness to non-distress did not. Moreover, although maternal sensitivity to distress and non-distress are often positively associated, they have more unshared than shared variance, and are predicted by different antecedents (Leerkes, Weaver, & O'Brien, 2012). In a meta-analysis of the research on features of parenting and children's delinquency, Hoeve, Dubas, Eichelsheim, Van der Laan, Smeenk, and Gerris (2009) reported that parental rejection and hostility predicted delinquency to a much greater extent than did lack of warmth and support, another indication that there are different forms of harsh parenting and that they are differentially related to child outcomes.

I turn now to a summary of recent studies reported by my colleagues and me which have addressed the issue of specificity. Each of these studies is briefly described with respect to domain and outcome.

Empathy, Prosocial Behavior, Discussion of Distressing Events, and Regulation of Negative Affect

The first four studies looked at outcomes relevant to the protection domain: empathy, prosocial behavior, disclosure about distressing occurrences, and regulation of negative affect. In the first study, using a variety of questionnaire, interview, and observational measures, Davidov and Grusec (2006a) assessed parents' responsiveness to their 6- to 8-year-old children's distress as well as their warmth. Mothers' and fathers' responsiveness to distress, but not their warmth, predicted children's regulation of negative affect. Maternal responsiveness to distress also predicted children's empathy and prosocial responding. The second study was concerned with the extent to which parents and children indicated their inclination to disclose about distressing events and about rule transgressions. Chaparro and Grusec (2014) found that mothers who talked about events they found upsetting had children who were more inclined to talk about similar distress-producing events (e.g., having a disagreement with a friend). Maternal disclosure about distressing events did not, however, lead to more disclosure concerning rule transgressions (e.g., forgetting to return a borrowed book). The fact that mothers indicated that a primary reason for disclosing to their adolescents was to encourage the adolescents to disclose to them supports the notion of causal direction – that is, from mother to adolescent. In the next study, Saritas, Grusec, and Gençöz (2013) focused on the relation between mothers' and adolescents' regulation of negative affect. In accord with expectation they found that maternal hostility and rejection mediated between mother and adolescent regulation, but that maternal lack of warmth did not. Finally, in a study that focused on the group participation and control domains, Grusec, Goodnow, and Cohen (1997) interviewed adolescents and their parents about household chores. They found that children who did work around the house on a routine basis, without being asked, displayed more prosocial behavior (assessed by mothers' daily record-keeping of their children's helpfulness as well as their displays of concern and sympathy) than children who performed chores when asked – that is, in the control domain.

Willing Compliance

In a study involving children between 6 and 9 years of age, Davidov and Grusec (2006b) assessed mothers for their general willingness to cooperate with their children's wishes. Additionally, mothers were asked to predict how their children evaluated different forms of discipline, an indication of the quality of maternal functioning in the control domain. Mothers were instructed to ask their children to clean up a playroom and then leave the child alone so that compliance in the absence of surveillance could be measured. Mothers who were high in willingness to cooperate with their children's reasonable requests had children who cleaned willingly. In contrast, mothers' knowledge of their children's reactions in the control domain was not a predictor of willing compliance.

Compliance in the Control Domain

Davidov and Grusec (2006b) found that mothers who were conversant with their children's evaluations of different discipline strategies (reasoning, power assertion, reflection of feelings accompanied by statements concerning appropriate behavior) were better able to gain their children's compliance in the cleanup task after the child's initial refusal. (The successful mothers addressed the refusal, offering reasons for why the child should comply, whereas mothers who were unsuccessful ignored the child's complaints or walked out of the room.) In contrast to mothers who knew how their children would react to different discipline interactions, mothers who were cooperative with their children's wishes were no more or less successful in obtaining their children's compliance after an initial refusal.

Peer Acceptance and Regulation of Positive Affect

Although, as noted above, Davidov and Grusec (2006a) did not find that parental warmth was a predictor of children's empathy and prosocial behavior, they did find it predicted children's acceptance by their peers (for boys) and regulation of positive affect (being cheerful, being able to control excitement) for both boys and girls.

Overview

This set of studies comes together to support the idea that different child outcomes can be linked to different domains of parenting. Events in the protection domain are more likely to involve the ability to regulate distress and to respond to the distress of others. Events in the mutual reciprocity domain are linked to willing compliance as well as competence in peer actions, and those in the control domain to compliance in response to reasoning. One interesting additional finding has to do with the group participation domain and the link between routinized work around the house and general helpfulness (not just helpfulness elicited by sympathetic distress). This finding highlights the important point that not all prosocial behavior is motivated by sympathy for the plight of others, but that it can also emerge from being part of a social group and finding one's identity as a member of that group in showing concern for others.

Some General Principles Involved in Successful Socialization

Although I have argued that socialization occurs in different domains that involve different actions and mechanisms, there are some overarching features of good parenting that apply across domains. These core skills are required no matter the domain in which socialization agent and child are operating.

Autonomy Support

The first core skill is autonomy support. For socialization to be effective children must not feel that they are being pressured to behave in a particular way, but that they have chosen to do so (Koestner, Ryan, Bernieri, & Holt, 1984). Autonomy support is operationalized as providing meaningful rationales for a particular action, giving choice and opportunity for initiative-taking within the limits of acceptable action, and acknowledgment of feelings (Deci, Eghrari, Patrick, & Leone, 1994). This definition overlaps to some extent with Baumrind's (2012) definition of confrontive power assertion, particularly in its inclusion of choice and the use of reasoning in the promotion of prosocial behavior. But the importance of autonomy support has also been demonstrated in the teaching of academic and other skills that occurs in the guided learning domain where discussion, exchange, and concern with the child's level of understanding are central (Grolnick, 2003; Joussemet, Koestner, Lekes, & Landry, 2005). And in the domain of protection, comfort and encouragement for self-regulation of distress must be applied in a gentle, sensitive, and non-coercive manner. Central to parenting action in all these domains is perspective-taking or willingness to take on the child's internal frame of reference (Long, 1990). The inability of a parent to try to understand the child's point of view leads to insensitive parenting in any domain as well as increased parent–child conflict (Belsky, 1984; Dix, 1992).

Knowledge of the Child

Another core skill involves knowledge of a particular child and of how that child will react to different forms of socialization. This skill goes beyond taking the child's perspective in a specific situation to a broader and more inclusive knowledge of the child. No two children are alike and, although it is possible to offer some general guidelines for socialization, it is still essential to realize that how those guidelines are effectively applied depends to a considerable extent on characteristics of the child. Hence, there is a growing literature showing interactions between children's genetically mediated characteristics and features of parenting, as well as between their temperament, age, and gender and parenting.

Smetana et al. (2015) provide one example of the importance of individual differences among children in how they respond to socialization interventions. Thus, they report that young children are more likely to see strong forms of power assertion as fair and more issues as being under parental as opposed to personal jurisdiction than are older children. This age difference in how children construe socialization interventions, then, requires that parents rely on more subtle techniques, such as monitoring and guidance, as children mature (Pettit, 1997). Temperament is a moderator that has been extensively studied, with one general conclusion being that children with difficult temperaments (that is, who are emotionally labile and have difficulty adjusting to routines) are more adversely affected by problematic parenting than are children with less difficult temperaments. It has also been suggested that some children are especially sensitive to both positive and negative forms of parenting (Belsky & Pluess, 2009).

It is these interactions, then, that necessitate knowledge of how different children will react to a particular form of parenting: whether or not children feel they are being treated fairly or non-coercively; whether what the parent believes is comforting is, in fact, perceived as such; whether the parents' action is seen as a result of caring or of rejection; or whether a parent's angry outburst is perceived as an indication of how important the issue is to the parent or as another indication of the parent's loss of control.

Conclusion

In this chapter I have offered a way of conceptualizing the socialization process that tries to move away from general terms for successful parenting, such as sensitive, responsive, warm, accepting, and harshly or gently controlling. The argument is that a more fruitful way of studying socialization requires acknowledgment that children behave in antisocial ways for a variety of different reasons and that the reason determines the nature of appropriate parenting. Also needing to be acknowledged is that parents do not have just one relationship with their children but, rather, a variety of different kinds of relationships, and that each of these relationships and interactions within these relationships will lead to different outcomes for the child. Children frequently operate in more than one domain at a time. Parents tend to favor or to be more comfortable in one domain than another. As a result, they may function better in some domains than in others. These are all assertions that need to be tested. But, in the course of that testing, we should move forward in understanding the most important task parents have, which is equipping their children to function in the wider social world and to make that world a better place.

References

Ainsworth, M. D. S., Blehar, M. C., Waters, E., & Wall, S. (1978). *Patterns of attachment: A psychological study of the strange situation*. Hillsdale, NJ: Erlbaum.

Bandura, A. (1977). *Social learning theory*. Englewood Cliffs, NJ: Prentice Hall.

Bandura, A., & Walters, R. H. (1963). *Social learning theory and personality development*. New York, NY: Holt, Rinehart, & Winston.

Barber, B. K. (Ed.) (2002). *Intrusive parenting: How psychological control affects children and adolescents*. Washington, DC: American Psychological Association.

Baumrind, D. (1967). Child care practices anteceding three patterns of preschool behavior. *Genetic Psychology Monographs*, *73*, 43–88.

Baumrind, D. (1971). Current patterns of parental authority. *Developmental Psychology, 4*, 1–103.

Baumrind, D. (2012). Differentiating between confrontive and coercive kinds of parental power-assertive disciplinary practices. *Human Development, 55*, 35–51.

Baumrind, D., Larzelere, R. E., & Owens, E. B. (2010). Effects of preschool parents' power assertive patterns and practices on adolescent development. *Parenting: Science and Practice, 10*, 157–201.

Bell, R. Q. (1968). A reinterpretation of the direction of effects in studies of socialization. *Psychological Review, 75*, 81–95.

Belsky, J. (1984). The determinants of parenting: A process model. *Child Development, 55*, 83–96.

Belsky, J., & Pluess, M. (2009). Beyond diathesis stress: Differential susceptibility to environmental influences. *Psychological Bulletin, 135*, 885–908.

Berry, J. W. (2015). Acculturation. In J. E. Grusec, & P. D. Hastings (Eds.), *Handbook of socialization*, 2nd edn. New York, Guilford Press.

Bowlby, J. (1969). *Attachment and loss (Vol. I. Attachment)*. New York, NY: Basic Books.

Bretherton, I., Golby, B., & Cho, E. (1997). Attachment and the transmission of values. In J. E. Grusec & L.Kuczynski, L. (Eds.), *Parenting and children's internalization of values: A handbook of contemporary theory* (pp. 103–134). New York, NY: Wiley.

Bugental, D. B. (2000). Acquisition of the algorithms of social life: A domain-based approach. *Psychological Bulletin, 26*, 187–209.

Bugental, D. B., & Goodnow, J. G. (1998). Socialization processes. In N. Eisenberg (Ed.), *Handbook of child psychology: Vol. 3. Social, emotional, and personality development*, 5th edn (pp. 389–462). New York, NY: Wiley.

Bugental, D. B., & Grusec, J. E. (2006). Socialization processes. In N. Eisenberg (Ed.), *Handbook of child psychology: Vol. 3. Social, emotional, and personality development*, 6th edn *(pp. 366–428)*. Hoboken, NJ: Wiley.

Chaparro, M. P., & Grusec, J. E. (2014). Parent and adolescent intentions to disclose and links to positive social behavior. *Journal of Family Psychology, 29*, 49–58.

Criss, M. M., Shaw, D. S., & Ingoldsby, E. M. (2003). Mother-son positive synchrony in middle childhood: Relation to antisocial behavior. *Social Development, 12*, 379–400.

Darling, N., & Steinberg, L. (1993). Parenting style as context: An integrative model. *Psychological Bulletin, 113*, 487–496.

Davidov, M., & Grusec, J. E. (2006a). Untangling the links of parental responsiveness to distress and warmth to child outcomes. *Child Development, 77*, 44–58.

Davidov, M., & Grusec, J. E. (2006b). Multiple pathways to compliance: Mothers' willingness to cooperate and knowledge of children's reactions to discipline. *Journal of Family Psychology, 20*, 705–708.

Deater-Deckard, K., & Petrill, S. A. (2004). Parent–child dyadic mutuality and child behavior problems: An investigation of gene–environment processes. *Journal of Child Psychology and Psychiatry, 45*, 1171–1179.

Deci, E. L., Eghrari, H., Patrick, B. C., & Leone, D. R. (1994). Facilitating internalization: The self-determination theory perspective. *Journal of Personality, 62*, 119–142.

Deci, E. L., & Ryan, R. M. (1985). *Intrinsic motivation and self-determination in human behavior*. New York, NY: Plenum Press.

Dix, T. (1992). Parenting on behalf of the child: Empathic goals in the regulation of responsive parenting. In I. E. Sigel, A. V. McGillicuddy-DeLisi, & J. J. Goodnow

(Eds.), *Parental belief systems: the psychological consequences for children* (2nd edn., pp. 319–346). Hillsdale, NJ: Erlbaum.

Gauvain, M., & Perez, S. M. (2015). The socialization of cognition. In J. E. Grusec & P. D. Hastings (Eds.), *Handbook of Socialization*. 2nd edn. New York, NY: Guilford Press.

Gershoff, E. T. (2002). Corporal punishment by parents and associated child behaviors and experiences: A meta-analytic and theoretical review. *Psychological Bulletin, 128*, 539–579.

Grolnick, W. (2003). *The psychology of parental control: How well-meant parenting backfires*. Mahwah, NJ: Erlbaum.

Grusec, J. E. (1992). Social learning theory and developmental psychology: The legacy of Robert Sears and Albert Bandura. *Developmental Psychology, 28*, 776–786.

Grusec, J. E., & Davidov, M. (2007). Socialization in the family: The roles of parents. In J. E. Grusec & P. D. Hastings (Eds.). *Handbook of socialization*. New York, NY: Guilford Press (pp. 284–308).

Grusec, J. E., & Davidov, M. (2010). Integrating different perspectives on socialization theory and research: A domain-specific approach. *Child Development, 81*, 687–709.

Grusec, J. E., & Goodnow, J. J. (1994). Impact of parental discipline methods on the child's internalization of values: A reconceptualization of current points of view. *Developmental Psychology, 30*(1), 4–19.

Grusec, J. E., Goodnow, J. J., & Cohen, L. (1997) Household work and the development of children's concern for others. *Developmental Psychology, 32*, 999–1007.

Haden, C. A., Ornstein, P. A., Eckerman, C. O., & Didow, S. M. (2001). Mother-child conversational interactions as events unfold: Linkages to subsequent remembering. *Child Development, 72*, 1016–1031.

Hoeve, M., Dubas, J. S., Eichelsheim, V. I., Van der Laan, P. H., Smeenk, W., & Gerris, J. R. (2009). The relationship between parenting and delinquency: A meta-analysis. *Journal of Abnormal Child Psychology, 37*, 749–775.

Hoffman, M. L. (1970). Moral development. In P. H. Mussen (Ed.), *Carmichael's manual of child psychology* (Vol. *2*, pp. 261–360). New York, NY: Wiley.

Joussemet, M., Koestner, R., Lekes, N., & Landry, R. (2005). A longitudinal study of the relationship of maternal autonomy support to children's adjustment and achievement in school. *Journal of Personality, 73*, 1215–1235.

Kagan, J. (1982). The emergence of self. *Journal of Child Psychology and Psychiatry, 23*, 363–381.

Kerns, K. A., Aspelmeier, J. E., Gentzler, A. L., & Grabill, C. M. (2001). Parent–child attachment and monitoring in middle childhood. *Journal of Family Psychology, 15*, 69–81.

Kochanska, G., Aksan, N., Knaack, A., & Rhines, H. M. (2004). Maternal parenting and children's conscience: Early security as moderator. *Child Development, 75*, 1229–1242.

Koestner, R., Ryan, R. M., Bernieri, F., & Holt, K. (1984). Setting limits on children's behavior: The differential effects of controlling vs. informational styles on intrinsic motivation and creativity. *Journal of Personality, 52*, 233–248.

Kuczynski, L. & DeMol, J. (2015). Dialectical models of socialization. In W. F. Overton & P. C. M. Molenaar (Eds.). *Theory and method. Vol. 1. Handbook of child psychology and developmental science*. 7th edn. Hoboken, NJ: Wiley

Laible, D., Thompson, R. A., & Froimson, J. (2015). Early socialization. The influence of close relationships. In J. E. Grusec, & P. D. Hastings (Eds.), *Handbook of socialization*. 2nd edn. New York, NY: Guilford Press.

Lansford, J. E., Malone, P. S., Dodge, K. A., Chang, L., Chaudhary, N., Tapanya, S., . . . & Deater-Deckard, K. (2010). Children's perceptions of maternal hostility as a mediator of the link between discipline and children's adjustment in four countries. *International Journal of Behavioral Development*, *34*, 452–461.

Leerkes, E. M., Blankson, A. N., & O'Brien, M. (2009). Differential effects of maternal sensitivity to infant distress and nondistress on social-emotional functioning. *Child Development*, *80*, 762–775.

Leerkes, E. M., Weaver, J. M., & O'Brien, M. (2012). Differentiating maternal sensitivity to infant distress and non-distress. *Parenting: Science and Practice*, *12*, 175–184.

Lindsey, E. W., Cremeens, P. R., & Caldera, Y. M. (2010). Mother-child and father-child mutuality in two contexts: Consequences for young children's peer relationships. *Infant and Child Development*, *19*, 142–160.

Long, E. C. (1990). Measuring dyadic perspective-taking: Two scales for assessing perspective-taking in marriage and similar dyads. *Educational and Psychological Measurement*, *50*, 91–103.

McElwain, N. L., & Booth-LaForce, C. (2006). Maternal sensitivity to infant distress and nondistress as predictors of infant-mother attachment security. *Journal of Family Psychology*, *20*, 247.

Parpal, M., & Maccoby, E. E. (1985). Maternal responsiveness and subsequent child compliance. *Child Development*, *56*, 1326–1334.

Pettit, G. S. (1997). The developmental course of violence and aggression: Mechanisms of family and peer influence. *Psychiatric Clinics of North America*, *20*, 283–299.

Puntambekar, S., & Hubscher, R. (2005). Tools for scaffolding students in a complex learning environment: What have we gained and what have we missed? *Educational psychologist*, *40*, 1–12.

Rogoff, B., Moore, L. C., Correa-Chavez, M., & Dexter, A. L. (2015). Children develop cultural repertoires through engaging in everyday routines and practices. In J. E. Grusec & P. D. Hastings (Eds.), *Handbook of socialization*, 2nd edn. New York, NY: Guilford Press.

Saritas, D., Grusec, J. E., & Gençöz, T. (2013). Warm and harsh parenting as mediators of the relation between maternal and adolescent emotion regulation. *Journal of Adolescence*, *36*, 1093–1101.

Schwartz, S. H., & Boehnke, K. (2004). Evaluating the structure of human values with confirmatory factor analysis. *Journal of Research in Personality*, *38*, 230–255.

Sears, R. R., Maccoby, E. E., & Levin, H. (1957). *Patterns of child rearing*. New York, NY: Row-Peterson.

Sheldon, K. M., Ryan, R. M., Deci, E. L., & Kasser, T. (2004). The independent effects of goal contents and motives on well-being: It's both what you pursue and why you pursue it. *Personality and Social Psychology Bulletin*, *30*, 475–486.

Smetana, J. G. (2011). *Adolescents, families, and social development: How teens construct their worlds*. West Sussex, England: Wiley-Blackwell.

Smetana, J., Robinson, J., & Rote, W. (2015). *Socialization in adolescence*. In J. E. Grusec & P. D. Hastings (Eds.), *Handbook of socialization*. 2nd edn. New York, NY: Guilford Press.

Trevarthen, C., Kokkinski, T., & Flamenghi, G. A., Jr. (1999). What infants' imitations communicate: With mothers, with fathers and with peers. In J. Nadel & G. Butterworth (Eds.). *Imitation in infancy: Cambridge studies in cognitive perceptual development* (pp. 127–185). New York, NY: Cambridge University Press.

Turiel, E. (1983). *The development of social knowledge: Morality and convention.* Cambridge, UK: Cambridge University Press.

Vygotsky, L. S. (1978). *Mind in society: The development of higher psychological processes.* Cambridge, MA: Harvard University Press.

Walker, L. J., Hennig, K. H., & Krettenauer, T. (2000). Parent and peer contexts for children's moral reasoning development. *Child Development, 71*, 1033–1048.

Wood, D., Bruner, J. S., & Ross, G. (1976). The role of tutoring in problem solving. *Journal of Child Psychology and Psychiatry, 17*, 89–100.

11 Mother–Child Conversations about Children's Moral Wrongdoing: A Constructivist Perspective on Moral Socialization

Cecilia Wainryb and Holly Recchia

Introduction

Research from a constructivist perspective has traditionally underscored children's active role in the process of developing moral understandings, but has had little to say about parents' contributions to this process. For example, research has shown that, starting at a young age, children consider and reflect on the consequences of simple exchanges involving sharing, helping, everyday misdeeds, and conflicts, and construct their own understandings of these sociomoral events (e.g., Eisenberg, Spinrad, & Sadovsky, 2006; Smetana, 2013). Research has also shown that in constructing their own understandings, children often face difficulties as they wrestle with the opacity of others' beliefs, with incompatible goals, or with the unintended or unforeseeable consequences of their own actions (e.g., Lagattuta, 2005; Wainryb & Brehl, 2006). But in spite of the abundant evidence concerning the complexities of moral life and children's struggles to balance competing and conflicting considerations, constructivist research has been largely silent about the types of scaffolding that parents may provide to their children along the way.

The reticence to examine parents' involvement in the process may be due to early claims (e.g., Piaget, 1932) that the hierarchical nature of the parent–child relationship does not support, but rather constrains, children's moral development; or perhaps it ensues from the longstanding assumption that the core of the moral development process lies in children's own evolving reflections about their experiences. In any case, such inattention to how parents may contribute to their children's moral development is both puzzling and untenable given that most parents seem to be deeply concerned about their children becoming good people and actively engage in guiding, supporting, and nurturing them. From our perspective, although parents are unlikely to be the only people who may have significant impact on the process of moral development, they are uniquely important by virtue of their role-related responsibility to teach their children right from wrong, their influential emotional bond, and their stable and ubiquitous presence in their children's lives. Thus, in this chapter we rely on a body of conversations that children (ages 7–16) and their mothers had about occasions when children had hurt a friend or sibling to outline a constructivist perspective on the moral socialization process. We examine these conversations to call attention to the multiple ways in which children frame and make sense of their hurtful actions; we also explore the more and less attuned manners in which mothers respond to their children's framings, alternatively soliciting, elaborating, affirming, challenging, or ignoring their children's meanings, and the more and less accepting ways in which children interact with their mothers' suggestions and contributions. More generally, we discuss how these bidirectional and co-regulated conversations may translate into the construction and elaboration of fresh moral understandings, thereby providing a window into the process of moral socialization in action.

The Bidirectionality of the Moral Socialization Process

In stressing the significance of parent–child conversations for moral development we are not suggesting that parents transmit their views on right and wrong to their children, who take it all in and adopt it wholesale. In the past, researchers understood the socialization process as largely unidirectional and deterministic; moral internalization was seen as stemming primarily from parents' transmission of values through discipline and other parenting practices, with the expected outcome being compliance. But contemporary approaches view parental influence in less unidirectional terms, though there is substantial diversity in the ways in which bidirectionality is conceptualized (e.g., Kochanska, Coy, & Murray, 2001; Kuczynski & Parkin, 2006).

In our view (see also Turiel, 2010), adopting a constructivist perspective on the moral socialization process requires thinking of socialization as a bidirectional process that implicates mutual influences and accommodations as well as reflection and meaning-making. As parents and children engage in this process, they may assert their own views and goals while also striving to make sense of the other's behaviors and perspectives; and they may adopt some aspects of the other's inputs and change their minds accordingly, but may also resist or challenge suggestions that violate their own understandings.

In spite of its bidirectionality, the parent–child relationship is not symmetrical; by virtue of their greater resources, knowledge, and authority, parents are better positioned to constrain children's behaviors than children are to compel their parents. And yet, both parents and children bring to bear on their interactions multiple goals that go beyond enforcing or resisting power. Parents may want to understand their children and may want their children to understand them; they may want to foster in their children a sense of autonomy and a sense of wellbeing; and they may desire to preserve their warm relationship with their children for the relationship's sake and because doing so would facilitate meeting other long-term objectives. As these and other parental goals come into play in parent–child exchanges about morally laden issues, they tend to moderate parental demands for compliance, affording children greater scope for negotiation (Kuczynski & Parkin, 2006). Children, on their part, may be motivated by more than a desire to evade parental demands. Children may enter these exchanges with a sincere trust in their parents' motivations and a desire to figure out how to meet their parents' demands without entirely giving up their own goals. They may also be driven by a genuine interest in gaining new insights about their own experiences, or by a desire to have their parents understand their point of view.

Therefore, conflicts that arise in the moral socialization process do not merely reflect children's failure to comply; rather, they are inevitable elements of interactions among people with complex goals and understandings, and can often (though not always) be understood and tolerated as such by both parties. Further, because this process is embedded within an ongoing, long-lasting, and evolving relationship, children's and parents' interpretations of what the other person says, wants, or demands are rarely limited to the immediate contingencies created in any given interaction. Rather, parents' and children's sense-making of the other's perspectives and behaviors is often informed by understandings and expectations each has developed based on their relational history; this, in turn, frequently (though not always) creates a deeper pool of shared experience within which disagreements are grasped and negotiated. Therefore, what is often at stake in moral socialization exchanges is not merely compliance understood as an exact match between the parent's demands and the child's behavior, but the co-regulated and non-deterministic construction of new understandings that may encompass some aspects of the give-and-take and negotiation between parents and children, including concessions, compromises, and resistances. Ultimately, the moral socialization process thus conceived incorporates the contributions and mutual adaptations of both parents and children, and may result in changed or new ideas and commitments among children as well as their parents.

Parent–Child Conversations as Unique Contexts for Moral Socialization

To date, most research on the contributions of parents to children's moral learning has focused on the impact of discipline and parenting strategies, and the quality of the parent–child relationship. Findings highlighted the ineffectiveness of power assertion and the effectiveness of strategies involving reasoning and induction, and underscored the facilitative role of warm and supportive relationships (Eisenberg et al., 2006; Grusec & Davidov, 2006; Thompson, Meyer, & McGinley, 2006). In comparison to the literature examining the strategies that parents use to promote their children's moral growth, researchers have paid relatively little attention to the sorts of conversations that parents and children actually have about morally laden events.

But conversations that parents and children have about moral experiences not only illustrate, but also constitute the critical features of the moral socialization process as we have defined it – its bidirectional quality, the prevalence of interpretations and meaning-making, the coexistence of multiple goals and perspectives, and its embeddedness within a relational context. Further, conversations are an essential vehicle through which the business of moral socialization is transacted. When children struggle to make sense of upsetting fights, admit to their own transgressions, or boast about their own good deeds, they tend to do that in the course of conversations. When parents teach their children about rules, talk to them about consequences of varied actions, scold them for their misdeeds, or praise them for their kindness, much of that also happens in and via conversations.

Recently, researchers began exploring moral socialization processes through the lens of parent–child conversations (Wainryb & Recchia, 2014b), but have largely used those conversations as a window into the forms and contents of the parents' activities. Collectively, this research has shown that parent–child conversations serve as an important platform from which parents convey moral messages to children, and that parents use diverse strategies during conversations to foster desired outcomes. They may discuss the effect of children's actions on others to induce empathy and psychological understanding; they may help children explore their own perspectives of why events happened; they may express feelings of disappointment and anger to induce shame or guilt; they may evaluate the child's actions; they may suggest possible paths for restitution or improved behavior in the future; and they may describe expectations or attempt to teach specific moral lessons. Research has also shown that the warmth and elaborative style of parents, as well as the strategies they deploy during their conversations with their children, are often associated with children's moral behavior and moral understanding. As a whole, this research has yielded a rich picture of how parental goals and practices get played out in actual conversations with their children, and has contributed to a better understanding of what processes such as induction, power assertion, love withdrawal, or shaming look like in action.

Nevertheless, the bulk of research on parent–child conversations about morally laden experiences has paid little attention to children's contributions to the conversations. Indeed, descriptions and prescriptions concerning parental styles and strategies and their effects on children have often been articulated without concomitant attention to children's contributions to the conversations; parental contributions have been depicted as though they work on their own, rather than in the context of and in response to specific meanings made by children. This is not to say that researchers simplistically assumed that conversations consist of parents teaching children moral lessons or that children are passive recipients of such lessons. In fact, researchers have explicitly acknowledged that children's contributions to conversations remain an important unexplored question and have speculated that children may shape the content and tone of conversations by switching topics, ignoring parents' requests for information, or challenging parents' interpretations (Callanan, Valle, Luce, & Rigney, 2014; Laible & Murphy, 2014). In some studies, the conversations between young children and their mothers have been examined for evidence of the extent to which children talk about moral dimensions of their everyday lives (e.g., Dunn & Hughes, 2014); yet, for the most part, this research served as a basis for analyzing individual differences in children's language use (e.g., Wright & Bartsch, 2008), rather than as a way to examine the give-and-take between children and their parents. With few exceptions (e.g., Miller, 2014; Sterponi, 2014), the simultaneous consideration of parents' and children's bidirectional contributions and mutual adaptations in morally laden conversations remains a largely neglected aspect of socialization research (see also Kuczynski & Parkin, 2006).

In our work, we focused on conversations precisely because conversations instantiate the bidirectional nature of the process. Conversations engender a shared psychological space where the topics and opinions being discussed may evolve and change with contributions from the two parties. Another way to put this is that conversations are much more than an exchange of information. As people talk with one another, they don't just swap facts: they may learn new facts, but they may also begin to view these facts in a new light, draw new conclusions from them, and engage in new trains of thought. This is likely to be especially significant in conversations between parents and children about morally laden issues.

Though parents are not arbiters of moral truth, by virtue of their continuous involvement in children's lives they often have unique knowledge concerning where "a story begins"; parents often know about circumstances preceding whatever incident they and their child are discussing. This "insider" knowledge may render them particularly valuable when helping their child consider, or reconsider, the facts and meanings surrounding complex events. Parents also know their children much better than most and they can, and often do, draw on this knowledge when discussing events with their child. Even if in such contexts parents at times assume a didactic tone, most parents don't *just* lecture, or at least they don't just lecture and then exit the stage. Parents, but also children, may at times enter into conversations with a goal in mind – a mother may want her son to understand that what he did was wrong, or may want him to comply with an expectation; a child may want to explain what made him angry, or may want to mitigate his responsibility for some wrong-doing. But it is often the case that goals and understandings evolve in the course of conversation. As conversations unfold, with each partner explaining, listening, arguing, elaborating, cajoling, insisting, and resisting, a new story is created and new knowledge is constructed. In these ways, conversations about morally laden experiences might create the space for a bidirectional process whereby the child's understandings are expanded and changed in ways that may integrate, albeit imperfectly, the parent's ideas and viewpoints.

But conversations are not only about the contents being transacted and constructed. When discussing morally laden experiences, including who did what to whom, why, what it felt like, what it meant, and whether it was right or wrong, a variety of emotions might also emerge. The sharing of emotion in conversation helps children to learn how to interpret and regulate their own emotional experience (Fivush, 2007; Thompson, 2010); conversations can thus serve to contain emotions that might otherwise be overwhelming. In this regard, it matters that these conversational exchanges are embedded within a close relationship. Especially in relationships characterized by warmth and trust, conversations with parents may provide an inimitable milieu for children to safely explore the difficult implications of their morally laden experiences, including uncertainties and regrets. When children discuss sensitive topics, parents may certainly challenge children's ideas or question their choices. In fact, by virtue of their special role, parents are more likely than other people to "tell it like they see it," even if the message is one that children will not be pleased to hear. Yet inasmuch as these conversations occur within a climate of positive regard, children receive powerful reassurance that they are accepted despite having done the wrong thing or having been a "bad person." Similarly, children also learn that they can disagree with their parents' stances on morally laden topics without risking the relationship. As a consequence, conversations with parents may provide a unique context for children to develop their own views and a sense of their own moral agency (Komolova & Wainryb, 2011).

The Importance of Conversations About Children's Own Moral Transgressions

Our decision to focus on the conversations that mothers and their children have about children's moral transgressions has to do with the centrality of those experiences for children's moral growth. The study of moral development has traditionally focused on children's moral concepts and judgments, with contemporary research showing that even young children know that it is wrong to hurt others (Smetana, 2013). Still, in the course of their everyday life, all children occasionally engage in behaviors that cause harm to others, such as hitting a sibling, excluding a peer from a game, or betraying a secret. Though these occasions may be thought of as failures in moral socialization, harm is an intrinsic part of interpersonal interactions and an inevitable dimension of moral life (Wainryb, Brehl, Matwin, 2005; Wainryb & Pasupathi, 2015). Consequently, being a moral person involves not only knowing right from wrong and trying to do the right thing, but also acknowledging one's capacity for harm and grappling with those instances when one has harmed another. And it is precisely those occasions when children's actions result in harm to others that may pose challenges to children's understandings of themselves as moral people, thus creating meaningful opportunities for moral growth.

It is hard to determine the extent to which children grapple with these situations on their own. Still, it is quite likely that children's ability to fully make sense of these experiences in ways that promote their understandings of their actions and the construction of a sense of themselves as moral people does not develop in a vacuum but is, rather, scaffolded by, and benefits from, conversations with other people. In some cases, children may choose to talk about these experiences to others, spontaneously sharing with friends or parents, but children are also habitually prompted to account for their wrongdoing.

As children wrestle with, and talk to their mothers (or others) about, how and why they hurt someone despite knowing that causing harm is wrong, they are likely to consider (or be encouraged or directed to consider) not only what they did, but also what they wanted, thought, and felt during that event. By connecting their own actions to psychological aspects of their experiences, children might come to understand their wrongdoing as being related to their own desires, beliefs, and emotions, and in so doing construct a sense of their own *moral agency* (Pasupathi & Wainryb, 2010a; Recchia & Wainryb, 2014; Wainryb et al., 2005). Relating their actions to what they thought, felt, or intended does not absolve children of responsibility or transform their hurtful actions into acceptable ones; rather, it helps children recognize that harm-doing can arise from their desires to harm others or their failures at managing their own anger, fear, or jealousy, but may also stem from their self-oriented or pro-social goals, from their imperfect attempts to balance their own and others' needs, or from their limited grasp of others' perspectives. Such understandings can help to contain the potentially negative impact of these experiences on children's broader self-views, by bracketing every instance of wrongdoing within a particular context, with its own motivations and reasons. This helps children to avoid constructing an essentialized understanding of themselves as bad or immoral people. In turn, this permits children to acknowledge the pain they caused and to recognize their potential for reparative action and their ability to behave differently in the future. Thus, by reflecting on their own moral agency in the context of particular experiences, children can ultimately come to understand themselves as imperfect but fundamentally moral people who are capable of growing and learning from their actions (Pasupathi & Wainryb, 2010a; Recchia & Wainryb, 2014).

Given the variety of children's harmful encounters and the complexity of internal and external factors bearing on the meanings of their actions, the task for mothers and children to jointly construct understandings of responsibility in their conversations about these events is far from straightforward. Much of the moral socialization literature might lead us to assume that, in conversations about moral transgressions, mothers would largely focus on issues of right and wrong and underscore the negative consequences of the child's actions for others. This literature might also suggest that, ideally, children would tend to internalize these suggestions and thus avoid engaging in similarly hurtful actions in the future due to an improved understanding of the effects of their actions on others. Our data, however, suggest that this is an oversimplification of what actually occurs in reflective conversations about children's past transgressions.

In the following sections, we use examples from our data to show how conversations about hurting others are an important vehicle whereby children, with their mothers' help and support, construct and adapt their understanding of their own transgressions. We focus on a corpus of conversations collected in a sample of approximately 100 mother–child dyads, evenly divided into three groups on the basis of the child's age (7, 11, or 16 years). Each child nominated events when he/she hurt or upset a friend and a younger sibling (see Recchia, Wainryb, Pasupathi, 2013), and subsequently each mother–child dyad was instructed to "talk about what [child] did, try to figure out everything that happened around it, and also see if there is something to be learned from it." In these conversations, children represented their experiences in varied ways (e.g., taking more or less responsibility for their actions; demonstrating more or less awareness of the effects of their actions on others) that often had a crucial impact on the direction that the conversations would ultimately take. In turn, mothers contributed to these conversations in ways that reflected a variety of goals. Often, mothers were responsive to children's particular ways of constructing their experiences, but other conversations were less well-coordinated. Last, we discuss how children responded to mothers' suggestions, sometimes accepting or elaborating on them, and sometimes resisting them. We explain how varied types of exchanges provide distinct types of opportunities for children to further their understandings of their experiences.

The Conversations: Children Frame Their Transgressions in Varied Ways, and Mothers Are Often Responsive to Children's Framings

By design, conversations in our dataset were initiated by the children. That is, each conversation invariably began with the child providing an account of his/her hurtful behavior. As such, the child's framing of his/her experience in the initial telling often served to guide the direction that the conversation would take. These framings could vary along multiple dimensions. For example, children positioned themselves in heterogeneous ways with respect to the psychological experience of hurting others (i.e., the cognitions, motivations, and emotions accounting for their harmful actions). In some cases, children described lashing out at others in angry or even calculated ways. However, more commonly, children described engaging in intentional behaviors that resulted in harm to others, but for which the harm itself was clearly not intended. In some situations, children described engaging in actions while knowing or suspecting that their behaviors would result in harm to others, due to imperfect attempts to balance their own needs and the needs of others (e.g., ignoring a friend's phone calls in order to spend time with a different person). Children also described unanticipated harms resulting from their own and others' divergent beliefs or understandings of specific situations. For example, children described peers reacting badly to insensitive comments (e.g., saying "Do I look fat in this?" to an overweight friend) or due to negative interpretations of more benign behaviors (e.g., a friend feeling slighted because the child chose to sit with another group at lunch).

There are at least three factors that might account for such variations in children's ways of narrating their transgressions. First, it is plausible that there are individual differences in children's ways of constructing meanings about their transgressions (e.g., describing more or less guilt/remorse, regardless of the circumstances), but our study was not designed to assess sources of individual variation. Second, children's constructions of meanings about their transgressions may also vary markedly across contexts. For instance, children's hurtful behaviors against their sibling are often described as more ruthless than those committed against friends (Recchia et al., 2013), and children's experiences of excluding others differ markedly from other types of hurtful behavior (Wainryb, Komolova, & Brehl, 2014). Third, children's constructions of meanings change substantively with age, as youth develop more sophisticated understandings of their social and psychological worlds. For instance, from early childhood to adolescence, youth demonstrate increases in their ability to recognize and coordinate their own and others' psychological perspectives (Pasupathi & Wainryb, 2010b; Wainryb & Brehl, 2006); and in adolescence, youth continue to struggle to grasp the broader implications of their actions for their understandings of themselves and their relationships (Hardy & Carlo, 2011; McLean & Pasupathi, 2012).

Importantly, our data suggest that mothers' contributions to conversations about children's transgressions are often sensitive to both developmental and contextual sources of variation in children's constructions of meanings about their experiences. To illustrate some of these patterns, below is an excerpt from a conversation between 7-year-old Walter and his mother (all names are pseudonyms), concerning an experience when Walter hurt a friend:

CHILD: Um, we were just playing a game on the tramp then we got in a fight and I keep kicking her and slamming her face to the ground . . . on the tramp, and she kicked me hard and I kicked her hard then she start crying [. . .]

MOTHER: Do you remember why you started fighting?

CHILD: No, but I remember when we fighted though.

MOTHER: You remember when you fought, but you don't remember what the fight was about?

CHILD: Like, we like messed up the game or something.

MOTHER: You were playing a game and it got messed up?

CHILD: Yeah

MOTHER: And you started hurting her?

CHILD: Yeah then she started hurting me.

MOTHER: Okay, tell me first what you did to her. (pause) And then I'll ask what she did to you.

CHILD: Um at first I slammed her head in the ground, then I kicked her really hard. Then she kicked me really hard.

MOTHER: (pause) You slammed her head into the tramp and kicked her?

CHILD: (smiles bashfully) Yeah . . .

MOTHER: You, well, why – Do you think that's okay?

CHILD: No! (says emphatically)

MOTHER: It's not?

CHILD: Uh uh. (shakes head)

MOTHER: Then why do you think you did it?

CHILD: She was hurting me?

MOTHER: But you said that you hurt her first, and then she hurt you.

CHILD: I don't know who like hurt us first, but we . . . but I know that we got in a fight.

MOTHER: So what do you think you could do next time? Cause you know it's not right, right? To hurt people?

CHILD: Yeah.

MOTHER: So what do you think you could do, to make sure you don't do that?

CHILD: Um, I could just tell her that it doesn't care, if we mess up the game, we could just start it over.

MOTHER: That'd be a good idea. But what if you're so so so mad, and she did something so wrong to you. Not hurt you, but what if she did something that made you so so mad? Would you be able to say, "It doesn't matter"? What if you're so so mad?

CHILD: I'd just say . . . it, doesn't care but I won't still fight you. I won't um, be mean, still.

MOTHER: Well sometimes when you get so so mad, and it's not okay what she did, I would just say, I would tell her that it made you mad and that your feelings were hurt, and then I'd say, "I need to go home for a little while." And then, when you're ready, when you're not so mad anymore – cause sometimes if you go away, like sometimes, have you done that when you go into your room? Like when you're really mad at me and dad and you go into your room, and you're there for a little while and then when you come out you're not as mad anymore right?

With respect to Walter's initial narration of the event, a number of features stand out. First, he largely fails to consider the psychological dimensions of his hurtful behavior: that is, he makes no reference to his own goals, thoughts, or feelings that might account for his actions. This type of pattern is particularly likely to characterize young children's descriptions of their transgressive behaviors, given their social-cognitive limitations and resulting tendencies to omit "landscapes of consciousness" from their narrative accounts (Pasupathi & Wainryb, 2010b; Wainryb et al., 2005). Perhaps partly as a result of this omission, Walter's behavior comes across as fairly ruthless, especially in light of the maximizing language he uses to describe his actions (e.g., "slamming" her face; kicking her "hard"). Thus, it is not surprising that his mother notes the negative moral implications of his actions ("do you think that's okay?"; "you know it's not right to hurt people"), albeit in a way that acknowledges Walter's existing moral capacities. In other words, Walter's mother does not appear to be trying to teach her son about moral concepts per se, but, rather, evoking and highlighting his own belief that it is wrong to hurt others. She also accompanies this judgment with a number of other developmentally appropriate contributions that may serve to further Walter's sense of his own moral agency. Specifically, one central line of the mother's inquiry concerns the reasons for Walter's behavior, helping him to recognize the situational and emotional dimensions of the event that might account for his harmful actions. She also goes on to help him consider strategies for how he might prevent similar instances from occurring in the future (i.e., when his emotions become overwhelming). Thus, although this conversation is characterized by a predominantly shared sense, between mother and son, of the son's wrongdoing, Walter is supported in his capacity to reflect on his goals and emotions that explain his actions, as well as provided with some tools to contain his aggressive impulses.

As we have noted above, much of the moral socialization literature might lead us to assume that parent–child conversations about moral transgressions would largely emphasize the child's wrongdoing. However, as discussed elsewhere (Recchia & Wainryb, 2014; Recchia, Wainryb, Bourne, & Pasupathi, 2014), our data also make clear that is not the only type of parenting goal that guides these discussions. Even in the conversation above, it is evident that Walter's mother is not *only* invested in noting her son's wrongdoing, but also in exploring her child's legitimate motives for his behavior, his positive moral qualities, and his capacity to behave differently in the future. Even more, it is sometimes the case that mothers in fact *minimize* their child's blameworthiness or responsibility for their morally laden actions – again, often in response to children's framing of events. Consider the following conversation between 7-year-old Natalie and her mother:

CHILD: What happened with me and Kelly and Joleen was we were going to the park last year and they were talking about their "days" [...] when like they're at school and they don't allow anyone else to play with them. [...] And I said "I don't think that is appropriate" and that really hurt them. [...] I said "excuse me, but I think that talking about 'days' is not okay with – is just not okay with me" [...] I just got really angry and they said "Well if you don't like our 'days' then maybe you should just like move to a different school."

MOTHER: They said that?

CHILD: Yeah

MOTHER: So, why don't you just go off and find another friend? Do something else? Do something different.

CHILD: A lot of times I don't think about that.

MOTHER: Well, you need to. You need to think outside the box about all the different things that you could be doing, instead of wasting your time with people who are just trying to bug you and hurt your feelings. There's 300 kids at that school. That gives you 300 opportunities to hang out with somebody else that appreciates you. Right? And that's what life's about, is different experiences and doing different things and learning about different people. Right?

In her initial account, Natalie describes her own comment to Kelly and Joleen as being very hurtful. However, she also clearly negatively evaluates her friends' exclusionary behavior ("Talking about 'days' ... is just not okay with me"), acknowledges her anger at the injustice ("I just got really angry"), and notes her friends' insensitive response to her criticism ("they said ... maybe you should just like move to a different school"). Therefore, it is perhaps unsurprising that her mother's response to this account implicitly underscores the acceptability of Natalie's resistance to her friends' actions, even though it resulted in their hurt feelings. That is, Natalie's mother helps her to coordinate her evaluation of her own behavior with the broader relational context in which it is occurring. More specifically, she emphasizes the role that Natalie's friends played in causing the conflict, and suggests that Natalie should seek out relationships with people who are more appreciative of her company.

As argued elsewhere, it is understandable that mothers occasionally respond to their children's acts of harm by minimizing their blameworthiness, as they wish to protect their children's positive self-views and to prevent them from becoming overwhelmed by guilt, especially in situations when mothers recognize factors that mitigate the blameworthiness of their children's actions (Miller, 2014; Recchia & Wainryb, 2014). That is, parents do not appear to believe that children should necessarily feel guilty every time that someone's feelings get hurt directly or indirectly by their actions. By the teenage years, youth may share this perspective (Wainryb & Recchia, 2012), but preschool and early-school-aged children tend to emphasize the moral dimensions of complex social experiences, often at the expense of other dimensions (Shaw & Wainryb, 2006). This may partially explain mothers' desires to be protective, particularly with their younger children. Thus, mothers' efforts to promote children's understanding of factors that might mitigate their responsibility (in this case, the inappropriate and hurtful nature of the friends' comments) may help children to reason about their own hurtful acts in ways that recognize the complexities of these social experiences, and thus support their ability to reason flexibly across different types of events. Nevertheless, if such protective responses were used consistently and exclusively by parents, this would become problematic inasmuch as it could undermine children's moral agency by minimizing their sense of responsibility for their own behavior and their consideration of the effects of their actions on others.

With age, children become increasingly able to consider the complexity of their morally laden experiences, and their conversations with their mothers also reflect these developmental shifts. For example, consider the following conversation between 11-year-old Laura and her mother:

CHILD: Okay so, one day, back in [city], with Jenny, we were walking to do a lap in school, and we were just walking together and Melanie was behind us, and all of a sudden Kristen walks past, and I say to Jenny and I said "Do you still like Kristen, um 'cause she's really rude to me and I don't like her." So Jenny thought that was offensive and so she just, she said, "Well I like um Kristen, and you shouldn't be saying that about her." So she walked up with Kristen and then Melanie came up with me, and then just walked with me for the rest of the way. [. . .]

MOTHER: So were you just talking about other things and then all of a sudden Kristen passed you

CHILD: Mm hmm

MOTHER: and then you just said that out of the blue?

CHILD: Well not out of the blue because we were kind of talking about Kristen, and so, and so then she passes by and I just say that. 'Cause she like she like passed by pretty much, and like, um bumps Jenny.

MOTHER: Oh, okay.

CHILD: So that's what brought it up, kind of

MOTHER: Did Jenny say something first?

CHILD: mm mm

MOTHER: Or you just brought it up?

CHILD: I just brought it up.

MOTHER: That was a hard situation

CHILD:	yeah
MOTHER:	back there, huh? [. . .] Um . . . (long pause) Are you glad that you said it?
CHILD:	I think so-
MOTHER:	Or do you wish you hadn't said it?
CHILD:	'Cause now now she knew how I felt about Kristen, so then um, later if she doesn't like Kristen then she can say, "Oh, well Laura doesn't like her either, so I'm not going to bring her up."
MOTHER:	(nods) [. . .] Let's see . . . did you learn anything from it?
CHILD:	I learned that I shouldn't say things about other people to people that I don't know if they really don't like the person or if they do, and I just don't know it.
MOTHER:	It's hard to know what to say because you kinda wanna be open but
CHILD:	you don't at the same time so you can be, still be friends with them if they like the person and you don't . . .
MOTHER:	Anything else?
CHILD:	(child shakes head no) Do you have anything else?
MOTHER:	But friends you're supposed to be able to talk to,
CHILD:	Yea
MOTHER:	but yeah it's kind of hard with girls, and
CHILD:	mm hmm. Because one minute they don't like the person, then the next minute they like them but you don't know.
MOTHER:	Right
CHILD:	So you never know
MOTHER:	You don't want people getting mad.
CHILD:	But like people like Melanie (giggles) you always know.
MOTHER:	You always know with Melanie.
CHILD:	Mm hmm

In Laura's account, she describes openly expressing her animosity toward Kristen, who has been unpleasant to her in the past. Her friend Jenny takes offense at her confession and chastises her for gossiping about Kristen. We don't get a clear sense from this initial telling about how Laura evaluates her own behavior. And, ultimately, the predominant impression conveyed in this conversation is that it is difficult to unequivocally evaluate Laura's actions as either the right or the wrong thing to do. Laura acknowledges that she was glad she told Jenny about her feelings regarding Kristen, as it resulted in her friend becoming aware of her perspective and potentially taking it into account in future interactions. Yet she also speaks of the potential pitfalls of sharing one's perspective with others when you don't know where they stand. Building on this, she and her mother conclude that being open with others can be a double-edged sword, especially with some kinds of girls who are hard to predict. They then conclude with some insights about friendship, implying that some kinds of people are simply more difficult to maintain relationships with. These nuanced psychological insights, lessons about relationships, and acknowledgment of complexity are features of conversations that become characteristic of discussions with the child's increasing age, as children become more sophisticated in their under-standings of the social and psychological world (Recchia et al., 2014).

In addition to age-related changes in the *content* of conversations, this example also highlights developmental shifts in their *process*. In particular, a salient facet of this conversation is the extent to which the emerging insights are jointly constructed: Laura literally finishes her mother's sentences on various occasions. Thus, while both parties are elaborating on each other's contributions, the conclusions about the complexity of the situation and its implications for navigating friendships emerge from the conversation. That is, both Laura and her mother seem to reach new understandings of this experience that neither would necessarily have drawn on her own. Such conversational synchrony may be a fruitful context for moral learn-ing, inasmuch as children may feel highly supported and thus more willing to participate and to take risks. Indeed, establishing shared meanings in conversations about challenging events has been shown to predict various indicators of moral development over time (e.g., Laible & Murphy, 2014).

Specifically with respect to developmental changes, younger children's contribu-tions are more often prompted and scaffolded by their mothers, whereas older children make more spontaneous contributions to discussions (Recchia et al., 2014). By the teenaged years, mothers often act as a sounding board for their children's independent narrations, asking occasional questions and offering insights but otherwise allowing children to structure experiences independently. Thus, this conversation reflects a middle ground between patterns with younger and older children, in that mothers and children are equally contributing to the discussion.

As one last example, to demonstrate how these conversations continue to shift in adolescence, we present excerpts from a discussion between 16-year-old Rita and her mother:

CHILD: [. . .] Thomas was like "so you want to come sit at this table with me? Like over there, at our usual table?" and I was like, "No I don't really want to," and I was like being pressured by other people around me, I was like "because we're not really friends," and that kind of stuff [. . .] I was being like really rude to him and he was like "fine" and he went and sat at the other table and I felt really bad about being so mean to him and I remember later that day I apologized to him and then sat at the table with him. But yeah [. . .]

MOTHER: Why do you think you were so mean?

CHILD: Um I, I don't know I think I, it was a lot of pressure, I think from the other kids, cuz nobody really liked him, but I think that's, I um I don't know, I was just being rude in general to him. I don't know why [. . .]

MOTHER: And . . . how do you think that made him feel?

CHILD: Really bad. I thought, he probably felt like "why have I been hanging out with her? Why did I buy her a birthday present when she's so rude to me all the time?"

MOTHER: When you apologized how did he respond?

CHILD: He was like, "Oh that's okay."

MOTHER: So he believed you?

CHILD: Yeah, cuz it was true.

MOTHER: Did you prove yourself then?

CHILD: Yeah I never did that again and I always sat with him.

MOTHER: Uh hmm. So what did you learn? In that situation?

CHILD: That trying to be um cool or popular is, can hurt people?

MOTHER: Did you hurt yourself too that day?

CHILD: Yeah I think so because I felt really bad. Like, I just felt so bad about saying that to him because I knew he was just confused about the thing he gave me and I was being mean.

MOTHER: Did you know too that that was not the kind of character that you wanted to have or be?

CHILD: Yeah . . . yeah

MOTHER: Uh huh. So are you tempted in situations like that? Now, currently?

CHILD: No. No, I think everyone is over that stage at this point of like, I mean there is certainly different groups but there aren't like shunning one person, like at this age so I, we don't really run into that problem.

We see in Rita's initial narration that she is highly capable of reflecting on the psychological and evaluative dimensions of her experience on her own, without any scaffolding from her mother. She describes engaging in hurtful exclusionary behavior due to feeling pressured by others, and then also describes her remorse in the aftermath, leading to her attempts at reparation. Although adolescents may still need some support in understanding psychological dimensions of experiences when they are particularly complex or opaque (Recchia & Wainryb, 2014), this conversation is typical of age-related changes in youths' social-cognitive capacities.

Her mother is largely responsive to Rita's initial framing of her actions; she builds on various dimensions of her child's account by exploring her motivations and the emotional effects of her actions in more depth, as well as relational implications of the event. As is characteristic of conversations with teenagers, she subsequently helps her daughter to explore self-related implications of her behavior and draw conclusions about the kind of person she wants to be and how she perceives that she has grown and changed since this experience. Adolescence is a particularly appropriate time for parents to explore these issues with their children, as it is during this period that youth are beginning to explore broader self-related meanings emerging from their life experiences and forming identity-related commitments (McLean & Pasupathi, 2012).

The Conversations: Failures of Coordination Between Children's and Mothers' Contributions

Thus far, we have presented examples that demonstrate the ways in which mothers' contributions appear to be generally responsive to children's initial framings of events. However, there are also instances in our data when mothers and children appear to be "talking past each other," so to speak, in the sense that mothers' contributions do not follow directly from the ways in which their children frame their conflict experiences. Consider the following example, involving a conversation between 16-year-old Todd and his mother, about a situation in which he harmed his younger sibling:

MOTHER: So what'd you do to Richard? (laughing)

CHILD: Uh . . . well it's happened multiple times, but it's just like me calling him stupid or slow when he, like asks me for help on his homework and he like didn't understand it. I'll just be like "how did you not understand that, that's extremely easy" and he just doesn't understand it cuz I guess it doesn't come as easy to him and I just I guess maybe I got to like got him a little down cuz I called him stupid or something and he maybe understands it, he doesn't under– get everything, but then coming from his older brother saying that makes it that much worse. So . . .

MOTHER: Cuz he looks up to you. But do you know why that doing these things hurts his feelings and makes him upset?

CHILD: Yea, that's why I haven't been doing it at all.

MOTHER: Okay I mean he . . . cuz he looks up to you. And besides those are the, those are words that are hurtful to anybody and make them feel bad. You know, belittle them. You know. So now you understand why we get so mad at you.

CHILD: Well, it hasn't happened in a while.

MOTHER: Alright, but now you know why we get so mad because of words. When you put somebody down like that it shuts their self-esteem down and could affect them in the long, you know, in the long run and so it's just extremely hurtful . . . you know?

CHILD: Yea (softly).

MOTHER: It doesn't get, you don't build them up. You should build somebody up, not always cutting them down, but sometimes you do that. (points at child with thumb)

CHILD: Alright.

Initially, Todd describes hurting his brother repeatedly by saying that the brother should succeed more easily on schoolwork. However, he also clearly underscores his understanding of the negative impact that his actions had on his brother, and implies a negative evaluation of his own actions ("coming from his older brother saying that makes it that much worse"). Shortly afterwards, he notes that he has stopped engaging in the behavior after reflecting on the harm it has caused. Thus, in many ways, this is the kind of narration we would hope to see in the aftermath of harm, reflecting Todd's view of himself as imperfect in his understanding of others' needs and his capacity to perspective-take, but also capable of trying to do better.

Given these features of Todd's account, his mother's contributions are somewhat jarring, in that she paraphrases what her son has said ("cuz he looks up to you") without acknowledging that he himself had reached these conclusions. She also emphasizes her anger and suggests that Todd has a tendency to behave in hurtful ways, implying that his actions are reflective of broader negative moral characteristics ("you should build somebody up, not always cutting them down, but sometimes you do that"). This leaves little room for more positive, redemptive lessons to be learned from this experience. It is worth noting that we do not have information about the larger history between Todd and his brother that may be leading his mother to respond in this way. Her initial query in the conversation ("so what did you do to Richard?") hints at her initial stance with respect to Todd's relationship with his brother, and it is clear from the conversation that this specific harm event is part of a series of recurring incidents. Nevertheless, Todd's mother's response to his account seems to be incongruent with Todd's description of his own perspective on events, and not likely to support Todd's emerging capacity to forgive himself (and perhaps others) in the aftermath of harm.

What follows is a second conversation between a 16-year-old boy (Ben) and his mother, also in which the mother's contributions seem to be out of synch with her child's narration:

CHILD: We were at the fireworks thing, me and Michael, my friend. And we were sneaking in the bounce houses cuz the person charged way too much. And we were at the slide and he kept pushing me. And it would make me mad, so one time, I pushed him and he got mad and then he called me a name, and then I called him a name. And I hit him in the mouth.

MOTHER: (pause) You did? (very surprised)

CHILD: It hurt me more than it hurt him, my fist. Cuz he had braces on and he cut my wrist.

MOTHER: Wow, I di– you never told me about that.

CHILD: (Shrugs) I don't know, it was just dumb and then we just laughed about it the next day and we were friends again. [. . .]

MOTHER: So, ww-what way could you have solved the problem, without calling each other names and doing that?

CHILD: uh, I could have said "stop pushing me please." [. . .]

MOTHER: And he could have too, right? So you both kinda were in the wrong.

CHILD: Yeah.

MOTHER: What did you learn?

CHILD: Ahh, not to hit people unless, not to, to say to say something nice, instead of hitting somebody, like say "please don't push me" instead of calling each other names and hitting me, and hitting him in the mouth.

MOTHER: (nods) Cuz then everybody feels bad, huh?

CHILD: Yeah.

MOTHER: That's, you know it's a good thing that, that in humans we feel bad like that. That we have a conscience.

CHILD: Yeah.

MOTHER: Cuz otherwise, I guess society wouldn't be the way it is.

CHILD: Yeah! Uh-

MOTHER: It means you have a heart of gold, you know that?

CHILD: yeah.

(Mom smiles and then child smiles back)

In his initial narration, Ben tells a different type of story from the one Todd told in the previous example. Ben describes an escalating conflict in which he and his friend mutually retaliated multiple times, culminating in him punching his friend in the mouth. However, rather than describing the hurt caused to his friend, Ben concludes that "it hurt me more than it hurt him." Although his mother appears to be understandably shocked by this event, her responses do not seem particularly in line with the relatively insensitive way in which her son narrated the experience. That is, she chooses not to challenge (or even directly acknowledge) his statement minimizing the harm he caused to his friend. Furthermore, after emphasizing the reciprocal nature of the harm, she also quickly shifts to noting the importance of remorse, and concludes that her son has a "heart of gold." It is difficult to see how the mother's conclusion emerges from Ben's contributions to the conversation, and, indeed, it seems largely based on her own suggestions rather than his own. We suggest that this exchange may be unlikely to support Ben's authentic experience of responsibility for his hurtful actions, in that this mother's redemptive conclusions are largely disconnected from her son's apparent perspective on the event.

We suggest this lack of coordination may lead to missed opportunities for moral growth. Certainly, all parents will occasionally misattribute intentions, dismiss emotions, or gloss over nuances. However, we suggest that these mistakes become especially problematic if they are characteristic of how mothers and children consistently talk about these issues. In some ways, they suggest failures of intersubjectivity, and may thus impede the contributions of parent–child conversations to children's moral learning (e.g., Laible & Murphy, 2014). From a relational perspective, consistent errors of this type are also problematic, in the sense that children may increasingly feel that their voices are not being heard or understood, and thus these failures may erode children's trust in their caregivers and their willingness to share openly in conversation.

Even so, it is possible that under some circumstances, when parents do not get things right, this may actually create the space for other dimensions of moral agency development (Wainryb & Recchia, 2014a; see also Nucci, 2014). While parents are generally more knowledgeable and more sophisticated than their children, they are not infallible (in either the moral or informational sense). We speculate that, rather than being "disasters," these imperfections in parents' understandings may be a crucial part of the give-and-take process of conversation. When parents occasionally get things a little bit "wrong," this provides opportunities for children to push back against the parent's perspective, elaborate on their own understandings of moral concepts, as well as to carve out their distinct stances on their experiences. More broadly speaking, children's gradual recognition of their parents' subjectivity and fallibility may constitute a crucial facet of the process of individuation. Nevertheless, to date, this represents a largely untested possibility that may be a useful direction for future research.

The Conversations: Children Respond in Varied Ways to Their Mothers' Contributions

Thus far, we have shown that mothers' contributions to conversations are often (but not always) framed and guided by children's constructions of meanings about their experiences. In turn, mothers' suggestions, comments, and explanations are among the stuff that children take in, test, push against, make their own, reject, and build on. In this section, we expand on this latter facet of parent–child conversations – that is, the ways in which children agree with and elaborate on versus reject or dismiss their parents' contributions to discussions.

In general, the moral socialization literature might lead us to assume that, ideally, children will internalize their parents' guidance. Presumably, this is especially the case in the moral domain, inasmuch as children from a young age tend to endorse moral concepts such as welfare and fairness, and thus would be expected to largely agree with their parents on these issues. Furthermore, research suggests that children tend to accept the legitimacy of their parents' authority in regulating behavior in the moral domain (Smetana, 2011). Nevertheless, the examples above illustrate that it is not a straightforward task for mothers and children to jointly construct understandings about children's hurtful actions, and that given the complexity of these experiences, there is considerable heterogeneity in how individuals attend to, understand, and prioritize various facets of these events. And indeed, our data do not suggest that mothers are necessarily focused on teaching a specific value or expecting perfect (or even imperfect) compliance with their own view of things. Rather, both mothers and their children seem to be authentically engaged in making sense of what happened, what the child's role was, and what the child can learn from that event.

Many of the excerpts in the preceding sections illustrate conversations in which children seemed to accept their mothers' suggestions, using them as a springboard for elaborating their understandings of events. For example, although Laura and her mother are generally on the same page across the entire conversation, her mother helps her broaden her view of the advantages and disadvantages of being honest with peers, and she ultimately draws a conclusion about friendship that she may not have reached without her mother's support. Similarly, Rita responds to her mother's questioning about identity-related implications of her experience by reflecting on her own personal commitments and self-improvement since the event. More generally, then, as children take in and reflect on their mothers' guidance in conversations, they may be learning to understand or recognize unfamiliar or opaque aspects of their experiences; to make sense of emotionally arousing experiences in which it is difficult for children to think things through and make reasonable decisions; and to make sense of their own transgressions in ways that help them forgive themselves, repair relationships, and make better decisions in the future.

Even so, there is also the potential for children to push back against their mothers' guidance, to make counterarguments, or to dismiss their mothers' perspectives. For instance, although children and their mothers almost certainly agree that it is wrong to harm others, there is nevertheless the potential for them to disagree markedly with respect to children's responsibility and culpability for their hurtful behavior. These disagreements can take various forms:

CHILD: I was looking at his coloring book.

MOTHER: Oh, was he mad at you?

CHILD: Yeah, because I accidentally ripped the page and then he got really mad […]

MOTHER: But didn't you guys both have the same coloring book?

CHILD: No

MOTHER: Did you think it was your coloring book?

CHILD: Yeah, I thought it was mine. I– I forgot that I left it at grandma's house.

MOTHER: Oh, well that's not your fault if you thought it was yours! You thought it was your coloring book.

CHILD: uh huh

MOTHER: Yeah, well then that's fine.

CHILD: But then he got really really mad at me.

MOTHER: Oh, Josh got mad at you? Oh, what'd he do? Did he pull your hair again?

CHILD: mm mm (no)

MOTHER: no? oh.

CHILD: He just got mad at me. He said he would never talk to me again.

MOTHER: He said he would never talk to you ever again?!

CHILD: Yeah, but he's still talking to me.

MOTHER: (laughs) Ohh, well that's good.

Beatrice initially describes her destruction of her brother's property as accidental. Her mother goes on to explore Beatrice's reasons for taking the coloring book, establishing that it was a misunderstanding (she had thought it was hers). As a result, her mother absolves her child of responsibility ("oh, well, that's not your fault if you thought it was yours"; "then that's fine"). However, despite Beatrice's initial mitigation of her responsibility, she resists this absolution by emphasizing her brother's anger as a result of her actions. Thus, Beatrice's goal seems to shift in the course of the conversation, moving away from mitigating her fault and toward highlighting the negative emotional effects of her actions on her brother. Interestingly, her mother also uses this statement as an opportunity to suggest that her brother also contributed to the conflict ("oh, what'd he do? Did he pull your hair again?"), and Beatrice once again does not accept this characterization of events ("he just got mad at me").

This example shows that children do not uncritically accept their parents' interpretations of their hurtful behavior even when such interpretations might absolve them of responsibility. In this example, the conclusion that appears to be drawn is that the siblings' relationship can withstand situations in which the child angers her younger brother; this conclusion seems to emerge more from the child's own contributions to the discussion than from those of her mother. Indeed, this conversation may also have served to give Beatrice's mother a new perspective on Beatrice's capacity to consider her own *and* her brother's needs in the context of sibling conflict.

However, when conversations about harm reflect disagreements between mothers and children about the child's culpability for hurting others, it is not always the case that children perceive their own actions as more blameworthy than their mothers do. Thus, as a last example, consider the following conversation between 16-year-old Quentin and his mother:

CHILD: The story was, we were upstairs, this is when you were yelling at us to go take a shower. Just non-stop yelling about taking a shower. [. . .] I got in the shower first, Zach was playing the Xbox. I got out of the shower and he was still playing the Xbox. I basically called him, uh, I think I said, "Hey grease ball why don't you get in the shower?" and, you know how he is about his hair, and so he threw a controller at me, or headphones. [. . .] He felt bad about it, and–

MOTHER: Yeah, well yeah you torture him. You always put him down! You called him a grease ball. But he did need to be thrown in the shower probably.

CHILD: Yeah he's disgusting. You've seen his–

MOTHER: Well he's your brother, you hurt his feelings.

CHILD: (makes mocking noises) It's initiative. I'm teaching him how to be man.

MOTHER: How is that teaching him to be a man?

CHILD: Well I don't know, when he gets older and he's working at McDonald's and he has his gross hair and his boss is like, "Zach go take a shower" and he's like, "No!"

MOTHER: His boss first of all wouldn't tell him to go take a shower, but (laughs)

CHILD: His girlfriend might.

MOTHER: his girlfriend might. [. . .]

CHILD: He's always filthy.

MOTHER: But you're always putting him down [. . .] He shouldn't have thrown the controller at you.

CHILD: He shouldn't have! (emphatically) It hurt (whispers).

MOTHER: It hurt? So what did you do to him?

CHILD: I think I, I think I just smacked him upside the head.

MOTHER: Okay, you started the fight, and then you ended it by hitting him?

CHILD: (pause) Isn't that, isn't that what everyone does? That's what governments do, that's what countries do.

MOTHER: Oh please

CHILD: Oh please. Don't get in this–

MOTHER: (laughs) Quentin, can you not throw things and hit him? You torture him, he looks up to you and you just torture him constantly. Not just that one time (laughs) but constantly you say things to him.

CHILD: Well it's cuz he deserves it.

MOTHER: No he does not deserve it. And you know he doesn't.

CHILD: Last night he flipped me off for no reason.

MOTHER: (pauses) There had to be a reason. Think of one reason.

CHILD: Oh you're right, remember it was the popsicles. He was like, "what flavor is that?" and I got it wrong and he flipped me off. Then I got it right– he flipped me off.

MOTHER: Yeah that was kind of ridiculous. He's feeling picked on. Let's just try not picking on him. And next time you get out of the shower don't call him a grease ball instead say, "it's your turn, mom's upstairs screamin'." […] Will you try and just tell him without insulting him?

CHILD: No. It's impossible. 'Cause most of the time he starts it. […] What's something you like and you don't want anyone else touching?

MOTHER: I'm the mother, there's nothing.

CHILD: Exactly. Let's say, let's say your car.

MOTHER: No, you guys drive my car.

CHILD: Let's say, no let's say even when you're at work, let's say when you're driving the car, I'm always calling you and I'm always asking, "can I just drive your car? I'm just gonna drive it for a minute." That's, that's him and my Xbox. […]

In this conversation, it is clear that Quentin evaluates his own actions less negatively than does his mother, as he vociferously argues in his own defense. For her part, his mother is also inclined to "tell it like she sees it," and she does not mince her words when she disagrees with Quentin's point of view. It should be noted that this is an unusually contentious conversation that seems to reflect a jocular style characteristic of the relationship between Quentin and his mother. And yet, neither Quentin nor his mother seems particularly troubled by the relentless disagreement. We suggest that a relatively high level of trust and warmth between parent and child may be a necessary condition for this level of comfort with disagreement and criticism. There is evidence of such warmth even in this combative conversation: for example, Quentin's mother tempers her strong criticisms of his sibling-directed behavior (e.g., "you torture him constantly") with her acknowledgment of the validity of some of his arguments (e.g., his brother probably did need to be thrown in the shower) and her self-deprecating humor (e.g., "mom's upstairs screamin'").

In an otherwise positive relationship, children's willingness to engage in conflict with their parents may serve adaptive developmental functions (Adams & Laursen, 2007). Regardless of whether children conceive of their own harmful behaviors as more or less blameworthy than do their mothers, these moments of disagreement may serve as important contexts for moral learning, inasmuch as they highlight for children the multiplicity of concerns that can be brought to bear on complex social events. Indeed, conflicts surrounding morally laden events serve as crucial contexts for supporting children's considerations of alternative viewpoints, their empathy for others' divergent perspectives, and their ability to find solutions to problems that take into account competing goals (Nucci, 2001; Wainryb & Recchia, 2014b).

In Quentin's case, the level of openness in this relationship means that it is possible for him to test out contentious ideas in a safe context. For example, he makes the claims that his hurtful behavior is "showing initiative" and "teaching his brother to be a man"; he also draws analogies between his aggressive behaviors and the actions of governments. Although his mother challenges and even scoffs at these suggestions, she effectively creates a space for her son to test his ideas and receive honest and informative feedback. Thus, through resisting, disagreeing with, and arguing against parents' perspectives, children may be furthering their understandings of their own unique stances on experiences, as well as their abilities to articulate those perspectives in dialogue with others. In turn, parents are also learning something new about their children's points of view, and likely developing richer understandings of their children's experiences and ongoing relationships with others. The result, then, when these conversations go well, is that both mothers and children construct new understandings of children's morally laden actions.

Conclusions

The conversational excerpts discussed in this chapter illustrate the myriad of meanings that children and their mothers construct about children's hurtful experiences as well as the bidirectional and co-regulated nature of the process. We have noted the marked heterogeneity in children's initial framings of their own experiences, as well as the varied ways in which mothers address their children's accounts and children respond to their mothers' contributions.

As suggested by these excerpts, along with related analyses (Recchia & Wainryb, 2014; Recchia et al., 2014), there is often a close relation between mothers' goals and contributions to the conversations and the specific meanings that their children construct about their transgressive experiences. For example, in some cases mothers' suggestions emphasized their children's wrongdoing, often by highlighting the negative effects of children's actions on others. Mothers' uses of this strategy seemed especially likely (and also particularly appropriate) when children's accounts of their own actions suggested a lack of concern for the other (e.g., because the harm was repeated or ruthless in nature). In other cases, mothers responded to their children's accounts by minimizing their children's wrongdoing or mitigating their responsibility for their actions. Mothers seemed most likely to use this strategy with young children, especially when their children appeared to be "overmoralizing" complex situations and overlooking other legitimate considerations. Finally, mothers also found ways to help children reconcile their hurtful behavior with a positive self-view. For instance, with younger children, mothers scaffolded children's capacities to anchor the harm in a particular context, by exploring children's psychological perspectives that explained their hurtful behavior in a given situation. With older children and adolescents, mothers engaged in strategies that helped their children explore connections between their morally laden actions and their broader identity-related commitments.

Although we underscored the many ways in which mothers often built on children's explanations of their own experiences, we also noted this was not invariably the case. In some instances, mothers' responses seemed to be out of synch with children's own accounts. We also noted cases in which mothers and children seemed to be responsive to one another, but were nevertheless in disagreement about children's culpability. We demonstrated that children do not unreflectively accept their mothers' interpretations and sometimes openly resist them; this was true not only at times when mothers stressed their children's wrongdoing, but even on occasions when mothers tried to mitigate their children's responsibility. These instances of open resistance on the part of children surely reflect only a small subset of children's noncompliant attitudes; research (Kuczynski & Parkin, 2006) indicates that children's unwillingness to adopt parental views often takes more covert forms, such as when children engage in passive noncompliance or when they privately or internally reject or ignore a parent's proposition.

When socialization is conceived of as parents teaching and children conforming, it is relatively easy to ascertain the success or failure of parents' socialization attempts in terms of the match between the two perspectives. Understanding socialization as a bidirectional and co-regulated process that implicates the interpretive capacities of both parents and children requires, instead, a fine-grained microgenetic exploration of communicative exchanges. Our excerpts illustrated the varied ways in which mothers and children, in conversation, framed their own understandings of events, considered the views and interpretations presented by the other, and engaged in fruitful give-and-takes that resulted in children, and sometimes also mothers, reaching new, more complete, or nuanced understandings of the events they were discussing.

Importantly, because this perspective on socialization does not aim for the child's submission to the parent's view, disagreements and conflicts do not necessarily signal a problem in the socialization process. Indeed, far from reflecting calamitous failures in socialization, moments of disagreement and conflict – whether they are instances when mothers' and children's contributions to a conversation do not seem well harmonized, when mothers miss their children's clues or misinterpret their mood or intentions, or when children reject mothers' suggestions or interpretations – may create space for children to 'flex their own muscles' so to speak, pushing back against the parent, standing their grounds, and finding their own voice. Therefore, it is not only those moments of attunement and synchrony that undergird and promote children's construction of more complex moral understandings; asynchrony and conflict may also usher in new moral learning. Ultimately, the constructive process embedded in conversation serves as an inimitably important crucible for moral development inasmuch as it provides support for children's ability to reflect on and make sense of their own morally laden experiences.

References

Adams, R., & Laursen, B. (2007). The correlates of conflict: Disagreement is not necessarily detrimental. *Journal of Family Psychology, 21*, 445–458.

Callanan, M., Valle, A., Luce, M., & Rigney, J. (2014). Discussions of moral issues emerging in family conversations about science. In C. Wainryb & H. Recchia (Eds.), *Talking about right and wrong: Parent-child conversations as contexts for moral development* (pp. 193–216). Cambridge, UK: Cambridge University Press.

Dunn, J., & Hughes, C. (2014). Family talk about moral issues: The toddler and preschool years. In C. Wainryb & H. Recchia (Eds.), *Talking about right and wrong: Parent-child conversations as contexts for moral development* (pp. 21–43). Cambridge, UK: Cambridge University Press.

Eisenberg, N., Spinrad, T., & Sadovsky, A. (2006). Empathy-related responding in children. In M. Killen & J. Smetana (Eds.), *Handbook of moral development* (pp. 517–550). Mahwah, NJ: Erlbaum.

Fivush, R. (2007). Maternal reminiscing style and children's developing understanding of self and emotion. *Clinical Social Work, 35,* 37–46.

Grusec, J., & Davidov, M. (2006). Socialization in the family: The role of parents. In J. Grusec & P. Hastings (Eds.), *Handbook of socialization: Theory and research* (pp. 284–308). New York, NY: Guilford.

Hardy, S., & Carlo, G. (2011). Moral identity: What is it, how does it develop, and is it linked to moral action? *Child Development Perspectives, 5,* 212–218.

Kochanska, G., Coy, K., & Murray, K. (2001). The development of self-regulation in the first four years of life. *Child Development, 72,* 1091–1111.

Komolova, M., & Wainryb, C. (2011). What I want and what you want: Children's thinking about competing personal preferences. *Social Development, 20,* 334–352.

Kuczynski, L., & Parkin, M. (2006). Agency and bidirectionality in socialization. In J. Grusec & P. Hastings (Eds.), *Handbook of socialization: Theory and research* (pp. 259–283). New York, NY: Guilford.

Lagattuta, K. (2005). When you shouldn't do what you want to do: Young children's understanding of desires, rules, and emotions. *Child Development, 76,* 713–733.

Laible, D., & Murphy, T. (2014). Constructing moral, emotional, and relational understandings in the context of mother–child reminiscing. In C. Wainryb & H. Recchia (Eds.), *Talking about right and wrong: Parent-child conversations as contexts for moral development* (pp. 98–121). Cambridge, UK: Cambridge University Press.

McLean, K., & Pasupathi, M. (2012). Processes of identity development: Where I am and how I got there. *Identity, 12,* 8–28.

Miller, P. (2014). Placing discursive practices front and center: A socio-cultural approach to the study of early socialization. In C. Wainryb & H. Recchia (Eds.), *Talking about right and wrong: Parent-child conversations as contexts for moral development* (pp. 416–447). Cambridge, UK: Cambridge University Press.

Nucci, L. (2001). *Education in the moral domain.* Cambridge, UK: Cambridge University Press.

Nucci, L. (2014). Conversations in the home: The role of dialogue and resistance in children's emerging understandings of moral, convention, and the personal. In C. Wainryb & H. Recchia (Eds.), *Talking about right and wrong: Parent-child conversations as contexts for moral development* (pp. 367–388). Cambridge, UK: Cambridge University Press.

Pasupathi. M., & Wainryb, C. (2010a). Developing moral agency through narrative. *Human Development, 53,* 55–80.

Pasupathi, M., & Wainryb, C. (2010b). On telling the whole story: Facts and interpretations in autobiographical memory narratives from childhood through midadolescence. *Developmental Psychology, 46,* 735–746.

Piaget, J. (1932). *The moral judgment of the child.* New York, NY: Free Press.

Recchia, H., & Wainryb, C. (2014). Mother-child conversations about hurting others: Scaffolding the construction of moral agency through childhood and adolescence. In C. Wainryb & H. Recchia (Eds.), *Talking about right and wrong: Parent-child conversations as contexts for moral development* (pp. 242–269). Cambridge, UK: Cambridge University Press.

Recchia, H., Wainryb, C., Bourne, S., & Pasupathi, M. (2014). The construction of moral agency in mother-child conversations about helping and hurting across childhood and adolescence. *Developmental Psychology, 50*, 34–44

Recchia, H., Wainryb, C., & Pasupathi, M. (2013). "Two for flinching": Children's and adolescents' narrative accounts of harming their friends and siblings. *Child Development, 84*, 1459–1474.

Shaw, L., & Wainryb, C. (2006). When victims don't cry: Children's understandings of victimization, compliance, and subversion. *Child Development, 77*, 1050–1062.

Smetana, J. (2011). *Adolescents, families, and social development: How adolescents construct their worlds*. West Sussex, UK: Wiley.

Smetana, J. (2013). Moral development: The social domain theory view. In P. Zelazo (Ed.), *Oxford handbook of developmental psychology, Vol. 1*, (pp. 832–866). NY: Oxford University Press.

Sterponi, L. (2014). Caught red-handed: How Italian parents engage children in moral discourse and action. In C. Wainryb & H. Recchia (Eds.), *Parent-child conversations as contexts for moral development* (pp. 122–142). Cambridge, UK: Cambridge University Press.

Thompson, R. (2010). Feeling and understanding through the prism of relationships. In S. Calkins & M. Bell (Eds.), *Child development at the intersection of emotion and cognition* (pp. 79–95). Washington, DC: APA.

Thompson, R., Meyer, S., & McGinley, M. (2006). Understanding values in relationships: The development of conscience. In M. Killen & J. Smetana (Eds.), *Handbook of moral development* (pp.267–298). Mahwah, NJ: Erlbaum.

Turiel, E. (2010). Domain specificity in social interactions, social thought, and social development. *Child Development, 81*, 720–726.

Wainryb, C., & Brehl, B. (2006). I thought she knew that would hurt my feelings: Developing psychological knowledge and moral thinking. In R. Kail (Ed.), *Advances in child development and behavior, Vol. 34* (pp. 131–173). New York, NY: Elsevier.

Wainryb, C., Brehl, B., & Matwin, S. (2005). Being hurt and hurting others: Children's narrative accounts and moral judgments of their own interpersonal conflicts. *Monographs of the Society for Research in Child Development, 70* (Serial No. 281).

Wainryb, C., Komolova, M., & Brehl, B. (2014). Being left out: Children's narrative accounts and judgments of their own experiences with peer exclusion. *Merrill-Palmer Quarterly, 60*, 461–490.

Wainryb, C., & Pasupathi, M. (2015). Saints, and the rest of us: Broadening the perspective on moral identity development. *Human Development, 58*, 154–163.

Wainryb, C., & Recchia. H. E. (2012). Emotion and the moral lives of adolescents: Vagaries and complexities in the emotional experience of doing harm. *New Directions in Youth Development, 136*, 13–26.

Wainryb, C., & Recchia, H. (2014a). Parent-child conversations as contexts for moral development: Why conversations, and why conversations with parents? In C. Wainryb & H. Recchia (Eds.), *Talking about right and wrong: Parent-child conversations as contexts for moral development* (pp. 3–20). Cambridge, UK: Cambridge University Press.

Wainryb, C., & Recchia, H. (2014b) (Eds.). *Talking about right and wrong: Parent-child conversations as contexts for moral development.* Cambridge, UK: Cambridge University Press.

Wright, J., & Bartsch, K. (2008). Portraits of early moral sensibility in two children's everyday conversations. *Merrill-Palmer Quarterly, 54,* 56–85.

12 Development in the Moral Domain: Coordination and the Need to Consider Other Domains of Social Reasoning

Elliot Turiel and Matthew Gingo

As the title of this chapter implies, explanations of the development of morality require attention to multiple factors. First, a central feature of human beings is that they engage in thinking, in reasoning (Nussbaum, 1999; Sen, 2006, 2009). Second, thinking can be about social relationships. Thinking about social relationships differs in qualitative ways from thinking about other realms, such as the physical realm. Moreover, thinking about social relationships is not of one kind but varies by domain, so that judgments in the domain of morality having to do with how people ought to relate to each other differ qualitatively from judgments about conventions in social systems, which in turn differ from judgments about persons and their arenas of choice and jurisdiction (Turiel, 1983a, 2015).

Extensive research conducted over many years in several cultures has provided a great deal of evidence for the proposition that the moral, social conventional, and personal domains of judgment have features distinct from each other. The configuration of moral judgments, based on understandings of welfare, justice, and rights, differs from the configuration of judgments about social organizations, with their systems of norms and conventions (as well as from judgments about the domain of personal jurisdiction). To state it briefly, judgments in the moral domain are not contingent on rules, authority dictates, or existing practices. By contrast, conventional norms are judged to be dependent on existing rules, the dictates of those in authority, and common practices in a social system. For the present purposes we present only these brief characterizations, which derive from much more extensive and detailed discussions and research documentation (for reviews, see Smetana, 2006; Turiel, 1983a, 1998, 2015).

A second central feature of human beings is that they undergo processes of development involving constructions through their interactions with the environment. In keeping with the distinction between thought about the physical world and social relationships, interactional processes with the physical environment differ in ways contributing to development from those with the social environment. In turn, in processes of development children experience different types of social interactions associated with each of the domains (Nucci & Turiel, 1978; Turiel, 1978, 1983a, 1983b).

The question of development in the moral domain raises the associated question of how development is related to the domains of morality, social convention, and the personal. Is it that the formation of these domains comes about through their differentiation with increasing age (see Kohlberg, 1971 and Piaget, 1932), or is it that each domain constitutes a separate developmental pathway? The same body of research that examined the domain distinctions provides a good deal of evidence for the proposition that, across cultures, by a relatively young age children form different configurations of thought within each domain and that such differences are maintained across ages. In other words, each domain of thought constitutes its own developmental pathway, and development is not accurately explained as entailing progressive differentiations among the domains (Turiel, 2010b; Turiel & Dahl, in press).

A third central feature of humans who develop distinctively different domains of social judgments through distinctively different types of social interactions is that they can reason about how the domains might relate to, or be in conflict with, each other. Reasoning about relations among the different domains is of significance for social decision-making because many social situations include different types of considerations and goals. Therefore, social decisions often involve weighing and balancing different considerations and goals – which we refer to as "processes of coordination" (Turiel, 2008a, 2015).

We can summarize the approach we take to moral and social development as follows: reasoning is central but emotions are part of it, without giving reasoning a minor or no role (Nussbaum, 2001; Turiel & Dahl, in press; Turiel & Killen, 2010); morality is a distinct domain of thought which develops through social interactions; and moral decisions entail coordination of different considerations and goals embedded in social situational contexts.

These propositions raise several questions of importance. First, with regard to the assertion that human beings are reasoning beings, a question can take the form of "why are you telling us this, is it not obvious that people think?" It seems to us that whereas it should be generally acknowledged that people engage in serious thought (as do psychological researchers), what makes it not so obvious is that many researchers make contrary assertions – especially that in the moral and social realms non-rationality or even irrationality predominates due to influences of, as examples, unconscious process and the overwhelming nature of emotions.

A second question bears on the development of morality. It might take the form of: "If children form their moral judgments through their social interactions (and are not genetically determined), how can it be that those growing up with different cultural norms and practices in different parts of the world develop similar moral judgments?" And a third question bears on our assertion that the evidence shows that individuals make moral judgments that are not contingent on rules, authority dictates, or existing practices. It would be in the form of: "Do we not know that people, for example, often obey authority in acting in ways that involve moral harm?" One example from research is the findings of "obedience to authority" in the experiments by Milgram (1963, 1974). More generally, "do we not know that individuals often do not make decisions consistent with the idea that morality overrides rules, authority, and common practice?"

In the remainder of this chapter we consider each of these questions, with an emphasis on the third one – and related evidence – as a means of explaining our position on morality, development, cultural practices, and decision-making as involving processes of coordination.

Human Beings are Above All Reasoning Beings

The heading of this section comes from a statement made by Nussbaum (1999, p. 71) in her discussion of the liberal political tradition from Greek and Roman Stoics to Kant, Smith, and modern moral and political thinkers such as Rawls (1971, 1993). However, Nussbaum does not by any means propose that emotions are irrelevant or independent of thought – as evidenced in her tome on *Upheavals of Thought: The Intelligence of Emotions* (2001). In her view, paralleled in psychological analyses (Frijda, 1986; Lazarus, 1991; Moors & Scherer, 2013), "Emotions are not just the fuel that powers the psychological mechanism of a reasoning creature, they are parts, highly complex and messy parts, of this creature's reasoning itself" (Nussbaum, 2001, p. 3).

In this view, therefore, emotional reactions function in concert with thought. Emotions involve evaluative appraisals in that they are guided by ways of thinking about social relationships; can be part of people's aims, purposes, and goals in life; and can be part of their understandings of others and events (Turiel, 2010b; Turiel & Dahl, in press). With regard to judgments in the moral and conventional domains, it has been found that children attribute positive emotions to actors, recipients, and observers in connection with positive actions such as helping and sharing (Arsenio, 1988; Arsenio & Fleiss, 1996). With respect to moral transgressions, children attribute hurt feelings to recipients of the acts and mixed positive and negative emotions to instigators of the acts (Wainryb, Brehl, & Matwin, 2005). By contrast, the emotions attributed to transgressors in the conventional domain are neutral emotions or feelings of sadness.

It has also been found that respect for persons, as a general sentiment, is one of the central organizing features of moral orientations (Piaget, 1932). Another central organizing feature considered in both philosophical (Dworkin, 1993) and psychological analyses (Turiel & Killen, 2010) is the value of life – in the sense that across cultures individuals are concerned with preserving lives, act to save lives when they can, hold strong judgments about the loss of life, and experience intense emotions such as grief at the loss of a loved one (Nussbaum, 2001). The dynamics of the issue of life are complicated since people do take lives in war and for reasons of self-defense, and it is one of the condoned ways, through capital punishment, of responding to murder. However, it is largely unheard of that nations do not have laws about killing.

Research on how individuals think and feel about the value of life is sparse. However, issues revolving around the value of life have been central in research stemming from the position that reasoning in the moral realm is, at best, secondary to the force of emotions. That research has examined evaluations about life from a neuroscience perspective by presenting individuals with so-called trolley car dilemmas. In several studies, participants are presented with what are labeled "trolley car bystander" and "trolley car footbridge" scenarios (Cushman, Young, & Hauser, 2006; Greene, Sommerville, Nystrom, Darley, & Cohen, 2001; Koenigs et al., 2007). One dilemma (bystander) depicts a runaway trolley that will kill five people unless a bystander throws a switch that will prevent killing the five but would kill one person instead. In another dilemma (footbridge), the actor has to decide whether to push a man to his death in order to save the five. While in an fMRI machine participants were only asked if it is permissible to throw the switch and push the man.

The findings that most participants judged it acceptable to throw the switch and that most judged that it is not permissible to push a man form the basis for the claim that emotions determine moral decisions (Cushman et al., 2006; Greene et al., 2001). Since both situations involve the same utilitarian calculation of saving five lives by sacrificing one life, the footbridge version is seen as evoking emotions that determine moral decisions. In turn, it is maintained that most moral decisions are non-rational, intuitive, and determined by unconscious processes. As evidence for this argument the authors point to research demonstrating that differential areas of the brain, associated with rationality and emotions are activated in the two scenarios.

The proposed dichotomy between reasoning and emotions that forms the basis for the interpretation that emotions are deterministic of decisions fails to account for the ways features of the trolley car situations are perceived by those asked to make judgments about them. First, these situations are complex in that they embed a conflict with regard to the value of life since participants are posed with problems containing multiple considerations that are difficult to reconcile without violating serious moral precepts in order to achieve serious moral goals. These situations are complex (and emotionally laden) because a strongly held value – the value of life – must be violated in order to preserve that very value (Turiel, 2010a).

Another problem lies in the idea that because the footbridge situation evokes emotions greater than the bystander situation the differences in decisions are accounted for by emotions. The intensity of the emotions in the footbridge situation is not the sole difference between the two. Although the footbridge situation is likely to evoke intense emotions (as well might the switch situation), the two situations are not otherwise the same. If we do not split emotions from judgments, then it is likely that people also make judgments about the act of physically pushing someone to his death. The footbridge situation constitutes a different context of evaluation from the bystander situation because in addition to the conflict involved in saving lives by repudiating the prohibition on taking lives embedded in the bystander situation, the footbridge situation entails judgments and emotions about actively and physically causing another's death. Reasoning in these situations does not solely entail utilitarian calculations. Judgments are also made about the fundamental conflict in values in the situations, and about the means used to achieve ends. Individuals take into account the different features of social situations, and attempt to coordinate different types of judgments relevant to those features.

Research that involves presenting participants with questions designed to assess their reasoning (which had not been done in the neuro-imaging studies) indeed shows that they attend to different features of the trolley car situations and attempt to coordinate those different considerations (Dahl, Gingo, Uttich, & Turiel, in preparation). For the present purposes, we present two types of findings indicating that differences in the features of these situations (e.g., throwing a switch or pushing another person) are construed in different ways, that there is cognizance of the conflicts embedded in the situations, and that participants attempt to coordinate the different components. One set of findings is that individuals do have reasons associated with their evaluations and that the value of life is salient in the varying decisions. However, other considerations also come into play. These include the actor's responsibility for the consequences of actions, and contractual obligations of all involved (e.g., workers in the railway enterprise). It is not the case that it is solely or primarily that emotions associated with physically pushing a human being are the determining factors. One of the variations introduced in this study was a situation in which someone has to decide whether to push another to save five lives, but the person pushed would only incur some non-life-threatening physical injuries. In that case, most judged it permissible to push the other person. In other situational variations that entailed saving the lives of family members (rather than strangers), most judged it acceptable to throw the switch or push another because of one's obligations to family. This body of findings indicates that the trolley car situations taken as a whole are perceived to have different dimensions from each other, dimensions taken into account in coming to decisions – decisions that usually entail conflicts, differing reasons, and differing emotional appraisals. A central component is that individuals struggle with contradictory moral goals involved in situations when asserting the value of life at the same time requires violating the value of life.

Common Moral Judgments and Variations in Cultural Practices: How Can It Be?

Of course, the types of conflicts involved in the trolley car situations are unusual in terms of the decisions people are asked to make (what philosophers label "hard cases"; see Walzer, 2007). Nevertheless, emotions are typically part of moral judgments and decisions. Moreover, emotions, including positive emotions such as affection, sympathy, and empathy, are part of the process in the development of morality. During childhood, in particular, experiences of being harmed, seeing others harmed, fair and unfair treatment, and unequal treatment all are likely to contribute to young children's development of moral judgments about welfare, justice, and rights.

It is these types of experiences and associated emotions that point to answers to the question, how can it be that children growing up with different cultural practices form similar moral judgments? There are two interrelated aspects to the answer to this question. One has to do with the theoretical proposition that children *construct* thinking through their interactions with the world (Kohlberg, 1969, 1971; Piaget,

1932, 1970; Turiel, 1983a, 2002; Werner, 1957). In this perspective, development is neither genetically nor environmentally determined, but involves constructions in efforts to make sense of experiences, social rules, roles of authorities, social institutions, and cultural practices.

The second aspect has to do with the types of experiences that centrally contribute to the development of moral judgments. A major source of moral development is children's everyday experiences with others of the same ages and of different ages (younger and older children, adults) having to do with harm, benefits, fairness, equality, and adjudication of disagreements and conflicts. Concretely, these types of experiences include, as a few examples, children hurting each other (physically and emotionally), helping and failing to help, sharing and failing to share, including and excluding others, cooperating and failing to cooperate, and treating people equally and unequally. Moreover, children are not solely recipients of "moral" messages from adults. They interact with adults over many of the same issues and observe adults interacting with each other harmoniously and with conflict – and sometimes around matters of harm, helping, sharing, cooperating, and equality. Wainryb and Recchia (Chapter 11, this volume) provide evidence that interactions between parents and their children revolve around concrete events and entail a good deal of explanation, negotiation, and scrutiny on the part of the children, as well as accommodation to children's concerns on the part of parents.

These types of experiences, social interactions, and observations are centrally involved in the formation of moral judgments, as evidenced by a number of observational studies with preschoolers (Nucci & Turiel, 1978; Nucci, Turiel, & Encarnacion-Gawrych, 1983; Nucci & Weber, 1995) and older children (Nucci & Nucci, 1982a, 1982b; Turiel, 2008b). The studies have documented that children's social interactions around events classified as moral differ from social interactions around events in the conventional and personal domains. Interactions around moral transgressions typically do not involve commands or communications about rules and expectations of adults. Interactions around moral transgressions are about the effects of actions on people, the perspectives of others, the need to avoid harm, the pain experienced, as well as communications about welfare and fairness. By contrast, interactions around conventional events revolve around adherence to rules, commands from those in authority, and an emphasis on social order.

It might even be – though at this point this is speculative – that morality involves thought, scrutiny, and reflection more directly from everyday experiences than in some non-social cognitive realms. To explain we refer to an observation made by Cole, Gay, Glick, and Sharp (1971, p. 219). In analyzing cultural contexts and cognitive activities, they pointed to the need to study familiar activities within cultures in order to accurately assess cognitive attainments: "The principle that says that people will be good at doing what is familiar to them then led us to the study of measuring and estimating quantities of rice. ... Rice farming consumes a great deal of every Kpelle person's time." Unlike rice farming, most children are directly familiar with activities and interactions involving harm, helping, sharing, inclusion and exclusion, and matters of equality and inequality. In that sense, the familiarity of certain types of activities pertaining to the development of morality are not so much related to a distinction between familiar and non-familiar culturally constituted activities.

Culture Works in Mysterious Ways

The question as to how growing up with possible differences in cultural practices can result in the formation of similar moral judgments can be addressed from another angle as well. If it is the case that the types of everyday activities we outlined result in moral judgments based on welfare, justice, and rights, then it should be the case that there would be opposition and resistance to cultural practices that violate these precepts. Such opposition and resistance to cultural practices are likely to occur since moral judgments would not represent replications of the values of the culture. Moreover, the development of moral judgments suggests that they would be applied not only to direct social interactions with others, but also to features of the system of social organization.

These questions have been addressed in a series of anthropological and psychological studies, conducted in patriarchal cultures, that examined the perspectives of adolescent and adult females on social hierarchical patterns of inequality between males and females (see also Way and Rogers, Chapter 13, this volume). As defined by Wikan (1982, pp. 55, 56), in patriarchal cultures "The male is considered superior, physically, morally, and intellectually," and "women must be constrained and protected by men." Wikan's characterizations are consistent with the characterizations by Shweder, Much, Mahapatra, and Park (1997) of relationships between males and females in India as involving unequal status in clearly demarcated status hierarchies. Shweder and colleagues regard the arrangements of patriarchy to be accepted by both females and males because they involve relationships of asymmetrical reciprocity by which females obey males and males take care of the needs of females and protect them. By contrast, Wikan regards the inequalities as subject to scrutiny, critique, and opposition by females. Wikan's position is based on her ethnographic studies in middle-eastern nations. For example, Wikan (1996) conducted extensive fieldwork with people living in conditions of poverty in urban areas (Cairo) in Egypt (see also Wikan, 1976/1980, 1996). Her work revealed that females, who do experience conflicts about social hierarchy and social inequalities, engage in opposition and resistance to practices that allow for male domination. Similar findings were obtained by Abu-Lughod (1993), in her ethnographic studies in a rural Bedouin village in northwestern Egypt. The Bedouin women, too, were critical of practices of male domination and unequal restrictions placed on the activities of females. Both Wikan and Abu-Lughod found that females engage in overt and covert actions aimed at asserting their freedoms, avoiding undue control by males, and changing cultural practices of gender inequality (including practices such as arranged marriages and polygamy).

As part of their reports of the ethnographic research, Wikan (1996) and Abu-Lughod (1993) describe in great detail aspects of the lives, including everyday events, of two women: one from Cairo and one from the Bedouin village. As put by Wikan (1996, p. 1):

> You will hear the voices of people living in poverty in a third world megacity, telling what it is like to be human in their world. It is an account of lives and living conditions, told from the perspective of a few real persons and in their own words, an account . . . of their concerns, struggles, dreams, and realities.

Although one study was conducted in a teeming megacity and the other in a rural, isolated village, there are striking similarities in the particular stories of the two women. In each case there is a combination of (a) living in the culture, concerns with participating with others in close relationships, fitting into the fabric of the society, and forging harmonious relationships, *and* (b) living apart from the culture, experiencing and expressing discontents with others in close and distant relationships, many frustrations and disappointments with others and with the ways cultural practices are set up to disadvantage certain people at the expense of others (especially females), experiencing many intense conflicts (including and especially with one's husband) and engaging in acts (overt and covert) to thwart and circumvent the expectations and demands of those in positions of power. In other words, life for these women is not by any means simple, straightforward, or free of conflict and contradictions. Wikan (1996, pp. 6–7) characterized one side of the situation for women – and for men as well – as follows: "these lives I depict can be read as exercises in resistance against the state, against family, against one's marriage, against the forces of tradition and change, against neighbors and society – even against oneself." However, all the resistance has a context of participation in Wikan's reading of their lives (pp. 6–7):

> But it is resistance that seems to follow a hidden agenda to manage and endure in ways that respect the humanity of others. It is this combination of respectability and resistance that makes the people in Cairo what they are: a people full of individuality and charm who delight in zest and humor, and whose hope of self-realization lies in honoring their social commitments.

The multifaceted nature of social lives among the Bedouin villagers was also evident to Abu-Lughod (1993, p. 14):

> In the face of the complexity of individual lives even in a single family, a term like "Bedouin culture" comes to seem meaningless, whether in the sense of rules that people follow or of a community that shares such rules. Individuals are confronted with choices; they struggle with others, make conflicting statements, argue about points of view on the same events, undergo ups and downs in various relationships and changes in their circumstances and desires, face new pressures, and fail to predict what will happen to them or those around them.

These characterizations, derived from ethnographic research and illustrated with stories of happenings of individuals and events told by them, are consistent with findings from the more usual type of research conducted in the field of psychology. Those findings come from studies of judgments about social hierarchies and gender inequalities conducted in India (Neff, 2001), Benin (Conry-Murray, 2009), Colombia (Mensing, 2002), and the Middle-East (Guvenc, 2011; Wainryb & Turiel, 1994). Those studies have shown that females are quite aware of the inequalities embedded in systems of social organization, including awareness of the independence and control granted to males over females. While in some respects females accept their designated social roles (especially because of fear of consequences of defiance), they also strive for greater freedom and equality. The findings also show that females regard many cultural practices of inequality to be unfair (see Turiel, 2002).

Significant portions of conflicts revolve around groups in different positions in social hierarchies. In addition to hierarchies based on gender, there are hierarchies based on social class, ethnicity, and race. The findings of conflicts within cultures suggest that some cultural practices, which can be considered collective practices, are simultaneously contested practices. This is because practices are collective in that they can be part of public pronouncements endorsed by those of higher status, but contested by those of lower status.

The proposition put forth by Abu-Lughod, that a term such as "Bedouin culture" seems meaningless, which surely would be endorsed by Wikan, is supported by the evidence we have considered and implies that one of the common ways of describing cultures is not valid. We are referring to descriptions of cultures as relatively homogeneous, harmonious, and reflecting shared meanings among its participants. Both the conflicts and forms of resistance found in the research mean that disagreements exist within cultures. In turn, disagreements and conflicts render as problematic some conceptions of cultural differences – as seen in the idea that differences exist *between* cultures and not *within* cultures. Instead, it is more accurate to say that there are some complex ways of characterizing cultural differences and similarities. As already noted, there are commonalities among cultures in moral conceptions. There can also be some commonalities in social perspectives among those in different cultures who occupy similar positions in their respective social hierarchies, which make for differences in perspectives of those in different positions within a culture. Figure 12.1 outlines some aspects of such relations of perspectives.

The general proposition is that there are multiple layers of similarities and differences between and within cultures. In some respects – though not all, by any means – there are more commonalities in perspectives of those in similar positions in different cultures than between those in different positions in the same culture.

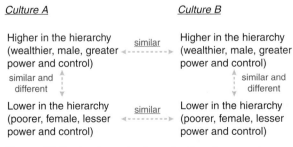

Figure 12.1. *A schematic view of cultural comparisons.*

Processes of Coordination: Context Matters

The findings from the anthropological research revealed that females, in addition to overt means, use deception as a means of resistance to circumvent perceived unfairness in cultural practices. These findings bear on our third question: is there not evidence indicating that individuals' decisions in morally relevant situations are not always based on morality and, furthermore, that individuals judge in accord with authority dictates (as in the findings of Milgram, 1974)? The findings from the anthropological studies bear on this question because a seeming violation of morality – of the value of honesty – occurs among females in patriarchal cultures. Along with the example from the studies by Milgram, our interpretation is that the findings actually suggest that moral judgments are applied in these situations, but that conflicting considerations exist in them and that decisions involve processes of coordination that result in different conclusions in different contexts.

First consider the structure and findings from the Milgram (1974) experiments. As detailed elsewhere (Turiel, 2015, in press), in several of the experimental conditions used by Milgram the large majority of participants refused to adhere to the instructions and commands of the experimenter and asserted that they would not inflict physical pain and harm on another. It was in one experimental condition (the most well publicized one) that a majority continued to administer electric shocks (which were not actually felt by the other person) to the end of the scale. Our explanation for these findings (Turiel, 2015) is that the experiments included multiple components that participants took into account. In particular, participants attended to the pain and harm experienced by the other person and the conflicting goals of the scientific enterprise. Participants in the experiments attempted to weigh and balance the moral and scientific goals, most frequently (but not always) giving priority to avoiding harm to another.

The actions of females as documented in the anthropological studies (Abu-Lughod, 1993; Wikan, 1996) appear to reflect decisions about conflicting moral considerations: honesty in conflict with preventing unfairness. The topic of honesty (and trust) seems to be one that poses contradictions and paradoxes for analyses of morality. On the one hand, honesty is often treated as a self-evident moral good requiring adherence. On the other hand, honesty is often regarded as requiring its violation for reasons other than self-interest or benefits to the actor.

The paradoxical nature of honesty and trust has long been part of philosophical discourse. One position, typified by Kant's (1788/1949) categorical and absolutistic view, was that lying can never be morally sanctioned. He maintained that the prohibition on lying could never be justifiably violated because all moral duty and reason are grounded in truth: "To be truthful, honest, in all declarations, therefore, is a sacred and absolutely commanding decree of reason, limited by no expediency" (Kant, 1788/1949, p. 347).

An alternative view holds that when honesty comes into conflict with an even greater duty, lying may be the moral course of action (Mill, 1896/2002; Sidgwick, 1874/1981). As an example, Sidgwick (1874/1981) and others taking a utilitarian stance have maintained that the moral implications of a lie depend upon its context. Therefore, when a lie will lead to greater good than honesty, the lie may be justified on moral grounds. It has also been proposed that categories of lies that entail positive values, such as "rectifying the equilibrium of justice" (Bok, 1978/1999, p. 83), should not be regarded as moral transgressions (Nyberg, 1993; Sweetser, 1987). In support of these positions, examples have been provided of instances in which honesty would lead to the violation of other moral prescriptions. A well-known example is the case of a murderer who comes to your door and asks if you know the location of his intended victim, who has taken shelter inside. This hypothetical case is meant to illustrate that honesty can come in conflict with other moral considerations and goals in ways such that many would regard dishonesty to be the moral course of action.

Examples of this sort are not confined to the musings of philosophers and other scholars about hypotheticals. In the United States there are the examples from past times in which slaves were helped to freedom in the north via surreptitious, deceptive activities. More recent examples come from the activities of those who attempted to save Jews and others from deportation by Nazis to concentration camps. Some, such as Raoul Wallenberg and Oskar Schindler, are well-known for the ways they engaged in complicated actions – often involving deception – to save Jews from deportation or from death while in camps. However, diplomats from many countries, government officials, and citizens engaged in deception to save lives during World War II.

In a different vein, but still involving conflicts between honesty and people's welfare, are frequent reports of physicians who engage in deception of insurance companies when they deem it necessary to prevent harm to their patients (see Wynia, Cummins, VanGeest, & Wilson, 2000, and Hilzenrath, *Washington Post*, March 15, 1998). Hilzenrath related several events recounted by physicians entailing deception on their part, necessitated by insurance company policies, which they deemed necessary in order to save patient's lives or even aid in their healing from severe illnesses. One example is of a physician whose impoverished patient required emergency treatment for a heart condition, which would not have been covered by insurance payments if she were not also admitted for a hospital stay. Although the hospital stay was unnecessary, the physician admitted her, stating, "I admitted her, and then, once she was admitted, as soon as she got to the floor, discharged her. It's a lie. What I would call a white lie" (*Washington Post*, March 15, 1998, p. H1). There is also research documenting that a majority of physicians judge it acceptable to deceive insurance companies when it is necessary for the health and well-being of patients (Freeman, Rathore, Weinfurt, Schulman, & Sulmasy, 1999).

An example closer to home comes from the decisions many psychologists make to engage in deception of participants in experiments on the assumption that it is warranted to achieve scientific goals. A clear and blatant example is the extensive steps of deception taken by Milgram (1974) in his studies – ranging from the content of advertisements to recruit participants to the many lies told to them during the course of the experiments. An ironic example is the myriad studies entailing deception of participants, including children, in order to study the participants' acts of deception.

In spite of these considerations, some psychologists and educators have treated honesty as a value or trait dictating behaviors in unequivocal ways. This has been so in spite of findings dramatically showing that children's cheating behaviors vary by situational contexts – such as in Hartshorne & May's (1928–1930) finding that most children cheat in some but not all situations. The Hartshorne and May studies are an example of researchers deceiving children in order to assess cheating behavior. They assessed the behaviors of large numbers of children in many settings (e.g., tests in schools, athletic contests, games) by deceptively leading the children to think their cheating would not be detected. For those who maintain that honesty is an inviolable value or trait, the findings are interpreted to signify that society (and parents) has not adequately instilled the value or trait. (In children, or in the researchers?)

However, other studies have approached honesty from the perspective of conflicting considerations and goals. For instance, research has been conducted with children and adults regarding so-called white lies, which have positive intentions because they are seen as intended to promote greater good (Bok, 1978/1999). A common finding across a range of studies on this topic is that beginning in early childhood children evaluate lies used to spare another's feelings (e.g., about the desirability of a gift) more positively than self-serving lies (Bussey, 1999; DePaulo, Kashy, Kirkendol, Wyer, & Epstein, 1996; Lewis, 1993). Correspondingly, it has been found that children and adults consider selfishly motivated lies to be worse than lies intended to spare the feelings of others (Bussey, 1999; Heyman, Sweet, & Lee, 2009; Peterson, Peterson, & Seeto, 1983; Talwar & Lee, 2008). In that line of research, it has been found that with increasing age, more children positively evaluate lies intended to benefit others (Lee & Ross, 1997; Talwar, Murphy, & Lee, 2007; Talwar, Lee, Bala, & Lindsay, 2002). Nevertheless, children as young as 3 years old rate lies that prevent harm more positively than self-serving lies (Fu & Lee, 2007). It has also been found that children at all ages judge selfishly motivated lies as wrong.

Another line of research shows that beginning in early childhood, judgments about the acceptability of lying take into account the intentions of those telling the lie (Hala, Chandler, & Fritz, 1991). When lies are told with the intent of acting politely or to maintain social harmony (e.g., "I don't mind waiting for you"; "I like your new haircut"), the majority of children (aged 3–7 years) judge deception to be permissible (Broomfield, Robinson, & Robinson, 2002; Talwar & Lee, 2008). The findings of these studies indicate that children assess intent in their judgments about the permissibility of a lie.

In our own research, we have focused on judgments about deception of parents, teachers, and peers in contexts placing honesty or trust in potential conflict with other moral goals, personals goals, or prudence and safety. Putting together findings from studies with children (Gingo, 2012) and with adolescents (Perkins & Turiel, 2007) shows that along with systematic contextual variations in judgments about the acceptability of deception, there are age-related commonalities and differences. In one study, the participants were children ranging in age from 7–12 years. They were presented with situations in which parents or teachers were depicted as directing a child to engage in acts considered morally wrong (e.g., cutting in line), acts in the personal domain (e.g., pertaining to choice of friends), and prudential acts (e.g., climbing a wall at a park); the child does not engage in the directed action, and then lies about it. Assessments were made of evaluations of the legitimacy of the directives of parents or teachers, the acts of non-compliance by the child, and the acts of deception on the part of the child. One set of findings is that children at all ages evaluated the directives from parents or teachers regarding the acts in the moral domain as unacceptable, coupled with positive evaluations of non-compliance with the directives. Nevertheless, the majority of children judge deception of parents or teachers as wrong. Some age differences were found in judgments about deception: 90% of the 7–8 year olds judged deception regarding the moral acts negatively, a percentage that decreased with age in that 70% of the 9–10 year olds and 50% of the 11–12 year olds judged deception as wrong.

The pattern of findings regarding situations involving acts in the personal domain differed from those involving acts in the moral domain. First, it was found that the younger children were more accepting of the directives from parents or teachers and more likely to negatively evaluate non-compliance than were older children. However, with age there was increased acceptance of deception regarding the acts involving personal choices (corresponding with the moral domain evaluations of deception). Judgments regarding the prudential acts were different in that at all ages the legitimacy of parental or teacher jurisdiction was accepted, and both non-compliance and deception were judged as wrong.

The findings of the research with children appears to demonstrate that there is a trajectory toward increasing priority given to adherence to moral considerations of preventing unfairness and to promoting legitimate personal choice over honesty. The study (Perkins & Turiel, 2007) with adolescents in two age groups (12–13 and 16–17 year olds) indicates that these patterns continue with increasing age. In that study, participants were asked to judge deception after directives from parents regarding acts in the moral, personal, and prudential domains. The large majority in both age groups did not accept the legitimacy of the parental directives in the moral domain and judged deception regarding those acts as acceptable. Therefore, among adolescents somewhat older than those in the Gingo (2012) study, moral considerations were given priority over honesty. It was also found that in these groups honesty is subordinated to fulfilling personal goals. Most of the 12–13 year olds judged deception of parents regarding the personal acts as acceptable (62%), and the large majority of the 16–17 year olds judged the deception as acceptable (92%). There were no differences in the judgments of the adolescents and younger children regarding the prudential acts since most rejected the legitimacy of deception.

It is not only adolescents who systematically give moral and personal consideration priority over honesty. We have also found that adults judge that deception is sometimes necessary to promote physical and emotional welfare and to assert personal choices in the context of marital relationships of inequality (Turiel & Perkins, 2004). Also engaging in processes of coordination, adults give priority to welfare over honesty or personal choices over honesty in situations entailing power differences and inequalities. The findings in the study with adolescents also showed that power differences and perceived social inequalities have a bearing on judgments about deception. It was found that the adolescents judged it more acceptable to deceive parents regarding acts in the moral and personal domains than it was to deceive their peers. Whereas the adolescents saw a need to use deception with parents, who are in positions of control and authority, they maintained that deception was not acceptable with peers, i.e., relationships viewed as based on equality and reciprocity.

Non-Relativism Without Moral Absolutism

The findings from both the study with adolescents and the one with adults brings us back to the findings discussed above: that females in patriarchal cultures engage in deception in order to circumvent power differences and practices of inequality. We interpret all these findings from Western and non-Western cultures to reflect that individuals engage in processes of coordination in coming to decisions in many situational contexts. The proposition that decisions in different situational contexts involve processes of coordination has implications for positions on perennial questions about moral universality and relativism – especially evident in philosophical debates. The relativist position, to put it simply, is that morality is specific to cultures, varying in ways that make cultural moral systems incomparable with each other. The universalist position, also put simply, is that aspects of moral judgments in social relationships are applicable to humans wherever they live, and therefore are not confined to particular cultures. Perhaps put a little less simply, these philosophical debates include considerations as to whether moral values are established by conventions or functions necessary within society, or are valid in that they represent "oughts" or "shoulds" that apply to all manner of social interactions. There is a third category – that of moral absolutism – that is contrasted with relativism but is sometimes associated with universality. As we discuss below, absolutism in the sense that moral judgments must always be applied in a certain way is not the same as universality.

Questions regarding universality, relativism, and absolutism are relevant for social scientific analyses as well. Many psychologists have, implicitly or explicitly, taken a relativistic position in assuming that the development of morality involves children's incorporation of values, standards, or customs of society mainly through their transmission especially by parents. The assumption of moral relativism stems from the proposed process of acquisition since the content of morality depends on the society one happens to populate. Consequently, moral values are particular to societies, incomparable with each other, and, in a sense, arbitrary but established by convention.

A related but different conceptualization of relativism comes from those proposing that cultures are cohesive and integrated, with differing patterns of organization. An example of early propositions of this sort was put forth by the cultural anthropologist Ruth Benedict (1934), who asserted that there is a great deal of variation in what might be considered fundamental moral values, such as in the "matter of taking a life." Recent formulations of integrated cultural patterns often identify two types of more or less homogeneous orientations labeled "individualist" and "collectivist," usually associated with Western and non-Western cultures (Markus & Kitayama, 1991; Triandis, 1990). In addition to identifying differences in specific social norms and cultural practices, characterizations of individualism and collectivism are meant to define respective general orientations to morality, the group, and persons (individualists emphasize independence, freedom of choice, and rights; collectivists emphasize the group, interdependence, moral duties and adherence roles in the social hierarchy).

By contrast, social and biological scientists implicitly take universalist positions insofar as morality is proposed to be biologically based. Such a position is taken by evolutionary psychologists, sociobiologists, and neuroscientists proposing that behaviors such as altruism and other traits or a universal moral grammar are genetically determined (e.g., Greene & Haidt, 2002; Hauser, 2006). Others have taken a universalist position with a decidedly absolutistic bent in proposing that morality entails acting upon a set of acquired traits of character (e.g., honesty, loyalty, responsibility) that must be categorically followed (Bennett, 1993; Ryan, 1989).

In the relativistic propositions that cultures embody varying and incommensurate moral positions, there has been reliance on the identification of differing practices and on the broad characterizations of cultural orientations. In biologically based universalist or absolutist propositions there is an assumption of fixed judgments and actions determined by evolutionary processes. We maintain that each of these views is inadequate because they fail to account for the development of social and moral judgments that make for different systems of thought within individuals, people's flexibility of mind in coming to social and moral decisions, the heterogeneity in judgments about persons and groups, and important commonalities across cultures. Our propositions are rooted in constructivist-relational explanations of processes of development. In this framework, development is due to reciprocal interactions of the individual and the environment (Overton, 2006; Piaget, 1932; Werner, 1957).

Whether comparing different situational contexts or different cultural contexts, it is necessary to consider how moral and other social judgments are applied. Looking at decisions from the perspective of the application of different types of judgments and how they are weighed and balanced in processes of coordination yields compelling evidence that there is not homogeneity within individuals or within cultures. Heterogeneity in social perspectives, domains of moral, social, and personal judgments, as well as reflections upon cultural practices and systems of social organization result in the complex and multifaceted similarities and differences among cultures we represented in Figure 12.1.

References

Abu-Lughod, L. (1993). *Writing women's worlds: Bedouin stories*. Berkeley: University of California Press.

Arsenio, W. (1988). Children's conceptions of the situational affective consequences of sociomoral events. *Child Development, 59,* 1611–1622.

Arsenio, W., & Fleiss, K. (1996). Typical and behaviourally disruptive children's understanding of the emotional consequences of socio-moral events. *British Journal of Developmental Psychology, 14,* 173–186.

Benedict, R. (1934). *Patterns of culture*. Boston: Houghton Mifflin.

Bennett, W. J. (1993). *The book of virtues*. New York, NY: Simon & Schuster.

Bok, S. (1999). *Lying: Moral choice in public and private life*. New York, NY: Vintage Books. (Original work published 1978)

Broomfield, K. A., Robinson, E. J., & Robinson, W. P. (2002). Children's understanding about white lies. *British Journal of Developmental Psychology, 20*(1), 47–65.

Bussey, K. (1999). Children's categorization and evaluation of different types of lies and truths. *Child Development, 70*(6), 1338–1347.

Cole, M., Gay, J., Glick, J. A., & Sharp, D. W. (Eds.). (1971). *The cultural context of learning and thinking*. New York, NY: Basic Books.

Conry-Murray, C. (2009). Adolescent and adult reasoning about gender roles and fairness in Benin, West Africa. *Cognitive Development, 24,* 207–219.

Cushman, F., Young, L., & Hauser, M. (2006). The role of conscious reasoning and intuition in moral judgment: Testing three principles of harm. *Psychological Science, 17,* 1082–1089.

Dahl, A., Gingo, M., Uttich, K., & Turiel, E. (in preparation) Reasoning about lives and deaths in trolley car dilemmas.

DePaulo, B. M., Kashy, D. A., Kirkendol, S. E., Wyer, M. M., & Epstein, J. A. (1996). Lying in everyday life. *Journal of personality and social psychology, 70*(5), 979–995.

Dworkin, R. (1993). *Life's dominion: An argument about abortion, euthanasia, and individual freedom*. New York, NY: Alfred A. Knopf.

Freeman, V. G., Rathore, S. S., Weinfurt, K. P., Schulman, K. A., & Sulmasy, D. P. (1999). Lying for patients: Physician deception of third-party payers. *Archives of Internal Medicine, 159,* 2263–2270.

Frijda, N. (1986). *The emotions*. New York, NY: Cambridge University Press.

Fu, G., & Lee, K. (2007). Social grooming in the kindergarten: the emergence of flattery behavior. *Developmental science, 10*(2), 255–265.

Gingo, M. E. (2012). The coordination of social contextual features in children's use and reasoning about honesty and deception. Unpublished doctoral dissertation. University of California, Berkeley.

Greene, J., & Haidt, J. (2002). How (and where) does moral judgment work? *Trends in Cognitive Science, 6,* 516–523.

Greene, J. D., Sommerville, R. B., Nystrom, L. E., Darley, J. M., & Cohen, J. D. (2001). An fMRI investigation of emotional engagement in moral judgment. *Science. 293,* 2105–2108.

Guvenc, G. (2011). Women's construction of familial-gender identities and embodied subjectivities in Saraycik, Turkey. Unpublished manuscript. Isik University, Istanbul, Turkey.

Hala, S., Chandler, M., & Fritz, A. S. (1991). Fledgling theories of mind: Deception as a marker of three-year-olds' understanding of false belief. *Child Development*, *62*(1), 83–97.

Hartshorne, H., & May, M. A. (1928–1930). *Studies in the nature of character. Vol. 1: Studies in deceit. Vol. 2: Studies in self-control. Vol. 3: Studies in the organization of character.* New York, NY: Macmillan.

Hauser, M. D. (2006). *Moral minds: How nature designed a universal sense of right and wrong.* New York, NY: Harper Collins.

Heyman, G. D., Sweet, M. A., & Lee, K. (2009). Children's reasoning about lie-telling and truth-telling in politeness contexts. *Social Development*, *18*(3), 728–746.

Hilzenrath, D. S. (1998, March 15). Healing vs. honesty? For doctors, managed care's cost controls pose moral dilemma. *The Washington Post*, p. H1.

Kant, I. (1788/1949). On a supposed right to lie from benevolent motives. In L. W. Beck (Ed. & Trans.) *Critique of practical reason and other writings in moral philosophy* (pp. 346–350). Chicago: University of Chicago Press.

Koenigs, M., Young, L. Adolphs, R., Tranel, D., Cushman, F., Hauser, M., Damasio, A. (2007). Damage to the prefrontal cortex increases utilitarian moral judgements. *Nature*, *446*, 908–911.

Kohlberg, L. (1969). Stage and sequence: The cognitive-developmental approach to socialization. In D. Goslin (Ed.), *Handbook of socialization theory and research* (pp. 347–480). Chicago: Rand McNally.

Kohlberg, L. (1971). From is to ought: How to commit the naturalistic fallacy and get away with it in the study of moral development. In T. Mischel (Ed.), *Psychology and genetic epistemology* (pp. 151–235). New York, NY: Academic Press.

Lazarus, N. (1991). *Emotion and adaptation.* New York, NY: Oxford University Press.

Lee, K., & Ross, H. J. (1997). The concept of lying in adolescents and young adults: Testing Sweetser's folkloristic model. *Merrill-Palmer Quarterly, 43*, 255–270.

Lewis, M., (1993). The development of deception. In M. Lewis & C. Saarni (Eds.), *Lying and deception in everyday life* (pp. 90–105). New York, NY: Guilford Press.

Markus, H. R., & Kitayama, S. (1991). Culture and the self: Implications for cognition, emotion, and motivation. *Psychological Review*, *98*, 224–253.

Mensing, J. F. (2002). Collectivism, individualism, and interpersonal responsibilities in families: Differences and similarities in social reasoning between individuals in poor, urban families in Colombia and the United States. Unpublished doctoral dissertation. University of California, Berkeley.

Milgram, S. (1963). Behavioral study of obedience. *Journal of Abnormal and Social Psychology*, *67*, 371–378.

Milgram, S. (1974). *Obedience to authority.* New York, NY: Harper & Row.

Mill, J. S. (1896/2002). *J S Mill: 'On Liberty' and other writings.* Cambridge, UK: Cambridge University Press.

Moors, A., & Scherer, K. R. (2013). The role of appraisal in emotion. In M. D. Robinson, E. R. Watkins, & E. Harmon-Jones (Eds.), *Handbook of cognition and emotion* (pp. 131–155). New York, NY: Guilford Press.

Neff, K. D. (2001). Judgments of personal autonomy and interpersonal responsibility in the context of Indian spousal relationships: An examination of young people's reasoning in Mysore, India. *British Journal of Developmental Psychology*, *19*, 233–257.

Nucci, L. P., & Nucci, M. S. (1982a). Children's reponses to moral and social conventional transgressions in free-play settings. *Child Development*, *53*, 1337–1342.

Nucci, L. P., & Nucci, M. S. (1982b). Children's social interactions in the context of moral and conventional transgressions. *Child Development, 53*, 403–412.

Nucci, L. P., & Turiel, E. (1978). Social interactions and the development of social concepts in preschool children. *Child Development, 49*, 400–407.

Nucci, L. P., Turiel, E., & Encarnacion-Gawrych, G. (1983). Children's social interactions and social concepts: Analyses of morality and convention in the Virgin Islands. *Journal of Cross-Cultural Psychology, 14*, 469–487.

Nucci, L. P., & Weber, E. (1995). Social interactions in the home and the development of young children's conceptions of the personal. *Child Development, 66*, 1438–1452.

Nussbaum, M. C. (1999). *Sex and social justice.* New York, NY: Oxford University Press.

Nussbaum, M. C. (2001). *Upheavals of thought: The intelligence of emotions.* Cambridge, UK: Cambridge University Press.

Nyberg, S. (1993). *Honesty, vanity and corporate equity: Four microeconomic essays.* Unpublished doctoral dissertation. Stockholm School of Economics.

Overton, W. F. (2006). Developmental psychology: Philosophy, concepts, methodology. In R. M. Lerner (Ed.), *Theoretical models of human development. Vol. 1 of the Handbook of Child Psychology* (6th edn., pp. 18–88). Editors-in-chief: W. Damon & R. M. Lerner. Hoboken, NJ: Wiley.

Perkins, S. A. & Turiel, E. (2007). To lie or not to lie: To whom and under what circumstances. *Child Development, 78*, 609–621.

Peterson, C. C., Peterson, J. L., & Seeto, D. (1983). Developmental changes in ideas about lying. *Child Development, 54*, 1529–1535.

Piaget, J. (1932). *The moral judgment of the child.* London: Routledge & Kegan Paul.

Piaget, J. (1970). *Psychology and epistemology.* New York, NY: Viking Press.

Rawls, J. (1971). *A theory of justice.* Cambridge, MA: Harvard University Press.

Rawls, J. (1993). *Political liberalism.* New York, NY: Columbia University Press.

Ryan, K. (1989). In defense of character education. In L. P. Nucci (Ed.), *Moral development and character education: A dialogue* (pp. 3–18). Berkeley, CA: McCutchan Publishing Corporation.

Sen, A. (2006). *Identity and violence: The illusion of destiny.* New York, NY: Norton

Sen, A. (2009). *The idea of justice.* Cambridge, MA: Harvard University Press.

Shweder, R. A., Much, N. C., Mahapatra, M., & Park, L. (1997). The "Big Three" of morality (Autonomy, Community, and Divinity) and the "Big Three" explanations of suffering. In A. Brandt & P. Rozin (Eds.), *Morality and health* (pp. 119–169). Stanford, CA: Stanford University Press.

Sidgwick, H. (1874/1981). *The methods of ethics.* Indianapolis, IN: Hackett Publishing.

Smetana, J. G. (2006). *Social domain theory: Consistencies and variations in children's moral and social judgments.* In M. Killen & J. G. Smetana (Eds.), *Handbook of moral development* (pp. 119–153). Mahwah, NJ: Erlbaum.

Sweetser, E. E. (1987). The definition of a lie: An examination of the folk models underlying a semantic prototype. In D. Holland (Ed.), *Cultural models in language and thought* (pp. 43–66). Cambridge, UK: Cambridge University Press.

Talwar, V., & Lee, K. (2008). Social and cognitive correlates of children's lying behavior. *Child Development, 79*(4), 866–881.

Talwar, V., Lee, K., Bala, N., & Lindsay, R. C. L. (2002). Children's conceptual knowledge of lying and its relation to their actual behaviors: Implications for court competence examinations. *Law and Human Behavior, 26*(4), 395.

Talwar, V., Murphy, S. M., & Lee, K. (2007). White lie-telling in children for politeness purposes. *International Journal of Behavioral Development, 30*, 1–11.

Triandis, H. C. (1990). Cross-cultural studies of individualism and collectivism. In J. J. Berman (Ed.), *Nebraska Symposium on motivation: 1989, Vol. 37. Cross-cultural perspectives* (pp. 41–133). Lincoln: University of Nebraska Press.

Turiel, E. (1978). Social regulation and domains of social concepts. In W. Damon (Ed.), *Social cognition: New directions for child development* (pp. 45–74). San Francisco: Jossey-Bass.

Turiel, E. (1983a). *The development of social knowledge: Morality and convention.* Cambridge, UK: Cambridge University Press.

Turiel, E. (1983b). Domains and categories in social-cognitive development. In W. Overton (Ed.), *The relationship between social and cognitive development* (pp. 53–89). Hillsdale, NJ: Erlbaum Associates.

Turiel, E. (1998). The development of morality. In N. Eisenberg (Ed.), *Social, emotional, and personality development. Vol. 3 of the Handbook of child psychology* (5th edn., pp. 863–932). Editor-in-chief: W. Damon. New York, NY: John Wiley & Sons.

Turiel, E. (2002). *The culture of morality: Social development, context, and conflict.* Cambridge, UK: Cambridge University Press

Turiel, E. (2008a). Social decisions, social interactions, and the coordination of diverse judgments. In U. Mueller, J. I. Carpendale, N. Budwig, & B. Sokol (Eds.), *Social life, social knowledge: Toward a process account of Development* (pp. 255–276). Mahwah, NJ: Erlbaum.

Turiel, E. (2008b). Thought about actions in social domains: Morality, social conventions, and social interactions. *Cognitive Development, 23*, 126–154.

Turiel, E. (2010a). The relevance of moral epistemology and psychology for neuroscience. In P. Zelazo, M. Chandler, & E. Crone (Eds.), *Developmental social cognitive neuroscience* (pp. 313–331). New York, NY: Taylor & Francis.

Turiel, E. (2010b). The development of morality: Reasoning, emotions, and resistance. In W. F. Overton (Vol. Ed), *Cognition, biology, and methods across the lifespan. Vol. 1 of the Handbook of life-span development.* (pp. 554–583) Editor-in-chief: R. M. Lerner. Hoboken, NJ: Wiley.

Turiel, E. (2015). Moral development. In W. F. Overton & P. C. Molenaar (Eds.), *Handbook of child psychology, Vol. 1: Theory & method*, 7th edn., Editor-in- chief: R. M. Lerner (pp. 484–522). Hoboken, NJ: John Wiley & Sons.

Turiel, E. (in press). Reasoning at the root of morality. In K. Gray & J. Graham (Eds.). *The atlas of moral psychology.* New York, NY: Guilford Publications.

Turiel, E., & Dahl, A. (in press). The development of domains of moral and conventional norms, coordination in decision-making, and the implications of social opposition. In K. Bayertz & N. Roughley (Eds.). *The normative Animal: On the anthropological significance of social, moral, and linguistic norms.* Oxford, UK: Oxford University Press.

Turiel, E., & Killen, M. (2010). Taking emotions seriously: The role of emotions in moral development. In W. Arsenio & E. Lemerise (Eds.), *Emotions, aggression, and morality in children: Bridging development and psychopathology* (pp. 33–52). Washington, D.C.: APA.

Turiel, E., & Perkins, S. A. (2004). Flexibilities of mind: Conflict and culture. *Human Development, 47*, 158–178.

Wainryb, C., Brehl, B. A., & Matwin, S. (2005). Being hurt and hurting others: Children's narrative accounts and moral judgments of their own interpersonal conflicts. *Monographs of the Society for Research in Child Development*, *70*, No. 3, Serial No. 281.

Wainryb, C., & Turiel, E. (1994). Dominance, subordination, and concepts of personal entitlements in cultural contexts. *Child Development*, *65*, 1701–1722.

Walzer, M. (2007). *Thinking politically: Essays in political theory*. New Haven: Yale University Press.

Werner, H. (1957). *Comparative psychology of mental development*. New York, NY: International Universities Press.

Wikan, U. (1976/1980). *Life among the poor in Cairo*. New York, NY: Tavistock Publications.

Wikan, U. (1982). *Behind the veil in Arabia*. Chicago: University of Chicago Press.

Wikan, U. (1996). *Tomorrow, God willing: Self-made destinies in Cairo*. Chicago: University of Chicago Press.

Wynia, M. K., Cummins, D. S., VanGeest, J. B., & Wilson, I. B. (2000). Physician manipulation of reimbursement rules for patients: Between a rock and a hard place. *Journal of the American Medical Association*, *283*, 1858–1865.

13 Resistance to Dehumanization during Childhood and Adolescence: A Developmental and Contextual Process

Niobe Way and Leoandra Onnie Rogers

Children develop within the macro-context of cultures and ideologies infused with a set of stereotypes about what it means to be a particular sex, race, nationality, religion, sexuality, and social class as well as beliefs about what it means to be a mature, successful, and happy adult (e.g., Bronfenbrenner, 1979; Coll et al., 1996; Harwood, Miller, & Irizarry, 1997; Spencer & Markstrom-Adams, 1990; Tamis-LeMonda et al., 2008; Turiel, 2003; Way, 2011). In American culture, children are taught – via the media, school, and family – gender stereotypes such as that being a "real man" entails being stoic, independent, and tough, and being a "good woman" involves sacrificing oneself for others (Brown & Gilligan, 1992; Gilligan, 1982, 2011; Kimmel, 2008; Pollack, 2000). They are also taught racial and ethnic stereotypes, such as that being "Black" or "Hispanic," especially from poor or working-class families, means not caring about school and only being interested in money, drugs, and sex (e.g., Cvencek, Nasir, O'Connor, Wischnia, & Meltzoff, 2015; Ghavami & Peplau, 2013; Spencer & Markstrom-Adams, 1990). Children are taught, furthermore, that the meaning of maturity, success, and happiness lies in being self-sufficient, autonomous, and financially well off (e.g., Bellah, Madsen, Sullivan, Swindler, & Tipton, 1985; Gilligan, 1982; Putnam, 2001; Rubens, 2008). Yet these stereotypes and beliefs fail to recognize the human potential, capacity, and needs of boys and girls, particularly those who are of color, poor, or working class, and thus dehumanize them (e.g., Gilligan, 1982, 2011; Hrdy, 2009; Putnam, 2001; Rubens, 2008; Turiel, 2003; Way, 2011). Believing that boys, including Asian American boys, are thinkers and not feelers and that girls are feelers and not thinkers or that Black boys, particularly from low-income families, are neither thinkers nor feelers, represent boys and girls, at best, as only partially human (they think *or* feel) or as not human at all (they neither think *nor* feel). According to a patriarchal and capitalist system that makes certain people (e.g., White, straight, rich, and Christian males) more human than others, the situation is much worse, of course, if the intersections of a child's social identities place her at the bottom of the "hierarchy of humanness" (e.g., Black, gay girls from working-class families) (See Way, 2014). In addition, believing that maturity, success, and happiness are solely contingent on independence and self-sufficiency denies the very real human need and capacity to belong, to be connected to a community, and to love, which have been consistently linked to longevity, health, and happiness (e.g., Cacioppo & Patrick, 2008; Hrdy, 2009; Lieberman, 2013; Putnam, 2001; Wilkinson & Pickett, 2009). There is, in other words, a disconnect or mismatch between American culture, with its damaging stereotypes and its privileging of the individual over relationships, and the very real capacities and needs of humans regardless of gender, race, ethnicity, social class, and sexual identity. Yet, we also know that humans resist such dehumanization, particularly during childhood and early adolescence.

Over the past three decades, researchers have consistently found that youth resist dehumanizing stereotypes and the privileging of the self over relationship (Anyon, 1984; Barker, 2000, 2005; Brown & Gilligan, 1992; Chu, 2004, 2014; Gilligan, 1982; 1990, 1996, 2011; Reichert & Ravitch, 2009; Robinson & Ward, 1991; Turiel, 2003; Turiel, Chung, & Carr, 2016; Ward, 1996; Way, 2011; Way et al., 2014; Way & Rogers, 2014). This growing body of research also suggests that such resistance is shaped by the context and is linked to psychological, social, and academic wellbeing (Gupta et al., 2013; Rogers & Way, 2016; Rogers, Yang, Way, Weinberg, & Bennet, under review; Santos, 2010; Santos, Galligan, Pahlke & Fabes, 2013; Way, 2011).

In this chapter, we present theoretical and empirical literature on the development of resistance to dehumanizing stereotypes and beliefs during childhood and adolescence; the role of the family and school context in the development of such resistance; and the links between resistance and individual-level wellbeing. Drawing from over thirty years of mixed-method research with children and adolescents, including our own, we reveal the importance of resistance in social and emotional development and suggest that interventions aimed at helping boys and girls thrive should focus on fostering resistance to dehumanization.

Resistance to Dehumanization

Resistance is a process by which individuals negotiate systems of oppression, including cultural norms, expectations, and stereotypes that dehumanize them (Anyon, 1984; Brown & Gilligan, 1992; Gilligan, 2011; Turiel, 2003; Way, 2011; Ward, 1996). Eugene D. Genovese (1976) writes of how resistance was a part of the daily lives of Black slaves during the 19th century: "Accommodation and resistance developed as two forms of a single process by which slaves accepted what could not be avoided and simultaneously fought [resisted] individually and as a people for moral as well as physical survival" (p. 658). Feminists and critical race scholars have extended the study of resistance to include an analysis of gender and race, exploring the ways in which oppressed groups (e.g., women, people of color) challenge normative beliefs and practices that undermine their humanity or their ability to see themselves and to be seen as fully human (Anyon, 1984; Gilligan, 1982, 2011; hooks, 1989; Tate, 1997; Way, 2011; West & Zimmerman, 1987).

Developmental psychologists, more recently, have investigated the ways in which children and adolescents resist stereotypes, expectations, and roles that undermine their humanity and how such patterns of resistance change from childhood through adolescence (e.g., Brown & Gilligan, 1992; Chu, 2004, 2014; Gilligan, 1990, 1996, 2011; Gupta et al., 2013; Rogers & Way, 2016; Santos, 2010; Santos et al., 2013; Turiel, 2003; Way, 2011; Way et al. 2014; Way & Rogers, 2014). Their studies suggest that resistance to dehumanization is a core part of healthy social and emotional development. Carol Gilligan (2011) describes the process of resistance:

> Like a healthy body, a healthy psyche resists disease. . . . It fights for freedom from dissociation, from the splits in consciousness that would keep parts of ourselves and our experiences outside our awareness. How else would women have found the will to secure agency, property ownership, the vote, fair pay, and freedom…? How would any people free themselves from psychological as well as political colonization?
> (pp. 32–33)

The study of resistance grows out of the recognition that children and adolescents are, from the beginning of life, active participants in their own socialization (Anyon, 1984; Brown & Gilligan, 1992; Chu, 2014; Gilligan, 1982, 1991; Turiel, 2003; Robinson & Ward, 1991). They are not simply passive recipients who accommodate to stereotypic messages received from parents, teachers, and peers about what it means to be a girl, with its emphasis on selflessness, a boy, with its emphasis on stoicism, toughness, and independence, or what it means to be Black or Latino, with its emphasis on "cool poses" and academic disengagement (Majors & Billson, 1992). They often resist these stereotypic messages and expectations (Brown & Gilligan, 1992; Chu, 2014; Gilligan, 1991, 2011; Robinson & Ward, 1991; Turiel, 2003; Way, 2011; Way et al., 2014; Ward, 1996).

Stereotypes are dehumanizing because they divide human beings into binaries (e.g., thinking or feeling), deeming them to be either *competent* or *incompetent* along social, emotional, moral, and cognitive domains. Some social groups are considered *entirely competent* in the cognitive domain and significantly less so in the social and emotional domains (e.g., White and Asian middle- and upper-class boys and men). Others are considered primarily competent in the social and emotional domains and less competent in the cognitive domain (e.g., White middle and upper-class girls and women), and still others are considered *incompetent* in the social, emotional, and cognitive domains (e.g., poor and working-class people and Black people). As these divisions suggest, stereotypes about social groups intersect with each other so that stereotypes about Black people, for example, are not the same as stereotypes about Black women, nor are stereotypes about Black women the same as those for White women (Ghavami & Peplau, 2013; Shields, 2008). For example, Ghavami and Peplau (2013) found that Black women were stereotyped as "promiscuous" and "overweight," while Black men were stereotyped as "rappers" and "quick to anger," but none of these stereotypes were used to describe Black people in general or White women. Yet regardless of the specificity of stereotypes, they dehumanize their recipients by suggesting that the stereotyped group is only half human or not human at all in that they are only competent in one or the other of the core domains that make us human.

While some stereotypes appear, or are considered to be, "positive" (e.g., Asian people are smart, boys are good at math, Black people are athletic), they position one group in opposition to another (Asian vs. non-Asian, boys vs. girls, and Black vs. White) in terms of social and emotional skills, intellectual ability, or physical prowess, and reify supposed differences. The implicit message of stereotyping is that members of a different ethnicity, race, gender, or social class than the stereotype do not possess those qualities or that those who are from the same ethnic, racial, gender, or class group as the stereotype but who do not possess those qualities are not true representations of that social group (Nasir, 2011). In this narrative, the Black male scientist who lacks athletic prowess is deemed "not Black enough" and the Asian American teen who struggles in math is "not really Asian" (Carter, 2006; Horvat & O'Connor, 2006; Nasir, Snyder, Shah, & Ross, 2012). In this way, *all* stereotypes are dehumanizing because they foster a binary that at its root is denying the full humanity of the individual. Thus, stereotypes dehumanize us and foster disconnections both within and between groups.

Decades of research have investigated how individuals conform or adhere to gender or racial stereotypes and perpetuate systems of inequality (Cournoyer & Mahalik, 1995; Fordham & Ogbu, 1986; Good et al., 1995; Hayes & Mahalik, 2000; Kimmel, 2008; Mahalik, Burns, & Syzdek, 2007; Ogbu, 1978; O'Neil, 2008; Pleck, 1981, 1995; Pleck, Sonenstein, & Ku, 1994; Wester, Kuo, & Vogel, 2006; Wong & Rochlen, 2008). Yet the empirical study of resistance or the ways in which people challenge gender or racial stereotypes attitudinally and behaviorally continue to be rare. There exists, however, a growing number of studies focused on resistance among girls and women (e.g., Anyon, 1984; Brown, 1999; Brown & Gilligan, 1992; Gilligan, 1996; Gilligan, 2011; Robinson & Ward, 1991; Turiel, 2003; Ward, 1996) and on boys and young men (Barker, 2005; Chu, 2014; Rogers, 2012; Rogers & Way, 2016; Way, 2011; Way et al., 2014). In our own longitudinal research with hundreds of Black, Latino, Asian American, and White adolescents from primarily working-class families, we find that the vast majority of boys and girls resist gender and racial stereotypes at some point in their development, particularly during late childhood and early adolescence (Rogers & Way, 2016; Santos, 2010; Way, 2011; Way, Hernández, Rogers, & Hughes, 2013; Way, Santos, Niwa, & Kim-Gervey, 2008; Way & Rogers, 2014) and that this resistance can take various forms, changes over time, is shaped by the family and school context, and is linked to psychological, social, and academic wellbeing (Rogers, Niwa, & Way, 2017; Rogers & Way, 2016; Rogers et al., under review; Santos et al., 2013; Way, 2011, 2014; Way et al., 2014).

Resistance to Dehumanization: Gender

Most of the work on resistance has focused on gender, with one of the earliest studies of resistance being conducted by sociologist Jean Anyon (1984), who examined resistance to gender stereotypes among girls. Her work underscored that gender socialization is not a one-way process of the society imposing values on children, but, rather, a process of children actively responding to the "social contradictions" of gender that culture imposes on them from a very early age. In her ethnographic research with fifth-graders, she finds that girls, across race and social class, both resist and accommodate to gender expectations and ideals. For example, when asked if she will work when she grows up, a fifth-grade girl responded:

> Yes, I want to be a violinist. But I don't know if he [my husband] would want me to work. Men are number one. I don't think I would like to be as strong as men. Strong women wouldn't be pretty.

This dance between resisting the cultural confines of femininity ("Yes I want to work ") and endorsing them ("Strong women wouldn't be pretty") illustrates the conflict that stereotypes place on girls' identities, the tension between what they *want* (and don't want) and what they *should* do. Anyon's (1984) study further shows that even when girls adhere to stereotypes they do not do so passively or without contest: "If you're a wife you've got to clean and cook. . . . I do not want to do that. But I'll probably be a wife and I'll work too." Exercising resistance by expressing her explicit dislike for the stereotypic role of wife (cooking and cleaning), this young girl indicates that she may acquiesce ("I'll probably be a wife") but not quietly ("I'll work too"). Rather than being passive recipients of gender socialization, girls actively engage with and resist cultural messages and expectations as they construct their identities. Anyon (1984) concludes that the processes of resistance and accommodation are evident not only among girls but among all children as they develop in cultures infused with contradictory values and dehumanizing stereotypes.

Developmental psychologists have also examined resistance to dehumanizing stereotypes and have found that resistance is particularly evident for girls in late childhood and for boys in both early childhood and early adolescence (Brown & Gilligan, 1992; Gilligan, 2011; Chu, 2014; Way, 2011, 2013; Way et al., 2014). The landmark study of girls' development by Carol Gilligan and Lyn Mikel Brown (Brown & Gilligan; 1992; Gilligan, 2011) tells a developmental story of resistance among girls and makes the distinction between *political* and *psychological resistance*. *Political resistance* entails resisting a patriarchal framework that silences girls and women by promoting a femininity focused on being "nice and kind" at the expense of saying what one knows, feels, and thinks. *Psychological resistance*, in contrast, is the resistance to knowing what one knows or going underground with one's knowledge in the name of being "a perfect girl" by not causing any disruption. They find in their 5-year longitudinal research with over one hundred girls that political resistance is evident especially during late childhood and that psychological resistance is evident during adolescence.

At 8–11 years of age across race and ethnicity, the girls in their study speak their minds freely, with a remarkable honesty and transparency, and resist the constraints of a femininity that tells them to be nice, kind, and complicit with the demands of the adult world. They speak what they know with their interviewers, underscoring the contradictions that they see and the honesty that they seek. Emma, one of the girls in their study, says at 10 years old, "my house is wallpapered in lies." Eleven-year-old Tessie says:

> When you are having an argument with your mother or brother and you just keep it inside and don't tell anyone, you never hear the other person's point of view. But if you tell your friend about the argument with your mother or brother, you are telling it from both sides and so you hear what my mother said, or what my brother said. And your friend can say, well, "you might be mad, but your mom was right," and you say, "yeah, I know." So when you say it out loud, you have to listen to both sides. (Brown & Gilligan, 1992)

The astute and honest responses of Emma and Tessie were typical of the girls during late childhood. They told it like it is with stunning clarity and resisted a culture that tells them to silence themselves or not know what they know to be true (Brown & Gilligan, 1992; Gilligan, 2011).

Once the girls in their study reached adolescence, however, they began to "discover that their honest voices jeopardize their relationships, not only their personal relationships but also their connection to the culture they are entering as young women" (Brown & Gilligan, 1992, p. 93). Consequently, the girls began saying "I don't know" in response to the interviewers' questions and claim not to know what they knew only a few years earlier. They experience a "crisis of connection" of whether to split from what they know and keep their "relationship" or speak what they know and risk losing relationship. Their political resistance heard so clearly during late childhood goes underground and turns into "dissociation or various forms of indirect speech and self-silencing" (Brown & Gilligan, 1992, p. 137). The researchers conclude that if girls' political resistance or, as we call it, resistance to dehumanization is not supported by parents, teachers, or peers, it becomes psychological with damaging consequences (e.g., eating disorders, cutting, depression).

In addition to the work on girls, there is a small but growing body of research focused on resistance among boys. The focus of this work is on norms of masculinity – the "boy code" (Pollack, 1998) or "the cool pose" (Majors & Billson, 1992) – that impose an implicit and explicit requirement on boys and men to be emotionally stoic, independent, and physically tough and to devalue emotional vulnerability, relationships, and softness (see Chu, Porsche, & Tolman, 2005; Chu, 2014; Way, 2011; Way et al., 2014). Examples of resistance to such norms, codes, or poses include boys openly expressing a desire for or having emotionally intimate friendships with male peers; expressing vulnerability with male and female peers; seeking and valuing interdependence; disliking aggression; and openly challenging the accuracy of gender stereotypes that boys, for example, are not emotional or do not "need" close friendships (e.g., Chu et al., 2005; Reichert & Ravitch, 2009; Way, 2011; Way et al., 2014). Resistance to norms of masculinity entails, in other words, the challenging of stereotypes about what it means to be a boy or a man.

Research has suggested that boys across race, ethnicity, and social class resist norms of masculinity in their romantic relationships, valuing emotional intimacy over sex in these relationships (Schalet, 2011; Smiler, 2008; Tolman, Spencer,

Harmon, Rosen-Reynoso, & Striepe, 2004). Smiler (2008) reports that the majority of his sample of tenth grade boys reported relational reasons for dating and having sex, including the enhancement of connection with their romantic partner (e.g., "I wanted to get to know the person better") and depth of feelings for their partner (e.g., "I liked the person more than I ever liked anyone"). Frosh, Phoenix, and Pattman (2002), in their examination of masculinity among working-class British boys, reinforce the stereotype of the hormone-driven, macho, working-class male, but also reveal the high levels of emotional intimacy that exist between adolescent boys. Other studies outside of the US have also found evidence of resistance to norms of masculinity among boys (e.g., Barker, 2005; Edley & Wetherell, 1997; Gough, 2001).

The developmental research with boys has found that resistance to dehumanization, or in Gilligan and Brown's framework "political resistance," is often evident in male friendships and can be implicit or explicit (Way, 2011, 2013; Way et al., 2014). Implicit resistance is the challenging of norms of masculinity in an indirect or unconscious manner and includes boys having emotionally intimate friendships and understanding and articulating the importance of such friendships. While these behaviors and attitudes implicitly challenge masculine stereotypes, they do not explicitly critique them. Explicit resistance, which is less common than implicit resistance, entails directly challenging or questioning such stereotypes. An example includes when a boy in one of Way's studies claimed that it "might be nice to be a girl, then you wouldn't have to be emotionless" (Way, 2011).

Additional examples of boys' implicit resistance include Pollack's (1998) research that finds that boys openly acknowledge "needing" someone to talk to, rely on their friends to share their secrets with, express their feelings with their closest friends, and tell each other "everything" (Pollack & Shuster, 2000). Chu also finds in her interviews with adolescent boys that they express their feelings of vulnerability and acknowledge their desire for intimate male friendships (Chu, 2004). They implicitly resist "the boy code" that label these behaviors as "gay" or "girly." Ethan, a tenth-grader in Chu's study (2004), describes the bond he has with his closest friend: "he really helped me – we helped each other a lot through our conversations "(p. 96). Chu concludes: "Contrary to popular discourse that tends to portray adolescent boys as emotionally deficient and relationally impaired, analyses of these data … revealed these boys to be clearly capable of thoughtful self-reflection and deep interpersonal understanding" (p. 83).

Similar to Gilligan and Brown's research on girls' resistance, the data suggest that boys' resistance to dehumanization declines as they grow older (Chu, 2004; Rogers & Way, 2016; Way, 2011; Way et al., 2014). In Chu's (2014) observational classroom study of 4- and 5-year-old boys over two years, she finds that four-year-old boys display a resistance to norms of masculinity that manifest in their school and peer group cultures. Demonstrating that their alignment with norms of masculinity is neither automatic nor inevitable, the boys in her study implicitly reject such norms by seeking out the friendship and support of other boys in the classroom and defending their peers when others are bullying them. Yet, Chu also finds that as the school year progressed the boys grew increasingly accommodating of masculine expectations, forming, for example, "the mean team" that pits them against girls and accentuates their aggression (Chu, 2014). While some of the boys in her study expressed the desire to maintain friendships with girls, they also expressed pressure from other boys to dislike the girls because they are girls. Like the girls in Gilligan and Brown's study, the boys in Chu's study begin to disconnect from what they know about themselves (i.e., that they like girls) and about girls (i.e., that girls like to be with them) and turn toward the cultural stereotype of "boys being boys" by being aggressive toward girls.

The developmental pattern of resistance among boys appears, however, to continue into adolescence. In her four-to-five–year longitudinal studies of primarily Black, Latino, and Asian adolescent boys from working-class families, Way (2011, 2013; Way et al., 2014) finds both resistance to the norms of masculinity, particularly during early adolescence, and the loss of such resistance as boys become men. The boys in her studies enter their teenage years with a tremendous desire to engage in intimate male friendships despite the masculine dictates that discourage such "girly" or "gay" behavior. They reject the masculine norms of emotional stoicism, autonomy, and physical toughness in their friendships and speak of revealing "one's heart" to their best friend so that "you won't go wacko" and "try to kill yourself." As Justin says in his sophomore year:

> [My best friend and I] love each other . . .. That's it . . .. You have this thing that is deep, so deep, it's within you, you can't explain it. It's just a thing that you know that that person is that person . . . and that is all that should be important in our friendships . . . I guess in life, sometimes two people can really, really understand each other and really have a trust, respect, and love for each other. It just happens, it's human nature. (Way, 2011, p. 1)

The boys also underscored the importance of "sharing deep secrets" with best friends for their psychological wellbeing. George, at 16 years of age, says that close friends are important because "I mean, if you have just have your mother and your parents [to talk to], then you're just gonna have all these ideas bottled up and you're just gonna go wacko because you can't express yourself even more." Chen, at 15 years of age, says that he needs a close friend so "you have someone to talk to, like you have problems with something, you go talk to him. You know, if you keep it all the stuff to yourself, you go crazy. Try to take it out on someone else." Approximately 85% of the boys in Way's studies, at some point during adolescence, indicated that they wanted or had intimate male friends with whom they could share their "deep secrets" (Way, 2011, 2013).

Yet as boys enter manhood, Way finds that they increasingly speak about the pressures to "man up" and not be "girly" or "gay"; their emotionally astute voices become fearful and wary and they begin to speak about the loss of their intimate male friendships – the very friendships that prevented them from going "wacko."

When asked how his friendships have changed since they were freshmen in high school, Justin says: "I don't know, maybe, not a lot. But I guess best friends become close friends. So that's basically the only thing that changes. It's like best friends become close friends, close friends become general friends and then general friends become acquaintances." Victor says:

> Like my friendship with my best friend is fading but I'm saying it's still there but . . . So I mean, it's still there 'cause we still do stuff together, but only once in a while. It's sad, 'cause he lives only one block away from me and I get to do stuff with him less than I get to do stuff with people who are way further so I'm like, yo . . . It's like a Dj used his cross fader and started fading it slowly and slowly and now I'm like halfway through the cross fade.

As the boys enter late adolescence, words such as "love," so pervasive in their interviews during early and middle adolescence, gave way to expressions of anger, frustration, or, simply, of not caring any longer. Boys began to disconnect from themselves and their friends in the name of "manhood" and maturity (Way, 2011, 2013). Way finds that loss of resistance among boys is due primarily to a homophobic American culture that sexualizes and thus pathologizes love between boys and defines maturity in terms of autonomy rather than relationships (Way, 2011; Way et al., 2014).

The research on resistance to dehumanizing notions of femininity and masculinity underscore the agency of boys and girls across race, ethnicity, and social class. Girls and boys actively resist the stereotypes of them and they tell it like it is despite a context and a culture that seeks to silence their voices.

Resistance to Dehumanization: Race

The notion of resistance to racial oppression has roots in the political sphere, with the Civil Rights Movement,[1] and is evident throughout the scholarly literature on slavery and antebellum history in America (e.g., Camp, 2004; Genovese, 1976; Turiel, 2003). Within psychology and child development, the study of race initially focused solely on the negative consequences of racism on the Black psyche. For example, in the landmark case *Brown vs. Board of Education* that mandated the desegregation of schools, Kenneth and Mamie Clark's (1947) "doll studies" were used to demonstrate that racism was psychologically harmful to the self-esteem of the Black child. Similarly, early theories of racial identity development focused on the process of "becoming Black" – that is, learning about and negotiating society's beliefs of, expectations for, and stereotypes about Black people from the perspective of mainstream cultural ideals (Cross, 1971, 1978, 1991). As evidence of internalized racism and self-hatred mounted, a counterargument ensued

---

1 During the 1950s and 1960s the African American community and civic leaders, including Martin Luther King, Jr. and Rosa Parks, challenged persistent inequalities in governmental laws and legislation. Major shifts included the legal case of *Brown vs. Board of Education* in 1954 to end "separate but equal" education, the Voting Rights Act of 1965 and the Civil Rights Act of 1965; see: www.history.com/topics/black-history/civil-rights-movement.

which made a simple but critical claim: Black people, while being subjected to racism, are not permanently damaged victims nor do they passively internalize racist ideologies; they are resilient and successful, crafting healthy identities in the face of racial oppression (e.g., Spencer & Markstrom-Adams, 1990; Tatum, 1997; Ward, 1996). In alignment with this counter-argument, scholars began to investigate how people of color negotiate their identities and sense of self-worth in a context of racial oppression. While the early conceptualization of racial identity assumed a largely unidirectional process whereby society exerts pressure on the individual and the individual copes with those expectations, the resistance framework for the analysis of both gender and race suggests a bidirectional interaction in which the individual actively contests and accommodates those messages that are projected onto him or her (e.g., Gilligan, 2011; Lei, 2003; Nasir, 2011; Robinson & Ward, 1991; Rogers & Way, 2016; Spencer, 1995; Turiel, 2003; Ward, 1996; Way & Rogers, 2014; Way, 2011; Way et al. 2014).

Robinson and Ward (1991) provide a useful framework of resistance to racial oppression based on their research with African American girls and women, in which they distinguish between *resistance for survival* and *resistance for liberation*. The first strategy, *resistance for survival*, is oriented toward quick fixes that offer short-term solutions. These strategies help youth to feel better for a time, but in the long run they are counterproductive to the development of self-confidence, positive identity, and community building. Examples of resistance for survival include substance abuse, early and unplanned pregnancies, school failure, and food addictions. When a Black girl, for example, becomes a teen mom and drops out of school, she may find purpose in motherhood but simultaneously reifies the very stereotypes that oppress her. Ogbu's (1978) "oppositional identity" is another example of resistance for survival: in the face of low expectations from teachers and unlikely economic rewards for academic achievement, a Black youth rejects education, dis-identifying with schooling and seeking alternate (deviant) paths for success (Fordham & Ogbu, 1986; Osborne, 1997). In short, youth respond to society's racial expectations in ways that are counterproductive and ultimately reinforce the stereotypes they should avoid in order to thrive.

Alternatively, youth may respond to racial stereotypes with *resistance for liberation* strategies, which serve to empower African Americans through confirmation of positive self-conceptions, as well as strengthening connections to the broader Black community (Ward, 1996). Examples include succeeding in school despite low expectations (Carter, 2008) or maintaining strong spiritual and community ties even while society undermines these ideals (Ward, 2000). Resistance for liberation is rooted in an "inner strength" of hope in the humanity of oneself and others (Robinson & Ward, 1991; Ward, 1996). Ward (1996) also shows that African American girls who respond to stereotypes using resistance for liberation report lower levels of psychological distress than those who use resistance for survival strategies. Suárez-Orozco (2004), in her investigation of how immigrant youth negotiate the stigma and stereotypes they encounter in American schools, distinguishes between two similar forms of resistance: one that is infused with a *hope* for "a better tomorrow" and one that lacks hope for change. Moreover, she finds that immigrant youth who respond to stereotypes with a hopeful resistance (i.e., resistance for liberation) often defy the odds, flourishing academically and psychologically, but when youth resist *without* the belief that their actions can bring about change (i.e., resistance for survival), it often leads to anger and delinquent behaviors, such as failing school or joining a gang (Suárez-Orozco, 2004).

Margaret Beale Spencer (1995; Spencer, Dupree, & Hartmann, 1997; Spencer, Dupree, Cunningham, Harpalani, & Munoz-Miller, 2003), in her *phenomenological variant of ecological systems theory (P-VEST)*, similarly argues that the healthy development of youth of color depends on countering cultural narratives and stereotypes about race and ethnicity that position them as inferior (Spencer et al., 1997). "The self," she argues, "is constructed in response to social stereotypes and biases" (Spencer et al., 1997, p. 817). Youth respond to stereotypes with "reactive coping" strategies, for example, reacting with anger and violence, or "proactive coping" strategies where they thoughtfully and purposely employ relational resources and problem-solving skills. Reactive coping is analogous to accommodation if used without "proactive coping" strategies as well. Used as the sole method to negotiate stereotypes, it undermines healthy development whereas proactive coping (alongside reactive coping or by itself) is likened to resistance for liberation because it functions to disrupt the stereotypes and opens alternative pathways for positive identity development and healthy community building.

Nasir's (2011) ethnographic analysis of how African American adolescents negotiate racial stereotypes in school reveals patterns that parallel the strategies of resistance outlined in these frameworks of resistance (Robinson & Ward, 1991; Spencer et al., 1997; Suárez-Orozco, 2004). In her school-based ethnography, Nasir's analysis identified some Black youth as "school oriented and socially conscious," resisting negative stereotypes and placing high value on education and belief in their ability to succeed. Others, however, responded to stereotypes by "taking up and reifying stereotypical aspects of the African American identity," such as acting out and failing classes (Nasir, 2011, p. 87). Studies on academically successful African Americans similarly argue that cultivating a "scholar identity" is an intentional act of resistance (e.g., Carter, 2008; Hrabowski, Maton, & Greif, 1998; Hrabowski, Maton, Green, & Greif, 2002; Whiting, 2006). In a small case study of high-achieving Black and Latino boys in a small charter high school, Conchas and Noguera (2004) also find that boys resist racial stereotypes that frame them as unintelligent by cultivating a community of support among themselves where academic success is valued. Whiting (2006), in his study of academically successful Black males, concludes: "They refuse to give in to low expectations and will work diligently to change such expectations" (p. 226). In other words, they are not just being scholars, they are *resisting* by being scholars.

Rogers (2013; Rogers & Way, 2016) conducted in-depth interviews with Black adolescent males during their first two years of high school and found resistance to racial stereotypes in an all-Black male high school where academic success was explicitly valued and expected. In this context, Black boys resisted stereotypes about the intellectual inferiority of Black people and believed in their ability to succeed in high school and college. For example, Michael, a 14-year-old Black male student, describes how he feels about the stereotype that Black people are seen as "unsuccessful" and not expected to do well in school: "Um, sometimes it hurts a little bit, but then I don't even think about it because as long as I know I'm not adding on to those stereotypes or adding a number to the statistics it doesn't bother me 'cause I know I'm doin' my part" (Rogers & Way, 2016, p. 277). The boys were able to name and challenge stereotypes. Marcus, another Black student in Rogers' study, said "Well I guess some people are so used to seeing the gang bangers and the gangsters and stuff like that on the outside, so they think that every Black male is like that. But that's actually a stereotype" (Rogers & Way, 2016, p. 281). In response to those stereotypes, Marcus explained:

> I try to focus it in, do my schoolwork, so I can like prove, like break the stereotype. And like, I'd like to get out into the community and like tell people that you know this is not how we act, you know, things like that, so I guess you could say, that I'm kind of inspired but then again I'm kind of like pissed off. That's kind of how I feel about it.

These adolescent boys were astutely aware of the prevailing racial stereotypes and believed in their ability to facilitate change, which supported a healthy resistance to such stereotypes.

Rogers (2012; Rogers & Way, 2016) also found that, counter to the patterns of resistance to norms of masculinity (Way, 2011; Way et al., 2014), resistance to racial stereotypes, specifically related to intelligence, education, and academic success, increased over time. Ronald at 14 years old explained that for him, "Being Black means bein' yourself, and bein' successful. We *need* to be successful. . . . '[C]ause a lot of people don't think we can do it. They don't think we're capable of excelling. But, um, I believe we are." Thus, rather than becoming increasingly oppositional toward or dismissive of school (Ogbu, 1978), the Black males in Rogers' study showed a greater resistance to cultural narrative that deemed them intellectually inept and unlikely to succeed in school and life (Rogers, 2013; Rogers & Way, 2016). The increase and maintenance of resistance to racial stereotypes suggests that youth are capable of resisting stereotypes throughout adolescence but that the patterns of resistance to norms of masculinity as boys become men may be harder to maintain than resistance to racial stereotypes about intellectual ability (Rogers & Way, 2016; Way et al., 2014).

Resistance to Dehumanization: Gender and Race

The studies reviewed thus far are examples of the ways in which adolescents are resisting gender *or* racial stereotypes in their daily lives. Yet adolescents encounter multiple dehumanizing stereotypes related to race, gender, sexuality, social class, and other social categories that they must negotiate simultaneously. It is less clear how resistance processes function across social categories, but there are a few empirical examples of resistance and accommodation that use an intersectionality lens. For example, Reichert and Ravitch (2009) reported on the ways in which Jewish-identified boys draw upon their Jewish heritage to resist conventions of masculinity that discourage their relationships and emotional acuity, and Barker's (2000; Pulerwitz & Barker, 2008) work focusing on boys living on the street in Brazil reveals how these boys construct an alternative masculinity that allows them to resist a set of masculine conventions that offer few paths out of poverty. Majors and Billson (1992) explore how Black males accommodate to stereotypes at the intersection of race and gender, revealing how racial stereotypes fuse with masculine expectations. Because of the way that stereotypes about race, gender, and sexuality intersect (e.g., Ghavami & Peplau, 2013), Black males who challenge gender stereotypes, for example, find that their race and sexuality is also questioned; they are deemed "soft," "girly," and "gay" (Davis, 2001; Pascoe, 2011; Waters, 1996; Way, 2011). Majors and Billson (1992) characterize Black masculinity as the "cool pose," a pattern of accommodation to stereotypes about being hyper-stoic and autonomous. They argue that Black males don the "cool pose" to enhance feelings of "social competence, protection, and convey a sense of pride" (p. 4). The reality, however, is that such accommodation impedes their abilities to achieve success in school, request help from others when needed, and be openly expressive in their relationships (Majors & Billson, 1992).

Ferguson (2000) conducted a rich ethnographic study examining how young Black males respond to the "bad boy" stereotype, which positions Black males as unintelligent, delinquent, and aggressive. Ferguson unveils two patterns of response. The "troublemakers" accommodated to the idea that they were "prison bound" rather than "college bound" – they acted out in school, spent more time in the principal's office than in their classrooms, were suspended repeatedly, and generally did not value education. The "scholars," in contrast, resisted these stereotypes, fighting against the negative expectations of teachers and peers to act out and underperform. Ferguson (2000) cautions, however, against categorizing them as two disparate groups, instead arguing that these groups of boys represented two ends of a continuum where "the 'schoolboys' were always on the brink of being redefined into the 'troublemakers'" due, primarily, to the force of racial and gender stereotypes that are working against them (p. 10). Similarly, Dance's (2002) ethnographic study of African American and Caribbean adolescents underscores the thin line between being "too hardcore" and being entangled with gang culture and failing school, and being "hardcore enough" to navigate the norms of neighborhood culture yet still succeed in school.

Robinson and Ward's (1991) analysis of Afro-centric cultural values and Black girls' development also makes explicit the tensions that necessitate resistance. For example, Robinson and Ward contend that Black girls' resistance to "excessive autonomy [in American Anglo culture]" is essential to resisting racial oppression. As an example, they quote Linda, an African American teenage girl talking about her racial identity: "when we used to drive through the bad parts of town or something, I would always see blacks out there and (think) I can't be a part of that, that's not me"

(Robinson & Ward, 1991, p. 91). Although Linda resists negative group identification, it is, they argue, a resistance for survival strategy marked by "cultural disassociation through psychological separation [which] . . . leaves her vulnerable to the destructive effects of emotional isolation and self-alienation" (Robinson & Ward, 1991, p. 91). That is, Linda, in her attempt to construct a counter-narrative of Blackness, exemplifies the dominant cultural narrative of individuality – separating the self from others ("I can't be a part of that"). Instead, they argue that women and girls must be supported in resisting "excessive individualism," as evident in mainstream masculinity, and embracing the collective "we" as the core of the self. Thus, in order to form healthy racial identities, girls must also resist masculine gender stereotypes.

Rogers (2013; Rogers & Way, 2016) also offers an explicit empirical analysis of patterns of resistance across racial and gender stereotypes and expectations. She finds that Black boys' resistance to racial stereotypes was more prevalent and consistent than was their resistance to gender stereotypes. That is, boys tended to challenge beliefs about the intellectual inferiority and incompetence of Black people while reinforcing the gender expectations for independence, heterosexuality, and emotional stoicism, endorsing the idea that such stereotypic masculine behavior "comes naturally." For example, Monte, a 15-year-old Black male, describes what he thinks *other people* think about Black people: "Society says that we are illiterate and that's not true" (p. 276). In contrast, in the conversations about gender, boys often viewed gender stereotypes as "normal": Ronald, a 14-year-old Black male, explained that getting into trouble and flirting with women "just comes naturally" to boys (Rogers & Way, 2016).

Furthermore, Rogers (2013; Rogers & Way, 2016) identified three resistance patterns among the Black boys in her sample that show how resistance functions across social stereotypes. The "accommodators" included boys who had glimmers of resistance but who, on the whole, reinforced gender stereotypes *and* racial stereotypes in their identity narratives. For example, Omar, the case study for the "accommodators," defines himself as the "hood guy" and when asked what he likes most about being Black, he said, "Oh like a lot of people are scared of us; that's great." This sort of taking on of stereotypes carried into gender as well, so that the "accommodators" sounded like caricatures of the tough Black guy who gets into fights and doesn't care about school. The majority of boys in Rogers' sample were characterized as the "exceptions" – boys who resisted racial stereotypes but accommodated to gender stereotypes. To oppose racial stereotypes, they positioned themselves as "exceptions" to racial stereotypes. For example, when Jaire, the case study for the "exceptions," was asked what he likes most about himself he said "I love the fact that people think of me to be a more complex individual and a more intelligent individual . . . Not just a regular Black guy". While challenging racial stereotypes, the "exceptions" simultaneously endorsed gender stereotypes of autonomy and stoicism:

> Um, the best part about being a young man is that we get to, like we're like the um, trendsetters of the world. You know what I'm saying, like the government, the

world is ran by men. Men run the world, you know what I'm saying. . . . And I don't think that a woman is fit to run a world. . . . Because men make hard decisions without emotion. And the women get emotional in certain situations. . . . Like their emotions are too high.

Thus, similar to Robinson and Ward's (1991) findings when girls separated themselves from "other Black people," as boys endorsed gender stereotypes, they separated themselves from negative racial stereotypes, and, at the same time, from other Black people.

The final pattern of resistance found in Rogers' study was the "resisters" – boys who were characterized as resisting racial *and* gender stereotypes (Rogers, 2013; Rogers & Way, 2016). In particular, the "resisters" stood out because they viewed challenging racial stereotypes as a collective effort rather than an isolated one, and for their resistance to gender stereotypes about emotionality and sexuality. Marcus, the case study for the "resisters," explained that boys should cry when they are sad or hurt: "of course you['re] gonna cry," Marcus is quoted as saying, "[be]cause that's like human nature, you're supposed to cry, that's why you have tear ducts in your body". The "resisters" identified and challenged systems of oppression and as a result resisted stereotypes about race *and* gender, a resistance that fosters humanity and benefits the self and others:

> 'Cause I guess society thinks that if men or boys act feminine that they're gay or they just assume that they're gay. And I think that's a bad stereotype because guys need to express their feelings too. I'm not going to say that guys are supposed to be tough all the time . . . and they're supposed to like man up and like cover that up with hardness or whatever. It's okay to let yourself cry and be heartbroken. I don't think that's a good stereotype because that's like telling kids not to care about anything that happens.

Resistance to gender and racial stereotypes allows adolescents to care, to feel and know, to be fully human.

Collectively, the growing evidence of resistance suggests that challenging stereotypes about race and gender are part and parcel of the process of being social and emotional development. The work on resistance rejects an "either/or" approach to understanding development. That is, youth are not "either" passively accepting cultural norms, stereotypes, or expectations (i.e., accommodation) or actively challenging all the messages they receive. Rather they are involved in a complex process of both accommodating and resisting norms, expectations, and stereotypes. It is also noteworthy that the commonality of these resistance frameworks grew out of research involving youth from a range of racial and socio-economic groups: Anyon's (1984) lower- and middle-class White girls and boys, Brown and Gilligan's (1992) middle- and upper-class girls from different racial and ethnic groups in private school, Brown's (1999) working-class White girls, Robinson and Ward's (1991; Ward, 1996) working-class Black girls and women, Chu's (2004, 2014) middle- and upper-class predominantly White boys, Way's (2011; Way et al., 2014) low-income, predominantly Black, Latino, and Asian American boys, and Rogers' (2013) low-income,

Black males. Such diversity in samples offers support for Anyon's (1984) claim decades ago: "Accommodation and resistance are an integral part of the overall processes that *all* children use to construct their social identities" (p. 44).

The Context of Resistance

While research has consistently revealed patterns of resistance among girls and boys across race, ethnicity, gender, and social class, what do we know about the context of resistance or what factors explain patterns of resistance in the midst of an American culture that discourages such behavior? The data suggest that the answers lie, as Urie Bronfenbrenner pointed (1979) out decades ago, in the contexts of youths' lives, including parent–child relationships and the academic, social, and cultural dynamics in schools.

Ward's (1996) analysis of the intergenerational transmission of resistance to racial stereotypes addresses the key role that parents can play in teaching and *modeling* "liberating truth telling" to their children (p. 97). Her research draws on the importance of voice – the need to speak out and be heard rather than be silent. "Black parents know," Ward (1996) argues, "that silence is often the voice of complicity" (p. 90). She finds, however, that not all "truth telling" is equal in terms of cultivating healthy resistance. There is "tongues-of-fire truth telling" which is characterized by harsh and blatant words aimed to "dismantle futile idealism" about how the world works (p. 94). The problem, however, is that the harshness can create a rift in the parent–child relationship, creating distance rather than intimacy. The alternative "resistance-building truth telling" requires neither "sugar coating nor avoiding the truth about racism" but the telling is done with care and attention to the child's self-esteem and character development (p. 97). Ward (1996) concludes the types of messages that adolescents receive from their parents directly influence their tendency toward resistance for survival versus resistance for liberation.

Data from Way's studies of boys' friendships show that those who reported having at least one parent who was emotionally engaged with them and offered a safe space for their sons to talk freely about their thoughts and feelings were often the boys who resisted conventions of masculinity and had intimate male friendships (Santos, 2010; Way, 2011). This is consistent with attachment theory, which reveals a significant link between security of attachment with parents and friendship quality during adolescence (e.g., Allen & Land, 1999; Hazan & Zeifman, 1999). And since parents are socialized into a culture in which mothers are considered the carriers of emotions and emotional talk and fathers are not, Way's studies found, unsurprisingly, that it is typically the mothers who are offering the space for boys to stay connected to and express their thoughts and feelings. Survey data from a middle-school sample of 400 boys indicate that boys' reports of high levels of maternal support in sixth grade predicted an increase in boys' reports of resistance to masculinity norms in their male friendships from sixth to eighth grade (Santos, 2010).

In addition to the family context, the school context plays a critical role in fostering or impeding resistance. As social institutions, schools often reproduce the dominant system of social inequalities, which is evident in the persistent educational disparities where Black and Latino males, for example, are the most likely to fail a grade, be suspended or expelled, and drop out of school (López, 2003; Noguera, 2008; Schott Foundation, 2015). At the same time, however, schools can function as sites of resistance with alternative norms – schools where Black males, for example, excel academically (e.g., Conchas & Noguera, 2004; Hilliard, 2003; Whiting, 2006), even in the STEM disciplines of mathematics and science (e.g., Hrabowski et al., 1998).

In her theoretical model of African American achievement, Theresa Perry (2003) uses the term "counterhegemonic communities" to refer to social spaces or institutions, such as schools, that exist to challenge hegemonic ideologies and beliefs. In order to successfully educate youth of color, schools, Perry (2003) argues, must be "counterhegemonic communities." Perry draws on historical accounts of the philosophy of education in African American communities in which education was synonymous with liberation – physical, psychological, and social. Education for African Americans has, since its inception, been about resistance: a refusal to accept the dehumanized position of inferiority society assigned to them through slavery and segregation (Du Bois, 1935; Perry, 2003; Nasir, 2011). The early schoolhouses for African Americans were constructed in ways that intentionally countered society's ideology; they were "figured worlds" where the dominant narrative of African American inferiority was defied and its members cultivated their identities as equal citizens. Today, where systems of oppression remain, "the act of constructing an institution whose organization and operation counter the larger society's ideology about an oppressed people is an act of resistance" (James Scott, quoted in Perry, 2003, p. 88). Today, successfully educating and promoting the healthy development of Black youth is an act of resistance.

Rogers' (2012; Rogers et al., forthcoming; Rogers & Way, 2016) analysis of an all-Black male school offers an empirical example of the ways that school messages and practices shape the pathways of resistance to stereotypes among Black adolescent males. This Black male school was designed as a "counterhegemonic community" to serve Black boys. The principal of the school explained:

> We want an environment where [students are] free to be who they are, where they don't have to live with these stereotypical ideas of what a Black man is, you know, I can only be a basketball player, I can only be a rapper, or a lot of machismo. We intentionally build . . . an environment where they really want to achieve and not feel like someone will call them lame or a nerd if they are achieving academically.

The importance of challenging stereotypes is woven into the teachers' goals as well:

> [Society] has created an image for us: that Black males are irresponsible . . . that we're sexual creatures that just spread our seed irresponsibly, that we deal drugs,

that we're not educated, those things. We have to fight that image. That we're rappers and basketball players and not scholars. These are the images that we have to tell them [the students], no, that's not the reality of who we are.

The school itself functioned as a site of resistance, a space where boys were intentionally given counter-narratives and counter-images of successful Black male teachers to use in defense against negative stereotypes. In alignment with Perry's (2003) model, the school enacted *ritualized culture, counter-narratives and counter-images, high expectations, and support*, which were targeted at challenging racial stereotypes.

At the same time, Rogers (2012; Rogers, Scott, and Way, 2015; Rogers & Way, 2016) finds that in this all-male school context, stereotypes about masculinity and sexuality were highly salient and particularly threatening, which seemed to undermine boys' resistance. For example, during survey administration the boys openly questioned whether they were being evaluated to see which students were gay (some of the students skipped questions and wrote "I'm not gay" on the survey). And during the interviews the boys repeatedly mentioned the absence of girls and expressed concerns about being seen as gay. Teddy, for example, at the start of his ninth grade year at this all-Black male school, answers what he thought about attending this particular high school:

> [My mom] She said did I want to go, I said no. It's [an] all boys' school.
> Q: Yeah and what didn't you like about that?
> A: 'Cause I heard a lot of stuff about all boys schools . . . People turn gay.
> Q: People turn gay from being around all boys?
> A: Mm-hmm. That's what I heard.
> Q: You think that's true?
> A: Probably so.

Kirk, also in the ninth grade, similarly explained that one reason boys did not want to attend this school is "you don't want to seem gay." When asked what was "gay" about going to school with boys he simply said: "Um, no girls." In other words, the mere absence of girls was a threat and perceived by some of the students as gay (Rogers & Nelson, 2010). Given this heightened awareness of masculinity in this all-male school environment, the social dynamics became essential. Boys who held social status were afforded more flexibility to challenge stereotypes.

The importance of school social dynamics with regards to race and ethnicity was also evident in Way's (2011) research, where boys' social status seemed to support their emotional and social skills and thus their resistance to conventions of masculinity. The boys who were most resistant to masculine stereotypes in Way's (2011) studies were those who had the most social power with their peers in school. Social power among peers was acquired through numerous routes, including the familiar ones such as being athletic, tall, conventionally good looking, and having a good sense of humor (Brown, Lamb, & Tappan, 2009).

Having these attributes resulted in greater social power which, in turn, appeared to lead to greater freedom to implicitly or explicitly challenge norms of masculinity. Boys in Way's studies (2011) who were talented basketball players or accomplished in other sports and were conventionally good looking were more likely to resist norms of masculinity in their friendships than those who were not. Felix, for example, was popular, funny, and confident in his ability to attract girls as well as in his ability to express vulnerability without being perceived as a "wuss." Brown and her colleagues (2009) note a similar pattern in their book *Packaging Boyhood*: "The good news for parents is that being successful at sports ... gives [a boy] permission to do well academically, show sensitivity, and stick up for kids who are bullied" (Brown et al., 2009, p. 222). The boys in Way's (2011) studies who succeeded in sports and/or who appeared "manly" by their physical size did not appear to feel as much pressure as the other boys to prove their masculinity or, as the case may be, their heterosexuality and thus they were more likely to resist norms of masculinity.

These contextual factors – including socialization, peer social status, and school norms and practices – weave together a web of support for adolescents to resist oppressive stereotypes and ideologies. Resistance, in other words, can be fostered, and as such it offers a practical tool for change – at both the micro-level of individuals and the macro-level of culture.

Resistance and Wellbeing

Resistance to dehumanizing stereotypes among both girls and boys has been consistently linked to positive psychological, social, and academic wellbeing (Blazina, Pisecco, & O'Neil, 2005; Brown & Gilligan, 1992; Chu, 2014; Cournoyer & Mahalik, 1995; Gilligan, 2011; Good, Heppner, DeBord, & Fischer, 2004; Gupta et al., 2013; Hayes & Mahalik, 2000; Mahalik, Pierre, & Wan, 2006; Rogers et al., under review; Santos, 2010; Santos, Way, & Hughes, 2011; Way, 2011, 2013; Way et al., 2014; Wester, Kuo, & Vogel, 2006). Just as girls' struggled at the edge of adolescence to resist the silencing of their voices, Brown and Gilligan also find that they experience depression, cutting, eating disorders and other forms of self-abuse (Brown & Gilligan, 1992; Gilligan, 2011). In a longitudinal analysis of 400 Black, White, and Latino boys from sixth to eighth grade, Santos (2010) examined the extent to which boys' resisted the masculine stereotypes of valuing emotional stoicism, independence, and physical toughness in their friendships and how such resistance is linked to wellbeing. He found that resistance to masculine stereotypes in friendships was associated with both high self-esteem and low depressive symptoms (Santos, 2010; Santos & Way, under review). As reports of resistance to masculine stereotypes in boys' friendships increased over time, so too did their psychological wellbeing. In a separate study, Santos reports that higher levels of resistance to masculine stereotypes in the friendships of boys is associated with higher levels of academic performance on standardized tests (Santos et al., 2013).

In a cross-cultural analysis in the USA and China, Gupta et al. (2013) find that resistance to masculine norms in boys' friendships is associated with lower levels of depression, higher self-esteem, and higher friendship quality among adolescent boys in both cultural contexts. In a separate analysis focusing only on the girls in USA and China, Rogers and colleagues (under review) find that girls' resistance to masculine norms of emotional stoicism, autonomy, and physical toughness is also linked to better mental health. Other studies have shown that men and boys who score lower on measures of adherence to conventional masculine norms (e.g., autonomy, emotional stoicism, toughness, dominance, and power) fare better on indices of wellbeing, such as lower levels of anxiety and psychological distress (Mahalik et al., 2006), higher levels of self-esteem (Good et al., 1995; Cournoyer & Mahalik, 1995; Chu et al., 2005; Mahalik et al., 2006), better coping skills (Cunningham, 1999; Wester et al., 2006), fewer behavioral problems at school (Pleck et al., 1994), and fewer health-care visits and increased likelihood of receiving preventative care (Lindsey & Marcell, 2009; Springer & Mouzon, 2008).

Research on racial identity also suggests a link between resisting mainstream racial stereotypes and positive outcomes. For example, Cross's (1991) seminal theory of racial identity development documents the transition from Eurocentric racial attitudes in the "pre-encounter" stage of racial identity, which are characterized by "self-hating" or a negative view of Black people, to an internalized racial identity where Blackness is viewed positively. Thus, in a culture plagued by racism, maintaining a positive evaluation of Black people is an act of resistance. Indeed, empirical studies have shown that individuals with stronger "pre-encounter" attitudes, which effectively show accommodation to mainstream ideals of Whiteness and negative beliefs about Blackness, have lower levels of self-esteem (Cross, 1991; Parham & Helms, 1985) and higher levels of psychological distress than individuals who resist the mainstream cultural narratives of oppression (Helms, 1995; Mahalik et al., 2006). Similar to Cross, Sellers and colleagues (1998) outlines four racial ideologies that can define one's racial identity. The "assimilation" ideology is characterized by the belief that the key to success for Black people is to "act more like Whites" and separate oneself from other Black people (Sellers, Chavous, & Cooke, 1998). Studies have shown that Black youth who endorse an assimilation racial ideology are less likely to be engaged in school (Smalls, White, Chavous, & Sellers, 2007) and report lower grade point averages then their peers who hold racial ideologies that are more positive and group-oriented (Sellers et al., 1998).

Ferguson (2000) finds that Black males who reject the "bad boy" stereotype in school do well academically – they achieve good grades and rarely get into trouble. In contrast, the "troublemakers" grounded their identity in acting out and doing poorly in school, they accommodated the stereotypes and reaped the consequences as they often spent more time in discipline than in their class-room. Nasir (2011) examined the experiences and narratives of African American youth in school with the goal of answering the question: what does it mean to be Black for these Black adolescents? Nasir finds that African

American youth who reject society's ideas about what it means to be (and not to be) African American, who resist the stereotypes, are able to carve out an identity that positions them jointly within the African American community and scholar community. In contrast, the "street savvy" youth in her study confined their identities to the stereotypes, relying on pre-paved pathways of being "Black." While those youth resisting stereotypes excelled academically, those who did not resist failed classes and often dropped out of high school before the end of Nasir's research. These studies offer evidence of the ways that resistance to stereotypes – or the absence of such resistance – directly shapes the wellbeing of youth.

Summary and Future Directions

Research over the past few decades indicates that resistance to dehumanization is a core developmental process, is shaped by familial and school contexts, and is linked to psychological, social, and academic wellbeing. Our studies have shown that when American children are young, they insist on their human capacities to think AND feel, to know what they know, and tell it like it is. Yet as they grow older, they increasingly silence themselves and succumb or accommodate to stereotypes and beliefs that disconnect them from themselves and each other. Thus, our challenge as educators, parents, and professionals is to nourish the resistance we hear in youth so that they maintain their ability to hold onto what they know and act in a way that protects and reaffirms their humanity.

While this growing body of research on resistance and accommodation has offered us new insights into the social and emotional development of children and adolescents, there are numerous remaining questions: What are the patterns of resistance to dehumanization during middle childhood or among children and adolescents who live in countries outside of the USA? How do LGBT or non-gender-conforming adolescents resist gender, racial, and/or sexual identity stereotypes? Does resistance to sexual identity stereotypes diminish or increase over time? What are the patterns of resistance to gender *and* racial stereotypes in co-ed schools? How can teachers, parents, and peers nourish such resistance in classrooms and homes? What does resistance look like for those with gender, racial, social class, and sexuality identity privilege versus those who do not share such privilege? Exploring these questions will help us better understand the role that resistance plays in social and emotional development and will help us better serve young people as they grow up in a culture and context that promotes messages that undermine their core humanity. Paolo Freire (1967) claimed that resistance is the "practice of freedom." The research on resistance to dehumanizing stereotypes among children and adolescents suggest that parents, family members, peers, and teachers should foster the practice of freedom in order to help young people of all races, classes, gender, sexual orientations, and religions thrive.

References

Allen, J. P., & Land, D. (1999). Attachment in adolescence. In J. Cassidy & P. R. Shaver (Eds.) *Handbook of attachment: Theory, research, and clinical applications* (pp. 319–335). New York, NY: Guildford Press

Anyon, J. (1984). Intersections of gender and class: Accommodation and resistance by working-class and affluent females to contradictory sex role ideologies. *Journal of Education, Boston, 166*, 25–48.

Barker, G. (2000). Gender equitable boys in a gender inequitable world: Reflections from qualitative research and programme development in Rio de Janeiro. *Sexual and Relationship Therapy, 15*, 263–282. doi: 10.1080/14681990050109854

Barker, G. T. (2005). *Dying to be men: Youth, masculinity and social exclusion*. New York, NY: Taylor & Francis Group.

Bellah, R. N., Madsen, R., Sullivan, W. M., Swindler, A., & Tipton, S. M. (1985). *Habits of the heart: Individualism and communalism in American life*. Los Angeles, CA: University of California Press.

Blazina, C., Pisecco, S., & O'Neil, J. M. (2005). An adaptation of the gender role conflict scale for adolescents: *Psychometric issues and correlates with psychological distress Psychology of Men & Masculinity, 6*, 39–45. doi: 10.1037/ 1524–9220.6.1.39

Bronfenbrenner, U. (1979). Contexts of child rearing: Problems and prospects. *American Psychologist, 34*, 844–850. doi: 10.1037/0003-066X.34.10.844

Brown, L. M. (1999). *Raising their voices: The politics of girls' anger*. Cambridge, MA: Harvard University Press.

Brown, L. M., & Gilligan, C. (1992). *Meeting at the crossroads: Women's psychology and girls' development*. Cambridge, MA: Harvard University Press.

Brown, L. M., Lamb, S., & Tappan, M. (2009). *Packaging boyhood: Saving our sons from superheroes, slackers, and other media stereotypes*. New York, NY: St Martin's Press.

Cacioppo, J. T., & Patrick, W. (2008). *Loneliness: Human nature and the need for social connection*. WW Norton & Company.

Camp, S. M. H. (2004). *Closer to freedom: Enslaved women and everyday resistance in the plantation south*. Chapel Hill, NC: University of North Carolina Press.

Carter, D. (2008). Achievement as resistance: The development of a critical race achievement ideology among Black achievers. *Harvard Educational Review, 78*, 466–569.

Carter, P. L. (2006). Straddling boundaries: Identity, culture, and school. *Sociology of Education, 79*(4), 304–328. doi: 10.1177/003804070607900402

Chu, J. Y. (2004). A relational perspective on adolescent boys' identity development. In N. Way, & J. Y. Chu (Eds.), *Adolescent boys: Exploring diverse cultures of boyhood*. (pp. 78–104). New York, NY: New York University Press.

Chu, J. Y. (2014). *When boys become boys: Development, relationships, and masculinity*. New York, NY: New York University Press.

Chu, J. Y., Porche, M. V., & Tolman, D. L. (2005). The adolescent masculinity ideology in relationships scale: Development and validation of a new measure for boys. *Men and Masculinities, 89*, 93–115.

Clark, K. B., & Clark, M. P. (1947). Racial identification and preference in Negro children. In T. M. Newcomb, & E. L. Hartley (Eds.), *Readings in social psychology.* New York, NY: Holt.

Coll, C. G., Lamberty, G., Jenkins, R., McAdoo, H. P., Crnic, K., Wasik, B. H., & Garcia, H. V. (1996). An integrative model for the study of developmental competencies in minority children. *Child Development, 67*(5), 1891–1914. doi: 10.2307/1131600

Conchas, G. Q., & Noguera, P. A. (2004). Understanding the exceptions: How small schools support the achievement of academically successful black boys. In N. Way & J. Chu (Eds.), *Adolescent boys: Exploring diverse cultures of boyhood* (pp. 317–337). New York, NY: New York University Press.

Cournoyer, R J., & Mahalik, J. R. (1995). Cross-sectional study of gender role conflict examining college-aged and middle-aged men. *Journal of Counseling Psychology, 42,* 11–19.

Cross, W. E. J. (1971). The Negro-to-Black conversion experience. *Black World, 20*(9), 13–27.

Cross, W. E. J. (1978). The Thomas and Cross models of psychological nigrescence: A review. *Journal of Black Psychology, 5,* 13–31.

Cross, W. E. J. (1991). *Shades of black: Diversity in African-American identity. Philadelphia.* PA, US: Temple University Press.

Cunningham, M. (1999). African-American adolescent males' perceptions of their community resources and constraints: A longitudinal analysis. *Journal of Community Psychology, 27,* 569–588.

Cvencek, D., Nasir, N. I. S., O'Connor, K., Wischnia, S., & Meltzoff, A. N. (2014). The development of math–race stereotypes: "They say Chinese people are the best at math." *Journal of Research on Adolescence, 25,* 630-637.

Dance, L. J. (2002). *Tough fronts: The impact of street culture on schooling.* New York, NY: Routledge-Flamer.

Davis, J. E. (2001). Transgressing the masculine: African American boys and the failure of schools. In W. Martino, & B. Meyenn (Eds.), *What about the boys?: Issues of masculinity in schools* (pp. 140–153). Maidenhead, UK: Open University Press.

Du Bois, W. B. (1935). Does the Negro need separate schools? *Journal of Negro Education, 4,* 328–335.

Edley, N., & Wetherell, M. (1997). Jockeying for position: The construction of masculine identities. *Discourse & Society, 8,* 203–217. doi: 10.1177/0957926597008002004

Ferguson, A. A. (2000). *Bad boys: Public schools in the making of black masculinity.* Ann Arbor, MI: University of Michigan Press.

Fordham, S., & Ogbu, J. U. (1986). Black students' school success: Coping with the "burden of acting White." *The Urban Review, 18,* 176–206. doi: 10.1007/BF01112192

Freire, P. (1967). *Education: The practice of freedom.* London, UK: Writers and Readers, Ltd.

Frosh, S., Phoenix, A., & Pattman, R. (2002). *Young masculinities: Understanding boys in contemporary society.* London, UK: Palgrave Macmillan Limited.

Genovese, E. D. (1976). *Roll, Jordan, roll: The world the slaves made* (Vol. *652*). New York, NY: Vintage.

Ghavami, N., & Peplau, L. A. (2013). An intersectional analysis of gender and ethnic stereotypes: Testing three hypotheses. *Psychology of Women Quarterly, 37,* 113–127. doi: 10.1177/0361684312464203

Gilligan, C. (1982). *In a different voice: Psychological theory and women's development.* Cambridge, MA: Harvard University Press.

Gilligan, C. (1990). *Joining the resistance: Psychology, politics, girls and women*. Ann Arbor, MI: University of Michigan.

Gilligan, C. (1991). Women's psychological development: Implications for psychotherapy. *Women & Therapy, 11*, 5–31. doi: 10.1300/J015V11N03_02

Gilligan, C. (1996). The centrality of relationship in human development: A puzzle, some evidence, and a theory. In G. Noam & K. Fischer (Eds.), *Development and vulnerability in close relationships* (pp. 237–261). Mahwah, NJ: Lawrence Erlbaum Associates.

Gilligan, C. (2011). *Joining the resistance*. Cambridge, UK: Polity Press

Good, G. E., Heppner, P. P., DeBord, K. A., & Fischer, A. R. (2004). Understanding men's psychological distress: Contributions of problem-solving appraisal and masculine role conflict. *Psychology of Men & Masculinity, 5*, 168–177. doi: 10.1037/1524–9220.5.2.168

Good, G. E., Robertson, J. M., O'Neil, J. M., Fitzgerald, L. F., Stevens, M., DeBord, K. A., et al. (1995). Male gender role conflict: Psychometric issues and relations to psychological distress. *Journal of Counseling Psychology, 42*, 3–10.

Gough, B. (2001). 'Biting your tongue': Negotiating masculinities in contemporary Britain. *Journal of Gender Studies, 10*, 169–185. doi: 10.1080/09589230120053292

Gupta, T., Way, N., McGill, R. K., Hughes, D., Santos, C., Jia, Y., . . . & Deng, H. (2013). Gender-typed behaviors in friendships and well-being: A cross-cultural study of Chinese and American boys. *Journal of Research on Adolescence, 23*, 57–68. doi: 10.1111/j.1532–7795.2012.00824.x

Harwood, R. L., Miller, J. G., & Irizarry, N. L. (1997). *Culture and attachment: Perceptions of the child in context*. New York, NY: Guilford Press.

Hayes, J. A., & Mahalik, J. R. (2000). Gender role conflict and psychological distress in male counseling center clients. *Psychology of Men & Masculinity, 1*, 116.

Hazan, C., & Zeifman, D. (1999). Pair bonds as attachments: Evaluating the evidence. In J. Cassidy & P. R. Shaver (Eds) *Handbook of attachment: Theory, research, and clinical applications* (pp. 336–354). New York, NY: Guildford Press.

Helms, J. E. (1995). Why is there no study of cultural equivalence in standardized cognitive ability testing? In N. R. Goldberger & J. B. Veroff (Eds.), *The culture and psychology reader* (pp. 674–719). New York, NY: New York University Press.

Hilliard, A. (2003). No mystery: Closing the achievement gap between Africans and excellence. In T. Perry, C. Steele, & A. Hilliard (Eds.), *Young, gifted and black: Promoting high achievement among African-American students* (pp. 131–165). Boston: Beacon Press.

hooks, b. (1989). *Talking back: Thinking feminist, thinking black*. Boston, MA: South End Press.

Horvat, E. M., & O'Connor, C. (2006). *Beyond acting White: Reframing the debate on Black student achievement*. Lanham, MD: Rowman & Littlefield Publishers.

Hrabowski, F. A., Maton, K. I., Greene, M. L., & Greif, G. L. (2002). *Overcoming the odds: Raising academically successful African American young women*. New York, NY: Oxford University Press.

Hrabowski, F. I., Maton, K. I., & Greif, G. L. (1998). *Beating the odds: Raising academically successful African American males*. New York, NY: Oxford University Press.

Hrdy, S. B. (2009). *Mothers and others: The evolutionary origins of mutual understanding*. Cambridge, MA: Harvard University Press.

Kimmel, M. S. G. (2008). *The perilous world where boys become men*. New York, NY: HarperCollins.

Lei, J. L. (2003). (Un) Necessary Toughness?: Those" Loud Black Girls" and Those" Quiet Asian Boys." *Anthropology & Education Quarterly, 34*(2), 158–181.

Lieberman, M. D. (2013). *Social: Why our brains are wired to connect*. New York, NY: Oxford University Press.

Lindsey, M., & Marcell, A. V. (2009). Help-seeking beliefs and perceptions of mental health and substance abuse services among urban males. *Paper presented at biennial Society for Research on Child Development Conference*, Denver, CO.

López, N. (2003). *Hopeful girls, troubled boys: Race and gender disparity in urban education*. New York, NY: Routledge.

Mahalik, J. R., Burns, S. M., & Syzdek, M. (2007). Masculinity and perceived normative health behaviors as predictors of men's health behaviors. *Social Science & Medicine, 64*, 2201–2209

Mahalik, J. R., Pierre, M. R., & Wan, S. S. C. (2006). Examining racial identity and masculinity as correlates of self-esteem and psychological distress in black men. *Journal of Multicultural Counseling and Development, 34*, 94–104.

Majors, R., & Billson, J. M. (1992). *Cool pose: The dilemmas of African American manhood in America*. New York, NY: Lexington.

Nasir, N. S. (2011). *Racialized identities: Race and achievement among African American youth*. Stanford, CA: Stanford University Press.

Nasir, N. I. S., Snyder, C. R., Shah, N., & Ross, K. M. (2012). Racial storylines and implications for learning. *Human Development, 55*, 285–301

Noguera, P. A. (2008). *The trouble with Black boys: And other reflections on race, equity, and the future of public education*. San Francisco, CA: Jossey-Bass.

Ogbu, J. U. (1978). *Minority education and caste: The American system in cross-cultural perspective*. New York, NY: Academic Press.

O'Neil, J. M. (2008). Summarizing 25 years of research on men's gender role conflict using the gender role conflict scale: New research paradigms and clinical implications. *The Counseling Psychologist, 36*, 358–445. doi: 10.1177/0011000008317057

Osborne, J. W. (1997). Race and academic disidentification. *Journal of Educational Psychology, 89*, 728–735.

Parham, T. A., & Helms, J. E. (1985). Attitudes of racial identity and self-esteem of Black students: An exploratory investigation. *Journal of College Student Personnel, 26*, 143–147.

Pascoe, C. J. (2011). *Dude, you're a fag: Masculinity and sexuality in high school, with a new preface*. Berkeley, CA: University of California Press.

Perry, T. (2003). Up from the parched earth: Toward a theory of African American achievement. In T. Perry, C. Steele, & A. G. Hilliard (Eds.), *Young, gifted, and black: Promoting high achievement among African-American students* (pp. 1–108). Boston, MA: Beacon Press.

Pleck, J. H. (1981). *Psychoanalysis and sex roles–yet another look*. Arlington, VA: American Psychological Association.

Pleck, J. H. (1995). The gender role strain paradigm: An update. In R. F. Levant & W. S. Pollack (Eds.), *A new psychology of men* (pp. 11–32). New York, NY: Basic Books

Pleck, J. H., Sonenstein, F. L., & Ku, L. C. (1994). Problem behaviors and masculinity ideology in adolescent males. In R. D. Ketterlinus & M. E. Lamb (Eds.), *Adolescent problem behaviors: Issues and research.* (pp. 165–186). Hillsdale, NJ: Lawrence Erlbaum Associates, Inc.

Pollack, W. S. (1998). *Real boys: Rescuing our sons from the myths of boyhood.* New York, NY: Henry Holt and Company, LLC.

Pollack, W. S. (2000). *Real boys: Rescuing ourselves from the myths of boyhood.* New York, NY: Owl Books.

Pollack, W. S., & Shuster, T. (2000). *Real boys' voices.* New York, NY: Penguin Press.

Pulerwitz, J., & Barker, G. (2008). Measuring attitudes toward gender norms among young men in Brazil: Development and psychometric evaluation of the GEM scale. *Men and Masculinities, 10*, 322–338. doi: 10.1177/1097184X06298778

Putnam, R. D. (2001). *Bowling alone: The collapse and revival of American community.* New York, NY: Simon and Schuster.

Reichert, M. C., & Ravitch, S. M. (2009). Defying normative male identities: The transgressive possibilities of Jewish boyhood. *Youth & Society, 42*(1), 104-130. First published on June 10, 2009 as doi: 10.1177/0044118X09338504.

Robinson, T., & Ward, J. V. (1991). "A belief in self far greater than anyone's disbelief": Cultivating resistance among African American female adolescents. *Women & Therapy, 11*, 87–103. doi: 10.1300/J015V11N03_06

Rogers, L. O. (2012). Young, Black, and male: Exploring the intersections of racial and gender identity in an all-Black, all-male high school. Dissertation; available from ProQuest Dissertation Abstracts (UMI No. 10197).

Rogers, L. O. (2013, March). Black males narrating identities and stereotypes in an all-Black male high school. In S. Sirin (Chair), *Negotiating cultural identities among youth.* Paper presented at biennial meeting for Society for Research on Child Development. Seattle, WA.

Rogers, L. O., & Nelson, J. (2010, March). "Masculinity when no girls are watching: Black adolescent males' experiences in all-male schools." *Poster session presented at the biennial meeting of the Society for Research on Adolescence*, Philadelphia, PA.

Rogers, L. O., Niwa, E. Y., & Way, N. (2017). The friendships of racial-ethnic minority adolescents in context: Identity and discrimination. Invited chapter in N. Cabrera & B. Leyendecker (Eds.) *Handbook of positive development of minority children.* The Netherlands: Springer.

Rogers, L. O., Scott, M. A., & Way, N. (2015). Racial and gender identity among Black adolescent males: An intersectionality perspective. *Child Development, 86*(2), 407–424.

Rogers, L. O., & Way, N. (2016). "I have goals to prove all those people wrong and not fit into any one of those boxes": Paths of resistance to stereotypes among Black adolescent males. *Journal of Adolescent Research, 31*(3), 263–298. doi: https://doi.org/10.1177/0743558415600071

Rogers, L. O., Yang, R., Way, N., Weinberg, S., & Bennett, A. (under review). Masculinity and psychosocial wellbeing among early adolescent girls in US and China. Manuscript under review.

Rubens, J. (2008). *OverSuccess: Healing the American obsession with wealth, fame, power, and perfection.* Austin, TX: Greenleaf Book Group Press.

Santos, C. E. (2010). The missing story: Resistance to norms of masculinity in the friendships of adolescent boys. Available from ProQuest Dissertations database. (UMI No. 3426967).

Santos, C. E., Galligan, K., Pahlke, E., & Fabes, R. A. (2013). Gender-typed behaviors, achievement, and adjustment among racially and ethnically diverse boys during early adolescence. *American Journal of Orthopsychiatry, 83,* 252–264. doi: 10.1111/ajop.12036

Santos, C., Way, N., & Hughes, D. (2011, April). Linking masculinity and education among middle school students. Paper presented at the biennial meeting of the Society for Research in Child Development, Montreal, BC.

Schalet, A. T. (2011). *Not under my roof: Parents, teens, and the culture of sex.* Chicago, IL: University of Chicago Press.

Schott Foundation (2015). *Black lives matter: The Schott 50 state report on public education and Black males.* Cambridge, MA: Schott Foundation for Public Education. Retrieved on October 15, 2016 from: www.blackboysreport.org/2015-black-boys-report.pdf

Sellers, R. M., Chavous, T. M., & Cooke, D. Y. (1998). Racial ideology and racial centrality as predictors of African American college students' academic performance. *Journal of Black Psychology, 24,* 8–27. doi: 10.1177/00957984980241002

Sellers, R. M., Smith, M. A., Shelton, J. N., Rowley, S. A., & Chavous, T. M. (1998). Multidimensional model of racial identity: A reconceptualization of African American racial identity. *Personality and Social Psychology Review, 2,* 18–39.

Shields, S. A. (2008). Gender: An intersectionality perspective. *Sex Roles, 59,* 301–311. doi: 10.1007/s11199-008-9501-8

Smalls, C., White, R., Chavous, T., & Sellers, R. (2007). Racial ideological beliefs and racial discrimination experiences as predictors of academic engagement among African American adolescents. *Journal of Black Psychology, 33,* 299–330. doi: 10.1177/0095798407302541

Smiler, A. P. (2008). 'I wanted to get to know her better': Adolescent boys' dating motives, masculinity ideology, and sexual behavior. *Journal of Adolescence, 31,* 17–32. doi: 10.1016/j.adolescence.2007.03.006

Spencer, M. B. (1995). Old and new theorizing about African American youth: A phenomenological variant of ecological systems theory. In R. L. Taylor (Ed.), *Black youth: Perspectives on their status in the United States* (pp. 37–69). Westport, CT: Praeger.

Spencer, M. B., Dupree, D., Cunningham, M., Harpalani, V., & Munoz-Miller, M. (2003). Vulnerability to violence: A contextually-sensitive, developmental perspective on African American adolescents. *Journal of Social Issues, 59,* 33–49.

Spencer, M. B., Dupree, D., & Hartmann, T. (1997). A phenomenological variant of ecological systems theory (PVEST): A self-organization perspective in context. *Development and Psychopathology, 9,* 817–833. doi: 10.1017/S0954579497001454

Spencer, M. B., & Markstrom-Adams, C. (1990). Identity processes among racial and ethnic minority children in America. *Child Development, 61,* 290–310. doi: 10.2307/1131095

Springer, K., & Mouzon, D. (2008, July). "Masculinity and health-care seeking among mid-life men: Variation by social context." *Paper presented at the annual meeting of the American Sociological Association,* Boston, MA.

Suárez-Orozco, C. (2004). Formulating identity in a globalized world. In, M. M. Suárez-Orozco & C. Suárez-Orozco (Eds.), *Globalization: Culture and education in the new millennium* (pp. 173–202). Berkeley, CA: University of California Press.

Tamis-LeMonda, C. S., Way, N., Hughes, D., Yoshikawa, H., Kalman, R. K., & Niwa, E. Y. (2008). Parents' goals for children: The dynamic coexistence of individualism and collectivism in cultures and individuals. *Social Development*, *17*, 183–209. doi: 10.1111/j.1467–9507.2007.00419.x

Tate, W. F. (1997). Critical race theory and education: History, theory, and implications. *Review of Research in Education*, *22*, 195–247.

Tatum, B. D. (1997). *"Why are all the black kids sitting together in the cafeteria?" and other conversations about race*. New York, NY: Basic Books.

Tolman, D. L., Spencer, R., Harmon, T., Rosen-Reynoso, M., & Striepe, M. (2004). Getting close, staying cool: Early adolescent boys' experiences with romantic relationships. In N. Way, J. Y. Chu (Eds.), *Adolescent boys: Exploring diverse cultures of boyhood* (pp. 235–255). New York, NY: New York University Press.

Turiel, E. (2003). Resistance and subversion in everyday life. *Journal of Moral Education*, *32*, 115–130.

Turiel, E., Chung, E., & Carr, J. A. (2016). Struggles for equal rights and social justice as unrepresented and represented in psychological research. *Advances in child development and behavior*, *50*, 1–29.

Ward, J. V. (1996). Raising resisters: The role of truth telling in the psychological development of African American girls. In B. J. R. Leadbeater, & N. Way (Eds.), *Urban girls: Resisting stereotypes, creating identities*. (pp. 85–99). New York, NY: New York University Press.

Ward, J. V. (2000). *The skin we're in: Teaching our children to be emotionally strong, socially smart, spiritually connected*. New York, NY: Simon and Schuster.

Waters, M. C. (1996). The intersection of gender, race, and ethnicity in identity development of Caribbean American teens. In B. J. R. Leadbeater, & N. Way (Eds.), *Urban girls: Resisting stereotypes, creating identities*. (pp. 65–81). New York, NY: New York University Press.

Way, N. (2011). *Deep secrets: Boys' Friendships and the Crisis of Connection*. Cambridge, MA: Harvard University Press.

Way, N. (2013). Boys' Friendships during Adolescence: Intimacy, Desire, and Loss. *Journal of Research on Adolescence*, *23*, 201–213.

Way, N. (2014). Getting to the root of the problem. Feminist.Com: www.feminist.com/resources/artspeech/genwom/totheroot.html

Way, N., Cressen, J., Bodian, S., Preston, J., Nelson, J., & Hughes, D. (2014). "It might be nice to be a girl . . . Then you wouldn't have to be emotionless": Boys' resistance to norms of masculinity during adolescence. *Psychology of Men & Masculinity*, *15*, 241–252. doi: 10.1037/a0037262

Way, N., Hernández, M. G., Rogers, L. O., & Hughes, D. L. (2013). "I'm not going to become no rapper": Stereotypes as a context of ethnic and racial identity development. *Journal of Adolescent Research*, *28*, 407–430. doi: 10.1177/0743558413480836

Way, N., & Rogers, L. O. (2014). "[T]hey say Black men won't make it, but I know I'm gonna make it": Identity development in the context of cultural stereotypes. Chapter in M. Syed & K. McLean (Eds.) *Oxford handbook of identity development* (pp. 269–285). New York, NY: Oxford University Press.

Way, N., Santos, C., Niwa, E. Y., & Kim-Gervey, C. (2008). To be or not to be: An exploration of ethnic identity development in context. *New Directions for Child and Adolescent Development*, *120*, 61–79. doi: 10.1002/cd.216

West, C., & Zimmerman, D. H. (1987). Doing gender. *Gender & Society*, *1*, 125–151.

Wester, S. R., Kuo, B. C., & Vogel, D. L. (2006). Multicultural coping: Chinese Canadian adolescents, male gender role conflict, and psychological distress. *Psychology of Men & Masculinity, 7*(2), 83.

Whiting, G. W. (2006). From at risk to at promise: Developing scholar identities among Black males. *Journal of Secondary Gifted Education, 17*, 222–229.

Wilkinson, R., & Pickett, K. (2009). *The spirit level: Why greater equality makes societies stronger.* New York, NY: Bloomsbury Press.

Wong, Y. J., & Rochlen, A. B. (2008). Re-envisioning men's emotional lives: Stereotypes, struggles, and strengths. In S. J. Lopez (Ed), *Positive psychology: Exploring the best in people, Vol 2: Capitalizing on emotional experiences* (pp. 149–163). Westport, CT: Praeger Publishers/Greenwood Publishing Group.

14 Racialized Learning Ecologies: Understanding Race as a Key Feature of Learning and Developmental Processes in Schools

Maxine McKinney de Royston and Na'ilah Suad Nasir

The United States is in an unprecedented era where income and resource inequality are more disparate than at any time in recent history (Hacker & Pierson, 2010). While many intuitively assume that broad societal trends such as these must have an impact on schools and on student achievement, these connections are rarely analyzed and made explicit within educational research. In part, this is because research on social and educational inequality that theorizes and examines such trends does not frequently occur in direct and close conversation with research on teaching and learning, and vice versa. Even teaching and learning scholars who examine racial and cultural processes in schools often do not explicitly discuss broader societal trends or make direct connections between their theories or findings and these trends.

We argue that this siloing of scholarship has dangerous consequences, especially for students who are from communities that have been historically marginalized in and out of schools. One example of this is that educational researchers have long developed nuanced insights into processes of learning and development and the optimal types of conditions that would effectively support these processes. This research continues to be refined, yet even that which has been repeatedly confirmed – such as the power of teacher–student relationships or the building up of and support for students' knowledge and interests – remains untapped and invisible within contemporary teacher education programs and classrooms. This is, in part, due to the current political climate in which educational contexts are encouraged to be market and data-driven, rather than developmentally appropriate. Pedro Noguera, Linda Darling-Hammond & Diane Friedlaender (2015) similarly argue for developmentally appropriate school contexts by encouraging educators and policy-makers to "align educational practices with what they know about child development and neuroscience" as a way to support schools in promoting equity and learning. Unfortunately, the educational by-products of the current political climate often disregard the best of what we know in terms of learning and development, and this neglect disproportionately affects and erodes resources from school districts and schools that predominately serve racially and culturally non-dominant students. As a result, the possibilities for creating optimal learning environments and enacting effective teaching in such schools and classrooms remain constrained and exponentially dwindle with every new neoliberal policy.

In line with many of the results from the last two decades of research on child and adolescent learning and development in relation to learning settings (see Eccles & Roeser, 2011 for a comprehensive review), we contend that the creation of productive learning environments requires that scholars, policy-makers, and practitioners understand that schools operate simultaneously as institutional spaces of knowledge acquisition, and as physically and discursively critical sites of human development. Eccles and Roeser articulate that schools must be understood as a critical context for development because:

> Adolescents spend more time in school than any other setting except their bed. It is the place where they are exposed to their culture's font of knowledge, hang out with their friends, engage in extracurricular activities that can shape their identities, and prepare for their future. Consequently, experiences at school influence every aspect of development during adolescence, ranging from the breadth and depth of their intellectual capital to their psychological well-being to the nature of peer influences on their development.
> (2011, p. 225)

The fundamental idea here is that adolescents spend most of their time in schools and that the context of school exposes them to and engages them in cultural practices and social interactions that lead the intertwined processes of identity formation, learning, and development (Vygotsky, 1978).

Throughout the 20th century, schools have toyed with the idea of being supportive sites for development and for the administration of developmentally necessary resources (Dryfoos & McGuire, 2002). One key example is that of full-service community schools. Consistent with theories of learning and development, full-service community schools are grounded in the belief that children learn best when: 1) their basic needs are met; 2) they feel socially connected to those around them; and 3) they have a personal interest (Dryfoos, Quinn, & Barkin, 2005). This means that in addition to functioning as a traditional school, full-service community schools also provide wrap-around services (healthcare, dental care, etc.) and comprehensive resources not only for the child that attends the school but also for the complete family. One tension, however, with the full-service community school model is the danger of schools being viewed as the sole institution that supports youth learning and development. Schools are but one, albeit critical, site of youth's day-to-day negotiations with their sociopolitical and physical realities and identities.

Ecological and sociocultural theories have been key to understanding how processes of development and learning are interwoven inextricably with the various physical contexts that youth navigate as well as the multiple social, cultural, and political contexts that surround schools and youth (Barron, 2006; Bronfenbrenner, 1994; Cole, 1996; Rogoff, 2003). Such an approach appreciates that schools are physical locations that are situated within specific geographies and communities and are often influenced and have to respond to the conditions and resources present there. At the same time, there is an awareness that processes of learning and development are not restricted to classrooms, schools, or other institutional spaces, but that these processes occur consequentially as youth navigate across institutional and local settings, and grapple with the various social messages and practice-based activities they encounter along the way.

In this chapter we build on these approaches to extend them into a sociopolitical inquiry: What does it mean to consider learning ecologies as racialized? To explore this question, we propose a multilevel framework for understanding how race organizes society and effectively structures and influences human development and learning. We then use it to analyze data from a case-study project of elementary, middle, and high schools in Oakland, California, that were selected because of their relative success with African American learners. Through the framework, we show how race was a salient aspect at each level of schooling even though it took shape differently in each unique school-centric ecology. We also examine how each school attended to the developmental, learning, and identity needs of their students given its resources, geographic location, and demographics. At the elementary school level, the school community was centered around a collective mission to create a safe environment and a kind of protection from racialized harm in the form of positive racial socialization experiences. At the middle-school level, there was also a focus on safety and supporting students in navigating a neighborhood where there were significant challenges, and lessons were organized in culturally relevant ways that provided points of entry for the specific racialized and classed student population. At the high school level, tensions arose around racial stratification with respect to access to rigorous instruction across different small learning communities within the school, and administrators were wrestling with how best to address these tensions, and in doing so, how best to undermine white privilege. We argue that these schools intentionally conceptualized race as a key feature of their learning ecology. This chapter has implications for how we theorize and study the ecological, cultural, and racialized nature of learning and development, and the affordances and constraints environments provide for identity and learning.

Conceptualizing Racialized Learning Ecologies

Cultural-ecological or sociocultural perspectives highlight the important ways that various layers of social and cultural – and, at times, political – context influences learning and development (Bronfenbrenner & Morris, 2006; Cole, 1996; Eccles & Roeser, 2011; Gutierrez & Rogoff, 2003; Nasir, Rosebery, Warren, & Lee, 2006; Weisner, 2002). Scholars that use these multiple level theories view learning and development as inherently cultural, in that they occur within socially and culturally designed activities, involve interaction with social others, require engagement with cultural artifacts and tools, and exist to meet culturally determined goals (Nasir & Hand, 2006; Saxe, 1999).

These scholars argue that in order to understand human development, and often learning, the broader ecological system in which an individual is situated needs to be taken into account. One example is the ecological framework theory of the developmentalist Bronfenbrenner (1979, 1994), who argued for conceptualizing the developing child as an individual nested within multiple layers of context that dynamically shift over the lifecourse. These contexts include the micro-context of institutions and groups, such as families and classrooms that have immediate and direct access and impact on the child; the meso-context or interconnections between the micro-contexts; the social, political, and economic exo-contexts that the child isn't directly involved in but which do impact them; and, finally, the macro-context that reflects the culture and ideologies of the society, state, country, etc., in which a child lives.

Multilevel models such as Bronfenbrenner's highlight how social, cultural, and political contexts are inextricably nested within one another and are connected to local, micro-genetic moments of interaction. These models have been critiqued for failing to explore the co-constitutive nature of each context (Cole, 1996; Rogoff, 2003; Vossoughi & Gutierrez, 2014). For example, while these models demonstrate how policy or discourse in city hall or in the school district often gets reproduced within schools and in the practices within classrooms, they do not capture how what happens in classrooms also shapes the political contexts of cities. We see this co-constitutive dynamic play out in cases such as the implementation of district-wide zero-tolerance discipline policies when an uptick in behavioral issues is perceived or when a given teacher implements a practice or lesson that gets taken up by the district or recognized at the state or federal level.

Another critique is that current models do not examine power dynamics in and across social, cultural, and political contexts that fundamentally influence ecologies of human development. Consider how current models talk about culture but do not sufficiently theorize race, even though in the United States race is a key determinant for social positioning and experience (Nasir & Bang, 2013; Omi & Winant, 2014). To address these critiques, we offer a multilevel framework for conceptualizing learning ecologies as racialized. We use the term *racialized* to highlight how historically situated discourses about race dynamically shift over time, and to recognize how racial discourses get enacted through macro- and micro-scales of activity – e.g. through interpersonal and institutional interactions and practices.

Figure 14.1 depicts this multilevel, sociopolitical framework. Although we view these levels as co-constituting and interactive, each level of context is displayed separately to make clear its distinct characteristics. The "social" level represents the racialized, dominant meanings and values, ways of being that pervade the social imagination and often guide how we conceptualize the "problems" in education. These are then transmitted through how our institutions are constructed and organized to differentially value and reproduce certain ideas, policies, and practices, and how these practices in turn shape our individual ways of being and knowing. This framework makes visible that seemingly local, idiosyncratic micro-interactions between individuals or specific contexts are, in fact, moment-by-moment reflections of larger social discourses or dynamics of power. It shows how dominant social narratives, institutions, and practices are reproductive and constrain individual development and learning.

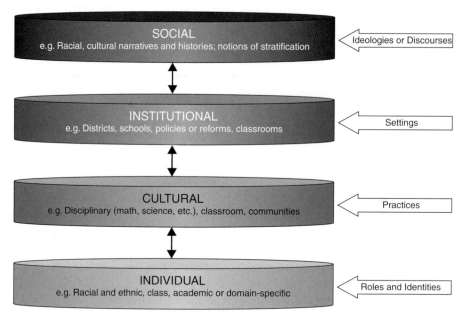

Figure 14.1. *Multilevel sociopolitical framework.*

Unlike prior cultural-ecological and sociocultural perspectives, however, this framework is distinctly sociopolitical because it accounts for the co-constructive, bi-directional nature of human learning and development that is indelibly ensconced within dynamics of power. It captures the reproductive, top-down nature of dominant forces that shape human development and learning, as well as the resistant, disruptive, and possibly transformative forces that emerge from the bottom up. There is thus an iterative feedback loop within and across the levels. Below, we explicate the conceptual underpinnings of each level of the framework. In the next section, we discuss Oakland as racialized learning ecology and demonstrate the co-constituting nature of the levels.

Social

At the top of the hierarchy and power dynamic is the "Social" level. This level is similar to the macro-context in Bronfenbrenner's model in that it deals with the broader attitudes, culture, and ideologies of a society or the "social imaginary" of a society (Nasir et al, 2016). This level represents the dominant socio-historical ideologies or discourses that physically and socially stratify our society. This includes discourses about socially constructed categories of distinction such as race, gender, class, etc., that articulate what is "normal," valued or appropriate in our society. Here we argue that race operates as a dominant discourse and that the USA is a racially organized society (Omi & Winant, 2014). In particular, we argue that race constantly structures our society via our interpersonal and institutional interactions even as the realizations and realities of race shift over time.

One way that race operates as a discourse in development and learning is through racial "storylines," or stereotypical artifacts (e.g., "Asians are good at math" or "Multiplication is for white people [not Black people]") that mediate how individuals make sense of themselves and how they position one another through their actions and interactions (Nasir, Snyder, Shah, & Ross, 2013). Storylines are often pervasive, unspoken, and unconscious ways of thinking that are assumed to be deterministic of individuals' or groups' abilities and ways of knowing. Racial storylines have distinct implications for students' perceptions of themselves as individuals and as learners, especially in domains such as mathematics where race stereotypes are especially pronounced and long-standing (Nasir & Shah, 2011). While some storylines are explicit, especially during different points of history such as narratives during the Jim Crow era, often racial storylines are implicit, rarely spoken beliefs and values that constitute our social imagination. As such, racial storylines are an undeniable aspect of life in schools and serve to racially and academically socialize students in ways that make available or close down certain identities that may be critical for engagement in learning settings, and ultimately for learning.

Recognizing the USA as a racialized society appreciates how racial storylines and other discourses of race serve to locate individuals "within a socially and historically demarcated set of demographic and cultural boundaries, state activities, 'life-chances,' and tropes of identity/difference/(in)equality" (Omi & Winant, 2014, p. 125). In this way race operates as a "frame" (Hand, Penuel, & Gutiérrez, 2012) or a tool of power that is employed by social actors to position individuals or group actors to achieve political ends. Frames help us understand the hierarchy and interconnectedness of the various contexts of human development and learning as it is often the frames that carry across the levels that we examine. Indeed, particular frames influence the way educational "problems" are identified, as well as how potential solutions are evaluated. Frames often motivate policy and activity in cities, districts, schools, and classrooms.

Outside of the frame of race itself, other "educational frames" (Hand et al., 2012; Nasir et al., 2016) intersect with discourses about race. We discuss two frames – colorblindness and neoliberalism – that are highly racialized and that carry across the multiple levels of human development and learning. Colorblindness (the ideology of not seeing or recognizing racial distinctions) often hinges upon the belief that the act of noticing race is problematic and perhaps racist. However, colorblindness is a myth because to enact it one would have to override the cognitive wiring that utilizes visual and social cues to guide human thought and action (Kang & Lane, 2010). Colorblindness also erases individuals' and groups of people's social and political histories and contemporary identities, practices, and everyday experiences that are linked to their racialized realities because as a strategy it must ignore that these social artifacts and experiences exist. Colorblind policies and practices thus operate under an abstract liberalist ideal that seeks to move us "beyond" race, but effectively (whether intentional or not) perpetuates and encourages racially disparate outcomes (Bonilla-Silva, 2006; Omi & Winant, 2014). For these reasons, a colorblind approach to human development is undesirable and impossible.

Another contemporary educational frame is the current national discourse around neoliberal reforms in education. In education, neoliberalism makes a set of core assumptions. The first is that educational contexts should be market driven. This marketized landscape stems from decades of policy that positioned the efficiency of the private sector as a superior social service model to the bureaucracy of the public sector. Previously education was viewed as an invaluable, non-quantifiable public investment, but the neoliberal frame portrays human development and learning as quantifiable in terms of human and material input and output. In so doing, a neo-liberalist frame codifies education as a social product and encourages a social and economic Darwinism in which those educational contexts, such as schools, that cannot thrive will die off and those students that cannot thrive will be pushed out to other places. This zero-sum modeling of educational success has largely benefited charter schools rather than public schools, the latter of which is mandated to serve and accommodate all students, regardless of performance, needs, and familial resources and involvement, rather than deliver high-efficiency schooling.

Yet, most research finds modest positive and negative results for charter schools and vouchers. Charter schools, on the whole, are not dramatically outperforming traditional public schools even though they contribute to the fiscal constraints in many urban districts by drawing students away from public schools. Moreover, research on high-stakes accountability tends to find negative shifts in instructional quality for children of color, English Language learners, and poor children (Booher-Jennings, 2005; Mathis, 2009; Valenzuela, 2004). Empirical studies also suggest that merit-pay systems have minimal impact in improving student outcomes and instead have largely negative effects on the working conditions of teachers, who often prefer to be assessed by more holistic measures (Glazerman & Seifullah, 2012; Johnson, Kraft, & Papay, 2012; Springer, Ballou, Hamilton, Le, Lockwood, McCaffrey, Pepper, & Stecher, 2011).

Second, the neoliberal frame is characterized by an emphasis on high-stakes, test-based accountability, for students and teachers. Increasingly, state and federal policy-makers are successfully tying teacher salaries to "value added" assessments of student test score performance, and sanctioning teachers who do not perform according to these metrics. More and more states find themselves unable to fund pensions, and additional efforts are underway to roll back teacher benefits or to further link teacher's career benefits, such as salary increases and tenure, directly back to student performance and teacher evaluation data (Rockoff, 2004; Rothstein, 2009). However, research on the efficacy of test-based accountability models for incentivizing teachers or improving student achievement are mixed, and many provide little support for such models (Baker et al., 2010).

These neoliberal reforms counter the best of what we know in terms of supporting optimal learning and development, and re-entrench racialized stereotypes because schools serving lower-income, and frequently racially non-dominant students are often presented as the "worst" schools in need of the harshest, most rigid market reforms. In this context, many Black and Latino students are cast as "underperforming" and the achievement of successful Black and Latino students is presented as newsworthy and exceptional. Consider the cases of two Black students – Akintunde Ahmad and Kwasi Enin – who made national news (Bhattacharjee, 2014; Toppo, 2014) when they were admitted to prestigious Ivy League universities. The way these cases are portrayed in the media reinforces the neoliberal false perception that the system is not broken, but that Black kids or Black families are – that if Black kids are resilient, work hard, and have "grit," educational and social mobility is guaranteed. Hence, the neoliberal frame is highly racialized because as a model of constructing schools and learning environments it disproportionately affects racially and culturally non-dominant students, and as a discourse it positions race as an individual issue of moral or social character and academic ability or effort, rather than a structural or systemic issue.

Institutional

Taking a top-down view, the next level of the hierarchy is the "Institutional" level, which is fundamentally about the settings in which human development and learning occur. This level correlates to various aspects of Bronfenbrenner's micro- and meso-contexts in that it fundamentally attends to the types of formal and informal institutional settings that an individual must navigate on a daily basis and that shape one's learning and development. This includes informal institutions such as one's family and other social networks (peers, etc.) as well as more formal social, political, and economic settings such as classrooms, schools, and districts. A key question for the institutional level is: How are districts, school, and classrooms racialized, and how do they mediate human development and learning?

Understanding the mediating function of institutions requires an appreciation of learning as a cultural process (Cole, 1996; Rogoff, 1990; Saxe, 1999). Lev Vygotsky, a Soviet psychologist of the early 1900s, articulated a view of culture as a system of meaning carried that is constantly being created and recreated in local contexts and across generations. These frameworks argue for the importance of local activity settings, including institutions such as schools and classrooms, where individuals participate in activities and draw on artifacts, tools, and social others to solve local problems. In considering the role of other people, such as teachers or peers, socio-cultural analyses can examine how institutions mediate learner's opportunities for participation. However, sociocultural perspectives do not explicitly attend to the power dynamics inherent to the participation opportunities that are created or foreclosed within institutions. Drawing upon sociopolitical perspectives, we understand institutions such as districts, schools, and classrooms as racialized sites that act as mediators of learning and development. Sociopolitical analyses attend to how race and power operate within institutional learning settings such that districts, schools, and classrooms are spaces of marginalization, positioning, and, potentially, empowerment where certain ways of being, knowledge, skills, and networks are perceived as legitimate and others are devalued or perceived as contradictory or oppositional (Nasir & McKinney de Royston, 2013).

The racial discourses within and across institutions are important to consider given the role of authority that social actors such as administrators, teachers, and paraprofessionals have within districts, schools, and classrooms. Institutional actors have power and authority over the movements of students' bodies, over what counts as "appropriate" behavior, over what counts as learning or domain-specific knowledge (e.g., what is/isn't "math"), and over which students are talked about and positioned as good students or as outcasts (Wortham, 2004). In this way, adults play a prominent role in creating the psycho-social climate for students, and the relationships that they develop with students are fundamental to how students experience schools and classrooms (McKinney et al., 2017). To demonstrate how institutions are racialized, we again draw upon the two frames of colorblindness and neoliberalism. In utilizing these frames we see how they mediate human development and learning through their infusion into the rhetoric, norms, artifacts, and forms of social interaction that are privileged within districts, schools, and classrooms.

Bonilla-Silva (2006) argues that as our society becomes more diverse, our institutions become more segregated and our national frame around race increasingly becomes one of colorblindness. We see these parallels within educational institutions, as the proportion of total enrollment in public schools of white students from 2000 to 2008 decreased from 61% to 56% and continues to decrease. During the same period, Hispanic or Latino school enrollment increased from 17% to 21%, Asian/Pacific Islander enrollment increased from 4% to 5%, and the percentages of Black (17%) and American Indian/Alaska Native (1%) students remained relatively unchanged. However, the teaching force has not grown comparably in racial and ethnic diversity, which raises questions about the degree to which teachers will be able to recognize the cultural strengths of the students they teach and respond to the racial, linguistic, and social-emotional needs of a more diverse body of students. White teachers, mainly women, are roughly 82% of the total teaching force and are evenly distributed across urban, suburban, and rural districts, while only 7–8% of teachers are Black and Latino and more than half of them are teaching in cities (Feistritzer, 2011; Goldring, Gray, and Bitterman, 2013).

The US Census Bureau (2012) projects that the white population will continue to drop and the Latino and multiracial populous will continue to grow, yet this demographic future has already arrived in many public schools, where "colorblind" choice policies have exacerbated existing patterns of residential and school segregation and inequality. Current patterns of racial and economic gentrification across cities in the USA evidence that predominately young, white, and upwardly mobile individuals and families are moving into cities, and corollary patterns of out-migration (or push-out migration) is happening by lower-income, non-whites to suburban and rural areas. Thus, segregative patterns within schools and systems have implications for development and learning in urban, suburban, and rural districts.

Many teachers, often less experienced ones, are with children who lack sufficient food, shelter, and medical and mental health care, and are within classrooms and schools that are not equipped to serve the wide range of student needs (Milner, 2015). These teachers do not have the pedagogical knowledge or other supports to teach in ways that respond to their students' social challenges and build on their unique strengths. Because of the segregative quality of schools, a contrasting set of teachers primarily exists within highly resourced schools with students whose parents have material and cultural capital that they leverage daily in support of high-quality education (Nasir et al., in press; Posey-Maddox, 2014). Without radical alterations in the Supreme Court's use of race in student assignment to schools, children will likely continue to attend schools and systems that are racially, socio-economically, and linguistically homogenous. Such a shift would require policy-makers to move away from a "colorblind" frame of school assignment and parental choice to race- and class-conscious frames.

Conceptually, neoliberal frames on education offer a narrow view of development and learning by limiting assessments of students' growth and success to test scores, measures of grade-level proficiency, or specific behavioral actions (such as KIPP's SLANT: Sit up; they Listen; they Ask and Answer questions; they Nod when it makes sense to nod; and they Track the speaker [Witney, 2013]) rather than appreciating the diversity of learning needs and participation styles that are inherent to any classroom or group of individuals. Because schools that use neoliberal frames largely serve racially and culturally non-dominant students, the implied racial discourse is that "these students" (read Black and Brown students) need such rigid structures. Such institutions also serve relatively fewer special education students than public schools because they are able to "cherry pick" students and push out underperforming ones (Furgeson et al., 2012; Nasir et al, in press). Research on educational market-based reforms largely concludes that they have heightened school resegregation patterns and create school environments that are more racially, linguistically, and economically homogenous (Darling-Hammond, 2010; Furgeson et al., 2012; Frankenberg & Kotok, 2013), particularly for White families who select into predominantly White schools and effectively circumvent efforts to desegregate traditional public schools (Renzulli & Evans, 2005).

Cultural Practices

Beneath the "Institutional" level in the hierarchy is the "Cultural" level or the level of practices and activities of practice-based communities, including those of academic disciplines, racial and linguistic groups, classrooms, etc. At this level, we try to understand the implications that schools and districts that serve as mediating institutions for social discourses and ideologies have for practices within schools. As with the prior two levels, sociocultural or ecological theories help to initially ground our understanding of the cultural level. While many psychological perspectives focus on human cognition and behavior as an in-the-head-phenomenon or one that occurs at the individual level, sociocultural theories locate the fundamental unit of analysis of human behavior in activity.

Much of this work builds on the theories of Russian psychologist Vygotsky (1962, 1978) and takes as a core unit of analysis the cultural practices that people engage in as they go about their daily lives (Kozulin, 2003). Vygotsky articulated a view of culture as a system of meaning carried that is constantly being created and recreated through activity and across generations. Sociocultural frameworks argue for the importance of understanding how individuals participate in activities and draw on artifacts, tools, and social others to solve local problems. These approaches rest on the idea that knowledge is socially constructed as individuals participate in culturally organized activities – activities that involve values, norms, goals, artifacts, and conventions and within which people co-create activity through talk and action. From this perspective, learning is as much about shifts in participation in social and cultural practices and activities as about shifts in ways of thinking (Lave & Wenger 1991; Rogoff 1993, 2003). In short, learning is considered a characteristic of practice (Wenger, 1998).

However, sociocultural perspectives do not explicitly attend to the power dynamics inherent in how opportunities to participate or engage in social and cultural practices are created or foreclosed within particular settings because of racialized discourses. Drawing upon sociopolitical perspectives, we understand cultural practices as inherently racialized mechanisms that mediate learning and development. Sociopolitical analyses attend to how racialized discourses shape which types of social and cultural practices are valued and privileged and the extent to which students' home and neighborhood cultural practices are welcomed/ attended to in school and classroom life or are marginalized as irrelevant or less sophisticated (Nasir & McKinney de Royston, 2013).

Colorblind and neoliberal frames often act in tandem and ignore the racialized nature of institutions in theory and practice. Neoliberal education reforms, by design, are colorblind and instead focus on increasing efficiency and equality as "sameness" by standardizing curricular practices, pedagogical practices, and disciplinary practices. By virtue of trying to offer all students a standardized curriculum and classroom experience, these frames necessarily devalue culturally open and responsive curricula and teaching that requires eliciting and incorporating student's cultural funds of knowledge, activities, and practices and supporting students' development of their own critical consciousness about the curriculum and about the world. A culturally relevant approach will necessarily vary based upon the experiences and lived realities of students and those of teachers. The lack of culturally relevant pedagogy within institutions based upon neoliberal reforms is doubly disturbing given that many such organizations generally serve large populations of students who live in poverty, as well as racially and culturally non-dominant students.

Individual Roles and Identities

Finally, the bottom level in the hierarchy is the "Individual" level or the level in which racial or ethnic identities, academic or domain-specific identities, and professional identities intertwine with processes of learning and development. Sociocultural or ecological theories have conceptualized identity as an aspect of social and cultural practice. For Wenger, both learning and identity have to do with shifting relationships to people and objects in a particular setting and involve membership in communities of practice. However, Wenger distinguishes between trajectories of identification and participation in communities of practice – such as inbound trajectories that involve newcomers "joining the community with the prospect of becoming full participants in its practice" (Wenger, 1998, p. 154) – and peripheral trajectories that never lead to full participation and keep certain participants marginal to the practice over time. These trajectories are composed of both learning opportunities and opportunities for the development of identity.

More recently, Holland, Lachicotte, Skinner, and Cain (1998) have argued that identity is constructed as individuals both act with agency in authoring themselves and are acted upon by social others as they are positioned (as members, nonmembers, or certain kinds of members of communities). They argue that identities are narrated through cultural practices that create "figured worlds" which carry with them a set of norms, expectations, and ideas that constrain and enable particular trajectories of participation and development. Through these acts of positioning, only certain cultural and identity trajectories may be offered and taken up. Consider the racial storylines "Asians are good at math" (Nasir & Shah, 2011) or "Multiplication is for white people" (Delpit, 2012) that often mediate how students and their forms of knowledge are positioned within mathematics classrooms in ways that shape the types of identity building and learning trajectories that students have access to.

Yet, a neoliberal frame places limitations on individual identity and learning by limiting who is positioned within a school or classroom as a "good" student based upon a narrow set of ideas about what it "looks like" to be engaged or to demonstrate one's learning. The rigid disciplinary and behavioral structures within most neoliberal institutional climates – from KIPP's SLANT to walking in the hall with one's arms crossed – more aptly reflect interactional models of physical compliance and submission than developmentally or cognitively appropriate learning models. Such models limit teacher's pedagogical approaches and strategies, including inquiry- or discussion-oriented activities that lend more power to students' actions, knowledge, and voice. They are also in stark contrast with approaches to learning and development that are found in classrooms in middle-class, affluent, and elite schools where the curriculum is less scripted and teacher-centric, and students are to able move about the classroom and the school unfettered (Anyon, 1980, 2014; Apple, 2013; Ellison, 2012; Lipman, 2013). Indeed, research on the learning and achievement of "minority" students implies the relation between processes of learning and development with identity processes (Conchas, 2001; Fordham & Ogbu, 1986; Ogbu, 1987) and suggests that racialized discourses and identities can constrain or enable opportunities to learn and be successful in school (Davidson, 1996; Ferguson, 2000; McDermott & Varenne 1995; Nasir, 2012). For example, within districts, schools, and classrooms racial storylines implicitly inform district policies and shape who has access to which curricula and classes based upon who is perceived to be able to benefit from high-status and advanced resources. In this way, individual students are racialized through how they are talked about and positioned vis-à -vis one another, the teacher, and the content.

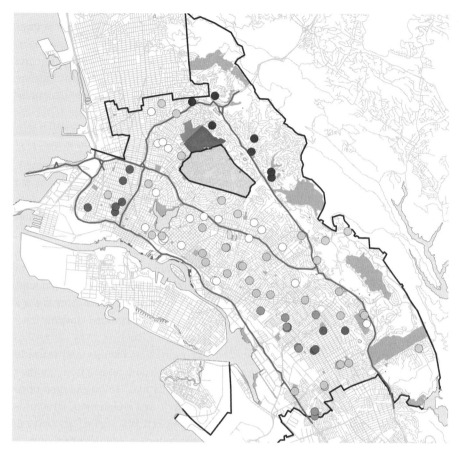

Map 14.1. *GIS stress mapping in Oakland, CA (OUSD, 2014)*

Oakland as a Racialized, Classed Learning Ecology

Thus far in this chapter we have offered a framework that attends to how discourses about race shift and get (re)constituted across timescales and across macro- and micro-scales of activity. In this section, we use this framework to demonstrate how local learning settings (e.g., a city, school, or classroom) operate as nested and co-influential learning ecologies within which discourses about race permeate and shift over time and scales of activity. Here, we apply our framework to considering Oakland, California – the city itself – as a racialized learning ecology and later use it to examine the school-centric ecologies of four schools in the city. We argue that Oakland is the broad learning ecology that students experience and that understanding school-level learning ecologies in Oakland requires attending to how young people in that city are differentially racialized (and classed, gendered, etc.) based upon where they live and where they go to school.

The above map (Map 14.1) shows the geographic layout and stress mapping of Oakland, CA. The area nearer the water in which a street grid can be seen, represents the "flats" or the flatland areas that have more families of color and a wider range of socioeconomic diversity. The flats is separated into two geographic areas – west and east – with the left or western one being much smaller than its eastern, oblong counterpart, which also encompasses the downtown area and lakeside areas. The demarcated area that runs alongside the eastern flats has a more hilly topography and is known as the "hills." The hills have the largest share of white affluent families and an overall population that is largely middle class or above.

Each dot on the map represents a composite measure of high or low stress indicators, including community violence and crime, income and unemployment, access to fresh food, and asthma and air quality, among other factors. The more deeply shaded dots in the flats indicate those areas that have a greater composition of high stress and low quality of life indicators. Conversely, the more deeply shaded dots in the upper hills represent areas that have a greater composition of little to no stress and high quality-of-life indicators. Not surprisingly, the dots in the western- and eastern-most areas where predominately racially and linguistically non-dominant communities live are precisely those zones in which environmental stressors are higher and quality of life indicators are lower. The focal schools we will discuss today come from these deeply shaded areas in the western- and eastern-most flats areas.

This map visually conveys that even the geography of Oakland is not post-race or post-class and that, like other cities, the quality of life indicators and outcomes of Oakland youth are largely based on their zip code. As one journalist said, "Children born in the flatlands are far more likely than children in the hills to suffer from poor nutrition, be victimized by violence, and lack decent health care. An African American child born in West Oakland is likely to die 15 years sooner than a white child of the Oakland hills" (Haddock, 2013, para 35). There thus exists a geography of educational and life opportunities that are highly racialized and classed (Tate, 2008).

By considering Oakland as a racialized learning ecology – as a site that consists of multiple levels of context that co-constitute one another – we can see how macro-narratives about race that appear in district-level and city-wide policies shape the city's educational landscape and are shaped by the physical and geographic tensions that divide the city into hills (richer, predominately white areas) and flats (poorer, predominately non-white spaces with enclaves of higher-income, white areas).

Oakland Unified School District as a Racialized Context

Oakland, like many urban centers, has struggled to maintain a robust public school system. Since the early 2000s, colorblindness and neoliberalism were framing ideologies that were reflected in Oakland Unified School District's (OUSD) policies, especially while under state receivership (2003–2009) due to fiscal insolvency. One result of the state takeover was to shift the institutional landscape and break up several larger schools, mainly those that had large number of racially and linguistically non-dominant students, into small schools and allow for a number of charter schools to be created within city limits. During this same period public school enrollment dropped by more than 17,000 students and charter school enrollment soared from 2,000 to 8,000 students (Trujillo, Hernández, Jarrell, & Kissell, 2014) and the budget deficit more than doubled before it was returned to the district in 2009 (Murphy, 2010).

Shifting ideological gears, in 2011 OUSD began to conceptualize its ongoing educational disparities as the result of interlocking racialized systems and structures that, as a whole in interaction, unevenly distributed and maintained opportunities for success. They implemented a strategic plan focused on addressing students' social, emotional, physical, and academic needs and on ameliorating the racialized inequalities in the district via 14 different task forces and initiatives, including the country's first African American Male Achievement Initiative (Nasir, Ross, McKinney de Royston, Givens, & Bryant, 2013). At the heart of the strategic plan, however, was an ideological shift from neoliberalism to a learner-centric model that takes into account "the whole child" as the focal unit of development and learning. The hallmark of this shift was OUSD's goal of becoming the nation's first full-service community school district, wherein each school would become a comprehensive site for students and their families to access not only academic services, but also wrap-around services such as health, housing, and other social service programs and resources (Haddock, 2013; Trujillo et al., 2014). See Figure 14.2: Oakland Unified School District's Community School Model for Change and Action.

Despite these ideological and policy shifts, OUSD continues to hold in tension neoliberalism as a framing ideology. This tension comes out through how individual students' test scores and schools' academic yearly progress scores continue to be the main measures of student and school success. While other measures are also collected in order to capture the quality of the school climate or the levels of teacher, student, and family satisfaction, the explicit linking of these non-test score measures to funding streams, teacher or administrator incentive programs, or other tangible markers of success or recognition remains unclear. This tension is an outgrowth both of local struggles within Oakland and its school district, but also reflects broader tensions within the state relative to these issues.

Likewise, within Oakland Unified School District, essentialized racial storylines about Black and Latino students continue to be bookended by narratives of failure and of exceptionality. Despite the commitments of the district, explicit attempts to disrupt such narratives are largely dependent upon the sociopolitical awareness of an individual teacher or administrator or program (such as the African American Male Achievement Initiative's programs) rather than as a holistic approach that manifests within and across all of the learning environments and approaches within the district. Similarly, the racialized and classed trajectories of students continues to remain, in large part, linked to the areas in which they live and the schools that they attend.

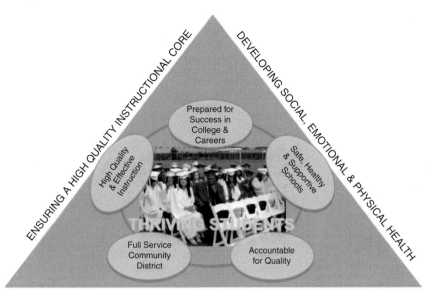

CREATING EQUITABLE OPPORTUNITIES for LEARNING

Figure 14.2. *OUSD's Community School Model for Change and Action (OUSD, 2011).*

Case Studies of Schools in Oakland as Racialized Contexts

To understand the racialized and classed trajectories of students further, we now turn to analyzing the school-centric ecologies of four case-study schools within Oakland. In particular, we examine how each of these schools navigates the racialized discourses and tensions present within the city of Oakland and it's school district, and how each school navigates these discourses and tensions differently given where they were located in the city and the specific needs of their student population and school community. The data we present come from a larger study situated in Oakland. As mentioned before, the city has grappled with problematic outcomes for Black students and other students from non-dominant communities, prompting the school district to develop a number of reforms. Our team of researchers was invited to conduct a series of case studies to examine how these initiatives were understood and taken up within schools.

This broad study centered on understanding the characteristics of each school that supported the relative success of its students, particularly its Black students. We sought out recommendations – from the district and other key educational stakeholders – for schools with significant populations of Black students that were recognized as either successful or as sites where positive change was underway. We defined "success" by normative academic measures (e.g., Academic performance index scores) and by an inclusive school climate for Black students, or both. Several elementary and middle schools were recommended, as were some high schools and schools that spanned across primary and secondary levels. After determining each school's willingness to participate, seven sites (two elementary, three middle, and two high schools) were selected.

During data collection, members of each school community referred to what was happening outside of each school as a way to talk about what needed to happen inside schools and classrooms. From these conversations we refined our rubric for classroom observations to describe the key participants, school setting, and the context and content of the class being observed. Particular attention was paid to pedagogical practices, such as the discourse or interactions related to student positioning and identity, discipline practices, teacher–student relationships, equity-oriented practices, and the quality of the academic content being taught. To better understand the history associated with the schools and their surrounding neighbor-hoods, we also utilized data from newspaper articles and from the school district and school websites.

For the purposes of this paper, we focus on four focal schools. These schools were chosen to represent each level of schooling (elementary, middle, and high school) and based upon the degree of communication and ongoing interaction that we were able to maintain at each of these schools. Other focal schools experienced turnovers in teachers, administrators, and other activities that limited the scope or duration of data collection. We also argue that at each of these four schools, race was intention-ally conceptualized as a key feature of their learning ecology. Table 14.1 provides an overview of each of the four schools, including their enrollment, demographics, and the school's designation as either a Science, Technology, Engineering, and Mathematics (STEM) school, a small school, or a larger school that was comprised of multiple academies. Given the high degree of teacher and administrator turnover that we observed at a number of schools – and that is arguably characteristic of schools serving racially and economically non-dominant students (Loeb, Darling-Hammond, & Luczak, 2005) – in Table 14.1 we also make note of the leadership model (i.e., strong or stable) that was present at each of the focal schools that we discuss.

Multilevel Analyses in Oakland

Our analyses of the four case-study schools demonstrate key ways that teachers, students, administrators, and parents experience their school sites as parts of a racialized ecology. Specifically, the school case studies illustrate the ways in which processes of human development and learning are cultural, and how learning spaces are inherently cultural and racialized. We present several findings from across the school sites – elementary, middle, and high schools – to show the multiple ways in which school ecologies are racialized in ways that support the engagement and achievement of Black students.

Our analysis relies upon our assertion about the co-constituting nature of the various levels in our framework, namely how each level operates within and (re) shapes local activity settings, like schools and classrooms, such that they act as micro-cosmic learning ecologies within a broader racialized context of a school district or school. In contrast to Figure 14.1, where each of the levels was represented independently, Figure 14.3 shows how the multiple levels of learning and

Table 14.1 *Four case study schools*

Parsons Elementary School	North Pineview Middle School	Molly Williams Academy	Pinehurst High School
Grades K–5	Grades 6–8	Grades 6–8	Grades 9–12
Stable leadership	Strong leadership	Stable leadership	Stable leadership
Small school	STEM corridor school	Small school	Academies; learning comm., 9th grade "houses"
Enrollment: 200	Enrollment: 220 students	Enrollment: 200	
66% AA; 25% Lat; 5% PI	81% AA; 10% Lat; 6% other	49.7% Lat, 45.9% AA, 2.3% PI, 2.1% Asian	Enrollment 1850
East Oakland	West Oakland	East Oakland	37% AA; 23% white; 18% Lat; 15% Asian; 5% PI
			North Oakland

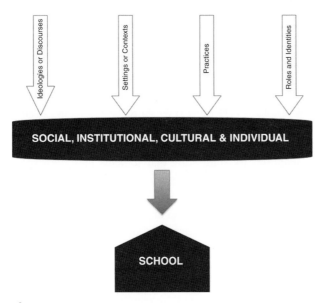

Figure 14.3. *Co-constituting levels.*

development (the arrows) that are central to our framework actually co-construct the sociopolitical context (Social, Institutional, Cultural, and Individual) of human learning and development that is infused into and shapes the racialized climate within micro-learning ecologies of schools and the spaces within them. We offer this representation as a race-conscious frame that challenges a colorblind, neoliberal model of education and schooling. We now use this frame to analyze each of the four case-study schools: Parsons, North Pineview Middle School, Molly Williams Academy, and Pinehurst High School.

276

Parsons Elementary School. At the elementary school level, "home grown" approaches aligned with district initiatives around creating schools as developmentally appropriate environments that responded to the racialized and classed geographic contexts in which students live. Administrators and teachers at Parsons saw it as their collective mission to create a safe physical and racial environment for their students, and to offer a kind of protection from racialized harm in the form of positive racial socialization and academic socialization experiences as Black students and as Parsons "scholars." The race consciousness, rather than colorblindness, of the Black educators and administrators at Parsons influenced how they interacted with and attended to their Black students' socioemotional needs and sought to nurture and protect their well-being. In describing what it is like to be a Black student at Parsons Elementary School, one administrator stated,

> I think they find this place to be home. . . . I feel like they're very comfortable here at Parsons. First, it's in their community, second they see a lot people who look like them . . . I feel like all of them feel like, "Hey, I can come here and people care about me" . . . I feel like the experience here is like you're comin' home, this is this my Parsons *family*, this is my Parsons *home*. [emphasis added]

In describing Parsons as a familial and comfortable environment for Black students, this administrator highlights three racialized features of Parsons as an institution. First, because the school is in their community, students likely know how to manage their physical location and the surrounding environment, a comfort they may not have in other schools or neighborhoods they are less familiar with, where they know fewer people, or where they are less likely to be known. Second, in highlighting the racial demographics of the school as a symbolically protective feature where students see "people who look like them," the administrator links the institutional care with students' identities by suggesting that students may not experience the racialized harm of isolation, stereotyping, or feeling like they have to be a "representative" of their race. Third, the administrator argues that students have a perception that "people care about" them at Parsons, which is in contrast to the lack of care Black students frequently experience in schools (e.g., Irvine & Fraser, 1998; McKinney de Royston et al., in press). Later in the interview the administrator shares that former students come back to visit and lament that they *had* to graduate and leave Parsons. His statements both suggest the presence of symbolically protective features at Parsons and allude to the potential for racialized harm when these features are absent.

Highlighting not only the symbolically racialized nature of Parsons, the Black educators, teachers, and parents at Parsons also spoke about the physical safety in and around the school as being critically important. Parsons community members, in general, commented on how their school contrasted physically with the neighborhood and areas around the school, and argued that the school offered the students a sense of physical safety. At the level of practice, this meant that Parsons educators sought to keep a "very clean," "orderly" school environment because they believed that it helps to create an "oasis" or safety net for students and avoids reproducing – visually or otherwise – the trauma of the poverty and violence in the surrounding neighborhood. Indeed, fieldnotes at each of the focal sites noted a marked distinction between the physical environment immediately around and inside of the school with that of the surrounding area. Consider the fieldnotes from one of the first visits to Parsons that marks the physical contrast between the neighborhood and the setting of Parsons itself: "It's strange, because while the neighborhood is considered 'deep East Oakland,' the school is almost spotless, both outside and within."

North Pineview Middle School and Molly Williams Academy. At the middle school level, there was also a focus on safety and supporting students in navigating neighborhoods where there were significant challenges based on historic racial and economic segregation. In taking up the full-service community model, at least at North Pineview Middle School, issues of access to necessary services was seen as the school's responsibility and not a shortcoming of the student or family. At the institutional level, there was a clear discourse and clarity about students' structural ecology. Consider the sentiments of one administrator:

> If the kids come to a place that's clean, that they feel like, "Alright I like this now 'cuz it's safe" . . . then it gives them a sense to come, but it also makes them feel like they can relax . . . 'Cuz I don't know where they're coming from, we don't know the hassle . . . . If at least they can come and breathe deep and be at peace for a good 6 to 8 hours, then we're helping them out. . . . Giving them things . . . if I can give you everything from food to clothes to health services – then, let me give it to you. . . . To me that gives an umbrella, a bubble of security around the kids. It gives them a place where they can take out some of the nonsense, some of the things that stress their life and more focus on getting better academically.

Responding to a question about how diversity or race was talked about at his school, Mr. Coles at North Pineville Middle School (NPMS) articulated the need for a race-conscious approach to teaching:

> You know, it's just embedded in the system . . ..It's [a race consciousness] in everything that we do. From the way we walk, to how we talk, it, it just is. I don't know how to explain it. It [race] has to be recognized. For a teacher to say everybody looks the same, or everybody, I see everyone the same . . . you mean to tell me you don't see color? And that's a problem. 'Cause everyone's not the same. So, you [the school administration and staff] need to address that.

Here, Mr. Coles stresses the importance of race consciousness or awareness by educators, and marks a colorblind frame as a "problem" that the administration at a school needs to "address." Implicit here is a recognition by Mr. Coles of the distinct sociopolitical realities of Black youth because they are Black. Foundational to Mr. Coles' argument is a racialized awareness that the work of teaching occurs *within* the broader context of structural and symbolic racism. In this view, teachers who employ a colorblind pedagogy could be reinscribing inside their classrooms the racialized harm that students experience outside school. Colorblindness, therefore, is a form of racialized harm.

Mr. Saunders, a middle school teacher at Molly Williams Academy (MWA), connected the problematics of not acknowledging race with students with his own practice of identifying his racial positionality with students:

I always identify myself as a Black man, and I feel like because I do that, I feel like kids internalize that as well and see themselves as Black. I've also had instructors tell me that . . . "Oh, well we feel like, you know, kind of like the Martin Luther King philosophy like, you know, people are not judging me [the student] by the color of my skin, but more the content of my character." You know, I would like to think . . . like that would be great if that was the case, but that's not the case. I try to be as realistic as possible with my kids. Like you should be judged by the content of your character and you should just have to look at yourself like a black kid, but you know, society has another view.

Mr. Saunders highlights colorblindness as a missed opportunity for educators to pre-emptively acknowledge their subjectivity with their students as a way to both align with their life experience and racially socialize them into what it means to be Black in the USA. He also argues that colorblind perspectives are inappropriate in a society that "has another view."

Earlier in the interview, Mr. Saunders talks about the killing of Michael Brown, an unarmed Black man who was killed in Ferguson, Missouri, by a white police officer, and connects it with stereotypes within schools: "race and ethnicity . . . plays out in the classroom . . . [and] a teacher's bias can gravely affect a student's achievement." In connecting Michael Brown's murder with teacher biases, Mr. Saunders argument suggests that a teacher's failure to acknowledge race effectively ignores the reality that Black youth may be subject to physical harm, including at the hands of police, *and* that this failure by teachers to acknowledge the racialized realities and forms of oppression their students experience can reproduce unchecked biases or stereo-types or otherwise position students racially. Like Mr. Coles, Mr. Saunders articu-lates the problematics of colorblind approaches to interacting with students and instead argues for explicit actions and practices that support students' positive racial identities.

In addition to creating symbolically and physically protective school environ-ments, the middle schools we studied in Oakland also operated as racialized learning ecologies in terms of the culturally relevant pedagogical practices and how lessons sought to provide points of entry for the specific racialized and classed identities of their student population. At Pinehurst Middle School administrators and teachers viewed their whole school as a racialized context and many educators tried to be culturally responsive and have a racialized clarity about how their students were perceived and positioned in and out of schools. This clarity was enacted through a degree of care for their students' academic and personal well-being, a need to protect and advocate for their students, and to prepare students to deal with bias and hold themselves up to higher expectations than others might. For example, the vice principal – who was subbing for the engineering class instructor – did a lot of explicit work to reposition students in taking up identities as engaged learners in the class-room. This included explicit repositioning (e.g., telling a student "you are a scholar," or that what they are doing is "what engineers do"). At other times it meant repositioning behaviors that tend to be viewed as antithetical to classroom engage-ment to be indicators of engagement.

Within the middle school, we also observed pedagogies and interactional practices that were intentionally constructed to counter dominant ideologies about race
and class and to instead support students' positive racial and domain identities. For
example, one day we observed Mr. Coles introducing his class to the next design
task: to create a gravity resistance box for an egg drop competition. The egg drop
competition is an NGSS-aligned activity that leverages the engineering design
process (Corbett & Coriell, 2013), with the aim being to create a container that
can protect a raw egg from cracking when it is dropped (Northeastern University
STEM Center, 2013; Tretter, 2005). Typically, when teachers introduce this task,
they discuss materials students might use to resist the force of gravity and assume
that students will gather these materials at home and complete the construction of the
box there. Instead, in this activity Mr. Coles talks to students about working with
what they have and seeing how the properties of those items will support their aim of
not letting their egg crack. In this way, he highlights their engagement in this project
as fundamentally about innovation and scientific thinking. For example, he remarks,
"I know my resources is [sic] limited, I have to use what I have" and positions
students as being able to "get billions for your ideas" if they are creative because
innovation is "what engineers do."

Engaging in role play, Mr. Coles tells students that he wants to take them "to the
Coles' household," where they are "broke." He moves across the front of the room as
if he is rummaging around a house for materials. He periodically calls out to his
mama to inquire about specific materials, to which she responds, "No!" He rum-
mages some more, mimics grabbing a stool – noting verbally that he's short and
needs a stool (students laugh) – and begins acting like he is opening cabinets and
pulling things out. While he is doing that, he's still in communication with his mama,

> "Mama, do we have napkins?" ("No!")
> "Mama, do we have cotton balls?" ("No!")
> "Mama, do we have styrofoam? ("No!")
> "Mama, do we have newspaper? Do we have
>   toilet paper?"

Here, Mr. Coles connects his awareness about the racialized, classed realities of his
students more explicitly to science. Considering the potentially limited resources
students may have access to, he notes that it is okay if "mama" – the students'
mothers or persons that care for them – do not have all the materials the students
think that they need to engage in science, and aligns himself with this reality in
saying that "the Coles' household" was "broke." This referencing of "mama" again
represents Mr. Coles' culturally relevant style, his humor, and his sociopolitical
awareness about what his students' out-of-school lives might entail. Mr. Coles
employs his cultural relevance and humor as a way to begin taking the material
constraints out of the picture and show his students different ways to make a gravity
resistance box. He reframes the day's task as one of scientific innovation and
improvisation and positions these practices as similar to the "hood skills" of working
with what one has access to. He is deliberately making explicit that students'
existing cultural capital and lived realities are applicable to and part of the skills

sets needed in science and engineering and that such realities do not preclude students from being scientists or engineers.

Pinehurst High School. Unlike at the elementary and middle school where school climate and students' racialized protection was prioritized, at the high school level tensions arose around racial stratification with respect to access to rigorous instruction across different small learning communities within the school. The administrators continue to wrestle with how best to address these tensions, and, in doing so, how to best undermine white privilege. Pinehurst High School is identified within the district as a school with tremendous potential that boasts one of the strongest academic profiles within its district. It has higher test scores and better graduation rates compared to other schools in the district. Moreover, unique within the district, Pinehurst offers a multitude of academic pathways and academies, such as the highly coveted Engineering Academy, and an intense humanities program. Some of these pathways have been in place for decades, and many families enroll their children at Pinehurst for the sole reason of gaining entrance into these rigorous academic spaces. Graduates of these programs often gain entrance into competitive post-secondary universities, from Ivy League Schools to the University of California system.

In many ways, Pinehurst defies common perceptions of dilapidated, run-down, and failing urban schools. However, while on the surface it offers expanded learning opportunities to racially and culturally non-dominant students, further analyses reveal that Black students, in particular, are largely excluded from the benefits widely attributed to the school at large. As an academy school, Pinehurst offers various pathways for students to engage in a more specified learning trajectory. For example, the Health Academy more deeply engages students on health-related issues, and may even connect some students with outside health-related opportunities, including internships.

Unfortunately, there are myriad ways that anti-Blackness operates institutionally and through practices of identification within Pinehurst to exclude Black students from the benefits largely attributed to the school. As one Black student notes:

> I know there is a lot of diversity, [but] in the higher classes it seems to be less. In the humanities program, there were two black people in my classes . . . And there are only two black people in the academy . . . Last year was stressful 'cause I did not know how to relate to others. It wasn't the same as if there were, you know, if was talking to a black person, I feel like they can relate to me more cause they have the same experiences. I would really relate easier. Yeah. So I felt kind of ostracized when I was in the humanities program. Like it was just . . . yeah.

Another student demonstrates how the racialized nature of the advanced classes creates tensions of racial and academic identity for students such that the two seem incompatible:

> yeah, but it's like when you're in there [the advanced class] you kinda have a feeling of like success in a way, cause when you're with white people, you feel like you're in a really good class, that's the same thing with my AP calculus class . . . but it's like, that's not how it should be in a way so that's why I kinda just left the class.

These findings highlight how tensions arose around racial stratification and around racialized access to rigorous instruction and content across different small learning communities within Pinehurst. Some of these tensions reified the neoliberal frame of Black exceptionalism or the idea of the "deserving Black" student as contrasted to those others who are not deserving. Students take up these problematics identities and position themselves with respect to them: "I need to surround myself with the better option, which is why I don't hang with African Americans especially boys." Many of the stakeholders' interviewed at Pinehurst offered various explanations to explain the large number of Black students who struggled academically, given the high academic profile of the school at large and the presence of prestigious academies.

Many of the high-achieving Black students interviewed then had to make sense of their personal success in relation to the larger number of underachieving Black students on their campus. For some, this was a constant struggle and a point of contention. For others, like that captured in the aforementioned quotation ("I need to surround myself with the better option. . ."), it literally becomes a question of how to relate to other Blacks on campus, and figuring out where they belong in relation to the Black community. In the process, stakeholders heavily employed meritocratic narratives that sought to explain Black academic achievement and failure according to students' possessing "exceptional" personal attributes or not. This racialized, bootstrap ideology, while not novel, obscures the structural barriers that contribute to Black student failure and fails to render institutional accountability. On this view, successful Black students merely possessed the individual attributes to work hard for success, whereas other Black students are assumed to not have them.

Implications

The sociopolitical framework that we present in this chapter has implications for how we theorize and study the ecological, cultural, and racialized nature of learning and development. Our findings demonstrate how race operates as a key feature of the broad learning ecology within a specific city – Oakland – and within the schools and classrooms in that city. These school case studies illustrate our argument that processes of development and learning are cultural in nature, and that learning spaces are always cultural and racialized. Another central point is that racial storylines are prevalent in society, and are taken up in schools. Societal storylines get reproduced and re-enacted (and resisted) locally and as they are invoked, academic and racial identities are made available, imposed, or closed down (influencing engagement and learning). Finally, a major point in considering learning ecologies as racialized and in considering schools within this framing is that schools must engage in active support for students to build counter-narratives of race and identity, in order to foster learning and present alternative developmental pathways to the stereotypes often present in schools.

In considering the ideological frames that guide our society, this study has implications not only for how we design classrooms and schools, but also for rethinking our views of education as a human endeavor and a growth opportunity. That is to say, what are the fatal consequences of colorblindness and neoliberal reform for learning and development? For example, one potential consequence is the pathologizing of students, families, and communities in focusing on individual-level factors and personal values. By contrast, considering learning ecologies as racialized requires moving beyond this individual-level analysis to a structural critique of factors in and outside of schools that influence racial discourses, school structures, and school policies, as well as teacher's practices and student engagement and identity formation. In considering learning ecologies as racialized, we are able to examine and respond to how racialized factors provide the preconditions for student learning, especially for students problematically positioned by racialized, classed narratives.

This lens presents a challenge for many of us to do well that which we are invested in, to examine the complexities of the human learning process, including its social, organizational, and cultural dynamics that play out at the multiple levels of context. To do this we will need to conceptualize learning as more than a set of cognitive processes within the minds of individuals or a cultural process that occurs through interaction. Instead, we need to consider the full sociality and socialization dynamics of learning as a process that is influenced simultaneously by micro- and macro-level discourses and positionings.

References

Anyon, J. (1980). Social class and the hidden curriculum of work. *Journal of Education*, Jan 1, 67–92.

Anyon, J. (2014). *Radical possibilities: Public policy, urban education, and a new social movement*. New York, NY: Routledge.

Apple, M. W. (2013). *Education and power*. New York, NY: Routledge.

Baker, E. L., Barton, P. E., Darling-Hammond, L., Haertel, E., Ladd, H. F., Linn, R. L., Ravitch, D., Rothstein, R., & Shavelson, J. (2010). Problems with the Use of Student Test Scores to Evaluate Teachers. EPI Briefing Paper# 278. *Economic Policy Institute*.

Barron, B. (2006). Interest and self-sustained learning as catalysts of development: A learning ecologies perspective. *Human Development, 49*, 193–224.

Bhattacharjee, R. (2014, April 23). Akintunde Ahmad, Oakland "Street Dude" with 5.0 GPA, Appears on "The Ellen Show," Announces He Will Attend Yale. NBC Bay Area. Retrieved from www.nbcbayarea.com/news/local/Akintunde-Ahmad-Street-Dude-From-Oakland-Ivy-Bound-Set-to-Meet-Ellen-256416751.html

Bonilla-Silva, E. (2006). *Racism without racists: Color-blind racism and the persistence of racial inequality in the United States*. Lanham, MD: Rowman & Littlefield Publishers.

Booher-Jennings, J. (2005). Below the bubble: "Educational triage" and the Texas accountability system. *American Educational Research Journal, 42*(2), 231–268.

Bronfenbrenner, U. (1979). Contexts of child rearing: Problems and prospects. *American Psychologist, 34*(10), 844.

Bronfenbrenner, U. (1994). Ecological models of human development. *Readings on the Development of Children*, *2*, 37–43.

Bronfenbrenner, U., & Morris, P. A. (2006). The bioecological model of human development. *Handbook of child psychology*, 6th edn, *Vol. 1*, 793–828: doi: 10.1002/9780470147658.chpsy0114

Cole, M. (1996). *Culture in mind*. Cambridge, MA: Harvard.

Conchas, G. (2001). Structuring failure and success: Understanding the variability in Latino school engagement. *Harvard Educational Review*, *71*(3), 475–505.

Corbett, K., & Coriell, J. (2013, October). STEM Explore, Discover, Apply-Elective courses that use the engineering design process to foster excitement for STEM in middle school students. *Institute of Electrical and Electronics Engineers Frontiers in Education Conference*, 1108–1110. New York, NY: IEEE.

Darling-Hammond, L. (2010). *The flat world and education: How America's commitment to equity will determine our future*. New York, NY: Teachers College Press.

Davidson, A. L. (1996). *Making and molding identity in schools: Student narratives on race, gender, and academic engagement*. Albany, NY: Suny Press.

Delpit, L. D. (2012). *"Multiplication is for White People": Raising expectations for other people's children*. New York, NY: The New Press.

Dryfoos, J. G., & Maguire, S. (2002). *Inside full-service community schools*. Thousand Oaks, CA: Corwin.

Dryfoos, J. G., Quinn, J. & Barkin, C. (2005). *Community schools in action: Lessons from a decade of practice*. New York, NY: Oxford University Press.

Eccles, J. S., & Roeser, R. W. (2011). Schools as developmental contexts during adolescence. *Journal of Research on Adolescence*, *21*(1), 225–241.

Ellison, S. (2012). It's in the Name: A Synthetic Inquiry of the Knowledge Is Power Program [KIPP]. *Educational Studies*, *48*(6), 550–575.

Feistritzer, E. C. (2011). *Profile of teachers in the United States*. Washington, DC: National Center for Education Information.

Ferguson, A. A. (2000). *Bad boys*. Ann Arbor: University of Michigan Press.

Fordham, S., & Ogbu, J. U. (1986). Black students' school success: Coping with the "burden of 'acting white'." *The Urban Review*, *18*(3), 176–206.

Frankenberg, E., & Kotok, S. (2013). Demography and educational politics in the suburban marketplace. *Peabody Journal of Education*, *88*(1), 112–126.

Furgeson, J., Gill, B., Haimson, J., Killewald, A., McCullough, M., Nichols-Barrer, I., ... Demeritt, A. (2012). Charter school management organizations: Diverse strategies and diverse student impacts. Princeton, NJ: Mathematica Policy Research. Retrieved from http://files.eric.ed.gov/fulltext/ED528536.pdf

Glazerman, S., & Seifullah, A. (2012). An evaluation of the Chicago Teacher Advancement Program (Chicago TAP) after Four Years. Final Report. *Mathematica Policy Research, Inc.*

Goldring, R., Gray, L., & Bitterman, A. (2013). *Characteristics of public and private elementary and secondary school teachers in the United States: Results from the 2011–12 Schools and Staffing Survey*. First Look. NCES 2013–314. National Center for Education Statistics.

Gutierrez, K. D., & Rogoff, B. (2003). Cultural ways of learning: Individual traits or repertoires of practice. *Educational Researcher*, *32*(5), 19–25.

Hacker, J. S., & Pierson, P. (2010). Winner-take-all politics: Public policy, political organization, and the precipitous rise of top incomes in the United States. *Politics & Society*, *38*(2), 152–204.

Haddock, V. (2013, Summer). The surprising Mr. Smith. California Magazine. Retrieved from http://alumni.berkeley.edu/california-magazine/summer-2013-new-deal/surprising-mr-smith

Hand, V., Penuel, W. R., & Gutiérrez, K. D. (2012). (Re)framing educational possibility: Attending to power and equity in shaping access to and within learning opportunities. *Human Development*, *55*(5–6), 250–268.

Holland, D., Lachicotte J.r, W., Skinner, D., & Cain, C. (1998). *Identity in cultural worlds*. Cambridge, MA: Harvard University Press.

Irvine, J. J., & Fraser, J. W. (1998). Warm demanders. *Education Week*, *17*(35), 56–57.

Johnson, S. M., Kraft, M. A., & Papay, J. P. (2012). How context matters in high-need schools: The effects of teachers' working conditions on their professional satisfaction and their students' achievement. *Teachers College Record*, *114*(10), 1–39.

Kang, J., & Lane, K. (2010). Seeing through colorblindness: Implicit bias and the law. *UCLA Law Review*, *58*, 465.

Kozulin, A. (2003). *Vygotsky's educational theory in cultural context*. New York, NY: Cambridge University Press.

Lave, J., & Wenger, E. (1991). *Situated learning: Legitimate peripheral participation*. New York, NY: Cambridge University Press.

Lipman, P. (2013). *The new political economy of urban education: Neoliberalism, race, and the right to the city*. New York, NY: Routledge.

Loeb, S., Darling-Hammond, L., & Luczak, J. (2005). How teaching conditions predict teacher turnover in California schools. *Peabody Journal of Education*, *80*(3), 44–70.

Mathis, W. (2009). NCLB's ultimate restructuring alternatives: Do they improve the quality of education? Boulder, CO, and Tempe, AZ: Education and the Public Interest Center and Education Policy Research Unit. Retrieved from http://nepc.colorado.edu/publication/nclb-ultimate-restructuring

McDermott, R., & Varenne, H. (1995). Culture as disability. *Anthropology & Education Quarterly*, *26*(3), 324–348.

McKinney de Royston, M., Vakil, S., Nasir, N., Ross, K., Givens, J. & Holman, A. (2017). "He's More Like a 'Brother' than a Teacher": Politicized Caring in a Program for African American Males. *Teachers College Record 119*(4).

Milner IV, H. R. (2015). *Rac(e)ing to class: Confronting poverty and race in schools and classrooms*. Cambridge, MA: Harvard University Press.

Murphy, K. (2010, March 26). Oakland school district: Is it better off after the state takeover? The Oakland Tribune. Retrieved from www.insidebayarea.com/ci_12753927?source=most_emailed

Nasir, N. (2012). *Racialized identities: Race and achievement for African-American youth*. Palo Alto, CA: Stanford University Press.

Nasir, N., & Bang, M. (2013). Conceptualizing cultural and racialized process in learning. *Human Development*, *55*(5–6), 247–249.

Nasir, N., Barron, B., Pea, R., Goldman, S., Stevens, R., Bell, P., & McKinney de Royston, M. (under review). Learning Pathways: A Conceptual Tool for Understanding Culture and Learning.

Nasir, N. & Hand, V. M. (2006). Exploring sociocultural perspectives on race, culture, and learning. *Review of Educational Research*, *76*(4), 449–475.

Nasir, N. & McKinney de Royston, M. (2013). Power, identity, and mathematical practices outside and inside school. *Journal for Research in Mathematics Education*, *44*(1), 264–287.

Nasir, N., Rosebery, A. S., Warren, B., & Lee, C. D. (2006). Learning as a cultural process: Achieving equity through diversity. In R. Keith Sawyer (Ed.), *The Cambridge handbook of the learning sciences (*pp. 489–504). Cambridge, UK: Cambridge University Press.

Nasir, N., Ross, K. M., McKinney de Royston, M., Givens, J., & Bryant, J. (2013). Dirt on my record: Rethinking disciplinary practices in an all-black, all-male alternative class. *Harvard Educational Review*, *83*(3), 489–512.

Nasir, N., & Shah, N. (2011). On defense: African American males making sense of racialized narratives in mathematics education. *Journal of African American Males in Education*, *2*(1), 24–45.

Nasir, N., Snyder, C. R., Shah, N., & Ross, K. M., (2013). Racial storylines and implications for learning. *Human Development*, *55*(5–6), 285–301.

Noguera, P., Darling-Hammond, L., & Friedlaender. D. (2015). *Equal Opportunity for Deeper Learning*. Students at the Center: Deeper Learning Research Series. Boston, MA: Jobs for the Future.

Northeastern University STEM Center (2013). Retrieved from: http://www.stem.neu.edu /programs/k-12-school-field-trips/egg-drop/

Oakland Unified School District, Research Assessment and Data (2014). *OUSD Environmental Factors Analysis in support of Budgeting for Equity.* Retrieved from https://drive.google.com/file/d/0B3_QaY7iAAQVdTY4a2N0UzY2dmc/ view?usp=sharing

Oakland Unified School District (2011). *Community Schools, Thriving Students: A Five Year Strategic Plan.* Retrieved from www.communityschools.org/assets/1/AssetManager/ Community-Schools-Thriving-Students-Strategic-Plan%20June%202011.pdf

Ogbu, J. U. (1987). Variability in minority school performance: A problem in search of an explanation. *Anthropology & Education Quarterly*, *18*(4), 312–334.

Omi, M., & Winant, H. (2014). *Racial formation in the United States*. New York, NY: Routledge.

Posey-Maddox, L. (2014). *When middle-class parents choose urban schools: Class, race, and the challenge of equity in public education.* Chicago: University of Chicago Press.

Renzulli, L. A., & Evans, L. (2005). School choice, charter schools, and white flight. *Social Problems*, *52*(3), 398–418.

Rockoff, J. E. (2004). The impact of individual teachers on student achievement: Evidence from panel data. *The American Economic Review*, *94*(2), 247–252.

Rogoff, B. (1990). *Apprenticeship in thinking: Cognitive development in social context*. New York, NY: Oxford University Press.

Rogoff, B. (1993). Children's guided participation and participatory appropriation in socio-cultural activity. In R. H. Wozniak & K. W. Fischer (Eds.) *Development in context: Acting and thinking in specific environments*, 121–153. Mahwah, NJ: Lawrence Erlbaum.

Rogoff, B. (2003). *The cultural nature of human development*. New York, NY: Oxford University Press.

Rothstein, J. (2009). Student sorting and bias in value-added estimation: Selection on observables and unobservables. *Education*, *4*(4), 537–571.

Saxe, G. B. (1999). *Cognition, development, and cultural practices*. In E. Turiel (Ed.), *Development and cultural change: Reciprocal processes* (pp. 19–35). San Francisco: Jossey-Bass.

Springer, M. G., Ballou, D., Hamilton, L., Le, V. N., Lockwood, J. R., McCaffrey, D. F., Pepper, M., & Stecher, B. M. (2011). Teacher Pay for Performance: Experimental Evidence from the Project on Incentives in Teaching (POINT). *Society for Research on Educational Effectiveness*. Evidence from the Project on Incentives in Teaching (POINT). Nashville, TN: National Center on Performance Incentives at Vanderbilt University.

Tate, W. F. (2008). "Geography of opportunity": Poverty, place, and educational outcomes. *Educational Researcher*, *37*(7), 397–411.

Toppo, G. (2014, April 2). He's all-Ivy – accepted to all 8 Ivy League colleges. USA Today. Retrieved from www.usatoday.com/story/news/nation/2014/03/31/ivy-league-admissions-college-university/7119531/

Tretter, T. (2005). Egg bungee jump. *Science Scope*, *28*(5), 12–18.

Trujillo, T. M., Hernández, L. E., Jarrell, T., & Kissell, R. (2014). Community schools as urban district reform analyzing Oakland's policy landscape through oral histories. *Urban Education*, *49*(8), 895–929.

US Census Bureau (2012). US Census Bureau Projections Show a Slower Growing, Older, More Diverse Nation a Half Century from Now. Retrieved from www.census.gov/newsroom/releases/archives/population/cb12-243.html

Valenzuela, A. (2004). *Leaving children behind: How "Texas style" accountability fails Latino youth*. New York, NY: State University of New York Press.

Vossoughi, S., & Gutiérrez, K. (2014). Toward a multi-sited ethnographic sensibility. *NSEE yearbook*, *113*(2), 603–632.

Vygotsky, L. S. (1962). *Language and thought*. Ontario: MIT.

Vygotsky, L. (1978). *Mind in Society*. Cambridge, MA: Harvard University Press.

Weisner, T. S. (2002). Ecocultural understanding of children's developmental pathways. *Human Development*, *45*(4), 275–281.

Wenger, E. (1998). Communities of practice: Learning as a social system. *Systems Thinker, 9* (5), 2–3.

Witney, E. (2013, April 11). Explaining KIPP's 'SLANT.' Retrieved from http://blogs.edweek .org/edweek/Bridging-Differences/2013/04/slant_and_the_golden_rule.html

Wortham, S. (2004). From good student to outcast: The emergence of a classroom identity. *Ethos*, *32*(2), 164–187.

15 Privilege and Critical Race Perspectives' Intersectional Contributions to a Systems Theory of Human Development

Margaret Beale Spencer

When considering the conceptual and intersecting contributions of privilege and critical race perspectives to the accrual of social science insights, too infrequently acknowledged is that each conceptual tradition uniquely and substantively provides understandings about human development across the life course. The frameworks both contribute insights about the variable levels of individual and group vulnerability given socially constructed differences in access to opportunity, and afford understandings concerning perceived coping needs, inferred identity formation statuses, and adaptive processes required of diverse citizens. Further, each contributes intuitions about patterned life-course successes as well as conditions that precipitate persistent states of challenge. Stigmatized and dissimilar relational and contextual processes and outcomes add to under-acknowledged *individual-context dissonance* producing experiences. Moreover, the recently recognized pattern of execution-like events involving black males and the parallel instigative functioning of the nation's justice system may provide fuel in support of the claim (e.g., see Stevenson, 2014). Although an uncomfortable acknowledgment for many American citizens, much of the latter circumstances may be associated with the observation that race remains salient – experienced as privilege or challenge – in everyday American discourse and traditional practices. The *status of privilege or challenge* is intersectionally linked with critical race views (e.g., see Harris, 1993; McIntosh, 2009; Roediger, 1999) which emphasize the problem of skin color associations with a knapsack of social benefits if you are white (i.e., the "wages" of whiteness) as well as the perceptions of blacks as property (see Harris, 1993).

Without question, and particularly when considered from a developmental perspective, the consequent intersectionality of the two also connotes a special quality of *identity formation challenge and confusion* (see reviews by Cross, 1991; Spencer, 1970, 1976, 1995; Spencer & Harpalani, 2008; Spencer et al., 2006; Spencer & Horowitz, 1973; Spencer & Swanson, 2015). The recent emergence, visibility, and cross-race instigation of the "Black Lives Matter Movement" have drawn attention to the social dilemma. The point is that diverse citizens navigate environments and attempt access to socially constructed supports which are constitutionally promised but are, in fact, differentially provided or made accessible due to the intersectionality of *unequitable conditions and impactful perceptions due to race, gender, skin color, and socioeconomic status influences and their interactions.* Particularly relevant for the factors noted, the conceptual orientations concerning daily experiences suggest both sources of between- and within-group varying processes (i.e., experienced both as trials and tribulations). Their overlapping influences function as myriad contributors to social incongruities. In addition, they are frequently referenced in media messages and journalistic reports as *gap findings.* Redundant reports of gap outcomes – which too frequently contribute to stereotyping – frame life-course group statuses (i.e., as "cradle to coffin" popular press-reported differences). The recently organized "Black Lives Matter" social movement in America and elsewhere highlights the unchallenged "normalization of police arrests and killings" and other situations that signal significant risk especially evident for brown, black, poor, and – independent of age – too frequently male citizens.

Introduction

The persistent conundrum addressed is that stigmatizing relational and contextual processes and outcomes contribute to under-acknowledged and unique individual-context cognition dependent *perceptions and commonplace objective experiences.* Much of the latter circumstances may be associated with the observation that race remains salient – experienced as privilege or challenge – in everyday American discourse and traditional practices. In fact, diverse citizens of color navigate environments and attempt access to socially constructed supports promised to US citizens as equitable conditions guaranteed by the constitution and associated with citizenship.

Formally integrated into educational curricula as instructions in citizenship, however – at the same time as daily discourse – democratic ideals (or their absence) are forcefully experienced and informally inferred as race-salient lessons. Across the life course, and within numerous contexts, citizens experience development-status-linked models and salient messages about *opportunity, power,* and *privilege* (see Spencer, 2008, 2011; Spencer & Swanson, 2015). The strength and clarity of status-relevant messages are evident even to preschool children, as indicated by the redundant findings that replicate the early studies by Mamie and Kenneth Clark and as footnoted in the *1954 Brown v. Board of Education Decision* (see reviews by Cross, 1991; Fegley, Spencer, Goss, Harpalani, & Charles, 2008; Harpalani, 2012; Spencer & Harpalani, 2008). As suggested, in practice (and by design) the nation's diverse citizens of color and those of low-income status experience unequal access to supports and opportunities. As a function of skin color and racial group membership, citizens lead lives wherein access to supports and exposure to chronic challenges actually function as vehicles *purposed for guaranteeing social inequality.* Legally designed and constitutionally assisted practices, unquestioned traditions, and the socially structured character of social assets (or their absence) differentially influence everyday practices. Accordingly, there is need for reactive coping and identity-relevant adaptations as a function of group membership. The character of actual experiences – no matter the democratic labeling for the political system in place, in fact – irrevocably guarantee the construction and sustainability of social hierarchies based upon socio-economically linked *disparate conditions of development*. These include stigmatiza-tion experiences associated with identifiability (e.g., skin tone, gender) and/or social identity (e.g., race, ethnicity, and immigration status, including country of origin, primary language usage, or some combination). Although all humans are vulnerable (i.e., unavoidably experience both risks and protective factors) (see Spencer, 2006, 2008; Spencer & Swanson, 2015), unequal societal experiences and socially con-structed conditions result in differences in risk and opportunity exposures. The primary point is that problems of inequality exacerbate the level of human vulnerability. Significantly *high levels of risk*, and, simultaneously, *inadequate access to assets and supports* result in **high or severe vulnerability**. At the same time, and given individual-context links, disproportionate supports represented as superordinate access to assets, on the other hand, *nullify some social risks*. This, in turn, *results in very low or a virtual imperviousness to acknowledging a shared state of human vulnerability*. The latter narcissism-associated or self-centered view of self and coping outcomes "as the norm" and belief of "earned superior social status" undergirds an assumptive perspective of privilege (see Spencer, 2011).

Human Vulnerability Perspective Overview

There are a variety of views about human vulnerability status. For example, Cardona (2013) characterizes vulnerability as *an internal risk* status and suggests that all forms of risk share a common division between *reality and possibility*. In other words, it might be inferred from Cardona's definition that social cognition processes are inextricably involved and that perception matters. Uniquely human perception-dependent phenomenological processes are involved in what might be referred to as one's "sense-making" of situations. Others have theorized vulnerability "as the risk of exposure and loss of control, as a construct through which to understand people's feelings of insecurity and unsafety" (Carlson, 2014, p. 64; Killias, 1990). Carlson's view may explain and make evident why it is difficult for particularly privileged groups to acknowledge and embrace – as a conceptual and intra-psychic awareness of differential opportunity – *a notion of shared vulnerability status which inescap-ably accompanies the human condition* (e.g., see Spencer, 2008, 2011, 2013; Spencer et al., 2006; Spencer & Harpalani, 2008; Spencer, Swanson, & Harpalani, 2015). The acknowledgment of both individual and societal statuses of *universal human vulnerability* invites the need for maintaining recursive self–other analytic and relational critiques vis-à-vis the impact of such conditions on conceptions of "self." The noted consideration suggests that a human-vulnerability perspective might serve as a policy-relevant heuristic device. Its inclusion may encourage engagement and analysis of the presence (or absence) of beliefs concerning mutual-ity particularly relevant when considering everyday societal experiences. Such understandings would include resource accessibility for those considered "the other" and, thus, have direct salience for espoused values of equality. Accordingly, the perspective may represent both *a moral stance as well as provide a point for ethical consideration and analysis*.

Of course, given the nation's history, relying on a moralistic stance alone is inadequate. As suggested by historian Howard Zinn and others, in fact, the nation's forefathers used biblically based interpretations to justify the institution of slavery (see Zinn, 2005). The subsequent and institutional custom of intergenerational transmission of wealth as a consequence of black slave labor remains an unapologetic and under-acknowledged aspect of the nation's history and, accordingly, serves as a fundamental (and inadequately addressed) aspect of an American identity (see Coates, 2015). That is, the nation holds as significant and indelible particular beliefs and perceptions vis-à-vis social relationships among citizens and their equal access to constitutionally guaranteed rights (see Spencer, 2011). However, as noted, recent national demonstrations illustrate the continuing American dilemma concerning *racial disharmony*; unfortunately, and as exemplars of the trend, the recent spate of male youth murders by police officers,[1] suggest the character of the troubling phenomenon at its core.

Critical race theory suggests that constitutional (property-based) protections virtually guarantee the long-term success and under-acknowledgment of privilege. Related American behavioral customs serve a foundational role in fomenting late-20th and early-21st-century life-course patterned disparities. Contemporary analyses by moral theorists indicate that possessing information and knowledge about morally relevant traditions alone is insufficient. Social science scholarship and theorizing indicate that intellectual prowess in and of itself is not enough for guaranteeing higher levels of moral behavior (see Kohlberg 1970; Piaget 1932). Thus, conceptual contributions from critical race scholars provide needed inputs for articulating policy-associated factors, remedies, and social requirements which coalesce well with an a priori view of shared human vulnerability.

At the same time, and similar to our own approach, Fineman (2008) argues that vulnerability should be viewed as a universal, constant, and inherent part of the human condition. In contrast to the traditional model of equal protection, he proposes:

> [a] post-identity inquiry in that it is not focused only on discrimination against defined groups, but concerned with privilege and favor conferred on limited segments of the population by the state and broader society through their institutions. As such, a vulnerability analysis concentrates on the structures our society has and will establish to manage our common vulnerabilities. This approach has the potential to move us beyond the stifling confines of current discrimination-based models toward a more substantive vision of equality.
> (Fineman, 2008, p. 1)

There are differences, including unique emphases in the myriad definitions and use of the construct; however, there are also overlapping grains of commonality.

---

1 See, for example, Ferguson, Missouri [re: Michael Brown]: www.nytimes.com/2014/08/31/opinion/sunday/nicholas-kristof-after-ferguson-race-deserves-more-attention-not-less.html; and Staten Island, New York [re: Eric Gardner]: www.nytimes.com/2014/07/19/nyregion/staten-island-man-dies-after-he-is-put-in-chokehold-during-arrest.html?_r=0

In this preliminary statement and introduction to the topic, first, we provided a very brief exemplar set of points of view about what is meant by human vulnerability. The next step requires providing a full review of the construct and then linking it with the phenomenological variant of ecological systems theory (acronym: PVEST) (see Spencer, 1995, 2006, 2008, 2011, 2013; Spencer et al., 2006; Spencer & Spencer, 2014; Spencer & Swanson, 2013). As a systems framework, PVEST describes an identity-focused culture- and ecology-acknowledging perspective of human development; as suggested; it reflects an undergirding belief concerning a *shared human condition (of a status or degree) of vulnerability.*

As an organizational structure, following the initial section which provided an overview of vulnerability as linked to a framework of human development, second, we review and integrate contributions from the privilege literature with PVEST, and, third, we present and synthesize the noted sections into the critical race theoretical perspective. Finally, the fourth section reports the benefits of the literatures reviewed (i.e., privilege and critical race perspectives) for systems theorizing (i.e., an integration with PVEST). The descriptive review and synthesis of perspectives with PVEST is designed to aid an understanding of human vulnerability as linked to under-analyzed American democratic traditions.

Diverse Perspectives Regarding Human Vulnerability

Hurst (2008) explores vulnerability in the context of research ethics and proposes a three-part taxonomy: consent-based, harm-based, and comprehensive. *Consent-based vulnerability* refers to those who are unable or limited in their ability to protect their own interests, thus rendering them at risk of abuse by others. *Harm-based vulnerability* refers to those social groups that are more susceptible to outside interventions (harms) because of physical or mental dispositions. *Comprehensive-based vulnerability* suggests a combination of the other two; thus, it emphasizes the limited ability of individuals to defend their interests as well as their own risks associated with group membership. Gilson (2011) agrees on the universality and pervasiveness of vulnerability, but suggests that it is neither positive nor negative. Instead Gilson suggests that vulnerability embodies conceptions of passivity, affectivity, openness to change, dispossession, and exposure. As a unique perspective, Gilson argues that in contrast to seeing vulnerability negatively, it actually represents a condition that makes other conditions possible.

Some have divided discussions of vulnerability into two broad categories: social and physical (Rader, Cossman, & Porter, 2012; Skogan & Maxfield, 1981). Physical vulnerability refers to physical characteristics that increase one's feelings of being vulnerable to victimization. Gender, age, and health are the most notable examples of this form of vulnerability. In contrast, social vulnerability involves social characteristics that enhance feelings of vulnerability at different levels. Contextually, this can include environmental hazards including neighborhood crime/violence (Rader et al., 2012) or areas prone to natural disasters or the impact of climate change (Carmalt, 2014). On the individual level, this can also mean race and socioeconomic status. There are areas where these forms of vulnerability overlap, as in, for example, the elderly during natural disasters (Gilson, 2011).

Rader et al. (2012, p. 135) suggest the importance of this interplay, noting that neighborhood conditions "may lead to an increased perception of social vulnerability which may, in turn, lead to increased levels of fear of crime. Likewise, existing physical vulnerabilities are likely to also be negatively affected by the existence of neighborhood disorder. Therefore, focusing on individual level vulnerability within a neighborhood disorder context is an important aspect of fear of crime research." They explore this idea in a nationally representative sample of Americans using self-reported feelings of being unsafe as a proxy for fear of crime. They found that physical vulnerability and social vulnerability are directly related to fear of crime, but the mediating effects highlight a relationship among the social and physical vulnerability indicators. They also suggest that the "effects of social vulnerabilities, in relation to their association with fear of crime, work indirectly through some physical vulnerability indicators and likewise the effects of some physical vulnerability indicators are directly linked to social vulnerability indicators" (p. 140).

As described elsewhere (e.g., see Spencer, 1995, 2006, 2008; Spencer et al., 2015), the conceptual strategy used in this chapter is informed by James Anthony (1974). It promulgates that human vulnerability suggests a tendency toward apprehension and fearfulness and is universally present. It implies the presence of conditions of risk and protection. As such, Anthony refers to highly vulnerable individuals as those who might not be indelibly injured as long as the environment is safe, responsive, and predictable (e.g., one may be highly impoverished, but psychological and physical safety serve as buffers). That said, PVEST capitalizes on Anthony's (1974) perspective and also represents elements of the previously reviewed perspectives referenced (also see Spencer, 2006, 2008; Spencer et al., 2006; Spencer, Dupree, & Hartmann, 1997; Spencer, Swanson, & Harpalani, 2013). As a developmental systems life course theoretical framework, PVEST serves as a heuristic device for understanding and demonstrating the unique and undergirding coping and adaptive processes which matter for an individual's stable identity process. The latter becomes associated with particularly patterned outcomes given the developmental tasks confronted at the various life-course stages. Using PVEST as a template, this chapter explores the role of privilege and the contributions of critical race theory for appreciating differences in human vulnerability.

Acknowledging Vulnerability and Conceding Privilege

The fact that all individuals are vulnerable due to an unavoidable fragile human status, interestingly, is an uncomfortable acknowledgment for many. Perhaps from a privileged-based identity perspective, a vulnerability-conceding psychosocial status fails to allow for a self-characterization as narrowly superior vis-à-vis others. For some, perhaps, vulnerability communicates (or may be inferred as suggesting) *characteristics denoting weakness*. Considered from a particular developmental systems framework (e.g., see Spencer, 1995, 2006, 2008), privilege indicates the significant presence of supports and protective factors which, if acknowledged at all, also suggest having been earned and, thus, reasons for a heightened "sense of self" or superior beliefs concerning the self. Importantly, at the same time, significant levels of protection, accessible assets, and myriad supports may also represent significant sources of risk and challenge (i.e., a "downside" of privilege given inadequate and positive coping opportunities). The dualistic function of *privilege excesses* is infrequently acknowledged or addressed. The "dual impact" of the privilege dilemma and its impact on the practice of democracy in the United States are made clearer when privilege viewpoints are synthesized from critical race perspectives. The differential level of resource accessibility (i.e., one's "knapsack of privileges") is not independent of race, ethnicity, gender, skin color, and other socially constructed and hierarchically organized indicators of status. Moreover, the socialized categories of human variance are observed and learned early from behavioral models as generously applied, informally communicated, and unchallenged messages about difference (i.e., including beliefs and assumptions about deviancy and deficit).

Introducing the Intersectionality of Privilege and Critical Race Theory Perspectives

Critical race theory (CRT) functions as an explanatory conceptual tool and heuristic device for exploring race/ethnicity-based individual-context experiences. It speculates about historical and race-relevant United States Constitution associations that become linked with stable traditions. Its legal linkages represented as policies virtually guarantee a state of high or substantial vulnerability for some which is based totally on minority status and identifiability (i.e., phenotypic-based recognition). At the same time, CRT unpacks the constitutionally supported conditions of privilege and its stable supports.

Social Privilege and Critical Race Perspectives: Reviewing and Describing a Status of Under-Acknowledged Opportunity

Social science has consistently noted that human societies have *always recognized variations in social status* (e.g., see review by Olson, Shutts, Kinzler, & Weisman, 2012). Thus, a global and historical framing of privilege may clarify its character and illuminate its persistency given its resistant and unique manifestation in the United States.

An Introduction and Historical Framing of Social Status and Privilege

Illustrations of privilege include the caste systems of India, New Spain, and Japan as well as the proximal and resistant customs of the USA's Jim Crow traditions. In fact, the current period overlaps with and highlights the very recent 150th anniversary of the Emancipation Proclamation penned by President Abraham Lincoln on January 1, 1863. As affirmed by students of American history, the Proclamation's issuance *was fraught with significant controversy from its earliest discussions between Lincoln and his Cabinet.* In reality, and as actually perceived in contemporary American life, for some American constituencies, it may be viewed as an accomplished feat. However, for others, it stands as an active, unconscious, and unacknowledged focus of resistance, and suggests a dismal social failure. These variously held views have co-existed for more than 150 years and represent the varied and diverse attitudinal stances noted. The fact of attitudinal differences is seldom explored from developmental perspectives. That is, infrequently explored by social science efforts is how the nation's state of dissonance or uncomfortableness concerning color, race and ethnicity is understood by the nation's diverse youth across racial and ethnic communities. Although generally not discussed, there continue to be different opinions regarding the intent of the Emancipation Proclamation and its contemporary impact in the 21st century within and between group relationships.

So, was the goal to free slaves, or to save the union and to communicate a particular message to the world? In fact, as some perspectives suggest, the Proclamation was successful in gaining official recognition from nations including the United Kingdom which had previously favored the Confederacy. Later in the year of the Proclamation's issuance in November 1863, Lincoln's Gettysburg Address indirectly referenced the issuance of the Proclamation by suggesting that the ceasing of slavery afforded the nation a "new birth of freedom." In fact, one hundred years later, then Vice President Lyndon Johnson noted while providing a speech on Memorial Day, 1963, specifically linked Lincoln's issuance with the fully in-swing civil rights resistance efforts. He noted:

> One hundred years ago, the slave was freed. One hundred years later, the Negro remains in bondage to the color of his skin. . . . In this hour, it is not our respective races which are at stake – it is our nation. Let those who care for their country come forward, North and South, white and Negro, to lead the way through this moment of challenge and decision . . . Until justice is blind to color, until education is unaware of race, until opportunity is unconcerned with color of men's skins, emancipation will be a proclamation but not a fact. To the extent that the proclamation of emancipation is not fulfilled in fact, to that extent we shall have fallen short of assuring freedom to the free.
> (Remarks of Vice President Lyndon B. Johnson, Memorial Day speech, May 30, 1963[2])

There may be consequences of unacknowledged and untoward social traditions. Unlike the public hearings held by the South African Truth and Reconciliation Commission following the end of that nation's Apartheid tradition, the United States has lacked formal and public opportunities to share the ways in which biased traditions impact the humanity of its citizens. Most importantly, the absence of the acknowledgment may well have contributed to the continuing salience of color *for the stable experience of opportunity and privilege for this nation's youth as well as the life-course experience of its citizens.* Of course, numerous points of view on privilege exist.

---

2 See Press Release, "5/30/63, Remarks by Vice President, Memorial Day, Gettysburg, Pennsylvania," Statements File, Box 80, LBJ Library.

A Perspective on Social Privilege

Black and Stone (2005) provide a particular lens for framing the concept of privilege and the various ways in which it is granted to some and denied to others. They believe that most academic discussions of privilege have centered upon race and gender, thus their conceptual approach is somewhat unique. Their definitional stance includes multiple categories of privilege frequently marginalized. In fact, their strategy attempts a dichotomous view of privilege which unpacks the various factors that shape and complicate one's identity and thus one's ability to access different forms of privilege. They speculate that a conceptually sophisticated approach for understanding human identity and its many sites of privilege and oppression aids the identification of each individual's unique needs. Broader forms of privilege considered (i.e., framed as social privilege) include race, gender, sexual orientation, socioeconomic status (SES), age, differing degrees of "ableness," and religious affiliation. In fact, each domain suggests differences by which the dominant groups acquired power and historically maintained their privilege while, at the same time, remained largely unaware of its existence. Importantly, Black and Stone suggest that accrued social privilege shapes the mentality of those who do or do not possess it. People with social privilege often deny the fact that they enjoy unearned advantages at the expense of others and maintain that they truly are more intelligent, hardworking, determined, etc. than the groups they dominate. It is probably fair to describe the identity dilemma as feeding into the belief that success is about meritocracy (i.e., that effort expended explains individuals' rise in the social hierarchy).

In fact, Black and Stone (2005) hazard that to avoid the dissonance and confusion that result from being confronted with one's social privilege, individuals must uphold a distorted/inflated view of their own innate value and justify their oppression (either overt and hostile or subtle and indirect) of others. According to this perspective, to become aware of one's social privilege is to accept one's responsibility to surrender unfair advantages and entitlements, recognize one's role in the oppression of others and, ultimately, to fight against the system that reinforces injustice – a feat that proves challenging for some people. Given the noted coast-to-coast recent reactions to black youth murders by white police offers (i.e., Black Lives Matter Movement), the response might suggest an effort to *resolve the dissonance of white participants by acknowledging their privilege of not occupying the position of serving as targets of white police officers.* That is, learning, growing, and navigating life without the burden of being perceived as an *everyday target of policing* matters at multiple levels of human functioning.

More to the point, people who identify partly or entirely with an underprivileged group experience many mental and physical consequences. Membership in multiple oppressed groups means that one experiences various kinds of oppression and, at the same time, persons with conflicting identities (i.e. partly privileged and partly underprivileged, as in the case of a black male, a rich woman, a gay white person, etc.) can feel confused, angry, and cynical about their standing in society. The experiences that come as a result of an underprivileged identity often have a highly negative general valence or effect on the overall well-being of the individual. A long-term assumption has been that members of disadvantaged groups may internalize their oppression and view themselves as inferior to others. However, more often than not, many are able to access *culturally specific* protective factors or internalize identifications which offset any potentially negative effect. Particularly, youth may take on environmentally associated, less adaptive coping responses and behaviors which may serve them in the short term but represent less efficacious coping in other contexts such as school settings (e.g., Spencer, Cunningham, & Swanson, 1995). Of clinical significance, individuals may manifest resistant behaviors required to cope with oppression and to gain some of the advantages lacking by virtue of their identity (see Stevenson, 1997).

Relatedly, and with regard to counselors/counselor educators and their patients, privilege studies have the potential to greatly enhance the effectiveness of the counseling relationship. Counselors and clinical supports are in a unique position that enables them to help their patients understand their experiences of privilege and the way they are negatively affected by it. Black and Stone (2005) affirm that it is the counselor's responsibility to engage in meaningful self-exploration, internal reflection, and processing of their various identities – counselors cannot afford to retain the privilege-blindness evident in some members of dominant groups. They must also examine the ways in which their individual identities influence their relationships with their supervisors (or supervisees) and patients. For example, a counselor who occupies a socially powerful position may be more likely to place exclusive blame on the patient for circumstances that resulted from the patient's underprivileged status. Black and Stone believe that counselors must be trained with an eye to their social identities, and a failure to do so will only strengthen unfair social hierarchies and reduce the effectiveness of counseling. It is critical to acknowledge that the approach taken by Black and Stone, like other privilege-focused efforts, is that the discussion could benefit from greater specificity concerning what it means to have social "privilege," and encourage exploration as to how this phenomenon differs from social "preference." Another possible priority in privilege studies could be to develop valid and reliable tools for measuring levels of privilege in individuals. It is only by educating people about the unearned advantages they possess which then could contribute toward the elimination of claims of ignorance. The unavoidable self-examination process ultimately encourages greater acceptance of responsibility for individual and systems change associated with the unfair accrual of significant benefits. The combination of concerns represents helpful illustrations of the interdependence between cognitive and affective processes.

Moreover, from a critical race perspective, the legal system plays a significant role in the perpetuation of social privilege. One may infer that the absence of biased or unfair treatment in the legal system is the most profound form of privilege. From a critical race perspective, one may infer that *the absence of legal abuses* is *a life impacting privilege*. Different from the protection of civil liberties enjoyed by whites, for black bodies – even children – living in the United States of America may represent a source of everyday risk and a lack of protection. The recent death of Sandra Bland, arrested for failing to indicate when changing lanes, is a case in point.[3] The protection of civil liberties is a privilege of American citizenship not necessarily bestowed on citizens of color. That is, becoming ensnared in the legal system as experienced by stereotyped minority-group members indelibly changes the life course process or potentially ends it. Not having to cope with this dilemma functions as an indelible privilege taken for granted. Importantly, CRT situates the privilege of citizenship within the context of a legal system burdened by problematic assumptions about minority status. Meaning-making processes are foundational for a phenomenological variant of the ecological system perspective. Inferences about the meaning of black bodies "tint" the interpretation of everyday practices. In fact, the recent death of Sandra Bland stemming from a preliminary car incident indicates a lack of attention to civil liberties for particular citizens, which in Bland's case resulted in an untimely death (see Gay, *New York Times*, July 24, 2015).

Critical Race Theory: Basic Tenets, Analytic Applications, Theoretical Renderings of Race

CRT has been described as a movement that is both theoretical and activist-oriented, and it arose from within the discipline of legal studies. CRT departs from many other disciplinary regimes in that it attempts to name the inequities in our current social structure and then re-envision the categories and assumptions that we as a society use to frame our world. The inequities experienced are the opposite of the privileges alluded to in the prior section. It is the absence of an invisible knapsack of privileges and supports which is inferable from the privilege literature (McIntosh, 1989).

As a perspective which unpacks impediments situated primarily in the legal system, the theoretical stance poses a critique that disrupts the blinders that our social systems have created – *blinders that make racism invisible and situate persons of color in their own struggles and confinement.* CRT forces an acknowledgment of the various ways in which discourse and social structure cooperate in the realization of societal inequities and racism. After the process of re-envisioning, theorists argue that change needs to take place as we forge ahead, casting aside the blinders, and attempting to recast society using race-conscious equitable means.

The critical race theoretical framing that follows first provides the historical foundations and basic tenets of the critical race theory movement, followed by several examples intended to demonstrate how CRT has been used to analyze current legal precedent and to suggest alternative conceptualizations. When considered from a phenomenological variant of the ecological system perspective (PVEST, a theoretical perspective with its assumption of shared vulnerability), the CRT stance – mainly addressing the inequality dilemma from a legal system context – demonstrates the sources of very salient risks and subsequent more severe levels of human vulnerability with which black bodies are burdened. Stated differently, from

---

3 See Roxane Gay, *New York Times*, July 24, 2015: www.nytimes.com/2015/07/25/opinion/on-the-death-of-sandra-bland-and-our-vulnerable-bodies.html

a justice system perspective, for people of color, CRT provides clear illustrations of the *risks and challenges associated with a system sworn to serve and protect the civil liberties of its citizens.* The last section of the overview examines theoretical renderings of race that have arisen both within and tangential to the CRT movement.

The approach termed "Critical Race Theory" formally began in the mid-1970s, through the founding work of Derrick Bell and Alan Freeman. The critical race theoretical approach arose primarily as a dialogue with and in response to the civil rights movement. The theorists were critical of the changes brought about by this movement, in particular the lack of steady advancement in racial reform in America and, in fact, the more recent retrogression of progress that had been made since earlier legal gains (Delgado & Stefancic, 2000). Bell (2000) indicates that "statistics on poverty, unemployment and income support the growing concern that the slow racial advances of the 1960s and 1970s have ended, and retrogression is well under way" (Bell, 2000, p. 2).

CRT, as a discipline, is based on the foundations laid by critical legal studies and feminism, and its intellectual ties extend back to American thinkers such as W. E. B. Du Bois and European theorists such as Gramsci and Derrida (see Delgado & Stefancic, 2000; Delgado & Stefancic, 2001). CRT questions the very foundations of legal reasoning. While CRT still predominantly produces new legal discourse, analysis is now applied more broadly in fields such as education, where the tenets of CRT are used to understand tracking, curriculum, and the history of IQ and achievement testing (Delgado & Stefancic, 2001). More recent work also analyzes its contributions for interpreting gap findings (see Tate, 2012).

CRT incorporates two main concepts from the field of critical legal studies. The notion of "legal indeterminacy" acknowledges the subjectivity of legal outcomes and maintains that "not every legal case has one correct outcome" (Delgado & Stefancic, 2001, p. 5). It is the insights concerning inherent intersubjective processes which aid a PVEST explanation of injustices as outcomes (Spencer & Swanson, 2015). Specifically, *the legal outcome depends upon whose interpretation is privileged, which is dictated by the power and authority* of various interpretations. Recent work examines the dilemma for minority men on death row (Stevenson, 2014.

The second concept from critical legal studies is that favorable precedents tend to erode over time due to the ways in which lower courts interpret precedents using narrower definitions and because of the general lack of enforcement of legal doctrine (Delgado & Stefancic, 2001).

CRT also incorporates concepts and terminology from feminism. CRT applies theoretical feminist views on power, the construction of social roles in society, and, in particular, its use of hegemony. The concept of hegemony was developed by Gramsci and is defined as "total social authority" acquired through the combination of *coercion* and *consent* at the economic, political, ideological, intellectual, and moral levels (Hall, 2002). From a PVEST perspective, the concept illustrates why ecology – given its ever-present character occupying multiple levels – is an imperative element to acknowledge. CRT also works within the feminist premise that legal and social theory have practical consequences within society and that these consequences must be addressed (Delgado & Stefancic, 2001; Armour, 2000). As a human development theory situated in a vulnerability framework which emphasizes risk and supports, PVEST is an ideal conceptual vehicle for demonstrating the practical consequences noted.

Delgado and Stefancic (2000, 2001) summarize four underlying tenets of CRT. As a first tenet, CRT maintains that "[R]acism is normal, not aberrant, in American Society" (Delgado & Stefancic, 2000, p. xvi). Racism is an intricate part of the everyday events in America and is woven into all institutions and social interactions. The tenet supports a PVEST assumption concerning the significance of context for making meaning of experience. Relative to an enveloping ecology, according to these theorists, racism is an ingrained aspect of our society to such an extent that racist practices and interactions are deemed "normal," and the roots of these injustices are ignored or frequently not even perceived. Formal equal opportunity rules and laws target extreme, overt injustices *but do not in any way address these micro everyday racisms*. For example, legal doctrine requires the demonstration of *intent* of racist action in order to litigate. However, this intent is often difficult to prove and racism is frequently built into the fabric of American social structures and institutions such that a specific intent is not immediately apparent. Most important from a vulnerability and coping perspective, *legal doctrine has no precedent for addressing these forms of racism*. In fact, privilege is not having to emotionally experience nor cognitively address – as coping responses – the myriad ingrained and multi-level forms of racism, socially constructed bias, and the micro-aggressions experienced in attempting to frame inferences regarding intent. Such significant risks and life-course experienced challenges are why severe or high vulnerability is a necessary perspective. As explained by a PVEST perspective, the view is needed for explaining "gap outcomes" when considering and comparing a severe vulnerability level against the experiences of low vulnerability individuals (i.e., those who enjoy significant privilege associated with protective factors and significant levels of accessible supports).

The second tenet assumes a critique of liberalism. According to Delgado and Stefancic (2000, 2001), liberals uphold the neutrality of the law and view it as objective and morally accurate. However, CRT questions these assumptions and the liberal notion of change in the law through the process of gradualism. CRT draws upon a term created by Derrick Bell – *"interest convergence"* – which describes a phenomenon in which *whites will only support black advances if these advances serve white interests*. Building upon this concept, critical race theorists contend that the civil rights movement and the current legal structure do not foster structural change, and that only through drastic alterations to systems, structures, and ideological foundations can true racial progress and equity ensue.

From a PVEST perspective, a CRT stance substantiates the critical role of risk as embedded everyday challenges that impact both developmental-stage-specific normative tasks and responsive coping processes and associated outcomes. Specifically, CRT posits and makes clear the deep and substantive role of supports required and acquired through racial progress. Critical race theorists maintain that "structural determinism" in society impedes racial reform through a variety of means. First, law

reform is difficult because the words, systems of thought, definitions, and categorizations developed by CRT do not easily become institutionalized within the discipline as general "tools" of the law. Second, reform is hindered by the "empathic
fallacy" which argues that racism can be corrected through response (written and
verbal) directed against racist messages. Of course, for learning contexts such as
schools and police academies, the instructor has to first understand the perspectives
and histories of their constituencies accurately enough to frame the messages in
ways which promote anti-racism interpretations. In other words, acknowledging and
addressing the character of meaning making of the instructors must consider those
for whom the "lesson" is directed (i.e., both as written and verbal messages).

However, CRT maintains that response is not always a valid or practical way of
diminishing racism. Learning environments such as schools and police academies
also represent socialization contexts and, thus, opportunities for the informal internalization of attitudes and values in addition to intended specific content. Moreover,
invasive and predominately placed stereotypes in the media do not lend themselves
to immediate response. Words alone cannot undo the meanings and prejudices that
are rampant in society.

As a third means noted, during the litigation process, commonly the lawyer and
the client are striving for alternative modes of change. Different constituents within
the struggle adhere to alternative definitions of what change should look like and
what implications should accompany such change. Finally and fourth, critical race
theorists characterize the law as a "*homeostatic device*" for race remedies. Freeman
argues that civil rights law enforces racial progress at a slow rate, thus creating
a social control mechanism that insures enough change to prevent civil uprising
while not actually altering the status quo (Delgado & Stefancic, 2001).

Critical race theorists question whether society-altering change can be made
through the legal system or whether new methods need to be envisioned. Under
liberal ideology, an extreme view has developed which maintains that it is wrong to
take any notice of race in the law. However, CRT acknowledges the historical details
and specific contexts of individual lives and contends that only through drastic
"color-conscious" efforts can we change the micro-aggressions of racism. From
a PVEST perspective, coping patterns (e.g., either with adversity or privilege)
become internalized and stable through identity formation processes, and thus,
would be more resistant to change.

The third major tenet of CRT establishes that race is a product of social construction. CRT maintains the premise that social reality is constructed and that, through
writing and speaking, one can critique common assumptions and false narratives,
imagine different forms of social interactions, and then articulate the shape that these
new equitable structures might take. For example, Richard Delgado, in *Rodrigo's
Eighth Chronicle: Black Crime, White Fears – On the Social Construction of Threat*
(1994), demonstrates the following:

> [T]he disproportionate criminalization of African Americans is a product, in large
> part, of the way we define crime. Many lethal acts, such as marketing defective
> automobiles, alcohol, or pharmaceuticals or waging undeclared wars, are not
> considered crimes at all. By the same token, many things that young black and

Latino men are prone to do, such as congregating on street corners, cruising in low-rider cars, or scrawling graffiti in public places, are energetically policed. Crack cocaine offenses receive harsher penalties than those that apply to powder cocaine. Figures show that white-collar crime, including embezzlement, consumer fraud, bribery, insider trading, and price fixing, causes more deaths and property loss, even on a per capita basis, than all street crime combined.
(Delgado & Stefancic, 1994, p. 113–14)

Prevalent definitions and assumptions in society are never innocent of the inequities shaped by power relations.

Related to this third CRT tenet is a fourth, which acknowledges the importance of context. The legal system works based upon the premises of generalizability and essentialized notions of right and wrong. These premises do not provide the legal space for consideration of the ways in which individuals – in unique ways as a function of developmental status – are inequitably influenced and shaped by their specific contextual factors. CRT uses the term "intersectionality" to acknowledge the complex, contradicting, and cumulative ways in which race, gender, class, and sexual orientation affect an individual's positioning within larger social structures. CRT contends that racism exists and continues in our society because the "mindset" of the majority of people in America has not changed, despite the civil rights movement. However, the traditional CRT perspective described, which considers the categories and intersectionality of race, gender, class, and sexual orientation, does not include the psychological additions and exacerbating intersectionality contributed by the human domains of cognition, affective, and biological processes; individuals unavoidably engage in cognition-based meaning processes which are affectively responded to and have physiological consequences that further exacerbate risk and, in fact, potentially compromise one's survival. Stemming from James' long-term scholarship, Sherman James et al.'s (1992) description of "John Henryism" provides the case in point. Thus, from a PVEST reframing of a traditional intersectionality perspective, a more inclusive approach includes linked external (i.e., traditional race, gender, class, and sexual orientation) contributors as well as impactful internal (i.e., cognitive, affective, and biological) processes contributing to more enhanced intersectionality. As illustrated by an op-ed by James Hamblin (2015) in describing the paradox of effort, and reporting on the seminal work of Sherman James, both levels of intersectionality (i.e., external and internal), considered jointly, may contribute important and dire consequences for not only the character of life but, moreover, an individual's very survival. With the external serving as context contributions, PVEST provides the vehicle for interpreting the "how" and "why" of particularly constructed outcomes.

Additionally, the presuppositions of dominant ideology and the resultant legal precedents are not frequently examined or contested. Based on these premises, CRT often takes the form of storytelling and counter-narratives (stories that emphasize alternative interpretations to "common sense" narrative, exposing the hidden/ignored underlying racist ideology) (Delgado & Stefancic, 2000, 2001). Delgado (2000), in *Storytelling for Oppositionists and Others*, maintains that through narratives and counter-narratives, the "out-group" builds consensus that subverts the myths of mainstream constructions and recreates alternative ways of understanding social realities. CRT argues that any event or occurrence can be interpreted in multiple ways. Through narratives, critical race theorists expose how our current mainstream assumed understanding is simply one way of making sense of our reality. Narratives demonstrate how the specific details of individual lives when brought to bear can both question and recreate our social understandings. The advantages of framing the latter from a PVEST perspective is that it provides strategies for discerning the constructs important for empirical testing as well as illuminative narrative. Unfortunately, and significantly, particularly for disciplines such as psychology, the narratives are too frequently ignored as fact and science, thus further delaying demonstrations of the dual level intersectionality, which then further slows potential impacts on problematic policies and practices.

Under the umbrella of CRT are other subsidiary studies, including critical White, Asian, and Latino studies, feminist studies, and queer critical studies. Asian studies look critically at the model minority stereotype, while feminist and queer studies look at "intersectionality." Critical white studies examine the ways in which whiteness is socially constructed and how groups have historically moved in and out of this category. For example, certain ethnic populations in America such as Jews, Italians, and Irish have moved into the category of white, after being labeled as non-white during their early history in the United States. Critical white studies also explore the ways in which privileges associated with the "white" label structure power relations and how discourse through literature and cultural forms powerfully reinforces stereotypes and the values associated with whiteness in contrast to color (Delgado & Stefancic, 2001).

Roediger (2002) looks at the social construction of whiteness and maintains that historically this category has been ignored. Additionally, Roediger cites Fusco, who contends that to ignore this category tends to "redouble its hegemony by naturalizing it" (quoted in Roediger, 2002, p. 327). Whiteness becomes further ingrained as the normative standard. Roediger explores the historical process by which immigrants earned their status as white. The process of Americanizing European immigrants ("white ethnics") allowed them to be accepted as white rather than Irish or Polish. There are specific examples of how the underlying premises of CRT are instituted to critique the justice system, the educational system, and policy affecting the broader society. However, from an "enhanced intersectionality" view consistent with a PVEST formulation, cognition-based identifiability and affective as well as physiological reactions to same-, whiteness-, or European-based ethnicities are absent the negative stereotypy of "dark skin tone." Data consistently demonstrate that children as young as 2.5 years have learned the negative attitudes and preferences associated with a dark skin tone, and studies have demonstrated the role of social cognition processes in the acquisition process (e.g., see reviews by Spencer, 1970, 1976, 1985, 1995; Spencer & Horowitz, 1973). Clearly, the latter demonstrates an "enhanced intersectionality" interpretation framed from a human-growth and development-sensitive perspective such as the one provided from PVEST.

In continuing the "whiteness" perspective, Armour (2000) states that "it has been well-documented that defendants in self-defense cases exploit racial prejudices of jurors in asserting the reasonableness of their fear of supposed assailants who are black" (p. 181). Essentially, in these cases, the jury must determine whether the defendant's self-defense claim is "reasonable." Armour (2000) maintains that claims of reasonable self-defense generally fall within three categories, which she terms "the reasonable racist," "intelligent bayesian," and "involuntary negrophobe." In his recent book, "Just Mercy," Bryan Stevenson provides numerous examples and narrative illustrations of the same for men of color on death row (Stevenson, 2014).

The reasonable racist acknowledges that he/she displays racial prejudices, believing that blacks are "prone to violence." However, he/she claims that since these prejudices are "typical" in American society, one's fears and actions are legally justifiable. A 1990 University of Chicago study found that more than 56% of Americans articulated their belief that blacks tend to be "violent prone." Also, news studies indicate that blacks are increasingly excluded from shops and taxicabs, based on the owners' explicitly stated "race-based assessments of danger." Hence, if the racial stereotype of black violence is typical, Armour asks the essential question as to whether the law defines typical beliefs as reasonable. The argument of the defendant in these cases is that typical beliefs are reasonable for the following two reasons: First, the beliefs are considered accurate: fear of black violence is supported by the statistics; second, wrong judgments are reasonable if most people would have made the same judgment under the same circumstances. Armour (2000) counters this argument, stating that "if we accept that racial discrimination violates contemporary social morality, then an actor's failure to overcome his racism for the sake of another's health, safety and personal dignity is blameworthy and thus unreasonable, independent of whether or not it is typical" (p. 185).

The intelligent bayesian rests his/her claim on generally recognized statistics, which indicate that blacks are disproportionately involved in crime and, hence, his/her assumption of crime is reasonable and logical. Armour (2000) counters that the use of race as a criterion of danger is not statistically justifiable for the following reasons. Foremost, for example, Blacks arrested for violent crimes in 1991 represented less than 1% of the entire black population in the United States at that time. Second, biases in the criminal justice system undermine the accuracy of statistics. Third, a Harvard Law Review survey (1988) found that racial discrimination by police officers in making arrests is significant to such an extent that the apparent divergence in crime between blacks and whites is skewed. Fourth, even after eliminating biases due to racial discrimination, if blacks are relatively more prone to violence, this behavior is not surprising considering the history of racial oppression that has existed in this country for hundreds of years.

Legal decisions based on stereotypical generalizations may "subvert the criminal justice system's promise that each individual defendant will be tried according to the specific facts of his case" (Armour, 2000, p. 187). These decisions will only further enhance and engrain racial stereotypes in our society, but will also create an atmosphere where blacks will avoid public places, not wanting to be mistaken for an assailant. Thus, legally justified use of racial stereotypes only serves to limit the ability of people of color to be active agents in their own lives, thereby not only restraining the spatial configuration of their engagement, but also limiting the range of their emotional engagement by instituting self-surveillance.

The involuntary negrophobe justifies his/her self-defense claim based upon past experience of violence by a black individual. The involuntary negrophobe claims that his/her present fear is justifiable because of the psychological trauma lingering from the past experience. The negrophobia claim can be treated like an insanity claim. Armour (2000) maintains that this is problematic because the extent to which the legal system accepts that either reasonable or pathological racists may act without fear of serious consequences ultimately limits the extent to which black individuals can participate in society. Armour claims that "instrumentalism" must be applied to look at the broader social implications of legal precedents in these cases. This practice calls attention to and articulates the social welfare implications of various legal precedents, maintaining the importance of recognizing these larger factors.

Lee & Zhou (2004) make similar claims to Armour, and contend that stereotypes factor into legal decisions for other Americans of color such as Asian Americans and Latino Americans. These stereotypes are implicated in cases in which self-defense is claimed. However, Lee also calls attention to the ways in which a focus on the black–white paradigm in the justice system ignores the racism that other minorities of color experience.

Butler (1995) employs CRT in his development of the concept of "jury nullification . . . [which] occurs when a jury acquits a defendant who it believes is guilty of the crime charged" (p. 195). Butler contends that it is the moral responsibility of black jurors to emancipate certain nonviolent guilty blacks, due to the fact that the system itself is biased. Black communities should not lose their members to a jail system in a society that has promoted black anti-social activities through institutional racism. The black prisoner is simply implicated in a system that has been set up by the status quo – individuals who do not have blacks' best interests in mind. The law uses punishment of individuals to deal with social problems that are the result of ingrained racism in society. Butler continues to argue that no general legal principle leads to justice in every case – legal principles are also based on socially constructed assumptions and sometimes these assumptions lead to inequitable racist outcomes. Hence, it is the moral responsibility of jurors to acquit guilty individuals based on the existence of unjust laws. The greater good of the black community should be considered in nonviolent cases. One may characterize these strategies as coping processes engaged at levels suggesting "enhanced intersectionality." That is, from a PVEST perspective, it is not just the intersecting issues of sex, race, and sexual orientation which determine the context; moreover, it is the ways in which they intersect with development-status-specific cognitive-, affective-, and physiologic-based stress-level processes given unavoidable biological contributors which unavoidably intersect with the context (see Hamblin, 2015 on Sherman James and "John Henryism").

CRT has also been useful to analyze the implications of various educational legal reforms, including integration and affirmative action (which affects a broad range of institutions, including the educational system). Derrick Bell (2000), in *Serving Two*

Masters, looks at the outcomes of integration mandates and asks a key question: Is racial balance in schools enough to provide educational equity? Bell contends that, since the 1930s, the approach of the National Association for the Advancement of Colored People (NAACP) has been to eliminate racial segregation across society. This approach took precedence in the education system, particularly with the passing of *Brown* in 1954. The subsequent lack of compliance with the legal precedent set by *Brown* led to a series of school litigation cases being filed. Bell explores the diverse expectations of the prosecuting lawyers and the clients they served. He establishes the ways in which their views on educational equity and approaches to change diverged.

The theory behind the integration approach is that "equal educational opportunity" can only be achieved *when black students have access to the resources of white schools and that only through integration can black students receive the same education*. However, Bell claims that this theory does not consider the effects of continued racism in society. *Brown* and the NAACP do not sufficiently address "state-supported subordination of blacks in every aspect of the educational process" (Bell, 2000, p. 240). Racial separation is only the most obvious expression of racism in the educational system. Even after integration, black children frequently have lower academic performance and a higher expulsion rate. Additionally, integration has been achieved only in smaller districts. Large urban areas have not been touched by the policy as these areas are frequently so drastically segregated that entire districts are racially separate entities. Bell (2000) maintains that alternatives to integration need to be imagined and implemented. He further asserts that enforcement is needed which pairs educational content and process with the constitutional rights given by *Brown*. Again, from a PVEST perspective which foments an "enhanced intersectionality stance," illuminating processes significant for training would include those at the internal level (i.e., cognitive, affective, and biological processes), which have implications for human meaning making, patterned coping processes, and physiologic reactions to same.

Johnson (2000) cites *Fordice* (1992) which found discrimination in Mississippi's post-secondary educational system, but rejected African American plaintiffs' requests to obtain equal funding for Mississippi's publicly funded historically black colleges. Rather, under *Fordice,* these colleges are merged into Mississippi's white college system under integration. Johnson argues that abolishing separate historically black colleges should not be considered advancement and that black students should have a choice about what type of college to attend. He maintains that many black students prefer all black colleges as immersion often presents a hostile environment to black students. An enhanced intersectionality explanation would suggest that merging contexts without addressing the climate character would serve as a diminution of perceived supports while increasing psychological risks, thereby, increasing severe vulnerability. In sum, it would serve to interfere with positive coping and productive outcomes, in fact, the opposite of the objective intent. The pattern to ignore the human development and unavoidable life-course meaning-making processes and preferences of individuals (i.e., both "white privilege denials" and black stereotyping) add to what has been framed as the American dilemma.

W. E. B. Du Bois named the educational dilemma for our society in 1935 and his concerns remain prevalent today. As indicated and referenced by Bell's analysis, integration has not proved to be the silver bullet for educational equity in our society. Reported as the seminal prediction by Du Bois, more comprehensive societal changes are needed before educational equity can be a reality. His analysis follows:

> [T]he Negro needs neither segregated schools nor mixed schools. What he needs is Education. What he must remember is that there is no magic, either in mixed schools or segregated schools. A mixed school with poor and unsympathetic teachers, with hostile public opinion, and no teaching of truth concerning black folk, is bad. A segregated school with ignorant placeholders, inadequate equipment, poor salaries, and wretched housing is equally bad. Other things being equal, the mixed school is the broader, more natural basis for the education of all youth. It gives wider contacts; it inspires greater self-confidence; and suppresses the inferiority complex. But other things seldom are equal, and in that case, Sympathy, Knowledge, and the Truth, outweigh all that the mixed school can offer.
> (quoted in Bell, 2000, p. 243)

In fact, Marable (2002) draws upon Du Bois' general argument as he articulates the two camps in the controversy of how to actualize racial equality. Marable maintains that in alignment with Du Bois, one camp argues that black culture and institutions in society should be maintained and that equality does not come from assimilation. Following Du Bois' concept of double consciousness, black Americans live with a double sense of how to function in American society and equity does not ensue from the erasure of Black knowledge. The other camp including civil rights activists tends to perceive equality as inclusion, which stems from a society that is "color blind". A critique in alignment with Du Bois would maintain that we have not reached the point in American society where a color blind culture is possible, despite the end of legal segregation. Racism is real and evident through structural inequities and white privilege. Consistent with an intersectionality perspective, Boykin (1983) would claim that the situation is made worse by gender given the patterned experiences of African American males. However, as referenced, the recent events including the death of Sandra Bland for failing to use lane changing signals would indicate otherwise.[4]

Marable (2002), as a critical race theorist, criticizes affirmative action as too conservative as he maintains that affirmative action "sought to increase representative numbers of minorities and women within the existing structure and arrangements of power, rather than challenging or redefining the institutions of authority and privilege ... affirmative action was always more concerned with advancing remedial remedies for unequal racial outcomes than with uprooting racism as a system of white power" (p. 351). Affirmative action quotas have resulted in the growth of the black middle class but have not restructured the ways in which systems continue to define and perpetuate racism. Delgado (2000), in *Affirmative Action as a Majoritarian Device*, is sympathetic to Marable's argument as he asserts multiple reasons why many scholars of color are critical of affirmative action. He maintains that inclusion of people in society through affirmative action is based on social utility

---

4 See Gay, cited in footnote 2.

and the discourse does not consider reparations or rights. Affirmative action is a stabilizing device and a system of social control and balance in American society. Delgado criticizes the ways in which the stamp of affirmative action is stigmatizing and ahistorical. It ignores the ways in which white men have benefited from their own affirmative action programs for hundreds of years since the inception of this country. Under affirmative action, black individuals are expected to be assimilationist, to serve as role models to uplift an entire people – examples to justify the myth that those who work hard will succeed. Additionally, Delgado maintains that fairness requires reallocation and this is not the way in which affirmative action is framed. He maintains that "by labeling problematic, troublesome, ethnically agonizing a paltry system that helps a few of us get ahead, critics neatly take our eyes off the system of arrangements that brought and maintained them in power, and enabled them to develop the rules and standards of quality and merit that now exclude us, make us appear unworthy, dependent (naturally) on affirmative action" (Delgado, 2000, *Affirmative Action as a Majoritarian Device*, p. 398).

As suggested, social privilege insights and CRT contribute recursively to developmental systems theorizing in particularly nuanced ways having to do with intersubjectivity and the critical role of developmentally linked perceptions.

Discussion and Conclusion of Privilege and CRT Recursive Influences for Vulnerability and Resiliency Theorizing

As described, PVEST as a human development framework provides specificity regarding the critical role of an individual's cognition dependent perceptions and the affect relevant meanings made of the inferences surmised. Physiologic processes are also involved due to unavoidable stress reactivity and cognition and maturation linked meanings made of experience. The outcomes have important implications for a subsequent level of human vulnerability as lives unfold across the life course. As suggested, there are also physiologic responses to the combination of domains of influence, which, collectively determine level of vulnerability as associated with context character (Spencer, 1995, 2008). As a vulnerability and resiliency acknowledging perspective, the framework focuses on identity formation while considering structural factors, cultural influences, and individual perceptions of one's self, significant others, life experiences, and the environments in which one lives and copes while navigating across myriad social and physical contexts. Privilege perspectives specify the contributions of having degrees of significant opportunity and CRT elucidates structural conditions and particularly those closely linked to the potentially life changing justice system.

Independent of whether one is considering social privilege insights or CRT conceptual contributions, what each perspective highlights is *the role of perception and implications for identity, beliefs of efficacy, and the challenge of stereotypes as associated with contextual conditions*.

PVEST emphasizes its identity-focused cultural ecological (ICE) attributes. Identity formation takes place across the life course and is especially relevant for adolescents given their heightened self-consciousness during a particularly challenging period of development. PVEST combines its emphasis on individual perceptions and unavoidable meaning-making with Bronfenbrenner's (1979) ecological systems theory, thus linking context and perception. While Bronfenbrenner's model provides a conceptual lens and means for describing the ways by which multiple levels of context can influence individual development, PVEST also directly illustrates life-course human development processes *within* context (i.e., given overlapping domains of human functioning). In doing so, as suggested, it emphasizes the individual's perceptions, which underlie *identity development* and behavioral outcomes, and which then influence subsequent levels of vulnerability as individuals traverse the life course (Spencer, 1995, 1999, 2007; Spencer et al, 1997). The characteristics of these processes and outcomes are associated with the developmental tasks and maturational themes associated with particular developmental periods. For example, given the identity emphasis of Erikson's theory, an infant's development of trust as linked to life-course identity issues is not independent of but is associated with the nature of identity achievement themes also of critical importance to the adolescent. An infant's and early-childhood youngster's capabilities are framed by the nature of experiences had by the adults who represent their context of development. Thus, the injustices of the legal system as described by Stevenson (2014) and CRT theorists have implications for parenting efforts and socialization processes given the problem of stereotyping and the disproportionate incarceration of minority adults. At the same time, privilege and disproportionate supports suggest different legal experiences for individuals privileged by less exposure to self-directed negative stereotyping. The implications for parenting and family life as sources of support are obvious and significant.

The public discussion of child-rearing tasks required of black parents in framing socialization messages needed particularly by black male youth to prevent their murder by police officers has only recently enjoyed "voice" as an aspect of the "Black Lives Matter" social movement. Social privileges enjoyed by white parents dispel the need for such protective strategies, thus diminishing the complexities and stressors associated with the parenting of white youth. Accordingly, as an under-acknowledged privilege, identity formation challenges do not hold sway in the same manner for white parents attempting to instill strategies for producing physically and psychologically healthy and competent youth. That fact represents an important illustration of McIntosh's (1989) view concerning white Americans' unacknowledged knapsack of privilege. We noted this pattern as one of "enhanced intersectionality." That is, on the one hand, and as described by CRT theory, the role of race, sex, and sexual orientation factors matter as part of the context.

Importantly, and to sum, PVEST reinforces the salience of the intersectional influences of the individual's cognitive, affective, and biologic processes as well as those linked to context. In reviewing the unique contributions of privilege and CRT literatures to PVEST, the synthesis of perspectives has the potential to enlighten several critical systems which contribute to and function as the context of life course development. Specifically, the "tri-component" synthesis of framing suggested better informs the justice, educational, and health systems and, thus, afford the creation of better policies and practices which potentially result in highly salient outcomes. Such results representing relationship-based practices and, thus, contextual conditions, have critical implications for life-course meaning-making processes unavoidably experienced from childhood through to adulthood.

References

Anthony, E. J. (1974). The syndrome of the psychologically invulnerable child. In: E. J. Anthony, & C. Koupernik, (Eds.) *The child in his family: Children at psychiatric risk.* International Yearbook *Vol. 3* (pp. 201–230). New York, NY: Wiley.

Armour, J. D. (2000). Race ipsa loquitur: Of reasonable racists, intelligent Bayesians and involuntary negrophobes. *Stanford Law Review 46,* 781–816.

Bell, D. (2000). After We're Gone: Prudent Speculations on America. In R. Delgado & J. Stefancic (Eds), *Critical Race: The Cutting Edge,* (2–8). Philadelphia: Temple University Press.

Black, L. L., & Stone, D. (2005). Expanding the definition of privilege: The concept of social privilege. *Journal of Multicultural Counseling and Development, Vol. 33*(4), 243–255.

Boykin, A. W. (1983). The academic performance of Afro-American children. In J. Spence (Ed.), *Achievement and achievement motives* (pp. 321–371). San Francisco: W. Freeman.

Bronfenbrenner, U. (1979). *The Ecology of Human Development: Experiments by Nature and Design.* Cambridge, MA: Harvard University Press.

Butler, P. (1995). Racially Based Jury Nullification: Black Power in the Criminal Justice System, *Yale Law Journal, 105,* 677.

Cardona, Omar D. (2013). The need for rethinking the concepts of vulnerability and risk from a holistic perspective: A necessary review and criticism for effective risk management. In G. Bankoff & G. Frerks (2013). *Mapping vulnerability: disasters, development and people* (pp. 37–51). London: Routledge.

Carlson, J. (2014). The equalizer? Crime, vulnerability, and gender in pro-gun discourse. *Feminist Criminology, 9*(1), 59–83. doi: 10.1177/1557085113502518

Carmalt, J. (2014). Prioritizing health: A human rights analysis of disaster, vulnerability, and urbanization in New Orleans and Port-au-Prince. *Health & Human Rights: An International Journal, 16*(1), 41–53.

Coates, T.-N. (2015). *Between the world and me.* New York, NY: Random House Publishing Group.

Cross, W. E. (1991). *Shades of black: Diversity in African American identity.* Philadelphia, PA: Temple University Press.

Delgado, R. (1994). Rodrigo's eighth chronicle: black crime, white fears. On the social construction of threat. *Virginia Law Review, 80,* 503–548.

Delgado, R., & Stefancic, J. (1994). Critical race theory: An annotated bibliography – 1993, A year of transition. *University of Colorado Law Review, 66,* 159–193.

Delgado, R., & Stefancic, J. (2000). *Critical race theory: The cutting edge.* Philadelphia: Temple University Press.

Delgado, R. & Stefancic, J. (2001). *Critical race theory: An introduction.* New York, NY: New York University Press.

Fegley, S. G., Spencer, M. B., Goss, T. N., Harpalani, V., & Charles, N. (2008). Colorism embodied: Skin tone and psychosocial well-being in adolescence. In W. Overton,

U. Mueller, & J. Newman (Eds.), *Developmental perspectives on embodiment and consciousness* (pp. 281–311). Mahwah, NJ: LEA Inc.

Fineman, M. A. (2008). *The vulnerable subject: Anchoring equality in the human condition* (SSRN Scholarly Paper No. ID 1131407). Rochester, NY: Social Science Research Network. Retrieved from http://papers.ssrn.com/abstract=1131407

Gay, R. (2015, July 24). On the death of Sandra Bland and our vulnerable bodies. *The New York Times*. Retrieved from www.nytimes.com/2015/07/25/opinion/on-the-death-of-sandra-bland-and-our-vulnerable-bodies.html

Gilson, E. (2011). Vulnerability, ignorance, and oppression. *Hypatia. 26*, 308–332.

Goldstein, J. & Schweber, N. (2014, July 18). Man's death after chokehold raises old issue for the police. *New York Times*. Retrieved from www.nytimes.com/2014/07/19/nyregion/staten-island-man-dies-after-he-is-put-in-chokehold-during-arrest.html?_r=0

Hall, S. (2002). Race, articulation, and societies structured in dominance. In P. Essed & D. T. Goldberg (Eds.), *Race critical theories: Text and context*. Malden, MA: Blackwell Publishers Inc.

Hamblin, J. (2015, July 16). The paradox of effort. *The Atlantic*, July 16, 2015, Retrieved from http://www.theatlantic.com/health/archive/2015/07/the-health-cost-of-upward-mobility/398486/

Harpalani, V. (2012). Diversity within racial groups and the constitutionality of race-conscious admissions. *University of Pennsylvania Journal of Constitutional Law, 15*, 463.

Harris, C. I. (1993). Whiteness as property. *Harvard Law Review. 106*(8), 1707–1791

Harvard Law Review (1988). Developments in the law – Race and the criminal process. *Harvard Law Review 101*(7), 1472–1641.

Hurst, S. A. (2008). Vulnerability in research and health care; describing the elephant in the room? *Bioethics, 22*(4), 191–202. doi: 10.1111/j.1467-8519.2008.00631.x

James, S. A., Keenan, N. L., Strogatz, D. S., Browning, S. R., & Garrett, J. M. (1992). Socioeconomic status, John Henryism, and blood pressure in Black adults: The Pitt County Study. *American Journal of Epidemiology, 135*, 59–67.

Johnson Jr., A. M. (2000). Bid whist, tonk, and United States v. Fordice: Why integrationism fails African Americans again. In R. Delgado & J. Stefancic (Eds.), *Critical race theory: The cutting edge* (pp. 404–415). Philadelphia, PA: Temple University Press.

Killias, M. (1990). Vulnerability: Towards a better understanding of a key variable in the genesis of fear of crime. *Violence and Victims, 5*(2), 97–108.

Kohlberg, L. (1970). Stages of moral development as a basis for moral education. In C. Beck & E. Sullivan (Eds.), *Moral education*. Toronto: University of Toronto Press.

Kristof, Nicholas. (2014, August 30). After Ferguson race deserves more attention not less. *New York Times*. Retrieved from www.nytimes.com/2014/08/31/opinion/sunday/nicholas-kristof-after-ferguson-race-deserves-more-attention-not-less.html?mtrref=undefined&gwh=45284BDCA3DDCAC73500FDDE7BAF8FDA&gwt=pay&assetType=opinion

Lee, J., & Zhou, M. (2004). *Asian American youth: Culture, identity, and ethnicity*. New York, NY: Routledge.

Marable, M. (2002). Affirmative action and the politics of race. In P. Essed & D. T. Goldberg (Eds.), *Race critical theories: Text and context*. Malden, MA: Blackwell Publishers Inc.

McIntosh, P. (1989, July-August). White Privilege: Unpacking the Invisible Knapsack, *Peace and Freedom Magazine*, 10–12.

McIntosh, P. (2009). White privilege and male privilege: A personal account of coming to see correspondences through work in women's studies. In K. Weekes (Ed. and preface) & P. McIntosh (foreword) (Eds.), *Privilege and prejudice: Twenty years with the invisible knapsack* (Vols. *1*–xvi, 1–182, pp. 7–18). Newcastle upon Tyne, England: Cambridge Scholars.

Olson, K. R., Shutts, K., Kinzler, K. D., & Weisman, K. G. (2012). Children associate racial groups with wealth: Evidence from South Africa. *Child Development*, *83*(6), 1884–1899. doi: 10.1111/j.1467-8624.2012.01819.x

Piaget, J. (1932). *The moral judgment of the child*. London: Routledge and Kegan Paul.

Rader, N. E., Cossman, J. S., & Porter, J. R. (2012). Fear of crime and vulnerability: Using a national sample of Americans to examine two competing paradigms. *Journal of Criminal Justice*, *40*(2), 134–141. doi: 10.1016/j.jcrimjus.2012.02.003

Roediger, D. R. (1999). *The wages of Whiteness: Race and the making of the American working class*. New York, NY: Verso.

Roediger, D. (2002). *Colored white: Transcending the racial past*. Berkeley: University of California Press.

Skogan, W. G. and Maxfield, M. G. (1981). *Coping with crime: Individual and neighborhood reactions*. Beverly Hills, CA: Sage Publications.

Spencer, M. B. (1970). The effects of systematic social (puppet) and token reinforcement on the modification of racial and color concept-attitudes in preschool aged children. Unpublished master's thesis, University of Kansas, Lawrence, Kansas.

Spencer, M. B., (1976). *The social-cognitive and personality development of the black preschool child: An exploratory study of developmental process*. Chicago, IL: The University of Chicago Press.

Spencer, M. B. (1985). Racial variations in achievement prediction: The school as a conduit for macrostructural cultural tension. In H. McAdoo, & J. McAdoo (Eds.), *Black children: Social, educational, and parental environments* (pp. 85–111). Beverly Hills: Sage.

Spencer, M. B. (1995). Old issues and new theorizing about African American youth: A phenomenological variant of ecological systems theory. In R. L. Taylor (Ed.), *African-American youth: Their social and economic status in the United States* (pp. 37–69). Westport, CT: Praeger.

Spencer, M. B. (1999). Transitions and continuities in cultural values: Kenneth Clark revisited. In R. L. Jones (Ed.), *African American children, youth and parenting* (pp. 183–208). Hampton, VA: Cobb and Henry.

Spencer, M. B. (2006). Phenomenology and ecological systems theory: Development of diverse groups. In R. M. Lerner & W. Damon (Eds.), *Handbook of child psychology, Vol. 1: Theoretical models of human development*, 6th edn. (pp. 829–893). New York, NY: Wiley Publishers.

Spencer, M. B. (2008). Lessons learned and opportunities ignored since Brown v. Board of Education: Youth development and the myth of a color-blind society (Fourth annual Brown lecture in education research). *Educational Researcher*, *37*(5), 253–266.

Spencer, M. B. (2011) American identity: Impact of youths' differential experiences in society on their attachment to American ideals. *Applied Developmental Science*, *15*(2), 61–69.

Spencer, M. B. (2013). Pursuing identity focused resiliency research post *Brown v. Board of Education 1954*. In J. Brooks-Gunn, R. M. Lerner, A. C. Petersen, & R. K. Silbereisen (Eds.), *The developmental science of adolescence: History through autobiography* (pp. 482–493). New York, NY: Psychology Press.

Spencer, M. B., Cunningham, M., & Swanson, D. P. (1995). Identity as coping: Adolescent African-American males' adaptive responses to high-risk environments. In H. W. Harris, H. C. Blue, & E. H. Griffith (Eds.), *Racial and ethnic identity* (pp. 31–52). New York, NY: Routledge.

Spencer, M. B., Dupree, D., & Hartmann, T. (1997). A phenomenological variant of ecological systems theory (PVEST): A self-organization perspective in context. *Development and Psychopathology, 9*, 817–833.

Spencer, M. B., & Harpalani, V. (2008). What does "acting White" actually mean?: Racial identity, adolescent development, and academic achievement among African American youth. In J. U. Ogbu (Ed.), *Minority status, oppositional culture, & schooling* (pp. 223–239). Mahwah, NJ: Lawrence Erlbaum Associates, Inc.

Spencer, M. B., Harpalani, V., Cassidy, E., Jacobs, C., Donde, S., Goss, T. N., Muñoz-Miller, M. M., Charles, N., & Wilson, S. (2006). Understanding vulnerability and resilience from a normative development perspective: Implications for racially and ethnically diverse youth. In D. Cicchetti & D. J. Cohen (Eds.) *Handbook of developmental psychology, Vol. 1: Theory and method*, 2nd edn. (pp. 627–672). Hoboken, NJ: Wiley Publishers.

Spencer, M. B., & Horowitz, F. D. (1973). Effects of systematic social and token reinforcement on the modification of racial and color concept attitudes in Black and in White pre-school children. *Developmental Psychology, 9*(2), 246.

Spencer, M., & Spencer, T. (2014). Invited commentary: Exploring the promises, intricacies, and challenges to positive youth development. *Journal of Youth & Adolescence, 43* (6), 1027–1035. doi: 10.1007/s10964-014-0125-8

Spencer, M., & Swanson, D. (2013). Opportunities and challenges to the development of healthy children and youth living in diverse communities. *Development & Psychopathology, 25*(4pt2), 1551–1566.

Spencer, M. B., & Swanson, D. P. (2015). Vulnerability and resilience: Illustrations from theory and research on African American youth. In D. Cicchetti (Ed.), *Handbook of developmental psychology, Vol. 4* (pp. 334–380). New York, NY: John Wiley & Sons.

Spencer, M. B., Swanson, D. P., & Harpalani, V. (2015). Conceptualizing the self: Contributions of normative human processes, diverse contexts and social opportunity. In Lamb, M., Coll, C. G., & R. Lerner (Eds.), *Handbook of child psychology and developmental science* (pp. 750–793). New York, NY: John Wiley & Sons.

Stevenson, B. (2014). *Just Mercy: A story of justice and redemption*. New York, NY: Spiegel and Grau.

Stevenson, H. C., Jr. (1997). "Missed, dissed, and pissed": Making meaning of neighborhood, risk, fear and anger management in urban Black youth. *Cultural Diversity and Mental Health, 3*(1), 37–52.

Tate, W. F. (Ed.) (2012). *Research on schools, neighborhoods, and communities: Toward civic responsibility*. Lanham, MD: Rowman and Littlefield.

United States v. Fordice 112 S.Ct. 2727 (1992) United States Supreme Court, 1 Race & Ethnic Anc. L. Dig. 39 (1995). Available at: http://scholarlycommons.law.wlu.edu/crsj/vol1/iss1/10

Zinn, Howard. (2005). *People's history of the United States*. New York, NY: Harper Collins.

16 Social Intelligence in a Multicultural World: What Is It? Who Needs It? How Does It Develop?

Richard A. Shweder

A Little Song on a Big Subject: Tolerance[1]

"George Washington liked good roast beef. Haym Solomon liked fish. When Uncle Sam served liberty they both enjoyed the dish." When I was a child growing up in New York City in the early days of television that jingle was part of a public service advertisement linking American patriotism to tolerance for differences in the beliefs and customary practices of ethnic and religious minority groups in the United States.[2]

George Washington, of course, is the iconic father of our country. In that jingle his food preference speaks for the habits of the dominant ethnic group: a White, Anglo-Saxon, Protestant population with a taste for bloody red meat. Nevertheless, following along with the lyrics of the song, the United States is represented as a complex multicultural society where its citizens (Haym Solomon, for example) have permission to be different from one another in their enjoyment of food and views about what is good to eat. Haym Solomon liked fish, not roast beef, and no one interfered with his pursuit of his preferences.

Haym Solomon, in case you did not know, was a personal friend of George Washington, a banker and a patriot who helped finance the American Revolution. My own knowledge of his biography and actual food preferences is quite limited. But, as you may have guessed, he was a Jew. His name and character appear in the verse as a symbol of the liberty of ethnic and religious minority groups to carry forward their way of life in the United States. The two revolutionary-era friends, one Protestant and one Jewish (yet both good Americans), were creatively appropriated as icons of an imagined national disposition to make space for the free exercise of

---

1 Sections of the essay concerning Montaigne and moral realism recapitulate or expand upon formulations in my essay "Relativism and Universalism" in *A Companion to Moral Anthropology*, Didier Fasson (Ed.), Wiley Blackwell, 2014, pp. 85–102 and in other essays of mine about the moral domain.

2 Recounting my memory of the song on another occasion (I have written about and narrated this memory before) it was suggested to me by someone who shared that memory that Levy's Rye Bread may have been the sponsor of the public service advertisement. This remains to be verified.

culture and religion, which is an outlook the public service advertisement encourages us to share. "Celebrate diversity" is its take-home message.

Recently I discovered that the George Washington/Haym Solomon verse comes from a book called "Little Songs on Big Subjects" which is full of morally loaded pluralistic and humanistic ditties about social understanding, the gist of which can be summarized by these lines: "Nature has no fav'rite nation, Color, creed, or occupation – Any place [on the globe] you point your finger to, There's someone with the same type blood as you!"

I have occasionally wondered if that rhyme about George Washington and Haym Solomon is one of the early influences on my much later decision to become a cultural anthropologist. Recently I have begun wondering whether the song's "everyone-is-the same-wherever-you-go" humanistic perspective is really reconcilable with its "different-but-equal" pluralistic message; after all, wherever you point your finger to on the globe, including fingering members of your own in-group, there will be many whose blood type is not the same as yours.

I have also wondered how far one can successfully extend the "to-each-his-own-bag" premise of moral subjectivism, or universalize its associated principles of liberty and expressive equality conveyed by the catchy lyrics of the song. That premise – of moral subjectivism – encourages a rather breezy and expansive sense of tolerance for variety in the customary practices of different ethnic groups. But it does so, one must admit, by indiscriminately (and presumptively) reducing cultural differences to the idea of taste, desire, or personal preference. And that is a problem.

"George Washington [the WASP] liked good roast beef. Haym Solomon [the Jew] liked fish. When Uncle Sam served liberty they both enjoyed the dish." Let's be a bit more discriminating, or at least discerning, in our food preferences. What if I were to interrogate the social intelligence of my Hindu Brahman informants in the temple town of Bhubaneswar in Orissa, India,[3] by asking them to react to that verse? They live in a coastal area of India where many of the local Brahmans customarily eat fish, but would never eat bloody red meat. In fact, it is precisely because of their fish-eating habits that Brahmans in the State of Orissa are viewed as somewhat lower in status by Brahmans from other regions of India who characteristically maintain a strict vegetarian diet.[4] And in rural Hindu India, including the state of Orissa, beef-eating of the sort indulged in by George Washington and his ethnic group is pretty much restricted to very low status castes, one of whom's specializations and caste duties is to undertake the spiritually polluting task of getting rid of dead "holy cows."[5]

---

3 This is a location where, beginning in 1968, and on and off over the decades, I have conducted research on cultural mentalities and social intelligence.

4 The local Brahmans are themselves differentiated into a series of hierarchically arranged Brahman sub-castes. The ranking is done on the basis of the importance and purity/sanctity not just of what they customarily eat but also of their family life practices and their social and traditional occupational duties. For example, manual labor is thought to be somewhat degrading compared to the reading of sacred texts or the performance of ritual activities in the presence of a god; hence (for example), one local sub-caste of Brahmans, who are believed to have historically engaged in farming, is ranked lower in the Brahman sub-caste hierarchy because they labored with a plow.

5 I realize of course that some of you may also be inclined to make degrading status and identity judgments about George Washington for not being a vegetarian or even a fish eater. The premise of

But let's go a step further and not just tip-toe around in the moral domain focusing merely on variations in food taboos. What if George Washington and Haym Solomon had different conceptions of marriage or gender relations or the meaning of bodily integrity or how to discipline children? What if George Washington liked monogamy and Haym Solomon liked polygamy? What if one of their wives liked to wear short dresses at social occasions while the other had a personal code of modesty and preferred to shield herself from the male gaze by wearing a burqa in the public square?[6]

Continuing for a moment with this interrogation of the moral implications of that rhetorically appealing punch line ("When Uncle Sam served liberty they both enjoyed the dish") what if we move from the choice between surf versus turf on the dinner menu to cultural "tastes" of a somewhat different sort? What if we discovered that George Washington (who one can reasonably assume was not circumcised by his parents) was personally disgusted by the very thought of neonatal male circumcision and judged the Jewish practice to be child abuse and a violation of various supposed inalienable human rights, such as the right to self-determination and the right to physical integrity? Possibly, Haym Solomon (who probably was circumcised) approved of the practice, and indeed might well have viewed the Jewish custom as an act of religious piety or at the very least as a significant sign of one's ethnic identity? Are you still prepared to say "When Uncle Sam served liberty they both enjoyed the dish?" And, one might ask, what should feelings of personal disgust or enjoyment have to do with judgments of right and wrong anyway?

Ultimately, if you are striving to develop your own social intelligence you might find yourself asking this question: If the United States is to be a genuinely multi-cultural society, what should be on your un-American cultural activities list, if anything at all, and why? That is the kind of question about social understandings addressed in this chapter. Increasingly, given the renewed challenge of cultural migration into various regions of North America and Europe, that is a question contemplated by at least some anthropologists in the sub-discipline increasingly known as "moral anthropology" or, alternatively, "the anthropology of morality."

---

moral subjectivism (which accords a privilege and authority to matters of taste or personal wants) is not necessarily taken for granted even in the coastal regions of the United States. Health has become a pervasive concept for hierarchically scaling and making "objective" moral judgments about the behavioral habits of individuals in our society. Public regulations (for example, prohibiting the creation of restaurants for smokers) and social judgments (for example, stigmatizing "fat people" on the assumption they are overweight because of what they eat) make one less and less free to choose what to ingest into one's own body. This type of moral mapping and grading of individuals and groups is even (or perhaps especially) commonplace within the most elite sectors of American society, where many tend to view themselves as superior to others because of their "enlightened" food habits.

6 If you drive 90 minutes North of the Upper West Side of Manhattan to the nearly 100% Jewish Satmar Hasidic village of Kiryas Joel in Orange County, New York, you will be greeted by a prominently displayed sign, sponsored by a local Jewish congregation, which reads as follows: "Welcome to Kiryas Joel, a traditional community of modesty and values. We kindly ask that you dress and behave in a modest way while visiting our community. This includes: wearing long skirts or pants, covered necklines, sleeves below the elbow, use appropriate language, maintain gender separation in all public areas. Thank you for respecting our values and please ENJOY YOUR VISIT!"

James Madison's Social Intelligence Concerning Factions in a Multicultural Society

James Madison, another founding father of the American experiment, had some profound things to say about the reasons for the persistence of group differences in social understandings in any complex multicultural society. He too was impressed by the role of liberty as a source of diversity, although he added two other factors as well, which he called "self-love" (and which we might gloss as visceral or affect-laden identity-maintenance) and the fallibility of reason. His observations appear in his famous treatise concerning factions in American society (in Federalist 10, originally published on November 22, 1787) – a "faction" being a sub-group of citizens, whether in the majority or in the minority, who are bound to each other by some shared interests, values, social understandings, passions, customary practices, or historical identity that sets them in contrast to the interests, values, social understandings, passions, customary practices, or historical identity of some other sub-group of citizens.

James Madison writes:

> There are two methods of removing the causes of faction: the one, by destroying the liberty which is essential to its existence; the other, by giving to every citizen the same opinions, the same passions, and the same interests. It could never be more truly said than of the first remedy [the tyrannical destruction of liberty], that it was worse than the disease. Liberty is to faction what air is to fire, an aliment without which it instantly expires. But it could not be less folly to abolish liberty, which is essential to political life, because it nourishes faction, than it would be to wish the annihilation of air, which is essential to animal life, because it imparts to fire its destructive agency. The second expedient is as impracticable as the first would be unwise. As long as the reason of man continues fallible, and he is at liberty to exercise it, different opinions will be formed. As long as the connection subsists between his reason and his self-love, his opinions and his passions will have a reciprocal influence on each other; and the former will be objects to which the latter will attach themselves.

I have brought forward the George Washington/Haym Solomon jingle from the early 1950s and those observations by James Madison from 1787 because they seem especially relevant for any cultural anthropologist interested in the development of social intelligence in a multicultural world. But what do I mean by a multicultural world? I mean the kind of world in which peoples who belong to different historical ethical communities (or to different value factions within a single society) seem to disagree with each other in self-involving and affect-arousing ways about the legitimacy of particular social norms and family life practices. And what do I mean by social intelligence? I mean everything a person thinks, feels, knows, and values that makes it possible for a member of an in-group to feel at home in that social group, to skillfully and effectively cooperate with its other members and be accepted as a party to an implicit agreement to uphold a particular way of life.

Feeling at Home in Your In-Group: Is Ethnocentrism a Vice or a Virtue?

As ironic as it may sound, social intelligence could not exist without a good deal of ethnocentrism – that is to say, ethnocentrism with a happy face. To be ethnocentric with a happy face means feeling at home in a particular way of life and embracing its local or parochial points of view about what is real and of value.

Nevertheless, that is just one side of the story of ethnocentrism in any society. Social intelligence in a genuinely multicultural society is also marked by the ability and willingness to de-center – to be at home with your ethnocentrism even while knowing when and how to step outside of it as well. In other words, to be socially intelligent in a complex multicultural society one must also be able to accurately and sympathetically comprehend the different ways of life of others and understand *their* parochial and historically situated point of view too. Perhaps you have already guessed where I am heading: While theorizing about social intelligence I am going to idealize the aims and methods of cultural anthropology and posit them as models for the development of social understanding.

If ethnocentrism is defined as the privileging of one's own habitual and familiar native point of view, then the sharing of a native point of view is probably essential for life among members of any cultural in-group. Members of a cultural in-group who feel at home in their way of life tacitly accept that they are parties to an agreement with other members of the in-group to uphold a particular way of life, picture reality in similar ways, and value the world in similar terms; and, in that sense, they must be ethnocentric if they are going to effectively function as cooperative and accepted members of their group. Ethnocentrism (the anthropologist's analogue to Jean Piaget's concept of ego-centrism) is thus not only pervasive but also unavoidable. Indeed, within any cultural group ethnocentrism is likely to be a starting point for the ontogenetic development of social understanding. In a purely mono-cultural world, ethno-centrism might even be an ideal (or at least defensible) endpoint for social development.

Nevertheless, ethnocentrism remains a potentially hazardous frame of mind. In a genuinely multicultural world, especially one with power imbalances between cultural groups, ethnocentrism can become a problem. Members of different ethnic groups or historical ethical communities living in multicultural societies are likely to customarily, habitually, or even deliberately do things that elicit spontaneous judgments of opprobrium (outrage, disgust, moral disapproval, condescension) from members of other historical ethical communities or ethnic groups. They may disagree, for example, about whether it is morally permissible to engage in sex-selective abortion, or about whether circumcising a male infant on the eighth day after birth is a legitimate parental right and morally defensible custom. In 2012, for example, an appellate judge in Cologne declared childhood male circumcision (as practiced by Jews and Muslims) unconstitutional in Germany (where male circumcision has never been customary, at least not among its dominant Germanic ethnic group), setting off a moral panic among Jews and Muslims around the world.[7]

Notably, overcoming ethnocentrism is the standard challenge confronting the cultural anthropologist in the field when seeking to understand other cultures from "the native point of view." Typically a cultural anthropologist conducting ethnographic field-work stands outside a form of life different from his or her own which initially he or she does not really understand. He or she must exercise considerable discipline and self-restraint to get beyond this type of epistemic subjectivity or ethnocentrism. Why? So as not to react to all the local things he or she does not really understand as if those things could be readily assimilated to one's native point of view and fairly judged by one's own self-affirming gut feelings. A willingness to bracket one's fast cognitions and gut reactions (thereby to temporarily set them to the side) and to leave oneself open to the much slower process of accommodative understanding of the point of view of others (the anthropologist's analogue to "decentering") is an essential feature of the anthropological process of understanding others.

When Even the Gods Don't Agree (About Moral Absolutes)

I would like to suggest that the development of social intelligence in a multicultural world is a process of keeping ethnocentrism and epistemic subjectivity in their proper place. The development of social intelligence in this respect amounts to a never-ending struggle to honor and make sense of two propositions.

The first proposition is nicely stated by the anthropologist Raymond Firth. He conducted field research on the island of Tikopia in the Southwestern Pacific Ocean and wrote the following about the moral beliefs of the Tikopia people: "The spirits, just as men, respond to a norm of conduct of an external character. The moral law exists in the absolute, independent of the Gods" (Firth, 1936/2004, p. 335).

That proposition – which abstractly stated postulates the existence of an objective moral charter for life in society comparable in ontological status to mathematical or logical norms – will be familiar to cognitive developmental theorists who study morality. You really cannot be a cognitive developmentalist, at least not in the tradition of developmental studies forged by Jean Piaget (1932/1997) and Larry Kohlberg (1981), if you believe that consensus makes something logical or that socially constructed judgments are self-validating. So-called "post-conventional" moral thinking is called post-conventional and is evaluated as a more advanced form of moral thinking because it was viewed by Kohlberg as a more rational expression of transcendental or objective moral truths; in that respect he subscribed to a metaphysical belief essentially the same as that of the natives of Tikopia: that there are normative moral truths which exist in the absolute, independent of both

---

7 Secular liberal progressive thinking of a sort (full of references to self-determination, human rights, beneficent safekeeping, and protection of the vulnerable from harm) went into the legal ruling. For further discussion of the German court decision banning male circumcision in Germany, see Shweder (2013).

humans and the Gods. Piaget's so-called constructivism is largely about the process of discovering those moral truths, which he assumed existed regardless of any assimilative or accommodative event leading to their discovery. Piaget's theory of constructivism is not about the creation, constitution, or invention of moral truths, for if that were the case then moral truth would be entirely subject-dependent. With due respect to social constructivists of an anti-realist stripe, Piaget himself was not an anti-realist and he assumed that moral truths, if they are truly true are also really real and must pre-exist their discovery by any individual or group.

Henry Sidgwick identifies this objectivism or realism presupposed by moral judgments. In his classic and highly influential 19th century text in moral philosophy *The Methods of Ethics* (1884) Sidgwick begins with an analysis of the key moral concept expressed in the English language by the word "ought." He argues that any expression of an attitude of approval for a social action that deserves to be called moral approval is "inseparably bound up with the conviction, implicit or explicit, that the conduct approved is 'objectively' right – i.e., that it cannot, without error, be disapproved by any other mind" (1884, p. 28).[8] That is precisely what Piaget and Kohlberg, and the Tikopia say too. You cannot be a socially intelligent and moral human being without making judgments of that sort, relying, rightly or wrongly, on some notion or other of universal moral truths or an objective moral charter for life in society.

The second proposition that plays a part in the struggle to develop one's social intelligence in a multicultural world is sometimes attributed to Socrates. That second proposition, unlike the first, is not a normative ontological assumption about the existence of the moral truths contained in some posited objective moral charter (for example, the Ten Commandments). Rather, it is an observation about diversity in social and moral judgments, which goes as follows: "There are some things about which even the Gods disagree."

So, my thesis is that the development of social intelligence in a multicultural world is the never-ending struggle to come to terms with those two propositions. This is one way to keep epistemic subjectivity and ethnocentrism in their proper place. It is the struggle to embrace some notion of an objective moral charter while trying to figure out what might explain apparent moral disagreements even among the Gods. If you are an attentive observer in a multicultural world you notice that among those who disagree in their moral judgments there are those who subject their attitudes or feelings of approval or disapproval to scrutiny and criticism and end up feeling justified and at home with their particular judgments of right and wrong. James Madison, as noted earlier, sought to explain the origin and persistence of ideological factions in any complex society by reference to the combination of liberty, the fallibility of reason, and self-love. His observations are profound. If you are going to develop your social intelligence in a multicultural society you cannot avoid wrapping your explanatory mind around the failure of moral judgments to converge, even among the Gods.

---

8 Sidgwick contrasts the expression of a genuine moral judgment to an expression of approval which is merely of personal liking, is a report about the shared opinions of the members of some group, or is the expression of nothing other than feelings of pleasure.

Two Visions of Social Intelligence: Currents and Counter-Currents

Perhaps it is obvious by now that my chapter is a play on two different visions of social intelligence. One of those visions is sometimes associated with theorists of the European Enlightenment. The other is sometimes associated with the romantic rebellion against the Enlightenment. If my effort seems dialectical, or perhaps just belabored and clumsy, it may be because I am trying to embrace the virtues (and avoid the vices) of each of those visions.

Isaiah Berlin draws the contrast between the two visions this way. For many progressive Enlightenment authors "there is only one universal civilization, of which now one nation, now another, represents the richest flowering." Berlin goes on to say that for the romantic authors (he has in mind German romantics such as Johann Herder, who had a big influence on my own discipline):

> [T]here is a plurality of incommensurable cultures. To belong to a given community, to be connected with its members by indissoluble and impalpable ties of a common language, historical memory, habit, tradition and feeling, is a basic human need no less natural than that for food or drink or security or procreation. *One nation can understand and sympathize with the institutions of another only because it knows how much its own mean to itself* [emphasis added].
> (Berlin, 1976, p. 122)

In line with that observation I wish to suggest that a highly developed social intelligence is one that is able to understand and sympathize with the unfamiliar and even ego-alien perspectives and attachments of the members of different cultural communities without shedding the attitudes, judgments, and feelings that give definition to one's own distinctive but culturally contoured and refined sense of self. The challenge or the trick is to figure out what type of multicultural experiences and understandings make that possible.

Of course, that first vision of social intelligence – the one associated with the Enlightenment – is consistent with the writings of Piaget, Kohlberg, and Leonard Hobhouse (1915/2015). Theirs are among the most influential (or at least well thought out) 20th century theories concerned with the development of social intelligence.

All three authors – Hobhouse, Piaget, and Kohlberg – were liberal progressives who believed that the social intelligence of both individuals and members of different historical communities could be ranked on a universal developmental scale. All three subscribed to the view that there exists an objective moral charter for the organization of an ideal universal civilization. That objective moral charter defined the normative endpoint for a fully realized social intelligence, which can and should be used as the global standard for judging the validity of diverse ways of life and ranking them in terms of their moral worth (for example, on a developmental scale from savage to civilized or backward to advanced). Developmental moral mappings of that sort get made all the time both within and across societies. Both (fast) visceral and (slower) reflective judgments get made about such things as whether monogamy is superior to polygamy, democratic governance superior to kingship or theocracy, or whether animism, Judaism, Christianity, Islam, and contemporary secular atheism can be lined up on some temporal developmental scale reflecting the supersession of superior forms and revealing historical progress in the human understanding of the God/Nature term.

This approach to the development of social intelligence is well-represented in the writings of Hobhouse, Piaget, and Kohlberg. All three theorists believed that liberal Enlightenment thinkers had come closest to discovering the terms of the one true charter for social intelligence. For example, all three viewed tribalism or in-group favoritism (which they judged to be incompatible with the principle of justice as equality) and deference to hierarchy (which they judged to be incompatible with individual autonomy) as lower forms of social understanding. All three argued that the social and moral consciousness of human beings had not only evolved over the course of cultural history, but should be encouraged to continue to develop in what they viewed as the progressive liberal direction, freeing the individual from the constraints of inherited tradition and the burdens of ancestry.

All three argued that the social understandings of the peoples of the world could be ranked from the earlier stages (in which there was blind or unreflective adherence to the acceptances of one's tribe and subordination of one's capacity for self-determination to the will of dead ancestors and the dictates of authority figures) to higher stages in which there was thoughtful and even self-critical reflection aimed at giving every person his or her rightful due with reference to impartial and objective standards of freedom, justice, and equality. All this they summarized in the pre-eminent principle of respect for persons and their self-determination or autonomy.

The Liberal Progressive Vision: From the Academy to the Invasion of Iraq

Echoes of this type of liberal progressive vision of social intelligence can be readily found not only throughout the academy in North America and Europe but also in contemporary public policy forums. Consider, for example, this resonant formulation by former United States President George W. Bush, which he voiced in his first "State of the Union Address to Congress and the Nation" after the terrorist attacks of September 11, 2001:

> America will lead by defending liberty and justice because they are right and true and unchanging for all people everywhere. No nation owns these aspirations and no nation is exempt from them. We have no intention of imposing our culture, but America will always stand firm for the non-negotiable demands of human dignity, the rule of law, limits on the power of the state, respect for women, private property, free speech, equal justice and religious tolerance.[9]

Those were weighty and portentous words expressing the foreign policy doctrine that American wealth and power should be used to make the world a better place by

9 https://georgewbush-whitehouse.archives.gov/news/releases/2002/01/20020129-11.html

upholding what many American activists and interventionists (both on the internationalist "left" and on the jingoistic "right") view as an incontestable universal framework for promoting the development of social understanding on a global scale.

And yet it remains a fact of life that there are some things about which even the Gods disagree. To pick a not-so-random example, one I have written about at some length but cannot discuss in any detail here, the peoples of the world are quite divided in their social norms concerning the potential reshaping of the genitals of children and youth, both males and females (e.g., Shweder, 2002, 2009). The typical customary European pattern where neither boys nor girls reshape their genitals and where both male and female genital reshaping for children are viewed with opprobrium by most members of dominant European ethnic groups (as among ethnic Swedes, Danes, Germans, and Italians) is not an empirical cultural universal. Despite the heightened media attention to campaigns against female genital reshaping in East and West Africa (and the associated moral panic over the imagined occurrence of the practice among African immigrant populations in Europe and North America) there are no ethnic groups anywhere in the world where only girls reshape their genitals. But there are many where both boys and girls do, and even more where genital reshaping is exclusively a male prerogative, such as in the United States, Israel, South Korea, the Philippines, most of the West Asian Muslim world, and many ethnic groups in Sub-Saharan Africa.

Cultural anthropologists of course spend much of their time documenting variability in social understandings and social norms across historical ethical communities (where one often finds that even the Gods disagree), but those are just descriptive facts, and not necessarily normative truths. When critiquing theories of social development it is surely important for cultural anthropologists to acknowledge the naturalistic fallacy and recognize that "is" does not imply "ought" and that the normative implications of their descriptive ethnographic research on diversity are far from clear.

How does one go about answering the following crucial question: with respect to the normative requirements of the one true and objective moral charter, which of those societies has got it right (for example, with regard to genital reshaping, or marriage customs, or food taboos, or the sexual division of labor, etc.)? At best, the descriptive anthropology is just the beginning of a conversation about the progressive development of social norms, precisely because when "red state" evangelical Christians condemn gay marriage and "blue state" secular liberals condone it the provocative difference in their judgments might merely be a sign of a developmental deficiency or fault in the social understandings of one or the other of the parties to the disagreement.

In other words, let us not forget that the premise that there are no faultless moral disagreements is an essential one for cognitive developmental theorists; at least, that is so if the disagreement is a genuine one concerning the demands of the objective moral charter or the requirements of some posited universal moral truth. Recall Sidgwick's point that an expression of *moral* disapproval is "inseparably bound up with the conviction, implicit or explicit, that the conduct approved is 'objectively' right – i.e., that it cannot, without error, be disapproved by any other mind." From the perspective of cognitive developmental theorists, the driving or motivating force behind the evolution of social intelligence is the force of self-critical reason to eliminate error, ignorance, and confusion from one's own picture of the world and to feel justified in one's social understandings. So, when the Gods disagree in their moral judgments, what are we to say? That some of them are in a state of error, ignorance, or confusion about the terms of the objective moral charter? That they don't possess enough local knowledge to allow them to correctly apply the terms of the objective moral charter to specific cases or local contexts? That their disagreements are not really moral disagreements at all, but, rather, about issues that are non-moral in character? Or that there is no objective moral charter after all? These are the types of questions that promote self-reflection and the development of social intelligence in a multicultural world.

Thinking Your Way Through Fast Cognitions and Visceral Responses in the Face of Apparent Barbarisms

One fascinating model for how to move from a descriptive to a normative mode in understanding exotic others while de-centering and getting beyond the dark side of ethnocentrism can be found in the famous and influential 16th century essay by Michel de Montaigne titled "Of Cannibals" (2003). In that essay, Montaigne, who was an early ethnographer of sorts, tries to come to terms with the then recently discovered cultural practices of the native Carib peoples of Brazil. He describes and morally evaluates the beliefs, values, and customs of a people who believed that hosting a captive of war and then killing, roasting, and making a common meal of him, and "sending chunks of his flesh to absent friends" (2003, p. 188), was right and good.

That particular practice, although customary and locally viewed as honorable and legitimate by both the natives and their captives ("you cannot find one [prisoner of war] who does not prefer to be killed and eaten than merely to ask to be spared," Montaigne recounts (2003, p. 190)) seemed shocking, repulsive, and backward to Portuguese and French moral and culinary sensibilities in the 16th century, just as many customary practices of peoples in the Southern and Eastern worlds (practices such as dowry, female genital reshaping, physical punishment, sex-selective abortion, arranged marriages, or animal sacrifice) seem barbaric, odious, and detestable to many peoples of the Northern and Western worlds today. Nevertheless, Montaigne dared to offer a critical (and ironical) response to the Portuguese and French opprobrium directed at the so-called under-developed cannibals of Brazil.

It is noteworthy that early in his essay Montaigne cautions the reader to step back and be reflective about his or her own aversive gut reactions to stories about Carib practices. It is also noteworthy that throughout there are many references to the universal virtues that are recognizable in their folkways and social norms but only if one makes the effort to be informed about the particular details of the Carib way of life: "their whole ethical science contains only these two articles: resoluteness in war and affection for their wives," which he also describes as "valor against the enemy and love for their wives" (Montaigne, 2003, p. 187). Writing as an ironist, a skeptic, and a detached observer of human behavior, Montaigne was prepared to morally complicate the European colonial encounter with alien societies. He was not inclined to let the righteous elite moralists of the metropols of the Western World make the world safe for condescension and for an imperial European rule justified under the banner of cultural superiority.

On the one hand, by means of various cultural comparisons he invited his readers to see the dark side of their own way of life. He writes:

> But there never was any opinion so disordered as to excuse treachery, disloyalty, tyranny and cruelty, which are our ordinary vices. So we may well call these people barbarians, in respect to the rules of reason, but not in respect to ourselves, who surpass them in every kind of barbarity. Their warfare is wholly noble and generous, and as excusable and beautiful as this human disease can be; its only basis among them is their rivalry in valor. They are not fighting for the conquest of new lands . . . they have no wish to enlarge their boundaries.
> (Montaigne, 2003, p. 189)

Commenting on the customary practice of polygamy by the Carib, he remarks favorably on the lack of jealousy among the women of the society and notes "Being more concerned for their husbands' honor than for anything else, they strive and scheme to have as many companions as they can, since that is a sign of their husbands' valor" (Montaigne, 2003, p. 192). And, perhaps most remarkably, he goes on to rebut the anticipated counter-claims (which are still commonplace today) that:

> all this is done through a simple and servile bondage to usage and through the pressure of the authority of their ancient customs, without reasoning or judgment, and because their minds are so stupid that they cannot take any other course.
> (Montaigne, 2003, p. 192)

In other words, for Montaigne the "cannibals" did not lack either agency or virtue, and by his lights their exercise of their agency was quite compatible with their embrace of the beliefs, values, and skills privileged and transmitted by and through their cultural tradition. He foresaw the objection of later liberal progressive thinkers (for example, John Stuart Mill) that tradition is a form of enslavement of the living by the dead, and he rejected it.

Montaigne's essay was written between 1578 and 1580. It is noteworthy that his take-home messages later became standard recommendations for researchers in 20th century cultural anthropology. I would like to suggest those take-home messages express a theory about how best to develop one's own social intelligence. The basic point is this one: participation (what anthropologists call "participant observation") in a thick cultural tradition is a necessary condition for recognizing the self-evident moral truths or moral absolutes (Montaigne called them "the rules of reason") that must be made manifest in any way of life with respect for which some group of human beings can feel at home. This is true not only for the individuals growing up and developing competencies in some cultural tradition different from one's own; it is also true for the outsiders (such as visiting anthropologists) trying to understand that cultural tradition. Even for individuals growing up in one's own cultural tradition, participant observation is a way of gaining insight into the social intelligence of alternative ways of life.

And Montaigne offers these cautions. When judging other cultures, beware of the illusory air of moral superiority that so naturally arises as you invest the popular acceptances of your own society with strong sentiment and experience them not only as familiar but as self-evident truths. Rushing to judgment can be hazardous. Be slow to demonize the way of life of little-known others. Distinguish facts from factoids. Try to see the world from the native point of view. Bracket your impulsive emotional reactions and visceral attachments. Have a closer look before arriving at strong moral conclusions.

Moral Anthropology and the Socratic Tradition

I believe Montaigne's recommendations for a critical moral anthropology are quite compatible with the Socratic tradition that has been so central to the mission of many contemporary cognitive developmental researchers. Within the terms of the Socratic research tradition, moral cultivation amounts to the preparation of an individual's mind to be receptive to the universally binding objective moral truths or moral absolutes (the "rules of reason") that are part of the natural order of things. Accordingly, to grow and become more sophisticated or developed in one's moral and social attitudes is to increasingly think for oneself, which is done by distinguishing objective moral knowledge from attitudes that have their source merely in personal desire, and by also distinguishing objective moral knowledge from attitudes that have their source only or merely in the received opinions and routine acceptances of one's local group.

Indeed, according to the Socratic–Piagetian–Kohlbergian–Turielian tradition (e.g., Turiel, 1983), it is only by becoming more and more able to draw such distinctions (between what is objective and what is subjective, between what is universal in scope and what ought to be restricted in its application to those who share a particular point of view) that a human mind can be in the position to feel at home in, and experience the legitimacy of, any deep tradition. It is only by appreciating (from both inside out and outside in) the manifestations of objective moral truths in one's own parochial patterns of behavior that one is able as a rational person to accept the authority of one's inherited way of life or defend its local or parochial requirements.

The aim of this type of social and moral development is to have one's personal desires aligned with (or at least compatible with) what is objectively desirable, to have preferences that are truly preference-worthy, and to live in a society where the customary practices of the group can be experienced as routine manifestations and habitual expressions of absolute moral truths or universally recognizable virtues. Understandably, it is a pre-requisite for that type of striving and growth of social understanding that one is able to draw the distinctions (between personal preferences vs. social preferences vs. objective goods) that make such developments possible.

No doubt the relationship between the objective moral charter and received custom, between moral theory and traditional practice, between knowledge and habit is a complex one. It seems safe to say that no human being lives a fully examined life in which, on the basis of pure reasoning and direct experience alone, and free of all external influences, they have become a fully autonomous arbiter of what is true, good, and beautiful. It also seems safe to say that no human being lives a fully unexamined mindless life in which their spontaneous attitudes of approval (and disapproval) are never objects of self-conscious reflection and auto-critique. There are processes for the acquisition of automated behavior (for example, processes of imitation, identification, and social referencing) by means of which one becomes fluent in and habitually respectful of a customary tradition. There are also processes of self-conscious reasoning for examining that received wisdom of the group, scrutinizing external authority, and making use of the dictates of reason to evaluate the moral claims of each and every tradition, including one's own.

Some Distinguished Distinctions: Genuine Moral Intuitions Versus Socialized Opinions

Henry Sidgwick, the great 19th century British moral philosopher mentioned earlier, gives voice in *The Methods of Ethics* to a conception of genuine moral development as a process of drawing relevant distinctions and putting them to work (1884, p. 340). He writes:

> most persons are liable to confound intuitions, on the one hand with mere impressions and impulses, which to careful observation do not present themselves as claiming objective validity; and on the other hand, with mere opinions, to which the familiarity that comes from frequent hearing and repetition often gives an illusory air of self-evidence which attentive reflection disperses.

In order to understand Sidgwick's distinctions between impressions, mere opinions, and what he calls "intuitions" (which have objective validity, an essential feature of which is their undeniable truth) it is essential to note that for Sidgwick and other British moralists of his era moral "intuitions" were included within the domain of human reason. Moral intuitions were definitely not equated with feeling, affect, impulse, emotion, or desire. Intuition referred to the direct, effortless, spontaneous human grasp of self-evident objective truths – undeniably true propositions about the world that required no further justification or deliberation. Moral intuitions were often likened by British moral philosophers in Sidgwick's era (and earlier) to rapidly grasped intuitions of a mathematical sort (for example, that two parallel lines cannot enclose any space or that a whole is greater than any of its parts). There was nothing dumb (or, for that matter, emotional) about them, except in the sense that to argue about their validity was both pointless and senseless. To the extent that there was a kind of silence associated with a genuine moral intuition, it was due to the absence of any credible spoken denial and the lack of any necessity for verbal justification.

Once a moral "intuition" had been identified or pointed to, the validity of the intuition is something that goes without saying because it is simply undeniable.

The category of rational (and hence genuine) moral intuitions (Montaigne's "rules of reason") was contrasted with learned habits, popular acceptances, and impulsive or affect-laden snap judgments that possessed an "illusory air of self-evidence." For those British moral philosophers a short list of stand-alone rational moral intuitions might include the following: one ought to speak the truth (veracity); one ought to give every person their due (justice); one ought to treat like cases alike and different cases differently; one ought to impartially apply rules of general applicability; one ought to requite benefits received as gifts or patronage (reciprocity); one ought to protect those who are vulnerable and in one's charge (beneficence); one ought to respond to the urgent needs of others if the sacrifice or cost to oneself is slight; one ought to pursue the more certain of two equal goods; one ought to select a greater good in the future over a lesser good now (if both are equally certain); one ought to never pursue a lesser good over a greater good (prudence)[10].

In that intuitionist tradition of moral philosophy the rules of reason and human rationality were not equated with slow and self-conscious mental processing, and fast processing was not equated with affect-laden or impulsive thinking. Unfortunately, those are the misleading and confusing equations that have become increasingly popular in some areas of contemporary moral psychology. In the discourse of contemporary moral psychology the very notion of a moral intuition has come to be used as a descriptor for mindless affect-laden visceral reactions of approval or disapproval. The moral intuition concept is thus theoretically employed in contemporary moral psychology to contrast fast vs. slow cognitive processing and to equate a moral intuition with affect (versus thought) or with initial fast spontaneous non-rational reactions of approval or disapproval detached from reflective judgments or later moral self-justification (which are now interpreted as mere rationalization).

Nevertheless, that said, it is certainly true of the Socratic–Piagetian–Kohlbergian–Turielian conception of the moral domain that genuine moral cultivation requires a certain degree of attentive self-reflection as to the source of, and authority behind, one's fast and spontaneous (and sometimes affect-laden) attitudes of approval and disapproval. According to that conception of the moral domain, the judgment (whether made hastily or slowly) that something is of value, good or bad, right or wrong, ought to be done or ought not to be done, is more than just a subjective declaration of value. The expressed attitude of approval (or disapproval) implies knowledge of something (the moral truth expressed in the judgment of approval or disapproval) and thus always invites the post-hoc interrogation of the substance and validity of that knowledge. In other words, it is precisely because a spontaneous moral judgment expresses an attitude of approval that it is inherently normative in character and hence subject to scrutiny and potential criticism. The Socratic tradition in moral philosophy wants to know whether the expression of approval is in fact moral approval

---

10 Of course, these moral intuitions might conflict with one another in particular moral decision contexts, raising questions about whether they are reducible to more general intuitions or should just be viewed as a base set of heterogeneous moral truths or absolutes.

(in contrast, for example, to mere personal liking) and, if it is, whether the moral approval (or disapproval) is justified by some rule of reason or not.

Sidgwick again gives us a roadmap. In this case he gives us a map for thinking about moral development as a process of self-reflection wherein and whereby our attitudes of approval (or disapproval) get scrutinized. That process of assessment and justification is presumably undertaken in anticipation of (or in response to) criticism. And the development or growth of social understanding occurs when and if certain fundamental distinctions get drawn and put in place: for example, the distinction between those of one's own attitudes of approval that are grounded in the objective moral charter versus those attitudes of approval that merely possess the semblance (the "illusory air") of a rational moral intuition but have no real objective authority at all.

Sidgwick begins the road trip by drawing our attention to attitudes of approval based on nothing other than personal passions and affections (1884, pp. 340–341). He writes:

> For, on the one hand, it cannot be denied that any strong sentiment, however purely subjective, is apt to transform itself into the semblance of an intuition; and it requires careful contemplation to detect the illusion. Whatever we desire we are apt to pronounce desirable; and we are strongly tempted to approve of whatever conduct gives us keen pleasure.

He then directs our attention to attitudes of approval based in such external authority as positive law or the legal code of a society. He writes (1884, p. 341):

> among the rules of conduct to which we customarily conform, there are many which reflection shows to be really derived from some external authority: so that even if their obligation be unquestionable, it cannot be intuitively ascertained. This is of course the case with the Positive Law of the community to which we belong. There is no doubt that we ought, – at least generally speaking, – to obey this [the law]: but what it [the law] is we cannot of course ascertain by any process of abstract reflection, but only by consulting Reports and Statutes. Here, however, the sources of knowledge are so definite and conspicuous, that we are in no danger of confounding the knowledge gained from studying them with the results of abstract contemplation.

Finally, Sidgwick has the following to say about attitudes of approval grounded in customary and traditional codes for behavior (1884, p. 341):

> The case is somewhat different with the traditional and customary rules of behavior which exist in every society, supplementing the regular operation of Law proper: here it is much more difficult to distinguish the rules which a moral man is called upon to define for himself, by the application of intuitively known principles, from those as to which some authority external to the individual is recognized as the final arbiter.

So far in this chapter I have tried to imagine some ways in which cultural anthropologists and developmental psychologists might need each other to fully understand what I take to be a general fact of life in human societies: namely, that most people much of the time feel at home in and affirmed by the many particularities of their distinctive way of life. If true, this is a remarkable fact of life. It calls out for explanation. If it is true, I wish to suggest that the received customs and social duties of any long-standing cultural tradition are generally in the service of some conception of natural moral law and, if understood from the "native point of view," the "native" generally experiences the cultural tradition as a manifestation of intuitive rules of reason of the sort mentioned earlier (e.g., treat like cases alike and different cases differently). The "I feel at home" acceptance of those customs and social norms is not merely an example of social conformity motivated by embarrassment, fear, or reward – and if that was all there was to it one would not feel at home in that tradition. For most people much of the time their received customs are experienced by those who feel at home with them as manifestations of "rules which a moral man is called upon to define for himself" (Sidgwick, 1884, p. 341). It is not simply a matter (sometimes dubbed "conventional" or a product of conditioning) whereby that which we find familiar and to which we have become accustomed is automatically judged acceptable. Indeed, I want to go further and suggest that participation in a thick cultural tradition may actually be a necessary condition or "affordance" for recognizing the self-evident moral truths or moral absolutes that must be made manifest in any way of life with respect for which some group of human beings can feel at home.

References

Berlin, I. (1976). *Vico and Herder*. New York, NY: Viking.

Firth, R. (2004). *We, the Tikopia*. London: Routledge. (Originally published in 1936)

Hobhouse, L. (2015). *Morals in evolution: A study in comparative ethics*. London: Forgotten Books. (Originally published in 1915)

Kohlberg, L. (1981). *The philosophy of moral development: Moral stages and the idea of justice*. New York, NY: Harper and Row.

Montaigne, Michel de (2003). Of cannibals. In D. M. Frame (Ed.), *Michel de Montaigne: The complete works, essays, travel journals, letters* (pp. 182–193). New York, NY: Alfred A. Knopf.

Piaget, J. (1997). *The moral judgment of the child*. New York, NY: Free Press. (Originally published in 1932)

Shweder, R. A. (2002). "What about female genital mutilation?" and why understanding culture matters in the first place. In R. Shweder, M. Minow, & H. Markus (Eds.), *Engaging cultural differences: the multicultural challenge in liberal democracies* (pp. 216–251). New York, NY: Russell Sage Foundation Press.

Shweder, R. A. (2009). Shouting at the Hebrews: Imperial liberalism v liberal pluralism and the practice of male circumcision. *Law, Culture and the Humanities, 5*, 247–265.

Shweder, R. A. (2013). The Goose and the Gander: The Genital Wars. *Global Discourse, 3*(2), 348–366. www.tandfonline.com/doi/abs/10.1080/23269995.2013.811923 #.VB9nyhZpKno

Sidgwick, H. (1884). *The methods of ethics*, 3rd edn. London: MacMillan and Company.

Turiel, E. (1983). *The development of social knowledge: Morality and convention*. Cambridge, UK: Cambridge University Press.

17 Cultural Neuroscience of the Developing Brain in Adolescence

Joan Y. Chiao

The United Nations Children's Fund in 2011 reported approximately 1.2 billion adolescents across the world, with nine out of ten youth living in developing nations (UNICEF, 2011). By 2025, the number of adolescents around the world will have increased by an estimated 600% over the preceding fifty years (Blum & Nelson-Mari, 2004). Adolescence represents a developmental period of opportunity for youth to gain educational, social, and occupational knowledge and resources to learn and mature into leaders of their generation. Preventative public policies that protect youth from risk factors associated with unintentional injuries from environmental influences may further enhance the ability of adolescents to enter into adulthood with strong intellectual, social, and professional resources.

Adolescence is a developmental period that serves as an important and protected time of cultural and biological change from childhood to adulthood. Adolescent youth are engaged in activities that engender social support and resources from family, community, and society. The adolescent brain during this time period has largely matured in cognitive capacities emerging during childhood, including motor, sensory, language, and spatial attention skills. The prefrontal cortex, which acts as a regulatory mechanism in the brain for cognitive, social, and affective information, matures during adolescence, allowing for greater regulation, selection, and inhibition skills in youth. Cortical connectivity between prefrontal cortex and cognitive, social, and affective brain regions, such as the orbitofrontal cortex, amygdala, and medial temporal lobes, may further prune during adolescence, allowing for cortical circuitry to refine and support enhanced cognitive and social behavior.

The introduction of the capacity for biological reproduction complements the cultural acquisition of reproductive rituals during adolescence, which represent novel challenges and opportunities for youth development. Societal education during adolescence typically emphasizes the cultivation and demonstration of the ability to culturally adhere to the values and beliefs of the community by young adulthood prior to the endorsement of rituals that support stable development and growth of the family. Public health policies that promote healthy living of youths may provide educational resources of cultural and biological social norms that protect reproductive health into adulthood. Both cultural and biological changes that support reproductive health during adolescence are associated with maturation of psychological processes and mechanisms in the developing brain. While much is known about the importance of understanding the risk and protective factors of adolescent health, less well understood is how the developing brain in adolescence is affected by and contributes to culture. By understanding the etiology of the cultural and biological mechanisms that contribute to adolescent health, we gain greater knowledge of how to protect youth during this important transition into adulthood. The majority of the psychology and neuroscience research with adolescents has been conducted in industrialized nations, although developing nations nurture the majority of the world's population of adolescents (Arnett, 1999; Henrich, Heine, & Norenzayan, 2010). Nine out of ten adolescents live in the developing world: approximately 60% live in Asia, 15% in Africa, and 10% in Latin America and the Caribbean, with only 15% in developed countries and regions (UNICEF, 2011). These scientific trends suggest that neuroscience research of youth may provide a valuable source of scientific knowledge that can guide public policy, and that expansion in the scope of research in adolescence is needed across the globe to ensure empirically based public policy about youth is possible for all (UNICEF, 2011; Patel, Fischer, Hetrick, &McGorry, 2007).

Adolescent neuroscience examines the integration of signaling from neuroendocrine systems with cortical circuitry (Blakemore & Mills, 2014), which occurs in response to environmental and cultural inputs (Telzer, Masten, Bermna, Lieberman, & Fuligni, 2010) and allows for the maturation of social and emotional behavior into adulthood (Pfeifer & Peake, 2012; Somerville, 2013). Advances in the neuroscience of youth indicate multiple neural systems that differ in structure and function in the transition from adolescence to adulthood, using longitudinal and cross-sectional design. These changes in the adolescent brain often accompany social and emotional maturation of behavior, albeit not necessarily in a linear fashion. Cultural expectations of fulfillment in social rituals and roles may alter neurodevelopmental pathways to adulthood. For instance, pubertal changes associated with acquisition of reproductive capacity may be accompanied by changes in cultural expectations in habits regarding use of tools and occupation of roles that protect the body from ecological challenges. Similarly, institutions and communities that foster adolescent growth may facilitate the cultural transmission of norms and rituals that guide psychological processes during neuroendocrine maturation toward adaptive behavior. Understanding how culture shapes neuroendocrine mechanisms in the production of adaptive behavior during adolescence is an important direction for future research. Broadly, by building scientific knowledge of the root causes and mechanisms underlying adolescent health across cultures, international policy-makers gain leverage on evidence-based rationale for behavioral guidelines and intervention strategies that prevent disease and promote health in youth.

Theories of Cultural Neuroscience of the Developing Brain in Adolescence

Cultural neuroscience is an interdisciplinary research field that addresses the origins of human diversity across multiple time scales, including phylogeny, ontogeny, and situation. This chapter addresses questions such as: where does human diversity come from, when and why? Theories and methods from anthropology, cultural psychology, neuroscience, and genetics may be integrated to understand diversity in human behavior from across multiple time scales (Chiao & Ambady, 2007; Chiao, Cheon, Pornpattananangkul, Mrazek, & Blizinsky, 2013). For instance, anthropology, with its emphasis of understanding others with empathy and perspective-taking, allows adults to provide insights into how adolescents navigate their social and educational world. Early anthropological studies highlighted adolescence as a period of "storm and stress," an important developmental period for understanding the influence of culture on social behavior (Arnett, 1999; Casey, Soliman, Bath, & Glatt, 2010; Mead, 1928).

The acquisition of biological reproductive potential represents a fundamental capacity that allows for vertical or linear transmission of cultural and biological heritage in future generations. The cultural and evolutionary investment in reproductive potential is immense and characterizes much of the unique ecological and environmental challenges facing fundamental units of society, including the individual, family, and community. For the individual, protecting the body from exposure to novel situations that may challenge the maturing person becomes a shared goal with family and community. For the family, providing youth with expectations, knowledge, and goals remains a significant and invaluable source of protection. For community, anticipating the needs of maturing youth and providing societal infrastructure to care for their growth is a fundamental requirement for their generation to adapt and fulfill their potential.

Distinct ecological challenges across geography may lead to the emergence of unique cultural norms, practices, and beliefs that interact with genetic inheritance to guide the mind and brain toward achievement and autonomy within the family and society. Culture–gene co-evolutionary theory posits that cultural and genetic transmission operate in parallel to affect the mind and brain throughout the course of development (Boyd & Richerson, 1985). Chiao & Blizinsky (2010) found cross-national evidence that cultural values of individualism and collectivism have co-evolved with the serotonin transporter gene in the production of social and emotional behavior of humans (see Figure 17.1). That is, both cultural and genetic pathways shape in parallel the psychological and neural mechanisms underlying social and emotional behavior. Individualistic cultures typically emphasize independence, autonomy, freedom of expression, and defining the self as distinct from others, whereas collectivistic cultures typically emphasize interdependence, hierarchy, and defining the self in relation to or as defined by roles with others. Historical and contemporary presence of disease or pathogens is thought to have exerted an environmental pressure within geographic regions, leading to an increase in behaviors that have cultivated collectivistic cultural norms, including adherence to authority, vigilance to environmental threats or pressures, and conformity (Fincher, Thornhill, Murray, & Schaller, 2008). The reliance on collectivistic cultural norms throughout evolutionary history has also led to a selection of the short allele of the serotonin transporter gene (5-HTTLPR), a gene previously associated with the regulation of social and emotional neural mechanisms in the human brain. The serotonin transporter gene contains a polymorphic region, known

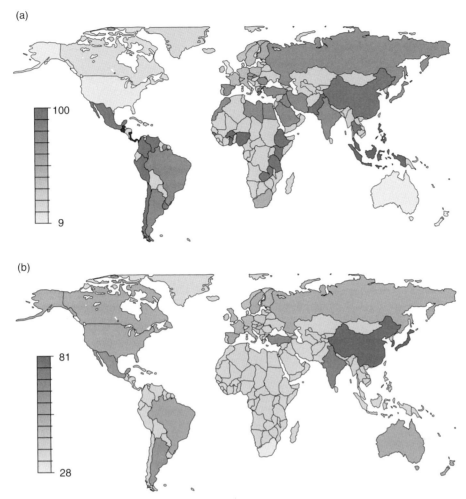

Figure 17.1. *Geographical coincidence between serotonin transporter gene and cultural values of individualism–collectivism across nations (adapted from Chiao & Blizinsky, 2010). (a) Geographic representation of individualism–collectivism across nations; (b) geographic representation of the frequency of the short allele (s) of the serotonin transporter gene (5-HTTLPR); (c) geographic representation of the prevalence of anxiety and; (d) geographic representation of the prevalence of mood disorders from the World Health Organization Survey.*

as 5-HTTLPR, with a short (s) and long (l) allele version that results in differential levels of 5-HTT expression and function (Lesch et al., 1996). Population geneticists have long documented differential prevalence of short allele carriers around the globe, with approximately 70–80% of individuals in the East Asian region carrying the short allele, compared to only 40–50% of individuals in the European region (Gelertner, Kranzler, & Cubells, 1997). The heightened prevalence of individuals who carry the

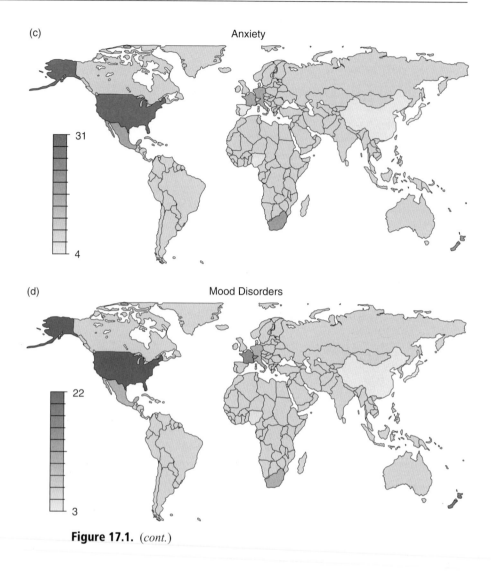

Figure 17.1. (*cont.*)

short allele within collectivistic cultures is thought to reflect the importance of interdependent psychological capacities valued or prized within these geographic regions faced with challenging environmental conditions.

Dynamic changes in ecology or environment may similarly lead to changes or shifts in cultural and biological experience. Migration across geography during adolescence may allow for experience with multiple cultural systems of knowledge that require the maturing youth to integrate beliefs and values from heritage and host cultures (Berry, 1997; Phinney, 1992; Telzer et al., 2010). While childhood is characterized by relative ease of cultural acquisition, adolescence represents a developmental period where acquisition of cultural norms during sociopolitical change can be complex, due to the universal importance of reproductive potential and the societal expectation for fulfillment of shared cultural rituals, including education, literacy, and status, in support of growth of the family. Maturation of prefrontal cortex during adolescence, as a biological adaptation, allows for the enhanced capacity to regulate social and emotional responses that may help to facilitate adaptation to ecological challenges within and beyond the developmental period for the individual. Dynamic patterns of neural activity across prefrontal cortical networks due to changes in epigenetic expression may similarly facilitate rapid cultural adaptation to novel ecological or environmental demands. For instance, parental care of youth, as a cultural adaptation, includes transmission of cultural expectations and habits that support performance and achievement in society into adulthood (Noble et al., 2015). Change in public policy, as a cultural adaptation – for instance, systematic school desegregation – allows for regulation of societal norms and provision of greater protections for students to fulfill their potential within their communities.

Empirical Progress in Cultural Neuroscience of the Developing Brain in Adolescence

Throughout the past two decades, there have been significant advances in understanding the developing brain in adolescence, particularly in Western developed nations. These novel insights demonstrate the importance of cultural and biological factors in the transition from childhood to adulthood for adolescence. Notably, how the brain develops during adolescence across cultures remains relatively unknown. In this section, the foundational mechanisms of social cognition that emerge by childhood and are continuously recruited while navigating sociality during adulthood are discussed, including the role of cultural and biological mechanisms during adolescence in the developmental trajectory of these social processes, such as self- and other-knowledge, emotion, empathy, and self- and other-emotion regulation.

Self- and Other-Knowledge

One important social capacity that emerges in the developmental transition from childhood to adolescence is self- and other-knowledge (Conway & Pleydell-Pearce, 2000, Pfeifer & Peake, 2012; Sebastian, Burnett, & Blakemore, 2008). During childhood, Western and Eastern children develop a self-concept through interactions with caregivers and parents, who guide children in their interpretation of events throughout the day (Wang, 2006). Western parents, for instance, may utilize phrases that emphasize core values of independence and individualism, highlighting the autonomy of objects and individuals in the environment. Eastern parents, on the other hand, may communicate with phrases that emphasize core values of interdependence and collectivism, such as an emphasis on relations between objects and individuals in the environment. With parental guidance, children learn to develop a social knowledge of self and others that is consistent with parental and community values. Autobiographical memories of early childhood already demonstrate cultural differences in self-concept. By young adulthood, early childhood self-concept has matured into an identity that largely conforms to the dominant culture within one's community. For instance, for Western young adults, self-concept is thought to comprise an individual with stable social traits and knowledge; by contrast, for Eastern young adults self-concept is thought to comprise an individual with relational social traits and knowledge (Wang, Shao, Li, 2010).

During the developmental transition from childhood to adulthood, the medial prefrontal cortex (MPFC) and other brain regions within the default mode network undergo significant changes in functional and structural connectivity or strength of communication between brain regions due to either neuroanatomy or neuropsychological function. For instance, connectivity within the prefrontal cortex, including the MPFC and the PCC (posterior cingulate cortex), is weaker in children compared to adults (Supekar et al., 2010). Throughout adolescence, the prefrontal cortex matures, including stronger connectivity across brain regions. By young adulthood, Western and Eastern young adults demonstrate a self-concept that reflects neural response within the MPFC. The MPFC shows greater response when adults think about themselves relative to thinking about others, including close or familiar others, particularly for Western young adults. For Eastern young adults, the MPFC demonstrates greater response when adults think about themselves in the context of close others.

While much is known about how culture affects the self in early childhood and where social knowledge is stored by young adulthood, little is known about how culture affects the adolescent social brain. During adolescence, social identity is a formative mechanism by which youth understand themselves and their relation to others within and across distinct social groups (Phinney, 1992). Belonging to a social group and having a social identity is one of the primary social goals for youth and may be composed of several facets. Having a sense of group membership and positive attitudes toward the group is one part of ethnic self-identification called affirmation and belonging. Another facet of ethnic self-identification is achievement. Experiencing success and achievement with one's ethnic identity may serve as an important developmental process for youth. Finally, engaging in activities or habits that are related to one's ethnic group also contributes to the development of an ethnic self-identity. The developmental process of ethnic identity formation during adolescence allows youth the opportunity to share roles and responsibilities with other's within a social group context, and to experience social success in coordination with others, thus preparing them for their subsequent mature social roles and responsibilities with a network of professional and social resources.

What brain mechanisms may support the development of ethnic identity during adolescence? For majority and minority youth, the maturation of the MPFC may allow for more sophisticated social interaction and networks amongst peers, family, and community. Peer influence increases as greater time is spent within schools and the community. Family influence also continues to play a large role throughout adolescence. The MPFC serves as a neural basis for social knowledge such that social representations of self and other are stored and recruited when people think of social attributes about themselves and others (Blakemore & Mills, 2014). By adulthood, cultural variation in self representations, such as an individualistic or collectivistic self, which may reflect social distance between self and others, is reflected in degree of neural response within this brain region. During childhood, connectivity between the MPFC and connected brain regions within the default mode network, specifically the PCC, is weaker in children compared to adults (Supekar et al., 2010). As the connectivity across the default mode network brain regions strengthens from childhood through adolescence into adulthood, it is possible that the default mode brain regions mature in a manner reflective of cultural and social identity.

By young adulthood, ethnic self-identity is correlated with brain activity with the default mode network, including the MPFC, anterior cingulate cortex (ACC), and PCC (Mathur, Harada, & Chiao, 2012, Figure 17.2). For instance, African Americans show increased neural response within the default mode network relative to Caucasian Americans, who show increased neural response within the medial temporal lobe, such as the bilateral hippocampus. Degree of ethnic identity across African Americans and Caucasian Americans predicts the degree of activation within the MPFC, ACC, and PCC during empathy for group members, suggesting that the social knowledge representation within the medial prefrontal and cingulate brain regions varies as a function of the experience with formation of an ethnic identity during adolescence. Hence, it is plausible that the cultural experience of belonging, affirmation, achievement, and community commitment for ethnic youth with their social group shapes the neural basis of self and identity during neuronal maturation in adolescence. Changes during cultural and biological maturation of self and identity during adolescence are likely important mechanisms that subsequently support psychological well-being (Roberts et al., 1999).

Emotion

From an early age, infants can detect differences in emotional expressions. The ability to perceive and express emotions continues to develop into childhood and adolescence. The experience of emotion changes during adolescence with the onset of puberty, with changes in hormonal levels that are gender-specific. By early adolescence, youth demonstrate the ability to recognize self-conscious emotions (Somerville et al., 2013).

By adulthood, limbic regions associated with emotion demonstrate differential response as a function of cultural learning. In cultures with a history of majority–minority group relations, unconscious or implicit associations may be reflected in limbic-region response to members of social groups. In the United States, amygdala response to Caucasian Americans and African Americans varies as a function of degree of unconscious or implicit association, likely due to the enhanced learning or familiarity with members of the majority group (Phelps et al., 2000; Cunningham et al., 2004). This enhanced amygdala response to members of minority social groups does not emerge until adolescence, providing support for a hypothesis of cultural learning of unconscious or implicit bias during youth (Telzer et al., 2013). Importantly, greater peer diversity is related to reduced amygdala response to faces of minority group members, likely reflecting the efficacy of ethnic group contact as a cultural treatment for social bias.

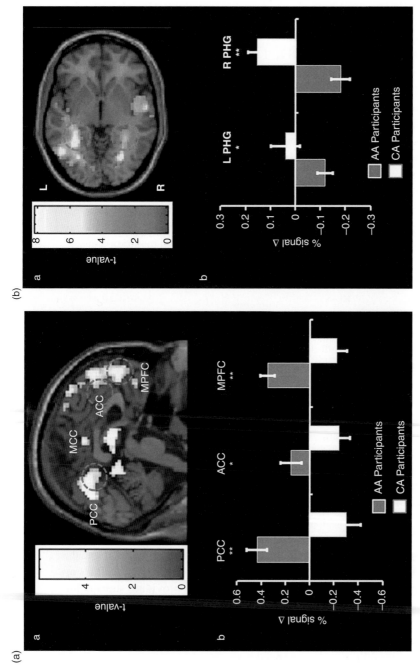

Figure 17.2. *Neural basis of ethnic identification in adults within the (a) default cortical midline structures and (b) bilateral parahippocampal lobes (adapted from Mathur, Harada, & Chiao, 2012).*

Notably, the amygdala also shows increased response to members of one's own cultural group when perceiving fear expressed by an adult group member (Elfenbein & Ambady, 2002). This heightened biological response for group members likely is due to the enhanced processing of group member's emotion when a social signal of threat to a group member is observed (Chiao et al., 2008, Figure 17.3). Both Caucasian Americans and Native Japanese show enhanced amygdala response to fear faces, indicating that this biological response for group members occurs across geography and culture. When viewing a group member who feels fear, others within the group may be more likely to infer that group members are in need of help.

The developmental trajectory of the cultural preference for recognizing emotion in group members remains relatively unknown. Little is known about whether or not this cultural preference is learned from parents, teachers, or peers. While the infant ability to detect emotions from the face occurs automatically, how infants differentiate emotions expressed from group members remains relatively unknown. Peer influence is an important mechanism of oblique and horizontal cultural transmission during development. Given that during infancy and early childhood, much of the emotional communication occurs between parents and child, it is plausible that the knowledge representations of self and others that emerge as a function of autobiographical memory in childhood integrates with knowledge representations of emotion through cultural learning with family and close others. By adolescence, the developmental experiences of forming an ethnic identity that emerges in context with the social group likely allows for the culturally learned psychological and biological preference for emotions expressed by group members. Maturation of functional connectivity within the cortical midline structures as well as with limbic regions, such as the amygdala, from childhood to adolescence likely allows for the heightened neural transmission and integration of social and emotional knowledge.

While the understanding of how culture affects the development of emotion recognition from early childhood to adulthood in the brain is not well formed, the role of culture in shaping emotional experience during development is better understood. Cultural transmission of parental values affects how the brain experiences reward. Family obligation in Latino culture reflects a set of cultural expectations that can affect how reward is subjectively experienced (Fuligni, 2001). The cultural expectation to help other family members, even when costly to oneself, reflects collectivistic cultural norms or family obligations. Latino communities that endorse collectivistic cultural values may experience rewards for others as rewards for the self, due to the overlap of self and other knowledge representation (Telzer et al., 2010). Telzer and colleagues (2010) recently showed that Latinos show greater response in neural reward regions during costly donation to family, rather than reward to the self, due to the collectivistic cultural norms that encourage an experience of reward for other family members as a reward to the self.

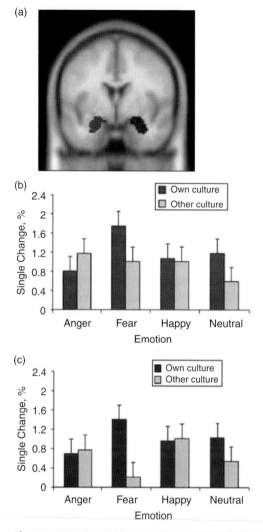

Figure 17.3. *(a–c) Greater bilateral amygdala response to fear faces expressed by group members (adapted from Chiao et al., 2008).*

Empathy

The experience of sharing emotion with one's self and others reflects the capacity for empathy. Affective empathy refers to the sharing of emotional experience, whereas cognitive empathy refers to the sharing of emotional knowledge. While the desire to alleviate the pain and suffering of others is universal, the ways that pain and suffering are alleviated may be distinct across cultures. Cultural values, practices and beliefs may regulate brain responses during observation of the pain and suffering of others as well as the extent to which empathy and altruistic responses readily occur.

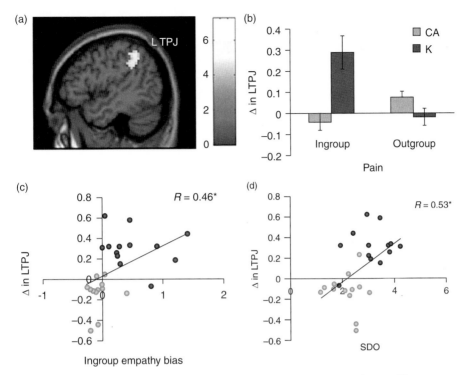

Figure 17.4. *(a–d) Greater left TPJ response to group members in Koreans predicts ingroup empathy bias and social dominance orientation.*

Cultural values modulate neural mechanisms of empathy. Hierarchical cultures that expect and value adherence to authority may encourage cognitive routes to empathy, including perspective-taking; by contrast, egalitarian cultures that expect fairness and reciprocity may emphasize affective routes to empathy, including affect sharing or simulation. In a cross-cultural neuroimaging study of young adult Koreans and Caucasian Americans, Cheon and colleagues (2011) found that hierarchical values predict neural response within the bilateral temporoparietal junction (TPJ) during intergroup empathy (Figure 17.4). In particular, people who endorse hierarchical values showed increased neural activity within the bilateral TPJ when empathizing with people from their culture relative to other cultures. Furthermore, left TPJ activity predicts the degree to which people report feeling empathy for cultural group members. The left TPJ has previously been implicated in conceptual understanding of other people's beliefs, or "theory of mind." Theory of mind represents a cognitive route to understanding others, including empathy, by inferring mental states of others from shared social rules or the social outcomes of others. In hierarchical cultures where adherence to authority is highly valued, the fact that the majority of social group members are behaving in accordance with social norms is more likely to encourage perspective-taking and shared cultural experience. These findings show for the first time that cultural values of social hierarchy shape empathic neural response.

Cultural values of other-focusedness also predict neural responses during empathy. Other-focusedness is a component of interdependence or collectivistic values that involves the extent to which a person is attentive and connected to other people's emotional experience and outcomes. By young adulthood, cultural differences in neural networks associated with other-focusedness occur when empathizing with group members living through a natural disaster (e.g., tsunami). Koreans, but not Caucasian Americans, show increased neural response within the affective empathy neural network as a function of other-focusedness. Koreans who demonstrate greater attentiveness or social connection with other people's emotions also show greater neural response when observing the emotional pain of others within several affective empathy brain regions, including the ACC, bilateral insula, right amygdala, and MPFC. By contrast, Caucasian Americans show increased neural response within brain regions associated with social cognition and self-regulation, including the left orbitofrontal cortex and right inferior frontal cortex. For interdependent cultures, the perception of pain and suffering of other group members during a natural disaster may readily elicit a strong emotional response that guides appropriate altruistic and helping behavior, such as approaching victims with disaster relief and aid. Because interdependent cultures emphasize the importance of other peoples' feelings and outcomes in how one's own self feels and behaves, the social goal to alleviate the pain and suffering in others may be more immediate and the psychological processes that guide behavior toward altruistic responses may be more readily responsive.

Neural networks associated with social cognition are largely mature during adolescence, but little is known about the extent to which culture affects the adolescent empathic brain (Choudhury, 2010). In Western individualistic cultures, adolescence is typically characterized by social interactions shaped through family, peer, and community influence. Community influences, including friends, teachers and peer groups, comprise a majority of social time for teens; the social environment for adolescents is unique and challenging in its emphasis on negotiating novel complex social interactions, involving greater autonomy from family and group decision-making with friends and peers, as well as negotiating the biological changes of the body associated with puberty that affect how others' perceive youth. Treating others with fairness and social affection while regulating emotional responses in situations involving unfairness or social exclusion encompasses a wide degree of adolescent social interactions. The enhanced sensitivity to social connection and a feeling of belonging (Somerville, 2013), including empathy for victims of social exclusion, during adolescence is associated with greater neural response within social cognitive brain regions typically observed in adults (Overgaauw, Guroglu, Rieffe, & Crone, 2014; Masten, Eisenberger, Pfeifer, & Dapretto, 2010).

Adolescents may be particularly sensitive to fairness and social connection across both intrapersonal and intergroup domains. Not only may the quality of peer interaction and friendships shape adolescent brain and behavior within a cultural group, it may also affect the quality of intergroup interactions with peers and friends of other cultures and ethnicities. In pluralistic societies, the frequency of social interactions with other teens who may have diverse cultural values and beliefs, as well as future orientations and goals, may present a unique challenge and opportunity, allowing for greater acceptance of nonconformity in teen social groups, while at the same time making social connection and empathy across majority and minority group members less automatic and more reliant on cultural cognition, including knowledge of others, perspective-taking, and theory of mind. A feeling of belonging may be more readily acquired in peer groups with other minority peers, particularly for youth with greater ethnic identity (Phinney, 1992). Similar to adults, teens may find inter-racial interactions challenging to navigate due to the need to balance competing social influences, such as the desire for egalitarianism and colorblindness, while acknowledging existing cultural stereotypes and biases of past generations (Killen, Henning, Kelly, Crystal, & Ruck, 2007; Shelton & Richeson, 2006). Successful development of close interracial relationships during youth may be effectively nurtured within educational communities by encouraging participation in shared school activities, including clubs, and close interracial friendships (Yip, Seaton, & Sellers, 2010).

Self- and Emotion Regulation

By adulthood, successful navigation of social interactions in diverse social environments is reliant on self-regulation (Richeson & Shelton, 2003) and emotion regulation (Goldenberg, Halperin, van Zomeren, & Gross, 2015; Halperin & Gross, 2011). Regulation of one's own desires and emotions requires a number of distinct strategies. Cognitive reappraisal represents a strategy whereby people rethink or reappraise a given emotion. For example, observing an expression of sadness may be reappraised into a more positive emotional state (e.g., a person is crying because they feel joy or relief after a school debate). By contrast, emotional suppression is a strategy whereby people suppress or control the physical expression or physiological manifestation of a given emotion. For instance, an arousing feeling of happiness or laughter may be suppressed if experienced in an inappropriate social context (e.g., receiving a personal note of congratulations or humor before math class). Emotion suppression occurs more readily in collectivistic cultures by adulthood and is thought to reflect an effective manner of emotional control. Asian adults show reduced parietal late positive potential (LPP) during emotional suppression, while European American adults show no LPP response during suppression (Murata, Moser, & Kitayama, 2013). The LPP may be interpreted as a late physiological index of emotional response. While Asians exhibit a down-regulation of emotion strategy when suppressing emotions, European Americans, who are culturally trained to express rather than suppress emotions, do not. These findings provide convergent evidence from behavior and physiology of a cultural difference in the psychophysiology of emotion regulation.

Regulating one's own social behavior may involve recruitment of cognitive resources associated with the prefrontal cortex, including executive function. For instance, maintaining and retrieving social information from working memory serves as one form of self-regulation; for adolescents, remembering the names and hobbies of peers in appropriate social situations may regularly recruit self-regulatory mechanisms. During interracial and intercultural social interactions, successful recruitment of executive function may be challenged possibly due to the quality of social relations which may enhance the ability to remember social information in an effective manner. The motivation to appear unprejudiced or unbiased may also serve as an important factor when navigating diverse social interactions. Heightened self-monitoring of communication to others, including regulating of possible expressions of cultural bias, may also present an important opportunity and challenge for youth.

During adolescence, the brain undergoes a number of structural and functional changes that facilitate effective navigation of the social environment. Brain regions within the frontal lobe, including the ACC, as well as the dorsolateral prefrontal cortex, undergo significant age-related changes during youth that are accompanied by increased cognitive control (Casey, Tottenham, Liston, & Durston, 2005; Fjell et al., 2012). The ability to exert inhibitory control, to filter irrelevant information from the environment, and to respond to relevant information enhances one's ability to conform to social norms and relies on prefrontal cortex. From childhood to adulthood, the recruitment of prefrontal cortex becomes more spatially focal and distinct during recruitment of cognitive control. During adolescence, higher education is an age-predictor of cognitive control ability, likely due to the habits and practices acquired at school (Noble, Korgaonkar, Grieve, & Brickman, 2013). By adulthood, cultural values of collectivism predict neural engagement of inhibitory control, particularly within the rostral ACC (rACC) (Pornpattananangkul et al., 2016). People who endorse higher levels of behavioral consistency as a cultural value show greater response within the rACC during an inhibition task. These findings reflect evidence for a cultural difference in the engagement of cognitive control brain regions during cognitive inhibition.

The ability to effectively regulate cognition is often accompanied by emotional signals that reinforce the appropriate deployment of cognitive inhibition in a given social situation. Self-conscious emotions, such as embarrassment, indicate to the self that cognitive inhibition or control may not have been appropriately engaged. For adolescents, the simple belief that a peer is watching them is a sufficient social situation to induce embarrassment, a feeling associated with increased response within the MPFC and connectivity between the MPFC and striatum (Somerville et al., 2013). Connectivity between the MPFC and the striatum represents self-relevant emotional cortical circuitry. These findings suggest that the regulation of a self-conscious emotion such as embarrassment may not occur as readily in youth relative to adults; the increased probability of the experience of embarrassment for youth due to social presence reflects the habit of enhanced social sensitivity or self-monitoring in youth.

By adulthood, cultural differences in self-conscious emotions, including the antecedents and consequences of feeling shame, guilt, and embarrassment, characterize a majority of social interactions. For collectivistic cultures, failure to fulfill social obligations or meet societal expectations may be accompanied by feelings of guilt and shame in one's self; by contrast, for individualistic cultures, failure to fulfill social obligations may be accompanied by self-conscious emotions accompanied by self-serving biases, which facilitate the attribution or cause of the negative event to an external factor. For adolescents, the extent to which culture shapes the engagement of self-conscious emotions and self-serving biases when responding to negative events or emotions remains unknown. How youth learn to respond to failures and successes may depend largely on their culture's attributional style, assigning responsibility for an event toward either internal or external factors. Cultural norms, practices, and beliefs guide youth toward factors that regulate the feeling of positive or negative emotions in response to positive or negative social outcomes.

Future Directions in Cultural Neuroscience of the Developing Brain in Adolescence

Youth represents a pivotal developmental period when cultural and bio-logical influences shape human experience. Much of adolescence is dedicated to the maturation of neurobiological mechanisms within prefrontal cortex that enhance the ability of teens to regulate and control their emotions and behavior. While a large degree of neural development during adolescence relies on cultural learning and experience through relationships with peers, teachers, and family, such social interactions also reflect complex neurobiological changes due to genetic and epigenetic factors. Social cognitive brain mechanisms in adolescents reflect similar circuitry as adults, although varying in size, degree of connectivity, and recruitment during social and cognitive tasks. Notably, cortical networks for social cognition are regulated by specific functional polymorphisms or genes that are known to modulate the degree of neurotransmission at the synapse. While much is known about gene x environment interaction in adult social behavior (Cheon & Hong, 2016), less well understood is how genetic and environmental factors interact in the adolescent brain and behavior. Even less well understood is how epigenetic and environmental factors interact in the brain and behavior during youth (Casey et al, 2010; Connelly & Morris, 2016; Viding, Williamson, & Hariri, 2006). Finally, recent demonstrations of cultural differences in gene x environment interaction in adult behavior (Kim et al., 2010; Sasaki, LeClair, West, & Kim, 2016) emphasize the importance of understanding the developmental trajectory of genetic, epigenetic, and environmental interaction in brain and behavior across cultures (Chiao & Blizinsky, 2013). Given the importance of culture and genes in the adaptive production of behavior from an evolutionary perspective (Boyd & Richerson, 1985), it is not surprising that dual inheritance influences the develop-mental processes during adolescence at the neural and behavioral levels of analy-sis. However, future cultural neuroscience research is needed to identify the specific cultural and biological mechanisms that predict successful functioning in youth social, cognitive, and affective development (Chiao, Li, Seligman, & Turner, 2016).

Implications of Cultural Neuroscience for the Developing Brain: Closing the Gap in Adolescent Health Disparities

Adolescence represents a developmental period of unique challenges, including the acquisition of cultural behaviors that may encourage social acceptance, but at a risk to physical and mental health, such as diet, physical inactivity, substance abuse, and obesity. National surveys indicate that risk for substance abuse varies across racial and ethnic youth groups. For instance, Whites and Hispanics are more likely to learn to smoke during adolescence compared to African Americans and Asian Americans (Ellickson, Orlando, Tucker, & Klein, 2004). Across multiple health risk behavior indicators, Whites and Asian Americans are at lower risk compared to Native American youth transitioning into adulthood (Harris, Gordon-Larsen, Chantala, & Udry, 2006). The engagement of increased health risk behaviors during adolescence represents an important and puzzling trend, suggesting the need for implementation of health promotion and interventions that are culturally and biologically effective for youth (Alegria, Vallas, & Pumariega, 2010; Lee et al., 2014). Understanding the cultural and biological factors that contribute to the commitment to healthy behavior from childhood to adulthood may help to close the gap in health disparities during adolescence. Research paradigms in cultural neuroscience that integrate cultural and neurobiological approaches to the study of the mind, brain, and behavior of youth aid in the discovery of novel models that predict adolescent health behavior, and effectively inform health promotion and intervention strategies for diverse, multicultural communities.

Acknowledgments

Special thanks to Genna Bebko, Vani Mathur, Bobby Cheon, Alissa Mrazek, Katherine Blizinsky, and Narun Pornpattananangkul for thoughtful discussion, Jennifer Pfeifer and Xinxin Chen from the 2012 Society for Research in Adolescence workshop on cultural neuroscience, and Eva Telzer, Liz Losin, and Carol Lee from the 2013 Jean Piaget Society symposium on social development and neuroscience for their helpful insights.

References

Alegria, M., Vallas, M., & Pumariega, A. J. (2010). Racial and ethnic disparities in pediatric mental health. *Child & Adolescent Psychiatry Clinics of North America, 19*(4), 759–74.

Arnett, J. J. (1999). Adolescent storm and stress, reconsidered. *American Psychologist, 54*(5), 317–26.

Berry, J. W. (1997). Immigration, acculturation, and adaptation. *Applied Psychology: An International Review, 46*(1), 5–68.

Blakemore, S. J., & Mills, K. L. (2014). Is adolescence a sensitive period for sociocultural processing? *Annual Review of Psychology, 65*, 187–207.

Blum, R. W., & Nelson-Mari, K. (2004). The health of young people in a global context. *Journal of Adolescent Health, 35*(5), 402–418.

Boyd, R., & Richerson, P. J. (1985). *Culture and the evolutionary process.* Chicago: University of Chicago Press.

Casey, B. J., Soliman, F., Bath, K. G., & Glatt, C. E. (2010). Imaging genetics and development: challenges and promises. *Human Brain Mapping, 31*(6), 838–51.

Casey, B. J., Tottenham, N., Liston, C., & Durston, S. (2005). Imaging the developing brain: what have we learned about cognitive development? *Trends in Cognitive Science, 9*(3), 104–10.

Cheon, B. K., & Hong, Y.-Y. (2016). The cultural neuroscience of intergroup bias. In Chiao, J. Y., Li, S.-C., Seligman, R., Turner, R. (Eds.). *The Oxford Handbook of Cultural Neuroscience.* New York, NY: Oxford University Press.

Cheon, B. K., Im, D. M., Harada, T., Kim, J. S., Mathur, V. A., Scimeca, J. M., Parrish, T. B., Park H. W., & Chiao, J. Y. (2011). Cultural influences on neural basis of intergroup empathy. *Neuroimage, 57*(2), 642–50.

Chiao, J. Y., & Ambady, N. (2007). Cultural neuroscience: Parsing universality and diversity across levels of analysis. In S. Kitayama & D. Cohen (Eds.), *Handbook of Cultural Psychology* (pp. 237–254). New York, NY: Guilford Press.

Chiao, J. Y., & Blizinsky, K. D. (2010). Culture-gene coevolution of individualism-collectivism and the serotonin transporter gene (5-HTTLPR). *Proceedings of the Royal Society B: Biological Sciences, 277*(1681), 529–37.

Chiao, J. Y., & Blizinsky, K. D. (2013). Population disparities in mental health: Insights from cultural neuroscience. *American Journal of Public Health, 103*(1), S122–S132.

Chiao, J. Y., Cheon, B. K., Pornpattananangkul, N., Mrazek, A. J., & Blizinsky, K. D. (2013). Cultural neuroscience: Understanding human diversity. In M. J. Gelfand, Y. Y. Hong, & C. Y. Chiu (Eds.) *Advances in Culture and Psychology.* Oxford, UK: Oxford University Press.

Chiao, J. Y., Iidaka, T., Gordon, H. L., Nogawa, J., Bar, M., Aminoff, E., Sadato, N., & Ambady, N. (2008). Cultural specificity in amygdala response to fear faces. *Journal of Cognitive Neuroscience, 20*(12), 2167–74.

Chiao, J. Y., Li, S.-C., Seligman, R., & Turner, R. (Eds.) (2016). *The Oxford handbook of cultural neuroscience.* New York, NY: Oxford University Press.

Choudhury, S. (2010). Culturing the adolescent brain: what can neuroscience learn from anthropology? *Social Cognitive and Affective Neuroscience, 5*, 159–167.

Connelly, J. J. & Morris, J. P. (2016). Epigenetics of social behavior. In J. Y. Chiao, S.-C. Li, R. Seligman, & R. Turner (Eds.). *The Oxford handbook of cultural neuroscience.* New York, NY: Oxford University Press.

Conway, M. A., & Pleydell-Pearce, C. W. (2000). The construction of autobiographical memories in the self-memory system. *Psychological Bulletin, 807*(2), 261–288.

Cunningham, W. A., Johnson, M. K., Raye, C. L., Gatenby, C. J., Gore, J. C., & Banaji, M. R. (2004). Separable neural components in the processing of black and white faces. *Psychological Science, 15*(12), 806–813.

Elfenbein, H. A., & Ambady, N. (2002). Is there an in-group advantage in emotion recognition? *Psychological Bulletin, 128*(2), 243–249.

Ellickson, P. L., Orlando, M., Tucker, J. S., & Klein, D. J. (2004). From adolescence to young adulthood: racial/ethnic disparities in smoking. *American Journal of Public Health*, *94*(2), 293–299.

Fincher, C. L., Thornhill, R., Murray, D. R., & Schaller, M. (2008). Pathogen prevalence predicts human cross-cultural variability in individualism/collectivism. *Proceedings of the Biological Sciences*, *275*(1640), 1279–1285.

Fjell, A. M., Walhovd, K. B., Brown, T. T., Kuperman, J. M., Chung, Y., Hagler, D. J. Jr., Venkatraman, V., Roddey, J. C., Erhart, M., McCabe, C., Akshoomoff, N., Amaral, D. G., Bloss, C. S., Libiger, O., Darst, B. F., Schork, N. J., Casey, B. J., Chang, L., Ernst, T. M., Gruen, J. R., Kaufmann, W. E., Kenet, T., Frazier, J., Murray, S. S., Sowell, E. R., van Zijl, P., Mostofsky, S., Jernigan, T. L., & Dale, A. M.; Pediatric Imaging, Neurocognition, and Genetics Study. (2012). Multimodal imaging of the self-regulating developing brain. *Proceedings of the National Academy of Sciences*, *109*(48), 19620–19625.

Fuligni, A. J. (2001). Family obligation and the academic motivation of adolescents from Asian, Latin American, and European backgrounds. *New Directions in Child and Adolescent Development*, *94*, 61–75.

Gelertner, J., Kranzler, H., & Cubells, J. F. (1997). Serotonin transporter protein (SLC6A4) allele and haplotype frequencies and linkage disequilibria in African- and European-American and Japanese populations and in alcohol-dependent subjects. *Human Genetics*, *101*, 241–246.

Goldenberg, A., Halperin, E., van Zomeren, M., & Gross, J. J. (2015). The process model of group-based emotion: Integrating intergroup emotion and emotion regulation perspectives. *Personality and Social Psychological Review*, *20*(2), 118–141.

Halperin, E., & Gross, J. J. (2011). Emotion regulation in violent conflict: reappraisal, hope and support for humanitarian aid to the opponent in wartime. *Cognition and Emotion*, *25*(7), 1228–36.

Harris, K. M., Gordon-Larsen, P., Chantala, K., & Udry, R. (2006). Longitudinal trends in race/ethnic disparities in leading health indicators from adolescence to young adulthood. *Archives of Pediatric Adolescent Medicine*, *160*, 74–81.

Henrich, J., Heine, S. J., & Norenzayan, A. (2010). The weirdest people in the world? *Behavioral and Brain Sciences*, *33*(2–3), 61–83.

Killen, M., Henning, A., Kelly, M. C., Crystal, D., & Ruck, M. (2007). Evaluations of interracial peer encounters by majority and minority children and adolescents. *International Journal of Behavioral Development*, *31*(5), 491–500.

Kim, H. S., Sherman, D. K., Sasaki, J. Y., Xu, J., Chu, T. Q., Ryu, C., Suh, E. M., Graham, K., & Taylor, S. E. (2010). Culture, distress, oxytocin receptor polymorphism (OXTR) interact to influence emotional support seeking. *Proceedings of the National Academy of Sciences*, *107*(36), 15717–21.

Lee, F. S., Heimer, H., Giedd, J. N., Lein, E. S., Sestan, N., Weinberger, D. R., & Casey, B. J. (2014). Adolescent mental health – opportunity and obligation. *Science*, *346*(6209), 547–549.

Lesch, K. P., Bengel, D., Heils, A., Sabol, S. Z., Greenberg, B. D., Petri, S., Benjamin, J., Muller, C. R., Hamer, D. H., & Murphy, S. L. (1996). Association of anxiety-related traits with a polymorphism in the serotonin transporter gene regulatory region. *Science*, *274*(5292), 1527–1531.

Masten, C. L., Eisenberger, N. I., Pfeifer, J. H., & Dapretto, M. (2010). Witnessing peer rejection during early adolescence: neural correlates of empathy for experiences of social exclusion. *Social Neuroscience*, *5*(*5–6)*, 496–507.

Mathur, V. A., Harada, T., & Chiao, J. Y. (2012). Racial identification modulates default network activity for same- and other-races. *Human Brain Mapping*, *33*(8), 1883–1893.

Mead, M. (1928). *Coming of age in Samoa*. New York, NY: Morrow.

Murata, A., Moser, J. S. & Kitayama, S. (2013). Culture shapes electrocortical responses during emotion suppression. *Social Cognitive and Affective Neuroscience*, *8*(5), 595–601.

Noble, K. G., Houston, S. M., Brito, N. H., Bartsch, H., Kan, E., Kuperman, J. M., Akshoomoff, N., Amaral, D. G., Bloss, C. S., Libiger, O., Schork, N. J., Murray, S. S., Casey, B. J., Chang, L., Ernst, T. M., Frazier, J. A., Gruen, J. R., Kennedy, D. N., Van Zijl, P., Mostofsky, S., Kaufmann, W. E., Kenet, T., Dale, A. M., Jernigan, T. L., & Sowell, E. R. (2015). Family income, parental education and brain structure in children and adolescents. *Nature Neuroscience*, *18*, 773–778.

Noble, K. G. Korgaonkar, M. S., Grieve, S. M., & Brickman, A. M. (2013). Higher education is an age-independent predictor of white matter integrity and cognitive control in late adolescence. *Developmental Science*, *16*(5), 653–664.

Overgaauw, S., Guroglu, B., Rieffe, C., & Crone, E. A. (2014). Behavior and neural correlates of empathy in adolescents. *Developmental Neuroscience*, *36*(*3–4)*, 210–219.

Patel, V., Fischer, A. J., Hetrick, S., & McGorry, P. (2007). Mental health of young people: a global public-health challenge. *Lancet*, *369*(9569), 1302–1313.

Pfeifer, J. H., & Peake, S. J. (2012). Self-development: Integrating cognitive, socioemotional, and neuroimaging perspectives. *Developmental Cognitive Neuroscience*, *2*, 55–69.

Phelps, E. A., O'Connor, K. J., Cunningham, W. A., Funayama, E. S., Gatenby, J. C., Gore, J. C., & Banaji, M. R. (2000). Performance on indirect measures of race evaluation predicts amygdala activation. *Journal of Cognitive Neuroscience*, *12*(5), 729–738.

Phinney, J. S. (1992). The Multigroup Ethnic Identity Measure: A new scale for use with diverse groups. *Journal of Adolescent Research*, *7*(2), 156–176.

Pornpattananangkul, N., Hariri, A. R., Harada, T., Mano, Y., Komeda, H., Parrish, T. B., Sadato, N., Iidaka, T., & Chiao, J. Y. (2016). Cultural influences on neural basis of inhibitory control. Manuscript under revision.

Richeson, J. A. & Shelton, J. N. (2003). When prejudice does not pay: effects of interracial contact on executive function. *Psychological Science*, *14*(3), 287–290.

Roberts, R. E., Phinney, J. S., Masse, L. C., Chen, Y. R., Roberts, C. R., & Romero, A. (1999). The structure of ethnic identity of young adolescents from diverse ethnocultural groups. *Journal of Early Adolescence*, *19*(3), 301–322.

Sasaki, J. Y., LeClair, J., West, A. L., & Kim, H. S. (2016). Application of the gene-culture interaction framework in health contexts. In J. Y. Chiao, S.-C. Li, R. Seligman, & R. Turner (Eds.). *The Oxford handbook of cultural neuroscience*. New York, NY: Oxford University Press.

Sebastian, C., Burnett, S., & Blakemore, S. J. (2008). Development of the self-concept during adolescence. *Trends in Cognitive Science*, *12*(11), 441–446.

Shelton, J. N., & Richeson, J. A. (2006). Ethnic minorities' racial attitudes and contact experiences with while people. *Current Diversity and Ethnic Minority Psychology*, *12*(1), 149–164.

Somerville, L. H. (2013). The teenage brain: sensitivity to social evaluation. *Current Directions in Psychological Science, 22*, 121–127.

Somerville, L. H., Jones, R. M., Ruberry, E. J., Dyke, J. P., Glover, G., & Casey, B. J. (2013). The medial prefrontal cortex and the emergence of self-conscious emotion in adolescence. *Psychological Science, 24*(8), 1554–1562.

Supekar, K., Uddin, L. Q., Prater, K., Amin, H., Greicius, M. D., & Menon, V. (2010). Development of functional and structural connectivity within the default mode network in young children. *Neuroimage, 52*(1), 290–301.

Telzer, E. H., Flannery, J., Shapiro, M., Humphreys, K. L., Goff, B., Gabard-Durman, L., Gee D. G., & Tottenham, N. (2013). Early experience shapes amygdala sensitivity to race: An international adoption design. *Journal of Neuroscience, 33*, 13484–13488.

Telzer, E. H., Masten, C. L., Bermna, E. T., Lieberman, M. D., Fuligni, A. J. (2010). Gaining while giving: An fMRI study of the rewards of family assistance among White and Latino youth. *Social Neuroscience, 5*, 508–518.

UNICEF (2011). Adolescence: An age of opportunity. *The State of the World's Children.*

Viding, E., Williamson, D. E., & Hariri, A. R. (2006). Developmental imaging genetics: Challenges and promises for translational research. *Development and Psychopathology, 18*, 877–892.

Wang, Q. (2006). Culture and the development of self-knowledge. *Current Directions in Psychological Science, 15*(4), 182–187.

Wang, Q., Shao, Y., & Li, Y. J. (2010). "My way or Mom's way?" The bilingual and bicultural self in Hong Kong Chinese children and adolescents. *Child Development, 81*(2), 555–567.

Yip, T., Seaton, E. K., & Sellers, R. M. (2010). Interracial and intraracial contact, school-level diversity, and change in racial identity status among African American adolescents. *Child Development, 81*(5), 1431–1444.

PART III

Language and Communicative Development

(Edited by Nancy Budwig and Katherine Nelson)

18 The Evolution of Linguistic Communication: Piagetian Insights

Eva Jablonka

I was first introduced to the work of Piaget in 1978, by Yehuda Elkana, a philosopher of science and a renaissance man, who became a lifelong friend. Yehuda knew that I was interested in evolutionary biology and in the then-raging sociobiology debate, and he brought me a new book that had just been translated into English: Piaget's *Behavior and Evolution* (the French original was published in 1976). I read the book overnight and filled it with notes. I was critical of some aspects of it, such as Piaget's interpretation of Waddington (my favorite evolutionist) and his misuse of "phenocopy," but overall I was very impressed with the insights and the approach, so I started reading his other books. Three years later, shortly after Piaget's death, Yehuda began planning a conference on Piaget's work, which was intended to discuss not only Piaget's great contributions to developmental psychology, but also his views about biology, anthropology, and philosophy. I was "responsible" for the biology part, and Emil Grunzweig, a young philosopher with an interest in the social sciences, was to organize the anthropology part. The conference never materialized. Emil was murdered during a *Peace Now* rally on February 10, 1983, when a right-wing thug threw a grenade into the crowd. The conference was cancelled, partly because we all lost heart. Participating, more than thirty years later, in a conference organized by the Piaget Society was, for me, the closing of an important circle.

I will discuss, in the context of the evolution of linguistic communication, several broad themes that were central to Piaget's constructive approach. Piaget, a structuralist and a system theorist, believed that adaptive and plastic adjustments in behavior – guided by the inherent constraints and affordances of the system (the systems' "laws") and mediated by learning, niche choice, and niche construction – precede genetic adaptation, and that through genetic assimilation, physiological, ontogenetically constructed adaptations become genetically entrenched. He also argued that processes of internal selection that are guided by the system's dynamic structure are involved in the developmental construction of phenotypic adjustments, and that there are therefore always two levels at which selection operates – by internal processes (developmental stabilization/selection processes) and by the external environment (classical Darwinian selection). In addition, a third level,

Dedicated to the memories of Yehuda Elkana and Emil Grunzweig.

that of cultural selection, has to be added when one is discussing human evolution. Cultural practices, including linguistic practices, are based on cooperation among individuals, and Piaget believed that the development of reason depends on communication and cooperation, an idea recently explored in depth in an evolutionary context by Michael Tomasello (2014). The status of human linguistic communication in the overall development and evolution of human reason was therefore an important issue for Piaget.

Constructive Development and Constructive Evolution

> [D]evelopments are subordinated from the outset to two teleonomies, one internal and the other related to the environment.
>
> (Piaget, 1978, p. 152).

In his writings about development and evolution Piaget highlighted the role of organizational laws that underlie the activity of developing and evolving biological systems, and the inherent activity and agency of the organism, especially the neurally mediated activity of animals.[1] His discussion of living organization and of the dynamic processes of integration that are involved in ontogenetic development was influenced by the work of developmental system biologists such as Paul Weiss and Conrad Waddington. Weiss underscored three related aspects of dynamic biological organization: (i) a biological system composed of multiple parts must embody overall system dynamics; (ii) the sum variability of the constituent parts far exceeds the variability of the system as a whole; (iii) perturbations of the system, and even loss of some parts, can be compensated by the system's cybernetic organization, so that the functioning of the system remains intact (Piaget 1978, chapter 5). The functional significance of any genetic change, random or directed, therefore depends as much on the internal organizational dynamics of the system as on the environmental conditions to which it responds. Similar ideas were presented by Conrad Hal Waddington, who emphasized the two complementary aspects of every developmental system: canalization and plasticity. *Canalization* is the process of adjustment of developmental pathways that bring about a uniform phenotypic result in spite of genetic and environmental variations (Waddington, 1957). *Plasticity* is the other side of the coin: it is the generation of variant forms of morphology, physiology, and/or behavior from the same genotype in response to different environmental circumstances. The two processes are intertwined: for plasticity to be manifest, some underlying processes must be canalized – for example, the production of diverse linguistic messages by humans depends on some developmentally canalized brain

---

1 Since a comprehensive discussion of Piaget's structuralist system approach to biology and psychology is beyond the scope of this chapter, I draw here mainly on *Behavior and Evolution* (1978), and on *Language and Learning: The Debate Between Jean Piaget and Noam Chomsky* (1980), because it was in these books that Piaget discussed most clearly and explicitly the evolution of behavior and the evolution of language. The structuralist position on which Piaget drew and to which he contributed is summarized by Goodwin (2009).

processes. Canalization, on the other hand, requires plasticity at an underlying level – for example, for normal behavior in a stroke victim to occur, there must be plastic compensatory mechanisms at the neural level in the non-damaged parts of the brain. Understanding behavioral responses requires an understanding of the complex, flexible, and adaptive organizational dynamics of the system.

The point of departure of Piaget's analysis of evolutionary change was the responsive, developing phenotype, especially plastic behavioral responses and learning. During development, variations in phenotypic responses to a new challenging environment (which can be the result of the organism's own activities) are selected if there is a hereditary (e.g., genotypic) basis for individual differences in responsiveness. In a normal, "standard" environment, phenotypic variation in a population is small and one often observes striking phenotypic uniformity (the famous "wild type"). Equilibrium is dynamically maintained in spite of inevitable fluctuations. However, once the environment drastically changes, development is decanalized and genetic variations that were previously cryptic (unexpressed) now have phenotypic effects and can be selected. The environmental conditions in this case are both inducing and selecting. This process can lead to the evolution of anatomical and morphological innate structures such as the calluses with which ostriches are born. Waddington (1957) called this process of induction followed by the selection of induced responses that culminated in a more canalized "innate" responses *genetic assimilation*. Piaget recognized that it could solve what was for him a big problem: that of the evolution of highly canalized cognitive structures that lead to the instinctive behaviors that scaffold all learning. He wrote:

> The most difficult problem raised – for the non-Lamarckian at any rate – is how to account for the fact that such behavior, which is endogenous inasmuch as it is hereditary, is nevertheless informed about the environment, even to the point of embodying a whole program of action directed toward objects or occurrences outside the organism.
> (Piaget, 1978, p. 73)

Genetic assimilation of effectively "blind" genetic variations can produce, within a few generations, an innate, highly canalized response that mimics a previously learned one – just what Piaget had been searching for.

What about the evolution of plasticity? West-Eberhard (2003) suggested a broader concept than Waddington's, which she calls *genetic accommodation*. Genetic accommodation includes not only the evolution of more canalized phenotypes, as Waddington had suggested, but also of more plastic ones. For example, if the environment becomes more fluctuating, with the different environmental phases inducing different adaptive phenotypes, organisms that express more reliably context-dependent traits will be selected. Importantly, both selection for increased canalization and for increased plasticity are likely to involve a "phenotype first" approach (Palmer, 2009): developmental induction exposes genetic variants to selection in the new inducing environment. As West-Eberhard (2003, p. 20) put it, "genes are followers, not leaders, in evolution." A similar view was advanced by the psychobiologist Gilbert Gottlieb, who developed a notion of plasticity as probabilistic epigenesis, and emphasized the diverse, multi-level, reciprocally interacting inputs into individual development that may be sometimes reconstructed across generations and genetically assimilated (Gottlieb 2007; Jablonka, 2007). This approach, which is close to Piaget's, was marginalized for many years, but has now become part of the current evolutionary-developmental biology (evo-devo) approach to evolution.

Piaget believed that the investigation of developmental adjustments and the developmental laws underlying them should be the starting point in analyses of both ontogeny and phylogeny. He regarded the progressive development of cognition in the child in terms of cumulative developmental adjustments. As the child develops, it goes through a series of stages. At each stage there are processes that change cognitive structures and others that assimilate information into existing structures. As information accumulates, these processes lead eventually to disequilibrium and "push" the developmental trajectory toward the next cognitive-developmental "attractor." These progressive developmental processes are not specific to one particular cognitive capacity (e.g., the linguistic capacity). They lead to coordinated changes in the general intelligence of the child. Piaget generalized this view and applied it not only to child development but also to the way evolutionary processes unfold, suggesting that behaviorally driven developmental adjustments become genetically entrenched during phylogeny, and hence enable the formation of new evolutionary trajectories (Piaget, 1971).

Piaget's view regarding evolutionary change resonates with West-Eberhard's and Gottlieb's more recent and more detailed suggestions. As they argued, when an environmental challenge is novel (for example, a drastic ecological change) there is no "genetic program" in place that can be activated upon encountering it, and the organism adapts phenotypically, mobilizing *general* strategies of adaptation. West-Eberhard called this phenotypic process of adjustment *phenotypic accommodation*. In Gottlieb's terms, this process of probabilistic epigenesis leads to changes in the construction of a "developmental manifold": a multi-level developmental system of interactions. Phenotypic accommodation and probabilistic epigenesis are therefore very close to Piaget's notion of constructive development. As West-Eberhard emphasizes, phenotypic accommodation is mediated through general biological properties such as mechanical flexibility and the multiplicity of partially overlapping regulatory elements that form regulatory, semi-stable networks, and through processes such as the selective stabilization of developmental variations that occur at the cellular, physiological, and behavioral levels (West-Eberhard, 2003). *Developmental selection* is therefore crucial for the adjustment of the animal to its novel environment.

Developmental selection is based on the generation of local variations and interactions, from which only a subset with functional effects is eventually stabilized or amplified. The states the organism reaches (the "attractors") are functional stable or semi-stable states that enable it to cope with its new environment. There are many examples, at every level of biological and social-cultural organization, of adaptive adjustments based on such exploration-stabilization strategies. Prominent examples include the generation of many variant antibody-forming cells in the adaptive immune system, with cells carrying antibody molecules that fit the antigen becoming preferentially amplified (Edelman, 1974); the formation of multiple labile synaptic connections in the brain, only a subset of which are stabilized during embryogenesis or learning following reinforcement (Changeux, Courrége, & Danchin, 1973); trial-and-error learning, with the stabilization of those behaviors that are rewarded or that avoid punishment (Skinner, 1981); and selection of particular technological products by human customers. For Piaget, the child's constructive cognitive development, like all developmental progressions, is based on transiently stabilized strategies of self-organization. Of course, the basic instincts and the processes underlying the general strategies of canalization and plasticity, which are the scaffolds on which learning is constructed, are products of evolution. But progressive development, especially cognitive development, must remain both highly adjustable and coordinated, so it is general rather than domain-specific adaptive strategies that must have evolved.

In addition to developmental considerations that led Piaget to a view of language as an outcome of the development of a general semiotic ability that is subordinate to thought, Piaget believed that his view was more evolutionarily plausible than the alternative view advocated by Noam Chomsky. In the famous debate between Chomsky and Piaget about the nature of language, Piaget suggested that the child learns language through innate *general* learning processes that construct linguistic competence, whereas Chomsky argued that the language capacity, the essence of which is syntax, is a unique and innate organ of the mind, and no learning occurs during language acquisition (Piattelli-Palmarini, 1980). Piaget also maintained that it is far easier to see how language evolved through an increase in general learning ability that was mobilized for both communication and reasoning, than to envisage an evolutionary trajectory leading to Chomsky's baroque, innate, and unique linguistic mental organ.[2]

There are many views today about the evolution of language, which has become a "hot" subject since the 1990s, with some people taking a more Chomskian view (e.g., Longa, 2013) and others a more Piagetian one (e.g., Christiansen & Chater, 2008). In what follows I outline a view of language evolution that tends toward the Piagetian end of the spectrum, describing the evolution of linguistic communication in terms of phenotypic accommodation mediated through cultural evolution and followed by genetic accommodation (Dor & Jablonka, 2000, 2010, 2014).

The Four Dimensions of Language Evolution

Although the genetic accommodation of linguistic capacities can help in understanding the evolution of complex developmental traits, Piaget wanted to go

---

2 Even Chomsky's more recent minimalist program, which requires far fewer innate elements than his previous theory, requires that humans have (i) a genetically coded universal inventory of certain linguistic lexical features (called "interpretable features"), (ii) an innate but input-dependent selection procedure of those features, (iii) another innate, but input-dependent operation of encapsulation within lexical items, and (iv) a set of innate computational operations (see Lorenzo & Longa, 2003, for a discussion attempting to minimize the innate "burden"). The debate between Chomsky and Piaget regarding the nature of language, language acquisition, and evolution is presented in Piattelli-Palmarini (1980).

beyond the Waddingtonian, selection-mediated link between development and evolution. He wanted developmental constraints and developmental affordances to contribute more directly to between-generation heredity, but without commitment to naïve Lamarckism. He therefore suggested that developmentally constructed phenotypic variations are selected ontogenetically, and that the effects of such selection then impinge on the organism's germ line and can become inherited. He was fascinated and encouraged by Temin's discovery of reverse transcription, and suggested that somatically selected RNAs find their way to the gametes and are reverse-transcribed into DNA, thus rendering a developmental response hereditary (Piaget, 1978). This was the weakest and most obscure part in his discussion of the relations between development, heredity, and evolution: Piaget did not really deal with the many limitations of this proposal. Nevertheless, he adhered to his intuition that there is some direct link between developmental and hereditary variation.

Piaget, like every scientist at that time (mid- to late 1970s), accepted the then universal premise that hereditary variation must involve variations in DNA base sequence, an assumption that became rectified only years later when the mechanisms of epigenetic inheritance – the inheritance of non-DNA variations – became understood. If epigenetic variations are not only part and parcel of developmental processes but can also be transmitted between generations, heredity can be developmentally constructed (Jablonka & Lamb, 1995). Moreover, the transmission of behavioral variations and, in humans, of cultural-symbolic variations is another route for the transmission of variations in information between generations. Marion Lamb and I have suggested that evolutionary analysis requires the consideration of several different dimensions of variation and heredity: genetic and epigenetic in all living organisms, behavioral in social animals, and cultural-symbolic in humans (Jablonka & Lamb, 2014). Considering these "four dimensions" in the case of the evolution of linguistic communication can help link development, social-cultural evolution, and genetic evolution.

The view of the evolution of communication that my colleagues and I have developed, and which I outline here, is based on Daniel Dor's functional characterization of language as a communication technology for the instruction of the imagination (Dor, 2014). Dor argues that the communicator produces a skeletal list of the basic co-ordinates of the private experience s/he wishes to communicate, which the interlocutor uses as a scaffold for the construction of a parallel experience in his or her own mind. This view of language is close to Vygotsky's understanding of language as a socially learned tool of communication (Vygotsky, 1978, 1986), and to Tomasello's framework, which emphasizes the guiding roles of cultural-learning processes in language evolution (Tomasello, 2008, 2011). This characterization of language as a *technology* leads to a scenario that starts from the *cultural construction and evolution* of this communication technology. Cultural linguistic evolution, based on collective, interactive practices among adults and children, shaped the plastic minds of communicators and listeners, and formed a social-cultural epistemological niche in which there was selection for good communicators and interlocutors. Changes in genes therefore followed cultural and developmental changes.

We argue that like the evolution of reading and writing, language evolution started through cultural evolutionary processes (Dor & Jablonka, 2000, 2014; Jablonka & Lamb, 2014). Literacy evolved culturally over several thousands of years, and until modern times was practiced mainly by individuals belonging to an elite class. It is clearly not the result of selection of genes *for* literacy, since people from illiterate societies can readily acquire the skill. Rather, the remarkable, adaptive, and specialized ability to read and write is the consequence of the learning-based recruitment and reorganization of existing neural structures and their new usage in a novel cultural-literacy context (Dehaene, 2009; Jablonka & Lamb 2014 and references therein). Learning to read and write changes not only brain activity, but also brain anatomy (Carreiras et al., 2009). At the cognitive level, the cultural technologies of reading and writing seem to have extended human memory, enabled abstract chains of reasoning, and guided new ways of scanning visual items, thus making humans even more cognitively plastic (Donald, 1991; Goody, 1977). More recently, learning to detect and discriminate among distant objects using echolocation, a new skill invented and propagated by blind individuals, was found to alter not only behavior but also brain function, recruiting some visual areas of the brain for echolocation (Thaler, Arnott, & Goodale, 2011). Hence, the acquisition of new skills through cultural learning leads to phenotypic accommodation that involves changed brain activity and brain anatomy, and leads to complex individual and social behaviors that increase the cognitive plasticity of the learner.

Although we cannot reconstruct the stages of early hominin language (proto-language), from what we do know about the history of social technologies we conjecture that if the first stages in the evolution of language were culturally driven, the cultural evolution of early linguistic communication involved incremental innovations and complexifications, and occasional losses (Mesoudi, 2011). As individuals and groups struggled to invent signs for things that had not yet been named, gave new meaning to existing signs, and arranged signs in new ways to reduce ambiguity, proto-languages diversified, increased in size and efficiency, and developed an internal structure. The process depended on cultural learning and cultural transmission, which were probably initially not very efficient, but which led to the formation of local linguistic traditions. According to this scenario, the (cultural) evolution of proto-languages preceded and drove the genetic evolution of the language capacity. There is therefore a clear relation between the cultural and genetic dimensions through genetic accommodation. But what do we know about the developmental foundation of this process?

We cannot study our ancestors and observe how their brains accommodated as they learned to communicate through language, but we do have some indirect evidence for phenotypic accommodation driven by language learning in language-instructed chimpanzees and bonobos. The question of whether or not their ability reflects "true" language capacities is beside the point. What is important is that these apes acquire an ability to use referential gestures and lexigrams sufficiently well to qualify as possessing proto-language capacities (Savage-Rumbaugh, Shanker, & Taylor, 1998), something they never display in the wild. The apes require the structured, humanly designed symbol system for that, but when this is given, their minds are plastic enough to be able to communicate through symbols. What they apparently cannot do is invent a symbolic system.

Humans, however, did not evolve directly from chimpanzees or bonobos. The evolution of the hominin lineage, beginning with *Homo habilis*, took more than 2.5 million years. Our more immediate ancestors, the large-brained archaic humans, lived in bands, used fire, colonized large parts of the globe, regularly made complex standardized tools that required motor control and an ability for motor imitation, had a social organization based on alloparenting that is uniquely human among the great apes, and engaged in cooperative foraging and hunting. All these cooperative practices, many of which can be seen already in the earlier hominin, *H. erectus*, require sophisticated information sharing. Most evolutionary linguists and cognitivists agree that erectile hominins, living some 800,000 years ago, probably used some form of proto-language (e.g., Donald, 1991). Crucially, the cooperative practices of our ancestors required a unique emotional profile. Hrdy (2009) argues that hominins became emotionally modern before they were anatomically and cognitively modern, and that inter-subjective sensitivity had already increased through alloparenting by 1.6 million years ago, in early *Homo erectus*. The psychological adaptations associated with alloparenting led to better theory of mind – to mind-reading, emotional control, empathy, and better cooperation – and there was selection for these traits in both alloparents and the cared-for infants. In addition, complex standardized tool-making, which appeared later, also required emotional control (e.g., patience, control of frustration) in both apprentices and demonstrators. The increased social sensibility that alloparenting, complex tool-making, and other cooperative practices such as collective foraging and hunting engendered led to the development of the social emotions of pride, shame, guilt, and embarrassment, which regulate cooperative alliances and establish and consolidate group organization. Since cooperative social practices require information sharing, communication must have co-evolved with the cognitive and affective capacities of these humans (Jablonka, Ginsburg, & Dor, 2012).

The idea that cooperation is the key to the development of human thinking is a central theme in Piaget's work. Piaget (1928) presciently wrote that "only cooperation constitutes a process that can produce reason" (English translation 1995, p. 200). He argued that the child's ability to take the perspective and role of the other enables the construction of normative rules of conduct and of rule-based reasoning. Tomasello (2014) has developed these ideas within an evolutionary framework, in the light of new empirical findings about cooperation in humans and apes, and theoretical considerations pertaining to the construction of shared, collective ("we") intentionality. He argues that the processes of off-line representation, inference, and self-monitoring that characterize what we call thinking evolved in a social-environmental context requiring the solution of social problems of coordination and collaboration. Human linguistic communication evolved in progressively more demanding social environments. Beginning with higher apes' communication, which is based on individual intentionality, communication evolved in small hominin groups into a simple symbolic proto-language based on joint intentionality, and, from that, in large sapiens groups into a conventional system of symbolic signals that created an epistemological common ground and enabled "objective" reasoning.

Increasingly sophisticated cooperation was not only a precondition and a driving force in human language evolution, it was also *shaped* by language (Jablonka et al., 2012). Once a rudimentary system of linguistic, imagination-instructing communication evolved in pre-sapiens hominins, it had profound effects on their cognitive and emotional evolution. Imagination-instructing communication required improved inhibition of action and of the emotional triggers for action – you should not run away from the leopard you were told about, however vividly you imagine it. Hence, the inhibitory control of emotions that were related to mental representations constructed through communication was a necessary facet of the evolution of imagination-instructing communication. This language-linked affective regulation allowed the control of aggression. It meant that aggression in humans could be inhibited in a new way, based on the newly formed links between emotions and language.

Enhanced emotional control was not limited to inhibitory control. Linguistic messages used during conversations and rituals reinforced the emotional contagion associated with the interaction, increasing the range of emotions in each individual human. Speech acts, a new kind of action made possible by language, reinforced the norm-related emotions of embarrassment, shame, guilt, and pride. The identification with the group, especially during rituals, created collective "we" emotions such as moral outrage, collective pride, fear, and joy. And the evolution of language into a conventional symbolic system that rendered propositions true or false generated the truth-associated emotions of doubt, suspicion, and certainty.

The greater control of emotions generated a new type of human emotional profile, and new types of cooperation of aggression. Both cooperation and aggression could be enormously enhanced as well as take completely new forms, becoming dissociated from personal experience. Neither the horrors nor the miracles of humans' collective behavior can be understood if the profound effect of language on the emotional basis of cooperation is not considered.

This view of human cognition suggests that language co-evolved with emotions and other human capacities. It suggests a link between the cultural evolution of languages and the genetic evolution of the speakers: language evolved through a process of genetic accommodation, with cultural and social changes preceding and guiding the selection of genes that foster linguistic communication. Waddington argued along these lines long ago:

> If there were selection for the ability to use language, then there would be selection for the capacity to acquire the use of language, *in an interaction with a language-using environment*; and the result of selection for epigenetic [developmental] responses can be, as we have seen, a gradual accumulation of so many genes with effects tending in this direction that the character gradually becomes genetically assimilated.
> (Waddington 1975, p. 306; my italics).

But what exactly was genetically assimilated or, more generally, genetically accommodated? If the use of language required combining and mobilizing the many different cognitive and affective capacities that co-evolved with it, then general aspects of development, affect, and cognition were most likely to become genetically accommodated. Tomasello (2009) has shown that very young human children cooperate and collaborate far more than other apes, and that they are exceptionally good at sharing information with others, so one of the things that seems to have been genetically accommodated is a tendency to cooperate and attend to others, beginning in early childhood. Other domain-general traits that were genetically accommodated are prolonged childhood, enhanced general memory, improved associative learning, a better ability for vocal and motor imitation, symbolic representation, and the construction of social emotions and their human-specific expression – the blush. Nevertheless, some language-specific capacities may also have become genetically assimilated and accommodated. Possible candidates are the ability to distinguish linguistic sounds or gestures from other types of sounds and gestures; more refined phonetic and phonological analysis of auditory signs and gestural analogues; an improved semantic-linguistic memory and episodic memory; and an earlier and more effective learning of language in infants (Ginsburg & Jablonka, 2014; Jablonka et al., 2012). In all cases, there must have been a premium on maintaining and extending plasticity, because cultures change relatively rapidly (especially as languages evolved); it is therefore unlikely that the neural basis of specific syntactic structures became genetically assimilated. Indeed, the variability exhibited by extant and past languages seems to preclude the genetic assimilation of syntactic structures (Dunn, Greenhill, Levinson, & Gray 2011; Evans & Levinson, 2009).

This evolutionary perspective is somewhat closer to Piaget's view of language evolution than to Chomsky's, although it does not exclude the possibility that some language-specific developmental predispositions may have evolved. The approach also opens up some additional questions that were important for Piaget: in what way are processes of cultural learning physiologically and biochemically instantiated? Are there developmental processes that can lead to transgenerational transmission of developmentally selected variation?

Piaget did not discuss cultural evolution, and he did not discuss the way in which a cultural variation, once introduced, can become entrenched through the interactions of the new practice with existing practices and institution. For example, the introduction of literacy became socially stabilized and extended through the effects it had on political and social practices that enabled better regulation of growing communities. It also led to the establishment of new practices of teaching and codification, which further expanded its range and advantages. In addition to such effects, which are best described in sociological terms, there were effects on the cognition of individuals, leading, for example, to the extension of memory, enhanced organization of visuospatial information, and better interpretation of the logical functions of language (Manly, Byrd, Touradji, Sanchez, & Stern, 2004). As mentioned earlier, literacy has neural correlates and it is obvious that its practice involves changes in gene expression in neurons. Although at present we do not know enough about these molecular neuronal correlates, the fact that identical twins can be discordant with respect to dyslexia suggests that literacy has developmentally persistent molecular correlates that do not depend on differences in the sequence of DNA – it has epigenetic correlates.

This brings me back to language development, the molecular-epigenetic correlates of linguistic culture, and the possibility of epigenetic inheritance of language-related developmental variations. Epigenetic inheritance occurs when phenotypic, developmental variations that do not stem from variations in DNA base sequence are transmitted to subsequent generations of cells or organisms. The mechanisms underlying epigenetic inheritance are complex and there are several classes of them. The most researched ones in mammals are DNA methylation, in which the addition of methyl to cytosines in DNA leads to changes in transcriptional competence; histone modifications, which chemically modify the histone proteins around which DNA is wound and alter the probability of gene transcription; and RNA-mediated regulation, which leads to gene silencing by affecting either translation or transcription (Jablonka & Lamb, 2014). Variations in DNA methylation, histone modifications, and the profiles of small RNAs can be inherited within and between generations, although the mechanisms are not yet entirely clear (Szyf, 2015).

Importantly, such inherited epigenetic variations can be associated with cognitive and emotional traits, and with learning. For example, male mice deprived of normal maternal care for a few hours each day for 14 days after birth display depression-like behavior and anxiety, and this behavior is transmitted through their sperm and persists to the third generation (Franklin et al., 2010; Gapp et al., 2014). Even more strikingly, mice that were conditioned to associate a specific odor (either acetophenone or propanol) with mild foot-shocks and became startled when they smelled the same odors in the absence of foot-shock transmitted the learned fear to their descendants. Their offspring and grand-offspring (the F1 and F2 generations) responded with a heightened startle-response to the odors to which their ancestors were conditioned (Dias & Ressler, 2014). In this case, too, it seems that the variations are transmitted through the gametes.

However, this need not always be the case. Through epigenetic mechanisms such as DNA methylation, histone modification, and small RNA regulation, parental behavior can alter the brains of offspring in a way that leads to the reconstruction of the parental behavior when the offspring become adults. For example, Weaver and his colleagues found that when a mother rat gave her biological or fostered offspring a low amount of licking and grooming they had an increased stress response and neophobia, and when these biological or foster daughters themselves become mothers they also exhibited low licking and grooming behavior, passed it on to their daughters, and so on. These developmental changes were associated with epigenetic changes in DNA methylation and histone modification in the rats' brains (Weaver et al., 2004).

The point I want to make here is that it is plausible that changes in the communication practices of distant ancestors, especially those that were related to cooperative practices that involved emotional and hormonal changes, contributed to the transgenerational transmission of the conditions that fostered proto-linguistic communication. Alloparenting, for example, is a plastic trait, dependent on the social context. It has been shown by cross-fostering experiments that polygynous meadow voles, which do not practice alloparental care, become caring fathers if they are exposed as neonates to the caring style of prairie voles, who do practice alloparenting. This suggests that altering the social/familial environment could trigger a developmental change in caring style, which could be the basis of further evolution of the trait (Avital & Jablonka, 2000). If, in early hominins, related females, as well as male and female young of different ages, stayed close together and alloparenting was socially encouraged and controlled, and if alloparenting was associated with an increased level of a hormone such as oxytocin that elicits caring, both the inclination to care and the learning of caring behaviors will be promoted (Hrdy, 2009) and socially transmitted between generations. Such a process is likely to involve epigenetic mechanisms.

It has been found that oxytocin has anxiety-inhibiting effects and that inducible epigenetic changes in the oxytocin receptor are involved in the modulation of emotions (Puglia, Lillard, Morris, & Connelly, 2015). If the hormonal effects are epigenetically reconstructed in descendants, either by promoting caring behavior through the reconstruction of social conditions or by the transmission of information through the gametes, it could further increase the cooperation-promoting alloparenting behavior and other pro-social behaviors that are important for complex communication. It is likely that other types of language-associated behaviors, such as those involved in planning a sequence of complex actions (e.g. the actions involved in making sophisticated tools), also have epigenetic correlates, but at present we know very little about the molecular basis of such behaviors, so I will resist the temptation to speculate about them.

Transgenerational inheritance, and especially gametic epigenetic inheritance, would no doubt have delighted Piaget. Since epigenetic mechanisms are involved in the stabilization of phenotypically accommodated traits, if the epigenetic variations that underlie the accommodated traits can be transmitted between generations (e.g., Stern, Fridmann-Sirkis, Braun, & Soen, 2012), then developmental selection can lead to the inheritance of developmental dispositions.

Let me sum up: I have presented an evolutionary-developmental approach to language evolution that suggests that language started evolving like literacy, through cultural evolution. The socially constructed language technology affected multiple social functions, mobilizing and modifying the development of many cognitive and affective capacities. The cultural evolution of language constructed a social and epistemological niche that selected developmental and genetic variations that fitted this niche, and epigenetic inheritance of some of the developmentally induced variations supporting the technology may have contributed to this process. Taking this view means that in order to understand the complex evolution of human linguistic communication we need to consider cultural evolution, behavioral transmission through social learning, and transmission through self-reconstructing hormonal modulations, epigenetic inheritance, and genetic inheritance.

Concluding Comments: Piaget, Popper, and the Extended Evolutionary Synthesis

I would like to end by positioning Piaget's developmental view of evolution within the emerging framework of the "extended evolutionary synthesis" that is being advocated by a growing number of evolutionary biologists (Jablonka & Lamb, 1995, 2007a, 2007b; Laland et al., 2014; Noble, Jablonka, Joyner, Müller, & Omholt, 2014; Pigliucci & Müller, 2010). In order to do so, it is necessary to try to understand why Piaget's views were dismissed by the biologists of his time. It is interesting that Karl Popper raised issues very similar to those discussed by Piaget, committed similar oversights, and had his views dismissed for similar reasons (for a comprehensive discussion of Popper's views, see Niemann, 2014; Vecchi & Baravalle, 2015). It is also interesting that these two influential scholars did not join forces to promote their very similar approaches to evolution.

I suggest that the dismissal of their views by biologists was the result of several mutually reinforcing factors. First, Piaget's and Popper's description of Waddington's genetic assimilation was not satisfactory. Piaget argued that genetic assimilation is not compatible with the plasticity seen in the populations of snails that he studied in Swiss lakes, and he ignored Waddington's response, which was that genetic assimilation need not lead to fixation, and is likely to lead to a different range of reaction in different populations (Waddington, 1975). Moreover, Piaget misused the term "phenocopy," which was coined by Richard Goldschmidt (1935) to describe an environmentally induced phenotype that mimics a phenotype that results from a genetic mutation (for example, a yellow body in the fruit fly *Drosophila* can be the result of a genetic mutation or it can be induced by feeding the larva of normal flies with silver salts). Piaget used the term in the exact opposite sense, to describe the phenotypic effects of a genetic mutation that mimics an environmentally induced phenotype, and stuck to his idiosyncratic misuse of the term in spite of the protests of biologists (Piattelli-Palmarini, 1980, pp. 59–62). Popper, too, seems to have ignored or misinterpreted Waddington's ideas. As Medawar pointed out to him in a long letter (Aronova, 2007), Waddington's evolution by genetic assimilation provides a modern interpretation of Baldwin's and Lloyd Morgan's ideas (which are very close to those of Popper), and Waddington's view is compatible with classical Neo-Darwinism (see Jablonka & Lamb, 1995, chapter 2, for a detailed explanation and discussion of Waddington's model).

Second, the general view prevalent among biologists at that time was that genetic assimilation cannot explain the growth in organismal complexity, and that reliance on it as a significant factor in evolution is therefore misguided (e.g., Simpson, 1953; Williams, 1966). In the Chomsky–Piaget debate, Simpson's and Williams' argument was reintroduced: It was suggested that genetic assimilation leads to the loss of genetic potentiality (plasticity) because an organism that was originally able to express either of two phenotypes, depending on the environment, after genetic assimilation can express only one phenotype, whatever the environment (Piattelli-Palmarini, 1980, pp. 195–196). However, although reduced responsivity and behavioral impoverishment is one possible result of genetic assimilation, genetic assimilation can lead to behavioral sophistication in several ways: (i) it need not be complete; it can be partial, leading to quicker and more efficient context-sensitive responses, so plasticity need not be compromised; (ii) even when fixation occurs, the internal factor that replaces and "simulates" the effect of the external environmental signs may be generated by a different biochemical pathway, thus forging a new functional link between previously independent processes and increasing the complexity of biochemical structures (Jablonka-Tavory, 1982); (iii) assimilation of a response that is part of a sequence of learned responses can lead to the lengthening of the behavioral sequence by enabling the animal to add, through learning, a new behavior to the existing sequence without an increase in its learning ability, something known as the assimilate-stretch principle (see Avital and Jablonka 2000, and Jablonka & Lamb, 2014, for details); (iv), genetic assimilation of plasticity-promoting strategies would increase rather than decrease plasticity (Dor & Jablonka, 2010). Hence, the argument that genetic assimilation necessarily leads to impoverished behavior and reduced responsivity is invalid.

Third, Piaget's (1978) and Popper's (see Aronova, 2007; Niemann, 2014; Vecchi & Baravalle, 2015) attempts to incorporate developmental selection into evolution did not take into account the considerable problems involved in the specific scenario they suggested, which was based on the suggestion that reverse transcription of the newly transcribed RNAs would lead to genetic inheritance. For such a process to occur, the environmental induction of transcription, which originates in somatic cells, must be accompanied by the successful transport of the transcribed RNAs to the germ line, the reverse transcription of these RNAs, and their incorporation into their DNA during gametogenesis. Although such a sequence of events is conceivable (Steele & Lloyd, 2015), Piaget's (and to a lesser extent Popper's) lack of detailed engagement with the plausibility of this chain of occurrences meant they were regarded as amateurish by biologists.

Fourth, evolutionary biologists thought that the perspective suggested by Piaget and Popper, which starts with the development of an active organism that constructs its niche rather than with a genetic change, makes no important difference to their own view. For most evolutionary biologists, the only thing that could lead to a significant change in their conception of evolution would be the discovery that the origin of heritable variations (which were universally considered to be variations in DNA base sequence) was non-random. Since there was no good evidence for directed mutations, and since epigenetic inheritance had not yet been explored, the assumption that the origin of variation is blind to function and is not affected by the developmental history of the organism was not challenged. The gestalt switch that Piaget and Popper advocated – starting evolutionary analysis with the responsive and active phenotype rather than with the mutated gene – was not considered significant.

The situation is different today, and Piaget's and Popper's views can be seen as historical precursors of the Extended Evolutionary Synthesis (EES), which is based on empirical and theoretical studies of development, heredity, and ecology, and the interrelations between them. The advocates of EES focus on insights derived mainly from research in four domains of study. The first is evolutionary-developmental biology (evo-devo), especially work on the chemical-physical and regulatory principles of embryological development. The second is the related investigation of developmental plasticity, which focuses on the range and type of the developmental responses organisms have to their changing environment. The third is research on inclusive inheritance – the study of the transmission of information through the often-interacting genetic, epigenetic, behavioral, and cultural systems. The fourth is the study of the activities and choices of organisms, which affect the selection acting on them and on other species. These studies suggest that developmental processes create novel variants, contribute to heredity, generate adaptive adjustments, guide the course of evolution, and are as important as natural selection in determining evolutionary history (Laland et al., 2014).

Piaget's neglected, and not always well-articulated, ideas about the active and constructive role of the organism in evolution, especially through its behavior, and his hunch that developmentally induced variations can contribute to heredity, have become areas of active research and fruitful debate. The application of this extended evolutionary theory to the evolution of language is a research project that is worth pursuing.

Acknowledgment

I am grateful, as ever, to Marion Lamb for her constructive comments on all aspects of the chapter.

References

Aronova, E. (2007). Karl Popper and Lamarckism. *Biological Theory, 2*(1), 37–51.

Avital, E., & Jablonka, E. (2000). *Animal traditions: Behavioural inheritance in evolution.* Cambridge, UK: Cambridge University Press.

Carreiras, M., Seghier M. L., Baquero, S., Estévez, A., Lozano, A., Devlin, J. T., & Price, C. J. (2009). An anatomical signature for literacy. *Nature, 461*, 983–986.

Changeux, J.-P., Courrége, P., & Danchin, A. (1973). A theory of the epigenesis of neuronal networks by selective stabilization of synapses. *Proceedings of the National Academy of Sciences USA, 70*, 2974–2978.

Christiansen, M. H., & Chater, N. (2008). Language as shaped by the brain. *Behavioral and Brain Sciences, 31*, 489–558.

Dehaene, S. (2009). *Reading in the brain.* New York, NY: Viking.

Dias, B. G., & Ressler, K. J., (2014). Parental olfactory experience influences behavior and neural structure in subsequent generations. *Nature Neuroscience, 17*, 89–96.

Donald, M. (1991). *Origins of the modern mind: Three stages in the evolution of culture and cognition.* Cambridge, MA: Harvard University Press.

Dor, D. (2014). The instruction of imagination: Language and its evolution as a communication technology. In D. Dor, C. Knight, & J. Lewis (Eds.), *The social origins of language* (pp. 105–125). Oxford, UK: Oxford University Press.

Dor, D., & Jablonka, E. (2000). From cultural selection to genetic selection: A framework for the evolution of language. *Selection*, *1*, 33–55.

Dor, D., & Jablonka, E. (2010). Plasticity and canalization in the evolution of linguistic communication, In R. K. Larson, V. Déprez, & H. Yamakido (Eds.), *The evolution of human language* (pp. 135–147). Cambridge, UK: Cambridge University Press.

Dor, D., & Jablonka, E. (2014). Why we need to move from gene-culture co-evolution to culturally-driven co-evolution. In D. Dor, C. Knight, & J. Lewis (Eds.), *The social origins of language* (pp. 15–30). Oxford, UK: Oxford University Press.

Dunn, M., Greenhill, S. J., Levinson, S. C., & Gray, R. D. (2011). Evolved structure of language shows lineage specific trends in word-order universals. *Nature*, *473*, 79–82. doi: 10.1038/nature09923

Edelman, G. (1974). The problem of molecular recognition by a selective system. In F. Ayala & T. Dobzhansky (Eds.), *Studies in the philosophy of biology* (pp. 45–56). Berkeley, CA: University of California Press.

Evans, N., & Levinson, S. C. (2009). The myth of language universals: Language diversity and its importance for cognitive science. *Behavioral and Brain Sciences*, *32*, 429–492. doi: 10.1017/S0140525X0999094X

Franklin, T. B., Russig, H., Weiss. I. C., Gräff, J., Linder, N., Michalon, A., Vizi, S., & Mansuy, I. M., (2010). Epigenetic transmission of the impact of early stress across generations. *Biological Psychiatry*, *68*(5), 408–415.

Gapp, K., Jawaid, A., Sarkies, P., Bohacek, J., Pelczar, P., Prados, J., Farinelli, L., Miska, E., & Mansuy, I. M. (2014). Implication of sperm RNAs in transgenerational inheritance of the effects of early trauma in mice. *Nature Neuroscience*, *17*, 667–669.

Ginsburg, S., & Jablonka, E. (2014). Memory, imagination and the evolution of modern language. In D. Dor, C. Knight, & J. Lewis (Eds.). *The social origins of language* (pp. 317–324). Oxford, UK: Oxford University Press.

Goldschmidt, R. (1935). Gen und Aatsseneigenschaft. *Zeitschrift für Induktive Abstammungs und Verebunglehre*, *69*, 38–131.

Goodwin, B. (2009). Beyond the Darwinian Paradigm: Understanding Biological Forms. In M. Ruse & J. Travis (Eds.). *Evolution: The first four billion years* (pp. 299–312). Cambridge, MA: Harvard University Press.

Goody, J. (1977). *The domestication of the savage mind*. Cambridge, UK: Cambridge University Press.

Gottlieb, G. (2007). Probabilistic epigenesis. *Developmental Science*, *10*, 1–11.

Hrdy, S. B. (2009). *Mothers and others: The evolutionary origins of mutual understanding*. Cambridge, MA: Harvard University Press.

Jablonka, E. (2007). The developmental construction of heredity. *Developmental Psychobiology*, *49*, 808–817,

Jablonka, E., Ginsburg, S., & Dor, D. (2012). The co-evolution of language and emotions. *Philosophical Transactions of the Royal Society B*, *367*, 2152–2159. doi: 10.1098/rstb.2012.0117

Jablonka, E., & Lamb, M. J. (1995). *Epigenetic inheritance and evolution: The Lamarckian dimension*. Oxford, UK: Oxford University Press.

Jablonka, E., & Lamb, M. J. (2007a). Précis of "Evolution in four dimensions." *Brain and Behavioral Sciences*, *30*, 353–365.

Jablonka, E., & Lamb, M. J. (2007b). Bridging the gap: The developmental aspects of evolution. *Brain and Behavioral Sciences*, *30*, 378–392.

Jablonka, E., & Lamb, M. J. (2014). *Evolution in four dimensions* (2nd edn.). Cambridge, MA: MIT Press.

Jablonka-Tavory, E. (1982). Genocopies and the evolution of interdependence. *Evolutionary Theory, 6,* 167–170.

Laland, K., Uller, T., Feldman, M., Sterelny, K., Müller, G. B., Moczek, A., Jablonka, E., & Odling-Smee, J. (2014). Does evolutionary theory need a rethink? Yes, urgently! *Nature, 514,* 161–164.

Longa, V. M. (2013). The evolution of the faculty of language from a Chomskyan perspective: Bridging linguistics and biology. *Journal of Anthropological Sciences, 91,* 1–48.

Lorenzo, G., & Longa, V. M. (2003). Minimizing the genes for grammar. The minimalist program as a biological framework for the study of language. *Lingua, 113,* 643–657.

Manly, J. J., Byrd, D., Touradji, P., Sanchez, D., & Stern, Y. (2004). Literacy and cognitive change among ethnically diverse elders. *International Journal of Psychology, 39*(1), 47–60.

Mesoudi, A. (2011). *Cultural evolution: How Darwinian theory can explain human culture and synthesize the social sciences.* Chicago, IL: University of Chicago Press.

Niemann, H-G. (2014). *Karl Popper and the two new secrets of life.* Tubingen, Germany: Mohr Siebeck.

Noble, D., Jablonka, E., Joyner, M. J., Müller, G. B., & Omholt, S. W. (2014). Evolution evolves: Physiology returns to centre stage. *Journal of Physiology, 592,* 2237–2244.

Palmer, A. R. (2009). Animal asymmetry. *Current Biology, 19,* R473–R477.

Piaget, J. (1928, Trans. 1995). Genetic logic and sociology. In L. Smith (Ed.), Piaget J., *Sociological Studies* (pp. 184–214). New York, NY: Routledge.

Piaget, J. (1971). *Biology and knowledge: An essay on the relations between organic regulations and cognitive processes.* Edinburgh, UK: Edinburgh University Press.

Piaget, J. (1978). *Behavior and evolution.* New York, NY: Pantheon Books.

Piattelli-Palmarini, M. (Ed.). (1980). *Language and learning: The debate between Jean Piaget and Noam Chomsky.* Cambridge, MA: Harvard University Press.

Pigliucci, M., & Müller, G. B. (Eds.). (2010). *Evolution: The extended synthesis.* Cambridge, MA: MIT Press.

Puglia, M. H., Lillard, T. S., Morris J. P., & Connelly J. J. (2015). Epigenetic modification of the oxytocin receptor gene influences the perception of anger and fear in the human brain. *Proceedings of the National Academy of Sciences USA, 112,* 3308–3313.

Savage-Rumbaugh, S., Shanker, S. G., & Taylor T. J. (1998). *Apes, language, and the human mind.* New York, NY: Oxford University Press.

Simpson, G. G. (1953). The Baldwin effect. *Evolution 7,* 110–117.

Skinner, B. F. (1981). Selection by consequences. *Science, 213,* 501–504.

Steele E. J., & Lloyd, S. S. (2015). Soma-to-germline feedback is implied by the extreme polymorphism at IGHV relative to MHC. *BioEssays, 37,* 557–569. doi 10.1002/bies.201400213

Stern, S., Fridmann-Sirkis, Y., Braun, E., & Soen, Y. (2012). Epigenetically heritable alteration of fly development in response to toxic challenge. *Cell Reports, 1,* 528–542.

Szyf, M. (2015). Nongenetic inheritance and transgenerational epigenetics. *Trends in Molecular Medicine, 21,* 134–144.

Thaler, L., Arnott, S. R., & Goodale, M. A. (2011). Neural correlates of natural human echolocation in early and late blind echolocation experts. *PLoS ONE, 6,* e20162. doi: 10.1371/journal.pone.0020162

Tomasello, M. (2008). *Origins of human communication*. Cambridge, MA: MIT Press.

Tomasello, M. (2009). *Why we cooperate*. Boston, MA: MIT Press.

Tomasello, M. (2011). Human culture in evolutionary perspective. In M. Gelfand, C.-y. Chiu, & Y.-y, Hong (Eds.) *Advances in Culture and Psychology* (Vol. *1*, pp. 5–51). New York, NY: Oxford University Press.

Tomasello, M. (2014). *A natural history of human thinking*. Cambridge, MA: Harvard University Press.

Vecchi, D., & Baravalle, L. (2015). A soul of truth in things erroneous: Popper's "amateurish" evolutionary philosophy in light of contemporary biology. *History and Philosophy of Life Sciences*, *36*, 525–545. doi 10.1007/s40656-014-0047-5

Vygotsky, L. S. (1978). *Mind in society: The development of higher psychological processes*, M. Cole, V. John-Steiner, S. Scribner, & E. Souberman (Eds.). Cambridge, MA: Harvard University Press.

Vygotsky, L. S. (1986). *Thought and language* (A. Kozulin, Trans.). Cambridge, MA: MIT Press.

Waddington, C. H. (1957). *The strategy of the genes*. London: Allen and Unwin.

Waddington, C. H. (1975). *The evolution of an evolutionist*. Edinburgh, UK: Edinburgh University Press.

Weaver, I. C., Cervoni, N., Champagne, F. A., D'Alessio, A. C., Sharma, S., Seckl, J. R., Dymov, S., Szyf, M., & Meaney, M. J. (2004). Epigenetic programming by maternal behavior. *Nature Neuroscience*, *7*, 847–854.

West-Eberhard, M. J. (2003) *Developmental plasticity and evolution*. New York, NY: Oxford University Press.

Williams, G. C. (1966). *Adaptation and natural selection: A critique of some current evolutionary thought*. Princeton, NJ: Princeton University Press.

19 Intuitive Psychology as Mind Designer: Scaffolding Cognitive Novelties in Early Childhood

Radu J. Bogdan

Intuitive psychology, also known as theory of mind or mindreading, has been a dynamic and expansive academic industry for almost forty years. Perhaps the most important insight of the multidisciplinary work undertaken in this area is how central and indispensable intuitive psychology is to social interactions, communication, cultural and language learning and transmission, and education. Less explored and less well understood is the crucial contribution of intuitive psychology to mental development and the very construction of the human mind. It is a contribution that takes the form of new (mostly) cognitive abilities that emerge at different stages of ontogeny and reshape the developing mind. I call this the *mind-design work* of intuitive psychology. In several past works I have explored this mind-design role of intuitive psychology in a few areas of cognitive development construed in evolutionary terms – reflexive thinking or thinking about one's own thoughts, learning word meaning and reference, predicative thinking, self-consciousness, and imagination (Bogdan, 2000, 2001, 2007, 2009, 2010, 2013). In sampling and expanding on key themes of this prior work, this chapter discerns several mind-design patterns through which intuitive psychology, in discharging its basic functions, *scaffolds* new cognitive abilities as ontogenetic adaptations to pressures arising at distinct stages of childhood.

The basic idea is this. The business of intuitive psychology is to register, represent, and interpret mental states of oneself and of others (cognitive component) and, as a result, guide appropriate reactions by way of thought, speech, and action, as part of one's goal-pursuing strategies (practical component). It is on the latter *practical* side, when in new domains children face new pressures on their actively initiated and pursued goal strategies, that the expertise of intuitive psychology is recruited to provide adaptive solutions that gradually end up scaffolding new cognitive abilities. The scaffolding follows several patterns that I call templates, matrices, assemblies, escalators and infrastructures. The earliest such scaffoldings, discussed below, occur in domains that generate some of the strongest pressures on young minds, such as meaning-based communication, learning word reference and mastering predicative communication and thinking.

The first part of the chapter provides a theoretical background for this basic idea. It introduces a certain conception of intuitive psychology and explains its mind-design potential, when its categories and abilities operate in mental rehearsals of goal strategies as scaffolders of new cognitive abilities. Several patterns of scaffolding in infancy and early childhood are then identified and briefly examined and illustrated in the second part of the chapter.

Theoretical Background

About Intuitive Psychology

If there is one feature shared by all organisms, it is their pursuit of goals, which I construe as the ability to aim at and bring about mostly external states of affairs that satisfy basic internal parameters such as homeostasis, metabolism, reproduction, defense, and more. In the interactions among and within species, it is also vital for organisms to *recognize* that other organisms are alive and pursue goals by acting accordingly. We may call this cognitive ability *intuitive biology*. Its importance resides in the fact that any major evolutionary advance in social cognition and (more narrowly) intuitive psychology is driven by the pressures to recognize and react to the goals of other organisms by representing and inferring them from various signals and symptoms: behavioral, communicational, and mental (Bogdan, 1994, 1997).

Building on their intuitive biology, a few intensely sociopolitical species (primates, elephants, dolphins) are also able to represent the *specific* goals and world-relations of others, and predict their actions, from a few overt signals and symptoms. This new cognitive ability may be called *intuitive teleology*. It represents and tracks the crude, observable agency of other organisms by recognizing their gaze, head and bodily posture, and direction of behavior, as well as what they perceive and know, and what they ignore (Bogdan, 1997, p. 71–84). We can think of intuitive teleology as joining a strict behaviorism and a minimal epistemology, both limited to what is observable about other organisms' behaviors and their overt relations to an environment. Missing in intuitive teleology is an awareness of the *mental* sources of those behaviors and relations (Bogdan, 1997, 2000; Csibra and Gergely, 2013; Gergely and Csibra, 2003; Tomasello and Moll, 2013).

Apparently only one species, the human one, shows awareness of *mental* states, such as attention, desires, beliefs, intentions, and emotions, and an ability to factor this awareness into its representing, predicting, and reacting to others. This new mind-sensitive competence is variously called intuitive psychology, mindreading, or theory of mind. Labels do not matter much as long as they simply name a competence or expertise, without further bias. Unfortunately two of these labels are much too suggestive and tend to bias the theorizing. Both mindreading and theory of mind suggest too passive a competence whose job is merely to represent and infer mental states. That is only half of the truth; there is, just as importantly, a practical, reactive, and action-guiding side to the competence. Furthermore, both mindreading and theory of mind are often applied to nonhuman species that do not and cannot detect and track mental states and are only capable of intuitive teleology and merely behavior-sensitive social cognition. Finally, the "theory" in "theory of mind" does not quite fit the procedural and skill-like nature of a good part of the human competence under discussion, particularly in its early ontogenetic stages. Hence, I prefer *intuitive psychology* for being less misleading and also in terminological tune with the popular labels of other functionally dedicated and domain-specific competencies attributed to humans and a few other species, such as intuitive physics, intuitive biology, or intuitive arithmetic.

Two major features of intuitive psychology, as I construe it, are particularly relevant to the argument of this chapter. The first concerns its tripartite constitution, the second its practical character and orientation.

Constitutionally, I think, intuitive psychology is not one single and unitary competence, maturing organically out of an embryonic and genetically dedicated core, but actually three fairly distinct though overlapping competencies, developing at distinct stages of ontogeny, with largely different (though, again, overlapping) domains of application and modes of operation, in response to ontogenetically distinct selection pressures. If we think of ontogeny in evolutionary terms, as we should (Bjorklund & Pellegrini, 2002, 2007; Bogdan, 1997, 2000, 2010; Nelson, 1996), these three competencies can then be regarded as distinct sets of ontogenetic adaptations.

What follows is a brief introduction to the three competencies, to be further elaborated and illustrated in the second part of the chapter, when we turn to their impact on mental development.

In early infancy, the first intuitive-psychological competence is exercised *bilaterally* in communication and overt exchanges of mainly affects, emotions, and intents to interact or socialize (Hobson, 1993; Meltzoff, 2013; Trevarthen, 1993, 2011). This is an extraordinary initial platform for intuitive psychology, since it provides infants with an incipient and implicit but very consequential *sense of the mental* in others, which detects and tracks *invariant* patterns behind various overt expressions of them (Bogdan, 2000, 2001, 2009). Mother, for example, can show joy (the mental invariant), which the infant detects through its various overt expressions, such as singing, lively eyes, smile, exuberant gestures, and so on. The point is not that infants know or are explicitly aware of mental states, but rather that they are primed to recognize and react to a common factor behind a variety of manifestations. Such is the entry of the mental in infant (and thus human) social cognition, turning it (likely for the first time in evolution) into an intuitive psychology.

This initial and exclusively bilateral grasp of the mental in others is an exclusively ontogenetic achievement, due to evolutionary pressures specific and possibly unique to human infancy. If intuitive psychology builds on and expands this infantile sense of the mental, and in so doing also redesigns a primate mind into a human one, as I argue here and elsewhere, then the human mind can be said to be the *evolutionary* (and not just maturational) product of a unique ontogeny. This building-on and expansion process occurs because the infantile sense of the mental in others is factored into as well as amplified by the successor competencies of intuitive psychology (Bogdan, 2009, 2010, 2013).

In a second stage of ontogeny, extending from late infancy to around age four, children develop a new competence to detect, represent, and react to the *world-oriented* mental states of others, and only of others, such as seeing, attending, simple desires, visually based beliefs, trying to do something, and the like. They also recognize when someone else has perceptual knowledge and when they are ignorant (i.e., lacking such knowledge)(Doherty, 2009; Perner, 1991). Some of these recognition abilities are also present in chimpanzees (their intuitive teleology, actually) but without a grasp of the *mental* component of world-directed states and actions. This asymmetry suggests that the initially bilateral infant sense of the mental is an evolutionary novelty that would later enable older children to engage in shared attention and joint action, in which two or more individuals interact in a shared world through a mutually acknowledged recognition of such trilateral or multilateral interactions – something that apes and other species apparently cannot do (Tomasello, 1999; Tomasello and Moll, 2013). I call this second competence *naïve psychology*. Its grasp of the mental is only *other*-directed and still dependent on its *overt* expressions. One's own mind is not yet explicitly on the radar of the young naïve psychology (Bogdan, 2010).

In a third stage, after the age of four, children develop a competence to represent, reason about, and react to subtler, conceptually networked, and not always overtly displayed attitudes, such as intentions, opinions, perspectives different from one's own, plans, complex emotions (e.g., hope, regret), and the like, of both other people and themselves. I call this third competence *commonsense psychology*. Dissenting from a widely shared view, I think that only older children (4 years or above), turn commonsense psychology toward their own minds and begin to represent their own thoughts and attitudes in the same (common or publicly shared) terms and under the same concepts as they represent those of others. Commonsense psychology is made possible by new post-four executive developments, such as inhibition, top-down control, a capacious working memory, offline thinking, and more, as well as cognitive developments, particularly metarepresentation, perspective-taking, and a suppositional stance. There is fairly solid evidence that I read as indicating that these latter cognitive abilities develop first in representing other minds before turning to one's own (Bogdan, 2010).

Parenthetically, but importantly, I think that commonsense psychology is ontogenetically the first and only competence that remotely resembles an intuitive "theory of mind" literally construed as concerned with understanding, explaining, justifying, and rationalizing the mental states and actions of others and oneself (concerns absent in earlier versions of intuitive psychology) and capable of representing mental states through well-integrated and flexibly deployed networks of concepts under systematic generalizations (Gopnik and Wellman, 1992). Projecting, even by weakening and miniaturizing, this late "theory of mind" back on earlier forms of intuitive psychology, and assuming a linear, organic, and merely maturational development of the former out of the latter, has been (in my view) an unnecessary and empirically unsupported position that violates the evolutionary dimensions of ontogeny and the significant reorganizations of young minds and their intuitive psychology.

Closer to our topic, this mistake also obscures the distinct mind-design contributions of the distinct competencies of intuitive psychology. This is because an important difference between the three versions of intuitive psychology, with implications for their mind-design work, is the nature and modus operandi of their respective abilities, both largely determined by the selection pressures of different stages of ontogeny.

Infancy is mostly about bilateral adult–offspring co-regulation, protection, and survival, and early childhood mostly a world-oriented, well-scheduled, and fairly tightly constrained initiation into language, regimented communication, basic cultural practices, and joint activities – all universal values strongly imprinted epigenetically in the species. This is why, not surprisingly from an evolutionary angle, the intuitive psychologies of infancy and early childhood are mostly procedural and implicitly formatted skills, whereas the later commonsense psychology leans much more on publicly shared concepts, explicit representations, and inference (Apperly 2010; Bogdan, 1997; Karmiloff-Smith, 1992).

This contrast suggests that the intuitive psychologies of infancy and early childhood result from a fairly tight co-evolution of a complex epigenetic bargain between what infant and young minds evolved to expect and are able to assimilate, on the one hand, and how adult parental and cultural practices in turn evolved to co-regulate, assist, and enculturate those developing minds, on the other hand. As telling examples, think of the unreflective spontaneity with which adults engage infants in baby talk or "motherese," to which infants respond equally spontaneously yet not imitatively, or a similar kind of spontaneous reciprocal interaction, this time imitative, in shared attention and joint actions. Both examples testify to evolved procedural and unreflective mechanisms in both parties. Understanding this co-evolutionary adjustment is still work in progress, as far as I can tell.

As intuitive psychology pursues its ontogenetic evolution and simultaneously its mind-design work, the inevitable impact of parental and cultural variability is bound to grow, as many studies have shown (summarized in Banaji and Gelman, 2013; Bjorklund, 2011; Nelson, 1996, 2007). This also makes evolutionary sense and reflects a more flexible co-evolutionary process than that of infancy and early childhood. Indeed, to become and remain successful, older children must inevitably adapt to the immense diversity of languages, cultures, and even civilizational stages that characterize human societies. As a result, more than its ontogenetic precursors, the commonsense psychology of late childhood and adulthood evolved to handle these diversities more flexibly, explicitly, and reflectively, with differential impact on how distinct genders or even ethnic groups, for example, perform some intuitive-psychological tasks, such as empathizing or figuring out complex emotions, or cognitive tasks, such as gossip, narration, or autobiographical recall – all deeply dependent on intuitive psychology (see Banaji and Gelman, 2013, for a review).

Despite their evolutionary and operational distinctness, what the three competencies have in common functionally, what makes them *psycho*logical, is (a) that they all recognize and track *mental* states behind their overt expressions, either minimally and in a mostly implicit (procedural) form in the first two versions or more probingly in an explicit (representational) form in the third version; and (b) that the successor

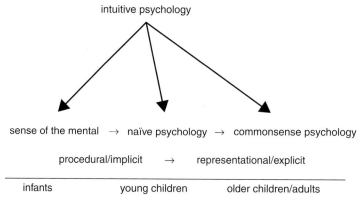

Figure 19.1. *Intuitive psychology.*

competencies incorporate, retool, and build on earlier acquisitions, perhaps through the "representational redescription" advocated by Annette Karmiloff-Smith (1992) and/or some internally operating scaffolding and assembly, along the lines suggested here, or some other appropriation process. Schematically, the picture of intuitive psychology drawn so far can be diagrammed as shown in Figure 19.1.

The second major feature of intuitive psychology relevant to what follows is this. Intuitive psychology is sensitive not only to how a mind relates to other minds and/or targets in the world, but also to the *affordances* or *implications* of such relations – mental, communicational, or behavioral – as grounds for action, reaction, and intervention. Far from being spectatorial, "theoretical," or merely "simulational," as most popular accounts assume, intuitive psychology is eminently practical, forward-looking, interventionist, and interested in, as well as shaped by, the implications and affordances for action or communication of the mental states it represents. In all its ontogenetic versions, intuitive psychology is a practically motivated set of abilities, and it evolved for this very reason. Natural and other forms of selection would not have it any other way (Bogdan, 1997). This critical point, all too often neglected, is crucial when examining the work of intuitive psychology as mind designer and its resulting impact on mental development, since that work and its impact emerge precisely on the practical side of the exercise of intuitive psychology, as noted next.

Rehearsing With Mental States

My conjecture is that the mind-design potential of intuitive psychology emerges on the practical or application side of intuitive psychology, when children rehearse mentally with representations of mental states in new domains they perceive as similar, close, or relevant to that of intuitive psychology. I will parse this conjecture in terms of its basic components. I begin with mental rehearsals.

As has become clear in recent years, brains are *projection engines* that anticipate states of the world, sensory inputs, and impending actions on the basis of prior expectations, habits, and accumulated experiences, and do so either automatically or deliberately. Such projections operate spontaneously and constantly, whether in sleep, dreaming, under anesthesia, in mind wandering, or in voluntary thinking (Hohwy, 2014). The mental projections of interest here operate either online, immediately preceding motor actions or various reactions (communicational, emotive, etc.), or offline, in deliberately anticipative thinking.

The mental projections with intuitive-psychological categories, representations, and schemes are *metamental* since the projecting states, themselves mental, are about or directed at other mental states, of other people and oneself – which means "mental about or involving mental," or, in short, "metamental." The metamental projections of interest here are most often conscious and voluntary, whether online, in infancy and early childhood, or offline, in late childhood and adulthood. When complex in structure and deployed sequentially and inferentially, such projections take the form of *metamental rehearsals* (Bogdan, 2007, 2010, 2013).

When the categories, representations, and schemes of intuitive psychology (which constitute its cognitive component) enter into metamental rehearsals that guide one's goal strategies and actions (which is the practical component) opportunities emerge for scaffolding new cognitive abilities. These opportunities become mental reality if and when at least two key conditions obtain:

(a) *subjectively*, children *perceive* an initial similarity, overlap, or proximity between the domain of intuitive psychology and a new domain, and hence perceive new challenges in the new domain as (more or less) *variations on familiar intuitive-psychological themes*; as a result, children's minds are prone to and likely to recruit familiar intuitive-psychological resources for new, stable, and routinized deployments in their online or offline rehearsals of goal strategies in the new domain, thus incorporating the intuitive-psychological resources into new cognitive capacities

and

(b) *objectively*, between intuitive-psychological abilities recruited by children's minds in their metamental rehearsals and the new cognitive capacities thus scaffolded in new domains, there is actually an *initial similarity* or *close proximity* of cognitive resources, modes of operation, and developmental schedules.

When these two key conditions are met, children's metamental rehearsals can be said to "mentalize" facts and patterns in new domains, such as those of communication, social interaction, and joint action, and often even in physical or biological domains as well as the cultural domains of artifacts, legends, and religion. As understood here, to "mentalize" is to represent facts and patterns in new domains in terms of mind-to-mind, mind-to-world, or mind-to-targets – or, in philosophical jargon, "intentional" relations. (The idea of mentalizing echoes in developmental and more general terms the well-known notion of "intentional stance" proposed by Dan Dennett many years ago as an explanatory and predictive strategy of (what is called here) commonsense psychology (Dennett, 1971)).

We can then say that the potential of intuitive psychology to scaffold new cognitive capacities derives from the propensity of children as intuitive psychologists to meet new challenges in new domains by mentalizing key aspects in those domains – that is, by representing them in terms of mind-to-mind and mind-to-target relations. Mentalization is what "exports" intuitive-psychological abilities to new cognitive capacities in new domains through scaffolding. If and when such mentalizations come under strong and persistent pressures to become mental skills or routines, the way is open to the scaffolding of new cognitive abilities in new domains, as argued in the second part of this chapter. Several patterns of such scaffoldings are briefly introduced next and illustrated later.

Patterns of Scaffolding

I use the notion of *scaffolding* in its original (dictionary) sense of an initial platform and basic skeleton of a building, which serves as the support and framework for further additions and enrichments. A scaffold may end up incorporated in the much-enriched and diversified building as final result or may be partly or entirely discarded as the construction expands its structure yet retains the shape of the scaffold. In the present context, the scaffolding is done by intuitive psychology and the final building is a set of novel cognitive competencies. The well-known Vygotskian notion of scaffolding by adults guiding children to a higher level of performance compatible with their potential is about improving a competence, whereas the more basic notion used here is about building a competence to begin with. The ability of intuitive psychology to scaffold new cognitive competencies through mentalization seems to follow several patterns, which I call template, matrix, assembly, escalator, and infra-structural scaffolding. They will be elaborated and illustrated in the next sections, after the following brief and informal definitions.

A *template* is an intuitive-psychological category or ability that is copied or emulated by a new category or ability operating in a new domain. Analogies and metaphors operate as conceptual templates. They abound in scientific thinking: the heart is almost literally represented as a pump; the planetary system provides an intuitive template for the structure of the atom; something hitting and moving something else is often an intuitive template for causation; and so on.

A *matrix* is an established inferential pattern in intuitive psychology that configures, partly or completely, a new inferential pattern in a new domain. Matrices are frequent in ordinary thinking, often by linking distinct templates, as for example in understanding natural phenomena in terms of what the gods are doing and then understanding the latter in terms of people's intentions and actions. (The latter understanding is an instance of mentalization.)

An *assembly* joins several abilities and categories in old domains to scaffold a new ability or category in a new domain. Reading and writing are examples of new abilities in new behavioral domains assembled out of prior visual, motor, memory, and conceptual abilities initially evolved or developed in other domains. Children's categories of right and wrong and other moral values, for example, are initially assembled out of prior and simpler categories they understand, such as "everybody does it," "it would displease father" or "displease the gods," or the like.

An *escalator* is a sequence of mental developments partly or entirely scaffolded by intuitive psychology along an ontogenetic sequence shaped by its advances. Differently said, an escalator operates along an ontogenetic staircase (so to speak) in which every important new step forward is made possible by a prior step largely or entirely shaped by earlier intuitive-psychological categories and abilities. As noted below, word acquisition is made possible by a prior platform of shared attention, which in turn is made possible by a still-earlier platform of recognition of gaze and pointing and their mental components (intent, interest, curiosity). Both platforms, as earlier steps, belong to intuitive psychology.

Finally, *infrastructural scaffolding* is at work whenever an initial competence – call it *incubator competence* – with its proprietary domain and tasks, provides an infrastructure or skeleton that is later enriched, diversified, and integrated with other competencies, and applied to new domains, the result being an *outcome competence*. Elsewhere, I argued that imagination (in a strong suppositional sense) is likely to have been infrastructurally scaffolded by the prior and more basic competence of strategizing (or thinking how to get the best results) in cooperative and competitive contexts of social interactions (Bogdan, 2013). In the same spirit, reasoning was theorized to have been infrastructurally scaffolded by the prior and more basic ability to evaluate arguments and evidence in communication (Mercier and Sperber, 2011).

The scaffolding strategies and nature of the scaffolded abilities are a function of the relevant resources operating in a particular intuitive-psychological competence at a given stage of ontogeny. This is to say that children mentalize in new domains and as a result develop (through scaffolding) new cognitive capacities at a given age-interval to the extent allowed and enabled by the mentalizing resources of the relevant competence of intuitive psychology. For reasons of space, I will illustrate this process only with some examples from infancy and early childhood.

Scaffolding Through Mentalization

Gricean Scaffolding: Sense of Mental → Meaning

As a reminder, a *sense of the mental* is an infant's bilateral grasp of "mental invariants" – initially mostly affects, emotions, and motives – detected behind a variety of overt expressions, such as facial, vocal, bodily, and gestural. This sense of the mental operates implicitly and procedurally in interactive and communicative acts exchanged between infants and adults (Adamson, 1995; Hobson, 1993; Trevarthen, 1993, 2011).

The major scaffolding contribution of this infantile ability is a grasp of communicative intent and of the reciprocal intent-recognition-and-acknowledgment loop that would become the *matrix* for producing and registering bilateral meaning, in a Gricean sense that I read in developmental and pre-linguistic terms as follows (where capital letters indicate the scaffolding intuitive-psychological categories and abilities and bold letters indicate the new scaffolded abilities):

i) communicators **mean** something by an act → is scaffolded by → communicators INTEND the act to produce a mental effect (e.g., attention, emotion, belief) in an audience by means of the audience's RECOGNITION of this INTENT (to produce the mental effect in question) and ACKNOWLEDGMENT of this RECOGNITION (original text: Grice, 1957; developmental accounts: Bogdan, 2009; Bruner, 1983; Tomasello, 1999)

(ii) communicative acts **mean** something → is scaffolded by → communicators **mean** something

This is a two-steps scaffolding enterprise. The first ontogenetic step, which is scaffolding a communicator's meaning in (i), is managed by an *assembly* of intuitive-psychological categories and abilities exercised bilaterally, namely, an *intent* to produce a mental state + *recognition* of that intent + *acknowledgment* of the recognition. The result is the initial *matrix of meaning*, as we may call it. The second step, in (ii), is a transfer from people meaning something to communicative acts and expressions, including words, meaning something, whereby the former (people) meaning becomes a *template* for the latter (acts) meaning. Three scaffolding strategies are at work here – assembly, template, and matrix.

The intuitive-psychological assembly and the resulting matrix in (i) are an indispensable ladder that enables infants to grasp personalized communicative meanings, before being discarded and replaced by impersonal and "fossilized" meanings attached to gestures, words, and utterances. As a skill installation, this process is not that different from impersonal routines, such as writing or driving, that eventually replace the initial personal instruction provided by scaffolding teachers and for a while may be literally remembered and rehearsed as the teachers instructed.

The earliest communicative exchanges between infants and adults are bilateral, face-to-face: this is the *initial domain* in which infantile intuitive psychology operates. Yet later on infants recognize the bilateral meaning of an expression of a mental state, even when the expression is decoupled from the physical presence of the adult; the gesturing mother may look elsewhere or vocalize from another room but in ways perceived by the infant as similar to those displayed in face-to-face communication. Such meaning-conveying but decoupled expressions as communicative acts constitute a *new* domain handled by infants in their comprehension mode with the *same* intuitive-psychological abilities initially used in face-to-face communication (old domain). In the production mode, involving metamental rehearsals and goal strategies, an infant's *intent* to catch an adult's attention and initiate communication may recruit the memory of a decoupled expression (gesture, vocalization) and project it online to *mean* "intent to communicate it" and expect the adult to recognize this intent and acknowledge the recognition (completing the bilateral meaning loop).

In sum, infants face a new challenge in a *new* domain when they have to grasp the meaning of a decoupled expression of a mental state in indirect (not face-to-face) communication. As subjectively perceived by infants, there is a close *proximity* or overlap of the domains involved (face-to-face interaction versus indirect communication). Furthermore, objectively, the *same intuitive-psychological resources* are employed in roughly similar ways through online metamental rehearsals servicing a goal strategy of initiating communication with or catching the attention of another person. The basic conditions of scaffolding through mentalization are met first by a matrix in which the initial sense-of-the-mental scaffolds an understanding of the bilateral meaning of a communicator, and then, in a fairly rapid developmental sequence, by a template that transfers the communicator's meaning to the impersonal meaning of a communicative act (Bogdan, 2009).

Scaffolding by Naïve Psychology: Shared Attention → Mastery of Word Reference

Naïve psychology is my label for the intuitive psychology operative from late infancy until around age four. Integrating the infantile bilateral sense of the mental, naïve psychology represents and reacts to the mostly visible, concrete, and behaviorally or verbally manifested mind-to-target relations of other people, as displayed in seeing, attending, simple desires, visually based beliefs, shared attention, and joint action (Apperly, 2010; Doherty, 2009; Perner, 1991; Tomasello, 1999). I will focus on what is perhaps the most momentous scaffolding in early childhood – namely, understanding word reference by way of shared attention. This, I think, is done in three major steps (Bogdan, 2009).

First step: a sense of co-referential intent in shared attention. The typical scenario operates roughly as follows. In a communication context, adult or child intends to refer through preverbal means (looks, gestures, vocalizations) to a shared target by making the intent manifest to the other party. The latter recognizes and acknowledges the intent. This intent to refer *and* its recognition and acknowledgment, resulting in a (mutual) sense of co-reference, are *scaffolded* by the new ability to share attention, which combines (i) the naïve-psychological representation of another person's attention to targets and (ii) a prior sense of bilateral meaning of communicative acts acquired earlier in infancy. For the child, this pre-linguistic scaffolding step, leading to a sense of co-reference, occurs in the already familiar naïve-psychological *matrix* of shared attention (Bruner, 1983; Tomasello, 1999).

Second step: acquiring the ability to direct attention co-referentially. The already acquired intent to co-refer pre-linguistically through shared attention *scaffolds* as a *template* a new ability to direct attention to a shared target by way of pre-linguistic co-reference through looks, head and eye movements, and hand gestures.

Third step: words that refer. The pre-linguistic co-referential work of directing attention to a shared target in turn *scaffolds* as a *template* the ability to comprehend and produce words as referential symbols. Children are likely to treat words initially as a new sort of attention directors, hence as part of a familiar game of shared attention, before regarding them as impersonal symbols (Bates, 1976; Bogdan, 2009; Bruner, 1983; Hobson, 1993; Tomasello, 1999).

Within naïve psychology as the old domain, shared attention itself is *assembled* out of prior abilities (namely, a bilateral sense of the mental plus representation of attention as mind-to-target relation) and in turn constitutes, in the new and later-developing domain of pre-linguistic and referential communication, a *matrix* that scaffolds children's sense of co-referential intent. The latter intent in the new domain of pre-linguistic co-referential communication is then recruited and actively projected, and often rehearsed online, to drive the child's goal strategy of directing another person's attention to a shared target by way of words – a still newer domain of linguistic communication.

The scaffolding conditions are therefore met: in children's minds, the old domain of shared attention to a target of mutual interest is close to the new domain of pre-linguistic co-referential triangulation, which in turn is close to the still newer domain of linguistic co-referential communication. The mental resources involved, from looks to gestures to words, are initially treated as attention directors and derive their functions from children's naïve psychology that manages interpersonal interactions to targets of mutual interest in a shared environment. Finally, the developmental advances occur in tight succession during the second and third year of life (Bogdan, 2009).

To sum up, once capable of shared attention, the young naïve psychologists initially acquire and treat words as co-referential attention directors, as they already treated looks and pointings in prior exercises of shared attention, before word acquisition and use become impersonally fossilized and routinized. These successive scaffoldings, which embed novelties in already familiar structures through templates, matrices, and assemblies, go a long way toward explaining why and how the immensely difficult and evolutionarily unprecedented task of learning word meaning and reference is carried out so speedily and apparently effortlessly in early childhood. The young children's minds come already well equipped and prepared for this task through earlier acquisitions initially evolved for handling challenges facing their intuitive psychology.

Scaffolding by Naïve Psychology: Shared Attention → Topic-Comment Predication

In doing its work, shared attention has another momentous implication: it scaffolds a unique format of communication and thinking, that of *topic-comment predication*. It is a format that is likely to be unique to human minds and, as far as I can tell, is not intrinsic to or simply maturing out of resources for grammar, semantics, and logic. Rather, it is an outcome of naïve-psychological scaffolding through mentalization (Bogdan, 2000, 2009).

In directing attention to a shared target, as a topic of mutual interest, and having such directing recognized and acknowledged, child and adult also exchange pre-linguistic *comments*, in the form of overtly expressed emotions, vocalizations, and gestures. As words begin to replace looks, head movements, and hand gestures as co-referential attention directors to shared targets as topics of mutual interest, the comments remain for a while pre-linguistic, before being gradually replaced by linguistic comments. The latter are likely to be *initially* viewed by young children as symbolic versions of pre-linguistic communicative interactions through shared attention (Bates, 1976; Bogdan, 2009; Tomasello, 1999). This scaffolding process can be analyzed as follows.

First step: shared attention as matrix scaffolds pre-linguistic predication. Words as attention directors (prior acquisition) operate as shared topic fixers. When words fix targets of interest as shared topics and comments are still pre-linguistic (inherited from shared attention interactions that are recognized and acknowledged), the result is a sort of half-linguistic topical predication.

Second step: pre-linguistic comments scaffold predicate phrases. The predicate phrases are intended, for a present or virtual audience, to add information about or reactions to a shared topic, with appropriate recognition and acknowledgment by the audience. My reading of the developmental literature is that in their earliest fully linguistic conversations with adults, once a topic is set, young children add or respond to earlier adult utterances with comments that are similar in tone and function to their pre-linguistic reactions, as comments, to shared items of interest (Bates, 1976; Bruner, 1983; Hobson, 1993; Nelson, 1996, 2007; Tomasello, 1999).

The scaffolding conditions posited by my analysis are met in this case as well: children perceive the old domain of shared attention to a target of mutual interest as similar or close to the new domain of exchanging reactive comments – first pre-linguistic and later wordy – to a shared topic. The resources employed belong initially to the infantile sense of the mental (as bilaterally shared meaning) and its successor, the young naïve psychology, in the form of shared attention, whose pre-linguistic resources become templates for the linguistically formed topics and comments. Shared attention itself becomes a matrix for early child–adult linguistic conversation. Finally, the developmental schedule for topic-comment predication overlaps with that of word acquisition by shared attention but extends into the third year of life, indicating a gradual incorporation of topic-comment predication initially based on shared attention into the emerging linguistic discourse (Bogdan, 2009).

Concluding Comments: Evolutionary Implications

I conclude with a few reasons why the mind-design work of intuitive psychology by way of scaffolding through mentalization makes evolutionary sense.

To begin with, not only does the human species rely essentially on intuitive psychology for its social and political (or competitive) interactions and cultural acquisitions and transmission, but the strongest pressures on young children – immature, helpless, and adult-dependent as they are – are also eminently social, political, and cultural. Children cannot respond and adapt to these pressures without access and reaction to the minds of others through intuitive psychology. For these reasons alone, intuitive psychology is in a uniquely strong evolutionary position to influence mental development, particularly in domains, such as those examined in this chapter, which initially require or encourage representations of mental states. This is what I think leads to opportunities for scaffolding through mentalization.

Second, natural and other forms of selection are known to be conservative and gradualist tinkerers: they tend to handle new selection pressures by modifying minimally, and building upon, existing and reliable resources. With social-cognitive precursors in nonhuman primates and archaic humans, intuitive psychology is older and more deeply grounded in the modern human mind than the cognitive novelties it scaffolds, such as word acquisition, predicative thinking, reflexive thinking, or imagining. This historical pedigree, earlier operation, and deeper evolutionary grounding again place intuitive psychology in a good position to scaffold more recent cognitive novelties through similarities of domains, modes of operation, and mentalizing resources employed.

Third, natural and other forms of selection act on overt behavioral interactions between organisms and their worlds, so that the impact of selection is first reflected in an organism's goal strategies that guide its behaviors. If an organism is capable of advance rehearsals of its goal strategies, as human children are, then these anticipatory resources will be the first in the mind to be subject to the forces of selection. And if mental rehearsals operate with and over representations of mental states, as they do in young (and adult) intuitive psychologists, then such metamental rehearsals hold the promise of turning to new domains and new challenges, and eventually evolve new (ontogenetic) adaptations, if the new domains and challenges are perceived subjectively by children as open to mentalizing – which is precisely what happens according to the argument of this chapter.

Finally, natural and other forms of (nonsexual) selection are first and foremost operative during *ontogeny*, for a simple reason: the forces of selection operate on phenotypes, not genotypes, and the latter *become* phenotypes during ontogeny; therefore, the work of selection is done through, during, and on development, including mental. Since the strongest and most urgent pressures on young human minds are bound to be sociocultural and later sociopolitical, children cannot respond to these pressures without access and reaction to other minds, namely through intuitive psychology. But since the pressures vary across age intervals, intuitive psychology as a generic know-how will respond with different resources (subsumed under the three competencies discussed here) and those resources in turn are bound to scaffold different new cognitive capacities. In evolutionary terms, therefore, intuitive psychology has the reasons, means, and opportunities to be a powerful and far-reaching mind designer.

References

Adamson, L. B. 1995. *Communication development during infancy.* Boulder: Westview Press.

Apperly. I. 2010. *Mindreaders.* New York, NY: Psychology Press.

Banaji, M. R. and S. A. Gelman (Eds.) 2013. *Navigating the social world*. Oxford: Oxford University Press.

Bates, E. 1976. *Language and context*. New York, NY: Academic Press.

Bjorklund, D. 2011. *Children's thinking*. Belmont: Wadsworth.

Bjorklund, D. and A. Pellegrini 2002. *The origins of human nature: Evolutionary developmental psychology*. Washington, D.C.: American Psychological Association.

Bogdan, R. J. 1994. *Grounds for cognition*. Hillsdale: Erlbaum.

Bogdan, R. J. 1997. *Interpreting minds*. Cambridge: MIT Press.

Bogdan, R. J. 2000. *Minding minds*. Cambridge: MIT Press.

Bogdan, R. J. 2001. Developing mental abilities by representing intentionality, *Synthese*, *129*, 233–258.

Bogdan, R. J. 2007. Inside loops, *Synthese*, *159*, 235–252.

Bogdan, R. J. 2009. *Predicative minds*. Cambridge: MIT Press.

Bogdan, R. J. 2010. *Our own minds*. Cambridge: MIT Press.

Bogdan, R. J. 2013. *Mindvaults*. Cambridge: MIT Press.

Bruner, J. 1983. *Child's talk*. New York, NY: Norton.

Csibra, G. and G. Gergely 2013. Teleological understanding of actions. In M. R. Banaji and S. A. Gelman (Eds.), *Navigating the social world*. (pp. 37–43). Oxford: Oxford University Press.

Dennett, D. 1971. Intentional systems. *Journal of Philosophy 8*, 87–106.

Doherty, M. 2009. *Theory of mind*. New York, NY: Psychology Press.

Gergely, G. and G. Csibra 2003. Teleological reasoning in infancy. *Trends in Cognitive Science 7*, 287–292.

Gopnik, A. and H. Wellman 1992. Why the child's theory of mind really is a theory. *Mind and Language 7*, 145–171.

Grice, P. 1957. Meaning. *Philosophical Review 66*, 377–388.

Hobson, R. 1993. *Autism and the development of mind*. Hillsdale: Erlbaum.

Howhy, J. 2014. *The predictive mind*. Oxford: Oxford University Press.

Karmiloff-Smith, A. 1992. *Beyond modularity*. Cambridge: MIT Press.

Meltzoff, A. N. 2013. Origins of social cognition. In M. R. Banaji and S. A. Gelman (Eds.), *Navigating the social world*. (pp. 139–144). Oxford: Oxford University Press.

Mercier, H. and D. Sperber 2011. Why do humans reason? *Behavioral and Brain Sciences 34*, 57–111.

Nelson, K. 1996. *Language in cognitive development*. Cambridge: Cambridge University Press.

Nelson, K. 2007. *Young minds in social worlds*. Cambridge: Harvard University Press.

Perner, J. 1991. *Understanding the representational mind*. Cambridge: MIT Press.

Tomasello, M. 1999. *The cultural origins of human cognition*. Cambridge: Harvard University Press.

Tomasello, M. and H. Moll. 2013. Why don't apes understand false belief? In M. R. Banaji and S. A. Gelman (Eds.), *Navigating the social world*. (pp. 81–87). Oxford: Oxford University Press.

Trevarthen, C. 1993. The self born in intersubjectivity. In U. Neisser (Ed.), *The perceived self*. (pp. 121–173). Cambridge: Cambridge University Press.

Trevarthen, C. 2011. The generation of human meaning. In A. Seemann (Ed.), *Joint attention*. (pp. 73–135). Cambridge: MIT Press.

20 Embrace Complexity! Multiple Factors Contributing to Cognitive, Social, and Communicative Development

Annette Karmiloff-Smith

In this chapter, I will first briefly examine domain-specific vs. domain-general explanations of human development, and suggest a third alternative, the *domain-relevant* explanation underlying neuroconstructivism, which allows for a greater degree of constrained flexibility. Touching on various aspects of developmental theory, I will examine how neuroconstructivism addresses them. Then, I will take language acquisition as an example and discuss motor, sleep-related, and environmental constraints on language. In the final section, I will examine what a domain-relevant view might contribute to claims about human evolution.

Domain-specific vs. Domain-general Explanations of the Infant Start State

The Nature *or* Nurture controversy has raged from time immemorial, particularly amongst the ancient Greeks. Its modern incarnation is often, although not inevitably, couched in terms of domain-specific versus domain-general explanations, in which some theorists claim that the infant brain comes equipped with primitive conceptual representations, domain-specific core knowledge, or domain-specific learning algorithms (Baillargeon & Carey, 2012; Carey, 2011; Spelke & Kinzler, 2007; van der Lely, 2005; van der Lely & Pinker, 2014), whereas others call on built-in domain-general learning mechanisms without the need for specific representational content (Elman et al., 1996; Kirkham, Slemmer, & Johnson, 2002; Lany & Saffran, 2013). Nowadays the majority of scientists recognize that evolution and ontogenetic development must be explained in terms of the very complex interactions of Nature *and* Nurture. Nonetheless, the Nature/Nurture dichotomy continues to sway debates about the structure of the human mind/brain (Pinker, 2002), how it evolved (Cosmides, Barrett, & Tooby, 2010), and how to interpret data such as the existence of domain-specific deficits in children and adults (Agrillo, Ranpura, & Butterworth, 2010; Clahsen & Temple, 2003; Cohen Kadosh et al., 2011). The debate still goes around in circles with regard to whether the infant brain constitutes an undifferentiated *tabula rasa* on which experience imprints itself via (innate) general learning mechanisms, or whether the infant brain comes innately equipped with specialized knowledge upon which further domain-specific learning takes place. Note that the innately specified perspective can, as Bates and colleagues stressed (Bates et al., 1998; Karmiloff-Smith et al., 1998), give rise to the conflation of innateness with: (a) *domain specificity* (outcome X is so singular that it must be innate), (b) *species specificity* (humans are the only species who do X, so X must be specified in the human genome), (c) *localization* (outcome X is mediated by a particular brain region, so X must be innate), and (d) *learnability* (we cannot establish how X could be learned, so X must be innate).

Studies of typically developing infants/children by researchers of a nativist persuasion (e.g., Baillargeon & Carey, 2012; Carey, 2011; Hyde & Spelke, 2011; Lee & Spelke, 2010; Spelke & Kinzler, 2007; Xu, Spelke, & Goddard, 2005) have often used the concept of innate, domain-specific modules. Rather than accounting for human development in terms of plasticity and a rich capacity for learning, early competences have frequently been explained in terms of built-in core knowledge/ conceptual representational primitives, i.e., infants are born with innately specified modules or sub-modules for processing specific types of input from each domain: number processing modules (Dehaene, 1997; Butterworth, 1999; Gelman & Gallistel, 1986), face-processing modules (Duchaine, 2000; Duchaine & Nakayama, 2005, 2006; Duchaine, Yovel, Butterworth, & Nakayama, 2006), grammatical sub-modules (van der Lely & Pinker, 2014), spatial cognition sub-modules (Landau, Hoffman, & Kurz, 2005), and modules containing core knowledge of the constraints governing the physical world (Spelke & Kinzler, 2007). Such reasoning led to the initial relegation of learning to a very unimportant role (Piattelli-Palmarini, 2001). However, as the importance of learning has been increasingly substantiated, researchers of the nativist persuasion have called on processes such as conceptual reorganization or the role of language to explain how domain-specific core knowledge of infant sensitivities to different cognitive domains becomes more abstract, adult-like knowledge (Baillargeon & Carey, 2012; Spelke & Kinzler, 2009).

Similar domain-specific claims have been marshaled by one brand of evolutionary psychology (Cosmides, Barrett, & Tooby, 2010; Duchaine, Cosmides, & Tooby 2001; Hauser & Spelke, 2004), contending that the association between human ancestral past and the human brain nowadays can be conceptualized in terms of innately specified, cognitive-level modules passed on through evolution (see discussion in Bolhuis, Brown, Richardson, & Laland, 2011), e.g., a cheater detection module, a grammar module, a face-processing module, a number module, etc., each coded for by specific sets of genes. Taking this stance, theorists conceptualize the brain in terms of the metaphor of a Swiss army knife, each tool (cognitive domain or sub-domain) being dedicated solely to carrying out a set of very restricted tasks, passed on by evolution from the hunter-gatherers of our ancestral past.

Some researchers studying neurodevelopmental disorders have also taken a strictly domain-specific, modular stance. For example, Baron-Cohen, Leslie, Frith, and colleagues claimed that autism could be explained because of impairments to a theory-of-mind module (Baron-Cohen, Leslie, & Frith. 1985; Leslie, 1992), due to the mutation of a specific gene or set of genes, which interfered with the development of the orbito-frontal cortex (Baron-Cohen et al., 1999). It was argued that this region was dedicated to computations involving the attribution of intentional states to others, an impaired ability in autism spectrum disorders. The explanatory framework of impaired versus intact modules or sub-modules has been extended to a wide variety of other neurodevelopmental disorders (Butterworth, 2008; Clahsen & Temple, 2003; Duchaine, Nieminen-von Wendt, New, & Kulomaki, 2003; Molko et al., 2003; Rice, 1999; Shalev, Manor, & Gross-Tsur, 2005; Temple, 1997), particularly those which present with uneven cognitive profiles, such as dyslexia (Castle & Coltheart, 1993), Specific Language Impairment (Gopnik, 1990; van der Lely, 2005; van der Lely & Pinker, 2014), Williams syndrome (Clahsen & Temple, 2003), developmental dyscalculia (Butterworth, 1999; Temple, 1997), and developmental prosopagnosia (Duchaine, 2000).

In general, then, early competences found in typically developing infants, deficits identified in brain-damaged adults or in children with genetic disorders, as well as arguments from evolutionary psychology all appear to corroborate the claim that the domain-general framework fails to explain both early domain-specific competences as well as atypical uneven cognitive profiles. Instead, theorists argued, the human mind/brain comprises highly specialized input/output systems, at both the perceptual and cognitive levels. So, what is wrong with this domain-specific framework? It can account for the profiles of typically developing children who show strong proficiency in, say, literacy and relative weakness in numeracy, or vice versa. It also seems an appropriate explanation for domain-specific deficits arising in adult neuropsychological patients. Similarly for atypically developing children: the domain-specific framework would seem to offer a plausible explanation for the existence of children with autism who may present with high abilities in, say, mathematics, but are incapable of dealing with the simplest of aspects of social interaction, or those with Williams syndrome who speak fluently but cannot do simple additions. How could a domain-general view explain such specificities? Is the only alternative to the domain-general approach that of innate, domain specificity? Not necessarily, because the domain-specific framework is itself problematic, ignoring, as it does, the developmental history of the organism, which Piaget deemed so vital.

The Neuroconstructivist Explanation of Human Development, Embracing the Domain-relevant Framework

We have hitherto discussed two alternatives for theorizing about human evolution and ontogenesis: the domain-general and the domain-specific frameworks. For some time, I have proposed a third alternative – a *domain-relevant* framework – that would likely be endorsed by several theorists working within a more domain-general framework. A domain-relevant approach to understanding specialization in adult brains argues that the brain starts out with a number of basic-level biases, each of which is somewhat more relevant to the processing of certain kinds of input over others, but which only *become* domain-specific over developmental time. This occurs, it is argued, through a process of neuronal competition and gradual specialization, localization, and modularization of function – a neuroconstructivist approach (Elman et al., 1996; Karmiloff-Smith, 1992, 1998; Mareschal et al., 2007; Westermann et al., 2007, 2010). Neuroconstructivism does not claim that the infant brain is an undifferentiated *tabula rasa* upon which experience simply imprints itself, nor does it rule out domain specificity; it argues that, when one discovers specialized functions in the adult brain, it cannot be taken for granted that the same automatically holds for the start state of the infant mind/brain (Karmiloff-Smith, 1998, 2013; Paterson et al., 1999). Rather, neuroconstructivism maintains that domain specificity, i.e., functional specialization, is the emergent *outcome* of developmental processes in interaction with the social and physical environments, rather than the start state.

It is within the neuroconstructivist account of development (Karmiloff-Smith, 1992, 1998; Elman et al., 1996; Johnson, 2001; Mareschal et al., 2007; Stiles, 2009; Thomas, Knowland, & Karmiloff-Smith, 2011; Westermann, Thomas, & Karmiloff-Smith, 2010) that domain-relevant approaches have been proposed, particularly in the clinical field of neurodevelopmental disorders. Neuroconstructivists explain such disorders at a very different level from the intact/impaired domain-specific cognitive modules discussed above. For the neuroconstructivist, atypical phenotypic outcomes are deemed to originate in perturbations in very basic processes early in development, such as a lack of/over-exuberant pruning, or differences in synaptogenesis, dendritic growth, the density/type of neurons, firing thresholds, poor signal to noise ratios, or generally in terms of atypical timing across developing systems. In other words, from a neuroconstructivist viewpoint, adult brain specialization *emerges developmentally* (Casey, Giedd, & Thomas, 2000; Elman et al., 1996; Johnson, 2001; Karmiloff-Smith, 1992, 1998). In this sense, it is probable that domain-specific outcomes may not be achievable at all in the absence of a gradual process of development over time.

But why does neuroconstructivism reject the notion that the infant brain starts out highly specialized with built-in conceptual knowledge, as some leading theorists (Carey, 2011; Spelke & Kinzler, 2007) maintain? This lies in the fact that multiple facets of early human development point instead to a flexible, plastic, self-structuring system, open to extensive environmental influences at the level of gene expression, brain, cognition, and behavior. Developmental change is the rule at every level, not the exception. Four facts clarify this point: (1) cortical areas are initially more highly interconnected in the infant brain than in the adult brain (Huttenlocher & de Courten, 1987; Huttenlocher & Dabholkar, 1997; Stiles, 2009), and it is only progressively, with the strengthening of some connections and the pruning of others, that localization and specialization of brain function occur (Johnson, 2001); (2) the ratio of white matter to gray matter is not static; it changes over development (Giedd et al., 1999); (3) the thickness of fiber bundles in the corpus callosum between the two hemispheres is different in infancy compared to later brain development (Giedd et al., 1996); and, (4) studies of neural processing of faces or language, for instance, reveal that initially in development neural activity is widespread across several cortical regions in both hemispheres. Only later does neural activity become progressively fine-tuned predominantly to one or other hemisphere (right hemisphere for face identification; left hemisphere for grammar production and phonemic processing) (Cohen Kadosh, Henson, Cohen Kadosh, Johnson, & Dick, 2009; de Haan, Humphreys, & Johnson, 2002; Johnson, 2001; Krishnan, Leech, Mercure, Lloyd-Fox, & Dick, 2014; Mills, Coffy-Corins, & Nevelle, 1997; Minagawa-Kawai, Mori, Naoi, & Kojima, 2007; Neville, Mills, & Bellugi, 1994; Stiles, 2012). As stressed by Stiles, multiple cross-sectional and longitudinal studies of children with peri-natal focal lesions (reviewed in Bates & Roe, 2001; Stiles, 2012) have yielded only very transient relationships between specific lesion sites and specific language deficits. Moreover, such relationships in children differ significantly from those found in adult aphasic patients. There is in fact no evidence of long-lasting language delays associated specifically with left versus right hemisphere perinatal focal brain damage (Stiles, 2012).

These four examples indicate that the brain's microstructure is neither pre-specified nor static. Cortical networks are not genetically determined, to be spared or impaired in genetic disorders. Rather, they emerge from progressively changing neural structure and functions (Casey, Tottenham, Liston, & Durston, 2005; Durston et al., 2006; Paterson, Heim, Friedman, Choudhury, & Benasich, 2006), which dynamically interact with one another and with environmental input, resulting ultimately in the structured adult brain. Emergent specialization of function is viewed by neuroconstructivists as the fine-tuning of initially diffuse, domain-relevant, but coarsely-coded systems, which *become* increasingly domain-specific over developmental time.

Of course, neuroconstructivism is not alone in taking a more dynamic approach to developmental change. For development, this holds for scientists espousing dyna-mical systems accounts (e.g., Smith & Thelen, 2003), although they tend to discount the notion of representational content. For healthy aging in adults, similar arguments have been put forward regarding the dynamic and changing nature of neural processes with respect, for instance, to grammatical processing (Tyler et al., 2010). Modules are now considered far less encapsulated, allowing them to operate in a relatively independent way in some circumstances, but modifiable by other processes in other circumstances (e.g., Dehaene & Cohen, 2007). However, whereas theorists such as Spelke or Pinker would be unlikely to adopt a strictly Fodorian view of modules (Fodor, 1983), their current theorizing continues to appeal to innate specification of highly specialized systems (Spelke & Kinzler, 2007; van der Lely & Pinker, 2014), a very different framework from that of neuroconstructivists.

The neuroconstructivist approach considers that mutations contributing to developmental disorders in infants are likely to affect widespread systems within the brain, some more seriously/more subtly than others, depending on their domain relevance (Karmiloff-Smith, 1998). This does not preclude that the outcome of the dynamic developmental processes might result in some areas being more impaired than others, due to the processing demands of certain types of input to those areas as well as to differences in synaptogenesis across various cerebral regions (Huttenlocher & Dabholkar, 1997). It is important to recall that gene expression in the brain (when a gene is expressed during day/night or across development, how much protein product is expressed, and in which brain region[s] it is expressed) is not predetermined, but also a function of environmental experience over developmental time. Studies of rodents nicely illustrate this point, highlighting the potential role of the environment in shaping patterns of gene expression (Kaffman & Meaney, 2007). The researchers tracked brain development in rodent pups and showed that differences in the amount of maternal postnatal pup grooming/stroking actually changed the amount and location of the expression of genes involved in the brain's responses to stress, which had lifelong effects on the animal's behavior and even on subsequent generations. Such dynamic environment–gene interactions are likely to be pervasive in mammalian brain development, including that of humans. In general, epigenesis is not deterministic under tight genetic control. Rather, epigenesis is probabilistic and only under broad genetic control (Gottlieb, 2007). So, if the architecture of the adult brain is highly specialized, this is likely to be the end-product of very complex gene–brain–cognition–behavior–environment dynamics (Scerif & Karmiloff-Smith, 2001), which give rise over developmental time to relatively domain-specific outcomes. And this flexible, dynamic framework makes evolutionary sense.

Neurocontructivism and Human Language: Motor, Sleep, and Environmental Constraints

Let us now take a concrete example and examine how the neuroconstructivist, in contrast to many other developmental psycholinguistic approaches, might think about human language acquisition and its disorders. Contrary to the notion that genetic mutations are the main cause of language disorders, the neuroconstructivist would consider this as merely one among many other dynamically interacting factors.

Always aiming to identify the roots of subsequent cognitive-level outcomes, the neuroconstructivist would examine research on the fetus in utero, because the auditory system is well developed by the final three months of intrauterine life. And indeed, numerous studies have shown that the fetus processes incoming auditory input – mother's voice, the intonation patterns of her mother tongue, the music she regularly listens to – altering its heart rate or leg kicking when noting a change in the input (Hepper, Scott, & Shahidullah, 1993). Moreover, using the non-nutritive sucking technique, researchers have shown that the newborn can already discriminate its mother's voice from that of other female voices (Moon & Fifer, 2000), despite it being very different ex-utero from in-utero, suggesting that the fetus has stored quite an abstract representation of the voice. Newborns also discriminate their mother tongue from languages from other language families (stress-based vs. syllable-based vs. mora-based languages) but not yet from those within the same language family (Gervain & Mehler, 2010). Newborns also recognize the music that their mothers listened to regularly, such as the theme tune of a soap opera. So, the baby comes into the world not only with genes that might be relevant to learning language, but also with quite a lot of prenatal auditory experience that would make the infant pay special attention to language at birth.

What else might the scientist pay attention to, outside obvious auditory stimuli, in the early development of communicative abilities? Attention and memory are clearly relevant, but what about motor development? The production of language involves a series of exquisitely-timed, coordinated oromotor movements, occurring at a rate of 3–4 Hz, much faster than other oral movements such as chewing (Ghazanfar et al., 2012). Speech involves a dynamic planning process in which the movements of various articulators – lips, tongue, soft palate, velum, and glottis – have to be finely inter-coordinated (Brownman & Goldstein, 1995). Moreover, babies have to *learn* to adapt their articulatory system to environmental language(s), a process that continues to develop well into childhood.

Many studies have shown that language delay is frequently accompanied by motor delay. And, while gross motor development does not predict language development, fine motor control has specific links with the onset of babbling and other language-relevant factors. Early mouthing predicts consonant production (Iverson, 2010), and non-linguistic oromotor control at 21 months predicts vocabulary production scores on the Communicative Development Inventory (CDI) for both vocabulary and sentence complexity (Alcock & Krawczyk, 2010). The popular Non-Word Repetition task (NWR) – repeating pseudowords that obey the phonotactics of English, such as /peplisteronk/ – involves not only phonological memory, as many have shown (e.g. Coady & Evans, 2008), but also complex motor planning. For instance, a recent study has yielded a strong correlation between oromotor praxis and NWR, not only in typical development (Krishnan et al., 2013) but also in children, adolescents, and adults with Williams syndrome (Krishnan et al., 2015). So, the motor system must be taken into account when thinking about how children acquire language in both typical and atypical development.

What other domains are relevant? What about sleep constraints on language and development? Previous assumptions about the role of sleep in development have been challenged by recent research. Whereas it was thought that sleep "comes naturally" to the infant, sleep is now considered part of cognitive development: babies have to *learn* to self soothe in order to pass between REM (rapid eye movement) and non-REM sleep states. It also used to be thought that when the newborn and young infants go to sleep, their brain takes a long rest to replenish energy stores. By contrast, it is now known that parts of the brain are more active during sleep than during the wake state (Foster and Kreitzman, 2010). This is due to the active process of sleep-dependant learning and memory, during which the brain replays the neural activity it had during wakefulness while strengthening connections within and across different brain regions. Recall the seminal study of Ruth Weir, where she recorded pre-sleep practicing of language sounds (Weir, 1962). Alone, in the dark, the baby emitted a series of language-like sounds as if practicing their discrimination. At that time, researchers were not sensitive to the role that sleep might subsequently play in strengthening these language-like representations, but more recently Rebecca Gomez and collaborators have shown how critical even a daytime nap is for the learning of grammatical structure (Gomez, Bootzin, &

Nadel, 2006; Hupbach, Gomez, Bootzin & Nadel, 2009). Indeed, this work has clearly demonstrated the long-term effects of sleep on memory for grammatical dependencies. The artificial language – *pel-wadim-jic-vot-kicey-rud-pel-deecha-jic-mut-kicey-den-pel –bisto-jic* – in which <pel> always predicts <jic> (rather like <is> predicts <ing> in the following English language example: *is*-play-*ing* / *is*-danc-*ing* / *is*-eat-*ing*) – was played to two groups of 15-month-old infants, one of whom had napped within 4 hours of the language exposure and the other who had stayed awake. Twenty-four hours later, the nap group discriminated the grammatical dependencies of language heard from new dependencies in a previously unheard language. By contrast, infants who had not napped shortly after familiarization showed no evidence of discriminating between the language heard and a new one (Gomez, Bootzin, & Nadel, 2006; Hupbach et al., 2009). Another group has recently shown similar findings with respect to the learning of new vocabulary, again comparing napping vs. awake infants (Horváth, Myers, Foster, & Plunkett, 2015).

What about environmental constraints on language and development? A cross-linguistic, longitudinal study examined perceptual narrowing for speech perception using native and non-native stimuli in the same infants at 6 and again at 10 months of age (Karmiloff-Smith et al., 2010; Elsabbagh et al., 2013). At the group level, the study yielded similar findings to those of other researchers, with 6-month-olds able to distinguish both native and non-native phonemes, whereas 10-month-olds had by then become specialized in their mother tongues (English, French, or German). However, when the groups were divided as a function of the style of mother–child interaction (from contingent to more controlling), babies of contingent mothers lost the ability to discriminate non-native phonemes significantly earlier than those of more controlling/directive mothers. We believe this can be explained by the fact mothers who were more contingent with their babies' activities tended to constantly adapt their speech to the level of their child's output, whereas more controlling mothers tended to speak at their child. However, this advantage was not a cross-domain, general advantage. Infants of mothers who were more controlling were in advance of those of contingent mothers with respect to understanding human goal-directed actions. We interpreted this in terms of the fact that sensitive mothers are always adapting to the goals of their infants, whereas infants of more controlling mothers have to work out what their mothers' goals are and are therefore in advance developmentally. So, the style of social interaction clearly plays a role in language development, and in developmental progress in general.

Environments can have, of course, more serious effects on development. A study comparing infants from low and high socio-economic-status (SES) backgrounds found that as early as 6 months, gamma-band activity in the prefrontal cortex was significantly less in those from low SES backgrounds (Tomalski et al., 2013), indicating that very early in development brain structure and function are being molded by environmental factors. If this holds for typical development, why does a positive, healthy, stimulating environment compensate only partially for genetic vulnerabilities? Is it just the mutated genes? In fact, while genes play a partial role, for the atypically developing infant there are also environmental vulnerabilities, even when parents believe that they are providing the most stimulating environment possible. This is because having a developmental disorder *changes the environment* (social and physical) in which the infant develops – i.e., differences in parental expectations of their child with a neurodevelopmental disorder change the environment very subtly.

Here are two examples. Carolyn Mervis and collaborators examined the role of parental interaction on overgeneralization in typical development and in infants with Down syndrome (Cardoso-Martins & Mervis, 1985). In typical development, when the child overgeneralized, say, the word /cat/ to other animals, the parent responded lightly, saying that indeed it was a bit like a cat but was called a /dog/. By contrast, the parents of toddlers with Down syndrome tended to correct immediately, not allowing the overgeneralization. Yet, overgeneralization can temporarily help the child form a broad category – <animal> in this case – and stopping overgeneralization could cause the child to learn much narrower mappings.

Another example comes from outside language, but again illustrates how subtle differences in parental behavior can affect development. Many children, both typically and atypically developing, come to our lab with their parents. We have consistently noted that when an atypically developing child crawls away, the parent is often quickly on their feet to pick up the child, due to a natural fear of danger. The same applies to objects placed in the mouth. When an atypically developing child sucks on an object, the parent is often quick to remove it, again due to a natural fear of greater danger for the child with a neurodevelopmental disorder.

Yet these naturally protective behaviors may actually thwart exploration: the nerve endings in the mouth are, early on, more sensitive than those of the fingers, so exploration by the mouth can provide important information on size, texture, shape, and temperature of an object. Likewise, crawling around a new environment can give rise to numerous discoveries and develop spatial maps. Thus, in their natural desire to help their infant, the parent of a child with a neurodevelopmental disorder is subtly changing his/her environment compared to that of a typically developing infant. We have recently been able to document these effects in twins discordant for Down syndrome: the mother turns out not to be intrinsically contingent or controlling. Rather, it is the dyad that counts, with the mother reacting differently to her typically developing twin vs. the one with Down syndrome. Clearly, a more dynamic view is required of how cultural, social, and physical environments interact with genetic vulnerabilities across developmental time.

Neuroconstructivism and its Relevance to Evolutionary Thinking

In their review of comparative neuroscience, Quartz and Sejnowski (1997) note that the degree of genetic pre-specification varies in non-random ways across species: highest in animals the most distant from humans, and lowest in our closest relatives. Of course, many species have complex special-purpose responses to the environment that human infants do not have (e.g., the spider's exquisite ability to weave a complex web). By contrast, humans develop an increasingly *flexible* cognitive system over time. Thus, rather than endow us with maximal pre-specified core knowledge (hyperspecialization), evolution may have leaned instead toward increasing plasticity for learning in the human case. So, instead of coming into the world as hyperspecialized, human infants are more likely born with a collection of reflexes together with some domain-general learning algorithms (for attention, discrimination, novelty detection, memory, etc.), but also some domain-relevant biases that provide not only a starting point but also an initial trajectory vector in cognitive space, one that will be affected not only by experience but also by interactions within and between levels of causal change (cellular, neural, body, environment; see Mareschal et al., 2007; Westermann et al. 2007, 2010). Interestingly, too, unlike other species, humans remain totally dependent upon their carers during a lengthy period of early development, allowing the social environment to impact significantly upon brain development.

So, instead of invoking a start state of innate, domain-specific modules handed down by evolution, the neuroconstructivist framework would argue that evolution may be driven predominantly by increased plasticity for learning (Finlay, 2007; Karmiloff-Smith, 2010, 2012; Karmiloff-Smith & Thomas, 2005), rather than increased genetic complexity, i.e., for a limited number of domain-relevant biases, which *become* domain-specific over developmental time via their competitive interaction with each other (Johnson, 2001; Karmiloff-Smith, 1998). Thus, evolutionary change can be looked upon as a trade-off between hyperspecialization but a relative lack of flexibility, on the one hand, and, on the other hand, maximum (but not unbounded) plasticity with some domain-relevant constraints (Karmiloff-Smith, 1992, 2009; Quartz & Sejnowski, 1997).

For the neuroconstructivist, plasticity is not simply the organism's response to injury; rather, it is the rule for development, normal or atypical (Bates & Roe, 2001; Bolhuis et al., 2011; Cicchetti & Tucker, 1994; Dehaene et al., 2014; Sur, Pallas, & Roe, 1990; Webster, Bachevalier, & Ungerleider, 1995). But plasticity is not, of course, unconstrained. As Hensch and collaborators (Bavelier et al., 2010; Hensch, 2005) have elegantly demonstrated in a series of molecular studies on the excitatory-inhibitory balance across brain regions and systems that place constraints on plasticity, it would make no sense in evolutionary terms to have unbounded plasticity. A developing organism needs to be both constrained and flexible (Karmiloff-Smith, 1992, 1994), and achieving that dynamic balance is what ontogenesis is all about.

Thus, theorists have several options to explain the start state of the human brain and its subsequent development, amongst which are the frameworks discussed in this chapter: (1) the domain-general framework of an initially undifferentiated brain which gains its structure solely from interacting with the environment; (2) the core knowledge or conceptual representations framework, where the brain starts out with very domain-specific knowledge upon which more abstract knowledge is built through, inter alia, language or conceptual reorganization; or, (3) the neuroconstructivist framework, together with a process of representational redescription (Karmiloff-Smith, 1992), which invokes domain-relevant – not domain-specific – biases to kick-start development, as well as initial neuronal competition and gradual emergent functional specialization, drawing a clear distinction between the developing brain and the developed brain. Nothing in biology or psychology is static: gene expression changes over time, brain structure and function change throughout development, cognitive processes change over time, behavior changes over time, and social and physical environments change dramatically over time. And as developmental scientists, we need to fully embrace developmental change in all its complexities.

References

Agrillo, C., Ranpura, A., & Butterworth, B. (2010). Time and numerosity estimation are independent: Behavioral evidence for two different systems using a conflict paradigm. *Cognitive Neuroscience, 1*(2), 96–101.

Alcock, K. J., & Krawczyk, K. (2010). Individual differences in language development: Relationship with motor skills at 21 months. *Developmental Science, 13*(5), 677–691. doi: 10.1111/j.1467-7687.2009.00924.x

Baillargeon, R., & Carey, S. (2012). Core cognition and beyond: The acquisition of physical and numerical knowledge. In S. Pauen (Ed.) *Early childhood development and later outcome* (pp. 33–65). Cambridge, UK: Cambridge University Press.

Baron-Cohen, S., Leslie, A. M., & Frith, U. (1985). Does the autistic child have a "theory of mind"? *Cognition, 21*(1), 37–46.

Baron-Cohen, S., Ring, H. A., Wheelwright, S., Bullmore, E. T., Brammer, M. J., Simmons, A., & Williams, S. C. (1999). Social intelligence in the normal and autistic brain: an fMRI study. *European Journal of Neuroscience, 11*(6), 1891–1898.

Bates E., Elman, J., Johnson, M. H., Karmiloff-Smith, A., Parisi, D., & Plunkett, K. (1998). Innateness and emergentism. In W. Bechtel and G. Graham (Eds.). *A companion to cognitive science* (pp. 590–601). Oxford: Basil Blackwell.

Bates E. & Roe, K. (2001). Language development in children with unilateral brain injury. In C. A. Nelson & M. Luciana (Eds.). *Handbook of developmental cognitive neuroscience* (pp. 281–307). Cambridge, MA: MIT Press.

Bavelier, D., Levi, D. M., Li, R. W., Dan, Y., & Hensch, T. K. (2010). Removing brakes on adult plasticity: from molecular to behavioural interventions. *Journal of Neuroscience. 30*(45), 14964–14971.

Bolhuis J. J., Brown, G. R, Richardson, R. C, & Laland, K. N. (2011). Darwin in mind: New opportunities for evolutionary psychology. *PLoS Biology, 9* (7), 1–8.

Brownman, C. & Goldstein, L. (1995). Dynamics and articulatory phonology. In R. Port & T. Van Gelder (Eds.). *Mind as motion: Explorations in the dynamics of cognition (pp. 175–193).* Cambridge, MA: MIT Press.

Butterworth, B. (1999). *The mathematical brain.* London: Macmillan.

Butterworth, B. (2008). State-of-science review: Dyscalculia. In Goswami U. C. (Ed.) *Foresight mental capital and mental wellbeing.* London: Office of Science and Innovation.

Cardoso-Martins, C., & Mervis, C. B. (1985). Maternal speech to prelinguistic children with Down syndrome. *American Journal of Mental Deficiency, 89,* 451–458.

Carey, S. (2011). The Origin of Concepts: A précis. *Behavioral and Brain Sciences, 34,* 113–167.

Casey, B. J., Giedd, J. N., & Thomas, K. M. (2000). Structural and functional brain development and its relation to cognitive development. *Biological Psychology, 54*, 241–257.

Casey, B. J., Tottenham, N., Liston, C., & Durston, S. (2005). Imaging the developing brain. What have we learned about cognitive development? *Trends in Cognitive Science, 9*(3), 104–110.

Castle, A., & Coltheart, M. (1993). Varieties of developmental dyslexia. *Cognition 47*(2), 149–180.

Cicchetti, D., & Tucker, D. (1994). Development and self-regulatory structures of the mind. *Developmental Psychopathology, 6*, 533–549.

Clahsen, H., & Temple, C. (2003). Words and rules in children with Williams syndrome. In Y. Levy & J. Schaeffer (Eds.). *Language competence across populations* (pp. 323–352). Mahwah, NJ: Erlbaum.

Coady, J. A., & Evans, J. L. (2008). Uses and interpretations of non-word repetition tasks in children with and without specific language impairments (SLI). *International Journal of Language and Communicative Disorders. 43*(1), 1–40.

Cohen Kadosh, K., Henson, R., Cohen Kadosh, R., Johnson, M. H., & Dick, F. (2009). Task-dependent activation of face-sensitive cortex: an fMRI adaptation study. *Journal of Cognitive Neuroscience, 22*(5), 903–917.

Cohen Kadosh, R., Bahrami, B., Walsh, V., Butterworth, B., Popescu, T., & Price, C. J. (2011). Specialization in the human brain: The case of numbers. *Frontiers of Human Neuroscience 5*: 62. doi: 10.3389/fnhum.2011.00062

Cosmides, L., Barrett, H. C., & Tooby, J. (2010). Adaptive specializations, social exchange, and the evolution of human intelligence. *Proceedings of the National Academy of Science, 107*, 9007–9014.

De Haan, M., Humphreys, K., & Johnson, M. H. (2002). Developing a brain specialized for face processing: A converging methods approach. *Developmental Psychobiology, 40*(3), 200–212.

Dehaene, S. (1997). *The number sense: how the mind creates mathematics*. Oxford: Oxford University Press.

Dehaene S., Charles, L., King, J. R., & Marti, S. (2014). Toward a computational theory of conscious processing. *Current Opinion in Neurobiology, 25*, 76–84.

Dehaene S & Cohen, L. (2007). Cultural recycling of cortical maps. *Neuron 56*(2), 384–398.

Duchaine, B. (2000). Developmental propagnosia with normal configural processing. *NeuroReport, 11*(1), 79–83.

Duchaine B, Cosmides L., & Tooby, J. (2001). Evolutionary psychology and the brain. *Current Opinion in Neurobiology, 11*(1), 79–83.

Duchaine, B., & Nakayama, K. (2005). Dissociations of face and object recognition in developmental prosopagnosia. *Journal of Cognitive Neuroscience 17*, 249–261.

Duchaine, B. & Nakayama, K. (2006). Developmental prosopagnosia: A window to content-specific face processing. *Current Opinion in Neurobiology, 16*(2), 166–173.

Duchaine, B., Nieminen-von Wendt, T., New, J., & Kulomaki, T. (2003). Dissociations of visual recognition in a developmental agnosic: Evidence for separate developmental processes. *Neurocase, 9*, 380–389.

Duchaine, B., Yovel, G., Butterworth, E., & Nakayama, K. (2006). Prosopagnosia as an impairment to face-specific mechanisms: elimination of the alternative explanations in a developmental case. *Cognitive Neuropsychology, 23*, 714–747.

Durston, S., Davidson, M. C., Tottenham, N., Galvan, A., Spicer, J., Fossella, J. A., & Casey, B. J. (2006). A shift from diffuse to focal cortical activity with development. *Developmental Science*, *9*(1), 1–8.

Elman, J. L., Bates, E., Johnson, M. H., Karmiloff-Smith, A., Parisi, D., & Plunkett, K. (1996). *Rethinking innateness: A connectionist perspective on development*. Cambridge, Mass: MIT Press.

Elsabbagh, M., Hohenberger, A., Herwegen, J., Campos, R., Serres, J., de Schoenen, S., Aschersleben, G., & Karmiloff-Smith, A. (2013). Narrowing perceptual sensitivity to the native language in infancy: Exogenous influences on developmental timing. *Behavioral Sciences*, *3*(1),120–132.

Finlay, B. L. (2007). E pluribus unum: Too many unique human capacities and too many theories. In S. Gangestad and J. Simpson (Eds.). *The evolution of mind: Fundamental questions and controversies* (pp. 294–304). New York, NY: Guilford Press.

Fodor, J. (1983). *Modularity of mind*. Cambridge, MA: MIT Press.

Foster, R., & Kreitzman, L. (2010). *The rhythms of life: The biological clocks that control the daily lives of every living thing*. London: Profile.

Gelman, R., & Gallistel, R. (1986). *The child's understanding of number*. Cambridge, MA: Harvard University Press.

Gervain, J. & Mehler, J. (2010). Speech perception and language acquisition in the first year of life. *Annual Review of Psychology*, *61*, 191–218. doi: 10.1146/annurev.psych.093008.100408.

Ghazanfar A. A., Takahashi, D. Y., Mathur, N. A., & Fitch, W. T. (2012). Cineradiography of monkey lipsmacking reveals putative origins of speech dynamics. *Current Biology*, *22*, 1176–1182.

Giedd J., Blumenthal, J., Jeffries, N., Castellanos, F., Liu, H., & Zijdenbos, A. (1999). Brain development during childhood and adolescence: A longitudinal MRI study. *Nature Neuroscience*, *2*, 861–863.

Giedd, J., Rumsey, J., Castellanos, F., Rajapakse, J., Kaysen, D., & Vaituzis, A. (1996). A quantitative MRI study of the corpus callosum in children and adolescents. *Developmental Brain Research*, *91*, 274–280.

Gomez, R., Bootzin, R. R., & Nadel, L. (2006). Naps promote abstraction in language-learning infants. *Psychological Science*, *17*, 670–674.

Gopnik, M. (1990). Genetic basis of grammar defect. *Nature*, *347*(*6288*), 26.

Gottlieb, G. (2007). Probabilistic epigenesis. *Developmental Science*, *10*, 1–11.

Hauser, M. D., & Spelke, E. S. (2004). Evolutionary and developmental foundations of human knowledge: A case study of mathematics. In M Gazzaniga (Ed.) *The Cognitive Neurosciences, Vol. 3*, pp. 853–864. Cambridge: MIT Press.

Hensch, T. K. (2005). Critical period plasticity in local cortical circuits. *Nature Reviews Neuroscience*, *6*, 877–888.

Hepper P. G., Scott, D., & Shahidullah, B. S. (1993). Newborn and fetal response to maternal voice. *Journal of Reproductive and Infant Psychology*, *11*, 147–153.

Horváth K., Myers K., Foster R., & Plunkett K. (2015). Napping facilitates word learning in early lexical development. *Journal of Sleep Research*, *24*(5), 503–509. doi: 10.1111/jsr.12306

Hupbach, A., Gomez, R. L., Bootzin, R. R., & Nadel, L. (2009). Nap-dependent learning in infants. *Psychological Science*, *12*(6), 1007–1012. doi: 10.1111/j.1467-7687.2009.00837.x

Huttenlocher, P. R., & de Courten, C. (1987) The development of synapses in striate cortex of man. *Human Neurobiology, 6*, 1–9.

Huttenlocher, P. R., & Dabholkar, A. S. (1997). Regional differences in synaptogenesis in human cerebral cortex. *Journal of Comparative Neurology, 387*, 167–178.

Hyde, D. C., & Spelke, E. S. (2011). Neural signatures of number processing in human infants: Evidence for two core systems underlying numerical cognition. *Developmental Science, 14(2)*, 360–371.

Iverson, J. M. (2010). Developing language in a developing body: The relationship between motor development and language development. *Journal of Child Language, 37(02)*, 229–261.

Johnson, M. H. (2001). Functional brain development in humans. *Nature Reviews Neuroscience, 2*, 475–483.

Kaffman, A., & Meaney, M. J. (2007). Neurodevelopmental sequelae of postnatal maternal care in rodents: clinical and research implications of molecular insights. *Journal of Child Psychology and Psychiatry 48*, 224–244.

Karmiloff-Smith, A. (1992). *Beyond modularity: A developmental perspective on cognitive science*. Cambridge, Mass: MIT Press/Bradford Books.

Karmiloff-Smith, A. (1994). Transforming a partially structured brain into a creative mind. *Behavioral Brain Sciences, 17(4)*, 732–745.

Karmiloff-Smith, A. (1998). Development itself is the key to understanding developmental disorders. *Trends in Cognitive Science, 2(10)*, 389–398.

Karmiloff-Smith, A. (2009). Nativism versus neuroconstructivism: Rethinking the study of developmental disorders. *Interplay of Biology and Environment, Developmental Psychology, 45(1)*, 56–63.

Karmiloff-Smith, A. (2010). Neuroimaging of the developing brain: Taking "developing" seriously. *Human Brain Map, 31(6)*, 934–941.

Karmiloff-Smith, A. (2012). Brain: The neuroconstructivist approach. In E. K. Farran & A. Karmiloff-Smith (Eds.). *Neuro-developmental disorders across the lifespan: A neuroconstructivist approach* (pp. 37–58). Oxford: Oxford University Press.

Karmiloff-Smith, A. (2013). Challenging the use of adult neuropsychological models for explaining neurodevelopmental disorders: Developed versus developing brains. *Quarterly Journal of Experimental Psychology, 66*, 1–14.

Karmiloff-Smith, A., Aschersleben, G., de Schonen, T., Elsabbagh, M., Hohenberger, A., & Serres, J. (2010). Constraints on the timing of infant cognitive change: Domain-specific or domain-general? *European Journal of Developmental Science, 4(1)*, 31–45.

Karmiloff-Smith, A., Plunkett, K., Johnson, M., Elman, J. L., & Bates, E. (1998). What does it mean to claim that something is "innate"? *Mind and Language, 13(4)*, 588–597.

Karmiloff-Smith, A., & Thomas, M. S. C. (2005). Can developmental disorders be used to bolster claims from Evolutionary Psychology? A neuroconstructivist approach. In S. Taylor Parker, J. Langer, and C. Milbrath (Eds.). *Biology and knowledge revisited: From neurogenesis to psychogenesis* (pp. 307–322), Mahwah, NJ: Lawrence Erlbaum Press.

Kirkham, N. Z., Slemmer, J. A., & Johnson, S. P. (2002). Visual statistic learning in infancy: evidence for a domain-general learning mechanism. *Cognition, 83*, B35–B42.

Krishnan S., Alcock, K. J., Mercure, E., Leech, R., Barker, E., Karmiloff-Smith, A., & Dick, F. J. (2013). Articulating novel words: children's oromotor skills predict nonword repetition abilities. *Speech Language and Hearing Research, 56(6)*, 1800–1812. doi: 10.1044/1092-4388 (2013/12–0206)

Krishnan, S., Bergström, L., Alcock, K. J., Dick, F., & Karmiloff-Smith, A. (2015). Williams syndrome: a surprising deficit in oromotor praxis in a population with proficient language production. *Neuropsychologia. 67*, 82–90. doi: 10.1016/j.neuropsychologia.2014.11.032. Epub 2014 Nov 27.

Krishnan, S., Leech, R., Mercure, E., Lloyd-Fox, S. O., & Dick, F. (2014). Convergent and divergent fMRI responses in children and adults to increasing language production demands. *Cerebral Cortex, 23*(9), 2261–2268. doi: 10.1093/cercor/bhs213

Landau, B., Hoffman, J. E., & Kurz, N. (2005). Object definitions with severe spatial deficits in Williams syndrome: sparing and breakdown. *Cognition 100*, 483–510.

Lany, J., & Saffran, J. R. (2013). Statistical learning mechanisms in infancy. In J. L. Rubenstein & P. Rakic, (Eds). *Comprehensive developmental neuroscience: Neural circuit development and function in the brain, Vol. 3* (pp. 231–248). Amsterdam: Elsevier.

Lee, S. A., & Spelke, E. S. (2010). A modular geometric mechanism for reorientation in children. *Cognitive Psychology 61*(2), 152–176.

Leslie, A. M. (1992). Pretense, autism, and the theory-of-mind-module. *Current Directions in Psychological Science, 1*, 18–21.

Mareschal, D., Johnson, M. H., Sirois, S., Spratling, M., Thomas, M. S. C., & Westermann, G. (2007) *Neuroconstructivism: Vol. I. How the brain constructs cognition.* Oxford, England: Oxford University Press.

Mills, D. L., Coffy-Corins, S., & Neville, H. (1997). Language comprehension and cerebral specialisation from 13–20 months. *Developmental Psychology, 13*, 397–445.

Minagawa-Kawai, Y., Mori, K., Naoi, N., & Kojima, S. (2007). Neural attunement processes in infants during the acquisition of language-specific phonemic contrasts. *Journal of Neuroscience, 3*, 315–321.

Molko, N., Cachia, A., Rivière, D., Mangin, J.-F., Bruandet, M., Le Bihan, D., Cohen, L., & Dehaene, S. (2003). Functional and structural alterations of the intraparietal sulcus in a developmental dyscalculia of genetic origin. *Neuron, 40*, 847–858.

Moon, C., & Fifer, W. P. (2000) Evidence of transnatal auditory learning. *Journal of Perinatology, 20*, S37–S44.

Neville, H., Mills, D., & Bellugi, U. (1994). Effects of altered auditory sensitivity and age of language acquisition on the development of language-relevant neural systems: Preliminary studies of William syndrome. In S. Broman and J. Grafman (Eds.). *Atypical cognitive deficits in developmental disorders: Implications for brain function* (pp. 67–83). Hillsdale, NJ: Erlbaum.

Paterson, S. J., Brown, J. H., Gsödl, M. K., Johnson, M. H., & Karmiloff-Smith, A. (1999). Cognitive modularity and genetic disorders, *Science, 286*, 2355–2358.

Paterson, S. J., Heim, S., Friedman, J. T., Choudhury, N., & Benasich, A. A. (2006). Development of structure and function in the infant brain: Implications for cognition, language and social behaviour. *Neuroscience Biobehavior Review, 30*: 1087–1105.

Piattelli-Palmarini, M. (2001). Speaking of learning: How do we acquire our marvellous facility for expressing ourselves in words? *Nature, 411*, 887–888.

Pinker, S. (2002). *The blank slate. The modern denial of human nature.* New York, NY: Penguin Group.

Quartz, S., & Sejnowski, T. (1997). The neural basis of cognitive development: A constructivist manifesto. *Behavioral Brain Sciences 20*, 537–596.

Rice, M. (1999). Specific grammatical limitations in children with Specific Language Impairment. In H. Tager-Flusberg (Ed.). *Neurodevelopmental disorders* (pp. 331–360). Cambridge, MA: MIT Press.

Scerif, G., & Karmiloff-Smith, A. (2001). Genes and environment: What does interaction really mean? *Trends in Genetics, 17*, 418–419.

Shalev, R. S., Manor, O., & Gross-Tsur, V. (2005). Developmental dyscalculia: a prospective six-year follow-up. *Developmental Medicine and Child Neurology, 2*, 121–125.

Smith, L. B., & Thelen, E. (2003). Development as a dynamic system. *Trends in Cognitive Science, 7*(8), 343–348.

Spelke, E. S., & Kinzler K. D. (2007). Core knowledge. *Developmental Science, 10*, 89–96.

Spelke E. S., & Kinzler, K. D. (2009). Innateness, learning and rationality. *Child Development Perspectives 3*, 96–98.

Stiles, J. (2009). *The fundamentals of brain development.* Cambridge, MA: Harvard University Press.

Stiles, J. (2012). *Neural plasticity and cognitive development: Insights from children with perinatal brain injury.* Oxford, UK: Oxford University Press.

Sur, M., Pallas, S. L., & Roe, A. W. (1990). Crossmodal plasticity in cortical development: Differentiation and specification of sensory neocortex. *TINS, 13*, 227–233.

Temple, C. M. (1997). Cognitive neuropsychology and its application to children. *Journal of Child Psychology and Psychiatry 38*, 27–52.

Thomas, M. S. C., Knowland, V. C., & Karmiloff-Smith, A. (2011). Mechanisms of developmental regression in autism and the broader phenotype: a neural network modeling approach. *Psychological Review, 118*(*4*), 637–654.

Tomalski P., Moore, D. G., Ribeiro, H., Axelsson, E. L., Murphy, E., Karmiloff-Smith A., & Kushnerenko E. (2013). Socioeconomic status and functional brain development – Associations in early infancy. *Developmental Science, 16*, 676–687.

Tyler, L. K., Shafto, M. A., Randall, B., Wright, P., Marslen-Wilson. W. D., & Stamatakis E. A. (2010). Preserving syntactic processing across the adult life span: The modulation of the frontotemporal language system in the context of age-related atrophy. *Cerebral Cortex, 20*(*2*), 352–364.

van der Lely, H. K. J. (2005). Domain-specific cognitive systems: Insight from grammatical specific language impairment. *Trends in Cognitive Science, 9*, 53–59.

van der Lely, H. K. J., & Pinker, S. (2014). The biological basis of language: Insights from developmental grammatical impairments. *Trends in Cognitive Science, 18*(11), 586–595.

Webster, M. J., Bachevalier, J., & Ungerleider, L. G. (1995). Development and plasticity of visual memory circuits. In B. Julesz & I. Kovacs (Eds.). *Maturational windows and adult cortical plasticity in human development: Is there reason for an optimistic view?* Reading, MA: Addison-Wesley.

Weir, R. (1962). *Language in the crib.* The Hague: Mouton.

Westermann, G., Mareschal, D., Johnson, M. H., Sirois, S., Spratling, M. W., & Thomas, M. S. C. (2007). Neuroconstructivism. *Developmental Science, 10*(1), 75–83.

Westermann, G., Thomas, M. S. C., & Karmiloff-Smith, A. (2010). Neuroconstructivism. In U. Goswami (Ed.). *Handbook of childhood development*, (pp. 723–748). Oxford: Wiley-Blackwell.

Xu, F., Spelke, E. S., & Goddard, S. (2005). Number sense in human infants. *Developmental Science, 8*(1), 88–101.

21 The Cultural Basis of Language and Thought in Development

Katherine Nelson

Language and culture are entangled in an ancient and endless interchange that has shaped the contemporary human mind and its development in both child and adult. As culture supports the child's entry into language, language becomes the major vehicle through which the child encounters cultural knowledge and practice. This chapter explores these relationships in terms of the continuously changing cultural perspective of the language-learning and language-using infant and child.

In Merlin Donald's account (Donald, 1991) the phylogenetic and cultural evolution of language and culture took place in three phases that resulted in three levels of culture and communication and in related changes in human cognitive systems. Specifically, Donald (1991) has proposed that three levels function within the brain in the context of environmental situations and demands involving distinct cognitive, communicative, and language systems specific to different aspects of contemporary culture. This proposal envisions the contemporary cultural environment as also layered, with different activities involving mimetic interpretation (i.e., sports, theater), oral language practice (everyday face-to-face interactions), and written language forms (notes, diaries, emails, and so on – as well as formal published texts such as newspapers, books, and scientific materials).

The Child in the Multi-Culture

The idea of cultural layers or levels is provocative for the present purpose in the following ways. The world that the infant is born into consists of cultural communicative – and thinking – layers: (a) basic person-to-person interactions often interpretable mimetically without language; (b) oral language interactions person-to-person or in groups, and through media such as television; (c) informal written language in script or print, used for various public communications or private purposes, and printed volumes and documents requiring literate skills of increasing facility supported through cultural institutions such as schools, universities, and libraries. Each of these involves different aspects of the available culture and communication. The first cultural layer (mimetic, in Donald's term) is limited to face-to-face interaction using facial expression, non-verbal sounds, imitation, and body language. The second becomes available to children as they first learn words and then continue learning, hearing, and interpreting more and more of the language in use. This is the level in focus here, but the child is also embedded in the first level, as well as in the third level involving written works that are characteristic of the surrounding literate culture as a whole. The general picture of the child in culture is thus that of movement from one limited aspect of culture mainly within the family, relying on the use of objects, mimetic gestures, and sounds, to a wider, more open oral-language culture that, over time and with increasing language competence, introduces a previously hidden vast world of experience and knowledge. From this perspective, the years of early childhood (roughly ages 2 to 4+) are in an ever-changing state of discovery and exploration of the unknown, using increasingly adequate language and the guidance of peers and adults, with accompanying changes in mental processing.

In this context, consider the powerful impact of language in its different phases on human cognition, according to Donald's analysis of the interplay between culture and mind. He writes (in press,) "material cultural innovations such as writing influenced the pattern of neural epigenesis and cognitive development ... eventually to such a degree that symbolic technologies now dominate the formation of the higher cognitive systems of the brain." These changes include: "(1) a greatly extended and differentiated working memory; (2) a capacity for multifocal attention;) lifelong plasticity; (4) a huge expansion of long term memory capacity; able to store thousands of neural word systems, in instantly retrievable form; and (5) a great increase in the amount of brain space devoted to semantic representation" (Donald, 2001, p. 293). The ways in which these various systems develop and become activated in the lives of infants and young children are not all well established at present. It is generally assumed that much of their development takes place in the years of late infancy and early childhood in the context of language learning and experience in oral language culture, and that their development continues into later childhood, adolescence, and adulthood. Donald's account implies the probability of a continuing state of cognitive expansion, accommodation, and empowerment in interaction with language use.[1]

These two basic insights – cultural layers related to language forms and uses, and cognitive adaptations with cultural change and individual development – have significant implications for how we view both language and cognitive development in the early years of childhood. I explored aspects of their development in two earlier books (Nelson, 1996, 2007). Here I discuss the implications for early child development implied by the ideas of layers of culture and mind established through different communicative practices.

The Cultural World of Infancy

The very small and helpless (compared with other primates) human newborn depends, for much of the first year at least, totally upon others for movement,

---

1 This account does not reach to the likely differentiation of mind as a result of internet use and widely available sources of reference, etc., that characterize the present environment. Given the premises of Donald's theory it seems likely that cognitive changes are involved at the present day, reflecting different habits of mind required for the new media. This probability is intriguing but will not be pursued further here.

nurture, warmth, and any other needs. Culture enters the infant's life in the form of the practices and materials that parents engage with in their caretaking roles. These involve things – food, clothes, furniture, toys, etc. – but also practices of child care: what and how to feed, when; how to handle toileting, and where and when; when and where to sleep; and so on. Each of these practices involves *routines* – ways of carrying out the practice – including the roles of parent and child, and their changes over the course of the first years. Within these routines are the social interchanges between adult and child, including both the verbalizations and vocalizations of mother and child, and the non-verbal gestures and actions that adults use in directing the activities as well as the reciprocal actions that the child comes to use in response.

Humans are "designed" as social, interactive creatures. Human adults in general are sociable chatty, compared with other non-human primates. They talk and sing to their infants as well as to other children and adults, regardless of the fact that the infant cannot understand the words. This social design, like culture, is necessary for survival of the species. The social environment of the long period of infancy (two years) and its relevance to language acquisition is now well-recognized in developmental work. It begins as an essential condition that mothers/parents and their infants are in more or less constant contact if the baby is to survive. Contact generally means comfort, nurture, warmth; and very soon after birth it typically involves the baby in back and forth social interchange through sound and gesture (Gallaway & Richards, 1994; Hobson, 2002). Such vocal exchange between mother and infants is common, and is recognized as a healthy sign that the child is "programmed for social engaging."

For all this social attention and support, it is the infant who negotiates the passage from neonate to cultural member. Whatever background organizing is provided by evolution does not predict the specifics of what surrounds her, with the probable exception of the pattern of human faces, bodies, and voices. S/he comes into a world that is furnished in cultural fashion with areas and materials, social partners, and a world of things and happenings that is totally unknown from prior experience in the world. Infants hear the speech around them, perhaps the music, and come to see the food and furnishings as their place in the world, together with their specific toys, stuffed animals, and baby equipment. Their understanding is restricted to those aspects that they encounter interactively (from a restricted physical position) in the mimetic cultural level. From birth the infant builds memory derived from sensory-motor interactions – about her partners, surroundings, and the routine activities they engage in together or separately. Memory of this kind becomes organized knowledge in the concepts of people, things, and actions (Bauer & Mandler, 1990; Mandler, 2004; Nelson, 1974). These serve as a basis for further knowledgeable participation in ongoing routines, as well as surprise or even distress at the unknown or unexpected. Conceptualization in infancy is the background knowledge that will later be used in learning words.

The basic unit of experiential cognition is assumed here to be the event, proposed from different perspectives: developmental (Nelson, 1978, 1986, Nelson & Gruendel, 1981), cognitive and social (Schank & Abelson, 1977; Shipley & Zacks, 2008), and evolutionary (Donald, 1991). The temporal dimension of change over time, of action, patterns of sound, and activity in the infant's environment, has received too little attention in developmental work, although it is the basis of measurement in many infant labs, from the habituation research of early infant sensory processes to the extended looking-time measures registering reaction to change or difference. These methods use the disposition of the infant to attend to the dynamics of the experiment; generally, however, they do not study the dynamics themselves. Infants listen to tunes, they watch actions. They also spend time examining objects, in a dynamic way – biting, mouthing, moving, rolling, and so on – investigating what it is and what it does (Mandler, 2004). Their interactions with other people are dynamic, changeable through time, both through actions and voices. It seems likely that the infant notices – and as a result knows more about – what things do than how they look. This observation was the basis for the theory of infant object concepts based on the dynamics and relations of objects in the child's experience, prior to attention to specific perceptual characteristics (Nelson, 1974).

During the last six months of the first year most infants are crawling, creeping over the spaces of their lives, have begun to stand, and in some cases have begun to walk alone. Thus, their views of the world expand considerably, and their ability to investigate new spaces leads to ever-new perspectives on the world (Campos et al., 2000). One can assume that the infant's memory and conceptual systems expand in concert. The child's relation with the social world keeps pace with her own abilities. As the infant grows in skills, parental practices change; social interchange proceeds from back and forth "cooing" and play to talk that accompanies practices, culturally attuned, as in feeding, bathing, and toileting. Thus, together adult and child engage in a transitional "mimetic world" where action is a communicative tool accompanied by the familiar sound of talk.

Launching into Language with Words

Language is used in communication at many levels – with individuals, in groups, and across communities – and learning these uses is tightly tied to the social environments of its learners. First word learning is the critical turning point, where infants emerge from embeddedness in the mimetic social-cultural environment of the family into the broad culture of oral language, the home culture of human activities. From the end of the first year, and for the rest of life, much of their time will be spent in the combined mimetic and oral language world. Evolutionary heritage and epigenetics (Jablonka, Chapter 18, this volume; Jablonka & Lamb, 2005) prepares children for entry to this part of the cultural world: through auditory discrimination of patterns of phonemes and words, imitative skills, and the emerging ability to produce verbal sounds in babble (see Jusczyk, 2000, for details and references on these epigenetic preparations). Vocal and verbal interchanges with familiar persons and accumulated experiential knowledge of the world of familiar people, things, and activities are critical to the next steps, as is joint attention of adult and child (e.g., Tomasello, 1995; Werner & Kaplan, 1963). The child's own disposition to learn, and to enter into the next level, is also relevant, as are any specialized talents or disabilities related to the area, and the fit of these to the social environments and interactions with others. As all of these conditions vary greatly across individuals, families, cultural settings, and languages, it is not surprising that the dynamic processes of acquiring vocabulary, comprehending, and producing sentences also vary widely in the speed and direction of achievement by individual children (Nelson, 1973).

Understanding the process of beginning to speak and understand words and sentences requires specification of what is involved in "learning" the language – that is, to begin with, how meaning in language is acquired. This is basically what the first steps of production and comprehension of words involves – as contrasted with hearing the pattern of sounds (already mastered), producing the sounds correctly (a long process), or acquiring the grammar (a later achievement). The research problem is to determine how and with what specific resources the child is able to acquire and use a vocabulary of 500 words or so by the middle of the second year (and thousands more in the subsequent 3 years). These words are of different kinds (nouns, verbs, adjectives, prepositions, conjunctions, pronouns) with different roles to play in making statements and questions. Only the first three kinds of these can be said to have meaning and to relate to the child's concepts; the others play structural roles in sentences. As most observers today assume that meanings for words are part of the conceptual base, a central question is how the child makes the connection between a new word and a relevant concept. Given this assumption, we can learn from the child's learning and use of words not only about the learning process, but also about the composition of her experientially derived meanings and concepts.

Learning Words for Meanings and Meanings for Words

Meaning is a concept that is not confined to language, but has many other interpretations (Nelson, 2007; see Millikan, 2004). Broadly speaking, meaning in the sense of significance exists for all creatures, not only humans. Thus, meaning exists for the infant prior to language. It guides and participates in the infant's developing memory and conceptual system, as well as in emotional systems. These systems are composed in terms of the mimetic context of infancy – that is, around concepts derived from action and social interaction in events of the mimetic world. For example, as previously proposed (Nelson, 1974), the infant initially finds meanings for object words in concepts formed on the basis of function, or what things do as the child observes and interacts with them (e.g., a ball is to roll).[2] Concept formation is an unconscious process based on the *meaningfulness* of experiences, and continues to be so throughout life, supplemented by conscious attention and effort through deliberate learning and thinking.

Most observers accept that meaning is in the head, in the form of concepts or semantic networks. Many adopt the idea of "mapping" a new word to a concept that implies a close word-to-concept fit. The assumption of a word-concept mapping in

---

2 Subsequently, such concepts were expected to be generalized on the basis of similarity of form or perceptual features. This function-to-form proposal was widely challenged, but has also been supported in recent research (e.g., Kemler-Nelson, 1999).

first language acquisition implies that the child has a store of "basic" concepts available for words to map to (e.g., Fodor, 1975; Macnamara, 1982; P. Bloom, 2000). Bloom accepts that a new concept may be constructed for a new word on the basis of instructive description combining already known words and concepts. But the mapping construct does not include context as a source for a possible new meaning/concept or construction. Strict word-to-concept mapping faces a problem that arose early in discussions of word learning (Macnamara, 1982), namely that words must mean the same thing for all users if they are to communicate. At first glance, this appears to be consistent with the idea that words and meanings are culturally held. However, this "same meaning" principle runs into the problem that meaning is *not* in the word – the word is but a symbol for the meaning. The meaning is in the mind of the user, the speaker, hearer, thinker, reader, or writer, and, ultimately, in the collective cultural minds of the community at large. For this purpose, common use establishes a modicum of cultural agreement on word meanings such that people can understand each other, even among strangers. In Deacon's (1997) account the word has a place in a broad network of symbolic relations that are gradually acquired or built up by users. Words derive meaning for users from their place in the network. The word is then a symbolic bridge in the exchange of meaningful messages. In itself it can "mean" different things in different contexts. As a culturally generated and shared symbol, only those who have acquired this bit of symbolism can use it knowingly in its cultural symbolic roles.

Thus, the word does not "mean" in the conventional sense; the speaker and hearer do. When a speaker uses a word, hearers refer it to their lexical-conceptual base; if it is found there in conjunction with a contextually appropriate meaning, all is well – but only if the meaning found coheres with that intended by the speaker. The hearer interprets *the speaker's meaning* in terms of his/her own meaning system, concepts, percepts, and context. Word-concept *mapping* as a learning process distorts this relation. It can only work after *meaning is given to the word* by the user; it cannot work to establish meaning initially, although the listener may tentatively assign a meaning on the basis of context and perceived intent. Moreover, even the simplest words often serve many meanings and purposes in both the same and different contexts. Thus, it is rare that a single use is definitive with respect to its meaning. Of course, once the word is entered into the learner's lexicon with its conceptual and contextual information noted, it appears to users to "mean" on its own, as that is what symbols do.[3]

A further consideration in contrast to the mapping idiom is that concepts are malleable, growable, and changeable. Does that suggest that the word's meaning itself may change? As implied above, words symbolize agreed-upon cultural meanings that users borrow, and these cultural meanings for words change over time and in different contexts. Moreover, the cultural meanings of words (all the meanings and uses that the word may serve) are usually multiple, many with intricate relations among other words, as Wittgenstein (1953) argued in his famous example of the word "game" and its multiple and seemingly miscellaneous applications. Many

3 For further discussion, consult Humpty-Dumpty in *Alice in Wonderland*.

complex words may be learned in simple applications; only later do children come to accept multiple interpretations of them. The word as *symbol* – not as a thing to be known in itself – accommodates this process and facilitates using words in abstract structures such as hierarchical categories.

In brief, children do not learn meaning from words but from the speaker's *use* of the word in context, or occasionally the speaker's deliberate teaching of the meaning implied (conceptual or perceptual) by a word.[4] However, given the cultural base of language, emphasized here, including the assumption that meanings of words and structures of language are culturally derived and maintained in cultural memory, it seems reasonable to assume, as Macnamara did, that children should learn the culturally accepted meaning for a word, not some unique meaning of their own, and this is what "mapping" seems to assume.[5] There are, nonetheless, numerous examples of children applying a word to meanings of their own or to things not included in its "rightful" use. Universality of meaning does not seem to be a guiding principle or "constraint." Indeed, children's "mistakes" and "over-generalizations" have revealed that infants and young children are often *unlikely* to share the exact meaning of a word-concept with that of the adult. As Mandler (2004) and colleagues have shown, the infant's concepts are likely to be more inclusive and general than those of adults. Indeed, in any given context both the meaning of the adult and the child are likely to be rather vague and perhaps off-target (see L. Bloom, 1973; Nelson, 1985, for examples). These observations nonetheless leave open the question of how the child's meaning system comes to "fit" that of the social world and the culture at large.

The realization that words do not "have" meanings but rather "serve," "trigger," or "point to" meanings and allow meaningful communication between those who have similar (if not identical) concepts related to the word/symbol provides a different view of word learning and use in childhood than is typically assumed. The question, then, is more complicated: How do children come to understand the meanings that others are conveying through their words? The emphasis here is on the child's interpretative abilities (Bogdan, 2003), that enable the deriving and sharing of meanings in context, without a requirement of exact matches to either the present speech environment or the culturally acceptable use of the word in different contexts. From this perspective the infant does not need to have a special ability for reading the intentionality of the speaker or to have in place a concept that matches that of the other. Rather, she can rely on the interactional mimetic context of infancy to bridge the gap toward a new phase of communication and conceptualization.

Words for the Bridge to Language Culture

To start, infants generally focus on one or more words used in connection with some aspect of her or his experientially based activity and attempt to verbalize it, using

---

4 As a reader you are the source of the meaning; the spoken message or the text you are reading is the context for its interpretation.
5 Although how the child acquires the cultural meaning prior to and independently of learning the word is not clear.

a small number of phonemes more or less mastered through babbling. Social partners use their knowledge of the child's interest and situations to interpret the child's intent. This is a cooperative process. A word is only successful as a communicative symbol if both speaker and listener access the same or similar meanings. It is obvious, however, that the concepts of child and mother (for example) may differ in breadth and depth, given that the early word learner's concepts must be derived from limited mimetic sources. Children do not simply learn the meanings of words, they learn parts of the meanings that their parents, or other speakers have for words. Faster progress can be made in finding words that others use for those relations, events, actions, appearances, and so on, that the child has already assimilated to the conceptual system. Then we can speak not of learning the meanings of words, but of *learning the words for meanings*.

Understanding of the reference of some words in comprehension typically precedes the child's own production of a "first word." *Matching meanings* is particularly easy for reference to objects, and the names of objects play a major part in the acquisition of early vocabularies. Indeed, it has long been noted – both by single observers and for samples of children and words – that many (perhaps most) of the child's first words are nouns, more specifically names of things, although other types also occur. Among the first 10 words of the 18 children in my early study (Nelson, 1973), the 5 most common were *Mama, Dada, ball, car, and Hi*. The first four of these are identified as nouns, but contrary to the usual generalization, only *ball* is a common noun and an object name. (*Mama* and *Dada* are proper nouns, i.e., names for people; car is typically used at this age in reference to an event of riding in the car or watching cars on the street.) Although there were children in this study (about half) who learned mainly object terms in this early period (10 to 18 months), others acquired a variety of kinds, including some phrases (e.g., "gimme," "go away"). Two of the major conclusions from this research were that (a) children were expressing aspects of their social experiences; and (b) variety in content and form within and across children was the norm. The variety of terms learned suggests that infants are learning the language that reflects their knowledge of the *mimetic world* of their lives, which varies in terms of their social interactions (e.g., siblings, relatives, parental practices, etc.).

In addition to the kinds of words learned, the pace of learning is also notably variable. While some children speed along, acquiring 50 words by the age of 15 months, others lag behind, often mainly silent (while understanding much that is addressed to them) until the age of 2 years or more. As previously noted, learning to produce words involves many systems – phonemics; social, cultural, sibling, and family structure; speed and articulation of the surrounding talk; infant processing speed – developing at different rates in different children and in different contexts. Thus, from a complex systems perspective the variability among learners in early language and learning is not surprising.

Research on mothers' styles of interaction with words – emphasizing names of things vs. focusing on the child's activities – identified a relation between the child's pace and type of word learning. In a study of 45 infants from 12 to 24 months of age (Hampson & Nelson, 1993) mothers' emphasis on names was associated with a greater number of words learned and more nouns learned by their children than by the children of mothers emphasizing more social interaction. The child's interest and growth along multiple dimensions together with the parental style of advancing language are both needed to account for this difference. There is scant evidence overall that early "noun learners" are more advanced in language and cognition than other learning styles.

The concepts entailed by the words that very young children learn are as interesting from the point of view of their expression of their experiential world, as is their relation with parental practices or teaching. Consider the following (non-object) nouns that were used by at least half the sample of the 45 children in the Hampson study at the 20-month vocabulary assessment:[6] *bath, home, kiss, money, outside, park, toy, walk.* Arguably, none of these words is an object name. In a child's use, *Bath* refers to the activity of having a bath; *home* generally to the target of returning from a venture; *kiss* may be a verb or noun and is clearly an activity; *money* typically refers to the change in Mother's purse that the child wishes to play with; *outside* (see *home*); *park* (see *home*); *toy* is usually plural and refers to a collection of playthings; *walk* can be a verb but is probably similar to *home, outside*, and *park* in being the target of or the activity itself. Whereas each of these words is used initially by the child in reference to her own sphere of activity, in the larger social and cultural sphere the same words may refer to different contexts, objects, and activities, thus inviting the child's attention to an originally unfamiliar experiential space. These activity words then help to close the gap between the mimetic world of experience and the oral language culture. I would argue that these words are important to understanding the child's perspective on the mimetic world of her experience and in preparing for the oral language world to come. They are representative of life in transition between two cultural domains, drawing on the familiar one as a bridge to the new.

In addition, event words such as *bath* and *park* illustrate the implausibility of the mapping paradigm for word learning. These words occur in the context of anticipated and ongoing familiar activities, words that children hear many times in these contexts, and that they appropriate for their own conceptualizations of what these activities involve. The adult listener must interpret the child's use in response. Such situational use requires a model of word learning that takes into account that children are aiming to communicate with others within a social-cultural environment where things happen that can be shared and even requested by beginning speakers.

Of course, many names of the objects involved in activities of the mimetic period are also learned during this transition. Much of the research on early words has focused on the analysis of how children learn the names of things and generalize the names to new items (Golinkoff et al., 2000; Nelson, 2014a). These words enable the essential function of reference, which, as Bogdan (2009) argues, is critical to predication and thus central to language. Predication enables "saying something about something" equivalent to Halliday's (1975) mathetic function. Halliday argued that every utterance by mature speakers involves both social and mathetic

---

6 The MacArthur checklist filled out by mothers (Fenson et al., 1994)

components, but beginning speakers tend to focus on one or another, and to use single words for these separate purposes before combining them in a single utterance.

The substantial focus of research on object naming in learning words has led many to the language, if not the belief, that words map onto the things they designate, forming a word-object mapping – in effect, that the object is the meaning of the word. This assumption lies behind the large research endeavor to decide the basis on which the child generalizes a name from the original object to others of the same appearance or kind. In the case of many event words such as "bath" and "walk" and other nouns (e.g., "wind," "rain") there is no object or set of objects to pin a word to. The language of actions and events requires a different strategy of generalization, based on the broad context of perception, action, and social interaction in everyday event contexts.

Event-based and other words not specific to objects must have a place in an emerging semantic network (e.g., Deacon, 1997) that enables using them for many purposes – to draw attention, to ask for things, to put words together to express a relation not in immediate evidence; and multiple other possibilities. The semantic network (words and possible meanings) may enable *thinking* as well as speaking about things, people, and events in a different way than personal experience only allows. Through this new level of semantic consciousness, precedent to the widespread cognitive changes of the succeeding period, the child can begin to take part in the larger community of language users and thereby encounter its community of minds.

The emerging access to words for expressing and sharing meanings marks an important change in the child's communicative and cognitive position in the world. Words for constructs that fit into the child's routines of mimetic life and have complex meanings within the oral world serve to bridge the cultural gap between the mimetic and the oral cultural community. While children still interpret experience from a basic personal observational perspective, supported by mimetic interaction, they also begin to interpret others' use of verbal symbols with meanings derived from a relatively closed communicative context. Clues for how language enhances the child's mimetic understanding can be glimpsed in the learning and use of categorical terms such as *toys* and *animals*, as well as terms for cultural roles such as *doctor* and *brother*, and the temporal designators of *morning* and *night* (Nelson, Hampson, & Kessler-Shaw, 1993). These words may begin with quite specific reference, but may then be generalized to fit their cultural meaning.

Transitioning to the Narrative Cultural World

A major transition in the child's cognitive and communicative life takes place during and after the early word using period. The acquisition of words and meanings sets the stage for and merges into experiential understanding within *oral language culture*, where other people's knowledge and perspectives are projected through their talk with the child. As anticipated in Donald's (2001) conception of levels of cognitive functioning that emerge with language in its different formats (oral and written), the child's experiences through language during this period (in stories, conversations, instructions, and play) contribute to the many significant developments in cognitive as well as social functions also in progress. Donald's (in press) recent summary of these developments include "a great increase in semantic representation," "differentiated memory," and "a capacity for multi-focal attention." These resonate with much recent developmental research, of which memory is of particular interest here.

Although research on language development has explored problems in semantics, syntax, and pragmatics in great detail over the last three decades, providing ample evidence of what children learn, less attention has been focused on how language functions in the life of the child and how children integrate language into their lives. How the functions of language expand and change over the years from 2 to 4, and how they relate to other social and cognitive changes in children's knowledge systems, are of central interest here. The basic claim is that during these years major psychological changes involved in understanding self and others, and the outside world, are fundamentally based in the experiential changes and ensuing possibilities opened through participation in the oral language culture of the *community of minds*. In this section the focus is on research revealing relations of different levels of mind and culture in the early childhood period.

Language Learning and Use in Post-Infancy

Speech in oral language culture, private or social, alone or in interaction with one or more others, is a novel form of the representation of meaning for the 2-year-old child, entering as it does into conscious, deliberative thought. Once acquired, language can amplify, specify, and manipulate thinking and keep it in mind in deliberate working memory. These benefits doubtlessly enable advances in the child's understanding of many heretofore unknown aspects of social and cultural life. As children become capable of engaging in conversation and listening to stories, they first encounter language about things, people, and phenomena that cannot be personally explored or experienced, opening up topics that may be initially mysterious. New words may lead to new thoughts and to the reconstruction of old conceptions. Narratives such as stories, personal tales, or talk about what will happen in the future can generate "knowledge" about things and events never actually experienced. Paul Harris (2012) has pioneered research into this aspect of young children's understanding of adult accounts and stories, as well as in children's own imaginative projections. Yet there is a continuing need for more systematic study of this kind over the developmental period that relates to children's understanding of complex concepts of time, space, and causal relations among events, as well as social relations among story characters. Learning in and through language is too easily taken for granted, although it is certainly one of the most important accomplishments of early childhood.

An under-explored aspect of early language is how children come to *comprehend* the complex language they hear in the oral language environment, as they listen to stories or to parents' explanations of shared plans and happenings. Comprehension ranges from the attribution of meaning to the use of novel words by the speaker, through the interpretation of explanation and narrative. The comprehension of novel words in this period is often thought to take place in "fast mapping" mode (discussed above) in which the child quickly learns a new word and induces its meaning. But as Ambridge and Lieven (2011, p. 101) have concluded, the development of word learning has been neglected: "The situation in which a new word's referent is first identified represents not the end but the *beginning* of the acquisition process." Previously "learned" words expand and change in meaning, and the child's growing accumulation of words, increasing knowledge, and changing social and cultural context implicate a dynamic continuing process in the developing child of 3 to 6 years and older.

There is an extensive literature on talk with children related to comprehension during this age period; notable are two volumes by Blum-Kulka and her colleagues (Blum-Kulka & Snow, 2002 on *Talking to Adults*; and Cekaite, et al. 2014, on *Children's Peer Talk*). These works illuminate the contemporary widespread political and educational concern with young children's adequate exposure to adult speech (now endorsed by the American pediatric community that recommends all parents read books to their children daily from birth). This concern is motivated by the well-established relation between the number of words spoken in the homes of children during the first three years and their later progress or lack of it in school (Hart & Risley, 1995; Snow, 2014). The concern is well-founded, but the "cure" is shallow at best: a kind of medicine designed to treat the symptoms but not the illness itself. When, how, and what children hear, and how they interact with the language, is likely to be of much greater importance to relevant learning and preparation for school than whether Mother began reading stories before or after birth (as recommended), or only when she judged that the child was interested. What Blum-Kulka and others emphasize is that talking with adults and peers (as well as listening to stories) is the context for both learning the language and acquiring the cultural modes of acting and thinking. These cultural modes demand new ways of thinking, specifically the cognitive changes and expansions that Donald emphasizes. We know of course that many changes are taking place in terms of brain development in this period; it seems inevitable that such changes develop in pace with changes in the social and cultural environment that accompany language acquisition and use.

It should be emphasized that no one questions whether language makes a difference in performance in the pre-school and school years. Language achievement correlates with all cognitive and social achievements studied at a level similar (but not identical) to that of age (Nelson, 2005). The question is *how* language makes a difference for different accomplishments. Children do not simply use language to advance cognitively. They need language to reason with, and they also need the background mentality in place prior to language (for example, in understanding events, forming concepts and categories) to interpret and extend narratives from memory and from stories. Thus, the claim to be made here is not that language possession makes one smart. As infant researchers have been demonstrating for decades, babies are competent in their own way within their own environment and culture. They use this competence to find their way initially into language mode, and then use those achievements to explore the social and cultural realms previously closed to those without language.[7]

Crossing the Cultural Border: A Private Venture

Some of the most compelling examples of the expansion of awareness, knowledge, and conscious thinking in this period are evident in the private pre-sleep monologues of a child, Emily, that were recorded by her parents when she was 2 to 3 years of age (Nelson, 1989). These private monologues were analyzed in different frameworks by eight researchers who each focused on a different aspect of the data. Emily's atypically advanced language at 2 years of age brought out a wide range of problems and challenges that any child might encounter and attempt to solve in the course of becoming part of the oral culture, albeit at an older age. They shed a singular light on how becoming part of the language community opens the mind to new ways of thinking and knowing.[8]

A major theme emerged from Emily's focus on sequences of daily events and routines of her life, provoking the hypothesis that she was in the process of developing a new way of thinking, drawing on and extending a basic orientation to events. Specifically, this focus suggested the emergence of the "narrative mind," proposed by Bruner (1986) as complementary to the traditional view of the rational mind, and implicated by Donald (1991) as the dominant mode of the oral language (mythic) level of culture and mind. Narrative builds on the earlier event focus but on "news," reaching beyond what is usually expected, thus requiring motivation and causation. Emily's earliest verbal accounts were of routine events, rather than of a specific episode. Specific memory accounts emerged later. Throughout, talk of future events (e.g., Christmas plans, a visit to the doctor, weekend activities), based on parental accounts, dominated the monologues in contrast to remembered events. Emily's talk about remembered events was rarely based on immediately prior conversations or accounts from parents, in contrast to their frequent pre-bed talk about coming events of the next day. In the last quarter of the year of recordings Emily's monologues began to include variations on stories from books that her parents had read with her, sometimes with the illustrated book in hand. And soon after she began telling stories of her own.[9]

Whereas early "proto-narrative" constructions appeared in Emily's private speech, similar proto-narrative constructions may be observed in the active play of less verbally advanced children of 2 to 3 years enacted with materials for both

---

7 For an insightful view of the extent of these realms see Schaller's (1991) account of *A Man Without Words*.

8 A brief account of Emily's early monologues may be found in Nelson (2015). See also Levy and McNeill (2015) on their relation to the development of narrative.

9 Emily's considerable advance in language compared to the typical 2-year-old level enabled these observations, but it seems reasonable to consider that her interests and efforts to represent and understand her daily experiences were not atypical of children in general.

familiar and imaginative scenarios, with or without a partner (parent, sibling, friend). Such play, sometimes considered as a stage mainly prior to the dominance of language, generally combines with language. Bogdan (2013) has argued that it appears as a platform for the emergence of the creative imaginative brain.[10] Observational studies[11] have also found that many children of 3 to 4 years of age, when left alone to play, carry on long explanatory tales of how the play characters are engaging with each other (reported in Winsler, 2009) and such play alone or with peers may be observed frequently in pre-school settings (Sawyer, 1997). In brief, the emergence of narrative in the speech and pretense of young children is commonly observed and deserves closer analysis to supplement studies of children's elicited story productions.

Emily's bedtime monologues are rightly viewed as a kind of private speech, which Vygotsky (1962) saw as a prelude to the interiorized speech/thinking that language makes possible. He attributed the diminishment of such speech later in childhood to the emerging dominance of silent interiorized speech for thinking. Following Vygotsky's model, most contemporary studies of private speech have focused on the self-regulating aspect of children's speech while solving problems, rather than in reflective or imaginative thought, such as in Emily's monologues. The latter kind of private speech appears to emerge *from* social speech to speech for self in the mode of narrative thinking that dominates in the newly entered oral culture. It may also be noted that Vygotsky's thesis that private speech *becomes* interiorized thought is difficult to reconcile with what is now understood as the relation between speech and conscious thought, and with the generally accepted assumption that (unconscious) thought exists prior to the acquisition of language.

Private speech may be best seen as using language to externalize thinking itself, thus enabling reflection on meaning. In general, speech may externalize thinking for communication and also for self-clarification and reflection. Thus, Emily's frequent repeating in private speech (to the best of her ability) what her parents have told her enabled reflection on what they meant. Without speech, both parental talk and the child's own thought may be fleeting in mind. Prior to the ability to bring thought to speech, conceptualization and memory may remain inchoate, unexamined. Private speech then may be seen as a useful mode of representing and reflecting, supporting memory and thought about the past, the present, and future, as well as aiding in learning and problem solving. Later, the same purpose may be served in silent but conscious thinking with language. Later still, such thinking may be expressed in written form.

Cognitive Challenges of the Language-Using Culture

Psychological researchers often include measures of language production and comprehension in studies of social and cognitive development in children of 3 to

---

10 As we did not assess Emily's engagement in play by herself or with others, the two situations could not be compared in her case.

11 Undocumented observations and unpublished documents by students.

5 years of age, usually as "control" variables to be distinguished from the experimental variable being investigated. Although language is not considered a contributor to the cognitive task under study, it is almost always found to be strongly correlated to the outcomes. These consistent findings led Janet Astington and her colleagues to organize a conference in 2002 focused on the question "Why does language matter for theory of mind?" addressed from different perspectives.[12] My work has been directed for many years toward this and the broader question: Why does language matter for many and perhaps *all* cognitive achievements of the pre-school period (e.g., Nelson, 1996)? I believe, like most of the contributors to the 2002 conference (Astington & Baird, 2005), that language opens the child's mind in many different ways that contribute to changes in cognition and social understanding. The problem is to be more specific with respect to what these changes are and how language contributes to them, mentally and in interaction. In the present context I note well-researched problems and achievements of the pre-school years that have provided insights into the overall solutions to this general question: emergence of autobiographical memory, information source attributions, theory of mind, and self.

What Kind of Memory When?

In the oral language culture talk of shared experience, verbal narrative and explanation makes demands beyond those of the former mimetic world. In the prior cultural milieu, direct learning from another of facts, ideas, stories, and experiences different from the self through the verbal medium was not possible. Keeping track of what is "my" experiential remembering and others' reporting then requires cognitive change of a major kind, distinguishing between self memory and other sources of knowledge. Exactly such a distinction is made in memory theory – namely, that between *episodic* and *semantic* memory. Semantic memory is held to consist of facts or knowledge in general (Tulving, 1993; Nelson, 2007), whereas episodic memory is autonoetic I or self-knowing (Tulving, 2005), emphasizing that its source is self-experience. This basic system has been maintained from infancy for keeping track of the relevant aspects of past experience and predicting the future (Nelson, 1993). In general, infant memory is believed to consist of procedural (perception-action) elements, whereas the semantic and episodic distinction appears post-infancy[13]. Although this description of the mature memory system might appear to indicate a reason for the "source blindness" discussed next, the picture is not so clear. Even infants clearly remember aspects of their prior experience, as extensive research from as early as 4 to 6 months of age has shown. Such memories do not persist in the long run (longer than a few months to a year at the age of 2 or 3 years). The young child's indifference to the source of knowledge or reported personal memory may be

---

12 Later published as *Why language matters for theory of mind* (Astington & Baird, 2005).
13 See Bauer, 2007, for a full account and different views. Also Bauer & Fivush, 2014, for detailed accounts and different views of many aspects of memory-development research.

held over from the conditions of infancy where memory and knowledge are attributable to only one source: the self (see next section). The overall picture is complex and autobiographical memory, the long-term retention of personal episodes of one's life, is late to develop.

In Donald's (2001, in press) account of the cognitive changes in human brains observed from mimetic to mythic to theoretic or modern culture, "massive" expansion of memory, and especially of semantic networks, were viewed as major effects, in addition to differentiation of memory kinds. As language is first acquired, it is obvious that memory must expand to accommodate its connections with expanding meanings. But beyond the simple acquisition of words and grammatical relations, language opens up a continuous exposure to a far larger world of knowledge than was accessible in the mimetic world. Both semantic (or factual) and episodic memory must expand as well.

Infant memory, although by definition about the past, is assumed to be timeless, reflecting the state of the infant self. This aligns with the view that basic memory is about what is known (from experience) to be the case, not about what happened in some imagined past time. Tulving (1983) made this case originally, stating that only humans are able to "travel into the past" through episodic remembering. This claim has raised the question of whether infants and young children have episodic memory distinct from semantic memory. Developmental research has clearly established that 2 and 3 year old children can report things from past experience, but the question remains, do they view them as being in a past existence of the self or simply as the "way of things" – established in memory, but not at a specific point in time? There is now a great deal of additional research on this and related issues (Suddendorf & Moore, 2011), but the questions are difficult to resolve. Studies of young children's memory up to the age of 3 years are relatively indecisive as to whether memory has differentiated into episodic (my memory from the past) and semantic kinds. The source of semantic knowledge – whether it is acknowledged or whether, once acquired the child claims to have always known it – remains indeterminate, as for many items in adult memory.

Differentiation of past personal experience in memory is culturally expected, and as research by Robyn Fivush and colleagues has illuminated, it is likely to be learned in the course of "past talk" with parents and others (Fivush, 2008). In the later preschool years parents and their young children may begin sharing memories, of their own or shared experiences. Such verbal sharing varies across cultures (Wang, 2014) in both its extent and content. Experience with shared talk about events is associated with more and better personal memories in the future; moreover, maternal styles of talk with the child about memories influences future memory retention (Fivush, 2011). As Fivush and I have argued (2004), autobiographical memory – a longitudinal accumulation of episodic memories comprising the personal stories of one's past life – is culturally defined and supported, beginning in the late preschool years (Nelson & Fivush, 2004; Nelson, 2014b). The general concept of the past, present, and future self, and its relation to other selves, is clearly relevant to these memory issues, and is recognized as an important area of development during the years of early childhood.

Whose Story?

Story memory and understanding has long been a topic of interest in developmental and educational studies. In recent years it has been enriched through the construct of narrative as a natural mode of language and of thought (Bruner, 1986; Donald, 1991). Narrative incorporates the beliefs and motivations of individuals, and the causal relations within and between events. Thus, the understanding of the importance of narrative, both in terms of fiction and of reports of personal experience, has become more relevant to the search for advances in social cognitive thinking. However, narratives of personal experience may contribute to the confusion of self and story that has been documented by a number of observers (e.g., Miller et al., 1990). Part of this confusion may reside in the original nature of memory exclusively for personal experience. Adding material to memory derived from language reports of others (including story books) is a novel contribution, perhaps easily confused as to its source. Indeed, the *sources* of talk for children are variable, including adults and peers, older siblings, television, and other media. These sources contrast with the restricted experiential domain of the pre-language infant. Thus, it may not be surprising that a specific weakness in the child's comprehension and interpretation of others' complex language is the distinction between *self and other sources* of what is currently in memory.

Confusion by the young as to the source of information in memory has been widely noted, with ample research from the laboratory as well as from observations of children's reports (e.g. Miller et al., 1990; Roberts & Blades, 2000). Children as old as 5 years are unreliable trackers of source, sometimes claiming that they have long known something that was only recently told to them, or repeating something as self-experience that was reported from someone else. This apparent deficiency may be understood in the context of the move from private experience of infancy to shared experience in the social language-using world of childhood. New sources in language format may simply be added to the growing memory for experience. We know more about source confusions than about how such confusion is overcome and when; it is reported to be developing in the later pre-school years and up to 8 years of age (Roberts & Blades, 2000).

Studies of young children's suggestibility, generally finding that they are surprisingly vulnerable to others' false post-experience suggestions, also indicate a gap in accurate source attribution. These lines of research imply that very young children often fail to make a distinction in memory between a self-experience and another's report of that (or of their own) experience, or between self-knowledge held in memory and factual knowledge conveyed from another. These errors tend to diminish or vanish toward the end of the pre-school period. It is likely that they are related to other changes – expansions and differentiations – in memory to which Donald (2001) refers. As already noted, a major differentiation between episodic and semantic memory places the self as source for episodic and autobiographical memories. The latter – the memories retained over a lifetime that locate the self in the past as well as the present and future – begin for most people sometime between 3 and 8 years, most frequently with more than a few memories a year from 5 to 7 years of age. This memory is a clear recognition of a unique self that comes into play toward the end of the pre-school period of development.

Whose Mind? What Self?

One of the most discussed aspects of the emerging self-concept has been the child's recognition that others' knowledge may differ from one's own, the topic of studies of "theory of mind." "Theory of mind" theorists have mainly argued either that children use their own mind as the model for attributing mind to others or that they construct a "theory" of other minds to explain others' behaviors. Both views invoke an inherent cognitive component that comes into play and guides the child's developing understanding of others' beliefs and desires or motivations. In these views, although the knowledge of how people's minds work is late in its full achievement, it is not presumed to be related in a significant way to either social processes or communication. In contrast, the social-cultural view emphasizes the role of social interaction and communication, reflected upon by the individual child, as critical to these developments. As argued throughout this chapter, language plays an essential part in this process.

The argument that language is the key to this development has been addressed from linguistic as well as philosophical and psychological positions (Astington & Baird, 2005; Nelson, 1996). A compelling argument has been made by Hutto (2010) that children acquire this distinction not through introspection but through experience with narratives offering different points of view on the same events. I believe that Hutto's case is persuasive, and that the child's increasing familiarity with narratives, personal and fictional, provides additional content for reflection and construction of one's own self and mind and the realization that these personal parts are components of the social and cultural world in which they live. Bogdan (2010), from a somewhat different position, also argues that children understand that others' have minds prior to, and as a basis for, understanding their own possession of "mind" as a key component of the maturing sense of self. In Bogdan's view, simply listening to adults talk of these matters may elicit the realization of one's own self and unique mind, beyond an earlier recognition of the taking of different perspectives. Experience with language in social context and in narrative formats is essential to these philosophical analyses, which both draw on psychological developmental research. Talking about unobservable selves and minds that may harbor knowledge, interests, and motives different from those of the self is a natural component of child–adult interaction in many cultures. Beyond the understanding of "mind" and "self" this process enables a child to see oneself as a member of a social and cultural community of minds, a major achievement of social and cognitive development in early childhood. The point here is that this achievement depends upon the exchange of talk about the unobservable – minds and selves – that lie behind the observable behavior of others.

The last sections have pointed to some of the research areas that have been addressed in relation to the learning and use of language in early childhood. They of course do not exhaust the possible relationship of language to cognitive achievements in this period. Among other topics that have been widely explored in this period are the development of concepts and categories relevant to different knowledge domains (such as biology, history, and astronomy) or the more domestic and familiar categories of food, clothing, and animals in everyday life, but I do not have room to consider this obvious but complicated area (see Nelson, 1996 and 2007 for earlier discussions).

Entry to the Cultural Community of Minds: What Lies Ahead

Throughout this chapter I have considered children's venture into communication and language within the context originally set forth by Merlin Donald (1991) in terms of related levels of mind, culture, and language. This is the background for the assumption that as children emerge from infancy they encounter simultaneously the complexities of language and those of the contemporary level of oral language culture. The background premise is that children's learning and use of language provides the opportunities for engaging with novel cultural contexts and materials that then contribute to advances in social and cognitive development that are typically observed during the pre-school years. The argument is not that language on its own achieves conceptual change, but that language used in interaction with others to understand the world, including the social and cultural as well as the material world, is essential to these changes.

Although the particulars of the "cultural levels" view may not be widely shared, the general emphasis on the social and cultural conditions of learning in this period of development is increasingly accepted. This social-cultural view has obvious connections to Vygotskian theory, but it relates to Piagetian theory as well in the sense that it assumes fundamental mental change, and not simply cultural learning, as the outcome of development. Its significance for further research directions lies in its integration of these classic approaches to developmental change. Its potential bearing on brain development may be less apparent than its relation to behavior, but understanding the biological base of mental change is a critical part of these developments especially relevant to issues of social and educational importance. Donald's (2001) projection of how brain structures and functions expanded and changed in response to language in its different formats and uses over the span of human existence provides a relevant model for developmental investigation. Are such changes evident in development as language is acquired, and do they relate to different aspects of knowledge?

Even the areas discussed briefly here – memory, source attributions, self, theory of mind – leave many questions to be addressed in this general framework. For example, although the relation of language achievement to theory of mind has been shown to exist at many levels, a detailed theory of how understanding progresses and the role of specific language input at different ages and levels of language has yet to be proposed and tested over developmental time. In fact, as noted earlier, there is a dearth of longitudinal investigation of how comprehension proceeds at different levels and with different support, as in the course of story understanding at different levels of language learning. Most research in developmental psychology follows the laboratory research model, illuminating a particular problem at a particular age, or sometimes comparison of two ages. This model has the advantage of clarifying our understanding regarding a specific effect. However, it needs to be supplemented, by observational studies of individual children over time (as with Emily) and by longitudinal samples that may address a multiple of individuals and observations, revealing individual patterns of development. Indeed, the social-cultural approach is only truly compatible with an individual differences account of development, one that marks not only differences in time course, but also differences in pathways. From this perspective the approach is also compatible with (indeed, inseparable from) a systems view of development.

To understand and refine such research it is important to have an overall model of how development proceeds. The mental- and cultural-levels approach – essentially social and cultural and centered on the role of language in its different formats – has proved useful in understanding developments in infancy and early childhood, as the previous sections discussed. I believe that it has the potential to guide further research in these areas as well as those that follow in the timeline of child development, providing needed insight into both problems for and achievements of children involved in formal education, en route to the "literate" or "theoretical" level of mind. In this projection, we need to be aware that culturally driven changes in minds – both child and adult – are very likely taking place now in many cultures of the world in ways not yet identified. Future research in this area will have to take account of how adult as well as child brains and minds may change in response to their encounters with cultural changes in semiotic and communicative tools.

References

Ambridge, B. & Lieven, E. V. M. (2011). *Child language acquisition: Contrasting theoretical approaches*. New York, NY: Cambridge University Press.

Astington J. W. & Baird, J., (2005). *Why language matters to theory of mind*. New York, NY: Oxford University Press.

Bauer, P. J. (2007). *Remembering the times of our lives: Memory in infancy and beyond*. Mahwah, NJ: Erlbaum.

Bauer, P. J., & Fivush, R. (2014). (Eds.). *The Wiley handbook on the development of children's memory*. New York, NY: Wiley Blackwell.

Bauer, P. J., & Mandler, J. M. (1990). Remembering what happened next: Very young children's recall of event sequences. In R. Fivush & J. A. Hudson (Eds.), *Knowing and remembering in young children*. New York, NY: Cambridge University Press.

Bloom, L. (1973). *One word at a time*. The Hague: Mouton.

Bloom, P. (2000). *How children learn the meaning of words*. Cambridge, MA: MIT Press.

Blum-Kulka, S., & Snow, C. E. (2002). *Talking to adults: The contribution of multiparty discourse to language acquisition*. Mahwah, NJ: Erlbaum.

Bogdan, R. J. (2003). *Interpreting minds*. Cambridge, MA: MIT Press.

Bogdan, R. J. (2009). *Predicative minds: The social ontogeny of propositional thinking*. Cambridge, MA: MIT Press.

Bogdan, R. J. (2010). *Our own minds*. Cambridge: MIT Press.

Bogdan, R. J. (2013). *Mindvaults*. Cambridge: MIT Press.

Bruner, J. S. (1986). *Actual minds possible worlds*. Cambridge, MA: Harvard University Press.

Campos, J. J., Anderson, D. I., Barbu-Roth, M. A., Hubbard, E. M., Hertenstein, M. J., & Witherington, D. (2000). Travel broadens the mind. *Infancy, 1*, 149–220.

Cekaite, A., Blum-Kulka, S., Grover, V., & Teubal, E. (2014). (Eds.). *Children's peer talk: Learning from each other*. Cambridge: Cambridge University Press.

Deacon, T. W. (1997). *The symbolic species: Coevolution of language and the brain*. New York, NY: Norton.

Donald, M. (1991). *Origins of the modern mind*. Cambridge, MA: Harvard University Press.

Donald, M. (2001). *A mind so rare: The evolution of human consciousness*. New York, NY: Norton.

Donald, M. (in press). The evolutionary origins of human cultural memory. In B. Wagoner (Ed.). *Oxford handbook of culture and memory*. Oxford: Oxford University Press.

Fenson, L., Dale, P. S., Reznick, J. S., Bates, E., Thal, D. J., & Pethick, S. J. (1994). Variability in early communicative development. *Monographs of the Society for Research in Child Development. 59(5)*.

Fivush, R. (2008). Remembering and reminiscing: how individual lives are constructed in family narratives. *Memory Studies, 1*, 45–54.

Fivush, R. (2011). The development of autobiographical memory. *Annual Review of Psychology, 62*, 559–582.

Fodor, J. A. (1975). *The language of thought*. New York, NY: Crowell.

Gallaway, C., & Richards, B. J. (1994). (Eds.). *Input and interaction in language acquisition*. New York, NY: Cambridge University Press.

Golinkoff, R. M., Hirsh-Pasekl, K., Bloom, L., Smith, L. B., Woodward, A. L., Akhtar, N., Tomasello, M., & Hollich, G. (2000). (Eds.). *Becoming a word learner: A debate on lexical acquisition*. New York, NY: Oxford University Press.

Halliday, M. A. K. (1975). *Learning how to mean*. London: Edwin Arnold.

Hampson, J., & Nelson, K. (1993). The relation of maternal language to variation in rate and style of language acquisition. *Journal of Child Language, 20*, 313–342.

Harris, P. L. (2012). *Trusting what you're told: How children learn from others*. Cambridge, MA: Harvard University Press.

Hart, B. & Risley, T. (1995). *Meaningful differences in the everyday lives of young American children*. Baltimore: Brookes.

Hobson, P. (2002). *The cradle of thought: Exploring the origins of thinking*. Oxford: Oxford University Press.

Hutto, D. (2010). *Folk psychological narratives: The socio-cultural basis of understanding reasons*. Cambridge, MA: MIT Press.

Jablonka, E., & Lamb, M. J. (2005). *Evolution in four dimensions: Genetic, epigenetic, behavioral, and symbolic variation in the history of life*. Cambridge, MA: MIT Press.

Jusczyk, P. W. (2000). *The discovery of spoken language*. Cambridge, MA: MIT Press.

Kemler Nelson, D. G. (1999). Attention to functional properties in toddlers' naming and problem-solving. *Cognitive Development, 14*, 77–100.

Levy, E. T., & McNeill, D. (2015). *Narrative development of young children: Gesture, imagery, and cohesion.* Cambridge: Cambridge University Press.

Macnamara, J. (1982). *Names for things.* Cambridge, MA: MIT Press.

Mandler, J. M. (2004). *The foundations of mind: Origins of conceptual thought.* New York, NY: Oxford University Press.

Miller, P. J., Potts, R., Fung, H., Hoogstra, L., & Mintz, J. (1990). Narrative practices and the social construction of self in childhood. *American Ethnologist, 17,* 292–311.

Millikan, R. G. (2004). *Varieties of meaning: The 2002 Nicod Lectures.* Cambridge, MA: The MIT Press.

Nelson, K. (1973). Structure and strategy in learning to talk. *Monographs of the Society for Research in Child Development, 38* (1–2, Serial No. 149).

Nelson, K. (1974). Concept, word, and sentence: Interrelations in acquisition and development. *Psychological Review, 81,* 267–285.

Nelson, K. (1978). How young children represent knowledge of their world in and out of language. In R. S. Siegler (Ed.), *Children's thinking: What develops?* Hillsdale, NJ: L. Erlbaum Associates.

Nelson, K. (1985). *Making sense: The acquisition of shared meaning.* New York, NY: Academic Press.

Nelson, K. (1986). *Event knowledge: Structure and function in development.* Hillsdale, NJ: Lawrence Erlbaum Assoc.

Nelson, K. (Ed.). (1989). *Narratives from the crib.* Cambridge, MA: Harvard University Press.

Nelson, K. (1993). The psychological and social origins of autobiographical memory. *Psychological Science, 4,* 1–8.

Nelson, K. (1996). *Language in cognitive development: The emergence of the mediated mind.* New York, NY: Cambridge University Press.

Nelson, K. (2005). Language pathways to the community of minds. In J. W. Astington & J. Baird (Eds.), *Why language matters to theory of mind.* New York, NY: Oxford University Press.

Nelson, K. (2007). *Young minds in social worlds: Experience, meaning and memory.* Cambridge, MA: Harvard University Press.

Nelson, K. (2014a). A matter of meaning: reflections on forty years of JCL. *Journal of Child Language, 14* (Supplement S1), 93–104.

Nelson K. (2014b). Sociocultural theories of memory development. In P. J. Bauer & R. Fivush (Eds.). *The Wiley handbook on the development of children's memory.* New York, NY: Wiley Blackwell

Nelson, K. (2015). Making sense with private speech. *Cognitive Development, 36* · October–December 2015, 171–179. doi: 10.1016/j.cogdev.2015.09.004.

Nelson, K., & Fivush, R. (2004). The emergence of autobiographical memory: A social cultural developmental theory. *Psychological Review, 1119,* 486–511.

Nelson, K., & Gruendel, J. (1981). Generalized event representations: Basic building blocks of cognitive development. In M. Lamb & A. Brown (Eds.), *Advances in developmental psychology, Vol. 1.* Hillsdale, NJ: L. Erlbaum Associates.

Nelson, K., Hampson, J., & Kessler-Shaw, L. (1993). The noun bias in early lexicons: Evidence, explanations, and implications. *Journal of Child Language, 20,* 61–84.

Roberts, K. P., & Blades, M. (2000). (Eds.). *Children's source monitoring.* Mahwah, NJ: Erlbaum Assoc.

Sawyer, R. K. (1997). *Pretend play as improvisation: Conversation in the preschool classroom.* Mahwah, NJ: Erlbaum.

Schaller, S. (1991). *A man without words*. New York, NY: Summit Books.

Schank, R. C., & Abelson R. P. (1977). *Scripts, plans, goals and understanding*. Hillsdale NJ: Erlbaum.

Shipley, T. F., & Zacks, J. M. (2008). (Eds.). *Understanding events: From perception to action*. New York, NY: Oxford.

Snow, C. (2014). Input to interaction to instruction: Three key shifts in the history of child language research. *Journal of Child Language, 14* (Supplement S1), 117–123.

Suddendorf, T., & Moore, C. (2011). Introduction to special issue: The development of episodic foresight. *Cognitive Development, 26*, 295–298.

Tomasello, M. (1995). Joint attention as social cognition. In C. Moore & S. Dunham (Eds.) *Joint attention: Its origin and role in development*. Hillsdale, NJ: Erlbaum (pp. 103–130).

Tulving, E. (1983). *Elements of episodic memory*. New York, NY: Oxford University Press.

Tulving, E. (1993). What is episodic memory? *Current Directions in Psychological Science, 2(3)*, 67–70.

Tulving, E. (2005). Episodic memory and autonoesis: Uniquely human? In H. S. Terrace & J. Metcalfe (Eds.) *The missing link in Cognition: Origins of self-reflective consciousness*. New York, NY: Oxford University Press (pp. 3–54).

Vygotsky, L. (1962). *Thought and language* (E. Hanfmann & G. Vakar, Trans.). Cambridge, MA: MIT Press.

Wang, Qi. (2014). The cultured self and remembering. In P. J. Bauer & R. Fivush (Eds.) *The Wiley handbook on the development of children's memory*. New York, NY: Wiley Blackwell (pp. 605–625).

Werner, H., & Kaplan, B. (1963). *Symbol formation*. New York, NY: Wiley.

Winsler, A. (2009). Still talking to ourselves after all these years: A review of current research on private speech. In A. Winsler, C. Fernyhough, & I. Montero, (Eds.). *Private speech, executive functioning, and the development of verbal self-regulation*. New York, NY: Cambridge University Press (pp. 3–41).

Wittgenstein, L. (1953). *Philosophical investigations*. New York, NY: Macmillan.

22 Children's Co-Construction of Sentence and Discourse Structures in Early Childhood: Implications for Development

Amy Kyratzis

From their earliest communication, children show sensitivity to patterning in the target languages to which they are exposed: to how words and morphemes go together into sentences, and how utterances combine and relate to one another in higher order discourse units. For centuries, psychologists, linguists, sociolinguists, and philosophers have wondered where this patterning comes from. Does it come from children's conceptual understandings of logical structures or events? Does it come from the input? From innate programming? Can wide (yet meaningful) cross-linguistic, community-based, and even situational variation be its source? In this review, I explore some possible social-interactive and functional supports that young children may receive, and agentively make use of, in assembling, applying, learning, and varying complex sentence structures (e.g., complement and causal constructions) and discourse structures (e.g., narratives) in their daily interactions.

The chapter is divided into two sections. The first section reviews studies that illustrate how children learn forms in particular pragmatic, social, and activity contexts that are meaningful from their point of view (Bahtiyar & Küntay, 2008; Budwig, 1995; Budwig, Stein, & O'Brien, 2001; Clancy, 2009; Ervin-Tripp, 1991, 1993, 1996, 2012; Küntay & Slobin, 1996; Kyratzis, 2009; Kyratzis, Ross, & Köymen, 2010; Slobin, 1985). Their own cognitive activity and social interactional pursuits help children select out and build the meaningful patternings of context (activity, speech act, etc.) and language forms that they articulate. The second section reviews studies that illustrate how children build grammatical constructions collaboratively in the discourse, recycling and repeating bits of others' (and their own) prior talk in order to align (and disalign) with others and take stances on what they or others have said in prior talk (e.g., Clancy, 2009; Du Bois, 2014; Ervin-Tripp, 1991; C. Goodwin, Goodwin, & Olsher, 2002; M. H. Goodwin, 2007; Köymen & Kyratzis, 2009, 2014; Küntay & Slobin, 1996; Kyratzis et al., 2010). Complex grammatical constructions can result from these dialogic processes. Taken together, these studies illustrate how children build and co-construct grammar and discourse structures in "socially organized interactive contexts" (Ervin-Tripp, 2012; Schieffelin & Ochs, 1996, p. 251) and dialogically, in concert with others (Du Bois, 2014; C. Goodwin et al., 2002), as they act to build particular forms of involvement and social organization (Goodwin & Goodwin, 2004) with adult caregivers, and with peers, during talk-in-interaction. Implications for broader developmental theories (Piaget, Vygotsky) and broader arenas of development (social, cognitive) beyond language are discussed.

Children's Patternings of Forms and Meanings – The Role of Context and Discourse

This section reviews studies that illustrate how children learn language forms in particular pragmatic, social, and activity contexts that are meaningful from their point of view. The studies come from a discourse- and function-based view of grammar acquisition. Researchers working within this theoretical perspective draw data from naturalistic samples of real conversations. According to this view (Budwig, 1995; Ervin-Tripp, 1993; Gerhardt & Savisir, 1986; Slobin, 1981, 1985), children learn particular grammatical contrasts and allocate forms so as to index particular clusters of semantic, pragmatic, and discursive notions that are meaningful from their point of view. According to Ervin-Tripp (1996, p. 21), "context permeates language" – that is, "contextual assumptions affect how we understand language, and . . . contexts of speech have to be better understood to develop realistic theories of language and language learning." In other words, patternings in grammar are appropriated by children to index patternings in contextual and discursive phenomena. A primary task for the researcher of language acquisition, then, is to discern the contrasts of context and discourse that are salient to children.

Many of the theorists who take the functional-basis approach are also researchers of developmental pragmatics – that is, investigate not only language forms, but also their use in social contexts. Developmental pragmatics examines "children's developing competence in the use of language within and across socially organized contexts" (Schieffelin & Ochs, 1996, p. 251), studying such skills as knowing how to address different interlocutors, make requests of peers versus superiors, and other social phenomena. Ervin-Tripp and Mitchell-Kernan (1977), and Ochs and Schieffelin (1979), were the first collections of studies that used the developmental pragmatics approach. Some of the theorists in the functional-discursive basis of forms perspective also adhere to language socialization theory. Studies of language socialization, like developmental pragmatics, also "examine children's skill to use language; however, the emphasis is on relating children's knowledge and performance to the social and cultural structures . . . and ideologies that give meaning and identity to a community" (Schieffelin & Ochs, 1996, p. 252; see also Ochs & Schieffelin, 1984, 2012).[1]

Activity type, agency/accountability, and discourse perspective are three features of context and discourse that seem to account for many of the grammatical contrasts that young children (and adults) make. For example, activity type has been found to

---

1 See also Cook-Gumperz & Kyratzis, 2001a; Kyratzis & Cook-Gumperz, 2015, for a history of these related fields of inquiry.

have a strong influence on the development of the ability to use causal and temporal clauses. Ervin-Tripp (2012, p. 94) examined a naturalistic database of videotaped talk in California families and found that "the first uses [by young children] in this large sample of use at the critical ages [2:0 to 5:0 years] shows that almost three-fourths of first uses were in Planning of future activity or in Control Acts. These, rather than Narratives, might be the optimal context for observing temporal clause development." That is, young children were more likely to use a temporal construction in the form of a Planning Sequence such as "First we put the hat on, then we will ready go," or a Bounded Control Act, such as "Can I have your worm when you get finished?" than they were to use a Sequential Narrative, such as "Paula put oatmeal in it, then put the water" (Ervin-Tripp, 2012, p. 91). In a similar vein, Kyratzis, Guo, and Ervin-Tripp (1990) reported that the youngest children in the same corpus of family data used codable causal clauses as adjuncts to directives and prohibitions, rather than for expressing ideational relations. For example, young children were more likely to produce utterances like "You have to hold onto him because you don't want him to fall" than "I sprained my ankle 'cause I was hitting my father's shoe" (1990, pp. 208, 206). Bahtiyar and Küntay (2008, p. 21) found that in a context in which children were told to "'ask [the confederate] nicely' for objects," 5 year olds were more likely to provide fuller, more mature referential constructions with discriminating adjectives than when they were not instructed that the confederate had this preference. Contexts in which children need to compel others to action, or in which politeness is required, call for different kinds of marking than ideational/narrative settings – that is, settings where pragmatic functions (i.e., requesting and politeness) are not emphasized. Young children seem to be aware of these differing demands and to be able to formulate grammatical constructions that are responsive to them.

Another feature of context that children attend to in making form contrasts is whether the speaker should emphasize accountability in the actor being described, or minimize it. Duranti and Ochs (1996), examining use of ergative and genitive constructions in Samoan, found that

> the use of ergative NPs seems associated in Samoan discourse with a stance that assumes or assigns accountability to the participant role . . . When the genitive phrase, as opposed to the ergative phrase, is used to refer to the putative agent, the description of the event seems to focus on the *product or result of the action* . . . rather than on the party who is responsible for the process.
> (Duranti & Ochs, 1996, p. 183)

Samoan children take a long period of time to fully acquire and exploit the genitive, possibly because of a subtle social feature: the need to minimize accountability that underlies its use, as well as its morpho-syntactic complexities. Budwig (1995) discovered an individual difference. She observed that some young US children use the contrast between "I-my" self-reference forms in first person to index a cluster of semantic/pragmatic features corresponding to the contrast between low and high agency/intentionality (e.g., using "I" for experiencing an event and "me-my" for acting to make it happen). Other children did not do so. This contrast turned out to be salient for children whose mothers characteristically emphasized the children's agency and accomplishment while de-emphasizing their own – what could be thought of as "self-esteem builder moms" (Ervin-Tripp, 1993) – implicating the role played by input.

Individual differences aside, low-transitivity marking can prevail in some pragmatic contexts. In another study, Budwig and colleagues found that "children acquiring both English and German made regular use of a variety of construction types to talk about nonagent subjects" (Budwig, Stein, & O'Brien, 2001, p. 64). For example, in contexts where they were being blocked from performing an action, they might choose to emphasize the result of the action ("it came off again"); in contexts where they were acting to shift the frame of play, they might also use a low transitivity form (e.g., "the ambulance came"). Thompson and Hopper (2001) reported that in face-to-face conversations, adult family members and friends used clauses with low Transitivity and concluded that "the low Transitivity in our conversational data is to a considerable extent determined by the kinds of things we are doing when we talk with friends and acquaintances. We do not seem to talk much about events … rather, our talk is mostly about 'how things are from our perspective'" (Thompson & Hopper, 2001, p. 53).

Kyratzis (2009) took this investigation to *children's* talk among friends, examining the verb constructions used by four target children in a specific category of peer disputes that were identified in a previously collected data set. These were video recordings of the naturally occurring interactions of children who attended two toddler-infant daycare centers. The children were aged between 12–30 months of age. She found that: 1) the verb constructions that the children utilized in the context of peer disputes were low in Transitivity, differing from the forms that young children were reported utilizing in early child language studies (e.g., Slobin, 1985), which were high Transitivity; 2) although accusing statements (e.g., "he take one of my tools!," "you push me!," "they knock off my truck"; Kyratzis (2009), p. 45) would have increased children's use of parameters of high Transitivity in their disputes, the children used this pragmatic function infrequently, preferring instead expressions with low Transitivity. These expressions mentioned feeling states or were statements of what they were doing cast with non-completive aspect (e.g., "I don't like it," "it's so loud," "I'm building"; Kyratzis (2009), p. 47). In accounting for this differential preference of children for perspective statements over accusing statements as speech acts to use in disputes, Kyratzis (2009) suggested some possible influences of caregiver practices and child-care ideologies utilized at the daycare centers at which these data were collected. To different degrees, these centers ascribed to a particular child-care philosophy whereby educators encouraged children to express their likes and dislikes ("tell [other child] that you don't like that"), and discouraged children from using accusing statements with other children; this was a means of de-escalating conflict by helping children become sensitized to one another's feelings. These practices may have accounted for young children's strong preference to use perspective statements and to use parameters of low Transitivity.

Another aspect of context that can influence children's syntactic choices is discourse perspective. Hopper (1979) argued that, depending on language, adult speakers make use of diverse form contrasts to mark a crucial and universal contrast of narrative discourse: foreground versus background – that is, the contrast between events speakers present as individualized and sequenced in a narrative, and those they present as commentary and background detail. For example, consider the following narrative sequence taken from a Swahili traveler's tale, translated to English, and cited in Hopper (1979, p. 214): "we returned to the camp, and ran away during the night, and we traveled for several days, we passed through several villages, and in all of them we did not have to pay tribute." Speakers of Swahili would make the following differentiation. They would put the prefix marker "ka" on the verbs of the main narrative – "returned," "ran away," and "traveled" – while putting the prefix "ki" on the verbs "passed through" and "pay," to denote that the latter two "amplify or comment on the events of the main narrative" (Hopper, 1979, pp. 214–215). In English, a speaker would use a finite verb form (e.g., the past tense -ed) for the events that "succeed one another in the narrative in the same order as their succession in the real world," and a non-finite verb form (e.g., -ing) for the backgrounded or amplifying events (e.g., "we traveled for several days, passing through several villages"). Such grammatical contrasts, Hopper argued, are not sentence-level, semantic phenomena, but are essentially discourse-level ones. In a related vein, Langacker (2001) argued for the influence of what he termed "viewing arrangement": "Inherent in every usage event is a presupposed viewing arrange- ment, pertaining to the relationship between the conceptualizers and the situation being viewed" (p. 16). Langacker argued that the progressive imposes a particular viewing arrangement. It involves "zooming in" and "taking an internal view" of a bounded event. This differs from the viewing arrangement characteristically taken in narrative, where events are told as though the narrator can view their endpoint (Benveniste, 1971; White, 1980). Cook-Gumperz and Kyratzis (2001b), studying tense-aspect marking in preschool children's pretend narratives, found that "between the ages of early three and late four," children showed developing "ability to shift among the simple present for temporally sequenced action and for giving a generic description and the progressive for achieving a zooming-in perspective" (2001b, p. 58). For example, a 4-year old narrated a part of her plan for circus play with her peer as follows: "and you're sitting where the man – where the lady zooms by, but she slows down when she gets to you. Okay? They say, 'who's that'" (p. 54). She encoded the phrases describing the temporally sequenced action – "where the man – where the lady zooms by," "she slows down," and "they say 'who's that'" – by using the simple present. In contrast, she used the progressive marker for the verb in the phrase "and you're sitting"– as this marking allows taking an internal view of the event from her peer's character's perspective (2001b, p. 54).

    Gerhardt and Savasir (1986), observing preschool-aged children organizing pre- tend play, found that children utilize the form contrast between simple present and progressive to mark a contrast between normativity and negotiation. More specifi- cally, Gerhardt and Savasir argued that if a child speaker used a simple present construction, such as "I *give* mommy back," the child was presenting the action as prescribed by a norm or standard; however, if they used a construction with the progressive, (e.g., "'I'm *puttin'* my shoes back on, mama'"), the child was presenting the action, in this case "puttin'," as "'open' for negotiation" with the interlocutor (1986, pp. 509–511, 516). In narrative discourse, Berman and Slobin found that children, with age, "make increased use of a productive system of verb morphology to present a non-agentive perspective on events as befalling the [main] boy-protagonist, rather than as prime activator of whatever happens" (Berman & Slobin, 1994, p. 311; see also Berman 2004). In general, different "types of non-agentive perspective are cognitively available to children long before they are used in narrative" (Berman & Slobin, 1994, p. 535). What develops, according to the authors, is in the domain of discourse function – that is, children's ability to take different narrative perspectives on a sequence of described events. "With age, the child comes to understand the varying ways that verbal accounts can be structured to bring about desired effects"; their grammatical markers become "the product of creative acts of perspective taking" (Berman & Slobin, 1994, p. 9).

In sum, the papers reviewed in this section illustrate how children can readily shift among grammatical forms of different types (e.g., using subordinate and temporal connectives vs. not using them, as well as shifting among low- vs. high-transitivity markers and tense-aspect forms of different types) to index differences in agency, accountability, activity type, and discourse or viewing perspective. Children show agency in attending to and choosing among the meanings that are salient to them, and the forms that mark these meanings. If they wish to conform to a school ideology that raises sensitivity to others' feelings, they can use a construction such as "I building this," but if they want to emphasize the peer's agency and responsibility and accuse that peer, they can use a high-transitivity form: "he took one of my tools!" They can shift among the simple present for temporally sequenced action and for giving a generic description or resort to the progressive for achieving a zooming-in perspective or more personal form of involvement in their pretend stories. Like the adults described by Hopper (1979), children are sensitive not only to sentence-level, semantic phenomena, but also to discourse-level ones going beyond individual sentences. We turn now to a discussion of how children attend to and themselves strategically manipulate features of discourse that go across utterances, as seen in their ability to tie to and reuse elements in prior talk.

Children's Co-Construction of Sentences with Others in Discourse: Reusing Elements of Prior Talk

This section reviews the relationship between discourse and grammar in another way. While the previous section explored how children select forms for, and build their utterances in such a way as, to express particular discourse functions, the studies in this section examine how children build grammatical constructions over sequences of turns by reusing elements provided in the prior talk and discourse. Complex grammatical constructions can arise through these dialogic processes, both for children as well as adults. Charles Goodwin (2013) has described how a 65+-year-old man, Chil (Goodwin's father), who had suffered a blood-vessel rupture on the left side of his brain and was able to produce only three words – "No," "Yes," and "And" – could nonetheless make himself understood and produce meaningful sentences by building on the resources of the prior talk of others (e.g., his family members) and having his points and words interpreted by those others in sequences of talk. In one example (C. Goodwin, 2013), Chil's son, Chuck, could not figure out what action was being requested when Chil repeatedly pointed to the remains of a grapefruit he had eaten which were currently in his lap, as well as pointing in front of him. Chuck makes a sequence of candidate proposals, with Chil uttering prosodic variants of "No No" until the two participants finally arrive at Chil's intended meaning. Chil builds his utterances by "performing systematic operations," namely, strong disagreement, on a publically available "substrate" (2013, pp. 8, 9, 11) consisting of prior talk produced by others. Through his analysis, Goodwin illustrates how "Chil is able to talk about many different things with fine precision" (2013, p. 11). "The meaningfulness of Chil's utterances are not 'encoded' in his talk alone. Instead the production of meaning and action draws upon resources provided by the sequential organization of the unfolding conversation he is contributing to" (C. Goodwin et al., 2002, p. 31) and the rich language structure others provide.

Charles Goodwin and colleagues note how the process of meaning construction among Chil and his family members "has clear structural affinities with events at the opposite end of the life cycle, the talk of caregivers with children just acquiring language" (Goodwin et al., 2002, p. 31). Indeed, for children, the prior talk of others, namely adults, has been found to provide a strong support for children's production of complex grammatical forms (Clancy, 2009; Ervin-Tripp, 1991; Ervin-Tripp & Miller, 1964; Keenan, 1977; Köymen & Kyratzis, 2009; Küntay & Slobin, 1996). Several studies have looked at the role of parental repetition in the input. For example, examining seven young English-speaking children's use of complement constructions in recordings of natural speech, Diessel and Tomasello found that the specific constructions used most frequently by the children were those used most frequently by parents, suggesting that the overall frequency of specific complement and other complex constructions in adult input to children can aid children's acquisition of these constructions (Diessel & Tomasello, 2001). In Turkish mother–child interaction, Küntay and Slobin (1996) observed mothers' use of repetition in "variation sets" – for example, a mother's successive uses of a verb through a series of related constructions ("I removed the pit from mine," "Will you remove too?," "Remove it, let's see"). They argued that such repetition and variation of verb constructions in child-directed discourse could help Turkish children compare across utterances and work out an aspect of the grammar of the Turkish verb system, namely, how it uses morphological agglutination. They concluded "that the child must learn to track lexical items across varying utterance positions, with different associated collections of agglutinated morphemes" (1996, p. 284).

Several studies have looked at the influence of mothers' priming of specific grammatical forms on their children's use of those forms *within the same conversation*. For example, Bloom et al. (1989) found that children used complement constructions with the matrix clause "I think," when this form was primed within five prior turns of the conversation. In her study of Korean mother–child conversations, Clancy (2009) found that when children were primed with the Korean accusative marker, they produced the same accusative marker on their own more frequently than they initially had. These studies suggest that children's syntactic constructions may serve the function of resonating caregivers' prior utterances *within the same conversation.* However, in the adult–child grammar acquisition literature, there has not been much attention paid to the discursive *functions* toward which children use such repetition.

In contrast, a long tradition of research on children's *peer* talk, or on children's peer talk involving an adult, has reported that young children do not passively imitate prior utterances. Children use repetition strategically in their talk (Corsaro & Maynard, 1996; de León, 2007; Ervin-Tripp, 1991; Goodwin, 1990, 2006; Keenan, 1977; Köymen & Kyratzis 2014). Marjorie Harness Goodwin has carried out the most systematic study of this phenomenon (1990, 2006, 2007). She identified a practice called "format tying." This construct takes a deeply functional view of children's repetitions (see also Corsaro & Maynard, 1996; de León, 2007; Evaldsson, 2002; Ervin-Tripp, 1991; Goodwin & Goodwin, 1987). Format tying is defined as participants' strategic use of the phonological, syntactic, and semantic structures of prior utterances through exact, partial, or elaborated repetitions (Goodwin, 1990).

In dispute sequences, children can tie to the format of their peer's prior utterance in order to use the peer's own words against them, in what Goodwin has termed the "boomerang effect" (see Goodwin, 1990, p. 180). Goodwin also studied format tying in assessment sequences. One of the most basic ways that children can "position those in their local social organization relative to one another and build their local social relations" (M. H. Goodwin, 2007, p. 354) is through assessment activity: "While assessing group members, attributing certain features or explicit terms to the participant being discussed, children can take up a common or divergent stance toward the target" (2007, p. 354). Through next moves to such assessments, participants can exhibit different forms of involvement or "participation" (Goodwin & Goodwin, 2004), expressing either "disdain or enthusiasm for the position of one's fellow interlocutors" (M. H. Goodwin, 2007, pp. 354–355).

Format tying can be a powerful resource in assessment sequences. For example, an extended conversation between two elementary-school-aged girls, Sarah[2] and Aretha, who were evaluating a non-present peer, the captain of the softball team, who had excluded them from a game (M. H. Goodwin 2007), contained many utterances with format tying. Goodwin extracted the following pair, the first produced by Sarah, the second by Aretha, and lined up the overlapping elements:

(1) Why would you wanna play with somebody   That's all mad at you[3]
      Why would you wanna play with somebody   Who only lets you play
                                                because his girlfriend
                                                suddenly-
                                                (M. H. Goodwin, 2007, p. 357)

---

2 All names of participants in this and other examples in this chapter, as in the original articles, are pseudonyms.
3 Underlining, as used in author's transcription system, denotes prominent syllable.

Goodwin describes how the lines of Aretha's talk are "built parasitically on prior ones" of Sarah, with Aretha repeating the frame of the start of Sarah's utterance, as well as mirroring the relative clause which follows. Producing assessments like this in overlap with one another is "one of the hallmarks of showing that people's minds are together" (M. H. Goodwin, 2007, p. 357; see also Goodwin & Goodwin, 1987).

In a large body of research on children's peer interactions reviewed recently by M. H. Goodwin and Kyratzis, children were observed using a broad range of cultural resources to negotiate "how they stand vis-à-vis one another" (Goodwin & Kyratzis, 2012, p. 366; Goodwin, 2007), and format tying was one of these resources (see also Goodwin & Kyratzis, 2007). In M. H. Goodwin's example above, the child speakers' format tying is part of their action of exhibiting different forms of involvement with one another (enthusiasm) and with the absent peer (disdain).

The work of Marjorie Harness Goodwin and Charles Goodwin on children's assessments and disputes underscores some of the discursive functions of format tying and how format tying relates to grammar. Similar to their proposal that child speakers use format tying to exhibit enthusiasm or disdain, alignment or disalignment with the expressed positions of their interlocutors (Goodwin and Goodwin 2004; M. H. Goodwin 1990, 2006, 2007), John Du Bois (2007, 2014) has invoked the construct of "Dialogic syntax." Dialogic syntax refers to the functional practice by which "a speaker constructs an utterance based on the immediately co-present utterance of a dialogic partner" (Du Bois, 2014, p. 359). Through strategically repeating the syntactic shape of a prior utterance in the talk, a speaker displays particular forms of engagement with their interlocutors (Du Bois, 2014). In repeating part of what was said, the speaker takes an evaluative stance toward the information conveyed. Regarding children and syntax, Du Bois claims that "whether intended or not, [adults'] dialogic actions frame an ideal site for the ongoing learning of linguistic structure by any young children in attendance (not to mention other adults). The connection of parallelism and reproduction across closely juxtaposed utterances can be mobilized to support children's learning processes" (Du Bois, 2014, p. 366). Language learners can rely on "dialogic bootstrapping" (Du Bois, 2014) "to produce their own utterances by reusing the forms and functions of the prior utterance" (Clancy, 2009, p. 114), thereby reducing their processing load. In the descriptions of studies which follow, I will attempt to illustrate how children together, beyond merely working out syntax from the talk of adults, can themselves produce and co-construct complex grammatical constructions, over sequences of turns, through the practice of format tying to others' speech (see also Du Bois, 2014; C. Goodwin et al., 2002; M. H. Goodwin, 1990, 2006, 2007; Köymen & Kyratzis, 2009).

In M. H. Goodwin's research on school-aged children's uses of assessment sequences (2006, 2007), she found that girls made frequent use of the practice of tying to one another's grammatical formats, such as Pronoun (Speaker) + Adverbial intensifier + Verb + Object (e.g., "*I ne*ver liked *them*," "I'm not *cra*zy about them," "I *ne*ver liked the Spice Girls," "*you* don't like things that are trendy") (Goodwin 2006, pp. 195–206). They did so in order to display their congruent view with that of co-present participants of some object of value, in this case, their shared dislike of the pop culture group the Spice Girls, while contrasting that view with the discongruent one held by absent peers, who they portrayed as liking the Spice Girls. "The activity of assessing objects provides a way for girls to make evaluations about present as well as non-present participants" (Goodwin 2006: 198) and to establish their relationships to one another.

With format tying, "because the structure of paired adjacent utterances remains similar with the exception of parts of the utterance which are replaced" (Goodwin, 2006, p. 201), the similarities among peer group members' assessments can be highlighted and "similar types of stances with respect to" a third party can be exhibited (Goodwin, 2006, p. 201). Very young children with limited linguistic resources can make similar uses of format tying, and, in the course of doing so, build up complex sentence structures in collaboration with their interlocutors. During disputes involving peers, a study by Köymen & Kyratzis (2014) observed very young children format tying to caregiver-provided expressions, as well as to their own earlier expressions. Through doing so, they attempted to influence the participation structure so that the caregiver would become aligned with them against the peer. They also built up a complex type of sentence construction: complement constructions, two-clause constructions with verbs of saying and feeling (e.g., "I want him move away"; "I don't like it he say 'Scott'"), across speaker turns. This was at a daycare center where toddlers aged 12–30 months were encouraged to "use your words" to convey their feelings to other children during peer disputes by way of de-escalating conflict. Caregivers would model expressions with verbs of saying and feeling ("are you saying 'no, don't stand on me?'") for children to use during their disputes. Children would tie to these expressions of the caregivers, and, in the process, build up complex constructions with complement verbs (verbs of saying and feeling such as "want," "need," and "say") over sequences of turns. Out of 151 complement constructions produced by seven target children (the most frequent matrix verbs were "let," "want," and "say," each accounting for between 15–18% of the constructions), 112 (or 74.17%) were primed within 20 clauses or fewer in the prior discourse, hence involved format tying (Köymen & Kyratzis, 2014).

Example 2 is one example of this practice. In the example, there is a conflict between two children, Scott and Sammy, because Scott attempts to hit Sammy. Both children sit on a couch. The caregiver intervenes in the conflict by encouraging Sammy to "use her words." She prompts Sammy to *tell* Scott to stop in lines 2 and 5 ("You can tell him to stop," "Tell him to stop"). In line 7, the caregiver models another directive for Sammy to use with Scott, saying "move away." In lines 9–12, Sammy ties to this directive that was suggested by the caregiver and uses it against Scott, telling him to "move away." However, Scott does not comply with her directive; he provokes Sammy further by putting his head on the pillow and smiling. In lines 13–14, Sammy ties to and expands her own earlier directive and embeds it into a complement construction with the stance verb "want." She says, "I want him move away" (line 13). In saying "I want him move away," Sammy is resonating elements of both her own prior utterance ("Move away") and the caregiver's ("Sammy you can tell him to stop") in line 2. She is using a complement verb as the caregiver had done, although it is a different one ("want") than the one the caregiver had used ("tell") to exhibit a congruent stance with the caregiver's and a negative stance toward the action of her peer. In line 14, when she recycles and repeats her construction, she adds the word "to" as the caregiver had used in line 2, heightening the resonance.

(2)   Children and ages: Sammy (female, 2;6); Scott (male, 1;8)
       ((SAMMY IS ON THE COUCH. SCOTT IS NEXT TO HER.))

1	((SCOTT TRIES TO HIT SAMMY))	
2	CG;	~Sammy you can tell him to stop.
3	((SCOTT GRABS THE TOY SAMMY WAS HOLDING.))	
4	SAMMY;	\<CRY\> A::h, \</CRY\>
5	CG;	Tell him to stop.
6	SAMMY;	Sto:p.
7	CG;	'Move away',
8		.. And then move away, ((SAMMY TO MOVE))
9	SAMMY;	Move away move away,
10	((SCOTT PUTS HIS HEAD ON THE PILLOW WITH AN ANGELIC FACE))	
11		Move awa:y move awa:y,
12		.. Move away.
> 13		((TO THE CG)) I want him move away.
> 14		I want him to move away.
15	CG;	If you don't like what he's doing, you can move away.
16	SAMMY;	No it's him.
17	((SAMMY TRIES TO PUSH SCOTT AWAY))	
18	CG;	He's not gonna move just 'cause you tell him.

(Köymen & Kyratzis, 2014, p. 507–508)

Du Bois (2007) uses "diagraphs" in stance-taking sequences, to highlight the resonance, as well as the contrast, across utterances. The diagraph below demonstrates several ways in which the speaker's (Sammy) complement construction is aptly designed to exhibit a negative stance toward her peer's action and a congruent view of it with the caregiver's. First, the embedded phrase "move away" ties to and embeds her own earlier request for Scott to move away in line 9. That request had itself resonated the caregiver's earlier utterance, "move away" in line 7. By format tying to her own earlier expression, Sammy expresses her stance on Scott's failure to comply with her earlier directive. By format tying to the caregiver's utterance, she also exhibits a view of Scott's action that is congruent with the caregiver's.

Diagraph 1

5	CG;	Tell	him	to stop		.
7	CG;			Move	away	,
9	SAMMY;			Move	away	,
13	SAMMY; I	want	him	move	away	.
14	SAMMY; I	want	^him	to move	away	.

(Köymen & Kyratzis, 2014, pp. 507–508)

Later, in lines 13–14, Sammy's use of ("I want X") resonates the caregiver's own use of a stance-indexing matrix verb ("Tell him to stop"), even though the stance verb that she uses ("want") is a different one from the one that the caregiver had used ("tell"). By resonating elements of the caregiver's utterances, Sammy, through her construction, is lending an air of adult-sanctioned legitimacy to her own complaint and is inviting the caregiver to take up a common stance toward the target being assessed (Goodwin, 2007), the peer's action.

In this example and many like it (Köymen & Kyratzis, 2014), toddlers formulated complex complement constructions by resonating their own directive from the prior talk (e.g., "move away"), converting its structure to a third-person description ("him move away"), and inserting a verb of intention (e.g., "I want") or speech in front of it, usually resonating a similar use of a verb of intention by the caregiver earlier in the talk. Through resonating elements of both the speaker's own and the adult audience members' prior talk, the emergent complement constructions emphasized the recalcitrance of the peer and exhibited a congruent view of it with that of the caregiver. In doing so, these constructions were carefully designed to solicit the involvement of the third party – the adult audience member – in the three-way participation structure.

Not only complement constructions, but also causal constructions can be built up by children over sequences of talk. Among friendship groups of preschool children engaged in peer pretend play, Kyratzis et al. (2010) observed a practice which we termed "validating justifications." In this practice, children would either expand a partner proposal by making a justification of that proposal, or they would make a similar proposal by tying to the format of the peer's proposal and follow that similar proposal with a justification. In both cases, the justification would get marked with "because." For instance, in Example 3 below, when Emily in a pretend play game of eating exotic international foods, proposes "pretend those are called rices," her friend Piper takes up this proposal of naming international foods by format tying to it and substituting her own food item ("And those are called chanizas"). The format tying exhibits alignment with Emily's proposal. Piper then validates this proposal of invoking a specific exotic food item by providing a reason: "because they're a special kind of tortilla." In other words, she justifies her own partial repetition of, and resonance with, Emily's proposal.

(3)   Children: Emily (4;7), Piper (4;9)
    Emily: Pretend those are called rices/
    Piper: *And those are called chaniza*s/
             because they're a special kind of tortilla
             and and we always need it/

                                    (Kyratzis, Ross, & Köymen, 2010, p. 134)

We found that validation of peers' prior talk was a supportive context for the use of the connective "because," as in Piper's use of the "because" construction in her turn: "*And those are called chanizas,* because they're a special kind of tortilla."[4] In

---

4 Italics, as used in author's transcription system, denotes the head act of the justification – that is, the statement justified .

including the connective, the speaker seemed to be marking the fact that the information in the main clause was a partial repetition of a co-participant's prior talk, thereby constituting presupposed information. Justifications which did not expand a partner proposal or the speaker's own repetition of a partner proposal, or which opposed a partner proposal (i.e., thereby constituting new information), on the other hand, were less likely to receive the connective "because." In the example below, a child, Bruce, opposes his peer Brad's move of stepping on a butterfly in a game of Step on Bees, saying "*when i say **don't.. step **on it/*" and follows his oppostional move with a justification "Those guys get mad easy/okay?"

(4) Children: Bruce (5;1), Brad (5;3)

     Bruce: [trying to make Brad let the butterfly go in a
                 game of 'Step on Bees']
                 when i say you can step on it, you step on it/
                 .. when i say **don't.. step **on it/
                 those guys get mad easy/ okay?

                          (Kyratzis, Ross, & Köymen, 2010, p. 127)

In this case, the justification does not get the causal marker "because." As studies like this illustrate, the use of connectives and discourse markers such as "because," as well as other markers (Köymen & Küntay, 2013; Kyratzis, 2007), rather than being influenced by sentence-level factors like causality per se, are serving a social-interactive purpose. Like format tying, the connectives are resources that child speakers can use to exhibit their support of their peers' play proposals and to exhibit that their own play proposals are congruent with and resonate with those of their peers during talk-in-interaction. Like the older children studied by Goodwin (2006, 2007), through format tying to prior talk and linking back to prior talk with connectives, young children are showing that "their minds are together" with their peers.

From such examples, it is evident that format tying is beneficial for grammar acquisition. Children's practice of creating resonance with the prior talk of others supports their production of complex constructions across turns, even though grammar acquisition is not the primary function of this practice. Format tying has been observed among young 2- and 4-year-old Tzotzil-Mayan children in Zinacantán, Chiapas (de León, 2007) and by immigrant children learning a second language in Sweden (Cekaite & Aronsson, 2004, 2014) and the US (Ervin-Tripp, 1986, 1991, 1996; Kyratzis, 2014). According to Cekaite and Aronsson (2014), "joint improvisations, based on playful recyclings or 'format tyings' (Goodwin, 1990), seem to be a core part of children's peer group encounters in creating sustained joint attention in peer and sibling teasing, disputes, and play" (2014, p. 201). These practices also support children's second- as well as first-language learning. In the case of very young children (de León, 2007; Köymen & Kyratzis, 2014), or children learning a second language (Cekaite & Aronsson, 2004, 2014; Ervin-Tripp, 1986, 1991; Kyratzis, 2014), the construction of utterances across different speakers can support learners in the formulation of utterances they most likely could not have produced on their own. Nonetheless, the pragmatic functions of format tying can be similar among children learning a language and those more competent in the language. For both younger and older children (and second language learners vs. native speakers), the main purpose of format tying seems to be to enable participation in playful, mocking exchanges and improvisations (e.g., through boomerang effects, e.g., Goodwin, 1990; Reynolds, 2007), in disputes to gain an upper hand and draw an audience (Köymen & Kyratzis, 2014; Goodwin, 1990), and in group-affirming assessment sequences (Goodwin, 2006; Evaldsson, 2002) and pretend play sequences (Kyratzis, 2014; Kyratzis et al., 2010) with peers and family members.

Format tying also enables collaborative narrative construction. In terms of collaborative *pretend* narrative construction, through close analysis of one very extended episode of birthday-party play among a peer group of Mexican-heritage girls that took place in a California preschool, Kyratzis (2014) illustrated how the children went to great efforts to sustain an overarching frame of birthday party in order to display their alignments to one another in the interaction. "Proposals were repeated, explicitly tied to and justified in terms of the overall frame of play" and there was "extensive use of format tying" (2014: pp. 145–146). In terms of collaborative *fictional* narrative construction, Nicolopoulou, Brockmeyer, de Sá, and Ilgaz (2014) describe how a peer-group story acting out activity involving public sharing of stories "allows narrative cross-fertilization" among preschool peers. In terms of collaborative *personal* narrative construction, Küntay and Şenay (2003) describe "rounds of narratives" being produced among peers in a preschool in Turkey in an effort to top one another.

In sum, the examples in this section underscore children's agency in building sentence (and narrative) structures in concert with their peers (Ervin-Tripp, 1991, 1996) and caregivers. Rather than complex constructions such as complement constructions or causal constructions arising solely as a reflection of the individual grammatical knowledge of child speakers, children's practices of "format tying" (Goodwin, 1990, 2006, 2007), of putting utterances into "dialogic juxtaposition" (Du Bois, 2014), and of expanding and "validating" peers' prior utterances and conversational contributions (Kyratzis et al., 2010) resulted in the collaborative construction of complex grammatical forms, over extended sequences of turns (Du Bois, 2014; Goodwin, 1990, 2006; Goodwin et al., 2002; Köymen & Kyratzis, 2009, 2014). Children engaged in these practices as they endeavored to negotiate how they stood relative to one another in the interactive encounter (Goodwin, 2007; Goodwin & Goodwin, 2004; Goodwin & Kyratzis, 2007, 2012). Children's actions of building sentences are multi-party and collaborative and go hand-in-hand with their actions of participating in conversation.

Conclusions

In the above two sections, I have attempted to show how a specific developmental outcome – the child's acquisition of grammar forms – is closely tied to discourse and social interaction. Children learn form contrasts in order to mark distinctions in discourse that are important and meaningful to them, and children use repetition and prior discourse as a resource to be able to construct their own sentences and discourse contributions and participate in conversation. In light of such evidence, it is difficult to assume that children's language-acquisition capacity is a free-standing module, and that other elements of children's understanding, including their social and cognitive knowledge, do not come into play.

In this review, I set out to explore some possible social-interactive and functional supports that young children may receive, and agentively make use of, in assembling, applying, learning, and varying complex sentence structures (e.g., complement and causal constructions) and discourse structures (e.g., narratives) in their daily interactions. To answer the question "Where does the sensitivity that children show to patterning in the target languages to which they are exposed come from?," I mentioned some sources that psychologists, linguists, sociolinguists, and philosophers have proposed, including: from conceptual understandings of logical structures or events, from the input, from innate programming, and from wide (yet meaningful) cross-linguistic, community-based, and even situational variation in the patterning. So which of these sources are influential for young children?

Across the studies that I have reviewed here, I barely implicated cross-linguistic factors, mentioning only how agglutinative Turkish verb morphology, for example, invokes different problems for language acquisition than the verb system in Romance and Western European languages (Küntay & Slobin, 1996) and how a language system that marks putative agent roles differently from English (the Samoan language, which uses ergative and genitive markers) presents different problems of language acquisition for the child (Duranti & Ochs, 1996). Although I focused this review on variation more specific than variation by language, emphasizing the role of context, cross-linguistic variation is exceedingly important, as a large number of child language-acquisition studies have shown (e.g., Berman, 2004; Berman & Slobin, 1994; Slobin, 1985, 1996).

The role of context has been shown to be exceedingly important in the language learning of young children (Ervin-Tripp, 1991, 1996, 2012; Nelson, 1973; Snow, 1999). In the first section of the chapter, I reviewed several studies illustrating how children can readily shift among grammatical forms of different types to index differences in context – that is, in agency/responsibility, activity type, and discourse or viewing perspective. These studies illustrated how, from a young age, children show agency in attending to and choosing among the meanings that are salient to them, and the forms that mark these meanings. If they wish to display conformity to a school ideology that raises sensitivity to others' feelings, they can use a low-transitivity construction like "I'm building this," but if they want to emphasize a peer's responsibility and accuse that peer, they can use a high-transitivity form, saying "he took one of my tools!" (Kyratzis, 2009). They can shift among the simple present for temporally sequenced action and for giving a generic description or, alternatively, resort to the progressive for achieving a zooming-in perspective in their pretend stories (Cook-Gumperz & Kyratzis, 2001b). Like the adults described by Hopper (1979), children are sensitive not only to sentence-level, semantic phenomena, but also to discourse-level ones extending beyond individual sentences (Ervin-Tripp, 1996, 2012).

Another way in which the role of context was shown to be important across the studies reviewed here was that in looking at the context of peers, as many of the studies that I reviewed did, we saw differences from studies which have focused on parent–child interactions. Studies around the world that examined transitivity in the expressions used by children interacting with their parents, for example, found a high transitivity in the constructions produced by the young children (Slobin, 1985), but a study that I reviewed of middle-class child peers in a California daycare setting (Kyratzis, 2009) found low transitivity in the children's marking. This seemed to be due to the kinds of pragmatic functions toward which children used language in the context of interacting with their parents (e.g., commenting on interesting, just completed events for the purpose of getting adults' attention) being different from those they used in the peer setting of the American daycare center (e.g., sharing feelings in accordance with the conflict management curriculum they were exposed to).

The role of input was very important. Parents' use of forms in the input was found to be related to children's uses (e.g., Budwig, 1995; Clancy, 2009). However, when we consider the role of priming and repetition in child-to-child rather than adult-to-child interaction, the role takes a quite different form, with repetition used differently in the case of children's peer talk (or peer talk involving an adult) than in one-on-one adult–child interactions. In peer talk, it is used mainly toward the purpose of building social alignments and influencing participation frameworks, while in adult–child talk, it is used mainly for teaching the child.

Another source of patterning in children's language acquisition was the pragmatic setting. In a case where children got "prompted by adults to use more polite language than they normally do" in getting a confederate to give them a sticker with certain features, they were more likely to use "more mature referential strategies" – that is, referring expressions with differentiating adjectival markers (Bahtiyar & Küntay, 2008, pp. 17, 7). Where children had to persuade addressees to do something rather than just describing events, they were more likely to use justifications and causal and temporal connectives (Ervin-Tripp, 2012; Kyratzis, Guo, & Ervin-Tripp, 1990). Social development and pragmatic development are very important in children's development of grammar, especially as complex grammar forms (e.g., adjuncts, modal verbs, complement constructions with embedding) seem to develop as part and parcel of children's ability and efforts to persuade others, get them to comply with their requests (Ervin-Tripp, 2012; Ervin-Tripp & Gordon, 1986; Snow, 1999), and exhibit forms of participation with them (Goodwin, 2007; Goodwin & Goodwin, 2004). Language does not develop in isolation from other systems of children's knowledge.

Another source of patterning was children's community-based understandings, the ideologies that they were socialized to in their communities (Ochs & Schieffelin, 1984, 2012). In a society which favors the use of the genitive constructions to express agency, hence enabling the mitigation of responsibility, children have to learn how to use such constructions (Duranti & Ochs, 1996). In a California daycare center where being sensitive to the feelings of others and not accusing them is emphasized, children learn to favor the use of low Transitivity expressions (Kyratzis, 2009).

A final source of patterning was children's efforts at building social organization and forms of participation with peers (e.g., Goodwin & Goodwin, 2004). " Playful recyclings or 'format tyings' (Goodwin, 1990), seem to be a core part of children's peer group encounters in creating sustained joint attention in peer and sibling teasing, disputes, and play" (Cekaite & Aronsson, 2014, p. 201), and in pretend play, assessment sequences, and story-telling. Through attending to grammatical formats and sequences used by their peers and other interlocutors in these peer-based speech events, and through permuting and recombining (Ervin-Tripp, 1991) elements of these formats in order to "tie" to what their peers had said, thereby influencing how they stood relative to one another (Goodwin, 2006, 2007; Goodwin & Kyratzis, 2007, 2012), children could extract much about the grammatical structures of their language. Moreover, they put this knowledge to use in their actions of format tying to their peers' and adult caregivers' utterances, thereby taking part in "the dialogic engagement that is an important part of everyday conversation" (Clancy, 2009, p. 114; Du Bois, 2014; Goodwin & Goodwin, 2004).

Vygotsky (1978) believed that children learn through participating in cultural activities in social interaction with more expert members of the community. Piaget also believed that peer interactions were important (1932/1997). However, neither of these developmental psychologists looked closely at how children learn through interaction on a moment-to-moment basis. In the research reported here, rather than complex constructions such as complement constructions or causal constructions arising solely as a reflection of the individual grammatical knowledge of child speakers, the children's conversational practices of "format tying" (Goodwin, 1990) and of putting utterances into "dialogic juxtaposition" (Du Bois, 2014) and "validating" peers' prior utterances and conversational contributions (Kyratzis, Köymen, & Ross, 2010) resulted in the collaborative construction of complex grammatical forms over extended sequences of turns (Du Bois, 2014; Goodwin, 1990, 2006; Goodwin et al., 2002; Köymen & Kyratzis, 2009, 2014). The activity of sentence construction, rather than being viewed as an activity carried out by individual minds, might better be viewed as a multi-party, collaborative activity drawing "upon resources provided by the sequential organization of the unfolding conversation" that children are participating in (Goodwin et al., 2002, p. 31). Video-analysis of how participants respond to one another and reveal and act on their understandings in sequences of talk moment-to-moment is needed (Goodwin et al., 2002).

In considering how children acquire grammar, a modern-day perspective would seem to require taking a multi-disciplinary approach. It would need to use video-analysis and consider naturally occurring conversations. It would need to look beyond linguistic competence to consider children's pragmatic and social knowledge – that is, "the acquisition of communicative competence, which is seen as the knowledge that underlies socially appropriate speech" (Kyratzis & Cook-Gumperz, 2015, p. 681). Pragmatic development is very important for grammar development (Snow, 1999; Ervin-Tripp, 2012). It would need to include knowledge of the ideologies and "ethnotheories" of the children's communities (Ochs & Schieffelin, 1984, 2012; Schieffelin & Ochs, 1996), which could only be ascertained through the use of ethnography. In keeping with Conversation Analysis, it would need to also consider the overall situation within which the individual grammatical construction arises – that is, the overall "unit that includes [the actor's] interlocutors, the sequential environment and a semiotically structured material setting" (Goodwin et al., 2002, p. 32), including the multimodal resources and actions that the child actor uses to exhibit particular forms of "participation" (Goodwin & Goodwin, 2004) in the discourse. In sum, it would need to consider the local particulars of what the child was doing in the sequence of interaction, as well as their whole development in their communities, including their peer group communities (Goodwin & Kyratzis, 2012). Such an eclectic, naturalistic approach would no doubt be useful for understanding the development and use of any human behavior.

References

Bahtiyar, S., & Küntay, A. C. (2008). Integration of communicative partner's visual perspective in patterns of referential requests. *Journal of Child Language, 35*, 529–555.

Benveniste, E. (1971). *Problems in general linguistics*. Coral Gables, Florida.

Berman, R. A. (2004). Between emergence and mastery: The long developmental route of language acquisition. In R. Berman (Ed.), *Language development across childhood and adolescence* (pp. 9–34). Amsterdam: John Benjamins.

Berman, R., & Slobin, D. I. (1994). *Relating events in narrative*. Hillsdale, NJ: Lawrence Erlbaum.

Bloom, L., Rispoli, M., Gartner, B. & Hafitz, J. (1989). Acquisition of complementation. *Journal of Child Language. 16*, 101–120.

Budwig, N. (1995). *A developmental-functionalist approach to child language*. Mahwah, NJ: Lawrence Erlbaum Associates.

Budwig, N., Stein, S., & O'Brien, C. (2001). Non-agent subjects in early child language: A crosslinguistic comparison. In K. E. Nelson, A. Aksu-Koc, & C. Johnson (Eds.), *Children's language, Vol. 11: Interactional contributions to language development* (pp. 49–67). Mahwah, NJ: Lawrence Erlbaum.

Cekaite, A., & Aronsson, K. (2004). Repetition and joking in children's second language conversations: Playful recyclings in an immersion classroom. *Discourse Studies, 6* (3), 373–392.

Cekaite, A., & Aronsson, K. (2014). Language play, peer group improvisations, and L2 Learning. In A. Cekaite, S. Blum-Kulka, V. Grøver, & E. Teubal (Eds.), *Children's peer talk: Learning from each other* (pp. 194–213). Cambridge: Cambridge University Press.

Clancy, P. M. (2009). Dialogic priming and the acquisition of argument marking in Korean. In J. Guo, E. Lieven, N. Budwig, S. M. Ervin-Tripp, K. Nakamura, & S. Özcalişkan (Eds.), *Crosslinguistic approaches to the study of language: Research in the tradition of Dan Isaac Slobin* (pp. 105–117). Mahwah, NJ: Erlbaum.

Cook-Gumperz, J., & Kyratzis, A. (2001a). Child discourse. In D. Schiffrin, D. Tannen, & H. Hamilton (Eds.), *A handbook of discourse analysis* (pp. 590–611). Oxford: Basil Blackwell.

Cook-Gumperz, J., & Kyratzis, A. (2001b). Pretend play: Trial ground for the simple present. In M. Putz, S. Niemeier, & R. Dirven (Eds.), *Applied cognitive linguistics I: Theory and language acquisition* (pp. 41–61). Berlin: Mouton de Gruyter.

Corsaro, W. A., & Maynard, D. (1996). Format tying in discussion and argumentation among Italian and American children. In D. I. Slobin, J. Gerhardt, A. Kyratzis, & J. Guo (Eds.). *Social interaction, social context, and language: Essays in honor of Susan Ervin-Tripp* (pp. 157–174). Mahwah, NJ: Lawrence Erlbaum.

de León, L. (2007). Parallelism, metalinguistic play, and the interactive emergence of Zinacantec Mayan siblings' culture. *Research on Language and Social Interaction*, *40*(4), 405–436.

Diessel, H., & Tomasello, M. (2001). The acquisition of finite complement clauses in English: A corpus-based analysis. *Cognitive Linguistics*, *12*(2), 131–152.

Du Bois, J. W. (2007). The stance triangle. In R. Englebretson (Ed.), *Stancetaking in discourse: Subjectivity, evaluation, interaction* (pp. 139–182. Amsterdam: Benjamins.

Du Bois. J. W. (2014). Towards a dialogic syntax. *Cognitive Linguistics*, *25*(3), 349–410.

Duranti, A., & Ochs, E. (1996). Use and acquisition of genitive constructions in Samoan. In D. I. Slobin, J. Gerhardt, A. Kyratzis, & J. Guo (Eds.), *Social interaction, social context, and language: Essays in honor of Susan Ervin-Tripp* (pp. 175–189). Mahwah, NJ: Lawrence Erlbaum.

Ervin-Tripp, S. M. (1986). Activity structure as scaffolding for children's second language learning. In W. Corsaro, J. Cook-Gumperz, & J. Streeck (Eds.), *Children's language and children's worlds* (pp. 327–358). Berlin: Mouton de Gruyter.

Ervin-Tripp, S. M. (1991). Play in language development. In B. Scales, M. Almy, A. Nicolopoulou, & S. M. Ervin Tripp (Eds.), *Play and the social context of development in early care and education* (pp. 84–97). New York, NY: Teachers College Press.

Ervin-Tripp, S. M. (1993). Constructing syntax from discourse. In E. Clark (Ed.), *Proceedings of the Stanford child language research forum* (pp. 333–341). Stanford, CA: CSLI.

Ervin-Tripp, S. M. (1996). Context in language. In D. I. Slobin, J. Gerhardt, A. Kyratzis, & J. Guo (Eds.), *Social interaction, social context, and language: Essays in honor of Susan Ervin-Tripp* (pp. 21–36). Mahwah, NJ: Lawrence Erlbaum.

Ervin-Tripp, S. M. (2012). Pragmatics as a facilitator for child syntax development. In M. Meeuwis & J.-O. Östman (Eds.), *Pragmatizing understanding: Studies for Jef Verschueren* (pp. 77–100). Amsterdam: John Benjamins.

Ervin-Tripp, S. M., & Gordon, D. (1986). The development of requests. In R. L. Schiefelbush (Ed.), *Language competence: Assessment and intervention* (pp. 61–95). San Diego, CA: College Hill.

Ervin-Tripp, S. M. & Miller, W. (1964). The development of grammar in child language. In U. Bellugi & R. Brown (Eds.), *The acquisition of language. Monographs of the Society for Research in Child Development*, *29*(1), 9–34.

Ervin-Tripp, S. M., & Mitchell-Kernan, C. (Eds.) (1977). *Child discourse*. New York, NY: Academic Press.

Evaldsson, A. C. (2002). Boys' gossip telling: Staging identities and indexing (unacceptable) masculine behavior. *Text*, *22*(2), 199–225.

Gerhardt, J., & Savasir, I. (1986). The use of the simple present in the speech of two three-year-olds: Normativity not subjectivity. *Language in Society*, *15*, 501–536.

Goodwin, C. (2013). The co-operative, transformative organization of human action and knowledge. *Journal of Pragmatics*, *46*(1), 8–23.

Goodwin, C., & Goodwin, M. H. (2004). Participation. In A. Duranti (Ed.), *A companion to linguistic anthropology* (pp. 222–244). Malden, MA: Blackwel.

Goodwin, C., Goodwin, M. H., & Olsher, D. (2002). Producing Sense with Nonsense Syllables: Turn and Sequence in Conversations with a Man with Severe Aphasia. In B. Fox, C. Ford, & S. A. Thompson (Eds.), *The Language of Turn and Sequence* (pp. 56–80). Oxford: Oxford University Press.

Goodwin, M. H. (1990). *He-said-she-said: Talk as social organization among black children*. Bloomington, IN: Indiana University Press.

Goodwin, M. H. (2006). *The hidden life of girls: Games of stance, status, and exclusion*. Oxford, UK: Blackwell.

Goodwin, M. H. (2007). Participation and embodied action in preadolescent girls' assessment activity. *Research on Language and Social Interaction*, *40(*4), 353–375.

Goodwin, M. H., & Goodwin, C. (1987). Children's arguing. In S. Philips, S. Steele & C. Tanz, (Eds.), *Language, gender, and sex in comparative perspective* (pp. 200–48). Cambridge: Cambridge University Press.

Goodwin, M. H., & Kyratzis, A. (Eds.) (2007). Children socializing children: Practices for negotiating the social order among peers. *Special issue of Research on Language and Social Interaction*, *40*(4).

Goodwin, M. H., & Kyratzis, A. (2012). Peer language socialization. In A. Duranti, E. Ochs, & B. Schieffelin (Eds.), *The handbook of language socialization* (pp. 391–419). Oxford, UK: Blackwell.

Hopper, P. (1979). Aspect and foregrounding in discourse. In T. Givon (Ed.), *Discourse and syntax* (pp. 213–241). New York, NY: Academic Press.

Keenan, E. O. (1977). Making it last: Repetition in children's discourse. In S. M. Ervin-Tripp & C. Mitchell-Kernan (Eds.). *Child discourse* (pp. 125–139). New York, NY: Academic Press.

Köymen, B., & Küntay, A (2013). Turkish children's conversational oppositions: Usage of two discourse markers. *Discourse Processes*, *50*, 388–406.

Köymen, S. B., & Kyratzis, A. (2009). Format tying and the acquisition of syntax in toddlers' peer interactions. *Proceedings of the 35th annual meeting of the Berkeley Linguistics Society* (pp. 202–210). Berkeley: Berkeley Linguistics Society.

Köymen, B., & Kyratzis, A. (2014). Dialogic syntax and complement constructions in toddlers' peer interactions. *Cognitive Linguistics*, *25*(3), 497–521.

Küntay, A., & Senay, I. (2003). Narratives beget narratives: Rounds of stories in Turkish preschool conversations. *Journal of Pragmatics*, *35*, 559–587.

Küntay, A., & Slobin, D. I. (1996). Listening to a Turkish mother: Some puzzles for acquisition. In D. I. Slobin, J. Gerhardt, A. Kyratzis, & J. Guo (Eds.), *Social interaction, social context, and language: Essays in honor of Susan Ervin-Tripp* (pp. 157–174). Mahwah, NJ: Lawrence Erlbaum.

Kyratzis, A. (2007). Using the social organizational affordances of pretend play in American preschool girls' interactions. *Research on Language and Social Interaction*, *40*(4), 321–352.

Kyratzis, A. (2009). "He take one of my tools!" vs. "I'm building": Transitivity and the grammar of accusing, commanding, and perspective-sharing in toddler's peer disputes. In J. Guo, E. Lieven, N. Budwig, S. M. Ervin-Tripp, K. Nakamura, & Ş. Özcalişkan (Eds.), *Crosslinguistic approaches to the study of language: Research in the tradition of Dan Isaac Slobin* (pp. 41–54). Mahwah, NJ: Erlbaum.

Kyratzis, A. (2014). Peer interaction, framing, and literacy in preschool bilingual pretend play. In A. Cekaite, S. Blum-Kulka, V. Grøver, & E. Teubal (Eds.), *Children's peer talk: Learning from each other* (pp. 129–147). Cambridge: Cambridge University Press.

Kyratzis, A., & Cook-Gumperz, J. (2015). Child discourse. In D. Tannen, H. Hamilton, & D. Schiffrin (Eds.), *The handbook of discourse analysis* (pp. 681–704). Chichester, UK: John Wiley & Sons, Ltd.

Kyratzis, A., Guo, J., & Ervin-Tripp, S. M. (1990). Pragmatic conventions influencing children's use of causal expressions in natural discourse. In *Proceedings of the sixteenth annual meeting of the Berkeley Linguistics Society, 16,* 205–215. Berkeley: Berkeley Linguistics Society.

Kyratzis, A., Ross, T S., & Köymen, S. B. (2010). Validating justifications in preschool girls' and boys' friendship group talk: Implications for linguistic and socio-cognitive development. *Journal of Child Language, 37*(1), 115–144.

Langacker, R. W. (2001). Cognitive linguistics, language pedagogy, and the English present tense. In M. Putz, S. Niemeier, & R. Dirven (Eds.), *Applied cognitive linguistics I: Theory and language acquisition* (pp. 4–39). Berlin: Mouton de Gruyter.

Nelson, K. (1973). Structure and strategy in learning to talk. *Monographs of the Society for Research in Child Development, 38*(1/2), 1–135.

Nicolopoulou, A., Brockmeyer, C., de Sá, A., & Ilgaz, H. (2014). Narrative performance, peer group culture, and narrative development in a preschool classroom. In A. Cekaite, S. Blum-Kulka, V. Grøver, & E. Teubal (Eds.). *Children's peer talk: Learning from each other* (pp. 42–62). New York, NY: Cambridge University Press.

Ochs, E., & Schieffelin, B. B. (Eds.). (1979). *Developmental pragmatics.* New York, NY: Academic Press.

Ochs, E. & Schieffelin, B. B. (1984). Language acquisition and socialization: Three developmental stories. In R. Shweder & R. LeVine (Eds.), *Culture theory: Essays on mind, self and emotion* (pp. 276–320). Cambridge: Cambridge University Press.

Ochs, E., & Schieffelin, B. B. (2012). The theory of language socialization. In A. Duranti, E. Ochs & B. B. Schieffelin (Eds.), *The handbook of language socialization* (pp. 1–22). Oxford: Blackwell.

Piaget, J. (1932, 1997). *The moral judgment of the child.* London: Free Press.

Reynolds, J. F. (2007). "Buenos dias/((Military salute))": The natural history of a coined insult. *Research on Language and Social Interaction, 40*(4). 437–465.

Schieffelin, B. B., & Ochs, E. 1996. The microgenesis of competence: Methodology in language socialization. In D. I. Slobin, J. Gerhardt, A. Kyratzis, & J. Guo (Eds.), *Social interaction, social context and language: Essays in Honor of Susan Ervin-Tripp* (pp. 251–64). Hillsdale, NJ: Lawrence Erlbaum Associates.

Slobin, D. I. (1981). The origins of grammatical encoding of events. In W. Deutsch (Ed.), *The child's construction of language* (pp. 185–200). New York, NY: Academic Press.

Slobin, D. I. (1985). Crosslinguistic evidence for the language-making capacity. In D. I. Slobin (Ed.), *The crosslinguistic study of language acquisition, Vol. 2: Theoretical issues* (pp. 1157–1256). Hillsdale, NJ: Lawrence Erlbaum Associates.

Slobin, D. I. (1996). From "thought and language" to "thinking for speaking." In J. J. Gumperz & S. C. Levinson (Eds.), *Rethinking linguistic relativity. Studies in the social and cultural foundations of language, 17* (pp. 70–96). Cambridge: Cambridge University Press.

Snow, C. E. (1999). Social perspectives on the emergence of language. In B. MacWhinney (Ed.), *The emergence of language* (pp. 257–276). Mahwah: Lawrence Erlbaum.

Thompson, S. A., & Hopper, P. J. (2001). Transitivity, clause structure, and argument structure: Evidence from conversation. In J. L. Bybee & P. J. Hopper (Eds.), *Frequency and the emergence of linguistic structure* (pp. 27–60). Amsterdam: John Benjamins.

Vygotsky, L. (1978). *Mind in society.* Cambridge, MA: Harvard University Press.

White, H. (1980). The value of narrativity in the representation of reality. In W. J. T. Mitchell (Ed.), *On narrative* (pp. 1–23). Chicago: The University of Chicago Press.

23 Developing with Diversity into the Third Decade of Life and Beyond

Colette Daiute

From Developing Language to Using Language for Development

Adolescents shift from developing linguistic and cognitive skills to *using* those skills in strategic ways. As older adolescents and adults interact in increasingly varied environments, challenges and opportunities in those environments elicit complex linguistic and other processes to mediate interactions with extant circumstances. For example, as an immigrant to the United States, 21-year-old Aida was especially attentive to how her American peers related to one another, the language they used to interact, and how those narratives interacted with personal, family, and public environments.

In a community-based research workshop in her town, Aida, like 133 other adolescents and young adults growing up during and after the wars that shattered the former Yugoslavia, wrote three narratives (Daiute, 2010). In response to a request to write about a conflict she or someone her age had experienced, Aida wrote the following:

> In high school American kids would always pick on Bosnians telling that we get everything for free from government, we don't pay taxes. They thought that they are right and that they know everything. I tried to explain the way it is but they didn't listen.

When asked to write about a conflict involving adults in her community, Aida shared the following narrative.

> My cousin got into a fight with my parents because we were going to visit Bosnia and my cousin's son was going to Hawaii because he's in the military and we didn't know that and we got mad because they didn't come to wish us luck with our flight. After we came back from Bosnia they still don't come over and we haven't seen them in 3 years.

Finally, Aida completed a brief fictional but realistic story starter, stating that members of the community had gathered to break ground for a new youth center. Aida entered the names of two protagonists and continued from the turning point, "Then someone came with news that changed everything!"

Nina and Elma
The news was that the mayor canceled the event. Everyone was so sad. They canceled it because they didn't like everybody in the community. Everyone went up against the mayor and they won and the mayor went to prison for discrimination.

Although narrative is often described as recounting memories or revealing developmental achievements (McAdams, 2005; Wertsch, 2002), theory and research on language use provide a foundation for studying narrative as a dynamic process (Bamberg, 2004a, 2004b; Wortham, 2001). Drawing on cultural theories of language development (Nelson, 1998; Tomasello, 2005), pragmatic philosophy (Austin, 1962; Wittgenstein, 1953), and research with adolescents and young adults (Daiute, 2010, 2014; Daiute & Kreniske, 2016; Lucic, 2013), I explain how socio-cognitive processes of language are developmental when people interact in, make sense of, and in some cases intend to change their environments. Complex genres such as narrating, writing commentaries in social media, and participating in myriad other communications are processes mediating human development. This theory of language use extends our focus from how cultural routines provide structures for language acquisition (Nelson, 1998) to a focus on how people use and expand linguistic achievements to interact in challenging environments (Daiute & Nelson, 1997). Aida thus mobilized the linguistic process of narrating to expand and reorganize the socio-cognitive process of monitoring self–other relations as she used different narrative genres to address the challenging circumstance of being an immigrant in the post-9/11 United States.

Although expressing her experience carefully, Aida was probably not managing the knowledge-in-context relation explicitly. This theoretical framework posits, instead, that we tend to share knowledge and experience in relation to everyday circumstances implicitly, drawing on social knowledge, such as what people in the environment might believe about us and how they are likely to respond to one version of our story or another. As threats, opportunities, and expectations of situations become explicit, we proceed with caution and craft narratives appropriate to each interactive situation. Based on her brief history in American schools, Aida, for example, was obviously aware that she, as an immigrant and practicing Muslim, was perceived by at least some locals with suspicion.

Differences across Aida's three narratives illustrate interacting *with* the social context – a context with audible chatter that the narrative genres invited her to adapt and transform to her own circumstances. For example, characteristic of first-person narratives in challenging situations (Daiute, Todorova, & Kovacs-Cerovic, 2015), Aida chose third persons, "American kids" and "Bosnians," as protagonists for a narrative about exclusion – in this case, discrimination against Bosnians, which she identified generally, rather than toward herself personally. In her second narrative, Aida shifted the focus to within the Bosnian community, positioning herself as involved (" . . . we got mad because . . . ") yet also as an observer of the family feud and suspending resolution ("We haven't spoken in 3 years"). In contrast, Aida used the fictional genre to express a more active narrator stance, creating a story of a protest and successful action against the mayor as an agent of discrimination. In this way, relational flexibility develops as afforded and provoked with, within, and between the narratives. That English is Aida's third language is notable, given her apparent skill at varying details with features of diverse narrative genres (autobiography, observation, and fiction). Given culturally diverse and challenging contemporary life circumstances, such use of symbolic genres for making sense of one's environment is a developmental requirement.

This chapter provides a foundation for defining human development as a process of reciprocal individual and societal activity, especially when maturing individuals use narrative genres to interact in diverse and challenging environments to make sense of what is going on around them, how they fit, and, sometimes, how they change situations. I draw on research in challenging circumstances in the United States and the Western Balkans to illustrate this process, and I connect the argument with theory and research on adult development processes (executive function, self-regulation, and reorganization). After explaining and illustrating the process of developmental genre use with examples from previous research, the chapter concludes with the observation that in spite of increasing evidence that adolescents and adults spontaneously demonstrate abilities such as those in Aida's narratives, relational flexibility benefits from support in education, community organizations, and research. In this process, we address the following questions: How do adolescents and adults use language genres – like narrative – to mediate changing and challenging circumstances? How might those genres be developmental processes? What does the proposal about developmental genres indicate for future research on the development of higher order cognitive processes?

Human Development in Global Systems

Contemporary dynamics of conflict, migration, and inequality are inextricably integrated in human development. Political-economic situations co-occur with individual development over the life course, rather than being local or temporary interruptions of norms (Daiute, 2010). These circumstances are not merely influences on development, but are also central in the developmental process. As has occurred for human civilizations across many troubled eras, people develop resources across the life span, to engage with the plights they face. By adolescence, a full range of capacities and responsibilities is typically available, so putting them to use and reorganizing those capacities has much to do with life purposes and supports. Nevertheless, the role of language *for* development has not been a major focus of developmental psychology.

Understanding the use of language for development in adversity is urgent. Global circumstances since 1989 define the current era as one of increasing violence, displacement, and inequality. Compared to the previous 40 years, the period since 1989 has involved increasing and ongoing changes in nation-states, global economic organization, and resident populations. A complete analysis of geo-political dynamics distinguishing the years after the Cold War is beyond the scope of this chapter, but the broadly defining characteristics have to do with a collateral rise in global capitalism, violent political changes, exacerbated economic inequalities, and resulting population shifts (Harvey, 2007; Sen, 2000, 2009; UNHCR). Like Aida, children born into situations of conflict, migration, and inequality suffer exclusions that endure into adulthood (Ogle, Rubin, & Siegler, 2013). Recent increases in violent conflicts, displacement, economic inequality, and societal reorganizations provide a foundation for the argument that developmental psychology must account for socio-cognitive mechanisms negotiating the interaction of human development and societal change. Because of the inter-connected nature of communication and thinking with economic and political dynamics, development cannot be considered primarily in terms of individual characteristics, such as vulnerability of character or developmental period. Instead, of utmost importance is inquiry into interdependent processes people use to engage with diverse environments where they live. Language is the major integrative process, especially when it occurs with positive engagement in stable institutions and collaborative projects for addressing problematic situations (Betancourt et al., 2015; Daiute, 2010).

With case studies in different settings characterized by conflict, migration, and inequality, I illustrate how symbolic genres – with a focus on narrating – become relationally flexible mechanisms of human development.

Language Genres Mediate Interactions and Development in Context

Socio-historical theory provides the foundation for considering the role of language in adolescent and adult development. A major tenet of this theory is that human development is an interdependent individual and societal process:

> Every function in . . . cultural development appears twice: first, on the social level, and later, on the individual level; first between people (interpsychological), and then inside the child/person (intrapsychological). . . . All higher functions [attention, logical memory, etc.] originate as actual relations between human individuals.
> (Vygotsky, 1978, p. 57).

More recently, developmental scholars have emphasized reciprocal actions or "co-actions" among similar bio-socio-behavioral dimensions of life (Overton & Lerner, 2014).

Language and other systematic symbolic media (such as sign language and certain ritual cultural practices) are, on this view, "cultural tools" developed in society, then used to enact and transform meaning in practice. "Language is the quintessential tool to "conduct human influence on the object of activity" (Vygotsky, 1978, p. 55). Language and other symbolic media are "externally oriented . . . aimed at mastering and triumphing over nature" (ibid.). Furthermore, purposeful uses of cultural media (newsletters, narratives, surveys, etc.) further human development as tool use becomes "a means of internal activity aimed at mastering oneself," thereby fostering "higher order consciousness" (ibid.).

The concept "genre" has been offered as a dynamic mechanism linking diverse spheres of meaning and behavior. "Genre" co-occurs with actions in life contexts as utterances in conversations do (Bakhtin, 1986; Bamberg & Georgakopoulou, 2008; Kress, 2014). Even extended novels have been defined as speech genres: "Any utterance is a link in a very complexly organized chain of other utterances" (Bakhtin, 1986, p. 69); "An essential (constituitive) marker of the utterance is its quality of being addressed to someone ... The utterance has both an author ... and an addressee" (p.95). Symbolic genres have regular formal features or affordances (Heft, 2007), including recognizable openings, such as "Once upon a time," or structural organizations, such as plots. Symbolic genres – including narrative, essays, news reports, friendly conversations, and presidential speeches – are culturally developed routines connected with the environments where they occur. Symbolic genres are material, like language, which one can hear, read, or see, based on at least some shared features and meaning. Genres also embed values and norms, such as what counts as interesting, satisfying, and ethical (Daiute, 2014). If genres are complex symbolic enactments, their use must be especially catalytic in the second, third, and later decades of life where experience provides a wide range of abstract and concrete stories as resources for making sense of the world and one's place in it.

The concept of genre posits that communication does not occur *through* language forms but *interactively* in terms of genres features, within social contexts (such as classroom, home, or community), purposes (such as to persuade, to figure out, to connect), and audiences (others in the context, others in the speaker's/author's history). In this sense, narrative is not only a format but also an integration of features (plot, time markings, characters, etc.) enacted in relation to situational qualities (audiences, expectations, taboos, prior histories) and available for relatively flexible use. For this reason, values, expectations, and a wide range of meanings in the context where a genre is developed and used are inextricable from meaning (Berkenkotter & Huckin, 1995; Kress, 2014).

Narrative is a genre especially implicated in human development (Bruner, 1986). Like all symbolic genres, narrative enacts meaning in context in a way that meaning is not only abstract but also integrated with goals, situations, and actual/imagined audiences at the time of telling (Bamberg, 2004a). Narrating, however, differs from other genres in its invocation of lifelike events, affective nuance, familiarity, and flexibility (Bruner, 1986; Nelson, 1998). In this way, narrating is less abstract than other genres, like paradigmatic genres, such as the essay or mission statement which have truth telling as a primary goal (Bruner, 1986). Narrating experience is, thus, developmental in process and not only indicative of developmental achievements.

Narrative is cultural in origins, in shared activities, beliefs, and intentions, conforming to and/or differentiating from norms. Narrative genres also entwine historical scripts in ways that are subjective, personally felt, understood, imagined, and recalled. With diverse invitations to narrate, research and practice designs reveal knowledge about relational strategies speakers/authors elicit *between* the narratives, provoking development *within* a time period. One way that we have identified these diverse relational dimensions of narrating during childhood, adolescence, and adulthood has been with research engaging diverse narrative genres – that is, not requesting a single narrative or explicit statement of one's experiences or knowledge but by inviting a range of narratives for a range of purposes, from diverse perspectives, and for different audiences.

The relational dimension is crucial in that narrating experience in adulthood must address changing circumstances. The importance of narrating experience is, in part, that it gives shape, significance, and, potentially, transformation to knowledge that might dissolve from memory or be integrated into ideology. For that reason, narrating from adolescence through adulthood is less about expanding linguistic and cognitive abilities and more about using those capacities in relation to diverse experiences, others, and situations.

As author, Aida, a refugee of war in her childhood, living temporarily in Germany, and then migrating with her family to the United States, used three different narrative genres (first-person autobiography, third-person observation, and fictional narrative) to offer three perspectives on conflicts in daily life. What she addressed cautiously as observations of unresolved conflicts in the first two narratives, Aida addressed directly and resolutely in the fictional story. Aida's stance as observer of "American kids" and "Bosnians" described discrimination, although not explicitly mentioned as her plight. Narrating conflicts among adults afforded a context for reflecting on difficulties within her community, and the fictional context, perhaps paradoxically, allowed Aida to name the problems and a remedy for discrimination. Those narrating activities indicate an ability to read the context, adjust one's narrations to it, and reflect on it. Such processes are, moreover, worth considering as advancing development.

A brief review of contemporary inquiry into adult development foregrounds the need to integrate language as a developmental mechanism.

Adult Development

Scholars refer to adulthood with a range of categories and chronologies. Some focus on age, some on biological factors such as puberty, functions such as neuroplasticity, or cognitive processes such as hypothetical-deductive thinking (Piaget, 1968). Others focus on cultural factors such as extended liminal periods in industrial societies where employment opportunities are scant (Arnett, 2004) and cultural rituals to gain entry into society as an adult (Honwana, 2006). Life activities have thus become central in defining and studying adult development, somewhat diminishing the emphasis on age and assumptions about psychological decline over the life course.

Adult development theory has identified the milestone of formal operational thinking in adolescence, as posited by Piaget (1968) and investigated by subsequent scholars (Kuhn, 2008). Characterizations of formal operations include "thinking able to take itself as the object" (Kuhn, 2008) and reasoning with contrary-to-fact propositions (Kuhn, 2008). The related process of executive function has been defined as "a broad attentional construct that commonly refers to goal-oriented, higher level cognitive processes, [and] executive processes refer to cognitive control" (Vaughn & Giovnello, 2010, p. 343). Given recent findings that neuroplasticity is a lifelong phenomenon, the nature of daily activities, attendant psychosocial requirements, and resources should become paramount in adult development research. Answering that need is research positing that development is an ongoing process mediated with complex symbolic artifacts that "comprise human culture, such as discourse, social representations, and symbolic resources (Gillespie & Zittoun, 2013). In active lives, this process progresses beyond adolescence as symbolic genres and requirements to use them expand and diversify.

A study of emotional competence in adulthood, for example, employed an intervention with a variety of linguistic measures, resulting in indications of improved emotional competence (Kotsou et al., 2011). The intervention involved "behavioral and experiential teaching methods (e.g., group discussions, role play, self-observation) and scale items, such as 'I often find it difficult to show my affection to those close to me' and 'I often pause and think about my feelings'" (Kotsou et al., 2011). The study design involved survey assessments and experimental comparison, so the researchers' interpretations about positive effects of the intervention seem appropriate.

Another study with people who had experienced extremely challenging situations used an array of survey measures to assess the impact of previous trauma on adult well-being (Ogle et al., 2013). Assessments of the time within five chronological periods (childhood [3–12], adolescence [13–19], young adulthood [20 – 34], midlife [35–54], older [55 +]) when participants had experienced traumatic events indicated that such events encountered early in life had the greatest negative impact on psychological and psychosocial functioning in older adulthood. The researchers explained that increasing social and cognitive capacities across the life span, especially in middle age, bolstered adaptation to adversity and minimized damaging effects of trauma. Although not addressed in that study, an implication is that social interaction with oral and written language could be such a bolstering factor. Consistent with this idea that narrating may be a developmental mechanism is a study indicating that writing a narrative about their experiences in an earthquake lead to improved well-being in the aftermath (Smorti, Del Buffa, & Matteini, 2007). Interestingly, although such studies employed linguistic measures to examine and sometimes to support adult development, the focus on language as means of development has yet to be fully realized.

Research on adolescent and adult development in dramatically changing life circumstances of conflict, migration, and inequality have shown remarkable changes in socio-cognitive orientations as groups experiencing those circumstances used a range of language activities to reflect on the challenging circumstances and their roles in them. One study with migrants to the United States, for example, showed that migrant youth wrote narratives of peer conflicts in much more context-sensitive ways than did US-born youth (Lucic, 2013). With this and research discussed below, I focus on the process of "relational complexity" to account for how individuals and groups situated differently within and across life contexts use linguistic genres strategically to think, feel, and act in relation to those contexts, especially threats and opportunities (Daiute, 2010, 2014; Lucic, 2013).

Relational complexity is a process whereby individuals perceive and interpret their experiences in terms of their cognitive and emotional interactions in events where they live. These interactions occur with symbolic resources, such as social media use and narrative, they have developed in their past histories, to address present others, events, and imagined futures. This process integrates individuals, collectives, and physical environments with language as the central mechanism and thus is neither top-down (from context to individual) nor bottom-up (from individual to context) (Overton & Lerner, 2014). This behavioral concept of relational complexity extends previous socio cultural research on the uses of symbolic means, such as cultural routines (Nelson, 1998) and pointing (Tomasello, 2005) with the developmental function of language. Language is a pivotal organizing mechanism in that it is developed in culture and becomes useful for developing culture (Bruner, 1986).

From the perspective of socio cultural theories, genres not only express meaning, but are also interactive mechanisms of meaning and action. In addition to serving cultural and group cohesion, genres are useful for making sense of what is going on, how we fit (Nelson, 1998), and what we can/should/want to change (Daiute, 2014). Relational complexity also addresses social structural factors as integral to meaning making. This integrative function involves a convergence of intentional factors (such as one's purpose in an activity or interaction), emotional factors (such as how one might feel about threats), and power relations (the magnitude of danger in a specific threat) in how one orients to the context. Given this broad account of higher order thinking, relational complexity is enacted with language by and across diverse institutions, groups, and individuals.

Adult development can be defined in terms of the uses of genres (beyond the sentence) as utterances (Bakhtin, 1986) to interact in the world, make sense of it, understand how one fits, and change it. Genres are, thus, actions in the world and in changing contexts. This definition is consistent with one by Overton and Lerner, stating that human "development occurs through its own embodied activities and actions operating in a lived world of physical and sociocultural objects, according to the principle of probabilistic epigenesis" (2014, p. 64).

Developmental genres play a role in relational complexity. Developmental genres do not only add skills to human repertoires, such as an addition of a new, more complex sentence structure or a new ability to coordinate one's understanding of a problem with a competing understanding. A developmental genre is, instead, characterized as employing existing skills across diverse situations to address diverse purposes, problems, and audiences. What may be natural would be to repeat familiar narratives such as "immigrants have taken jobs from people born here," while developmental uses of narratives would engage issues of immigration from diverse perspectives, such as those of immigrants. In this way, developmental genres reorganize capacities in adolescence (Amsel & Smetana, 2011), and such development is horizontal rather than progressing toward a hierarchically superior process. Orienting to her context and herself in different ways afforded by three narrative genres, Aida, for example, used the different narratives to extend observation to critique and to productive solutions. This integrative nature of genre is central to the premise that adverse environments do not only affect individuals, but that purposeful uses of language can change understandings in ways that affect the environment.

In the next section, I offer examples from three studies across the adolescent to adult life course in different contexts defined by conflict, migration, and inequality to explain how participants used diverse genres in developmental ways.

Considering Relational Developmental Methods in Practice and Research

Contexts of major social change from war, migration, and increasing inequality threaten human development and require ongoing individual development. Research in three such contexts occurred in the former Yugoslavia, community colleges in the United States, and Roma communities in Europe. Brief descriptions of the designs, research questions, and findings from these studies illustrate the concept of developmental genre.

Table 23.1 presents design features of three studies examining how adolescents and adults in dramatically changing and challenging circumstances used various narrative genres to make sense of their environments. These designs consider individuals' narratives in relation to diverse societal dimensions, such as political changes and reform policies. Each of those contexts listed across the top row in Table 23.1 was in the process of major societal change.

As shown in Table 23.1, in "dynamic storytelling research workshop" studies, we worked with communities in the midst of change whereby a youth center or educational practice involved a nexus of activities by individual and societal actors. Dynamic storytelling activities relevant to participants and the research questions (workshop in a community center, evaluation of a community college, professional development workshop) involved several narrative genres (first-person autobiography, third-person observations of others, and fictional narratives), as well as other genres (such as letters and policy statements). Because the narrative genres provided a range of features and connections, I focus here on how the narrating activities were developmental. Developmental dimensions of the dynamic storytelling activities across the environments (in column one of Table 23.1) note the context, the individual–society relation, diverse narrative genres, the mediating role of the genres for youth/adult development, and a brief summary of evidence of how participants used these genres.

Study 1 involved community centers devoted to youth and society development in the aftermath of the Yugoslav wars. Study 2 sampled immigrant and US-born students across four community colleges in New York City. The individual–society relation came to life in workshops for Study 3 with Roma adults in the new role of Pedagogical Assistant designed to increase participation of Roma children across the eastern European region in public education.

Table 23.1 *Mediating uses of symbolic genres across four studies*

3 studies >>> with narrative genres to mediate changing and challenging environments	Study 1 = Youth and young adults growing up in violent conflict	Study 2 = Younger and older adults negotiating the contemporary community college	Study 3 = Roma professionals participating in education reform in Eastern/Central Europe
Developmental context and challenge	Youth growing up during and after Yugoslav wars (N=134)	Community college students across New York City (N=384)	Roma Pedagogical Assistants in Serbia (N=174)
Individual–society relations	Adolescents interacting with different positions and circumstances of war	Students make sense of higher education institution	Pedagogical Assistants make sense of reform designed for their group
Narrative genres highlighting relational qualities in practice-based research	1st person, 3rd person and fictional narratives	Narratives of best and worst experiences (among other genres)	Narratives of personal journey, of a Roma child & letter to future PA
Mediating use of narrative genres = using genres to express different knowledge and experiences	Participants use 1st person narratives to conform to expectations; 3rd person and fictional narratives to express taboo circumstances	Older students & immigrant students emphasize different values than younger & US-born students	PAs enact professional and community solidarity in different ways across genres
Evidence of relational complexity = using genres to enact context-sensitive experience/knowledge	Accounting for global and local war narratives	Addressing adult life experiences and personal sense	Enacting professional role in the relation to extreme poverty and exclusion

Study 1 – Youth and Young Adults Growing Up in Violent Conflict

Young people growing up during and after the 1990s wars that broke apart the former Yugoslavia continued to face difficulties as the newly formed countries defined themselves politically, economically, and socially (Daiute, 2010). Many non-governmental community centers across post-war countries worldwide have been devoted to helping young people cope with changes during their lives and to develop strategies for participating in political, economic, and social structures very different from those experienced by their parents, teachers, and political leaders.

The study beginning several years after acute Yugoslav conflicts involved 134 participants aged 12 to 27 in community centers across post-war Bosnia, Croatia, Serbia and a refugee community in the United States sharing their perspectives on contemporary life.

The primary research question of this study was "How do youth growing up during and after political violence narrate conflict in the present realities to make sense of what is going on around them and how they fit?" To avoid the assumption of direct consequences of war on the participants and the assumption that their major response to war was trauma, the study method asked participants to narrate experiences of conflict in their everyday lives. As outlined in Table 23.1, three narrative genres were varied for author stance, author–audience relation, and affordances of each narrative genre.

The first-person narrating activity asked participants to "Write about a time when you or someone your age had a conflict or disagreement with another adult in your community. What happened? Who was involved? Where was it? How did those involved think and feel about the conflict? How did you (they) handle it? How did it all turn out?"

The prompt suggests a personal stance with a framework for narrating an event involving characters, a turning point, and resolution. Based on previous research (Daiute, 2004), our hypothesis was, moreover, that this prompt would be useful for presenting an acceptable account of conflict in the context, given that a first-person stance reveals the author as character, available for connection and possibly judgment by readers, near and far.

Another activity invited participants to use the narrative affordance of the third-person perspective, which shifts from focus on the author to focus on another. That prompt echoed the one above, however, asking about "a time when an adult had a conflict or disagreement with another adult in your community." This activity allowed for a more distant stance on the issues at hand, so speakers and writers could express different – and possibly critical – knowledge and experiences.

Finally, as narrating conflict in a war zone, even in the post-war years, is fraught with potential judgment, the following fictional prompt was included as a potentially powerful genre:

> ___ and ___ (from two groups) met at a ground-breaking of the new town center building. Everyone at the event had the opportunity to break the earth for the foundation and to place a brick for the building. It was an exciting community event and everyone was pleased that the new building would mark a new future. As they were working to begin the new foundation, ___ and ___ had a conversation about how they would like to make a difference in their town so children could live happily together. All of a sudden, someone came with news that changed everything! What was the news? How did everyone involved think and feel? How did it all turn out?

This fictional story starter provided the affordance for engaging experience from yet another perspective, one that allows authors to take an omniscient stance on events.

Analyses of the narratives indicated very different orientations to conflict across the genres and across the country contexts (Daiute, 2010). For example, a plot analysis (Daiute, 2014) focusing on the high point/turning points and resolution strategies of each genre (first-person narrative; narrative of conflict among adults; fictional narrative) revealed that participants across age groups narrated a wide range of interpersonal issues in the first-person peer narratives, narrated issues of property, differences of opinion, or silly reasons in the third-person adult conflict narratives, and relevant political issues in the fictional narratives (Daiute, 2010).

Narratives by Thor, aged 21, in Serbia bring this pattern to life. Across Thor's narratives, like those by Aida, differences between the narratives of conflicts among adults and the fictional narratives revealed participants' strategic uses of narrative genres.

> One day the neighbor "A" parked his car where the "B" neighbor usually parked his. They started to argue and swear hard. The children were looking at them and laughing; their mothers cried: "Oh, my God!" Some people didn't even notice that something was going on. The conflict has never been resolved, because after the incident, they started puncturing tires on each other's cars and scraping the other's car with keys.

In contrast, fictional narratives revolved around issues of political structure, roles, or dilemmas in political relations such as political roles (mayor, government) interacting via power dynamics (protests, edicts) and resolved via an intervention, such as collective action, a new law, or a new strategy. Thor's fictional narrative illustrates this with imagery and metaphors depicting a dangerous scene like a battle.

> Rockers and posers . . .
>   An anxious guy came running. He was breathing so heavily that he could hardly speak. "Fire," he whispered. Both rockers and posers started to run, trying to rescue the people who were in vicinity. The fire was approaching us. They took to a safe place all the onlookers. They redirected their attention to a construction site. They were trying to redirect the fire digging trenches. Alas, nothing could help –the fire was gigantic. When the fire ceased, they came to where the construction site used to be. The sight was devastating. For the rockers, it was like a battlefield where their destiny was completed. For the posers, it was like a destroyed path. They went their own separate ways. They no longer hated each other, but they didn't love each other either. There's still hope.
> (By Thor, in Daiute, 2010, p. 135)

The importance of these findings is that the shifts of meaning between narrative genres indicate authors' and speakers' interactions with broader societal narratives, which differed across Bosnia, Croatia, Serbia, and the US refugee community. While youth in Serbia used the fictional narrative to express their sense of victimization in a masked way, such as in Thor's story evocative of the bombing of Belgrade, which he experienced as a teenager, participants in Bosnia tended to use fiction differentially to express happiness and hope. These strategies are consistent with understandings about aggressors and victims in each country and in the region. Serbian youth presumably used fiction to narrate their plight because they knew their country had been the aggressor, while Bosnian youth presumably used fiction to narrate hopefulness because they knew their country had been the major victim. This study thus revealed participants' strategic uses of the narrative genres in relation to their personal presentations with narrative genre features. These are developmental uses of the genres because they organize and employ linguistic skills in relation to diverse contexts, thereby drawing on socio-politically sensitive metacognitive knowledge.

This brief review of uses of narrating to engage with histories of war and the aftermath is consistent with findings of another study in a large urban context in the United States.

Study 2 – Making Sense of the Contemporary Community College

Although community colleges in the United States differ in many ways from community centers across the former Yugoslavia, the United States community colleges also enact tensions in the broader society. Community college is presented as a relatively low-cost option for training in vocational, English-language, computation, and critical thinking skills, as well as a pathway to four-year college. Because those promises have not materialized for many students, the community college is an institution in transition. This issue led to our research on the meaning of the college for students.

A study with 342 community college students attending four colleges across New York City addressed the question "How do students of different backgrounds make sense of the community college to mediate their own and institutional development?" (Daiute & Kreniske, 2016). The study asked students to "Write about your *best* experience in community college" and to "Write about your *worst* (most difficult) experience in community college." Narratives of best and worst experiences are diverse narrative genres because they engage different author/speaker stances on the phenomenon of inquiry – in this case, the meaning of the community college. Best experience narratives are available for aligning with the institution, while worst experience narratives allow for critiquing. This may be obvious, but whether and how students used such narrative genres in those ways was an empirical question. To include perspectives of other stakeholders in the development of the contemporary community college, we also sampled mission statements from college websites, policy statements from public officials, faculty narratives, and media reports.

Values analysis revealed shared and diverse meanings across the students' best and worst experience narratives and across statements about the college by public officials and college administrators. Values Analysis examines organizing principles, beliefs, and norms, apparently guiding what to write/say, what not to write/say, and how to do that. Values analysis is a systematic process (Daiute, 2014), achieving at least 85% reliability. Results of the values analysis revealed four major values with several values related to each. Major values emerging across the narratives include: "Participating in academics is important"; "Connecting is important, with various participants, in various ways"; "It is important to acknowledge lack of connection and sometimes to disconnect, from various others, in various ways"; and "Human development is important, mine and others'."

The major value of the following narrative is "developing is important," with related sub-values including "developing collectively is important" and "education is important in relation to this broader context."

> I'm an international student in LG College and my best experience so far on campus was in my urban sociology classes because it helped me to understand

better how America is and why America became the country it is today. I've been taking good grades in this course and I feel really motivated to watch the classes since they are about what I see in real life.

This narrative emphasizes the value of attending community college as a way to develop understanding of the society and how one fits was unique among students.

Given our focus on adult development, we compared uses of narrating to make sense of the community college by younger (aged 18–22) and older (aged 23+) students, as their histories of coming to college and the relevant political, economic, and social factors over their lifetimes were likely to have differed. Younger students' narratives emphasized the importance of doing academics and connecting more than older students' narratives (77% and 57% of academic values narratives, respectively). Older students, in contrast, wrote more narratives than younger students, expressing the importance of developing (68% and 59%, respectively) and the importance of disconnecting (73% and 68%, respectively).

Specific values within the major categories also revealed different older and younger student orientations to community college. In addition to writing more narratives that emphasized the importance of developing, older students emphasized developing collectively (24% compared to 14%, respectively), while also developing the self somewhat more than younger students (45% compared to 40%). These and other differences suggest that older students brought a broader perspective or social frame to their experiences in college. Emphases across younger students' narratives included the importance of developing independence (24% compared to 8% in older students' narratives), struggling with academics [29% compared to 18%], success with academics [24% compared to 21%], and supports in academic endeavors [13% compared to 7%]). The broader perspective by older students who emphasized collective development could be wrought of expanded metacognitive orientations and/or life experience in later adulthood. This interpretation is similar to that of others who are exploring advances in middle age (Ogle et al., 2013), and merits further inquiry.

Immigrant and US-born participants organized narratives around some different values. Immigrant students emphasized, more than US-born students, the importance of connecting (29% and 25%, respectively) and acknowledging disconnects (30% and 25%, respectively). Immigrant students also emphasized the importance of acknowledging disconnects due to essentials such as financial obstacles. Although US-born students organized their narratives around the importance of developing more than did their immigrant peers (25% and 18%, respectively), immigrant students expressed values related to developing skills (such as language skills) more than their US-born peers (30% and 15%, respectively). The US-born students emphasized the importance of disconnecting with the college (26% of US-born students' narratives, compared to 16% of immigrant peers' narratives), even though their immigrant peers emphasized disconnecting more overall. Another difference had to do with US-born students tending to emphasize the importance of developing one's self (38% compared to 33%), while developing collectively was emphasized by immigrant students (20% to 14%).

These differences across students' histories – their countries of origin (US-born and immigrant) and general life experiences (younger and older) – support the flexible use of genre as a developmental mechanism for relating to environmental circumstances. In order to vary narrative meanings in such nuanced ways, one must be able to direct language skills toward relevant dimensions of the environment. Even though English-language and academic writing skills were relatively rudimentary for many of the participants, they directed their narrating skills toward circumstances evocative of challenges they faced. Immigrant students, in particular, narrated issues of connecting to American culture, while US-born students emphasized other factors, such as college life more generally and relationships with peers.

Study 3 – Roma Adults Narrate a Program to Mediate Poverty and Discrimination

The professional role of Roma Pedagogical Assistant in Serbia, one of 12 countries across the Eastern and Central European region to ratify the "Decade of Roma Inclusion" policy, occurs in the midst of broader societal change. Even though there are 11 million Roma living across Europe, circumstances conspire to confine Roma lives to the margins of society. Systematic exclusion of the Roma occurs due to lack of access to public resources, including lack of access to preschool through college, lack of financial resources and aid, no monitoring of programs that are in place to help Roma communities, discrimination, special "culturally adjusted" programs, untrained teachers, and brief vocational schools. The Roma PA program was created to comply with the national commitment to improve the situation of Roma in education (as well as in housing and health).

The Roma Pedagogical Assistant (PA) program in Serbia was designed to promote social inclusion through increased participation in education from preschool onward, with the support of the small percentage of high-school-educated Roma adults (4% of Roma adults). This research highlights the perspectives of 174 PAs (aged 20–42 years) from Roma communities across Serbia. Pedagogical Assistants participated in a one-day storytelling workshop embedded in one of the six training modules required for their certification as teaching assistants. The dynamic storytelling workshop research design involved sampling a range of individual and collaborative, oral and written activities. A primary research question guiding the study was "How do adults positioned via education between a highly marginalized community and the majority community evaluate a reform program designed for them? How do they use narrating to mediate this challenge/opportunity?" (Daiute et al., 2015).

The focus of this action research has been to highlight the experiences and reflections of those who have been previously left out of political-economic reform, as well as those with resources and power to make policy. Involved in this workshop were individuals and institutions with much at stake in the reform process –Roma PAs, policy makers of the Decade of Roma Inclusion Treaty, a Serbian national stakeholder, and a Roma advocacy organization. For purposes of this discussion, I highlight differences across two age groups and parental status – two dimensions especially relevant to adult development. Younger PAs were aged 20–25 and older PAs aged 26–42; in terms of parental status, 48.35% have children.

Three narrating activities provided different affordances and assumptions to use for enacting knowledge and experience relevant to participants' professional activities as minorities in public educational institutions. One narrating activity asked participants to "Write about your journey to becoming a PA." In this activity, the author as first person is presumed to be on stage and appropriately narrating as a professional. Another narrative prompt asked the participants to "Write a story about a Roma child in education." The narrative genre implied by this prompt provided a context for participants to relate to their profession and the attendant activities in a different way than in the first-person narrative. The authors could thus observe the situation of their community and the children on whose behalf they are working. A third activity invited participants to "Write a letter to a future pedagogical assistant." This letter is a frame for a future narrative, although the author may choose to write in a more expository way, such as to provide a list of suggestions. The major purpose of this activity was to provide the explicit stance of expert so the participants might directly address an audience of those who will be in their roles. Participants' writings were transcribed and translated, with examples of the three genres below.

Example of Genre 1: Personal journey to becoming a PA:

> It started with my acknowledgement that the Roma population belongs to the lowest class in education, and that in my street, there live many who are uneducated and very poor. I had a desire to do something for my people, to help them. I applied for the vacancy for PA, together with my best friend, who also wanted to do something for our people. We collected necessary documentation and submitted it to the committee. We were accepted! (Smiley).
>
> Today I work as a PA in a preschool institution. I primarily help children and their parents persuading them that education is essential. Also, I related to the NGOs and the local institutions. I use all possible ways to help my people. I use all institutions for which I know. I created a circle of people around me who are willing to help.

Example of Genre 2: Story of Roma Child:

> One day a father appeared at the door of the institution, with his daughter in torn dress and slippers.
> "Good morning," he said to me.
> "Good morning," I answered. "How can I help?"
> Her father said: "I want to register my daughter for kindergarten; I could not bring her earlier. You know how it is. I work collecting metal the whole day, and there is nobody else to bring her."
> "Super!" said the assistant-pedagogue. "Please, sit down. Of course, you can register her; it is good that you took her here because she can learn a lot,

and there are many children here to befriend with her. What do you think,
Marija?"

"Well, super! I'd like to come here every day!" Marija happily responded.

Father: "But, you know, I have no money to buy her shoes or books; all
I earn goes for food."

PA: "Don't worry. I will provide all that. I only ask that she regularly comes
to school."

Example of Genre 3: Letter to a Future PA:

> Dear colleague, the job of the assistant-pedagogue is not easy but is interesting.
> You are going to work in preschool institution and your task is as follows. As you
> know yourself, PA is a link between the institution you work in, the parents and
> the other institutions as NGOs, for example. Essential is to establish a good
> cooperation with them all because their support will be important for your future
> work. Since the Roma children are in educational institution for the first time, very
> important is to keep them there and make their stay there easier; they will then
> attend regularly. These first steps are important for their further schooling and for
> formation of their habits. If this is not clear enough, please, call me. Good luck!
> PA 100% sure

Achieving over 90% agreement analyzing 20% of the 6,000 sentences in the
database, five researchers identified six major values (24, if including sub-
categories) guiding narratives and letters by the PAs and policy makers.

Younger and older PAs used narrative genres differently. The older cohort
(aged 30+) emphasized collaboration more than the younger (aged 20–25)
group (25% to 20%, respectively). Within collaboration values, however,
older participants emphasized collaboration among the majority and Roma
communities, while younger participants emphasized collaborations with
families and parents. The younger cohort emphasized the importance of PA
roles, in particular, to meet expectations, more than the older cohort, who
emphasized the role of working on behalf of children. Both older and younger
PAs emphasized education, but the younger group emphasized learning while
the older group emphasized teaching. Both older and younger cohorts also
emphasized the importance of acknowledging and addressing obstacles similarly, the importance of personal qualities, and the importance of successful
outcomes,

Parents and non-parents used narrative genres differently. Parents emphasized systemic issues (such as social exclusion) and the importance of collaborating with family and with organizations. In contrast, narratives by non-
parents emphasized the importance of collaborating with community and
collaborating with parents. These differences in emphasis underscore the role
of life experience in the narration of professional development activities.
Greater experience in the professional role and as a parent was enacted with
diverse narrative expressions from relatively broader perspectives, such as
recognizing systems of social exclusion and the importance of organizations
in overcoming the Roma plight.

Discussion

This discussion is organized around questions about the role of symbolic genres in adult development and research with narrative genres.

How Do Older Adolescents and Adults Use Language Genres to Mediate Changing and Challenging Circumstances?

Research across different settings within the global processes of conflict, displacement, and socio-economic inequality indicates that adolescents and adults use language to mediate interactions in their challenging and changing environments. Analyses showed that several hundred adolescent and adult participants across a range of challenging circumstances used different genres to engage with different aspects of experience and knowledge in context-sensitive ways. Differences within as well as across groups with different histories coming to the study activities indicated the creative use of genres to interact with local issues and contexts. Groups with different histories used narrative genres to connect with specific social conventions and avoid taboos relevant to their situations, thereby demonstrating the power of language in adult life. Use of the genres relevant to actual circumstances was developmental in that the genre features provoked expanded participant orientations to extant plights and possibilities. Such horizontal development – applying complex language genres to numerous diverse contexts – extends beyond understandings of development as a sequence of achievements to an understanding of development as the flexible use of achievements for diverse relationships.

How Might Such Genre Use Be a Developmental Process?

Participants' uses of diverse narrative genres to express different experiences and knowledge support the argument that symbolic genres function as developmental mechanisms in adulthood. This ability to use the features of diverse narrative genres to interact with context norms appears to come with experience and, thus, adult life. Some findings, such as the older community college students' greater emphasis on collective development and the younger students' greater emphasis on developing their own independence, show a broadening of perspective as one matures.

What seems especially interesting is the horizontal development demonstrated by these participants across the studies. Horizontal development, defined as sensitivity to expectations in a context as enacted with the affordances of the different genres, involves a process of relational flexibility. Adult development may, thus, progress with relationally complex – that is, flexible – uses of symbolic genres. This extension into relational complexity includes attention to and integration of social structures as well as actual or hypothetical individuals. As a process of adult development, narrating must involve expanding narrative stances – that is, actual and imagined *purposes* for sharing experience (such as not only to justify one's actions but also to imagine new reasons to act); *audiences* with which to share experiences (such as not only those we know but those we perceive to be different from us); and *perspectives* on life (such as not only first person[al] perspectives but also third [other]personal and fictional perspectives).

Given culturally diverse and challenging contemporary life circumstances, such uses of symbolic genres for relational interactions with diverse others is a developmental requirement. Those with language and life experience can rise to that requirement, if they care to. Professional, educational, and research activities among adults can foster such developmental narrating – narrating not only from the "I" perspective, but also from the "not-I" perspective, and not only from assumptions about "facts" but also for hopes of the "possible." Because relational flexibility addresses social structural differences, such as understanding forces of injustice and inequality in which individuals are embedded, it compounds notions of interpersonal perspective-taking and thus requires new inquiry.

What Does This Proposal About Developmental Genres Indicate for Future Research on Higher Order Socio-Cognitive Processes?

Considering such processes in situations of adversity that provide social support has offered preliminary evidence for future developmental inquiry to study humans at their best rather than as already defeated. Given the contemporary prevalence of conflict, migration, and inequality, developmental psychologists should address the increasing need for complex symbolic processes. I have argued that there is much at stake in social-relational sensitivity, and the lack of it. Because narrating enacts meaning in terms of norms, power relations, prejudices, and other social relations in actual and virtual contexts, individuals must share their experience and knowledge in ways that allow them to connect, disconnect, reflect, and, ideally, to develop.

Such a dynamic enactment of older adolescents' and adults' uses of narrative genres is evident when research designs, like those presented here, invite participants to narrate from diverse perspectives as provided in narrative features. When we acknowledge that the explicit content, structure, and implications in a narrative are inextricably entwined with what goes on before, during, and after the performance of each narrative, we observe that narrating is a cultural tool whose working parts require detailed examination. It takes cultures a long time to create their devices, like marking intensity, focus, and structure, for doing things with language, and individuals use them as elements to combine strategically when sharing experience and elements to pay attention to when trying to understand others.

If human development means, at least in part, transforming canons, developmental uses of story are those that can imagine new possibilities. Inviting research participants, students (and ourselves as researchers) complexity, contradiction, and multiple takes opens possibilities, like using fiction to express what we decide to silence in autobiography. When research emphasizes only a singular story, what else can we expect but canonical stories?

A strategy to explore in research and practice is what we refer to as "dynamic storytelling," defined as narrating from diverse stances to foster development across the lifespan. Several principles define this approach: 1) invite complexity of narratives in context by always asking participants to narrate more than once; 2) engage narrators in various relational stances, with various purposes, and audiences, such as employing fiction, which allows more freedom to explore and critique, as well as autobiography, which involves aligning with the context; and 3) involve narrators in re-visiting and reflecting on their narratives, with others and on their own in relation to issues in their society.

When analyzing narratives and narrating contexts, the details of language help us unlock "magic ... beyond banality into the realm of the possible" (Bruner, 2002, p. 10). "To advance narrative inquiry and developmental uses of narrating, we must, in brief, ask for trouble with multiple diverse narrating activities. Rather than reducing the story and the story-maker as mirror images, we then join with others to use narrating and enjoy it" (Daiute, 2011, pp. 334–335). In this chapter, I have argued that dynamic storytelling can be especially powerful in adulthood when we have linguistic and cognitive complexities to use in narrating for development by extending our skills to broader social and political complexities. By "broader," I mean different from what we know – maybe even different from what we think we want – resulting in ongoing development and connection.

Conclusion

Human development occurs well into and across adulthood, especially when interacting with challenges and new goals. Adolescents and adults have the ability to use a range of resources to interact with negative changes, as well as to identify and take advantage of positive changes. Understanding how people address issues of diversity, power relations, and other inter-subjective functions is increasingly important in contemporary globalization. These roles of diversity and adversity seem especially important to pursue. Maintaining cultural diversity across the globe is important, but mutual understanding has become essential to the possibility for individuals to live into adulthood. Narratives can reduce humanity to conflicting ideologies or, as we have seen in a small way in this chapter, can be sensitive means to connect with new, different, and even challenging situations and other people and, as such, to foster positive development.

Acknowledgments

Former Yugoslavia Research: Luka Lucic, Maja Turniski, Maja Ninkovic, Group Most, Suncokret-Gvozd; Community College Research: Phil Kreniske, David Caicedo, Ralitsa Todorova; Education Reform for Social Inclusion of the Roma in Serbia: Tinde Kovacs-Cerovic, Ralitsa Todorova, Aysenur Ataman, Tijana Jokic, Phil Kreniske; National Council of Teachers of English, PSC-CUNY, Spencer Foundation, UNICEF, OSCE-Serbia, Roma Education Fund, William T. Grant Foundation; Thank you also to Herb Saltzstein and Jessica Murray for their assistance with this chapter.

References

Amsel, E., & Smetana, J. (Eds.). (2011). *Adolescent vulnerabilities and opportunities: Developmental and constructivist perspectives*. New York, NY: Cambridge University Press.

Arnett, J. J. (2004). *Emerging adulthood: The winding road from the late teens through the twenties*. New York, NY: Oxford University Press.

Austin, J. L. (1962). *How to do things with words*. Cambridge, MA: Harvard University Press.

Bakhtin, M. M. (1986). The problem of speech genres. In C. Emerson & M. Holquist (Eds.), *Speech genres and other late essays* (pp. 60–102). Austin: University of Texas Press.

Bamberg, M. (2004a). Considering counter-narratives. In M. Bamberg & M. Andrews (Eds.), *Considering counter-narratives: Narrating, resisting, making sense* (pp. 351–371). Amsterdam: John Benjamins.

Bamberg, M. (2004b). Positioning with Davey Hogan: Stories, tellings, and identities. In C. Daiute & C. Lightfoot (Eds.), *Narrative analysis: Studying the development of individuals in society* (pp. 135–158). Thousand Oaks, CA: Sage.

Bamberg, M., & Georgakopoulou, A. (2008). Small stories as a new perspective in narrative and identity analysis. *Text & Talk, 28*(3), 377–396.

Berkenkotter, C., & Huckin, T. (1995). *Genre knowledge in disciplinary communication*. Hillsdale, NJ: Erlbaum.

Betancourt, T. S., Ito, B. S., Lilienthal, G. M., Abdi, S., Agalab, N., & Ellis, H. (2015). We left one war and came to another: Resource loss, acculturative stress, and caregiver–child relationships in Somali refugee families. *Cultural Diversity and Ethnic Minority Psychology, 21*(1), 114–125.

Bruner, J. S. (1986). *Actual minds, possible worlds*. Cambridge, MA: Harvard University Press.

Bruner, J. S. (2002). *Making stories: Law, literature, life*. Cambridge, MA: Harvard University Press.

Daiute, C. (2004). Creative use of cultural genres. In C. Daiute & C. Lightfoot (Eds.) *Narrative analysis: Studying the development of individuals in society* (pp. 111–134). Thousand Oaks, CA: Sage Publications.

Daiute, C. (2010). *Human development and political violence*. New York, NY: Cambridge University Press.

Daiute, C. (2011). Trouble – In, around, and between narratives. *Narrative Inquiry, 21*(2), 329–336. doi 10.1075/ni.21.2.11dai

Daiute, C. (2014). *Narrative inquiry: A dynamic approach*. Thousand Oaks, CA: Sage Publications.

Daiute, C., & Kreniske, P. (2016). Hopes, misunderstandings, and possibilities of narrating for inclusive education. In A. Surian (Ed.), *Proceedings of "Open Spaces for Interaction and Learning Diversities"* (pp. 53–67). Rotterdam, The Netherlands: Sense Publishers.

Daiute, C., & Nelson, K. A. (1997). Making sense of the sense-making function of narrative evaluation. *Journal of Narrative and Life History, 7*(1–4), 207–215.

Daiute, C., Todorova, R. S., & Kovacs-Cerovic, T. (2015). Narrating to manage participation and power relations in an education reform program. *Language & Communication, 45*, 46–58.

Gillespie, A., & Zittoun, T. (2013) Meaning making in motion: Bodies and minds moving through institutional and semiotic structures. *Culture & Psychology, 19*(4), 518–532.

Harvey, D. (2007). *A brief history of neo-liberalism*. New York, NY: Oxford University Press.

Heft, H. (2007). The social construction of perceiver-environment reciprocity. *Ecological Psychology, 19*(2), 85–105.

Honwana, A. (2006). Child soldiers: Community healing and rituals in Mozambique and Angola. In C. Daiute, Z. Beykont, L. Nucci, & C. Higson-Smith (Eds.), *International perspectives on youth conflict and development* (pp. 225–245). New York, NY: Oxford University Press.

Kotsou, I., Nelis, D., Gregoire, J., & Mikolajczak, M. (2011). Emotional plasticity: Conditions and effects of improving emotional competence in adulthood. *Journal of Applied Psychology, 96*(4), 827–839.

Kress, G. (2014). Genre as social process. In B. Cope & M. Kalantzis (Eds.). *The powers of literacy (RLE Edu I): A genre approach to teaching writing* (pp. 22–37). Oxon, UK: Routledge.

Kuhn, D. (2008) Formal operations from a twenty-first century perspective. *Human Development, 51,* 48–55.

Lucic, L, (2013). Use of evaluative devices by youth for sense-making of cultural diverse interpersonal interactions. *International Journal of Intercultural Relations, 37*(4), 434–449. doi: 10.1016/j.ijintrel.2013.04.003

McAdams, D. P. (2005). *The redemptive self: Stories Americans live by.* New York, NY: Oxford University Press.

Nelson, K. (1998). *Language in cognitive development: The emergence of the mediated mind.* New York, NY: Cambridge University Press.

Ogle, C. M., Rubin, D. C., & Siegler, I. C. (2013). The Impact of the developmental timing of trauma exposure on PTSD symptoms and psychosocial functioning among older adults. *Developmental Psychology, 49*(11), 2191–2200.

Overton, W. F., & Lerner, R. M. (2014). Fundamental concepts and methods in developmental science: A relational perspective. *Research in Human Development, 11*(1), 63–73.

Piaget, J. (1968). *Six psychological studies.* New York, NY: Random House.

Sen, A. (2000). *Development as freedom.* New York, NY: Anchor Press.

Sen, A. (2009). *The idea of justice.* Cambridge, MA: Harvard University Press.

Smorti, A., Del Buffa, O., & Matteini, C. (2007). Narrazione autobiografica di eventi dolorosi: Analisi degli aspetti formali e contenutistici del testo [Autobiographical narrative of the painful events: Analysis of the formal aspects and content of the text]. *Rassegna di Psicologia, 24*(3), 11–33.

Tomasello, M. (2005). *Constructing a language: A usage-based theory of language acquisition.* Cambridge, MA: Harvard University Press.

Vaughn, L., & Giovanello, K. (2010). Executive function in daily life: Age-related influences of executive processes on instrumental activities of daily living. *Psychology and Aging, 25*(2), 343–355.

Vygotsky, L. S. (1978). *Mind in society: The development of higher psychological processes.* Cambridge, MA: Harvard University Press.

Wertsch, J. V. (2002). *Voices of collective remembering.* New York, NY: Cambridge University Press.

Wittgenstein, L. (1953). *Philosophical investigations.* Oxford: Basil Blackwell.

UNHCR.org (2014). The world at war: Global trends, forced displacement in 2014: www .unhcr.org.

Wortham, S. (2001). *Narratives in action: A strategy for research and analysis.* New York, NY: Teachers College Press.

Index

Abu-Lughod, L., 215–217
academic success
  critical race perspective on, 298, 299–300, 304–307
  executive functioning and, 47–48
  language development in home environment and, 412–414
  neoliberal educational reforms and, 263–265
  in Oakland school case study, 270–281
  poverty and predictions of, 132
  psychological health and, 247–249
  racism and, 237–240
  resistance and, 237–240, 247–249
  self- and emotion-regulation and, 343–345
accommodation
  developmental change and, 73–75
  gender development and, 145–148
  genetics and, 355–356
  language evolution and, 358–360, 362–364
  resistance to, in girls, 232–237
  resistance to racism and, 239, 242–243, 249
  slavery and role of, 230–232
accountability
  contextuality in discourse and, 196–199
  discourse construction and, 426–430
  moral accountability in robots, 115–117
  neoliberal educational reforms and emphasis on, 263–265
active memory, representation and, 22
adaptation
  cultural modeling and, 4
  reciprocity and, 170
  seeking comfort and, 169
additive factors, velocity-time-distance relations inference and, 18–20
adolescents/young adults
  accountability in humanoid robots, study involving, 115–117
  brain development in, 335–345
  conversations on moral socialization with, 195–196
  diversity development in, 447–466
  emotional development in, 337–339
  empathy development in, 340–343

failures of coordination in conversations with, 196–199
future research issues on brain development in, 345
health disparities for, 346
identity-focused cultural ecological attributes in, 307–309
intersectionality of race and gender resistance in, 240–244
language use by, 8, 447–449, 464
lying and honesty in, 219–222
narrative by, 451–452
neuroscience of brain development in, 330–346
population demographics, 330–331
productive learning environments for, 258–260
racialized learning ecologies for, 280–281
relational development research in, 455–463
resistance to dehumanization in, 230–232
resistance to gender stereotypes in, 232–237
resistance to racism in, 237–240
school environment for, 459–461
self- and emotion-regulation in, 343–345
self- and other-knowledge development in, 335–337
violent conflict and development in, 456–459
adults
  development in, 452–455
  honesty and lying in, 219–222
  implicit racial bias in, 30–32, 39–40
  racism in, 27–28
  Roma narrative on poverty and discrimination of, 461–463
Advanced Telecommunications Research Institute International (AtR), 107–113
adversity, language development and, 449–450
affect
  control and, 171
  empathy development in adolescents and, 340–343
  positive affect and peer acceptance, 175
affiliative preference
  in adolescents, 335–337
  gender development and, 150–151

469